Political Development in Hong Kong

Political Development in Hong Kong

Joseph Yu-shek Cheng

NEW JERSEY · LONDON · SINGAPORE · BEIJING · SHANGHAI · HONG KONG · TAIPEI · CHENNAI · TOKYO

Published by

World Scientific Publishing Co. Pte. Ltd.
5 Toh Tuck Link, Singapore 596224
USA office: 27 Warren Street, Suite 401-402, Hackensack, NJ 07601
UK office: 57 Shelton Street, Covent Garden, London WC2H 9HE

British Library Cataloguing-in-Publication Data
A catalogue record for this book is available from the British Library.

POLITICAL DEVELOPMENT IN HONG KONG

Copyright © 2020 by World Scientific Publishing Co. Pte. Ltd.

All rights reserved. This book, or parts thereof, may not be reproduced in any form or by any means, electronic or mechanical, including photocopying, recording or any information storage and retrieval system now known or to be invented, without written permission from the publisher.

For photocopying of material in this volume, please pay a copying fee through the Copyright Clearance Center, Inc., 222 Rosewood Drive, Danvers, MA 01923, USA. In this case permission to photocopy is not required from the publisher.

ISBN 978-981-120-143-1

For any available supplementary material, please visit
https://www.worldscientific.com/worldscibooks/10.1142/11311#t=suppl

Typeset by Stallion Press
Email: enquiries@stallionpress.com

Desk Editor: Karimah Samsudin

Preface

Hong Kong is a rather unique political entity. It was a British colony before 1997, and it has been a Special Administrative Region (SAR) under Chinese sovereignty since. Its economic takeoff in the 1950s transformed it from an entrepôt into a manufacturing base; and making use of the opportunities offered by China's economic reforms and opening to the external world since 1979, it has become an international financial centre and business services centre.

During this development process, the Hong Kong people gradually developed their own identity and political values. The territory's new generation of political elites emerged in the 1970s as student activists and organizers of non-governmental organizations. They exerted pressure on the British administration and learnt to articulate the community's interests. Later, they had to face the Chinese authorities, though they had no formal role in the negotiation process on Hong Kong's future.

While a considerable segment of the population might not be enthusiastic in the struggle for democracy, the Hong Kong people have always been keen to uphold their values, and maintain the rule of law and the freedom of information flow. When they protested, they normally did so peacefully. Their actions often attracted the attention of the international community too.

As one of the first batches of political science graduates from the University of Hong Kong in 1972, I have been a concerned observer of the territory's political developments. I researched on them, and published my works in newspapers, magazines, international journals, and academic books. Now in retirement, I intend to present a volume of my past publications revised and edited, so as to offer a relatively complete view on Hong Kong politics from the 1970s till now.

This book is a collection of academic papers which had appeared as international journal articles and book chapters based on research. My values are clear though; I support the democratization of Hong Kong and hope to see that its people can enjoy the basic political rights they deserve. I have been a political activist, and my publications embody these experiences.

The political crisis in Hong Kong in the summer of 2019 again places it in the headlines of the international media. Hong Kong is a small place, its people embrace universal values, and they hope to have the support of all those who support democracy and human rights. It is hoped that this book may help to enhance the understanding of Hong Kong people's aspirations.

I would like to take this opportunity to express my gratitude to World Scientific for this book's publication, especially Karimah Samsudin who has helped to make many valuable improvements. The author alone, however, has to be responsible for the volume's inadequacies.

Joseph Y.S. Cheng
July 2019

About the Author

Joseph Yu-shek CHENG is the retired Professor of Political Science and Coordinator of the Contemporary China Research Project, City University of Hong Kong. He is the founding editor of the *Hong Kong Journal of Social Sciences* and the *Journal of Comparative Asian Development*. As researcher and writer, he publishes widely on the political development in China and Hong Kong, Chinese foreign policy, and development in southern China. His recent books include *China's Japan Policy: Adjusting to New Challenges* (2015), *The Use of Mao and the Chongqing Model* (2015), *China's Foreign Policy: Challenges and Prospects* (2016), *The Development of Guangdong: China's Economic Powerhouse (2018)*, and *Multilateral Approach in China's Foreign Policy* (2018). He was the Convener of the Alliance for True Democracy in Hong Kong and a trustee of the Justice Defense Fund in Hong Kong.

Contents

Preface		v
About the Author		vii
Chapter 1	The Goals of Government Expenditure in a *Laissez-faire* Political Economy: Hong Kong in the 1970s	1
Chapter 2	Political Modernization in Hong Kong	17
Chapter 3	The Future of Hong Kong: Surveys of the Hong Kong People's Attitudes	53
Chapter 4	The 1988 District Board Elections: A Study of Political Participation in the Transitional Period	93
Chapter 5	The Post-1997 Government in Hong Kong: Toward a Strong Legislature	127
Chapter 6	Prospects for Democracy in Hong Kong After the Beijing Massacre	149
Chapter 7	The Basic Law: Messages for the Hong Kong People	171
Chapter 8	Values and Attitudes of the Hong Kong Community	207
Chapter 9	Political Participation in Hong Kong: Trends in the Mid-1990s	239

Chapter 10	Political Changes Since the Establishment of the Hong Kong Special Administrative Region, 1997–1999	273
Chapter 11	Administrative Performance and the 2000 LegCo Elections	303
Chapter 12	Elections and Political Parties in Hong Kong's Political Development	323
Chapter 13	Hong Kong: Democratization at a Critical Stage	361
Chapter 14	Hong Kong Since Its Return to China: A Lost Decade?	379
Chapter 15	The Pro-Democracy Movement: A Lost Decade?	421
Chapter 16	Hong Kong District Councils: Political Development and Community Building	441
Chapter 17	Challenge to the Pro-democracy Movement in Hong Kong: Political Reforms, Internal Splits, and the Legitimacy Deficit of the Government	467
Chapter 18	Has He Got the Job Done: An Evaluation of Donald Tsang's Administration	509
Chapter 19	The 2012 Chief Executive Election in Hong Kong and the Challenges for the Chinese Authorities	539
Chapter 20	Power, Transparency, and Control: The Hong Kong People's Adaptations to Life	557
Chapter 21	New Trends of Political Participation in Hong Kong	579
Chapter 22	Democratization in Hong Kong: A Theoretical Exception	607
Chapter 23	The Emergence of Radical Politics in Hong Kong: Causes and Impact	637
Chapter 24	Assessing the C.Y. Leung Administration	673

Chapter 1

The Goals of Government Expenditure in a *Laissez-faire* Political Economy: Hong Kong in the 1970s

In the late 1970s, Hong Kong was already one of the few developing areas in the world whose people are rapidly growing richer. The fast growth of its economy and the steadily improving quality and variety of its exports impressed an increasing number of consumers and manufacturers in industrial countries. Since the establishment of the People's Republic of China (PRC), Hong Kong had been successfully transformed from a colonial entrepot into a modern industrial colony. This development was possible, first of all, because the government of the PRC, in the past three decades and in the foreseeable future, had made and would make it a policy to keep Hong Kong economically viable. The status quo was obviously economically beneficial to the PRC, more so then because of its "four modernizations" program; and not surprisingly the PRC government had been tolerant of the classical *laissez-faire* philosophy that had been guiding the colonial government of Hong Kong in the past century or more.

In the early 1970s, however, international and domestic factors began to pose a serious challenge to this *laissez-faire* philosophy. For one thing, the Governor, Sir David Trench, retired in 1971 after seven and a half years in office, and he was replaced by Sir Murray MacLehose, the new governor who, unlike his postwar predecessors, was a professional diplomat with no previous experience in colonial administration. Sir John Cowperthwaite, the ultra-conservative Financial Secretary, whose long tenure had left his personal stamp on almost every aspect of government policy in the 1960s, also retired, and was replaced by his deputy, Philip Haddon-Cave.

This change of guard was by no means the only factor that prompted the Hong Kong government to make a thorough reappraisal of its policies. Two important developments — namely, the rise of protectionism and the coming of age of the postwar generation — made such a reappraisal unavoidable. The purpose of this chapter is to examine the impact of these developments on Hong Kong's politics and economy, and, above all, on the government's response as revealed in its expenditure patterns.

In the economic field, the newly appointed Financial Secretary Philip Haddon-Cave sounded a sharp note of caution on Hong Kong's future economic prospects in an address on November 12, 1971:

> The world trading system, which has served Hong Kong so well over the past 20 years, is threatened. The United States and Britain, our two biggest markets, are experiencing serious economic difficulties.... The uncertainty over the outcome of the international monetary crisis is inhibiting trade. And the dangers of a trade war are increasing every month the monetary crisis remains unresolved.[1]

This increasing danger of restrictions on world trade was perhaps best demonstrated by the pressure the Nixon administration applied on Hong Kong, Japan, Taiwan, and South Korea to sign a "voluntary" agreement severely limiting their exports of non-cotton textiles to the United States (U.S).[2] Such an agreement was of major significance to the future economic prospects of Hong Kong, not only because the U.S. was the largest market of Hong Kong products, but also because the agreements

---

[1] See *Far Eastern Economic Review Yearbook: Asia 1972*, p. 164.
[2] The former Governor, Sir David Trench, commented acidly on the "voluntary" agreement: "We were invited to conduct negotiations...in a way a highwayman negotiates with a stagecoach driver." It was certainly an unprecedented comment from any British colonial official. See *ibid.*, p. 168.

violated the basic principles of free trade and created a dangerous precedent for Hong Kong's other trade partners.

At the same time, Britain's entry into the European Economic Community also created some uncertainty in Hong Kong's business world over its Commonwealth preferential status in the British market. However, this had long been anticipated, and the British negotiators managed to get more out of the Europeans than Hong Kong had been expecting. In February 1971, the European Economic Community finally agreed to classify Hong Kong as a developing country in granting tariff preferences to imports from developing economies, though special restrictions were to be imposed on the territory.

By the early 1970s, Hong Kong also had become aware that it was no longer alone (with Japan) in the export of textiles and consumer goods on a large scale to advanced countries. Instead, it was facing increasing competition from countries and regions such as Taiwan, South Korea, Singapore, Yugoslavia, etc. Hong Kong's competitive edge would certainly diminish unless it could be strengthened by more technical training and education, higher productivity, diversification of industries and markets, and perhaps by the government's playing a more active role in bringing about the above. Indeed, Hong Kong's entrepreneurs could well point to the fact that their counterparts in Taiwan, South Korea, and other developing countries received much greater help from their respective governments than they could expect in Hong Kong. At this time, the governments in Taiwan, South Korea, and Singapore were actively promoting the development of heavy industries and providing the infrastructure required for such development.

The coming of age of the postwar generation meant that the Hong Kong government could no longer take for granted that the refugees from Mainland China would be satisfied with economic survival and law and order. As published statistics showed, in mid-1977, the estimated population of Hong Kong was 4,513,900; and 29.1% of the population was below the age of 15, 41.2% below 19, and 60% below 29.[3] The figures showed that over half of the population of Hong Kong was born

---

[3] *Hong Kong's Population*, a pamphlet published by the Hong Kong Government Information Services, Hong Kong, September 1978.

after the establishment of the PRC and that they sorely needed an identity with Hong Kong; this situation created a serious problem as well as a valuable opportunity for the Hong Kong government.

The diplomatic achievements of the PRC in the early 1970s strongly appealed to nationalistic sentiments in the Chinese community in Hong Kong, indicating that something more than economic survival and law and order was required to hold the allegiance of the Chinese population. Surely, it was no mere coincidence that three important campaigns occurred in 1971, involving a major portion of the student and youth activists in Hong Kong, and attracting the sympathy of most Chinese in the colony. They were (i) the strike of the blind workers at the factory operated by the Hong Kong Society for the Blind; (ii) the campaign to have the Chinese language legalized as an official language of the Hong Kong government; and (iii) the demonstrations to support the PRC's claim over the sovereignty of the Diaoyutai (Senkaku) Islands.

All these demonstrated the urgency of the basic task of establishing and strengthening the sense of identity of the local population as citizens of Hong Kong; and this important task simply could not be accomplished by organizing a Hong Kong Festival once every two years. A solution was suggested by the new Governor, Sir Murray MacLehose, in his first policy speech to the Legislative Council on October 18, 1972: "I have therefore concentrated on defining broad objectives in three fields where this seemed particularly necessary at this juncture — housing, education and social welfare. I have also spent much time and thought on the two prerequisites of the very continuance of our community — on the one hand the prosperity that has provided everything that has been done or whichever will be done and, on the other, public safety."[4]

Public safety became a serious concern for the Governor in 1972 because, in the previous four years, key major crimes had increased by 40% and violent crimes by 135%; and the proportion of young people committing such crimes had also steadily increased. The prevalence of

---

[4] *Address by H. E. the Governor, Sir Murray MacLehose, at the opening session of the Legislative Council — October 18, 1972*, Hong Kong Government Information Services, p. 3.

corruption also prompted the introduction of the Prevention of Bribery Bill in December 1970, which came into force the following May. The prevention of crime and corruption was necessary because they threatened to destroy law and order in the community, one of the two basic conditions that had served to retain the local population's allegiance to the colonial government. Furthermore, in the longer term future, crime and corruption would also affect the investment climate and hinder the development of tourism, the second largest industry in the colony.

The Hong Kong government's expenditure on housing, education, and social welfare represented an attempt of the *laissez-faire* government to help provide an ideal environment for investment and thus promote prosperity in the colony. Various public housing schemes helped to ensure a cheap labor supply, for the majority of Hong Kong's labor force simply could not afford the expensive rent charged by the private sector. The government's expenditure on social welfare, together with public housing, helped to provide a decent living standard for the labor force and indirectly contributed to a reduction of crime, especially juvenile delinquency, which, as in most parts of the world, flourished in slums and squatter areas. Expenditure on education, as indicated in the government's White Paper on Education in 1974, was largely an investment on the part of the community to promote future prosperity in the colony. A hardworking and highly skilled labor force, in addition to a corps of efficient, intelligent, and highly educated managers and executives, was Hong Kong's most important asset; and it was largely in this area that Hong Kong could hope to maintain the edge over its competitors and to satisfy the demand for higher wages through the achievement of even higher productivity.

In order to attract the loyalty of the local population, to ensure the maintenance of an ideal investment environment, and to retain Hong Kong's competitive edge, the Hong Kong government in the early 1970s not only felt that it should increase its expenditure in the fields of housing, education, and social welfare, but also felt the need to plan with a time horizon of 10 years or more. Regarding housing, for example, the Governor made it very clear on October 18, 1972 that "the target taken, which I repeat is as a basis for calculation, is 10 years and has as its objective to build on such a scale that, with the contribution of the private

Table 1.1: Total Expenditure on the Gross Domestic Product in Hong Kong, 1970–1977 (HK$ Million)

Year	Private Consumption Expenditure Current	Constant	Government Consumption Expenditure Current	Constant	Gross Domestic Fixed Capital Formation Current	Constant	Total Expenditure on Gross Domestic Product Current	Constant
1970	13,942	12,828	1,190	1,023	3,565	2,893	18,760	15,211
1971	15,967	13,631	1,269	1,028	4,768	3,465	20,976	15,704
1972	17,308	14,204	1,581	1,101	5,339	3,653	24,156	16,838
1973	22,844	16,204	1,952	1,254	6,637	4,195	30,736	19,229
1974	26,520	16,475	2,493	1,385	7,683	4,175	35,252	19,657
1975	28,505	17,062	2,711	1,451	7,798	4,062	37,268	20,230
1976[a]	33,102	19,197	3,120	1,570	9,727	4,793	47,329	23,655
1977[b]	39,663	22,087	3,724	1,767	12,996	6,005	54,444	26,408

Note: Current = Current Market Price; Constant = Constant (1966) Market Prices.
[a] provisional estimates.
[b] preliminary estimates.
Source: *The 1978–79 Budget: Economic Background,* Hong Kong: The Census and Statistics Department, January 1978, pp. 6–7.

sector, there will be sufficient permanent self-contained accommodation in a reasonable environment for every inhabitant of Hong Kong."[5]

The same ambition was found in the government's policies in other sectors. A careful examination of Tables 1.1, 1.2, and 1.3 reveals that government expenditure in Hong Kong increased from HK$2,718 million in 1971–1972 to HK$10,266 million in 1978–1979 — that is, by 278%.[6] In terms of constant market prices, the increase was less impressive but was still considerable. However, government expenditure in 1977–1978 was only 15% of the gross domestic product (GDP) of 1977; and this percentage, when compared with the government expenditure in 1971–1972, which amounted to 13% of the GDP of 1971, did not show any significant increase over the years. Meanwhile, per capita GDP in Hong Kong in the period 1970–1977 showed an increase of 156% when

---

[5] *Ibid.*, p. 4.

[6] The fiscal year in Hong Kong begins on April 1 and ends on March 31 of the next calendar year.

Table 1.2: Per Capita Gross Domestic Product in Hong Kong, 1970–1977

Year	Current Market Prices (HK$)	Constant (1966) Market Prices (HK$)
1970	4,716	3,842
1971	5,185	3,882
1972	5,869	4,091
1973	7,296	4,565
1974	8,161	4,551
1975	8,478	4,602
1976[a]	10,651	5,323
1977[b]	12,061	5,850

Sources: *Estimates of Gross Domestic Product*, Hong Kong: The Census and Statistics Department, 1978, p. 26; *The 1978–79 Budget: Economic Background*, Hong Kong, The Census and Statistics Department, January 1978, p. 6.

[a] provisional estimates.
[b] preliminary estimates.

calculated in current market prices and an increase of 52% in constant market prices. Certainly the increase in government expenditure was impressive in absolute terms in the period 1971–1979, but government expenditure as a percentage of GDP showed only a very modest increase.

Moreover, this increase in government expenditure did not cause any rise in the standard tax rate in the colony, which remained throughout the period at the low rate of 15%; and the government throughout the period enjoyed a budget surplus almost every year. The increase in government expenditure, at constant tax rates, was therefore largely financed by the growth of the economy, which expanded at almost 8% per annum in real terms in the 1970s. All public works programs were also implemented with a considerable measure of flexibility so that constant tax rates could be maintained and the completion of the programs rescheduled in case of need.

All these revealed that the Hong Kong government was still reluctant to adopt a more progressive system of taxation to finance an expansion of government services; it still refused to dilute its basic principle of *laissez-faire* and continued to maintain an ideal investment climate in Hong Kong by imposing a low standard tax rate and leaving the initiative largely to the

Table 1.3: Summary of the Hong Kong Government's Expenditures by Groups of Services, 1971–1972, and 1974–1975 to 1978–1979, in HK$ Millions

	1971–1992 Adjusted Actual	1974–1975 Adjusted Actual	1975–1976 Actual	1976–1977 Actual	1977–1978 Revised Estimates	1978–1979 Draft Estimates
Total	2,718	5,973	6,032	6,591	8,160	10,266
General services	527	950	986	1,303	1,624	1,918
% of the Total	19.4	15.9	16.4	19.8	19.9	18.7
Economic services	321	533	553	560	650	720
% of the Total	11.8	8.9	9.2	8.5	8.0	7.0
Community services	534	1,653	1,274	1,431	1,778	2,092
% of the Total	19.7	27.7	21.1	21.7	21.8	21.4
Social services	1,057	2,202	2,637	2,647	3,249	4,375
% of the Total	38.9	36.9	43.7	40.2	39.8	42.6
Education	587	1,145	1,268	1,403	1,680	1,918
Medical and health	305	560	562	648	750	891
Housing	101	219	439	217	406	998
Social welfare	55	262	352	359	407	535
Labour	9	16	16	20	6	33
Common supporting services	160	318	245	270	349	400
% of the Total	5.9	5.3	4.1	4.1	4.3	3.9

Note: This table excludes the items unallocable expenditure and other financial obligations, therefore expenditures by groups of services do not add up to the total.

Source: The 1978–79 Budget: Speech by the Financial Secretary, moving the Second Reading of the Appropriation Bill, 1978, Hong Kong: The Hong Kong Government Printer, p. 124.

entrepreneurs. The system of taxation in the 1970s, however, became slightly more progressive because of inflation, and the tax burden of the salaried middle class was considerably increased because of the increase in their monetary income.

A detailed examination of the Hong Kong government's expenditure by groups of services showed that expenditure on social services expanded fastest relative to the expenditure on other groups of services. Among social services, expenditures on housing and social welfare showed the most remarkable increases: from fiscal year 1971–1972 to fiscal year 1978–1979, they increased by 888% and 873% respectively. Expenditures on these two items probably contributed most to providing a decent standard of living to the general public, as well as removing the most conspicuous hardships in the community, and thereby helped to maintain law and order in society and strengthen the sense of identity of the local population with the existing government. Direct expenditure on law and order also expanded considerably, showing an increase of 259% in the same period, reflecting the government's concern, as well as that of the public, with the prevalence of violent crimes and corruption. Expenditures on transport, roads, and civil engineering, as well as on education also demonstrated considerable increases of 430% and 227% respectively in the same period. These two items might be interpreted as the community's investment in building the infrastructure of the economy and providing a well-trained labor supply. Expenditure on education also provided the most important channel of upward social mobility and thereby contributed to the stability of the political system.

The construction of an efficient and relatively cheap transportation system in the New Territories was particularly important in the 1970s, because the supply of land in the easily accessible urban areas had been exhausted and the opening up of the still relatively sparsely populated areas in the New Territories to public and private housing would have to depend on an adequate transportation system. The government could also reasonably hope that expenditure on this transportation system could be partly recovered from the sale of newly available land. Another intangible benefit would be the sense of confidence created in the business community, which would stimulate further investment and expansion of economic activities.

The Hong Kong government achieved universal free and compulsory primary education in 1971, and since September 1980, universal free and compulsory education to the age of 15 or Form III has been provided. The fact that education was the largest single expenditure item certainly demonstrated the government's awareness that a well-trained labor force was the most important asset of Hong Kong's economy and the traditional importance the local Chinese population attached to education. More important still, as the structure of Hong Kong's economy was gradually transformed from one emphasizing labor-intensive industries to one emphasizing technology-intensive industries and professional services, the provision of education and training programs was a responsibility that could be borne only by the government. The major objective of the government's education policy in the 1970s was to provide nine years of free and compulsory education as the basis for further education, while the emphasis in senior secondary and tertiary education would be gradually reoriented to technical education, which would contribute in a more direct way to the growth of Hong Kong's economy.

While expenditure on social and community services as a percentage of total expenditure expanded in the period being considered, those on general services declined slightly and those on economic services were reduced significantly. This showed that the size of the government bureaucracy expanded at a slightly slower rate when compared with the economy, and that the role of the government in regulating the economy did not expand at the same pace as the growth of the economy. These observations supported the hypothesis that the Hong Kong government in the 1970s still observed the basic principles of *laissez-faire*.

There were occasions, however, when the government was forced to intervene. After the disastrous crash of the local stock market in the first half of 1973, when the Hang Seng Index dropped from its peak of 1774.96 points in March to 492.01 points in July, the government introduced a Securities Bill and a Protection of Investors Bill. Described as "historic," these two pieces of legislation, among other things, established a Securities Commission with statutory powers. At the end of 1978, because of the drastic fluctuations in the local stock market and the sharp rise in interest rates, as well as the increasing trade deficit and the continual devaluation of the Hong Kong dollar, there were talks of the desirability of establishing a central bank in Hong Kong. Up till the late 1970s, however, interest rates were still determined by the Exchange Banks' Association, which was dominated by an oligopoly of private commercial banks.

Since the government maintained a budget surplus every year in the 1970s except 1974–1975, it lacked both the fiscal and the monetary policy mechanisms to intervene in the economy. The government, however, was an important consumer and investor through its massive public works programs. It would be an exaggeration to suggest that the government intervened in the economy by means of these programs, but there was an increasing tendency for the government to schedule its public works programs in accordance with the tempo of the economy to avoid overheating the economy and exacerbating a recession. The construction of the mass transit railway system was a good example. Contracts were signed for the system's HK$5,800 million initial stage at the end of 1975 when Hong Kong, like most parts of the world, was suffering from an economic recession. The mass transit railway system was certainly built on its own merits, but the commitment was made at a time when a massive public works program would not overheat the economy. Furthermore, as indicated by the Governor in his policy speech on October 8, 1975: "Commencement of construction will provide direct employment for at least 4,500 people and indirectly for many more. The project will certainly stimulate international interest in Hong Kong and enhance its reputation."[7] The last statement, in fact, meant that the project would enhance the confidence of foreign investors in Hong Kong and help to increase the flow of foreign investment into the colony.

The mass transit railway system was in full operation in the urban area in 1980 and the second stage of the system in 1982. Anticipating the completion of the system and a slowdown in the growth of Hong Kong's exports, the Hong Kong government considered the development of Lantau Island in the 1980s, and projects under consideration included a second airport on the island and a bridge linking the island to Tsing I and Tsuen Wan.

---

[7] *Address by H. E. The Governor, Sir Murray MacLehose, at the opening session of the Legislative Council — October 8, 1975*, Hong Kong Government Information Services, p. 17.

In the second half of the 1970s, the Hong Kong government launched a scheme of industrial estates. The first of these was completed in Tai Po at the end of 1977, and the possibility of building similar estates in the New Territories was also examined. The supply of relatively cheap land for the development of certain selective industries represented the first attempt on the part of the government to provide direct aid for industrial development. The government acknowledged that if this was not done, Hong Kong would lose new industries and technology to its competitors. The important role assumed by the governments of other developing countries finally forced the Hong Kong government to act, albeit reluctantly.

Two streams of thinking gradually emerged in Hong Kong, although their respective lines of argument were not made explicit. One group argued that the *laissez-faire* philosophy had served Hong Kong well in the past decades, and that there was no compelling reason why this should be changed. No doubt the government should continue to expand its social and community services, particularly in the fields of housing, education, social welfare, and the construction of the infrastructure of the economy; but this expansion should be financed predominantly by economic growth, and not by an increase in taxation. The government's role in the economy should still be kept to a minimum and the initiative should be left to the entrepreneurs. This stream of thinking agreed that future economic growth in Hong Kong would have to depend on diversification of industries and markets, but this could be accomplished largely through the efforts of the private sector. In the past decades, entrepreneurs in Hong Kong had demonstrated a remarkable ability to adapt to the changing external environment; any attempt on the part of the government to intervene would probably do more harm than good.

The above was the orthodox view of the government and the business establishment in the colony. However, in the 1970s it was being challenged by another stream of thinking, supported by elements of the bureaucracy (probably including the Governor) and the business world, the academics, and the more articulate elements of the general public. This group believed that the expansion of social and community services by the government was absolutely necessary in the 1970s, not only to promote economic growth, but also to retain the support of the local population for the existing regime — particularly that of the postwar generation, which increasingly doubted whether law and order plus economic survival provided an adequate basis for legitimacy. The riots in 1966 and 1967 were lessons that should constantly be borne in mind. The expansion of social and community services anticipated was to be financed largely by economic growth, but the government should be explicitly committed to the cause and should have long-term plans with definite targets set for the 1980s. Such plans naturally would have to be rescheduled during years of adverse economic conditions, but limited increases in taxation were tolerable. In fiscal year 1975–1976, the profits tax rate for corporations was raised from 15% to 16.5%, and was later further raised to 17%. In his policy speech on October 11, 1978, however, the Governor revealed that the Hong Kong government expected that in the next six years, the average growth rate of the economy would be about 9% per annum in real terms.[8] On this basis, the government's ambitious plans would be achievable at constant growth rates. It would therefore be pure speculation to suggest that the government might have to increase taxation during years of adverse economic conditions. One thing was certain though — namely, that any increase in taxation must not be allowed to jeopardize the investment environment and erode Hong Kong's competitive edge over its neighbours in attracting foreign investment.

The later stream of thinking tended to believe that in the 1980s and beyond the government should play a more active role in regulating the economy, especially in the adjustment of interest rates. Diversification of industries and markets also required greater government assistance, and the industrial estates scheme was probably an important step in the proper direction. The schedule of public works programs might also be utilized to regulate the tempo of the economy, especially to avoid overheating the economy and massive unemployment — the latter being particularly intolerable.

So far, the Hong Kong government had largely followed a *laissez-faire* policy line, although this had come under increasing pressure in the second half of the 1970s. Except for mild setbacks after the 1973–1974 oil crisis, Hong Kong's economy was growing at extremely healthy rates. The

---

[8] *Address by H. E. the Governor, Sir Murray MacLehose, at the opening session of the Legislative Council — October 11, 1978*, Hong Kong Government Information. Services, p. 42.

crucial test for the *laissez-faire* policy line would probably come in the event of a major recession. The government would then have to face the following important tasks: (1) to maintain a reasonable expansion of social and community services, and to increase its social welfare expenditure because it could no longer afford to disappoint the expectations it had created; (2) to restructure the economy in a more drastic manner so that Hong Kong could regain its competitive edge over those neighbors in which the governments assumed much more important economic roles, and so that Hong Kong could switch to more appropriate technology-intensive industries in a more planned manner. These two tasks definitely would lead to an overall reappraisal of the existing *laissez-faire* policy line and might lead to more interventionist orientations in the government's policy program. Meanwhile, the Hong Kong government only made minor adjustments whenever it was compelled to do so, and such compulsions so far were weak because of Hong Kong's remarkable economic health in the 1970s.

Two developments in Hong Kong in the late 1970s seemed to indicate that the advocates of a more active governmental role in regulating the economy were gaining ground. The Advisory Committee on Diversification completed a report in the middle of 1979 on whether there was a case for modifying existing government policies and/or extending them to facilitate diversification of the Hong Kong economy; the report recommended a more active governmental role regarding this vital issue. Perhaps more important still, the Financial Secretary, Sir Philip Haddon-Cave, in his speech moving the second reading of the Appropriation Bill 1979 on February 28, 1979, indicated for the first-time that "in certain circumstances, namely, a slowing down in the growth rate of the economy and/or a situation of threatened demand-pull inflation, the need to ensure compatibility between budgetary policy and the process whereby the economy adjusts to changing internal and external influences assumes *a critical importance*" (emphasis added);[9] and that he was prepared to adopt fiscal, economic, and monetary policies to ensure this compatibility.

---

[9] *The 1979–80 Budget: Speech by the Financial Secretary, moving the Second Reading of the Appropriation Bill, 1979*, Hong Kong: The Hong Kong Government Printer, pp. 1–2.

Acknowledgement

Originally published as Cheng, Joseph Y.S., "Goals of Government Expenditure in a Laissez-Faire Political Economy: Hong Kong in the 1970s", *Asian Survey*, Vol. 19, No. 7 (July 1979), pp. 695–706. Reproduced with kind permission from the publisher.

Chapter 2

Political Modernization in Hong Kong

I Introduction: Modernization and Political Modernization

Modernization is a complicated process involving changes in many areas of human thought and activity. Most scholars agree that the important aspects of modernization are urbanization, industrialization, secularisation, democratization, the spread of education and mass media, etc. In the socioeconomic development of the West, these aspects of modernization are closely interrelated. After the Second World War, however, in the modernization process of many developing countries, special emphasis has been put on economic development. The "Four Modernizations" of China in the 1980s, for example, referred to the modernization of agriculture, industry, national defence, and science and technology.

Though democratization, the so-called "fifth modernization" in China, remains the ideal of a minority of intellectuals in many developing countries, modernization nonetheless has its psychological and educational aspects, and it involves a fundamental shift in values, attitudes, and expectations. In the process of modernization, knowledge about the human environment expands rapidly, and this knowledge is quickly diffused throughout society through the increase in literacy rate, development of education, and the spread of mass media.

Huntington considers that in the process of modernization, social mobilization and economic development have a major impact on political stability.[1] According to Deutsch, social mobilization is the process by which major clusters of old social, economic, and psychological commitments are eroded or broken, and people become available for new patterns of socialization and behaviour.[2] Economic development, on the other hand, normally relies on the growth in the gross national product of the particular country concerned as the chief indicator, though per capita gross national product, level of industrialization, and level of individual welfare gauged by such indices as life expectancy, calorie intake, supply of hospitals and doctors, ownership of consumer durables, etc., are often taken into consideration as well.

Huntington's hypothesis may be summarized as follows — social mobilization increases the expectations of the individual and the community as a whole, and therefore enhances social frustration as well as exacerbates the contradictions in the community; while the fruits of economic development satisfy the demands of the individual and the community, and therefore reduce social frustration and social contradictions. In the process of modernization, social frustration and social contradictions often promote political participation, whereas economic and social mobility opportunities reduce the demand for political participation. In the circumstances of inadequate political institutionalization, political participation may lead to political instability.[3] It is believed that Huntington's hypothesis contributes to an understanding of political modernization in Hong Kong, as the following discussion demonstrates.

The definition of political modernization is usually based on a comparison between modern political systems and traditional political systems. Using the concepts of Max Weber, political modernization involves the rationalization of authority, traditional authority, and the charismatic authority of political leaders being replaced by legal–bureaucratic authority.[4] In history, political modernization normally

---

[1] See Samuel P. Huntington, *Political Order in Changing Societies*, New Haven: Yale University Press, 1968, pp. 33–34.
[2] See Karl W. Deutsch, "Social Mobilization and Political Development", *American Political Science Review*, Vol. 55, No. 3, September 1961, p. 494.
[3] See Huntington, *op. cit.*, pp. 33–59.
[4] See Max Weber, *The Theory of Social and Economic Organisation*, translated by A.M. Henderson and Talcott Parsons, edited with an introduction by Talcott Parsons, New York: Free Press, 1964, Section III, pp. 324–407.

follows the establishment of the modern state, the sovereignty of which is recognized by the international community and is realized domestically through the organization of a government with ultimate authority. To meet the demands of modernization, the organization of government becomes complicated and hierarchical. In response to the increase in government activities and the accompanying detailed division of labor, government departments multiply and the size of government expands. There is no lack of organization theories such as Parkinson's law to explain this. The establishment of a civil service system provides fair competition for public offices and allows the government to recruit the necessary talents.

Political modernization certainly involves increases in political participation on the part of the individual and the community. A high level of political participation strengthens society's supervision of the state; but in authoritarian countries, this may well enhance the state's control of society. In all modern states, citizens cannot avoid being involved in public affairs and affected by government policies.

To study political modernization in Hong Kong, it is perhaps important to examine the relationship between urbanization on the one hand, and political participation and democracy on the other. Weber, one of the pioneering scholars of the sociology of the city, held that the city as a political community was a peculiarly Western phenomenon and the source of the modern conception of "citizenship", and the latter was the source of democracy.[5] Later, Harold Laski's view that "organized democracy is the product of urban life" was further elaborated by Lipset.[6]

It does not follow, however, that what holds true of the historical relationship between urbanization and democracy is necessarily true in the cities of the Third World. Hong Kong probably fits well into McGee's description of the "colonial city".[7] According to Berger, the cities of the Third World are in a situation "that is congenial not to democracy but rather to political demagoguery, or to radical movements, and to the

---

[5] See Mas Weber, *General Economic History*, Glencoe, Illionis: Free Press, 1950, pp. 315–318.

[6] Harold Laski, 'Democracy', in *Encyclopaedia of the Social Sciences*, New York: Macmillan and Co., 1937, quoted in Seymour Martin Lipset, *Political Man*, Garden City, New York: Anchor Books, 1963, pp. 34–38.

[7] See T. G. McGee, *The Southeast Asian City*, London: Bell 1967, Chapters 3 and 4.

eruption of mob violence".[8] There are many factors that make Western urban political life different from that in Third World cities. However, the principal cause is that the rapid increase of population living in urban settlements in the Third World means that the major sociopolitical transformation process takes place within a much shorter period of time. Applying Huntington's hypothesis, the gap between rapid socioeconomic changes and the slower process of political institutionalization is the source of political instability in Third World cities.

II Postwar Political Development in Hong Kong

After the Second World War, Hong Kong's population grew rapidly.[9] In the mid-1980s, Hong Kong, with an area of 1,071 square kilometres, has a population of about 5.5 million. In terms of the urban areas and the new towns in the New Territories, population density in Hong Kong was the highest in the world.[10] Its economic development had been outstanding.[11] The potential for social mobilization was also very considerable — Hong

---

[8] See Brigitte Berger, *Societies in Change: An Introduction to Comparative Sociology*, New York Basic Books, 1971, p. 160.

[9] In 1841, Hong Kong's population was mere 12,000. It then grew to 300,000 at the beginning of the 20th century, and expanded rapidly to 1.64 million in 1941. Japan's invasion of Hong Kong led to the dispersal of the residents into Mainland China. But when the war ended, Hong Kong's population quickly increased from 0.6 million to 1.55 million in 1945–1946. It then continued to expand to 2.24 million in 1950, 3.17 million in 1961, 4.05 million in 1971 and 5.15 million in 1981. At the end of 1987, Hong Kong's population was 5.66 million. See Government Information Services, *Hong Kong 1988*, Hong Kong: Government Printer, 1988, p. 302.

[10] At the end of 1987, Hong Kong's overall population density per square kilometre was 5,252; *ibid*. According to the 1986 By-census, the population density for the metropolitan areas of Hong Kong Island, Kowloon, New Kowloon, and Tsuen Wan was 20,811 people per square kilometre, but for the New Territories it was 1,449 per square kilometre. See Government Information Services, *Hong Kong 1987*, Hong Kong: Government Printer, 1987, p. 291.

[11] In 1987, Hong Kong's total expenditure on gross domestic product at current market prices amounted to HK$360,237 million, while its per capita gross domestic product at current prices amounted to HK$64,174 (US$1 = HK$7.80). See Government Information Services, *Hong Kong 1988*, *op. cit.* p. 332.

Kong people had a very high literacy rate, they were quite well educated (since the 1970s, the government had been providing nine years of free compulsory education), and the mass media were well developed (almost every family had a television set and a radio, and local newspapers and magazines enjoyed wide circulation). Yet, until the early 1980s, the community's political participation was very limited, the constitutional structure of the colonial government had not experienced any major reforms, and there was little political modernization to speak of.

How could we explain this almost unique phenomenon? The first general explanation was the refugee mentality among the Hong Kong population after the Second World War. From the late 1940s to the early 1950s, most people came to Hong Kong as refugees. They obviously did not have much sense of belonging, and lacked any consciousness of being citizens of Hong Kong. They would be satisfied as long as they could make a living, with the colonial government maintaining law and order. Living in a refugee settlement, one's demand for political participation could not be high. Colonial rule was an affront to national pride, but when compared with the rampant warlordism, chaos, corruption, and the abuse of power in China in the first half of the 20th century, it was quite acceptable.

Language and law were important factors that could not be overlooked. The official language in Hong Kong was English, and the law was English common law. Without an adequate grasp of the official language and the legal system, it would almost be impossible to engage in peaceful political struggles. The independence movement in India was a good example. Many political leaders of the independence movements in former British colonies were graduates of Oxford and Cambridge, and quite a few of them had law degrees. In the 1970s, most activists of the political groups in Hong Kong graduated from the colony's two universities earlier in the decade; they had an adequate command of English, and understood the colony's political economy and the legal system well. Many of them came from the lower-middle socioeconomic strata too. On the other hand, the 1961 Census showed that Cantonese (a southern Chinese dialect) was the mother tongue of the majority of the urban population, with 806 out of every 1,000 inhabitants of Hong Kong, Kowloon and New Kowloon speaking Cantonese, while only 13 people in every 1,000 spoke English.[12] At that time, most people believed that the pressure of public opinion had to work through the English mass media, and only "letters to the editor" in the English press would receive the attention of government officials. It was not surprising that the lower socioeconomic strata such as hawkers often sought the help of a British missionary worker, Mrs. Elsie Elliott, and of a British barrister, Mr. Brook Bernacchi.

The refugee mentality under colonial rule was a kind of political alienation. This political alienation made ordinary Hong Kong people feel that they had no channel of political participation, and that they could not influence government policy and administration. As commonly conceived by political sociologists, the term "alienation" describes three different but related sets of attitudes, namely, (i) the sense of powerlessness, (ii) the sense of meaninglessness, and (iii) the sense of isolation.[13]

The only quantitative data concerning political participation in Hong Kong in the 1950s and 1960s were the voting figures of the Urban Council elections. According to a study by Aline K. Wong, from 1952 when the elections were re-instituted to 1967, the highest turnout was in 1967 when 10,189 voters voted; and they constituted about 0.3% of the population then.[14] Admittedly, voter qualifications and registration procedures were complicated, but the low participation rate and the general lack of interest in the electrons were largely due to the following factors: (a) the powers of the Urban Council were very limited; (b) people felt that the promises made by the candidates had little to do with their daily life; and (c) people did not perceive much competition and they believed that the same group of candidates would get the seats.[15]

In September 1966, a local Chinese newspaper, *Kung Sheung Yat Po*, conducted a public opinion survey, and the respondents were selected roughly in accordance with the categories of the electorate under the new

---

[12] See Alice K. Wong, "Political Apathy and the Political System in Hong Kong", *United College Journal* (Hong Kong), Vol. 8, 1970–1971, p. 19.

[13] See Lewis Feuer, "What is Alienation? The Career of a Concept", in Maurice Stein and Arthur Vidich (eds.), *Sociology on Trial*, Englewood Cliffs, New Jersey: Prentice-Hall, Inc., 1963, pp. 127–147.

[14] See Wong, *op. cit.*, p. 4.

[15] *Kung Sheung Yat Po* (a Hong Kong Chinese newspaper) editorial, July 31, 1966.

franchise qualifications of 1965. The results of the survey indicated that the majority of the respondents considered that under the existing political system, voting was a "meaningless" act. People who replied that they "lacked interest" in the elections complained most that the Urban Councillors did not have power. The survey showed that the majority of the respondents knew exactly the procedures for registration; the fact that they did not register was not because of the troublesome or complicated procedures, but because they had "no interest".[16] On the other hand, an earlier opinion poll in 1966 showed that only 51% of the population had heard of the Urban Council, and that only one Urban Councillor was known to more than 6% of the population.[17]

Though many people regarded the Urban Council elections as meaningless there was, however, still a segment of the population who showed an interest in political reforms. In June 1949, the Governor, Sir Alexander Grantham, followed the footsteps of his predecessor, Sir Mark Young, and proposed the establishment of a municipal council. The proposal met with severe opposition from the unofficial members of the Legislative Council (all of whom were appointed) who had another plan for constitutional reform. In general, they urged that the Legislative Council itself should first be reformed before a municipal council was to be set up. Some even doubted if there existed any popular demand for constitutional reform at all, as they believed that the majority of the population was absorbed by the turmoil in China and was not interested in local reforms.[18]

These unofficial members were proved wrong. There were substantial public discussions on constitutional reform. In the following July, 142 Chinese organizations claiming to represent 142,000 people presented a petition to the Governor requesting more thorough political reforms. Public opinion supported the demand of the unofficials for immediate reform of the Legislative Council, but did not approve of their suggestion

---

[16] *Ibid.*, September 12, 1966.

[17] "Raising the Rates", *Far Eastern Economic Review*, Vol. LIV, No. 2, October 13, 1966, p. 109.

[18] See G.B. Endacott, *Government and People in Hong Kong, 1841–1962*, Hong Kong: Hong Kong University Press, 1964, Chapter 11; and Wong, *op. cit.*, pp. 5–6.

to delay the setting up of a municipal council. In May 1950, the Governor announced that he had sent various views on constitutional reform, together with those of his own, to be studied by the British government. However, London indicated in 1952 that the colony was not yet ready for major constitutional reforms. Henceforward, and especially in the late 1970s, senior officials of the Hong Kong government often hinted that Beijing would not approve of any major constitutional reforms in Hong Kong. Apparently, the community also feared that any important change in Hong Kong would lead to interference from the People's Republic of China (PRC), to the extent of regaining control over the colony. This vague fear helped to explain why an independence movement had never emerged in the territory.

The above discussion serves to demonstrate that the low demand for political participation in the territory could not be adequately explained solely in terms of the refugee mentality of Hong Kong people in the early post-war years and their traditional lack of interest in politics. The lower socioeconomic strata did not know English, did not understand the law, and suffered from a sense of political impotence. They moved from the Chinese Mainland to Hong Kong, abandoned their traditional rural and lineage organizations, and felt acutely isolated in a big city. They made no significant demand on the colonial government, and the latter's performance was also acceptable to them.

Since the establishment of the PRC, the Hong Kong government had been attempting to suppress the activities of the Kuomintang and the Communist Party of China (CPC). Occasionally, the Hong Kong government exercised its emergency powers and exiled some political activists. A vast majority of Hong Kong people did not want to get involved in the political struggles between the Kuomintang and the CPC, and were afraid of retaliation from the government. In the 1950s and 1960s, many people in Hong Kong believed that besides the sanction of exile, those with connections to the Kuomintang and the CPC would not be admitted into the civil service, would not be granted British nationality, etc. Even in the 1980s and 1990s, those applying for the posts of administrative officers and police inspectors had to go through political checks. These vague fears were obviously exaggerated and generated considerable misunderstanding, but the end result remained that many people were deterred from any form of political participation. Before the 1970s, the colonial police were also quite rough towards those from the lower socioeconomic strata; taking part in petitions demonstration, etc., would have involved some risks.

The refugee mentality and the lack of interest in politics could not explain the political behavior of the political activists. In the decade after the Second World War, the constitutional reform programmes of Sir Mark Young and Sir Alexander Grantham aroused their interest, but they soon realized that the British government had no intention of introducing major political reforms, and they were not interested in the Urban Council which had little power. The middle class was also afraid that serious political changes in the territory would lead to interference from Beijing and its regaining control of the colony. The local middle class was quite well educated and enjoyed relatively high incomes; it had no great expectations of the Hong Kong government and was generally satisfied with the *status quo*. After all, the middle class and professionals in Hong Kong had been enjoying the highest living standards in Asia.

The colonial education system played a significant role in suppressing the potential demand for political participation from the middle class.[19] As in other societies in East Asia, education provided the most important channel for upward social mobility in Hong Kong. A university graduate almost automatically became a member of the middle class, and those with a law degree or a medical degree had a fair chance of moving into the upper strata of society.[20] The open, fair, and competitive education system provided hope for the hardworking parents; those with high expectations for their children tended to identify with the existing systems, and their dissatisfaction and social frustration were to a large extent reduced.

It was an exaggeration to describe this education system as indoctrination, but this system never attempted to encourage students to

---

[19] There are no concrete published materials on the subject. On the development of Hong Kong's education system, see Yee-wang Fung, 'Education', in the author's edited work, *Hong Kong in Transition*, Hong Kong: Oxford University Press, 1986), pp. 300–330.

[20] There are again no concrete published materials on the subject. One may refer to Alice K. Wong, *The Study of Higher Non-Expatriate Civil Servants in Hong Kong*, Hong Kong: Social Research Centre, Chinese University of Hong Kong, June 1972.

become interested in public affairs, and no efforts were made to cultivate a sense of citizenship and a critical attitude. The Chinese history curriculum, for example, covered only the period up to the overthrow of the Manchu Dynasty in 1911; what happened afterwards was a blank. Naturally, English was very much emphasized. Those who managed to succeed through this channel of upward social mobility were readily accepted by the elites, and the former in turn became inclined to support the existing systems. The rich men in Hong Kong differed from their counterparts in Europe in that they would not stress their family background; they were usually proud to talk about their childhood poverty. The successful products of the territory's education system normally had a better command of English than of Chinese; and from their individual career's point of view, they could strive for the acceptance of the establishment and naturally had little motivation to push for reforms through political participation.

To the business community, the market economy of Hong Kong was probably the freest in the world and experienced the least interference from the government. In the past, the freedom of the market economy had been effectively protected by government officials.[21] To a large extent, senior officials of the British administration in Hong Kong were a neutral administrative elite without direct ties to the business community. Appointed by the British government, they were constitutionally accountable to the British government. In practice, in the post-war years up to the beginning of the Sino-British negotiations, the Hong Kong government had encountered little interference from London. Even in the 1960s and 1970s when the British Labour Party was in power, the Hong Kong government was able to resist pressure from London to follow its "welfare state" policies.[22] Senior bureaucrats of the British administration in Hong Kong respected the rule of law and were guided by the political philosophy of *laissez-faire* (or positive non-interventionism in its final years), and ultimately, they had to be responsible to a democratic government in London.

---

[21] See N.J. Miners, *The Government and Politics Hong Kong*, Hong Kong: Oxford University Press, 1986, 4th ed., Chapter 4, "Economic Constraints and the Government's Ideology".

[22] *Ibid.*, pp. 147–148.

The post-war economic development in Hong Kong differed from that in the other "little dragons" of Asia post-war (Singapore, Taiwan, and South Korea). The major enterprises in the territory had not received any direct assistance from the government. Part of their capital came from the Chinese entrepreneurs (mostly from Shanghai) who fled to Hong Kong in 1949–1950, and the rest from the banking system in Hong Kong in which a firm foundation had been established when the territory served as an entrepot, as well as from the subsequent accumulation of the enterprises themselves. On the other hand, much of the capital of the major corporations in Taiwan and South Korea came from government-owned financial institutions, and the corporations maintained close ties with the respective governments and ruling parties.[23] The governments in Taipei and Seoul assumed a considerable guidance role in their respective market economies; and in the 1950s and 1960s, various regulatory and control schemes hindered the operation of the free markets. The business communities were forced to maintain cordial relations with the government officials, and it was not uncommon to offer political donations in exchange for favoured treatment from the government authorities. Even in Singapore, the guiding hand of the government was obvious in the market economy: the priority accorded to the "strategic industries" of electronics, petrochemicals, etc., in the early 1970s was a good example.

In Hong Kong, a basic separation between economics and politics had been maintained, and the business community had full confidence in the government's observance of the operational principles of a free market economy. Business leaders, having made their fortunes, could easily gain honors (such as knighthoods from the Queen) and social status through donations to respectable philanthropic organizations, and were generally not interested in politics. This was not to deny the fact that until the mid-1980s, major British corporations such as the Hongkong and Shanghai Banking Corporation and the Swire Group had been offered seats in the Executive Council (equivalent to the Governor's cabinet) so that their interests would be safeguarded. In the past decades, the business community

---

[23] Regarding the situation in South Korea, see Mark Clifford, 'Filing for divorce' and 'Playing the game', *Far Eastern Economic Review*, Vol. 140, No. 16, April 21, 1988, pp. 58–60.

was satisfied with the positive non-interventionist political philosophy of the government, and it had not raised specific demands for direct assistance from the government. Since the late 1960s, the establishment of the Hong Kong Trade Development Council, the Hong Kong Productivity Council, the Hong Kong Export Credit Insurance Corporation, and the Hong Kong Industrial Estates Corporation had been designed to serve the long-term economic interests of the territory, through the offer of the necessary infrastructure by the government for the smooth functioning of the private sector. Owing to its small and open nature, Hong Kong's economy was vulnerable to external factors, and government action to offset unfavorable external factors was often of limited effectiveness. The government was of the view that, except where social considerations were regarded as overriding, the allocation of resources in the economy would normally be most efficient if market forces were relied on and government intervention in the private sector was kept to a minimum. The government considered that the narrowly based tax structure with relatively low tax rates provided incentives for hard work and investment, and that the primary role of the government was to provide the necessary infrastructure and a stable legal and administrative framework conducive to economic growth and prosperity.[24]

Though the free market economy led to the concentration of wealth and the unequal distribution of income, yet in a colonial political system, power had been highly concentrated in the senior officials of the colonial government and had not been affected by economic development. This separation of political power and wealth in fact constituted a form of checks and balances. The considerable gap between the rich and poor too had not paved the way for a strong labor movement. The sense of political impotence, isolation, and alienation on the part of ordinary people, the lack of support from middle-class intellectuals in the organization of workers for their rights, and the general fear of involvement in politics suppressed the demand for political participation among the lower socioeconomic strata. More important still, the spectacular economic growth in Hong Kong since the 1950s improved the community's living

---

[24] Government Information Services, *Hong Kong 1987*, Hong Kong: Government Printer, 1987, p. 55.

standards significantly, and provided ample white-collar jobs and opportunities for starting small businesses. Together with the vast expansion of the education system, all these made the people realize that they could solve their problems through their own efforts without having to exert pressure on the government by political participation. These factors also constituted the basis of a political culture depicted by S.K. Lau as "utilitarian familism".[25]

According to a survey of young adults from urban households by the Sociology Department of the University of Hong Kong published in 1973, 62.7% of the young adults interviewed agreed that "Hong Kong is truly a land of opportunity and people get pretty much what they deserve here".[26] Despite the considerable gap between the rich and the poor and the juxtaposition of luxurious apartments and squatter huts, the young adults still held such a view. No wonder Hong Kong remained politically stable and demand for political participation was low.

III Changes in the 1970s

After 1970, those who had been born in Hong Kong and grew up in the territory gradually became the majority in the population. They did not share the refugee mentality with their parents, they had a strong sense of belonging to the territory and were proud of its achievements. Secondly, the spread of education and economic development created a significant middle-class; many citizens also began to have a good understanding of their rights and obligations. After fulfilling the obligations of paying taxes and obeying the law, it was natural that people started to demand political rights. Further, in a modern metropolis, the daily life of the citizens was closely related to government policies. As government expenditure on social services expanded, its ability to interfere in the economy also

---

[25] Siu-kai Lau, *Society and Politics in Hong Kong*, Hong Kong: Chinese University Press, 1982.

[26] 31.2% of the young adults interviewed disagreed with the statement, while 6.1% did not reply or indicated that they did not know. See D.C. Chaney and D.B.L. Podmore, *Young Adults in Hong Kong: Attitudes in a Modernising Society*, Hong Kong: Centre of Asian studies, University of Hong Kong, 1973, p. 60.

increased. Policies related to the provision of public housing and nine years of free education affected almost every family. It was a natural and inevitable development that people would demand to take part in policymaking in order to protect their own rights. These factors also became the foundation for various campaigns for citizens' rights.[27]

Such campaigns developed at two levels. Regarding issues with a direct impact on their daily life, people from the lower socioeconomic strata gradually learned to organize themselves to appeal to public opinion, to petition, and to engage in various forms of protect activities to protect and promote their interests. Social workers from voluntary agencies funded by Western churches and student activists from the tertiary educational institutions also began to take part in these campaigns. The most obvious examples of these *ad hoc* campaigns were the protests and petitions organized by the government. In the late 1970s, the development of grassroots pressure groups reached the stage when territory-wide campaigns for citizens' rights could be organized. Classical examples were campaigns against the raising of bus fares and those demanding citizen supervision of the monopolistic electric power companies. These territory-wide campaigns finally led to the establishment of the Coalition for the Monitoring of Public Utilities. It demonstrated that *ad hoc* territory-wide campaigns against the raising of prices by public utilities finally developed into a permanent organization with well-defined long-term objectives, though admittedly such an organization possessed meagre resources and was highly dependent on a small number of charismatic pressure group leaders.

The problem for such grassroots pressure groups was that people were as yet reluctant or unable to fight for their interests from a macro point of view instead of a micro one. Great difficulties existed in mobilizing people to become concerned with and to supervise the government's major policies. This showed that ordinary people were only willing to fight for immediate interests directly related to their daily life, and they were not concerned with the government's decision-making process.

---

[27] See the author's "Hong Kong Citizens' Push for Power", *Asiaweek*, Vol. 8, No. 51, December 24–31, 1982, pp. 49–50.

At the same time, student movements developed in the tertiary educational institutions. They played an important role in the campaign for Chinese as an official language.[28] However, their ideals and concerns for global developments and their understanding of the motherland (People's Republic of China) obviously could not appeal to the grassroots pressure groups. In the second half of the 1970s, political groups such as the Hong Kong Observers emerged. They represented the local-born generation of middle-class intellectuals, hoping to supervise and criticise the government through objective research, and exerting pressure on the government by influencing public opinion.[29]

Such campaigns for citizens' rights and political groups basically accepted Hong Kong as a free market economy, and did not demand reforms of the existing economic system. The former asked the government to do more for the lower socioeconomic strata, but they did not have a blueprint for a welfare state. The latter requested the government to be more responsive to public opinion and be accountable to the community, but they too did not have a plan for the development of a system of representative government. These limited attempts at political participation involved groups of moderate reformists. They did not have clear ideologies, though concepts of liberty, human rights, rule of law, democracy, responsible government, etc., as practised in Western democracies were attractive to them. They realized too that no radical ideologies could attract a sizeable following in the territory.

Hong Kong is a small place; unlike Taiwan and South Korea, there were no regional rivalries. Class consciousness was weak, even blue-collar workers had no strong sense of class identification and were reluctant to join trade unions.[30] Most parents in the lower socioeconomic

---

[28] See King-cheung Chan, "Hong Kong's Student Movement" (in Chinese), in the author's edited work in Chinese, *Hong Kong's Political System*, Hong Kong: Cosmos Books, 1987, pp. 289–314; and Hong Kong Federation of Students (ed.) *Review of Hong Kong's Student Movement* (in Chinese), Hong Kong: Hong Kong Federation of Students, 1983.

[29] See the Hong Kong Observers, *Pressure Points*, Hong Kong: Summerson, 1983, enlarged and updated edition.

[30] According to the July–September 1987 General Household Survey, Hong Kong's workforce was estimated to be 2.7 million. At the end of 1987, there were 458 unions, comprising 415 employees' unions with about 368,090 members, 29 employers'

strata hoped that their children would become middle-class professionals. They themselves could easily leave the ranks of the proletariat; it was not too difficult to become hawkers, street-stall owners, or purchase a taxi.

In response to rising demands for political participation in the 1970s, the British administration in Hong Kong become much more active in the provision of social services and in the process of "administrative absorption".[31] The former satisfied the demands of the community, solved the daily problems of the citizens, and reduced the contradictions in society. It certainly weakened the tendency of the lower socioeconomic strata to fight for their rights through political participation. While protecting the functioning of the free market economy, the government began to promulgate labor legislation in the 1960s to protect the rights of laborers and improve their working conditions and environment.[32] The government probably anticipated the pressure of international public opinion, and tried to improve Hong Kong's image as a manufacturing centre while opening up overseas markets. It obviously wanted to avoid being attacked for exploiting of Sir Murray MacLehose (1971–1982), the government made substantial commitments in public housing, education, and social welfare. In the early 1980s, government expenditure accounted for almost 20% of Hong Kong's gross domestic product. The size of the public sector and the amount of the social services provided by the government did not quite square with the official political philosophy of positive non-interventionism.[33]

---

associations with some 3,000 members, and 14 mixed organisations of employees and employers with about 22,010 members. See Government Information Services, *Hong Kong 1988, op. cit.*, pp. 86 and 88.

[31] See Ambrose Yeo-chi King, "The Administrative Absorption of Politics in Hong Kong", *Asian Survey*, Vol. 15, No. 5, May 1975, pp. 422–439.

[32] See Sek-hong Ng, "Labour", in the author's edited work, *Hong Kong in Transition*, *op.cit.*, pp. 268–299.

[33] In the fiscal year 1972–1973, Hong Kong's public sector was 12.8% of the territory's gross domestic product. This percentage gradually rose to 14.6% in fiscal year 1979–1980, and rapidly increased to 19.1% in fiscal year 1982–1983. It then declined to 16.5% in fiscal year 1985–1986, and has stayed at this level in recent years. See Shu-hung Tang, "The Role of the Hong Kong Government in Regulating the Economy" (in Chinese), in the author's edited work in Chinese, *Hong Kong's Political System and Politics, op. cit.*, Table 1, p. 214.

In the 1970s, social services provided by the government expanded rapidly. They served to improve the community's quality of life (especially public housing), offer opportunities for upward social mobility (especially the provision of nine years of compulsory education and the expansion of tertiary educational institutions), establish a social security net (through the Public Assistance Scheme and related social welfare programmes), etc. What Huntington considered to be the source of political instability was largely eliminated, and the demands for political participation and democracy failed to lead to a strong movement.

In fact, when the Hong Kong government presented its district administration scheme and proposed the election of district boards in June 1980, 20 years had already passed since the community last demanded constitutional reforms.[34] In 1960, the Civic Association and the Reform Club had sent a joint memorandum to the Colonial Office in London, demanding additional seats in the Urban Council and the creation of a number of elected seats in the Legislative Council. They also requested an extension of the franchise. Their proposals, however, were totally rejected by the British governments.[35] Since then, political activists in the territory had not presented any comprehensive constitutional reform proposals. In the late 1970s, the Governor, Sir Murray MacLehose, occasionally hinted to political groups such as Hong Kong Observers that Beijing would object to any political reforms in Hong Kong; this undeniably constituted an effective deterrence. After the fall of the Gang of Four, relations between Hong Kong and China were vastly improved. In the spring of 1979, the Governor was officially invited to visit China. He was received by Deng Xiaoping, and the two parties even discussed the future of the territory. China therefore was no longer a taboo; it was an important factor to be considered in Hong Kong's various developments. In the same year, the government's industrial diversification plans treated China as a positive factor.[36]

---

[34] *Green Paper: A Pattern of District Administration in Hong Kong*, Hong Kong: Government Printer, June 1980.
[35] See Wong, "Political Apathy", *op. cit.*, pp. 6–10.
[36] *Report of the Advisory Committee on Diversification*, Hong Kong: Government Printer, 1979.

On the other hand, the Hong Kong government learned a lesson from the riots in 1966 and 1967, and became more responsive to public opinion. It even claimed to be a "government by consultation". The system of advisory committees following the British tradition was further developed to involve community leaders of the upper socioeconomic strata, and such "administrative absorption" was used to strengthen the colonial government's representativeness. In his analysis of Hong Kong government's administrative absorption", Ambrose Y.C. King borrowed the concept of "synarchy" from John King Fairbank.[37] "Synarchy" did not mean equal sharing of power. It referred to Britain's traditional colonial policy of consistently emphasizing the absorption of the local elite into the colonial government so as to reduce the resistance of the governed and to increase the legitimacy of the colonial government.

"Administrative absorption" by the colonial regime had a long history in Hong Kong. The first Chinese, Ng Choy (or Dr. Wu Ting-fang), was appointed to the Legislative Council in February 1880, because of the belief of the then Governor, Sir John Pope Hennessy, that since the Chinese outnumbered the foreigners in Hong Kong, they should be allowed a share in the management of public affairs. Then Sir Shouson Chow was made the first Chinese member of the Executive Council in 1926. After the Second World War, the proportion of Chinese unofficial members in the Legislative Council increased steadily from less than 50% in 1945–1950 to 62.5% in 1960–1963, 77% in 1964–1967, 77% in 1968–1969, and 84% in 1970. According to a study by Ambrose King, the unofficial members of the Legislative and Executive Councils were, with few exceptions, very rich. Before 1964, over 90% of the Chinese unofficial members came from the established rich families of the territory. Since the mid-1960s, members of the "new rich" — the industrialists who made their fortunes after the Second World War — began to be appointed to the legislative and Executive Councils. Of the non-Chinese unofficial members of the two Councils, about three-quarters held the rank of executive director or its equivalent in major banks and industrial/ commercial enterprises.[38]

---

[37] John K. Fairbank, "Synarchy Under the Treaties", in John K. Fairbank (ed.), *Chinese Thought and Institutions*, Chicago: University of Chicago Press, 1957, pp. 163–203.

[38] See Ambrose Yeo-chi King, *op. cit.*, pp. 426–427, 429–430.

Although constitutionally, power was highly concentrated in the hands of the Governor, yet in general, he would not go against the opposition of a majority of unofficial members in the two councils on important issues. In deference to local Chinese opinion, legislation concerning Chinese custom was unlikely to be proposed except on the initiative of the Chinese unofficial members. "Synarchy", or "government by consultation", basically meant that on important policies, the government had consulted the elites of the society and largely secured their consent.

In the 1970s, the government's consultative network expanded considerably. After the "new rich" industrial elite, established professionals in their 30s and 40s also became targets of "administrative absorption". Senior government officials attached much significance to the process, the chosen few were each admitted to an important advisory committee or its sub-committee, and their performance was carefully monitored. Those who demonstrated a positive attitude, whose work proved to be constructive, and whose values were in accordance with the political philosophy of the colonial government would stand a good chance of being appointed as unofficial members of the Legislative Council. In the early 1980s, some pressure group leaders who established themselves as respectable critics of the colonial regime were also admitted into some important advisory committees, and they were often invited to meet the visiting Members of Parliament from London to demonstrate the magnanimity of the colonial government in treating its critics.

The City District Officer Scheme, which started in 1968 as a response to the 1966–1967 riots, also expanded in the 1970s. This enabled the government's consultative network to reach the grassroots and facilitated the absorption of the activists at the grassroots level into its system of advisory committees.[39] In 1972, each City District Office set up within the district a number of area committees whose members were community leaders nominated by the City District Office. In the following year, the government encouraged residents of public housing estates to form mutual aid committees in support of its Fight Crime Campaign and Clean

---

[39] *The City District Officer Scheme, A Report by the Secretary for Chinese Affairs*, Hong Kong: Government Printer, January 1969.

Hong Kong Campaign. Earlier, the government also persuaded the owners of private housing to organize owners' corporations to promote better building management and security.[40] At the informal level, senior government officials entertained activists at small dinners in the Governor's House or large-scale cocktail parties during the Chinese New Year. The granting of honors and medals became more generous, and the lists often included citizens from the lower socioeconomic strata.

In the 1970s, the composition of the Legislative Council also demonstrated marked changes. Unofficial members included almost every profession and social stratum, and the trade unionists, social workers, and church leaders were regarded as spokesmen for the poor. The government also offered leaders of the two established political groups, the Civic Association and the Reform Club, seats in the Legislative Council, though it refused to recognize them as representatives of their respective organizations. Attitudes of government officials towards citizens showed considerable improvement, and the former acquired a better understanding of their status as "public servants". Since the establishment of the Independent Commission Against Corruption in 1974, the problem of corruption had largely been contained. At the same time, remuneration for the civil service, especially the police force, was raised significantly.

On the whole, in the 1970s, demand for political participation among the young generation began to germinate, and ordinary people also learned how to get organized to protect their rights. However, spectacular economic growth and the development of social services offered by the public sector much weakened the community's demand for political participation; and the government's aggressive "administrative absorption" and expansion of its consultative network also softened such demands from the political activists. Throughout the decade, development in political participation was limited to supervision and criticism of the government, influencing government policies and exerting pressure on the

---

[40] See Cho-bun Leung, "Community Participation: The Decline of Residents' Organisations", in the author's edited work, *Hong Kong in Transition, op. cit.*, pp. 354–371; see also David K.K. Chan, "Local Administration in Hong Kong", in Alex Y.H. Kwan and David K.K. Chan (eds.), Hong *Kong Society — A Reader* (Hong Kong: Hong Kong Writers' and Publishers' Cooperative, 1986), pp. 111–135.

government through mobilizing public opinion, organizing pressure groups and *ad hoc* campaigns. There were no strong demands for constitutional reforms from the community, and the government was not tested by any serious challenge.

IV "Self-administration" and the Development of Representative Government

During the Sino-British negotiations on Hong Kong's future, the Chinese leaders promised "*gangren zhigang*", or "self-administration" to the community. In its *Green Paper: The Future Development of Representative Government in Hong Kong* released in July 1984, the Hong Kong government pledged "to develop progressively a system of government the authority for which is firmly rooted in Hong Kong, which is able to represent authoritatively the views of the people of Hong Kong and which is more directly accountable to the people of Hong Kong".[41] The respective positions of the Chinese and British governments then greatly boosted the morale of the advocates for democracy in Hong Kong. Even ordinary citizens without much interest in political participation realized that as colonial rule was to be terminated in 1997, and none of the parties concerned wanted the future Hong Kong Special Administrative Region (HKSAR) to be directly administered by Beijing, the establishment of an HKSAR government with a high degree of autonomy, as stipulated in the Sino-British Joint Declaration, would be a natural development. A government with a high degree of autonomy, it was hoped, would be an important guarantee for the maintenance of the status quo for 50 years.

The Sino-British Joint Declaration promised that the "current social and economic systems in Hong Kong will remain unchanged", and this was welcomed by all parties concerned and by the people of Hong Kong.[42] However, political reform became a source of controversy, not

---

[41] *Green Paper: The Further Development of Representative Government in Hong Kong*, Hong Kong: Government Printer, July 1984.
[42] *A Draft Agreement between the Government of the United Kingdom of Great Britain and Northern Ireland and the Government of the People's Republic of China on the Future of Hong Kong*, Hong Kong: Government Printer, September 26, 1984, p. 12.

only between Beijing and London, but also within the Hong Kong community itself.

After the release of the Green Paper in July 1984, some business leaders openly opposed direct elections to the Legislative Council which the Green Paper had proposed. A few even want so far as to indicate that they would prefer Beijing's appointees to those directly elected to administer Hong Kong. These businessmen had probably made the logical choice to protect their interests. They believed in the Chinese leadership's sincerity and determination to maintain stability and prosperity. They were therefore confident that the Chinese authorities would respect and promote their interests. An elected government, accountable to the electorate and hoping to win the next election, would find it difficult to resist the pressure to offer more social services, which in turn would damage business interests.

Further, it was thought that a Hong Kong government appointed by Beijing would be more stable and predictable than an elected one (Lee Kuan Yew and his colleagues thought likewise).[43] Many business leaders believed that they had the experience and ability to deal with Beijing's appointees, but lacked the confidence to bargain with an elected administration accountable to the electorate. They harbored deep suspicions of the leaders of grassroots pressure groups, and felt that they had no values in common with them. Finally, these businessmen felt that a government appointed by Beijing would be able to maintain a direct dialogue with Chinese leaders and would therefore be in a better position to withstand pressures from cadres of Chinese organs in Hong Kong, from the Guangdong provincial government, or from the relevant ministries in Beijing.

On the other hand, Hong Kong's younger generation and intelligentsia argued that only an elected administration could effectively maintain the territory's international status and promote the interests of its citizens.

---

[43] In 1990s, Lee Kuan Yew and some other leaders of Asia supported those "Asian values", which were more appropriate for Asia country than Western liberal democracy with its emphasis on elections and individual freedoms. See for example Fareed Zakaria, "Culture is destiny — A Conversation with Lee Kuan Yew", *Foreign Affairs*, March/April 1994, https://www.foreignaffairs.com/articles/asia/1994-03-01/conversation-lee-kuan-yew-0.

After 1997, substantial co-ordination between the central government in Beijing and the government of the HKSAR would become essential. In handling this relationship, the people of Hong Kong would need a government directly accountable to them. Further, the territory's economic development depended on the maintenance of its existing international status and identity. In order to maintain this status and to be able to negotiate with other governments on economic and trade issues, Hong Kong, as SAR under Chinese sovereignty, had to be recognized and accepted by the international community. An elected government would be best placed to win this recognition and acceptance, and be able to safeguard and promote Hong Kong's interests in non-political international negotiations unrelated to China's sovereignty. Most important of all, self-administration was what attracted them most in the return of the territory to China.[44]

In fact, if Hong Kong was to develop a genuine system of representative government, the local business leaders would be prepared to imitate their counterparts in the West and form political parties to articulate their interests. In 1984–1985, two members of both the Legislative and Executive Councils, Maria Tam and Allen Lee, were making preparations to form political groups which would develop into political parties. Such political groups would include the central figures in the establishment as well as representatives from the established rich families and major business conglomerates. Maria Tam even formally launched the Progressive Hong Kong Society.[45] Nevertheless, if the political system of the future HKSAR did not differ too much from the existing colonial political system, the above preparations would become unnecessary.

In 1982–1985, concern for the future of the territory and the challenge posed by the development of representative government contributed to the organization and development of many political groups and grassroots pressure groups. At the time of Mrs. Margaret Thatcher's visit to China in September 1982, many Hong Kong people wanted a leader like Prime

---

[44] See the author's "Case for democracy", *South China Morning Post*, December 11, 1986.
[45] See the author's "The Present Situation of the Development of Hong Kong's Political Forces" (in Chinese), *Hong Kong Economic Journal Monthly*, Vol. 9, No. 2, May 1985, pp. 25 and 34.

Minister Lee Kuan Yew of Singapore. Two years later, concerned citizens were raising a more sophisticated question — could a strong political party emerge that was acceptable to the Chinese authorities, the British administration in Hong Kong, and the local business community? The hope was that this party could encompass respected figures from all social strata and therefore be in a position to win the community's confidence, emerge victorious in all major elections, and then form a government capable of maintaining the territory's stability and prosperity.

In the district board elections in March 1985, the number of voters reached a record high of 476,500, a milestone in Hong Kong's political development. Assuming that each of the 501 candidates had recruited 100 friends to campaign for him or her, the number of activists participating in the elections would have been 50,000. These figures reflected a considerable degree of politicisation of the community.[46]

The September 1985 elections to the Legislative Council were based on the electoral college, comprising members of the district boards, the Urban Council, and the Provisional Regional Council, and the functional constituencies.[47] Qualified voters therefore only numbered about 70,000 and those who actually voted amounted to about 25,000. The scale of political mobilization was limited as many people were unaware of the elections, but they were nevertheless a significant step in Hong Kong's political development. Twenty-four of the 56 Legislative Councillors had to be accountable to their respective constituencies, unlike the appointed unofficial members, who were accountable to the Governor of Hong Kong (who made the appointments). Even the oath of allegiance was changed — it might then be directed to the citizens of Hong Kong or to the Queen. In fact, most of the newly-elected unofficial members opted for the former.

---

[46] See the author's "The 1985 District Board Elections in Hong Kong", in his edited work, *Hong Kong in Transition, op. cit.*, pp. 67–87.

[47] The nine functional constituencies returning 12 unofficial members comprised the commercial, industrial, financial, labour, social services, educational, legal, social services, educational, legal, medical, and engineering and associated professions. See *White Paper: The Further Development of Representative Government in Hong Kong*, Hong Kong: Government Printer, November 1984, p. 17.

These elections facilitated the development of political groups in Hong Kong. Middle-class political groups were prompted to develop their organizations at the grassroots level and establish close ties with the grassroots pressure groups. At the same time, they became concerned with the social issues at the district level and took part in the related campaigns for citizens' rights. This process contributed to the expansion of almost all political groups.

Elections to the Legislative Council based on the electoral college, as well as the elections of district board chairmen and committee chairmen within the district boards, exposed the limitations of the elected members operating on an individual basis and encouraged various forms of coalitions within the district boards. The government, through the appointment of one third of the district board members, exercised considerable influence in the above elections. In fact, the grassroots pressure groups and the middle-class political groups had limited success in the elections of district board chairmen and the following elections to the Legislative Council based on the electoral college. In all the elections in 1985, both Maria Tam, leader of the Progressive Hong Kong Society, and Allen Lee, who was then organizing a political party were in active support of many candidates. In fact, some of the candidates took the initiative of enlisting their support. Such campaign activities naturally played a role in extending party politics into the new Legislative Council.

In response to this accelerated politicisation and increase in political participation, the Chinese officials responsible for Hong Kong and Macau affairs attempted to cool down the political fever through various channels. Officials of the New China News Agency in Hong Kong also tried to convey two messages in their contacts with the local community. The first was that, according to the Sino-British Joint Declaration, the British government's commitment was to return the sovereignty and administration of the territory to China, not to the people of Hong Kong. The second was that when the Chinese authorities promised to maintain the status quo for 50 years after 1997, they were referring to the status quo at the time of the conclusion of the Joint Declaration, not to the situation in 1997.

The Chinese authorities' dissatisfaction with the rapid process of political reforms and their suspicions of the intent of the Hong Kong government finally led to the public warning issued by Xu Jiatun, head of the Hong Kong branch of the New China News Agency, in November 1985. In his first press conference held since his arrival two years earlier, Xu warned that political reforms in the territory in the transitional period should converge with the Basic Law. Since then, it appeared that both London and the British administration in Hong Kong had abandoned the initiative regarding political reforms in the transitional period, and their officials only emphasized a convergence with the Basic Law.[48]

By the spring of 1988, it was clearly revealed that the mainstream view within the Basic Law Drafting Committee favoured an "executive-led" government for the future HKSAR, with power concentrated in the hands of the Chief Executive.[49] In accordance with the Sino-British Joint Declaration, the Central People's Government in Beijing would appoint the Chief Executive and the principal officials of the HKSAR government, and the exercise of the power of the appointments would be "substantial" rather than symbolic. The Chief Executive would be elected by a grand electoral college of about 600, which would also have the power of electing representatives to one-quarter of the seats in the legislature. Further, the first government and legislature of the HKSAR would be elected by an Election Committee formed by a Preparatory Committee appointed by the National People's Congress, thus giving Beijing a large measure of control. A leader of the local "democratic camp", Szeto Wah, attacked the system as "dictatorship of the grand electoral college", and he asked members of the "democratic camp" to be prepared to remain in opposition for 20 years. On the other hand, Ronald Li, then chairman of the Hong Kong Stock Exchange, made a statement at an international investment conference which perhaps best reflected the conservative business community's attitude. Li declared: "Hong Kong is a colony. It is a dictatorship, although a benevolent one. It is and has been a British

---

[48] See the author's "Hong Kong: the pressure to converge", *International Affairs* (London), Vol. 63, No. 2, Spring 1987, pp. 271–283.

[49] See the Drafting Committee for the Basic Law, *The Draft Basic Law of the Hong Kong Special Administrative Region of the People's Republic of China (for solicitation of opinions)*, Hong Kong: Basic Law Consultative Committee, April 1988.

colony, and it's going to be a Chinese colony, and as such it will prosper. We do not need free elections here."[50]

In the 1980s, the development of social services provided by the public sector entered a stage of consolidation. The rapid economic growth in the 1970s and the ambitious programs of the MacLehose administration had largely satisfied the community's basic demand for social services. Anticipating slower economic growth in the future, and in view of the natural expansion of the existing programs, the government has had to reconsider its various social service commitments. The increase in the ratio of Hong Ownership Scheme flats to rental public housing flats, the doubling of rents for public-housing tenants whose incomes exceeded the income limits for applicants and who had been residing in public housing for more than 10 years, the establishment of an independent Hospital Authority to manage public hospitals, etc., all demonstrated the government's intention to limit its social service commitments. Due to the uncertainty over Hong Kong's future, Beijing and all parties concerned wanted to maintain the territory's attraction to investors, and thus much weakened the demand for more social services and a greater degree of income redistribution. A good example was the government's plain rejection of the proposal for a central provident fund scheme.

The conservative business leaders' attacks on "free lunches" (social service programs of the public sector) resulted in considerable self-restraint among the pressure groups within the "democratic camp". In the five years since the Sino-British Joint Declaration, the government offered no new major social welfare programs, nor had the community made any specific demand. The proposed central provident fund scheme involved no direct financial burden on the part of the government. The local community was aware of Beijing's demand for balanced budgets, and in the late 1980s, the Governor and the Financial Secretary indicated that the expenditure of the public sector should be kept at the level of about 16% of the territory's gross domestic product.

Besides the above factors, Hong Kong's traditional political culture encouraged self-reliance, and the past spectacular economic growth, as well as the anxiety over the future, had lowered the community's

---

[50] *South China Morning Post*, June 17, 1987.

expectations of social services from the government. Hence, the contraction of the public sector and the reduction in the growth of social services had not caused much dissatisfaction in the community, and there were no indications that people were prompted to satisfy their demand for social services through political participation. Unless Hong Kong's economy deteriorated severely, the situation would probably remain unchanged.

Regarding the development of representative government, the Chinese authorities' strong position and the Hong Kong government's concessions successfully suppressed the community's expectations of a democratic political system. A survey in 1985 conducted by H.C. Kuan and S.K. Lau of the Chinese University of Hong Kong indicated that only 22.3% of the respondents believed that China would genuinely let Hong Kong people administer Hong Kong.[51] The percentage was probably much lower in 1988. In the second half of the 1980s, because of the concern over the territory's future, the Hong Kong people demonstrated a fairly high degree of acceptance of such concepts as representative government, democracy, political participation, etc., but those who were committed to the cause of democracy were a very small minority. The above survey also showed that a majority of the respondents strongly hoped to maintain social stability in Hong Kong. Such fears of change and of political confrontation were certainly not encouraging for the further development of representative government in the territory.

The community's response to Beijing's opposition to the development of representative government was an upsurge of interest in emigration. On May 16, 1988, *Ming Po* (a Hong Kong Chinese newspaper) published the results of an opinion survey indicating that 24% of the respondents wanted to emigrate. Among those with tertiary education, the percentage was as high as 45.5%.[52] The irony was that most people did not want to emigrate because there would not be democracy in Hong Kong. Rather,

---

[51] 43.9% of the respondents indicated that they had no faith in the Chinese authorities' promise, and 33.8% remained undecided. See Hsin-chi Kuan and Siu-kai Lau, "The Civil Self in a Changing Polity: The Case of Hong Kong", in Kathleen Cheek-Milby and Miron Mushkat (eds.), *Hong Kong: The Challenge of Transformation*, Hong Kong: Centre of Asian Studies, University of Hong Kong, 1989.

[52] The survey was commissioned by the newspaper and conducted in early May 1988.

they had no confidence in Hong Kong's future and China's promises. They obviously did not accept the socialist system in China. It appeared that businessmen wanted to emigrate for the same reasons, not because they feared that Hong Kong might become a welfare state as a result of the development of representative government in the territory. After all, the vast majority of them were emigrating to the English-speaking democracies of the U.S., Canada, and Australia.

At least 90% of the population could not emigrate, and they could only hope for the best. To them, the maintenance of their existing lifestyle — without democracy — was quite acceptable. There were already signs that the traditional political apathy had gradually returned. In March 1988, the voter turnout rate dropped considerably in the district board elections; and people showed little interest in the discussions about the Basic Law and the development of representative government.[53] The total circulation of serious news magazines and political publications was also in decline.

The controversies relating to political reforms, however, led to a confrontation between the so-called "conservative camp" and the "democratic camp". Serious cleavages existed within the strata of political activists, and destroyed any consensus regarding the political system of the HKSAR and future political development. Moreover, the positions of Beijing and London on Hong Kong in the second half of the 1980s made many local people felt that they had been betrayed, and this had damaged the legitimacy of the existing British administration and the future HKSAR government.

On May 31, 1987, *South China Morning Post* published the results of an opinion survey on the recently released *Green Paper: The 1987 Review of Developments in Representative Government*. In response to a question on whether or not they believed that public opinion would affect the government's decision on the options regarding political reforms listed in the Green Paper, only 47% of the respondents gave a positive answer, 36% said no, and 16% gave no views. What deserved attention was that the following categories of respondents showed a below average level of

---

[53] On the March 1988 district board elections, see Emily Lau, 'One point for democracy', *Far Eastern Economic Review*, Vol. 139, No. 12, 24 March 1988, pp. 25–26.

confidence in the influence of public opinion: 41% of those in the age group of 18–24 gave a negative answer; 42% of those in the age group of 25–34 did likewise, and the same applied to 50% of those with tertiary education and 44% of those who earned HK$7,000 or more per month. Why was this sense of political impotence so widespread in a society with freedom of speech and the rule of law? The survey results also cast considerable doubt on the Hong Kong government's claim as a "government by consultation", at least when China's interests were at stake.

V Conclusion

Huntington's hypotheses on political participation in developing countries to a certain extent helped us to understand why the desire for political participation remained low in Hong Kong in the post-war period. The refugee mentality under colonial rule was a kind of political alienation. In the lower socioeconomic strata, this political alienation generated a sense of political impotence, resulting in little desire for political participation. The feeling of isolation among those who had moved to the big city from the rural areas in China and the failure to understand English also strengthened this sense of political impotence. Among those in the upper-middle and upper socioeconomic strata, the limitations of political reform produced another type of political alienation, the feeling that political participation was meaningless. This minority was largely the beneficiary of the status quo, and naturally, they had no strong commitment to work for constitutional reforms. Situated at the periphery of China also brought uncertainty to the prospects of any thorough constitutional reform; this fear of the unknown prompted the majority of the people to opt for the maintenance of the status quo. After all, rapid economic growth and stable colonial rule made Hong Kong people the fortunate ones in Asia. Moreover, behind the benevolence of the colonial administration, there was also a strong "stick" of suppression.

The post-war education system had a significant impact on the territory's political culture and political participation. Education produced the professionals and skilled workers who worked for the economic development of Hong Kong, which in turn reduced the desire for political participation. The open and competitive education system also offered an important channel for upward social mobility which much weakened class-consciousness. Those who had succeeded in the education system joined an English-speaking elite which was also proud of its acquaintance with the British culture. This elite was then gracefully incorporated by the establishment. This process much reduced the contradiction between the colonial government and the local elite, and enhanced the former's legitimacy. The education system had therefore contributed significantly to the elimination of the two major contradictions most likely to emerge in the colony.

The education system had successfully suppressed any nationalist sentiments too. Its pragmatic, utilitarian values and emphasis on self-reliance were important factors behind the territory's political culture depicted as "utilitarian familism". An elite with such values could easily be co-opted by the government through the process of "administrative absorption"; and before the end of the 1960s, politically ambitious members of this elite failed to cooperate with the lower socioeconomic strata.

The nature of the colonial government denied the business community most channels of gaining political power. The political philosophy of the colonial regime also gave no such incentive to the business leaders. Hence, senior government officials were in general left undisturbed by vested interests, and could maintain law and order in a fair and neutral manner. Since the 1960s, they could also take the initiative in improving labour legislation and providing social services.

Demands for political participation began to emerge in the 1970s. At the same time, the government vastly expanded its social service commitments, and its "administrative absorption" evolved to encompass the elites from all social strata. Its image was also improved by attempts to be a "government by consultation", while the China factor continued to block demands for thorough political reforms. Economic development consistently raised the people's living standards and lowered their demand for political participation, and the community was even proud of not being affected by the "British disease", the symptoms of which included too much social welfare, militant trade unionism, frequent labor disputes, decline in economic competitiveness, etc. As no obvious contradictions existed, radical ideologies were unattractive to the community. In sum, the dominant values in society and the education system prevented the emergence of a "participatory" political culture.[54]

The Sino-British negotiations generated expectations of autonomy and democracy, but Beijing's position soon suppressed the community's demand for democracy. However, the process also created a confidence crisis and an upsurge in emigration; it also damaged any consensus on the political system of the future SAR and the legitimacy of its government.

Hong Kong's prevailing political culture offered meagre support for the advocates of representative government. When the emerging enthusiasm for political participation in 1984–1985 encountered strong resistance from Beijing and the conservative business community, it wilted rapidly. In contrast to Taiwan and South Korea, the sub-culture in support of political participation and democracy in Hong Kong was very weak. The local movement for democracy could mobilize at most only about 20,000 people for a peaceful gathering. To a certain extent, the Hong Kong people realized that the future of the territory was not in their hands, but was largely determined by political and economic reforms in China. This sense of political impotence, as well as the emigration opportunities available for the middle class, effectively eroded whatever forces the democracy movement could gather.

The more than 90% of the population who could not emigrate simply hoped to maintain their existing lifestyle; those who were preparing to emigrate also wanted to maintain the status quo to facilitate the withdrawal of their assets. Fear of change and confrontation, along with eagerness to compromise, became the dominant values of the society, and they were reinforced by the self-censorship of the mass media. Lowering one's demands or emigration became the natural choices of the politically alienated.[55]

Many people failed to realize that in the absence of democracy, liberty and the rule of law were mere gifts bestowed on the people by their rulers and liable to be withdrawn by them at will. Those who opposed democracy

---

[54] See G.A. Almond and S. Verba, *The Civic Culture*, Princeton; Princeton University Press, 1963.

[55] See Albert O. Hirschman, *Exit, Voice and Loyalty: Responses to Decline in Firms, Organisations and States*, Cambridge: Harvard University Press, 1970.

and direct elections in Hong Kong often argued that despite the absence of constitutional democracy in the territory, there was ample liberty and the rule of law was observed. What they failed to notice was that the colonial government in Hong Kong ultimately had to be accountable to a democratic government willing to defend freedom and the rule of law. Many Third World countries experienced an erosion of their democratic political systems after independence. Under such circumstances, they might be able to retain their stability and prosperity, but liberty and the rule of law were bound to be adversely affected. Those who wanted only liberty and the rule of law, but not democracy, should ponder these historical lessons.

As can be seen from the above, Huntington's gap hypothesis was obviously useful in explaining political participation in developing countries, including Hong Kong. The gap hypothesis proved to be more powerful when the relationship between the gap and the shaping of the political culture had been further analyzed. This in turn introduced an evolutionary and dynamic aspect to the gap hypothesis. The lack of development of a participatory political culture in Hong Kong and Singapore was certainly a very important factor in explaining why democracy failed to develop in these two Asian dragons despite the fact that the normal pre-requisites for a democratic political system had all existed.

On the other hand, Hong Kong had a unique external factor. The accountability of the colonial administration to the democratic government in London served as an assurance, making benevolent despotism almost a blessing. A change of this external factor would certainly have serious repercussions, and that was why the Chinese leaders made the offer of "one country, two systems".

Student demonstrations in Beijing since the death of Hu Yaobang, former general secretary of the Communist Party of China, on April 15, 1989, and subsequent developments leading to the brutal military crackdown on Beijing students of June 3–4 highlighted in the strongest possible way the importance of democracy and freedom in China and Hong Kong. Since 1984, the Hong Kong people had become increasingly aware that their destiny was no longer entirely in their hands, and that much depended on developments in China. In the wake of the Tiananmen

Incident, they established a very strong identity with their compatriots in China while intensely following the recent tragic events there. A conviction emerged that while freedom, human rights, and democracy could not be guaranteed in China, they could not be well protected in Hong Kong after 1997. When over one million people in Hong Kong marched for democracy and freedom in China and against the suppression of the student movement on May 21, 1989, 90% of the participants were marching for the first time in their lives. They were strongly motivated by anger and shock at what was happening in China, and at the same time, struck by a sense of despair and insecurity regarding the territory's future. The vast majority of them marched again on the two following Sundays.

Before the massacre in Beijing on June 3–4, 1989, the Hong Kong people's confidence was largely based on the Chinese leadership's goal of modernizing China. The local community considered this a legitimate goal widely supported by the Chinese people, and believed that maintenance of the status quo in Hong Kong would enable the territory to contribute to China's modernization. This was the foundation of the confidence in the Sino-British Joint Declaration and various promises made by the Chinese leaders to Hong Kong. The developments in China in the summer of 1989 showed that the Chinese leadership could totally disregard this goal and related priorities. This meant that trust in the Chinese leadership, the Sino-British Joint Declaration, and the draft Basic Law had been badly shaken.

In response to the developments in China, it was expected that the proportion of the population seeking emigration would significantly expand, a prediction which was substantiated by the marked increase in emigration-related enquiries received by the consulates general of countries like the U.S., Canada, and Australia in the second half of 1989. Demand for the right of abode for the 3.25 million holders of British Dependent Territory Citizen (BDTC) passports was stepped up, while attempts were also made to seek some form of international guarantee for Hong Kong people's rights and freedoms beyond 1997. At the same time, there emerged a broad consensus for the acceleration of the development of representative government in the territory in the transitional period before 1997.

The major challenge to the democracy movement at this stage would be to channel the energy of the awakened people to constructive work. Obviously, mass rallies could not be organized every Sunday. The movement should as soon as possible launch a political party which would offer a constructive program based on the new consensus in support of a more democratic system of government.

Discussions on the future political system of the HKSAR, however, would be meaningful only when the following two conditions are met. The first was that there would have to be demonstrable political consensus in Hong Kong on which an appeal to Beijing and, to a lesser extent, the international community could be based. The second was that before 1997, there would have to be a credible and legitimate government in China which considered modernization the most important goal of the nation and values Hong Kong's actual and potential contribution to its modernization programme.

Acknowledgement

Originally published as Cheng, Joseph Y.S., "Political Modernisation in Hong Kong", *The Journal of Commonwealth & Comparative Politics*, Vol. 27, Iss. 3, 1989, pp. 294–320. Reproduced with kind permission from the publisher.

Chapter 3

The Future of Hong Kong: Surveys of the Hong Kong People's Attitudes

In the late 1970s and early 1980s, there was a great deal of discussion about the future of Hong Kong and the lease of the New Territories.[1] A number of civic groups, academics, and legal experts in Hong Kong suggested ways whereby a settlement could be negotiated, but the main purpose of this chapter is to study the attitudes of the Hong Kong people on the territory's future through studying and analyzing a number of well conducted polls carried out in 1982–1983. Five surveys, each polling a separate sample and using different approaches to the questions, will be summarized and analyzed in this chapter.

Since all parties concerned wanted to maintain the stability and prosperity of Hong Kong, any arrangement to be reached therefore had to satisfy the desire and demands of the Hong Kong people. Otherwise, there would certainly be an exodus of talent and capital; even for those who could not afford to emigrate, morale and enthusiasm for socioeconomic development could no longer be guaranteed. Stability and prosperity could hardly be maintained under such circumstances. Rigorously conducted opinion surveys presented a reliable indicator of the attitudes of the Hong Kong people who, largely due to political apathy and a sense of political

---

[1] David Bonavia, *Hong Kong 1997*, Hong Kong: South China Morning Post, 1983 and the author's "The Future of Hong Kong: A Hong Kong Belonger's View", *International Affairs* (London), Vol. 58, No. 3, July 1982, pp. 476–488.

impotence, and in the absence of an elected government, were reluctant to articulate their interests.[2] They should be carefully studied and might well serve to generate international support for a settlement in accordance with the desires of the five and a half million people. After all, though China and Britain might come to a settlement through a process of negotiation, the people of Hong Kong would be informed only when all details had been finalized, and it was hard to have full confidence that the two countries would keep the Hong Kong people's interests at heart. Finally, as shown below, there was a considerable shift of attitudes within a fairly short period of time, and it would be interesting to attempt to explain this shift.

I Preparations for Sino-British Negotiations

In September 1982, the British Prime Minister, Mrs. Margaret Thatcher, visited Beijing and came to an agreement with the Chinese leaders to "enter into talks through diplomatic channels with the common aim of maintaining the stability and prosperity of Hong Kong."[3] Nonetheless, serious differences between the two sides on the questions of the "unequal treaties" and sovereignty over Hong Kong, Kowloon, and the New Territories were revealed.[4] This conflict severely shook business confidence in Hong Kong, and the local stock market as well as the value of the Hong Kong dollar plummeted, drawing international attention to the uncertainty over Hong Kong's future as a capitalist enclave.

The Chinese leaders resolutely stated their intention to regain sovereignty over all three areas, as well as their view that the treaties signed by the Qing Dynasty government and the British Empire

---

[2] For studies of Hong Kong people's political apathy as well as their political values and behavior in general, see S.K. Lau, *Society and Politics in Hong Kong*, Hong Kong: The Chinese University of Hong Kong Press, 1982 and Ambrose Y.C. King, "Administrative Absorption of Politics in Hong Kong: Emphasis on the Grass Roots Level", *Asian Survey*, Vol. 15, No. 5, May 1975, pp. 422–439.

[3] Reuter (Beijing), September 24, 1982, in *South China Morning Post* (Hong Kong), September 25, 1982.

[4] For a good analysis of the questions of the "unequal treaties" and sovereignty over Hong Kong, Kowloon and the New Territories, see Anthony Dicks, "Treaty, Grant, Usage of Sufference? Some Legal Aspects of the Status of Hong Kong", *China Quarterly*, No. 95, September 1983, pp. 427–455.

relinquishing Hong Kong and Kowloon and leasing the New Territories were unequal treaties that China should not recognize. The British side, on the other hand, persisted in its belief that the treaties were legal and valid.

From the British government's point of view, the New Territories lease was based on the second Anglo-Manchu Convention of Beijing, concluded in 1898, which together with the first Anglo-Manchu Convention of Beijing in 1860 (ceding the Kowloon Peninsula) and the Anglo-Manchu Treaty of Nanjing in 1842 (ceding Hong Kong Island), provided the legitimacy for British rule over Hong Kong. The British government could not therefore ignore the New Territories lease, or any of the clauses of the Treaty of Nanjing and the First and Second Conventions of Beijing. Theoretically, it could choose to return to China only the New Territories and continue its rule over Hong Kong and Kowloon after June 30, 1997, when the lease expired; in practice, however, according to the development plans of the Hong Kong government, over half of the total population and a large portion of the industrial plants would be in the New Territories by 1997. It was simply impossible to move the Hong Kong–Guangdong border southward to Boundary Street in Kowloon.

To recognize the treaties and the lease, not to say extend the latter (as some had suggested), would be contrary to the Chinese government's declared goal to terminate all unequal treaties, an important aim of the Chinese Communist revolution. The Chinese Communist leaders believed that they had to be accountable to the whole Chinese nation for this, and it was difficult to imagine that any Chinse leader would sacrifice a principle of such importance for the sake of economic advantage.

The British government was also reluctant to acknowledge Chinese sovereignty over Hong Kong, partly because of its insistence that the treaties were valid, and more importantly still, it appeared that the British government wanted to use this as a bargaining chip, for Mrs. Thatcher indicated that the treaties might be revised through negotiations.

In response to the British negotiating positions, the Chinese government's stand hardened, rejecting any suggestion of retaining the British administration beyond 1997, and presenting its own scheme of "*gangren zhigang*" (Hong Kong people governing Hong Kong) which amounted to Hong Kong becoming a Special Administrative Region (SAR) under Chinese sovereignty, enjoying the privileges of self-administration and retaining its current systems.

Under the existing circumstances, the interests and rights of Hong Kong citizens were obviously not well protected. The Chinese government having then stated its position definitely, the people of Hong Kong generally felt very uncertain about their future, as change appeared inevitable. The middle class preferred to emigrate, given the opportunity. At least they would like their children to study and settle abroad, so that the next generation would not be affected by the current uncertainties. Many had also begun to invest in real estate in countries like Canada and the United States (U.S). There were no statistics available; but, to judge by the pages and pages of overseas real estate advertisements in the local newspaper, such investments had become highly popular. Even a small country like the Dominican Republic set up an office in Hong Kong to sell property, and it automatically granted any real estate owner the right of permanent residence. This person could even become a citizen after staying in the country for half a year; further, it was possible to hold the Dominican passport concurrently with another issued, say, by the British government. Such terms seemed to suggest that the buyers were concerned more about the right of permanent residence in a foreign country than with real estate investment.

Those Hong Kong citizens who had travelled abroad could see that living standards in Hong Kong compared very favorably with those of advanced countries (though housing and transport continued to be problems); moreover, Hong Kong was famous for fashion and entertainment, and at reasonable prices too. Most of those who had migrated overseas were professionals and technicians, and their occupational options after emigration were limited; nor could they take much part in the politics and public affairs of their countries of residence. Their mental and psychological satisfaction was often lower than before. Furthermore, the opportunity cost of migration was very high, and this was common knowledge. Indeed, the main reason for so many middle-class people migrating overseas was simply lack of confidence in the future of Hong Kong.

Owing to this lack of confidence, most citizens did not take much interest in public affairs. They suspected that both the British government and the British authority in Hong Kong had already been preparing for the worst, and meanwhile were merely making use of Hong Kong and would not commit themselves with regard to the future. The new British Nationality Act (which came into force on January 1, 1983) was a good example of the minimization of British responsibility towards Hong Kong.[5] Under the Act, Hong Kong's 2.6 million Chinese who were registered as British subjects would no longer be thus designated and would instead become "citizens of the British dependent territory of Hong Kong". This meant that when Hong Kong ceased to become a British dependent territory, these people would become stateless. It was natural that the people in Hong Kong could not develop a sense of belonging, and did not feel part of a community that enjoyed citizens' rights and responsibilities.

Even when negotiations between China and Britain were being conducted on Hong Kong's future, they were held in top secrecy, and the citizens of Hong Kong were not informed until an agreement had been reached. The people would simply have to accept this. If the negotiations were made public, the complicated process would merely arouse unnecessary speculation and worry in the community. Negotiations, then, had to be conducted in secrecy. Since Hong Kong did not have any elections (except the unimportant Urban Council elections and the District Board elections), Hong Kong's citizens could not choose representatives to articulate and safeguard their interests in the negotiations. Even if they were to elect representatives, it seemed unlikely that China and Britain would accept their legal status and allow them to participate. Opinion surveys therefore appeared to be the most important indicator so far of the Hong Kong people's attitudes towards the future of Hong Kong.

II Important Opinion Surveys Regarding Attitudes on Hong Kong's Future: Hong Kong Reform Club's Survey

The first important poll was a telephone survey carried out by a market research firm, Survey Research Hong Kong Ltd., for the Hong Kong Reform Club in March 1982.[6] The survey was designed so that the findings were representative of the Hong Kong adult population (aged 20 or over) living in homes with a telephone (93% of families in Hong Kong had

---

[5] See the author's "The British Nationality Bill and Hong Kong Citizens' Rights and Future" (in Chinese), *Ming Pao Monthly* (Hong Kong), No. 186, June 1982, pp. 33–36.

[6] The author would like to thank the Hong Kong Reform Club for allowing him the use of the data in the full report of the survey which had not been published, though summaries of the report appeared in major newspaper in Hong Kong.

telephone then). The objectives of the survey were to establish: (a) the level of knowledge regarding the New Territories lease, (b) the perceived outcome and preferred outcome of the future of Hong Kong after 1997, and (c) attitudes towards and preference between living in Hong Kong and China.

Field work was carried out during March 4–12, 1982. A total of 998 people aged 20 or over were selected for interview by a probability sampling method using the telephone directory as the sampling frame.

The level of knowledge about the New Territories lease was summarized as follows:

	%	Projected Number of People Aged 20 Years or Over
Knew about the lease of the area north of Boundary Street	49%	1.6 million
Knew about the lease but did not know which area	19%	0.6 million
No idea about the lease at all	32%	1.0 million

The level of knowledge was much higher among men than women, and much higher among the young, those with higher income, white-collar workers and students, the better educated, those born in Hong Kong, and holders of British passports issued by the Hong Kong government.

Regarding the perceived outcome and preferred outcome of the future of Hong Kong after 1997, the responses were as follows:

After 1997, Hong Kong	Probable Outcome (%)		Preferred Outcome (%)	
To maintain the *status quo*	43	76	70	85
To become a British trust territory	33		15	
To be taken back by China and under Chinese administration	6		4	
None of the above	1		2	
Don't know	16		9	

Three in four adults expected that Hong Kong would remain under British administration after 1997, either by maintaining the status quo or by becoming a British trust territory. An even higher proportion (85%) preferred Hong Kong to be under British administration after 1997, with 70% in favor of maintaining the status quo, though only 43% predicted this as the most probable outcome.

There was a significant proportion (33%) who expected Hong Kong to become a British trust territory, a solution advocated by the Hong Kong Reform Club. Such an expectation was considerably higher among adults with the highest monthly household income (51%) and adults with tertiary education (49%). The better educated groups expected that a settlement would have to be reached between the British and the Chinese governments, as the expiry of the New Territories lease and the subsequent removal of legitimate British administration there would make it difficult for the status quo to be maintained, and they therefore opted for Hong Kong to become a British trust territory as the best device to maintain the status quo. Two-thirds of the respondents who believed that Hong Kong would remain under British administration after 1997 expected that it would further continue for over 20 years.

If China was to take over Hong Kong in 1997, 58% if the respondents would still prefer to stay Hong Kong, 28% would hope to emigrate overseas, while 4% would return to China. As can be expected, the younger generation, professionals and white-collar workers, and the better educated displayed a considerably greater tendency to emigrate. Among those who would prefer to stay in Hong Kong, the reasons were mainly a matter of habits or emotional ties rather than dissatisfaction with life in China or overseas. On the other hand, the wish to emigrate was mainly related to preference for a freer and more comfortable lifestyle, and a dislike for the Chinese Communist system.

On the question of preferences for living in Hong Kong or China, 86% of the respondents preferred to live in Hong Kong rather than in China. Even among those who preferred to live in Hong Kong to be returned to China and placed under direct Chinese administration after 1997, 76%

still preferred to live in Hong Kong. The major aspects liked about living in Hong Kong were as follows:

	%
Freer life/more liberal	40
Better food	19
Can buy/do anything you like when you have money	13
Better entertainment	9
Everything is available	9
More job opportunities	9
As long as you work, you will get paid	8
Used to living in Hong Kong	8
Freedom of speech	7
Economically more prosperous	7
Convenient transportation	7
Convenient to buy things	6
Better enjoyment	6
Better/fashionable clothing	6
Better living environment	6

There were certainly dissatisfactions about living in Hong Kong, and they were summarized as followers:

	%
High crime rate	27
Poor transportation/congested roads	20
Small living area/poor living environment	20
Too crowded/too many people	20
Life is too tense/hectic	11
High cost of living	6
High rent	6
Air/noise pollution	5

The things that the respondents liked about living in China were:

	%
Spacious home	18
Fresher air	15
Life is less tense/hectic	13
Better scenery/famous landmarks	9
Better living environment	9
Less materialistic/simpler life	7
Homeland/have a sense of belonging	6
Quieter	6

Though the living environment in China was well appreciated, there were serious complaints too and the major dislikes about living in China were as follows:

	%
No freedom/many restrictions	22
Low standard of living	13
Not enough food for everyone	12
Few consumer goods available	7
Too authoritative	7
No liberty to buy things distribution by ration	6
Technology not yet developed	6
Unstable government/policies	5
Inconvenient transportation	5

The data provided by this survey showed that most people in Hong Kong wanted to maintain the status quo after 1997, and there was a general optimism that this could be accomplished, perhaps by turning Hong Kong into a British trust territory. There was obviously inadequate understanding and concern for the issue even in early 1982, as indicated by the level of knowledge of the New Territories lease. That was probably why the Hong Kong community was quite shocked by the Chinese government's subsequent rejection of the retention of the British administration after 1997.

The general optimism prevalent in Hong Kong then was in part based on a blind faith in the survival of Hong Kong. As the status quo had been tolerated by Beijing since 1949, why should the Chinese leadership want to take back Hong Kong by 1997? Further, after the fall of the "Gang of Four" and the shift in emphasis to the Four Modernization, the Chinese leadership began to understand the importance of foreign trade and the introduction of advanced technology and capital from the West; Hong Kong's contribution to China's economic development accordingly became more significant. In addition, the Chinese leaders then were less dogmatic than their predecessors, and seemed likely to adopt a more pragmatic attitude towards the question of Hong Kong. The possibility of China and Britain coming to a negotiated settlement over this historical legacy was therefore correspondingly higher. Consequently there were high hopes before Mrs. Thatcher's visit to China that substantive progress would be achieved during her talks in Beijing on the question of Hong Kong's future.

III The Hong Kong Observers' Poll

The findings of the Hong Kong Reform Club survey were corroborated by those of the Hong Kong Observers poll which was conducted slightly later.[7] The Hong Kong Observers poll was also conducted by Survey Research Hong Kong Ltd., and was probably the most detailed and the best survey ever carried out on this subject.

After a year's preparation, the actual fieldwork was carried out between May 10 and June 11, 1982. One thousand people between the ages of 15 and 60 were interviewed face to face. The people questioned

---

[7] The author was the Chairman of the Hong Kong Observers when the poll was conducted, and he was responsible for the design and the supervision of the poll. He would nonetheless like to thank the Hong Kong Observers for allowing him the use of the data in the full report of the survey which had not been published, though summaries of the report appeared in major newspaper in Hong Kong.

were chosen randomly from sampling frames developed from census data and which divided Hong Kong into eight strata — three each from Hong Kong Island and Kowloon, according to upper (quality) private and lower private housing and public housing, and two from the net territories, lower private and public housing. Households were first chosen at random and one member selected by the Kisch grid method.

A total of 71 questions was asked and each interview lasted about 40 minutes. The information gathered by such a sampling method could be taken to represent the views of 3.3 million people in the 15–60 age group with an accuracy margin of plus or minus 3% at a confidence level of 95%.

The survey initially asked the respondents what importance they attached to money, material comforts, and freedoms; whether their attitudes to life were predicated on the uncertainty of the territory's future, what they liked and disliked about life in Hong Kong, where they considered their roots to be, and what links they had with China. It was believed that these questions would put the respondents at ease and prepare them to answer the most testing questions on the future of Hong Kong; more importantly still, the Hong Kong Observes also considered that the data collected would provide valuable background material to analyze the responses to the questions on Hong Kong's future.

The findings showed that the aspirations of the Hong Kong community were similar to those of people in developing countries — Hong Kong citizens wanted a future. Also, money was not the most important thing in life, nor would all the people want to leave, even if they had the chance. There were obvious trends revealed too — the younger, better educated generation was far more critical, and more demanding. Despite the higher level of awareness existing channels of communication with officialdom among this group, its feelings that these channels were inadequate were also greater.

Money was important to 79% of the respondents, but more to the 25–44 age group and with less education (primary or below). The opportunity to make money is slightly more important (82%). Its importance was almost equal to that of freedom of speech (83%), but is outranked by "comfortable living environment" (85%) and "freedom of choice" (86%), with "a meaningful life" (77%) coming close to the importance of money. Good food was more important (65%) than (other) material comforts (36%). Good clothing was important to 21% of the respondents.

The younger and better educated placed greater importance on intangible like "a meaningful life", while material comforts were more important to the less educated and lower income groups.

The greater importance attached to opportunity to make money, freedom of speech and choice, and a comfortable living environment explained why 86% of the respondents said they liked living in Hong Kong. However, among these, 56% also disliked some aspects of life in the territory. Only 2% of those interviewed had an unmitigated dislike of life in Hong Kong.

When asked for reasons why they liked living in Hong Kong, the main reasons cited were that they were used to life there (27%), they were born there (21%), freedom of speech (12%), and "many job opportunities and good income" (11%).

Aspects which this group disliked were mainly housing (19%), traffic (15%), crime (13%), over-crowding (12%), and the hectic pace of life (6%).

To assess the respondents' attitudes towards the future, interviewers read seven statements and asked respondents whether they agreed or disagreed. Eighty-nine percent agreed that they were trying to save as much as they avoided thinking about the future of Hong Kong because there was nothing they could do about it; 77% agreed that although the future of Hong Kong was uncertain, they were still planning for their own future; 78% agreed that no matter what happened in 1997, people could work hard and create a good future; 73% agreed that regardless of what would happen in 1997, they had to make some contribution to Hong Kong. Only 17% agreed with the statement: "I want to spend as much money as I can now as it may not be useful in future".

When asked whether they regarded Hong Kong as home, 89% said yes — 41% because they were born or had grown up there, but only 11% because they felt a sense of belonging. Among the minority (11%) who did not regard Hong Kong as home, reasons cited include "no sense of belonging", that they were Chinese and regarded China as home, and that Hong Kong was not a country but a colony.

Ethnicity, nationality, and roots were obviously not clear in the respondents' minds. While 65% considered their roots to be in Hong Kong, only 33% said they were "*Heung Kong yan*" (Hong Kong citizens); 61% said they were Chinese, though only 24% considered their roots to be in China; 5% said they did not know where their roots were, while 3% said they were rootless. Predictably, most of those who considered their roots to be in Hong Kong were in the 15–34 age group while those who had their roots in China were mostly from the 35–60 age group. Eighty-two percent of the people had relatives or friends in China.

Regardless of whether they regarded Hong Kong as home or where their roots were, 57% said they would emigrate if they had the chance, against 36% who said they would not.

The survey then went on to probe the respondents' evaluation of the Hong Kong government. There were more people who thought the government was doing a good job looking after the public's interest (36%) than those who thought it was not (24%). However, 23% thought the government's performance was ordinary, while another 17% felt it was good and bad in parts.

Areas where people thought the government had done a good job, in descending order, were housing (30%), the welfare system (22%), education (12%), and the medical system (12%). Only 2% each thought the government was doing a good job in crime and corruption control, and in responding to public opinion. However, housing was also highest on the list of bad performances (24%), followed by crime control (17%) and traffic (15%).

Awareness of existing channels of communication with the government was generally low. People were most aware of two channels — the District Board and the City District Office, but, even so, only 30% of the respondents were aware of them. As for the adequacy of the existing channels of communication, 28% thought they were inadequate, 14% thought they were "all right", while 36% thought they were inadequate. Furthermore, a significant proportion (47%) felt official explanation of politics and measures to the public to be inadequate (particularly among the 15–34 age group and the better educated), compared with 22% who thought they were adequate, and 24% who rated them as "average".

Regarding the questions on Hong Kong's future, the survey first set out to find out the respondents' spontaneous reaction to the term "the future of Hong Kong". Twenty-six percent said it meant the return of Hong Kong to China, 18% referred to 1997 and the New Territories lease, 10% took the phrase to mean economic development, while 29% did not know what it meant. The highest percentages of "don't knows" were among those in the 45–60 age group, with six or less years of schooling and from households with monthly incomes of less than HK$3,000.

The interviewers then read a short statement explaining to the respondents the 1898 Convention of Beijing and asked whether they were concerned about the expiry of the New Territories lease in 1997. Forty-nine percent said they were concerned, 31% not quite, 17% not at all, and 3% said it was beyond their concern.

When asked for reasons, 34% of those expressing concern said it was because their lifestyles or the political/social system would change; 10% said they were concerned about their children's as well as their own future; and 2% each said that Hong Kong would be returned to China, China was not democratic, and they were worried about Hong Kong's economic development as well as employment opportunities.

Among those who were not concerned, 23% said it was because they did not know how to show concern or that it was beyond their concern, 21% said that it only concerned the government, 26% left it to fate, while 7% said 1997 was still a long time away.

As for attitudes towards the issue of Hong Kong's future, 53% said they had never discussed it, 28% seldom did, and 19% often talked about it.

When asked if 1997 was a problem which needed solving, 82% said yes, 9% said no, and 9% replied "don't know". When asked if they had taken precautionary measures, 97% said "no"; and of these, 33% gave as their reason an inability to do so, another 30% were resigned to fate, and 21% said they did not know what to do. The rest were "don't know".

Of the 3% minority who said that they had taken precautionary measures, 48% said they would leave Hong Kong, 19% said they were only "psychologically prepared for whatever will happen", while 10% said they were saving more money.

When asked if the 1997 lease had any effect on the people of Hong Kong, 51% of the respondents said "no", 41% said "a little", while 3% said "a great deal"; and 5% were "don't knows". Among those who thought there were effects, 49% said it was "worrying", 39% said that economic development and investment were affected, 10% said that emigration would increase, and 6% said that property and land values would fall (the total adds up to more than 100% because some mentioned more than one effect).

When asked if the uncertainty was affecting their own lives, 84 said "no", 14% said "yes" while 2% were "don't knows". Among the 14% who said yes, 40% said they would make less long-term investment, 13% said their future was uncertain, 9% talked of emigrating and 8% said they did not dare buy properties. The uncertainty was also a "psychological burden" to 17%.

When asked which of the following five solutions to the 1997 issue they thought were possible, 19% picked maintenance of the status quo, 3% expected Hong Kong to remain under British administration but under Chinese sovereignty, 3% thought of a return of Hong Kong to China, 2% said that Hong Kong would become a Special Economic Zone (SEZ) of China, and 2% said that it would become an independent city-state. However, some respondents also suggested other possible solutions, such as "negotiations between Britain and China" (11%), and the renewal of the New Territories lease (7%), etc. The "don't know" totaled 56%.

When asked which of the five solutions they preferred most as well as least and which they thought most likely, the status quo solution registered the highest percentage in the most preferred (69%) and most likely (39%) categories. "Return to China" was the least preferred (55%) and fourth in the most likely category (7%). Independence was thought most likely by only 3%.

When asked how acceptable they thought each of the five solutions, 95% said maintenance of the status quo was acceptable (figures included who thought the solution was "all right"); 64% felt that way about Hong Kong remaining under British administration but under Chinese sovereignty; 42% about Hong Kong becoming a SEZ; 87% about independence; and 26% thought a return to China acceptable. However, three of the suggested solutions were not understood by some respondents: SEZ (32%), independence (17%), and Hong Kong remaining under British administration but under Chinese sovereignty (15%).

No one thought any of the options, except independence, impossible. Three percent said independence was impossible.

Table 3.1: Solutions Preferred Most and Least

	Total	Sex		Age				Monthly Household Income			Education		
		Men	Women	15–24 Years	25–34 Years	35–44 Years	45–50 Years	Under HK$3000	HK$3000–4999	Over HK$5000	Primary or Below	Secondary	Post-Secondary
	%	%	%	%	%	%	%	%	%	%	%	%	%
Preferred most													
Return Hong Kong to China	3	3	3	3	2	2	6	4	2	3	4	2	3
Special Economic Zone of China	5	6	4	4	6	4	5	4	5	6	4	4	11
Maintain *status quo*	69	71	67	68	68	72	72	67	72	69	72	67	66
Independence	11	9	14	15	14	10	5	13	9	12	9	14	8
Remain under British administration with sovereignty belonging to China	9	11	7	10	10	10	7	8	11	9	6	12	11
Don't know	3	1	4	1	1	3	6	3	2	*	6	*	1
Preferred least													
Return Hong Kong to China	55	51	60	56	59	58	49	56	57	56	57	55	53

(*Continued*)

Table 3.1: (Continued)

	Total	Sex		Age				Monthly Household Income				Education		
		Men	Women	15–24 Years	25–34 Years	35–44 Years	45–50 Years	Under HK $3000	HK $3000–4999	Over HK $5000	Primary or Below	Secondary	Post-Secondary
	%	%	%	%	%	%	%	%	%	%	%	%	%
Special Economic Zone of China	5	5	5	6	3	3	6	5	6	6	5	6	1
Maintain *status quo*	1	1	1	2	1	—	1	*	1	1	1	1	1
Independence	25	32	17	26	25	24	22	25	25	25	20	27	31
Remain under British administration with sovereignty belonging to China	6	4	8	8	5	7	4	7	4	8	5	6	13
Don't know	9	8	9	3	7	8	19	9	8	5	14	5	3

*Less than 0.5%
Based: All aged 15 to 60 years old (3 299 000)
Source: See footnote 7

The main reasons for the acceptability of the status quo solution were satisfaction with the existing situation, that there would be no change, and the freedoms enjoyed at this time. The main reasons given by the minority (5%) who thought the status quo solution unacceptable were poor administration and welfare, inflation, the fact that the lease issue was not yet solved, and that Hong Kong should belong to China.

When asked why Hong Kong remaining under British administration but under Chinese sovereignty was acceptable, the main reasons given were familiarity with British rule and that it meant "no change". Among the 17% who felt this solution was unacceptable, their main reasons were the confusion such a system would create, and that Hong Kong should belong to China.

No clear reasons were given for the acceptability of Hong Kong becoming a SEZ, but among the 23% who thought this unacceptable, the main reasons cited included an end to freedoms, poor Chinese administration, and that economic development would cease.

Among the 37% of respondents who felt that independence was acceptable, an overwhelming 53% gave "freedom from control by others" as the reason. However, an equal 37% said independence was not acceptable. The main reason (56%) was the territory's lack of natural resources.

Those who felt it was acceptable that Hong Kong be returned to China gave no particular reason. Among the 67% who thought this was unacceptable, poor Chinese administration, an unfamiliar new lifestyle, lower living standards, and "no freedom" were the main reasons cited.

When asked what the respondents would do if each of the five solutions materialized, 95% said they would stay in Hong Kong if the status quo was maintained, 2% said they would not worry, 196 said they would try means to go abroad, and 2% said "don't know". When asked if they would emigrate if the chance was provided, 43% of those polled said yes.

Seventy-two percent said they would stay in Hong Kong if it remained under British administration but under Chinese sovereignty, 5% said they would try every means to leave. Three percent said they would not worry and 4% were "don't knows." Fifteen percent did not understand the solution. Again, just under half (46%) of those who had not mentioned leaving said they would emigrate if given the chance.

Table 3.2: Solutions Most Likely to Happen

Preferred most	Total %	Sex Men %	Sex Women %	Age 15–24 Years %	Age 25–34 Years %	Age 35–44 Years %	Age 45–50 Years %	Monthly Household Income Under HK $3000 %	Monthly Household Income HK $3000–4999 %	Monthly Household Income Over HK $5000 %	Education Primary or Below %	Education Secondary %	Education Post-Secondary %
Return Hong Kong to China	7	6	8	8	6	4	6	9	8	4	7	7	—
Special Economic Zone of China	15	16	14	16	15	17	11	13	14	18	11	16	26
Maintain *status quo*	39	40	38	39	41	37	39	40	39	39	40	39	38
Independence	3	3	2	3	3	3	2	3	3	2	3	3	2
Remain under British administration with sovereignty belonging to China	25	28	21	31	24	27	16	22	23	31	15	32	33
Don't know	12	7	17	3	10	12	27	14	13	6	23	3	2

Based: All aged 15–60 years (3 299 000)
Source: See footnote 7

If Hong Kong became independent, 64% would stay, 7% would try every means to leave, 5% said they would not worry, 1% would go to China, 4% said "don't know", and 17% did not understand the term. Forty-five percent of those who had not mentioned leaving would emigrate if they had the chance.

If Hong Kong was to be returned to China, 58% would stay, 22% would try every means to leave, 11% would not worry, 3% would go to China, and 4% were "don't know". Fifty-three percent of those who had not mentioned leaving would emigrate if they had the chance.

It was believed that it was important to define what respondents thought were the most important aspects of the status quo. Eight aspects were mentioned: (1) economic system (37% thought this was the most important), (2) lifestyle (35%), (3) housing (18%), (4) employment (16%), (5) trade (15%), (6) freedom of speech (11%), (7) adequate supply of goods, and (8) freedom to shop and transportation (9%). However, respondents on their part named two other aspects: (1) the political system (10%) and (2) democracy (6%).

When asked when they thought was the latest time for an announcement of a solution, 33% of the respondents said within two years, 20% said within five years, and 18% said within 10 years; 25% said the timing did not matter.

When asked who the respondents thought had the greatest influence in solving the problem of Hong Kong's future, China came out on top with 44%, followed by investors in Hong Kong (23%), and Hong Kong citizens (19%). Only 1% thought the Hong Kong Governor had the greatest influence.

Sixty-two percent of the respondents thought that assurances given so far by Chinese leaders — that investors needed not worry about the future of Hong Kong — were inadequate. Only 32% thought they were adequate; 6% were "don't knows".

Among those who thought that the Chinese assurances were inadequate; 21% felt that if China and Britain were to sign a new agreement, people would cease to worry about the future. Another 19% thought it would be reassuring if China and Britain were to formally announce a solution.

There was a strong reluctance, particularly among the younger generation (the 15–34 age group), the better-off (household incomes exceeding HK$5,000 a month) and the better educated, to purchase flats in China or abroad. A large majority (76%) would buy a flat in Hong Kong if they had the money, but the majority would not buy a flat in China (70%), or in a foreign country (60%) even if they had the money.

Sixty-four percent of the respondents agreed that Hong Kong was of vital importance to China, 9% disagreed; 63% also agreed that Hong Kong relied heavily on China, and 29% disagreed.

While 95% agreed that Hong Kong citizens should play a role in deciding the future of Hong Kong, only 38% thought they would have the ability to influence any decision.

On the whole, the findings of the Hong Kong Observers' survey not only confirmed the prevalent preference of the Hong Kong community for the maintenance of the status quo, but also helped to explain why, namely, that the people in Hong Kong were happy with their existing lifestyles despite the usual complaints of life in a metropolis. It was perhaps significant to note that independence was the second most preferred solution, though it was also believed to be the least likely.

When presented with all the five solutions and asked to predict the most likely solution, only 39% believed that the status quo would be maintained, while 40% considered that some forms of compromise, namely, under British administration with sovereignty belonging to China or becoming an SEZ of China, would be most likely.

Again, a general optimism was revealed in the respondents' attitudes towards the future; and the uncertainty over 1997 at this point still had very little effect on the community. Though 82% of the respondents believed that 1997 was a problem which needed solving, and 49% said that they were concerned with the expiry of the New Territories lease, the level of awareness and understanding of the issue was surprisingly low, and 97% of the respondents had taken no precautionary measures. The reason was simple — they did not know what to do and they felt powerless to do anything. The respondents probably over-estimated Hong Kong's importance to China, as 64% of them agreed that Hong Kong was of vital importance to China while only 9% disagreed; this incidentally could be another cause for the optimism revealed.

Ethnicity, nationality, and roots probably were not only conceptually, but also emotionally confusing for the respondents. Sixty-one percent said they were Chinese; identification with Hong Kong was not strong, less so with the Hong Kong government; there was no attempt to reject China's claim for sovereignty; and the vast majority simply hoped that the status quo would be maintained or that some sort of compromise could be worked out between the Chinese and the British governments. No wonder 57% of the respondents said they would emigrate if they had the chance.

IV Dr. Kenneth Leung's Survey

In the above survey, 23% of the respondents shrewdly calculated that the investors in Hong Kong had the greatest influence on solving the problem of Hong Kong's future. Given the common goal of the Chinese and the British governments to maintain the stability and prosperity in Hong Kong, they certainly had a point. An opinion poll on the "best possible arrangement for Hong Kong's status after 1997" among the influential Hong Kong business community conducted by Dr. Kenneth Y.Y. Leung in May 1982 provided valuable information on their attitudes.[8]

Dr. Leung used self-administered mailed questionnaires which were sent to 2,906 companies. The companies were selected by the systematic probability sampling method from "the list of manufacturers" and "the list of services" in the *Business Directory of Hong Kong* 1981, published by the Current Publications Company, Hong Kong. Within a specified period of 29 days, a total of 545 usable questionnaires was returned, producing a return rate of 19%. The 545 companies had an estimated total investment of over HK$6,713.5 million in Hong Kong, and had more than 100,050 employees. Two major weaknesses of this survey, however, were a low return rate and the lack of guarantee that the questionnaires were completed, as requested, by the companies' policymakers.

---

[8] The author would like to thank Dr. Kenneth Y.Y. Leung for allowing him the use of the data in the full report of the survey which had not been published, though summaries of the report appeared in major newspapers in Hong Kong.

The survey mainly concentrated on three questions. The first question was on the best time as perceived by the respondents for Beijing to announce its decision/position regarding the political future of Hong Kong after 1997, and the responses are summarized as follows:

Best Time	No. of Companies	%
Before the end of 1982	240	44
In 1983	106	19
In 1984	34	6
In 1985	59	11
Between 1986 and 1987	63	12
After 1987	37	7
Others	2	0 (0.37%)
No answer	4	1
Total	**545**	**100**

The second question was on the impact of the uncertainty over Hong Kong's future political status on the investment planning of the business community in Hong Kong, and the responses are as follows:

Degree of Impact	No. of Companies	%
The uncertainty has **no effect** on our investment planning. We believe the arrangement will made to benefit all the parties concerned, especially the investors. We will continue to expand our business in Hong Kong.	136	25
This uncertainty has **a little effect** on our investment planning. Though we believe that the arrangement will be made to benefit most of the parties concerned, we will freeze the expansion of our business in Hong Kong, at least until this uncertainty has been cleared.	246	43

(*Continued*)

(*Continued*)

Degree of Impact	No. of Companies	%
This uncertainty has **some effect** on our investment planning. We will freeze our expansion plans in Hong Kong and at the same time begin to consider diverting our investment to other places.	138	25
This uncertainty has **great effect** on our investment plans. We have already scaled down the size of our business in Hong Kong and have already diverted some of our capital to other places.	18	3
Others	14	3
No answer	3	1
Total	**545**	**100**

The third question was on "the best possible arrangement for Hong Kong's status after 1997" as perceived by the business community in Hong Kong. Dr. Leung offered nine options and the respondents were asked to pick the best, the second best and third best arrangement. The nine options were:

1. that Beijing announce officially that China will not consider the issue of the expiry of the 1997 New Territories lease for another 30 to 50 years, beginning in 1997, so that the present model of government and relationship between Beijing, London and Hong Kong would not be changed for another 30 to 50 years.
2. that a Pact of Arrangement be signed between Beijing and London so that Hong Kong's present constitutional status would remain the same for the next 30 to 50 years after 1997.
3. that Beijing and London sign a lease for a period of 30 to 50 years, beginning in 1997, which would cover the whole of Hong Kong, including Hong Kong Island, the Kowloon Peninsula, the New Territories, and the outlying islands.

4. that Hong Kong be returned to China, but as a Special Economic Zone (SEZ), having a different set of laws, rules, and regulations, so that the Hong Kong people would be willing to stay, and foreign investment will continue to flow into Hong Kong.
5. that Beijing reclaim the sovereignty of Hong Kong, but Britain be asked to continue to govern Hong Kong for a period of 30 to 50 years.
6. that Beijing reclaim the sovereignty of Hong Kong, but Britain be asked to continue to administer and manage the internal affairs of Hong Kong, and all matters related to its finance/business/trade/commerce/industries for a period of 30 to 50 years. The Beijing government, however, would take care of external defence and diplomatic matters.
7. that Beijing reclaim the sovereignty of Hong Kong, but Britain be asked to jointly administer and manage the internal affairs of Hong Kong, and all matters related to its finance/business/trade/commerce/industries for a period of 30 to 50 years, The Beijing government, however, would take care of external defence and diplomatic matters.
8. that Beijing announce officially that Hong Kong be made an international free port for 30 to 50 years, beginning in 1997. The Beijing government, however, would retain the sovereignty of Hong Kong, and choose at its own will to take it back at the end of period. It might also choose to further extend the period for another specified duration. During the period, Britain would be asked to continue to administer and manage the affairs of Hong Kong.
9. that Beijing announce officially that Hong Kong be made a trust territory under British administration for 30 to 50 years, beginning in 1997. At the end of the entrusted period, the Beijing government might choose to extend the period for another specified duration, of choose to end this form of arrangement by taking back Hong Kong as part of its territory. In case of the latter, an advance notice of 10 years would be given.
10. Others (please specify).

The responses of the respondents are summarized as follows:

Arrangement	Best No. of Companies	%	Second Best No. of Companies	%	Third Best No. of Companies	%
1	221	41	82	15	50	9
2	111	20	135	25	43	8
3	47	9	57	10	106	19
4	30	6	20	4	43	8
5	36	7	57	10	59	11
6	5	1	18	3	34	6
7	6	1	7	1	27	5
8	77	14	61	11	72	13
9	52	10	48	9	74	14
10	4	1	0	0	0	0

This simple, straightforward survey clearly showed that the business community in Hong Kong wanted the elimination of uncertainty over Hong Kong's future as soon as possible. Forty-four percent of the responding companies indicated that the most appropriate time for Beijing to announce its official decision/stand on the 1997 issue was before the end of 1982. Eighty percent of them desired an announcement in or before 1985.

This desire to remove the uncertainty was natural, as over 71% of the eight responding companies revealed that uncertainty over the political status of Hong Kong had an adverse effect on their investment planning, ranging from freezing their business expansion plans in Hong Kong to diverting some of their capital to other places. Only one out of four responding companies indicated that they would continue to expand their business in Hong Kong.

Regarding the business community's perception of the "best possible arrangements", it might be noted that the most popular "five best possible arrangements" had three things in common:

1. the status quo of Hong Kong was maintained,
2. Beijing only indirectly reclaimed its sovereignty over Hong Kong,
3. Britain was allowed to continue to govern Hong Kong legally.

As expected, the two least preferred "best possible arrangements", arrangement (f) and arrangement (g) did not have any of above elements. On the contrary, these two arrangements shared exactly the opposite characteristics:

1. the status quo of Hong Kong is not maintained,
2. Beijing only indirectly reclaimed its sovereignty over Hong Kong,
3. Britain only had a limited involvement in the administration of Hong Kong's internal affairs.

V Another Opinion Poll by Student Activists

Within the specified time frame, the findings of the above three surveys produced a very similar picture of the Hong Kong community's and its business community attitudes towards the uncertain future of the territory. However, the visit of Mrs. Thatcher to Beijing in 1982 caused a great shock to the people of Hong Kong. For the first time, they learnt that serious differences existed between the positions of the Chinese and British governments on the future of Hong Kong, and that the likelihood of their coming to a satisfactory compromise — especially satisfactory to the local people who wanted the maintenance of the status quo — was not as great as previously imagined.

In fact, before Mrs. Thatcher's visit, in about June 1982, reports about China's position on Hong Kong's future began to come out from Beijing. Statements attributed variously to Chinese leader Deng Xiaoping that China would recover sovereignty over Hong Kong in 1997, to the General Secretary of the Communist Party of China, Hu Yaobang, and Premier Zhao Ziyang that a "one-country, two-systems" approach would resolve the problem of Hong Kong's future, and the suggestion of Peng Zhen (Politburo member in charge of the draft of the new state Constitution) to compatriots in Hong Kong, Macau, and Taiwan to study Article 30 of the draft constitution of the People's Republic of China providing for the setting up of Special Administrative Regions, all contributed to a vague definition of the Chinese government's position.[9]

---

[9] For a brief summary of the events, see the section on *Hong Kong in Far Eastern Economic Review: Asia 1983 Yearbook*, pp. 145–149.

With apparent disregard for the Hong Kong community's preference for the status quo, a top Chinese official reportedly told British journalists in early October 1982 that "sovereignty includes territorial sovereignty and management sovereignty", indicating that Beijing did not want to tolerate the retention of the British administration after 1997.[10]

It was under such circumstances that a group of pro-China student activists ventured to conduct a poll on Hong Kong citizens' attitudes towards the proposal of self-administration.[11] This group, known as the Investigatory Group on Public Opinion Concerning Hong Kong's Future, claimed that based on informed sources, they believed that the future model of Hong Kong administration would be "Hong Kong people governing Hong Kong" — China would recover sovereignty over Hong Kong which would become a special zone politically and economically, a local Chinese resident would be chosen to administer Hong Kong, while the socioeconomic system would remain entirely unchanged.[12]

The telephone interview method was used, and the respondents were invited to answer a set of questions over the telephone. All respondents were over 17 years of age — people aged 18 or above comprised 68% of Hong Kong's population, and they numbered 3.4 million according to the latest statistics provided by the Census and Statistics Department of the Hong Kong government. The stratified random sampling approach was adopted. Hong Kong was divided into Kowloon, the New Territories, and Hong Kong Island, and the sampling was based on the telephone directory. By using the random number table approach, telephone numbers were chosen. When each telephone number was rung, the interviewer would ask how many people aged 18 and above were living in the household, then they were arranged in order of age and one out of four was chosen to be an interviewee.

---

[10] *Ibid.*, p. 146.

[11] The author had discussions with the Investigatory Group on Public Opinion Concerning Hong Kong's Future regarding its survey, and would like to thank the group for allowing him the use of the data in the full report of the survey which had not been published, though a summary and an analysis of the data appeared in *Wide Angle Monthly* (a Chinese magazine in Hong Kong), No. 121, October 16, 1982, pp. 10–16.

[12] *Ibid.*, p. 10.

The formal interviews were conducted in the evenings of September 25 to October 5, 1982; and in terms of the statistics, the sample of 418 interviews provided a level of confidence of 90%, with an accuracy margin of plus or minus 5%.

Of the 418 people interviewed, 257 (62%) said they supported the policy of "Hong Kong people governing Hong Kong". Thirteen percent opposed the idea, while 19% "would accept whatever comes their way". While sex was not a variable affecting the respondents' answers, age and socioeconomic status were. A higher percentage of the younger respondents supported the policy. Those in the higher socioeconomic strata showed a greater inclination to oppose the concept, while those in the lower socioeconomic strata tended more to support it or "accept whether comes their way".

The reasons for supporting the policy were:

Hong Kong belongs to China/Hong Kong people are Chinese	33%
Hong Kong will have no change	33%
Can allow the spirit of self-rule by Hong Kong people to materialize	19%
Better than being ruled by the British	5%
Society will be much more equitable	2%
No comments	2%
Others	6%

On the other hand, the major causes for opposing the policy were:

No confidence in Communist China	32%
Cannot do without the British	18%
Social instability	14%
Lowering of living standards	13%
No freedom	5%
No comments	5%
Others	13%

If self-administration were to be implemented, 3% of the respondents believed that Hong Kong would become much better, 15% believed that Hong Kong would still be quite good, 16% believed that Hong Kong would remain the same as before; 17% on the other hand, believed that Hong Kong would become a bit worse off, and 7% believed that it would become much worse; 36% stated that they could not foretell, and 3% offered no comments.

Regarding the practicality of the policy, respondents were equally divided. Thirty-two percent believed that it would be practicable, another 32% believed that it would be impracticable, while 30% stated that they could not foretell. In terms of age and socioeconomic status, the older and less well-off tended to avoid any forecast, while a higher proportion (51%) of those in the higher socioeconomic status considered the policy to be impracticable.

Most respondents reacted passively to the implementation of the policy: 45% would live as usual, as if nothing had happened; 22% adopted a wait-and-see attitude; 10% would react as other people do; only 6% would attempt taking part in the administration of Hong Kong; 1% would actively try to understand more about China; and 5% would leave Hong Kong.

On the question of the ideal Hong Kong governor, 47% of the respondents thought that he should be knowledgeable, 12% thought that he should command great respect, and 9% thought he should have a good relationship with China. Wealth, social status, etc., did not appear to be significant considerations. Apparently a leadership vacuum existed, as 53% of the respondents thought they could not come up with a suitable candidate to be the governor of Hong Kong, 26% offered no comments, and 14% thought there was no suitable candidate, while only 7% could come up with specific names.

The findings of the survey showed a distinct change of attitudes of the Hong Kong community since Mrs. Thatcher's visit to China. In view of the demonstrated differences between the Chinese and the British governments on the questions of sovereignty and unequal treaties, Hong Kong people felt they could neither support nor accept the British position that the unequal treaties concluded between the British Empire and the Manchu Dynasty were still valid and that the sovereignty of Hong Kong belonged to Britain. Largely because of such nationalistic feelings, they accepted the Chinese offer of self-administration as the best alternative to maintain the status quo.

There was much confusion and hesitation, however. Though 62% of the respondents supported the policy of self-administration with only 13% opposing the proposal, they were still very divided on the practicality and possible impact of the policy. This hesitation and confusion could further be exacerbated by their perception of a leadership vacuum.

VI Further Survey by a Student Group

The final survey to be examined in this article was conducted in April 1983 by the Undergraduate Students' Social Research Group.[13] Between 1983 by the Un April 1983 and Mrs. Thatcher's visit to China, the question of the future of Hong Kong attracted much attention from the Hong Kong community, and Beijing's policy of self-administration became the focus of the discussion. Further, considerable elaboration on the policy of self-administration was made by Chinese officials while receiving various delegations of businessmen, academics, etc., from Hong Kong. Basically, the Chinese leadership reaffirmed that China would recover the sovereignty and the administration of Hong Kong by 1997, and that Hong Kong would then become a Special Administrative Region (SAR) as stipulated by Article 31 of the Chinese Constitution promulgated in December 1982. As a SAR, Hong Kong would enjoy a large measure of autonomy and the policy of administration would be implemented; Beijing promised that it would not send any officials or the People's Liberation Army to Hong Kong. The capitalist system, the legal system, and the lifestyles of the people would be maintained, Hong Kong would continue to function as a free port and an international financial centre, and the Hong Kong dollar would still be circulated as an international currency.

---

[13] The author had discussions with the Undergraduate Students' Social Research Group regarding its poll, and would like to thank the group for allowing him the use of the data in the full report of the survey which had not been published, though a summary and an analysis of the data appeared in *Qishi Nianda* (*The Seventies*, a Chinese monthly in Hong Kong), No. 161, June 1983, pp. 9–12 and No. 162, July 1983, pp. 39–42.

At the same time, the Hong Kong government also attempted to improve its image and counter the propaganda offensive from Beijing and pro-China mass media. Public opinion became more clearly divided, and the mass media, opinion leaders, and civic groups began to take sides, either supporting — with qualifications — the policy of self-administration under Chinese sovereignty, or rejecting it, claiming that the retention of the British administration would be essential to the maintenance of Hong Kong's prosperity and stability.

Such was the context in which the poll of the Undergraduate Students Social Research Group was conducted. The methodology was similar to that of the previous poll, although the age limit was lowered to 15 this time. The sample covered 3.75 million people, about three-quarters of the people in Hong Kong. The second minor difference was that this poll used the random number table to pick the pages of the telephone directory, and 15 telephone numbers were located from a specific portion of each page chosen.

The questionnaire was designed in mid-April 1983, and the telephone interviews were conducted in the five evenings of April 18–22 by 71 well-trained interviewers. Valid respondents numbered 1,128. When the sample is compared with the 1981 census of the Statistics Department of the Hong Kong government, it was found that the sample was younger, better educated, with a slightly higher income, and contained a higher proportion of males. Such biases are obviously anticipated using the telephone interview method in a Chinese society.

The questionnaire mainly concentrated on five questions. Regarding the ideal solution to the question of Hong Kong's future, 41.8% opted for the maintenance of the status quo. Their main reasons were that they would not want to change their existing lifestyle (53.7%), and they believed that this would be the only way to maintain the prosperity and stability of the territory (30.1%).

About a quarter (24.3%) opted for self-administration under Chinese sovereignty. Their three main reasons were: (1) Hong Kong people were more familiar with Hong Kong (36.9%), (2) Hong Kong basically belonged to China (26.3%), and (3) that they would not want to change their existing lifestyle (25.2%). The option of remaining under British administration with sovereignty belonging to China was supported by

17.4% of the respondents, and their reasons were: such a solution would benefit Britain, China and Hong Kong (29.1%), they would not want to change their existing lifestyle, and it would best maintain Hong Kong's stability and prosperity. Independence and a return of sovereignty and administration to China, however, attracted 7.4% and 4.8% of the respondents respectively. One could observe that if sovereignty of Hong Kong were to be returned to China, more people favoured self-administration than British administration; and slightly more people preferred independence than direct administration by China.

On the probability of the options, only 8.3% of the respondents thought that the maintenance of the status quo was most probable, despite the fact that 41.8% believed it to be the ideal solution; 42.8% considered self-administration under Chinese sovereignty to be most likely, 18.6% thought so about Hong Kong remaining under British administration with sovereignty belonging to China, 14.9% thought so about Hong Kong returning to China and under direct Chinese administration, while only 1.2% thought independence most likely.

When confronted with the sole option of self-administration under Chinese sovereignty, 55.3% of the respondents supported the policy, a percentage considerably higher than those who thought this to be the ideal solution (24.3%) and those who considered this the most likely outcome (42.8%) 20.4% of the respondents opposed the idea, 16.8% responded with nonchalance, while 7.5% made no comments. For those who supported the policy, their main reasons were that Hong Kong people would be more familiar with Hong Kong (47.8%), Hong Kong people could then maintain their own lifestyle (16.1%), and Hong Kong belonged to China (12.5%). Among those who opposed the policy, their main reasons were that there was no confidence in Communist China (26.8%), the inability to maintain the existing lifestyle (19.5%), and a decline in living standards (12.1%). For those who responded with nonchalance, their main reasons were that they could not do anything (34.4%) they could adapt (21.7%), and they expected no major change in Hong Kong (15.3%).

Concerning individual plans in response to the implementation of self-administration under Chinese sovereignty, 68.7% would react with passivity, 18.4% would behave as if nothing had happened, 29.6% would wait and see, and 20.7% would simply follow the others. Only 9.3% would take part in the administration of Hong Kong, while 6.1% would actively try to leave Hong Kong. The "don't knows" amounted to 13.5%.

On the assessment of impact of the implementation of self-administration under Chinese sovereignty, 43% believed that they could not make any forecast, 18% believed that Hong Kong would become better, 24.2% believed that Hong Kong would be worse off, while 12.7% predicted that there would be no changes. The results of this poll reinforced the findings of the previous survey. The responses also showed considerable confusion and helplessness.

VII Some Observations

The above poll data reflected a very considerable and rapid shift in the attitudes of the Hong Kong community since Mrs. Thatcher's visit to China, a realization that the status quo could not be maintained indefinitely and an inclination to accept self-administration under Chinese sovereignty.

The following reasons may help to explain this shift of attitudes. In the first place, most people in Hong Kong did not have an adequate understanding or a firm position regarding the issue of Hong Kong's future, hence their attitudes could change easily. In the abovementioned survey of the Hong Kong observers, 53% of the respondents revealed that they had never discussed the issue. Twenty-eight percent indicated that they seldom discussed it, and only 19% occasionally or often talked about the issue. This was the case with the fairly well educated too. The author was one of the markers of the Economics and Public Affairs paper of the entrance examination of the Chinese University of Hong Kong in the summer of 1983, in which one of the examination questions was on the treaties relating to Hong Kong between the Qing Dynasty government and the British Empire. Less than 5% of the candidates could correctly provide the names and dates of all three of the treaties. This lack of understanding and concern was certainly startling the blame. Part of the blame should fall on the education system which almost ignored civic education and avoided discussion of controversial policy issues. Not surprisingly, the government, at least until the early 1980s, had similarly never encouraged the community to discuss the future of Hong Kong.

A considerable segment of the mass media and opinion leaders also shared the view that the topic should be avoided as much as possible.

Secondly, the vast majority of Hong Kong people were politically apathetic and did not like to be involved in politics. They desired stability and feared change, and therefore hoped for the maintenance of the status quo. This was quite understandable. When stimulated by the appeal to nationalism and under the pressure of the Chinese government's firm stand on the recovery of sovereignty, they began to realize the infeasibility of the maintenance of the status quo, though they still wanted to avoid any major change of their lifestyle, so they had come to accept self-administration under Chinese sovereignty as a feasible and realistic compromise. As indicated in the poll of the Undergraduate Students' Social Research Group, 82.2% of the respondents (including the "don't knows") had no positive plans regarding self-administration under Chinese sovereignty.

Thirdly, people in Hong Kong also felt impotent and helpless in deciding their future. In the survey of the Hong Kong Observers, 97% of the respondents revealed that they had made no preparations for the evolution of Hong Kong's future. Regarding the reasons, 33% indicated that they lacked the capability, 30% were resigned to fate, and 21% indicated that they did not know how to prepare. When asked which side would have the largest stake in determining Hong Kong's future, 44% of the respondents indicated China, 23% indicated the investors in Hong Kong, only 19% indicated the people of Hong Kong, while 1% indicated the governor of Hong Kong. This sense of impotence and helplessness obviously was a major cause of apathy.

Finally, there was also a widespread optimism within the community on the future of Hong Kong before Mrs. Thatcher's 1982 visit to China. Until then, Hong Kong people generally believed that a satisfactory agreement could be reached between Beijing and London on the future of Hong Kong. They turned pessimistic when serious differences emerged between the two governments on the questions of sovereignty and unequal treaties. Optimism returned on July 1, 1983, when it was announced that the second round of Sino-British negotiations would begin on July 12, only to be destroyed again the following September. To some extent, the optimism was based on a blind faith in the survival of Hong Kong, though it was also founded upon the belief that since all parties concerned wanted to maintain the stability and prosperity of Hong Kong, there was no reason why a satisfactory settlement could not be reached.

From the point of view of maintaining Hong Kong's stability and prosperity, the factors underlying the attitudes of Hong Kong people towards their future discussed above produced two, not undesirable results. The first was that majority of the people in Hong Kong did not actively fight for a say in determining their future. Since they did not have a good grasp of the complexity of the issue and felt impotent, they prefer to leave things as they were and tried to be optimistic. Most people in the lower socioeconomic strata considered that the issue was of no concern to them, that it was something to be settled by the Chinese and British governments, and only the rich need to be worried. The second result was that the society and economy were still relatively stable despite the uncertainty over the territory's future.

Among those in the upper socioeconomic strata, including large investors and financial groups, an exodus of capital and talent had definitely occurred. However, the situation then was a bit different from that in 1967 when riots occurred in Hong Kong in emulation of the Cultural Revolution — the wait-and-see attitude and attempts to seek some form of insurance were the predominant mood. Many middle-class families purchased properties overseas, enquired about emigration opportunities, sent their children to study abroad, and encouraged them to settle overseas, but after making the above arrangements, they were still in Hong Kong. Major investors naturally had even better arrangements. They swapped equities with foreign corporations, so that their properties would be transformed into foreign assets without outright sales. They could also easily obtain foreign passports through overseas investment; and after setting up holding companies registered in the countries where they had obtained their passport, their assets in Hong Kong would become those of foreign holding companies. In this way, they felt they had adequate security even when China recovered the sovereignty of Hong Kong.

All these ways enabled the economy of Hong Kong to continue to function as before in the uncertain period of Sino-British negotiations. Obviously, if the negotiations could lead to a satisfactory agreement, the exodus of capital and talent would be sharply accelerated. For example, one estimate suggested that 80% of medical doctors in Hong Kong had made preparations for emigration. As they could earn better incomes in Hong Kong, the preferred to stay on; but if the existing situation deteriorated further, then the people of Hong Kong might suffer from a shortage of doctors.

In 1982–1984, especially since Mrs. Thatcher's visit to Beijing visit to Beijing, the outflow of capital from Hong Kong had led to the devaluation of the Hong Kong dollar, a fall in capital formation, and recessions in the stock exchanges and the property market. These phenomena might well have their economic causes, but it could not be denied that the uncertainty over Hong Kong's future had a very significant factor.

This actual and potential exodus of talent and capital, however, had also been compensated by an inflow of foreign capital and graduates returning from overseas studies. Executives of major multinational corporations all over the world certainly found investment in Hong Kong a bargain today at that time because of the recession and the considerable devaluation of the Hong Kong dollar; and if a satisfactory settlement could be reached in the foreseeable future, the potential for a substantial appreciation of such investments would be likely. In terms of risks, investment in Hong Kong were just as safe as in any Third World country. Foreign investors today certainly have no fear of nationalization by China even in the event of its recovery of the sovereignty of Hong Kong. Investing a small percentage, say, less than 5% of its assets in Hong Kong then seemed a wise decision to a multinational corporation intending to tap the vast potential development of China and the Asia-Pacific region. It was fact that American and Japanese investors were fairly bullish in Hong Kong today, though admittedly their investments were predominantly short-term deals.

In the late 1960s and early 1970s, most of the more outstanding students from Hong Kong studying overseas tended not to return. In the early 1980s, however, because of high unemployment in the developed countries and their much more restrictive policies, nearly all of them had to return to Hong Kong to seek employment. It was possible, too, that the actual and potential exodus of professionals might be exaggerated. The employment situation in the English-speaking developed countries at this time was such that few professionals in Hong Kong could find comparable employment overseas; further, the quotas for emigration granted to Hong Kong by such countries were by no means large and they were being reduced in favour of investors.

This compensatory inflow of foreign capital and returning graduates not only helped maintain stability and prosperity in Hong Kong, but also strengthen bargaining position of the Chinese government which, apart from its general propaganda campaign, mainly concentrated on cultivating and wooing the major local investors who were mobile and whose departure could do Hong Kong's economy considerable damage. There were hints already that the Chinese government would be more accommodating with regard to their demands concerning Hong Kong's authority to handle foreign economic issues, banking and currency, travel documents, etc.

Another important target for Chinese cultivation should be the young intelligentsia who, in various surveys, showed a stronger than average inclination to accept self-administration under Chinese sovereignty as the ideal and the most likely outcome. They demonstrated the strongest identification with Hong Kong and, unlike their senior counterparts, lacked the financial means and the qualifications to emigrate. It was no surprise too that those in the higher income brackets showed a stronger inclination to opt for the retention of British administration.

If the Sino-British negotiations could reach a compromise on the questions of sovereignty and unequal treaties, which appeared much more likely since early 1984 as the British government softened its position, then the focus of the negotiations would naturally be shifted to the maintenance of Hong Kong's international and genuine autonomy. To satisfy those who tentatively accepted the Chinese policy of self-administration under Chinese sovereignty as well as those who accepted it as Hobson's choice, it was essential that the Chinese government should provide concrete guarantees, including formal stipulations in the Constitution and in law, a formal agreement between the Chinese and British governments, and a complete plan accepted by the majority of the Hong Kong people after consultations with them. If this concrete plan of Hong Kong's future could be made part of the Constitution of the PRC as well as the formal Sino-British agreement (or treaty), plus a provision that it would not be changed for certain period of time, say, 50 years, then the confidence of Hong Kong people would be considerably strengthened.

Nonetheless, it had to be realized that the ultimate guarantee of self-administration lay on the Hong Kong people themselves. They had to be organized and, through democratic channels, establish their own local government. Only a government directly elected by the people of Hong Kong can truly express the popular will of Hong Kong, struggle for the interests of Hong Kong people, and play an active role in designing the concrete arrangements for an effective Special Administrative Region. More importantly, only such representatives will be able to resist external interference to the greatest possible extent. Unfortunately, apart from a small minority of the well-educated young people, few in Hong Kong were ready to accept the challenge then.

Acknowledgement

Republished from Cheng, Joseph Y.S., "The Future of Hong Kong: Surveys of Hong Kong People's Attitudes", *The Australian Journal of Chinese Affairs*, No. 12 (July 1984), pp. 113–142, © 1984 University of Chicago Press.

Chapter 4

The 1988 District Board Elections: A Study of Political Participation in the Transitional Period

On March 10, 1988, 424,000 people cast their votes in the territory's third district board elections. The voter turnout was 30.3% of the 1.4 million registered voters, indicating a drop of 7.2% compared with the previous elections in March 1985.[1] The Governor, Sir David Wilson, who was in Japan promoting trade on election day, said that there was "great enthusiasm" for the elections and that the turnout rate was "reasonable". Sir David did not consider that the release of the White Paper entitled "The Development of Representative Government: The Way Forward" in February 1988 which rejected direct elections to the Legislative Council in 1988 had any adverse effect on the turnout.[2] Commentators and the territory's pro-democracy movement, however, disagreed.

I The Decline of Political Expectations and Confidence

Political participation at the previous district board elections was high-water mark as it took place six months after the initialing of the

---

[1] Joseph Y.S. Cheng, "Drop in Voter Turnout Comes as No Surprise," *South China Morning Post*, March 12, 1988.
[2] Emily Lau, "One Point for Democracy," *Far Eastern Economic Review*, Vol. 139, No. 12, March 24, 1988, p. 25.

Sino-British Joint Declaration.[3] At that time, even ordinary citizens without much interest in political participation realized that as colonial rule was to be terminated in 1997, and none of the parties concerned wanted the future Hong Kong Special Administrative Region (SAR) to be directly administered by Beijing, the establishment of a Hong Kong SAR government with a high degree of autonomy, as stipulated in the Joint Declaration, would be a natural development. They also believed that they had something to contribute by fulfilling their obligation to vote.

Political activists in various social strata began to organize to meet the challenge of democratization and political reform. Many political groups, most of which also intended to develop into political parties, emerged in 1984–1985.[4] In the district board elections in March 1985, the number of voters reached a record high of 476,530 (a turnout rate of 37.5%), a milestone in Hong Kong's political development.[5] Assuming that each of the 501 candidates had recruited 100 friends to campaign for him (which appeared to be the average), the number of activists participating in the elections was 50,000. These figures reflected a considerable degree of politicization of the community attained within a short period of time.

In response to the accelerating politicization in the territory in 1984–1985, the Chinese authorities attempted to cool down the political fever through various channels.[6] The showdown came in November 1985. It was reported then that the Chinese representatives had asked to discuss Hong Kong's political reforms at the second round of meetings of the Sino-British Joint Liaison Group, scheduled for the end of November 1985 in Beijing. This request was turned down. Beijing felt that Xu Jiatun, director of the Hong Kong branch of the New China News Agency, should

---

[3] *A Draft Agreement between the Government of the United Kingdom of Great Britain and Northern Ireland and the Government of the People's Republic of China on the Future of Hong Kong*, Hong Kong: Government Printer, September 26, 1984.

[4] Joseph Y.S. Cheng, "Dangqian Xianggang Zhengzhi Shill Fazhan de Xingshi (The Present Situation of the Development of Hong Kong's Political Forces)," *Hong Kong Economic Journal Monthly*, Vol. 9, May 1985, pp. 21–25 and 34.

[5] Joseph Y.S. Cheng, "The 1985 District Board Elections in Hong Kong," in his edited work *Hong Kong In Transition*, Hong Kong: Oxford University Press, 1986, pp. 67–87.

[6] See Joseph Y.S. Cheng, "Hong Kong: The Pressure to Converge", *International Affairs*, Vol. 63, No. 2, Spring 1987, pp. 271–283.

issue a public warning. In his first press conference in Hong Kong on November 21, Xu warned of the danger of Hong Kong's political reforms and the Basic Law not converging. He indicated that he "did not want to see major changes in the twelve years [to come], transforming the fundamental system in Hong Kong, and then no more changes in the following fifty years." Finally, Xu sternly indicated "Now we cannot help noticing a tendency of doing things that deviate from the Joint Declaration."[7]

Under such pressure from Beijing, London agreed to discuss the issue of political reform in the Sino-British Joint Liaison Group. British and Hong Kong government officials also changed their line on the issue since the end of 1985. After his visit to Beijing in January 1986, Timothy Renton, Minister of State at the British Foreign Office in charge of Hong Kong affairs, emphasized that it would be Britain's job to ensure a smooth transfer of power in 1997, and to do this it would be necessary to bring about a convergence of the Hong Kong and Chinese systems. He also admitted that political reforms in the territory had probably been too rapid.[8] In his end-of-year press conference in December 1985, Sir David Akers-Jones, the Chief Secretary, elaborated on the theme that "the systems must converge." He also revealed that the Hong Kong government's political reform proposals in 1987 would be presented to Beijing before their release to the local community for comment in the form of a Green Paper.[9]

It appeared that senior members of the Executive and Legislative Councils were also feeling the pressure. At the end of December 1985, Allen Lee, a member of both Councils, indicated that his plan to organize a political party was to be shelved for the time being. In an interview with the *Hong Kong Standard*, published on December 29, 1985, Lee stated that he did not believe China would allow genuine self-administration in Hong Kong. He said that the chief executive of the future SAR government would be appointed by the central government in Beijing. While a political

---

[7] *Ta Kung Pao* (a Hong Kong Chinese newspaper), November 22, 1985.
[8] Emily Lau, "Wrenching Words of Woe," *Far Eastern Economic Review*, Vol. 131, No. 6, February 6, 1986, p. 18.
[9] Emily Lau, "Telling Big Brother," *Far Eastern Economic Review*, Vol. 131, No. 3, January 16, 1986, pp. 37–38.

party, he said, had been intended to fill the vacuum, there was no longer a vacuum to fill, and hence forming a political party was meaningless. At about the same time, the senior unofficial member of the Legislative Council, Lydia Dunn, stopped talking about the introduction of a ministerial system in Hong Kong. In fact, since then the majority of the unofficial members of both Councils no longer played a leading role in community discussions on political reforms, nor did they carry out much consultation with the public.

One could speculate about the reasons why London and the British administration in Hong Kong yielded to the pressure from Beijing. One line of thinking was that the British government had been eager to ensure a smooth transfer of sovereignty and thus minimize its responsibility to Hong Kong people. Engaging in a confrontation with Beijing involved raising the political expectations of Hong Kong people and the burden of granting asylum to them, or at least to the political activists in the community. There was naturally the speculation too that the British government was more interested in a good relationship with China and the expansion of economic exchanges with it than Hong Kong people's political rights.

Since the 1966–1967 riots, the colonial government in Hong Kong had claimed to be "a government by consensus," implying that while it lacked the legitimacy of an elected government, it made efforts and took pride in consulting the public concerning its major policy proposals. Since the 1970s, attempts had been made to decentralize the delivery of social services. Unfortunately, in the second half of the 1980s, while it was troubled by its "lame duck" image and discovered that it had less social services to offer to the community, it also appeared to be much less sensitive to the values and feelings of the community.

In the 1980s, Hong Kong's public sector had entered a period of consolidation. The rapid economic growth in the 1970s and the other ambitious initiatives of the MacLehose administration (1971–1982) provided a basic network of social services for the community. Slower economic growth in the following decade, together with the natural tendency for various social service programs to expand continuously, resulted in an increased financial burden on the government throughout this decade. It was natural for the government to re-assess its commitments in various social services and cut back those that were perceived to be unnecessary or luxurious. At the same time, the political uncertainty of the territory's future and the eagerness of Beijing and indeed of all parties concerned to attract and retain investors had seriously eroded the bargaining position of the advocates for more social services and a greater redistribution of wealth.

On the other hand, though democracy had yet to develop in Hong Kong, the people had long treasured their various freedoms which made Hong Kong one of the freest places in Asia, second only to Japan. With the conclusion of the Sino-British Joint Declaration, concerned citizens and the intelligentsia in general were nervously speculating whether freedom of expression and freedom of the press would evaporate by 1997. Within the mass media, there was a general tendency to please Beijing, or at least not to antagonize or embarrass it, and cases of self-censorship were on the increase. A series of political rows that broke out in the past three years or so, however, demonstrated that the administration and the Legislative Council (with 24 indirectly elected members since late-1985) were highly insensitive to the public's awakening concern to retain its freedom of expression, resulting in a string of confrontations with pressure groups claiming to represent the views of the people. As could be expected, conspiracy theories also emerged suggesting that the British administration was cooperating with Beijing to "prepare" the territory's return to China.[10]

In line with the government's intention to strengthen the legislature, a bill on the powers and privileges of the Legislative Council members was introduced in anticipation of the introduction of an elected element and its gradual expansion. The bill, however, appeared to be too eager to protect the legislators' privileges at the expense of the freedom of the press. It aroused much opposition and was subsequently amended. Then the Attorney-General, in an attempt to speed up the judicial process, proposed to do away with juries in complex commercial crime cases, replacing them with qualified assessors. The proposal encountered strong opposition from the legal profession and the concerned public, which

---

[10] Derek Davies, "Stopping the Rot," *Far Eastern Economic Review*, Vol. 136, No. 16, April 16, 1987, pp. 38–40.

considered the upholding of the existing judicial system in the transitional period of paramount importance. The Attorney-General's proposal was seen as a dangerous step to weaken a cornerstone of the system. The proposal was subsequently shelved. Not too long afterwards, however, in a campaign against pornography, the government came up with a system of censoring what were "deemed" to be "objectionable" publications. The system granted the administration wide-ranging powers without proper safeguards for the protection of the freedom of publication. After much protest, this plan was amended also to the satisfaction of the public.

Finally came the amended Public Order Ordinance which was rushed through the Legislative Council in early 1987 despite widespread objections that some of its provisions presented a threat to press freedom. The core of the issue was again the anxieties of those who did not really believe that the existing British administration would misuse its new powers, but worried that the rulers of the future Hong Kong SAR might well find the ordinance useful to control the press.

The Chinese decision to go ahead with the construction of a nuclear power plant at Daya Bay next to the Shenzhen Special Economic Zone (SEZ), 50 kilometers from the centre of Hong Kong, further eroded the confidence of the Hong Kong community.[11] Despite the collection of over a million signatures against the project by a local anti-nuclear group, the Chinese authorities concluded the major contracts in September 1986. The community took the futility of the signature campaign as evidence that Chinese interests would prevail in all future conflicts of interests between Hong Kong and China. It was even suggested that the Chinese authorities had wanted to show that they were the true masters of the territory. In general, the local community felt that the government and most Legislative Council members had not defended its interests, and the introduction of direct elections to the legislature was considered all the more necessary.

Nevertheless, once agreement was reached in the second meeting of the Sino-British Joint Liaison Group in late-1985 that London would consult Beijing on the territory's political reforms in the transitional period, the British administration abandoned its initiative in shaping those

---

[11] See *Far Eastern Economic Review Asia 1987 Yearbook*, p. 141.

reforms and retreated to a neutral position. Its promise to review the progress in the development of representative government in the territory in 1987 made in the government White Paper entitled *The Further Development of Representative Government in Hong Kong,* published in November 1984, however, presented the British administration with a dilemma.[12] Under the pressure of converging with the Basic Law, it wanted to maintain a neutral position and avoid being accused of trying to present Beijing with another *fait accompli.* Yet it fully appreciated that unless a genuine review was held as scheduled, it would be difficult to shed its "lame duck" image.

Its steps therefore coincided with those of the Chinese authorities — attempts were made to lower the community's expectations for democracy. In 1986, the public gradually came to realize, through piecemeal messages from senior government officials, that the Green Paper entitled *The 1987 Review of Developments in Representative Government* to be published in the following spring would, unlike its predecessor in July 1984, provide no major breakthroughs nor indeed contain any surprises.[13] The Green Paper would not deal with the respective powers of the executive and legislature, nor the relationship between them. The only important proposals would be those concerning changes in the composition of the Legislative Council, including the introduction of direct elections. The British administration would simply list all possible options in the Green Paper for the community to choose so as to maintain its neutral stance, though it was at pains to convince the public that the review was a genuine one and that public opinion would be respected.

At least to the pro-democracy movement, the British administration apparently had not kept its pledge. On November 4, 1987, the Survey Office set up by the Hong Kong government to collect public opinion on the Green paper published its report.[14] The findings came as a surprise to the

---

[12] *White Paper: The Further Development of Representative Government in Hong Kong,* Hong Kong: Government Printer, November 1984.

[13] *Green paper: The 1987 Review of Developments in Representative Government,* Hong Kong: Government Printer, May 1987.

[14] *Report of the Survey Office — Public Response to Green Paper: The 1987 Review of Developments in Representative Government,* Hong Kong: Government Printer,

community because the results of the government polls were widely at variance with those revealed by surveys conducted by other independent survey companies. The two opinion polls commissioned by the government showed only 12% to 15% support for direct elections to the Legislative Council in 1988. On the other hand, surveys conducted by three other market research companies indicated support for direct elections of between 41% and 62%, while those opposing amounted to less than 25%. Further, more than 230,000 names, supported by identity card numbers, gathered in a signature campaign in support of direct elections in 1988, were not counted as submissions by the Survey Office, thus allowing the report to claim that 39,000 people favoured direct elections in 1988 while 94,000 did not.[15]

The pro-democracy movement reacted to the report with shock and dismay. It certainly felt betrayed by London and the British administration in Hong Kong for failing to respect public opinion and to faithfully develop a system of representative government in the transitional period so that the territory achieve democracy and a high degree of autonomy by 1997. It also considered it could no longer trust the British administration in Hong Kong and that maintaining a dialogue with local government officials would be futile.

The vast majority of Hong Kong people, however, took little interest in the survey as they had already been psychologically prepared to expect no direct elections to the Legislative Council in 1988. The community's attention instead concentrated on the stockmarket crash.

The release of the White Paper entitled, *The Development of Representative Government: The Way Forward*, in February 1988 contained no surprises.[16] The Hong Kong government accepted that the

---

October 1987. The full text of the report may also be found in *South China Morning Post*, November 5, 1987.

[15] Emily Lau, "A Matter of Opinion" and "'Lies...and Surveys'," *Far Eastern Economic Review*, Vol. 138, November 19, 1987, pp. 26–29. The magazine also asked Norman Webb, the Secretary General of Gallup International, to examine the opinion surveys on representative government sponsored by the Hong Kong government, and the expert found them to be "inadequate" and "deeply flawed"; see Emily Lau, "'Liew, Damn Lies and Statistics'," *Far Eastern Economic Review*, Vol. 139, March 10, 1988, pp. 32–33.

[16] *White Paper: The Development of Representative Government; the Way Forward*, Hong Kong: Government Printer, February 1988. See also Joseph Y. S. Cheng, "Political Reform

public supported in principle the concept of direct elections, but believed that it was "sharply divided" over their timing. The government therefore decided that 10 seats in the Legislative Council would be directly elected in 1991, replacing the 10 indirectly elected by the 19 District Boards at this stage.

In his speech to the London Royal Institute of International Affairs on March 21, 1988, the Governor, Sir David Wilson, hinted that in 1991 the Legislative Council would still have 56 seats with about 18% of its members directly elected.[17] The White Paper earlier suggested the introduction of a "grand electoral college" which was proposed by the mainstream of the Basic Law Drafting Committee to elect the chief executive of the future Hong Kong SAR and a quarter to one half of the members of the SAR legislature.

The White Paper was hardly a step forward and it showed that the British administration had abandoned its pledge made in the July 1984 Green Paper "to develop progressively a system of government the authority for which is firmly rooted in Hong Kong, which is able to represent authoritatively the views of the people of Hong Kong."[18] The White Paper in 1988 instead limited the government to the objective "that the system in place before 1997 should permit a smooth transition in 1997 and a high degree of continuity thereafter."

II The Voter Turnout Rate and the Political

The above developments helped to explain why expectations of and confidence in achieving democracy and a high degree of autonomy in the territory were considerably eroded. The lower voter turnout rate in the 1988 district board elections (see Table 4.1) was one of the indications of a gradual return to traditional political apathy among Hong Kong people.[19]

---

is at a Standstill," *South China Morning Post*, February 11, 1988.

[17] *South China Morning Post*, March 22, 1988; see also *Ming Pao*, March 22, 1988.

[18] *Green Paper: The Further Development of Representative Government in Hong Kong*, Hong Kong: Government Printer, July 1984.

[19] For a good analysis of the traditional political apathy of the Hong Kong community, see Lau Siu-kai, *Society and Politics in Hong Kong*, Hong Kong: Chinese University Press, 1982.

Table 4.1: Registered Voters, Actual Voters, and Voter Turnout Rates of the 19 Districts in 1982, 1985, and 1988 District Board Elections

	Registered Voters			Actual Voters			Voter Turnout Rates* (%)		
	1982	1985	1988	1982	1985	1988	1982	1985	1988
Urban Districts									
Central and Western	49,968	53,778	59,179	16,402	16,267	13,876	33	30	23
Wan Chai	46,952	59,364	50,484	12,824	17,870	10,437	27	30	21
Eastern	101,527	128,171	142,945	32,561	41,331	34,419	32	32	24
Southern	48,680	48,795	79,955	23,809	18,498	25,526	45	38	32
Yau Ma Tei	31,398	44,025	44,135	7,755	11,389	9,347	25	26	21
Mong Kok	42,329	72,361	40,087	10,585	17,773	6,598	25	25	17
Shan Shui Po	87,063	78,351	115,965	30,387	28,978	32,243	35	37	28
Kowloon City	80,540	97,491	98,798	27,934	28,766	21,896	35	30	22
Wong Tai Sin	98,830	116,397	130,216	33,627	39,762	38,275	34	34	29
Kwun Tong	119,546	148,780	148,818	49,578	53,518	44,824	42	36	30
Sub-total	706,833	847,513	910,562	243,862	274,152	237,441	35	32	26

Table 4.1: (*Continued*)

	Registered Voters		Actual Voters		Voter Turnout Rates*(%)	
New Territories						
Sha Tin	15,673	61,751	7,105	31,234	45	51	38
Sai Kung	5,912	12,448	3,539	7,396	60	59	52
Tsuen Wan	70,675	51,019	26,307	20,994	37	41	32
Kwai Chung & Tsing Yi	70,675	90,853	26,307	37,400	37	41	32
Tuen Mun	25,551	72,196	13,819	36,950	54	51	40
Yuen Long	28,337	55,366	17,377	28,546	61	51	41
North	19,311	34,542	12,265	17,044	64	49	46
Tai Po	12,564	27,850	8,099	12,434	64	45	40
Islands	14,703	17,754	8,825	10,380	60	58	48
Sub-total	197,726	423,879	97,336	202,378	51	48	38
Total	899,559	1,271,392	341,398	376,530	38	37	30

Note: In some cases, the voter turnout rates should have been slightly higher as some seats were uncontested and therefore some registered voters did not vote because they were not given the opportunity.

Source: City and New Territories Administration, Hong Kong Government, 1988.

On the other hand, the 30.3% turnout rate was not too disappointing for elections to local advisory bodies which had no control over issues of top priority in the voters' mind such as housing, education, transport, and taxation. The turnout rate compared favourably with similar local elections in Western democratic countries, especially the U.S.

The turnout rate also reflected the lack of participatory political culture in Hong Kong;[20] demonstrating that interest in politics and knowledge of the political system remained weak. A survey conducted by the Student Union of the Chinese University of Hong Kong on the polling day of the second district board elections in 1985 (March 7) indicated that 22% of the voters were not clear about the work of district boards and another 37% were not aware of what the district boards had done.[21] As the voters were the politically more active citizens, the general level of knowledge of the district boards among ordinary citizens might even be lower. Other polls, mostly conducted by student groups of local tertiary educational institutions, also revealed that about 50% of the respondents could not name one district board member from their own district.[22]

The situation did not seem to have been improved two years later. A poll conducted by Survey Research Hong Kong during July 6–12, 1987 and published in *Ming Pao* (an influential Chinese daily) on July 24, 1987 showed that 64% of the public clearly indicated that they were not concerned with the contents of the Green Paper reviewing the development of representative government in Hong Kong. Further, 80% of the respondents said that they had no understanding of what was meant by "representative government", and that a minuscule 1% had actually read the complete text of the Green Paper.

---

[20] Gabriel A. Almond and Sidney Verba, *The Civic Culture*, Princeton: Princeton University Press, 1960.

[21] See *Ming Pao*, March 12, 1985.

[22] Most of these polls were small in scale and not very vigorous in methodology. For a summary of them, see Chung Lok-chung, "Behind the Voting — A Preliminary Study of the Voters' Political Attitudes (in Chinese),' *Pai Shing Semi-Monthly* (a Hong Kong Chinese magazine), No. 92, March 16, 1985, p. 58.

When asked to respond to the following statement:

"I am not concerned with the political system, I am only concerned with my own life."

Fifty-four percent of the respondents agreed that it applied to them, while 42% disagreed. The pro-democracy movement was certainly discouraged by the survey's discovery that 32% of the respondents wrongly believed that there were already directly elected members in the Legislative Council.[23] Another survey indicated that only 11% of those over 15 years of age had read all or most of the text of the Green Paper, despite the fact that a million copies in Chinese and 356,000 copies in English had been taken by the public from various distribution centres.[24]

In contrast to South Korea and Taiwan, there was still widespread political apathy in Hong Kong. The movement for democracy had only a very small core of dedicated academics, social workers, trade unionists, and grassroots pressure group activists. The political culture in Hong Kong frowned upon confrontation and tended to support the status quo which, after all, had been able to provide rising standards of living for Hong Kong residents. There was a strong sense of political impotence, as the community accepted that the fate of Hong Kong was not in the hands of Hong Kong people but was largely determined by what went on in Beijing. Given the brittle nature of the local economy, the "don't rock the boat mentality" was very strong. It was widely considered counterproductive to exert pressure on the Chinese government whose gerontocratic leadership was most concerned with "face". At the same time, the socioeconomic strata most committed to democracy were those who could easily emigrate and were likely to exercise that option.

In a survey published in the *Sunday Morning Post* on May 31, 1987, the respondents were asked the following question:

"Do you believe that public opinion will influence the decision of the options for future democracy that are to be selected from the Green Paper?"

---

[23] The telephone survey was based on a random sample of 1,012 people above 18 years of age; see *Ming Pao*, July 24, 1987.
[24] The poll was conducted by Market Decision Research for the *South China Morning Post*. It took place at the end of June and in the first week of July 1987, interviewing a random sample of 1,041 people; see *South China Morning Post*, July 15, 1987.

Forty-seven percent of the respondents' answers were positive, 36% negative, and 16% said "don't know". It was significant to note that the following groups appeared to be more cynical and a higher than average proportion of them did not believe that public opinion would influence the democratization process: age group 18–24 (41%), age group 25–34 (42%), those with post-secondary education (50%), and those earning HK$7,000 or more a month (44%). In a society where there was freedom of speech and where the rule of law was respected, the widespread sense of political impotence was extraordinary. Such a phenomenon also cast doubts upon the British administration's claim of being "a government by consensus", at least on issues where China's interests were at stake.

Under such circumstances, emigration naturally became an attractive option. A survey published by *Ming Pao* on July 16, 1987 indicated that 11% of the households interviewed revealed that they or some of their family members had obtained rights of abode in foreign countries, and a further 11% expressed a desire to emigrate. In this survey, 78% of those queried said they intended to stay in Hong Kong, 5% less than in February of that year. Confirming the general impression, the survey also showed that 22% of the professional, entrepreneurs and executives were seeking homes in foreign countries, while 16% had already acquired the necessary documents. Ironically, the poll also revealed that political confidence had been restored after a dip earlier in the year which was partly related to Hu Yaobang's purge and the political struggles in China. Economic confidence remained buoyant. Hence, the accelerating expansion of the potential exodus was not much affected by short-term fluctuations in political and economic confidence.

Such survey results received further support from government sources. In March 1988, the Police Identification Bureau indicated that the number of Hong Kong residents applying for certificates of no criminal record was expected to double in the coming summer, increasing from 200 to 400 a day. These documents were needed as proof that people were law-abiding and were only issued in connection with visa applications. The bureau confirmed that applications for the certificate had soared in the four years since the signing of the Sino-British Joint Declaration in 1984. It was estimated that students made up only 20% of the total applicants.[25]

---

[25] *South China Morning Post*, March 31, 1988.

So far, the closest the Hong Kong government had come to acknowledging that there was a brain-drain was an attempt to provide an accurate figure for those leaving. The Governor, Sir David Wilson, admitted that the net outflow of Hong Kong citizens from the territory was 27,000 in 1987 compared with 14,000 in 1986 and 11,000 in 1985.[26] This increase in emigration was also related to the relaxation of immigration policies by countries such as Canada, Australia, and New Zealand which wanted to attract wealthy and professionally-qualified immigrants.[27]

While emigration continued to increase, the local mass media then turned their attention to the departure of talented senior civil servants to the private sector, which was considered to be the beginning of a major exodus. In the last nine months of 1987, 3,344 civil servants (including five at the directorate level) left the civil service, which stood at 179,053 on April 1, 1987.[28]

While there were many reasons that people emigrated and civil servants resigned, they were certainly not encouraging signs, and were largely perceived as a vote of no-confidence on Hong Kong by 1997. While the decline of political expectations and confidence, together with the characteristics of an immature participatory political culture, served to explain the relatively low and declining level of interest in political participation in district board elections, an explanation had to be made to account for the 424,000 voters who turned out to vote in March 1988.

Many surveys and mass media interviews demonstrated that most voters in district board elections did not have a good understanding of the work and authorities of the district boards, nor did they have an adequate understanding of the candidates and their platforms. Most voters went to vote to fulfill their obligations as citizens, reflecting the fact that modern ideals such as democracy and citizens' rights had made inroads into the minds of the Hong Kong people. It appeared, however, that voting was seen more as an obligation rather than as a right, an obligation whose fulfillment, like paying taxes, required some persuasion and reminding.

---

[26] *Ibid.*

[27] See Chris Pomery, "Leaving...on a Jet Plane," *Far Eastern Economic Review*, Vol. 140, April 7, 1988, pp. 66 and 71–72.

[28] *South China Morning Post*, March 12, 1988 and *Sunday Morning Post*, March 20, 1988.

They were all the more necessary because failure to vote, in contrast to failure to pay taxes, was not penalized. This persuasion mainly came from two sources: the government and the candidates.

In the first district board elections in 1982, the government almost shouldered the burden of the publicity campaigns all by itself to encourage qualified residents to register and to vote, and in some instances, senior government officials even encouraged community leaders to stand as candidates. The government then indicated that such involvement would not be repeated in the following elections, and voter registration as well as voting would have to rely on voluntary efforts of the citizenry. The government, however, was again substantially involved in the 1985 elections. Such involvement was generally accepted, and even perceived as necessary in view of the community's general political apathy and the absence of well-organized political groups. The government also considered that it should help prepare the foundation for the development of representative government in the territory after the conclusion of the Sino- British Joint Declaration. This time, the mass media and various newly-formed political groups were very active in promoting voter registration and encouraging voters to vote.

Government efforts tended to be more low-key in the district board elections in 1988. While routine programs were run as before to promote voter registration by the City and New Territories Administration, Radio Television Hong Kong, and other government agencies, senior government officials generally avoided the subject. As indicated earlier, the government had abandoned taking the initiative to shape political reforms in Hong Kong and the community was then involved in heated debates on the introduction of direct elections to the Legislative Council in 1988. In the month before the district board elections, governmental publicity programs on the district board elections were smaller in scale and the mass media in general appeared to be considerably less interested. In response to this lack of interest, the government stepped up its efforts in the last week or so, and the Secretary for District Administration, Donald Liao, was much relieved when the voter turnout rate finally passed the 30% mark which he had earlier predicted. It was said that community workers were sent to districts like Mong Kok where turnout was particularly low, to mobilize voters to vote in the evening of the polling day.[29] The initiative was probably taken by the District Officers concerned.

In the three district board elections, it was clearly established that the rural areas had higher voter turnouts than urban areas; and in urban areas, districts with a greater proportion of public housing residents usually achieved higher voter turnout rates (see Table 4.1). This was mainly because face-to-face contacts by grassroots neighborhood groups remained the most effective channel to mobilize voters to vote. In the rural districts like Sai Kung, North and Islands, there existed a traditional system of electing village representatives and the residents knew each other and the candidates well, hence voters could easily be reached by the candidates and the peer group pressure to vote was high. In Yuen Long and Tai Po where a number of public housing estates had been built in recent years, the voter turnout rates showed an above average decline in the last two elections combined. The oldest new towns in the New Territories, Tsuen Wan, Kwai Chung, and Tsing Yi, consistently registered the lowest turnout rates in the New Territories, which were only slightly above the territory-wide averages. The new towns of the recent decade, Sha Tin and Tuen Mun, had voter turnout rates higher than those of Tsuen Wan, Kwai Chung, and Tsing Yi, but lower than those of the other more rural districts of the New Territories.

Grassroots neighborhood groups, mainly mutual aid committees of public housing estate blocks and various district-level groups with such names as "Concerned Group for the People's Livelihood of X District" were more active in the new towns and public housing estates. In the former, there was often a need to get organized to solve the problems of community building and to redress the grievances caused by the inadequacies of town planning. Similarly, the mutual aid committees in most public housing estates had been active in various "Clean Hong Kong Campaigns" and "Fight Violent Crime Campaigns", and had good access to the residents. This was why new towns and urban districts with a greater proportion of public housing residents usually achieved higher voter turnout rates that old urban districts where such grassroots

---

[29] *Ming Pao*, March 11, 1988.

neighbourhood groups were not well developed. As expected, Kwun Tong, Wong Tai Sin, Sham Shui Po, and Southern (where there is located the traditional fishing port of Aberdeen) consistently attained higher than average voter turnout rates.[30]

In line with the above, voters in the lower socioeconomic strata tended to be more enthusiastic in district board elections. In comparison with middle-class voters, they had a greater need for district board members who were expected to articulate their interests, help to redress their grievances, explain to them government policies, and show them the proper channels to obtain the necessary services from relevant government departments. As the pro-democracy movement admitted after the 1988 district board elections, the lower socioeconomic strata also had greater expectations from the district boards concerning cultural and recreational services which the movement had relatively neglected.[31] This utilitarian element of participation in district board elections not only partially explained the motivation to vote but also helped to answer why voter turnout rates were usually lower in middle-class urban districts.

III The 1988 Campaign

Altogether there were 493 candidates standing for 264 seats in 19 district boards. As 34 candidates were returned unopposed, 459 candidates competed for 230 seats; and in 1982, there were 404 candidates standing for 132 seats.[32] There were also seven Legislative Councilors, 10 Regional Councilors, and eight Urban Councilors taking part in the 1988 elections, the latter were hastily forced to stand as they would otherwise lose their seats in the respective district boards in March 1989 according to the new rules of composition of the urban district boards.

On the surface, the number of candidates was less than in 1985 and the number of elected seats slightly higher, but the extent of competition

---

[30] See Janet L. Scott, *Local Level Election Behaviour in an Urban Area*, Hong Kong: Centre for Hong Kong Studies, The Chinese University of Hong Kong, January 1985.

[31] Based on the author's interviews of leaders of the pro-democracy movement.

[32] See Joseph Y.S. Cheng, "The 1985 District Board Elections in Hong Kong," *op. cit.*, and Emily Lau, "One Point for Democracy," *op. cit.*

was considerably keener. In the first elections in 1982, the district boards were a political vacuum and not many community leaders were interested in running. In 1985, many political groups participated on a more limited scale (see Table 4.2), but the number of elected seats available had more than doubled from 132 to 237. In other words, there were many new vacant seats to accommodate interested candidates.

This was certainly not the case in 1988. To adjust for population growth, there was a slight increase of elected seats from 237 to 264, but 212 incumbents aimed for re-election, leaving only 52 vacant seats to be freely contested. Further, incumbents enjoyed a number of significant advantages compared with new candidates: (a) they could normally claim credit for all the work done by the respective district boards; (b) they had better mass media exposure and their names therefore were better known to the voters; (c) they had better contacts and access to the various groups in their respective constituencies; and (d) their votes in the respective district boards could win them many influential supporters in the elections. In short, a conscientious, hardworking incumbent should have no great difficulty in getting re-elected. In fact, 163 of the incumbents (76.9%) were successful in their bid for re-election.

As there was a general expectation that competition would be keen, the vast majority of the candidates were well prepared which in turn ensured that most contests would be tough. A record number of 218 candidates registered on the opening day of nominations (compared with 82 contenders in 1985).[33] This showed that many candidates sought an early start in view of the anticipated keen competition; in fact, many of them had banners and posters put in place the night before the first day of nominations, an act which was technically illegal. This fully demonstrated the eagerness of the candidates.

Unlike the previous district board elections, a vast majority of the candidates belonged to a territory-wide group which had quite well-defined political platforms, embracing at the least, a clear stand on the most controversial political issue — direct elections to the Legislative Council in 1988. This was evidenced by the number of candidates endorsed by various' political groups listed in Table 4.2; furthermore,

---

[33] *South China Morning Post*, January 9, 1988.

Table 4.2: The Performance of Various Political Groups in the 1985 and 1988 District Board Elections

	Number of 1985 Candidates	Number Elected	Success Rate (%)	Number of 1988 Candidates	Number Elected	Success Rate (%)
Hong Kong People's Association	8	8	100.0	Inactive in 1988		
Meeting Point	4	4	100.0	23	17	73.9
Hong Kong Affairs Society	3	3	100.0	21	16	76.2
Association for Democracy and People's Livelihood	Not yet formally established then			32	27	84.4
Progressive Hong Kong Society	Not yet formally established then			49	41	83.7
Hong Kong People's Council On Public Housing Policy	11	9	81.8	70	60	85.7
Hong Kong Professional Teachers' Union	30	24	80.0	125	92	73.6
Reform Club	33	17	51.5	7	2	28.6
Civic Association	54	21	38.9	33	15	45.5

Source: Based on the author's own data, derived from interviews and reports of major newspapers and magazines.

a government source indicated that the Communist camp had fielded nearly 100 candidates, of whom 50 were believed to have solid left-wing connections.[34]

As a result, the candidates could be easily categorized into a pro-democracy camp and a conservative camp (ironically, the Communist camp was included in the latter, reflecting the "unholy alliance" between Beijing and the conservative business community). There were intense canvassing and political mobilization by the Communist-backed organizations, traditionally conservative political groups, and residents' bodies (the *kaifongs* in the urban areas and the Heung Yee Kuk plus the rural committees in the New Territories), and the liberal pro-democracy groups. The latter formed a loose coalition advocating democracy which was mainly composed of the following three political organizations: Meeting Point, the Association for Democracy and People's Livelihood, and the Hong Kong Affairs Society.

This division of candidates into two camps to some extent reflected the polarization in the territory-wide political spectrum, especially in the Legislative Council. The division was also a result of the development of parliamentary politics in the district boards since 1985 when district board members acquired the power to elect their own board chairmen and 10 members to the Legislative Council. The district boards in the New Territories had the additional privilege of electing a Provisional Regional Council member each. These elections and the formation of committees within each district board as well as the associated election of committee chairmen meant that group politics developed and had become entrenched in most district boards. District board members and candidates in district board elections naturally fell in line with the divisions among major political figures in the political community.

The division was very much affected by the pattern of political mobilization in district board elections. Candidates' election platforms were remarkably similar, concentrating on such local issues as hygiene, security, transport, the environment, and the availability of medical, educational, and recreational facilities, etc. Moreover, few voters were willing to spend the time to study the qualifications and past performance

---

[34] Lau, "One Point for Democracy," *op. cit.*, p. 25.

of the candidates; at any rate, data available were limited, and the mass media were not very helpful. Most voters' choices therefore were decided on the basis of the following considerations: the academic and professional qualifications of the candidates, the district-level groups and territory-wide political groups to which they belonged, and the major political figures endorsing them. The latter two criteria helped the voters to decide whether the candidates' political orientations were in accordance with theirs and to verify the candidates' past records of performance. These two criteria were also important factors in enabling the candidates to recruit campaign workers and gain access to the grassroots groups such as the mutual aid committees and owners corporations which were crucial channels of directly mobilizing voters.

The mass media provided little guidance to the voters. A number of major newspapers gave considerable coverage to the district board elections, but their coverage mainly concentrated on the political affiliations of the candidates and their respective chances of winning, with very little scrutiny of their past records of performance, thus reinforcing the mode of voter choice described above.

The liberal pro-democracy movement attached much significance to the district board elections. As it had failed to secure direct elections to the Legislative Council in 1988, the district board elections in March 1988 and the Legislative Council elections in the following September were the only opportunities for them to demonstrate their political prowess. Due to the decline of political expectations and confidence in the past two or three years, the three major political groups in the pro-democracy movement largely failed to make much headway in expanding their organizations. The district board elections were vital to new recruitment and a boost of morale which had suffered in the series of political setbacks.

Under such circumstances, the groups could not afford to be too selective in endorsing candidates. They basically welcomed all candidates who were willing to join them, offering the candidates the general blessing of the movement, limited financial assistance, and the endorsement of their leading figures such as Legislative Councillors Martin Lee, Szeto Wah, and working-class champions such as Lau Chin-shek, director of the Christian Industrial Committee. Candidates of the pro-democracy movement usually lacked social status and financial resources, but they had excellent support from effective grassroots groups. They managed to recruit well-educated campaign workers from the tertiary educational institutions, and their key campaign managers were the most experienced in the territory. Obviously, their youth, academic, and professional qualifications, and the campaign efforts of Martin Lee and company were valuable assets. The three groups reached an agreement to coordinate nominations so as to avoid clashes among their candidates, but they stopped short of pooling resources.

Opposing the pro-democracy movement was the conservative camp which, in the district board elections, was largely represented by the traditional community leaders of the *kaifongs* in the urban areas, and the Heung Yee Kuk and rural committees in the New Territories. They were usually better off economically and conservative in political outlook. Naturally, they were favored by the government and were cultivated by the officials of the local district offices. They tended to be appointed to the local area committees and other committees, and played a supportive role in activities and campaigns initiated or sponsored by the government. Many of these traditional community leaders were businessmen and above 40 years of age. Among this group, however, there was an increasing number of school principals, lawyers, business executives, and other professionals who were similarly conservative in political outlook, and they were actively co-opted by government officials.

The conservative cause's main champions were Legislative Councillors Maria Tam, Selina Chow, and Stephen Cheong. Maria Tam was also a member of the Executive Council and the Basic Law Drafting Committee, as well as Head of the Progressive Hong Kong Society. The group was formed in 1985 and had the foundation of a conservative political party. It then adopted a very low political profile when Beijing made it clear that it objected to the rapid development of representative government and the emergence of political parties in the territory. It seemed that, like the political groups in the pro-democracy movement, the Progressive Hong Kong Society could not afford to abandon active participation in the district board elections. It supported 49 candidates (see Table 4.2, another report indicated that it supported about 70 candidates), and actively campaigned for them, enlisting the help of beauty queens and television stars.[35] The conservative camp also vastly improved its campaign strategies, imitating many of the effective tactics of the pro-democracy movement. With much more financial resources at its disposal, it presented a formidable threat to the pro-democracy movement.

Participation on a considerable scale by pro-Communist organizations was an interesting phenomenon in the 1988 district board elections. In many cases, pro-Beijing candidates, who included bankers and other professionals, camouflaged their backgrounds, stressing their credentials as local residents who only wanted to serve the community. In the rural areas in the New Territories, pro-Beijing candidates were bolder and publicly admitted to being linked with China. The left-wing Hong Kong Federation of Trade Unions indicated that 12 of its members stood for the elections (compared with 10 in the 1985 elections), but it revealed only two names. Presumably, these two were very strong candidates and they did get elected.

In some cases, prominent conservative political leaders endorsed candidates from the pro-Communist camp, which was also against the rapid development of representative government in Hong Kong. In return, left-wing organizations, in their letters to members, instructed them to vote for candidates from the conservative camp as well. The Progressive Hong Kong Society reached an agreement with the Civic Association too to coordinate nominations so as to avoid clashes, they also pledged to support each other's candidates.[36] They admitted, however, that contest between the two groups might still emerge in one or two constituencies.

Participation by pro-Communist organizations became a cause of concern because the Communist Party of China had been stepping up its activities in the territory and was seeking to establish itself as the dominant political force.[37] It began publicly building its community network and influence in 1985 when the Hong Kong branch of the

---

[35] *Ibid.*, p. 26; see also *South China Morning Post*, March 16, 1988.

[36] *Ming Pao*, January 17, 1988.

[37] Emily Lau, "Positioning for Power" and "Grasping the Grassroots", *Far Eastern Economic Review*, Vol. 137, August 6, 1987, pp. 26-29; see also Loong Sin (pseudonym), *Xianqang de Linyige Zhengfu*, A Shadow Government of Hong Kong, Hong Kong: Haishan Tushu Gongsi, no publication date given, probably in 1986.

New China News Agency opened three district offices in Hong Kong, Kowloon, and the New Territories. Pro-Beijing political forces mounted a campaign to block the introduction of direct elections to the Legislative Council in 1988. They too began to organize grassroots neighborhood groups in districts like Kwun Tong and Wong Tai Sin. These groups would have considerable resources from China at their disposal and would constitute unfair competition in various elections. In some constituencies in Hong Kong Island, China Resources (Holdings) Co. Ltd. and China Merchants Steam Navigation Co. Ltd. provided transport to support the pro-Beijing candidates on election day. These two were major Chinese corporations in Hong Kong and were directly accountable to the Chinese Ministry of Foreign Economic Relations and Trade, and the Ministry of Communications respectively.

During the campaign period, there were several complaints made to the Independent Commission Against Corruption alleging inaccurate voter registration. In one case, 40 people were said to have registered a school as their home, and the school supervisor was a candidate.[38] Similar complaints were made in the previous elections, and the authorities in charge of elections failed to take measures to deter such acts. This negligence might well be due to the eagerness to boost up the voter turnout rate as prosecutions might scare qualified voters away from registration.

Moreover, some candidates appeared to have exceeded the spending limit of HK$20,000. Again the election authorities were too lax to sanction the irregularities. One or two public relations companies offered to run a campaign for candidates. Though they did not reveal their price tags, any candidate employing them would be bound to spend beyond the ceiling.

IV Results of the Elections

The elections did not produce many surprises. A profile of the successful candidates reveal that they appeared to be younger, with 59% 40 years of age and under (see Table 4.3). The proportion of those who were over

---

[38] Lau, "One Point for Democracy," *op. cit.*, p. 25; see also *Ming Pao*, March 8 and 9, 1988.

Table 4.3: Age of the Elected Members of the 1982, 1985, and 1988 District Boards (Percentage of Total)

Age	1982	1985	1988
20–30 years	8.3	19.4	19.3
31–40 years	25.8	36.3	39.8
41–50 years	25.0	19.0	23.9
51–60 years	31.8	19.0	13.3
61–70 years	6.8	5.0	3.4
71–80 years	2.3	1.3	0.4

Source: Based on the author's own data, derived from the candidates' campaign pamphlets and newspaper reports.

50 years of age showed a considerable decline. In the previous elections, it was already demonstrated that age was not an asset, voters appeared to favour younger candidates as they probably would be able to devote more time to community service. As district board work had become more strenuous, some senior traditional community leaders also chose to abdicate in favour of younger professionals who shared their conservative political views.

A study of the occupations of the elected members showed that the proportion of businessmen continued to decline (see Table 4.4). Many of them simply could not afford the time, and they were increasingly reluctant to stand as they were aware that their image was generally unattractive to voters. Professionals performed well again. There was a higher proportion of business executives and white-collar employees, social workers and professionals, and a slight decline in the proportion of educators. Lawyers, in particular, tended to do well. As explained above, voters preferred someone young, well educated, and with the relevant professional expertise to represent them and help to solve their problems. Free legal advice offered by lawyer candidates was especially attractive; and school principals and social workers too were often rewarded for their services to the constituencies.

The proportion of social workers was probably somewhat exaggerated, as a number of young full-time district board members registered their occupation as community work. A controversy concerning social workers

Table 4.4: Occupation of the Elected Members of the 1982, 1985, and 1988 District Boards (Percentage of Total)

Occupation	1982	1985	1988
Businessmen	43.9	28.3	19.3
Educators	16.7	17.7	15.2
Business executives and white-collar employees	11.4	14.8	20.1
Professionals	3.8	12.6	13.6
Social workers	3.0	8.4	14.8
Workers and technicians	4.5	3.4	3.4
Retirees	2.3	3.0	1.9
Others	14.4	11.8	11.7

Source: Based on the author's own data, derived from the candidates' campaign pamphlets and newspaper reports.

standing as candidates in the constituencies where they worked emerged in the campaign period. More than 30 social workers sent "letters to the editors" to major newspapers protesting that such social workers had transformed their daily work and the associated community ties into their personal political assets. It was also argued that social workers had the duty to encourage local residents to stand in the elections. In practice, many major voluntary organizations did not favor their social workers to stand in the constituencies where they worked. Those who did so would be transferred to work in other districts.[39]

It was certainly the performances of various political groups in the election outcomes that attracted the most media attention (see Table 4.2). Meeting Point, the Hong Kong Affairs Society, and the Association for Democracy and People's Livelihood all did well in the elections. Many of their successful candidates were also endorsed by Hong Kong People's Council on Public Housing Policy and Hong Kong Professional Teachers' Union.[40] Roughly, the pro-democracy movement gained between one-third to 40% of the elected seats.

---

[39] *Ming Pao*, January 8, 1988 and March 9, 1988.
[40] *Ming Pao*, March 12, 1988, and *South China Morning Post*, March 16, 1988; also based on the author's interviews of candidates and survey of the candidates' campaign pamphlets.

This was certainly a victory, and victory was badly needed for the pro-democracy movement in Hong Kong. The election results were a morale-booster, not so much for the core members, but for the less committed. Election victory will also strengthen the financial resources of the groups, thanks to the generous allowances for district board members from the government. Further it would also enhance the groups' political appeal and viability.

This victory, however, should not be exaggerated. One had to bear in mind that a very large segment of the conservative business community did not take part, and the pro-Beijing forces apparently were far from being fully mobilized. After all, direct elections to the Legislative Council in 1991 would be a very different game. One should remember too that the pro-democracy movement could often muster the support of about 100 district board members in various protest movements and signature campaigns even before the 1988 elections.

The pro-democracy movement was concerned that many of their candidates, though re-elected, saw their previous large winning margins considerably eroded. They might blame the drop in voter turnout rate, as they believed their opponents' votes were sure votes based on connections and mobilization, while their higher popularity should have attracted a much larger proportion of the voluntary, uncommitted voters had they voted. They also had to admit that their opponents had become much more sophisticated in election strategies and tactics. The latter's patient yet less conspicuous work in cultural and recreational activities began to pay off, an area where the pro-democracy district board members tended to neglect. In general, the movement anticipated tough times ahead.

The Progressive Hong Kong Society also performed well in the elections.[41] Introduction of parliamentary politics into the district boards and the polarization of politics in Hong Kong pushed the conservative forces in the district boards to coalesce into a loose alliance. This spontaneous alliance, with the help of the appointed members, was quite successful in limiting the liberal, pro-democracy district board members to winning no more than two seats (plus three sympathizers) in the Legislative Council and only one district board chairmanship in 1985.

---

[41] *Ming Pao*, March 12, 1988.

The Progressive Hong Kong Society offered a natural rallying point for the otherwise disorganized conservative district board members, despite the dwindling popularity of its leader, Maria Tam.[42]

The pro-Beijing forces attempted to gain experience in district board elections. Their campaign appeared to be a manoeuvre in preparation for more important contests to come. In some instances, they worked very hard to get their candidates elected, especially those whose ties with China were clear to all. In a very small number of constituencies, they also campaigned hard to unseat unfriendly incumbents. In the urban districts of Kwun Tong and Wong Tai Sin, it appeared that their grassroots neighborhood groups earlier established began to pay handsome dividends.[43] On the whole, about a third of their nearly 100 candidates were returned.[44]

Generally, their strategy was one of denial. They were not yet well prepared to field too many candidates. To do so would also be counter-productive as this would alarm the public. United-front work was probably being stepped up after the elections, and the pro-Beijing forces concentrating on ensuring that candidates unacceptable to them would not be elected district board chairmen or to the Legislative Council.

On March 24, 1988, the government announced the appointment of 141 members (about a third of the total) to the 19 district boards.[45] Eighty-eight of them were incumbent appointed members, some of whom were appointed to their fourth term of office; and five of them were incumbent elected members who opted not to stand again in the elections held earlier in the month. Among the appointments, there were six Legislative Councillors and 48 new faces (34%). Forty-four of the incumbent

---

[42] Incidentally, Allen Lee, who publicly admitted abandoning the formation of a political party in late 1985, formed a Hong Kong Economic Research Centre in 1987 with Stephen Cheong, a conservative Legislative Councillor. The center planned to imitate Japan's Keidanren (Federation of Economic Organizations), the most powerful business lobby in Japan. It appears that both Maria Tam and Allen Lee still wanted to keep their options open concerning the formation of political parties.

[43] Emily Lau, "China derails 'through train' reform plans," *Far Eastern Economic Review*, Vol. 140, April 7, 1988, p. 56.

[44] Emily Lau, "One point for democracy," *op.cit.*

[45] See *Ming Pao* and *South China Morning Post*, March 25, 1988.

Table 4.5: Age and Occupation of the 141 Appointed Members of the 1988 District Boards (Percentage of Total)

Age	Percentage	Occupation	Percentage
21–30 years	2.1	Businessmen	28.4
31–40 years	36.9	Educators	22.7
41–50 years	29.8	Business executives & white-collar employees	17.0
51–60 years	16.3	Professionals	10.6
61–70 years	13.5	Social workers	7.8
71–80 years	1.4	Others	13.5

Source: City and New Territories Administration, Hong Kong Government, 1988.

appointed members were not reappointed, including four district board chairmen. A small number of those not re-appointed had earlier indicated their intention not to accept re-appointment.

A government spokesman said that the overall objective of the appointments was to achieve a balanced representation in each of the boards with regard to sex, age, social, and educational background of the members. He also indicated that consideration was given on an individual broad basis and account was taken of the appointees' performance in community service and their links with the respective districts. He further commented that "results of the elections and the need to inject new blood into the district boards are also considered", but no reference was made to the appointed members' political affiliations as a criterion for appointment.[46]

Table 4.5 shows that the appointed members were considerably older than the elected ones. They usually had successful careers and were conservative in political outlook. Even the educators and the social workers among them were often conservative secondary school principals and senior administrators of major voluntary social welfare organizations.

The pro-democracy movement took the appointments as "an expected disappointment."[47] Even though it managed to win a majority of the elected seats in Tuen Mun, Sha Tin, Wong Tai Sin, and Sham Shui Po, it was still in a minority in these district boards. The movement was particularly angry with the appointment of an extra member to the Central

---

[46] *Ibid.*
[47] *Ibid.*

and Western District Board, and the original arrangement of adding the Sai Kung and the Islands District Boards to the Tsuen Wan and the Kwai Chung and Tsing Yi District Boards to form the South New Territories geographical electoral college; these two arrangements were instrumental in depriving it of the chairmanship of the Central and Western District Board and the Legislative Council seat from South New Territories in 1988.

In the election of district board chairmen and Legislative Councillors, the traditional and conservative community leaders, the appointed members and the pro-Beijing forces appeared to have endorsed the same candidates. The pro-democracy movement was more interested in Legislative Council seats than district board chairmanships, as the Legislative Council provided a much better forum to articulate its interests and the district board chairmen were expected to remain neutral most of the time. In 1985, the pro-democracy movement won two seats (plus three sympathizers) in the Legislative Council through the electoral college system and only one district board chairmanship. In 1988, however, it could only secure one solid sympathizer in the Legislative Council through the electoral college system and just one district board chairmanship. The alliance of conservative forces proved to be more aggressive and effective.[48]

V Conclusion

The district board elections in 1988 gradually came to reveal the basic cleavages of politics in Hong Kong. All parties concerned believed that the electoral contests were preparations for the 1991 direct elections to the Legislative Council, and that future elections would anticipate keener competition and greater demand for resources.

This politicization of the district board elections and the developing confrontations involved might, ironically, have the same effect as the decline of political expectations and confidence discussed earlier, resulting in further disincentive to take part in elections. The greater amount of

---

[48] See Joseph Y.S. Cheng, "The Democracy Movement in Hong Kong: Difficulties and Prospects" (unpublished paper), January 1989, pp. 21–24.

resources spent and the resultant higher capacity of mobilization on the part of the candidates might not be able to counter-balance the general tendency of Hong Kong people to avoid political confrontation. Lower political participation would hurt the pro-democracy movement more.

The keen competition between the pro-democracy movement and the conservative camp in the district board elections was in fact further complicated by the involvement of the Kuomintang forces. The Kuomintang was generally regarded as a disorganized political force adopting a low profile, but a Hong Kong government source revealed that it had participated significantly in the elections and worked hard to support many candidates fielded by the pro-democracy movement.[49] This strategy was adopted probably because the Kuomintang realized that the public was no longer enthusiastic about its message of fighting Communism and that it had little financial support to offer. This aspect was still little known to the community, but, if widely recognized, would most likely discourage voting and political participation in general.

Hong Kong government officials have privately expressed concern over the mobilization of the Communist Party of China in the 1988 district board elections. They believed that election on a "one-person one-vote" basis would be an easy way for the Communists and their sympathizers to enter the Hong Kong government structure, given their extensive network in the community. It was said that this was a key reason why some government officials opposed direct elections to the Legislative Council.[50] An editorial of the local Communist paper, Wen Wei Po, on the other hand, said that the poor turnout in the district board elections indicated voter apathy and inadequate civic education. It therefore implied that the decision to delay direct elections to the Legislative Council till 1991 was correct.[51] Earlier, in response to the Hong Kong government's White Paper in February 1988 indicating the above decision, an editorial of the newspaper praised the White Paper as a balanced and fair conclusion to the debates in recent years and a reflection of the spirit of the Sino-British Joint Declaration.[52]

---

[49] Emily Lau, "China derails 'through train' reform plans," *op. cit.*
[50] Emily Lau, "One point for democracy," *op. cit*, p. 26.
[51] Wen Wei Po (a Hong Kong Chinese newspaper), March 11, 1988, editorial.
[52] *Ibid.*, February 11, 1988, editorial.

The keen competition and the campaign irregularities noted before naturally called for a stronger and more neutral watchdog organization than the existing group of government officials from the City and New Territories Administration. Members of the judiciary might well be involved though unfortunately, even they had an image problem then. An independent electoral commission should also be given the responsibility of drawing the boundaries of electoral districts to avoid gerrymandering. Such a commission would gradually gain credibility and experience through being in charge of electoral affairs beginning from 1989 when Urban Council and Regional Council elections would be held. It would, hopefully, serve to remove the suspicions of the Chinese authorities concerning elections held under the British administration, an argument used by Ji Pengfei, chairman of the Basic Law Drafting Committee, to reject the election of the first chief executive (and probably the first legislature as well) of the Hong Kong Special Administrative Region government in a meeting of the committee held in December 1987.[53]

To demonstrate its sincerity, or at least its neutrality, in the development of representative government in the territory, the Hong Kong government should allow all district boards seats to be directly elected in 1991. However, in order to attract talents and services which might not be obtained through elections, the government could choose to retain the existing system of appointments, but appointed members should no longer be given the right to elect district board chairmen and Legislative Councillors. Otherwise, the government would be perceived as deliberately and unfairly diluting the electoral gains of the pro-democracy movement.

The mass media certainly could do much to promote meaningful political participation. More detailed coverage of the past performances and social service records of the candidates, more careful scrutiny of their platforms and analysis of their solutions offered to handle community problems would help voters understand their candidates better and hence make their decisions more intelligently. Unfortunately, the mass media showed even less interest in the 1988 district board elections than in 1985.

To the pro-democracy movement, a more important challenge than the election of district board chairmen and Legislative Councillors was how

---

[53] Emily Lau, "China derails 'through train' reform plans," *op. cit.*, p. 54.

to influence the Basic Law. In attempting to secure a more democratic political system for the future Hong Kong Special Administrative Region, the movement had yet to present itself as an effective and credible political force.

Acknowledgement

Originally published as Cheng, Joseph Y.S., "The 1988 District Board Elections: A Study of Political Participation in the Transitional Period", in *Hong Kong: The Challenge of Transformation*, ed. Kathleen Cheek-Milby and Miron Mushkat, HKU Centre of Asian Studies Occasional Papers and Monographs, No. 82, pp. 116–149. Hong Kong: University of Hong Kong, 1989.

Chapter 5

The Post-1997 Government in Hong Kong: Toward a Strong Legislature

Student demonstrations in Beijing since the death of Hu Yaobang, former general secretary of the Communist Party of China (CPC), on April 15, 1989, and subsequent developments leading to the brutal military crackdown of Beijing students in June highlighted, in the strongest possible way, the importance of democracy and freedom in China and Hong Kong. Before the massacre in Beijing, the confidence of Hong Kong people was largely based on the People's Republic of China (PRC) leadership's goal to modernize China. The local community considered this a legitimate goal that was widely supported by the Chinese people, and it believed that maintenance of the status quo in Hong Kong after its return to China's jurisdiction after 1997 would enable the territory to contribute to the modernization. This was the foundation for confidence in the Sino-British Joint Declaration on the Future of Hong Kong, the Draft Basic Law, and various promises made by Chinese leaders.

Events in China in 1989 showed that power struggles within the Chinese leadership could cause the goal of modernization and related priorities to be totally disregarded. It was also demonstrated that since power had been so highly concentrated in the hands of a few gerontocratic leaders, a system of checks and balances did not exist and even the CPC Politburo could be ignored. This meant that Hong Kong people's trust was badly shaken and that a meaningful dialogue with Beijing would be difficult and might even lack legitimacy. This chapter analyzes the terms of the Draft Basic Law following the Sino-British Joint Declaration with respect to the governmental system in Hong Kong before and after 1997, emphasizing the importance of a system of checks and balances. It explores the concerns of the Hong Kong people who were increasingly agreeing on the need to accelerate the development of representative government in the territory before 1997.

During negotiations leading to the initialling of the Sino-British Joint Declaration, the PRC government indicated that the optimum outcome would be one that would re-establish Chinese sovereignty over the territory, with local Chinese residents responsible for its administration. In July 1984, the Hong Kong government published a Green Paper entitled *The Further Development of Representative Government in Hong Kong*, and the community itself realized that, as none of the parties concerned wanted the future Hong Kong Special Administrative Region (HKSAR) to be directly administered by Beijing, the establishment of an HKSAR government with a high degree of autonomy — as subsequently stipulated in the Sino-British Joint Declaration — would be a natural development. The future political system, however, became probably the most controversial issue, as revealed later in the drafting of the Basic Law, partly because the Joint Declaration did not provide for one. While the community was divided on direct elections, political parties, and other issues, a consensus on certain basic principles formed soon after the initialling of the Declaration.

In the first place, almost no one opposed a gradualist approach. There was also general agreement that the existing political institutions should be respected in the transitional period and that, as far as possible, they should serve as a basis for political reforms, with the aim of preserving their strong points. Understandably, gradualism was often a catchword used to camouflage the differences between the pro-democracy movement in Hong Kong and the conservative business community.

Second, the political system of the HKSAR should be designed to achieve a high degree of stability. A presidential system, for example, gives the chief executive security of tenure and is therefore a relatively stable system. An electoral system based on proportional representation, however, encourages a multi-party system; if this were combined with a parliamentary system, Hong Kong might well encounter a situation where shifting coalitions of political parties would result in frequent falls of government and general elections. Hong Kong could ill afford such a scenario, which might well lead to an early termination of whatever autonomy the territory might have gained. Indeed, in its very early stage, the Basic Law Drafting Committee (BLDC) unanimously agreed on a system of separation of powers that implied adoption of a presidential system. The phrase "separation of powers" was no longer mentioned after Deng Xiaoping's rejection of the U.S. political system as a model for China, but consensus on a presidential system with its checks and balances had not been affected.

Third, a future HKSAR government should be efficient. Over-emphasis on separation of powers as well as checks and balances could lead to deadlock and confrontation among different sections of the government, resulting in political crisis and paralysis. A relatively independent chief executive with sufficient powers would help to guarantee the dedication and devotion of department heads and other civil servants in his government and thereby maintain high efficiency. While the pro-democracy movement did not object to this emphasis on efficiency, it considered that the HKSAR government must be subject to effective democratic supervision to prevent abuse of power.

According to a study of Hong Kong's civic culture by researchers at the Chinese University of Hong Kong, people in the second half of the 1980s, because of their concern over the territory's future, demonstrated a fairly high degree of *acceptance* of concepts such as representative government, democracy, and political participation, but those who were *committed* to the cause of democracy were still a very small minority.[1] A major public opinion survey sponsored by Hong Kong newspapers on the attitudes of residents to the first draft of the Basic Law also reflected this fairly high degree of acceptance of a system of representative

---

[1] Kuan Hsin Chi and Lau Siu Kai, "The Civic Self in a Changing Polity: The Case of Hong Kong," in *Hong Kong: The Challenge of Transformation*, edited by Kathleen Cheek-Milby and Miron Mushkat. Hong Kong: Centre of Asian Studies, University of Hong Kong, 1989, pp. 93–96.

government.[2] Seventy percent of the respondents endorsed the statement: "The Chief Executive and principal officials of the legislative authorities should be elected by universal suffrage to reflect local opinions." Only 5% of the respondents said that the practice of democracy would cause social unrest and damage the capitalist system; the remaining 25% had no comment. Further, about 60% of those surveyed opted for the election of the chief executive by universal suffrage, while only 16% favoured election by an electoral college, and 4% supported selection by an advisory group. The respondents, however, were quite confused with the various proposals on the electoral system put forward by the pro-democracy movement, the conservative business community, and other groups. This was understandable as only 1% of the respondents had read through the complete draft Basic Law.

On the basis of this vaguely defined consensus, a modified presidential system appeared to suit Hong Kong's needs best. To ensure the stability of the HKSAR government, security of tenure for the chief executive, whose term might be limited to four or five years, was an important condition. The legislature's ability to check and balance the executive lies mainly in its authority to appropriate money, to legislate, and to approve government appointments. To ensure effective supervision of the executive, the Basic Law should provide the legislature with the power to question, investigate, and impeach principal officials of the government, including the chief executive. In the event of a violation of law or serious neglect of duty, the central PRC government might remove from office any principal official, including the chief executive, acting on an impeachment resolution passed by the local legislature.

Such a system seemed to be the logical outcome of the general consensus, and it was disappointing to discover that the Draft Basic Law of the Hong Kong Special Administrative Region of the People's Republic of China (for solicitation of opinions) (henceforth referred to as the draft Basic Law) released on April 28, 1988, did not provide for adequate

---

[2] *South China Morning Post* (Hong Kong), September 19, 1988, and *Ming Pao* (a Chinese newspaper in Hong Kong), November 11, 14–17, 1988. The survey covering 2,359 respondents was conducted by Survey Research, Hong Kong, from July 29 to August 31, 1988.

accountability of the chief executive and the executive authorities to the legislature. The latter, in turn, was given insufficient powers to establish a system of healthy checks and balances so as to realize the effective supervision of the chief executive and the executive authorities.[3]

I Relationships Among the Chief Executive, the Executive Authorities, and the Legislature

Article 45 of the draft Basic Law reaffirmed what was stipulated in the Joint Declaration: "The Chief Executive of the HKSAR shall be selected by election or through consultations held locally and be appointed by the Central People's Government." It had been hoped that this appointment would be a mere formality to demonstrate China's sovereignty over Hong Kong; however, Chinese officials responsible for Hong Kong affairs indicated that the appointment would be a "substantial" one, implying a veto power in the hands of the PRC government. If the latter refuses to appoint the chief executive elected by universal suffrage in the manner outlined by Alternative 2 of Annex 1 to the draft Basic Law, there will be a constitutional crisis with a serious adverse impact on the stability and prosperity of the territory.

To be in line with the above method of selection, the chief executive "shall be accountable to the Central People's Government and the HKSAR in accordance with the provisions of this Law" (Article 43). Nowhere in the section on the chief executive does it mention that he has to be accountable or responsible to the Legislative Council. On the other hand, Article 64 of the following section on the executive authorities stipulates: "The executive authorities of the HKSAR must abide by the law and shall be accountable to the Legislative Council of the HKSAR." It appears therefore that the chief executive does not have to be accountable

---

[3] The draft Basic Law was issued by the Basic Law Drafting Committee, while the Introduction and Summary were compiled by the Basic Law Consultative Committee. The whole set of documents, appearing in pamphlet form with separate Chinese and English versions, has been distributed freely since April 29, 1988, in Hong Kong. The Chinese version is the official version, while all quotations of the Law in this article are from the English version.

to the Legislative Council, but the executive authorities (treated in a separate section of the draft Basic Law) do.[4] This certainly is not in accordance with the general understanding of the Hong Kong community concerning the promise in the Joint Declaration that "the executive authorities shall abide by the law and shall be accountable to the legislature." On the other hand, Article 59 of the draft Basic Law states that the government of the HKSAR is the executive authorities of the Region, and Article 60 states that the chief executive of the HKSAR is the head of the government of the Region. This may be interpreted to mean that the chief executive is part of the executive authorities and therefore has to be accountable to the Legislative Council.

Obviously, the ambiguity has to be removed. In fact, a member of the BLDC proposed that Article 60 should be rewritten as follows: "Members of the executive authorities shall include: (1) The Chief Executive; (2) Principal Officials nominated by the Chief Executive and appointed by the Central People's Government (officials corresponding to the Secretary level); (3) the Executive Council, including the Chief Executive and members of principal officials appointed by him." In this connection, it was also suggested that Article 43 be revised to read: "The Chief Executive of the HKSAR is the head of the Region and the head of the executive organs of the Region, representing the Region and leading its executive organs, and shall be accountable to the Central People's Government, the HKSAR, and the legislature of the Region in accordance with the provisions of this Law."[5]

Article 43 also raises the following question — the chief executive's accountability to the central PRC government can be well defined as the central government is a concrete entity and controls his appointment; on the other hand, the chief executive's accountability to the HKSAR is

---

[4] Li Hou, a deputy director of the Hong Kong and Macau Affairs Office, State Council of China, told a visiting delegation of the Hong Kong Christian Industrial Committee in Beijing on July 6, 1988, that it would be more appropriate for the chief executive to be accountable to the HKSAR than to the Legislative Council, as "this accountability is much broader than the scope of the 'legislature'." *South China Morning Post*, July 8, 1988.

[5] "A Collection of Opinions and Suggestions of Some Members in Regard to the Articles Drafted by Their Respective Special Subject Subgroups" (henceforth "Collection of Opinions and Suggestions"), draft Basic Law pamphlet, English version, pp. 99 and 96.

largely symbolic and has not been defined by the Basic Law. Article 48.8 further states that the chief executive has "to implement the directives issued by the Central People's Government in respect of the relevant matters provided for in this Law." The constitution of the PRC promulgated in 1982 clearly stipulates that the State Council is "the highest organ of state administration" and it has the power "to exercise unified leadership over the work of local organs of state administration at different levels throughout the country, and to lay down the detailed division of functions and powers between the Central Government and the organs of state administration of provinces, autonomous regions and municipalities directly under the Central Government."[6]

It is not sufficiently clear in what way and to what extent the HKSAR differs from the provinces, autonomous regions, and municipalities in its accountability to the central government. Is the HKSAR government also one of the "local organs of state administration" as defined by the PRC constitution? Moreover, the State Council is one of the three parties that have been empowered by the Basic Law to propose amendments to the law. With the consent of the National People's Congress, it can seek to expand its power *vis-à-vis* the HKSAR government (Article 170). Article 1 of Annex 1 of the Joint Declaration is equally unclear. On the one hand, it states that the "HKSAR shall be directly under the authority of the Central People's Government," and on the other, it stipulates that "the executive authorities shall abide by the law and shall be accountable to the legislature."

Article 48 defines the powers and functions of the chief executive. The HKSAR political system, as outlined in the draft Basic Law, conforms to the view that the chief executive should be a very strong leader. His powers and functions are similar to those of the president of the U.S., though the powers probably are even greater *vis-à-vis* the legislature. According to Articles 48 to 52, bills passed by the Legislative Council have to be signed by the chief executive before being promulgated as laws (Article 48.3). If the chief executive considers that a bill passed by the

---

[6]Articles 85 and 89.4, *The Constitution of the People's Republic of China*, adopted December 4, 1982, by the Fifth National People's Congress in its Fifth Session, Beijing: Foreign Languages Press, 1983 (henceforth The Constitution), pp. 63 and 66.

Legislative Council is not compatible with the overall interests of the HKSAR, he may return it to the Council within three months for reconsideration. If it passes the original bill again by no less than a two-thirds majority, he must sign and promulgate it within one month (Article 49). The chief executive, however, has one further option which is not available to the U.S. president — he may still refuse to sign the bill and dissolve the Legislative Council instead. He may also dissolve the Council when its members refuse to pass the budget or other important bills and consensus cannot be reached after consultations. Before dissolving the Legislative Council, which he may do only once in each term of office, the chief executive should ask for opinions from the Executive Council (Article 50).

This power to dissolve the Legislative Council is supposed to be balanced by the risks that the chief executive has to take into consideration: he must resign (1) if the new Legislative Council again passes with a two-thirds majority the original bill that the chief executive twice refused to sign, leading to dissolution of the previous Council; or (2) if the new Legislative Council still refuses to pass the budget or any other important bill that the previous Council refused to approve (Article 52). The risks, however, will be very limited. The chief executive, in fact, controls the introduction of the budget and important bills to the Legislative Council; and if he perceives that he will not be supported on the disputed original budget or important bill, he simply has to alter it to the satisfaction of the new Legislative Council. Then he will not be forced to resign and his tenure will not be threatened. Similarly, if the chief executive has twice refused to sign a bill, leading to dissolution of the previous Council, he will simply have to assess the extent of support he gets from the new Council, make concessions, and reach a compromise with it when necessary. It should not be too difficult for the chief executive to avoid a scenario in which the new Legislative Council again passes the original bill in dispute with a two-thirds majority, thus leading to his resignation.

A simpler and more balanced arrangement could be as follows — a bill passed by the Legislative Council would have to be endorsed by the chief executive before its formal promulgation. If he refuses to do so within a specified period of time, it would be returned to the Legislative Council, which may choose to pass the bill again by a two-thirds majority.

The bill will then become law even without the endorsement of the chief executive. This arrangement follows the American system of separation of powers and checks and balances. The chief executive may refuse to endorse a bill that is considered incompatible with his policy program, but two-thirds majority support in the Legislative Council would fully demonstrate the popularity of the legislation, and the chief executive would have to accept it.

Article 72.9 of the draft Basic Law does provide the Legislative Council with the power to impeach the chief executive. This is a very important characteristic of a system of separation of powers. It states: "In the event of serious breach of law or dereliction of duty by the Chief Executive, an independent investigating committee, to be chaired by the Chief Justice of the Court of Final Appeal, on the motion jointly initiated by one-fourth of the members of the Legislative Council and passed by the Council, may be established to carry out investigations and to report its findings to the Council. If the committee considers the evidence sufficient, the Council may pass a motion of impeachment with a two-thirds majority and report it to the Central People's Government for decision." The above impeachment procedure is appropriate, and it can only be hoped that the central PRC government's decision to remove an impeached chief executive would be just a formality demonstrating China's sovereignty over Hong Kong. It is difficult to imagine how an impeached and therefore totally discredited chief executive could be allowed to retain his office through the support of the central government without severely damaging political stability in Hong Kong. Also, if the PRC government wants to retain the chief executive, its lobbying efforts certainly would take place before formal impeachment procedures. Under such circumstances, the last clause of Article 72.9 "and report it to the Central People's Government for decision" should be amended to read "and report it to the Central People's Government for the removal of the Chief Executive."

In order to ensure smooth functioning of the government when disagreement arises between the chief executive and the Legislative Council, Article 51 also provides that if the Council refuses to pass the budget bill or when it is impossible to approve any appropriation of public funds because the Council has already been dissolved, the chief executive may, during the interim period prior to the formation of a new Legislative

Council, approve temporary short-term appropriations in accordance with the level of expenditure of the previous fiscal year.

The strength of the chief executive and weakness of the Legislative Council are further demonstrated by the chief executive's power to approve the introduction of motions to the Council on revenues or expenditure (Article 48.10), and to decide, in the light of security and public interest, whether government officials or other personnel in charge of government affairs should testify or give evidence before the Legislative Council (Article 48.11). If the chief executive can, without having to give reasons, reject any motion presented to the Legislative Council regarding revenues and expenditure, then basically the Council can respond only to the chief executive's proposals on budgetary matters. It is not sufficiently clear whether the Council can reject certain items of the budget, though it does not appear likely. If it can only accept or reject the budget as a whole and the refusal to pass the budget will lead to its dissolution, the Legislative Council's power over government revenues and expenditure will be very limited indeed. Under such circumstances, the Council may have to rely largely on the pressure of public opinion to persuade the chief executive and the executive authorities in the process of consultation between the two branches of government. This was the actual situation under the British administration in its final decade.

The extensive powers of the chief executive and the narrow definition of accountability of the executive authorities (which most probably do not include the chief executive) to the Legislative Council considerably limit the Council's powers and functions; Article 73 further reinforces such limitations. Bills relating to revenue and expenditure, to government policies, and to the structure and operation of the government may only be introduced by members of the Legislative Council with the prior written consent of the chief executive (Alternative 1 of Article 73). Alternative 2 of the same article appeared to be more lenient, stating: "Bills which do not relate to public expenditure or public policies may be introduced individually or jointly by members of the Council." However, along with the impotence of the Council to control government revenue and expenditure, there also will be a danger that "government policies" or "public policies" may be so broadly defined as to render members of the Legislative Council almost powerless to introduce bills. The author therefore supported the suggestion of a member of the Basic Law Drafting Committee that bills relating to public expenditure or public policies should be jointly proposed by no less than one-tenth of the members of the legislature, but that the prior written consent of the chief executive should not be required.[7]

The chief executive's power to exempt government officials or other personnel responsible for government affairs from testifying or giving evidence before the Legislative Council would severely hamper the latter's function as a watchdog of the executive. Considerations of security and public interest are not sufficient reasons for preventing the Legislative Council from calling government officials or personnel to testify or give evidence, especially if this can take place in closed sessions. The provision in the draft Basic Law assumed that the chief executive has a greater concern for security and public interest than members of the Legislative Council; such an assumption was obviously subject to dispute. The author therefore supported the proposal of a member of the Basic Law Drafting Committee that Article 72 defining the powers and functions of the Legislative Council should include the following clause: "The legislature and its subordinate committees shall have the power to summon the person concerned to appear before them to testify and give evidence."[8] This power was in fact implied and restricted by Article 48.11 that granted the chief executive the power to "decide, in the light of security and public interest, whether government officials or other personnel in charge of government affairs should testify or give evidence before the Legislative Council." As the power was already implied, it might as well be clearly stated in Article 72, and Article 48.11 should be deleted. It should be noted that the committee system and its power to summon witnesses have contributed much to the effective role assumed by the American Congress in a system of separation of powers.

In this connection, a member of the Basic Law Drafting Committee suggested that a provision for the establishment of standing committees

---

[7] "Collection of Opinions and Suggestions," p. 101; see also Martin Lee and Szeto Wah, *The Basic Law. Some Basic Flaws*, Hong Kong: Martin Lee and Szeto Wah, June 1988, pp. 57–58.
[8] "Collection of Opinions," p. 56.

and ad hoc committees should be added to Article 72. Experiences of legislatures in various countries have well demonstrated that a system of standing committees and ad hoc committees allows members of a legislature to specialize and cultivate their expertise *vis-à-vis* the executive branch of the government and the civil servants, and thereby enable them to play a more effective role in policymaking as well as supervision of the executive branch. After all, Article 70 of the PRC constitution promulgated in 1982 provides for the establishment of standing committees by the National People's Congress, and the Legislative Council in Hong Kong at that time revealed a similar trend.

In spite of his extensive powers, the chief executive is quite limited in appointing and dismissing the principal officials of the HKSAR government. He may nominate them and report such nominations to the central government for appointment; and he may, in the same manner, propose the removal of principal officials (Article 48.5). The draft Basic Law did not specify the criteria by which the PRC government would approve the chief executive's nominations and proposals for dismissals. If the central government withholds approval, it will cause substantial difficulties within the HKSAR government. A better arrangement would be to give the Legislative Council the power to endorse the chief executive's nominations of principal officials, with refusal of endorsement limited to the following two conditions: (1) when the portfolio of a nominee involves an obvious conflict of interest, for example, if the nominee to head the transport portfolio comes from a family having a substantial stake in an important corporation in the public transport sector; and (2) when the nominee's qualifications and credentials fail to meet the requirements of the post. This would enhance the Legislative Council's power *vis-à-vis* the chief executive and act as a healthy means of checks and balances. The chief executive, however, should have full authority to dismiss principal officials. It could only be hoped that the central government's power to approve nominations and proposals for dismissal would be only a formality to demonstrate China's sovereignty over Hong Kong, as any rejection of the chief executive's nominations, and especially proposals for dismissal, would compromise the HKSAR government's autonomy.

The section on the legislature did not touch the power of the legislature to impeach members of the executive authorities and the Executive

Council. Neither did it mentioned the power of a certain number of members of the Legislative Council to call special meetings during the recess. (This power seemed to lie solely in the hands of the president of the Legislative Council, according to Article 71.) It was therefore hoped that amendments would be made to provide such powers to the Legislative Council and its members. It was reasonable that the same power and procedure of the Legislative Council to impeach the chief executive should be extended to include at least all principal officials of the executive authorities.

The accountability of the executive authorities to the Legislative Council was too narrowly defined. Article 64 states: "The executive authorities of the HKSAR shall abide by the law and shall be accountable to the Legislative Council of the HKSAR in the following respects: they shall implement laws passed by the legislature and already in force; they shall present regular reports on their work to the Legislative Council; they shall answer questions raised by members of the Legislative Council; and they shall obtain approval from the Legislative Council for taxation and public expenditure." Implementation of laws passed, and presentation of regular reports are by no means effective measures of enforcing accountability on the part of the executive authorities. The powers of the chief executive to approve the introduction of bills on revenues and expenditure and on government policies as well as to decide, in the light of security and public interest, whether government officials should testify before the Legislative Council would severely circumscribe the remaining two measures of accountability of the executive authorities to the Council.

It was significant to note that some members of the BLDC objected to this narrow definition of accountability and attempted to broaden it by suggesting that Article 64 be amended to read: "The executive authorities of the HKSAR must abide by the law and shall be accountable to the legislature of the Region. They shall: (1) implement laws passed by the legislature and already in force; (2) present regular reports on their work to the legislature; (3) be subject to supervision by the legislature; (4) answer questions raised by members of the legislature, and be subject to or assist in investigations by the legislature on special issues; and (5) obtain approval from the legislature for taxation and public expenditure, and be subject to supervision by the legislature in respect to public expenditure."[9]

II Infringements on the Principles of Separation of Powers

The political system as outlined in Chapter IV of the draft Basic Law is fundamentally a modified presidential system based on the principles of separation of powers and checks and balances. The chief executive and members of the Legislative Council have respective fixed tenures, they are elected by separate electoral methods and different constituencies, and the Legislative Council has the power to impeach the chief executive while the latter can dissolve the Council. Yet, there were certain provisions in the draft Basic Law that violated these principles. In the first place, according to Article 55, members of the Executive Council, an organ for assisting the chief executive in policy making (Article 54), might include members of the Legislative Council (Article 55). This violated the principle of separation of powers and the provision in the Sino-British Joint Declaration that "the executive authorities shall…be accountable to the legislature."

If the purpose of the above arrangement was to improve coordination between the legislative and executive branches of government, as indicated by some members of the BLDC, then the objective might be better fulfilled by the following formal and informal arrangements: (1) scheduled sessions between the Executive Council and the committee chairmen of the Legislative Council; (2) executive as well as informal sessions of individual committees in the Legislative Council inviting principal officials (and their subordinates) concerned to attend; (3) advisory bodies established under the executive authorities (Article 65) involving both senior members of the Legislative Council interested in a certain policy area and principal officials responsible for the same policy area; and (4) all kinds of informal communications between the two branches of government.

Secondly, in view of the extensive powers of the president of the Legislative Council (Article 71), and in view of the chief executive's

---

[9] *Ibid.*, p. 99; see Lee and Szeto, *op.cit.*, pp. 45–46.

power to dissolve the Legislative Council (Article 50) and the Council's power to impeach the chief executive (Article 72.9), it would be highly inappropriate for the chief executive to serve concurrently as president of the Legislative Council (Alternative 2 of Article 70). This not only violated the principles of separation of powers and checks and balances, but even in the Westminster model, the British prime minister does not serve concurrently as speaker of the House of Commons. It was therefore much more appropriate for the president of the Legislative Council to be elected from among members of the Council (Alternative 1 of Article 70).

Finally, Note 6 of the draft Basic Law raised a similar question. It stated that whether or not members of the legislature should be required to resign after being appointed principal officials in the executive remained to be studied. As the executive authorities shall be accountable to the legislature according to the Joint Declaration and Article 64 of the draft Basic Law, it was only natural that members of the legislature should have to resign after being appointed principal officials in the executive branch. Moreover, the Legislative Council has the power to impeach the chief executive (and, it was hoped, all principal officials of the executive branch and members of the Executive Council as well). Further, it was already suggested that a number of formal and informal arrangements be established to improve coordination between the legislative and executive branches of the government without violating the principles of separation of powers and checks and balances.

III "Executive Dominant" Political System and Control from China

The political system outlined in Chapter IV of the draft Basic Law presented an "executive dominant" system in which the chief executive would have powers similar to those of the existing British governor. The Legislative Council, constituted by a combination of direct and indirect elections, would only have limited powers. As analyzed above, its initiatives on proposing legislation as well as on revenues and expenditure of the government would be very limited; and if it rejected the budget introduced by the chief executive and the executive authorities, it would be dissolved. The Legislative Council would have no control over appointments by the chief executive nor the removal of principal officials; further, its watchdog role would be circumscribed by the chief executive's power not to allow government officials to testify or give evidence before the Legislative Council.

As the chief executive must be accountable to the central PRC government but not to the Legislative Council of the HKSAR, and the appointment as well as removal of the chief executive and principal officials must be approved by the central government, the autonomy of the HKSAR would certainly be affected. According to Article 101 of the 1982 PRC constitution, local people's congresses, at their respective levels, "elect, and have the power to recall, governors and deputy governors, or mayors and deputy mayors, or heads and deputy heads of counties, districts, townships and towns."[10] Article 104 further provides that "the standing committee or a local people's congress at and above the county level...decides on the appointment and removal of functionaries of state organs within the limits of its authority as prescribed by law."[11] Such appointments and dismissals only have to be reported to the local people's government at a higher level for record-keeping purposes.[12] Similar provisions exist for the organs of self-government of national autonomous units. It did not seem logical that the central PRC government should have more control over the appointment and dismissal of the chief executive and principal officials of the HKSAR than their counterparts in other local people's governments within the PRC, while the chief executive and principal officials of the Region should be less accountable to the Legislative Council of the HKSAR than their counterparts in other local people's governments within the PRC to their corresponding local people's congresses.

---

[10] *The Constitution*, p. 74.

[11] *Ibid.*, p. 76.

[12] "The Organic Law of the Local People's Congresses and the Local People's Governments of the PRC" was adopted by the Second Session of the Fifth National People's Congress in 1979. It was revised according to "Resolution on Certain Revisions of 'The Organic Law of the Local People's Congresses and the Local People's Governments of the PRC'" adopted by the Fifth Session of the Fifth National People's Congress in 1982. For the text of the revised law, see *Renmin Ribao* (Beijing), December 16, 1982.

More significantly, it appeared that the Chinese authorities wanted to have a certain measure of control over the formation of the first government and the first Legislative Council of the HKSAR (Annex III). Articles of the Basic Law, like any constitution, can only provide the bare skeleton of the political system, which also involves numerous precedents, conventions, practices, and regulations to be established through actual implementation of the Basic Law. The first two or three years after 1997 were therefore crucial. If in the first two years, both the chief executive and members of the Legislative Council were selected and elected respectively by the same election committee, it would be difficult for a system of checks and balances to function properly, and consequently the evolution of the political system of the HKSAR would be adversely affected.

A careful study of Article 56 of the draft Basic Law might provide a hint. It states: "Except for the appointment, removal and disciplining of public officers and the adoption of measures in emergencies, the Chief Executive shall consult the Executive Council before making important decisions, introducing a bill to the Legislative Council, enacting subsidiary legislation, or dissolving the Legislative Council. If the Chief Executive does not adopt a majority opinion of the Executive Council, he must put his specific reasons on record." This was a superficial and largely meaningless replication of the existing colonial system. In the existing British administration, appointments to the Executive Council were made by the Crown, i.e., the secretary of state for Foreign and Commonwealth Affairs; and the commander British Forces, the chief secretary, the financial secretary, and the attorney general were ex-officio members of the Executive Council. The appointments of these senior government officials also had to be approved by the secretary of state according to *Civil Service Regulations*. In this way, the need for the governor to consult the Executive Council on all important matters of policy constituted a means of check and balance, which was especially significant in view of the almost dictatorial powers of the governor. In the case of the chief executive of the HKSAR, he has full authority to appoint and dismiss members of the Executive Council, and it is difficult to see how the need to consult the Executive Council will similarly constitute a means of check and balance. It should be noted, however, that an earlier draft of the

Basic Law stipulated that members of the Executive Council should be nominated by the chief executive and appointed by the central government, and that if the chief executive did not adopt a majority opinion of the Executive Council, he should register his specific reasons and report them to the central government for record purposes.[13]

There was obviously an attempt to retain the political structure of the existing colonial government as both Beijing and the conservative business community see it as part of the foundation for Hong Kong's economic success and political stability. A statement by the former chairman of the Hong Kong Stock Exchange, Ronald Li, at an international investment conference perhaps best reflected the conservative business community's attitude. Lee declared: "Hong Kong is a colony. It is a dictatorship, although a benevolent one. It is and has been a British colony, and it's going to be a Chinese colony, and as such it will prosper. We do not need free elections here."[14] The colonial government in Hong Kong was certainly a benevolent one; there was ample liberty in the territory and the rule of law was observed. This colonial government, however, had to be accountable ultimately to a democratic government willing to defend freedom and the rule of law; this was the guarantee of its benevolence.

V Conclusion

The survey conducted in 1985 by Kuan Hsin Chi and Lau Siu Kai of the Chinese University of Hong Kong revealed that only 22.3% of the respondents believed that China would truly let Hong Kong people rule Hong Kong, as against 43.9% who expressed no confidence in the Chinese promise, and 33.8% who had not made up their mind. In addition, 62.3% of the respondents agreed or strongly agreed with the general statement

---

[13] Articles 9 and 10, Section 1, Chapter 4, "The Political Structure of the HKSAR" in the draft articles presented by the Subgroup on the Political Structure of the HKSAR to the Basic Law Drafting Committee meeting in August 1987; the text of these draft articles is in *Ta Kung Pao* (a Hong Kong Chinese newspaper), August 25, 1987.
[14] *South China Morning Post*, June 17, 1987.

that the political fate of Hong Kong people was beyond their control.[15] Since 1985, it appeared that political expectations and confidence had been on the decline.[16] Survey results released in mid-May 1988 indicated that 56.7% of the respondents who had picked up copies of the draft Basic Law had not read the document, while 35% had read a small part of it. Among those who knew of the draft Basic Law, only 6.9% said they were ready to comment on various articles of the draft.[17] To some extent, neither Beijing nor the Basic Law Consultative Committee (BLCC) had convinced the community of their eagerness to listen to the views of the Hong Kong people.[18] Meanwhile, a survey conducted in early May 1988 reflected that 24% of the respondents wanted to emigrate, and the percentage went up to 45.5% among those who had tertiary education and above.[19] A return to traditional political apathy and preparations to emigrate (among those who had the means to do so) were natural responses.

To arrest these trends, the Chinese authorities had to refrain from too much interference in the territory's political development. Their attempts to reserve in their own hands the final say in all important matters unfortunately created such an impression, and the draft Basic Law only reinforced it. Beijing had to also demonstrate once again China's willingness to listen and respond to the community's demands. Not too many people in Hong Kong would take part in open demonstrations to fight for democracy, but many well-educated citizens were aware that measures of checks and balances were essential for the future political system. Given that the powerful chief executive will have to be acceptable to Beijing, freely contested elections based on universal suffrage to an adequately empowered legislature would remain the most effective means

---

[15] See Kuan Hsin Chi and Lau Siu Kai, *op.cit.*, p. 105.

[16] See Joseph Y.S. Cheng, "Hong Kong: The Decline of Political Expectations and Confidence," *The Australian Journal of Chinese Affairs*, No. 19/20, January–July, 1988, pp. 241–267.

[17] *Ming Pao*, May 16, 1988, and *South China Morning Post*, May 16, 1988.

[18] 18. Andy Ho, "Confused DB Members to Put Their Case to Drafters," *ibid.*, May 17, 1988, and "Some Basic Mistakes," *ibid.*, May 18, 1988.

[19] *Ming Pao*, May 16, 1988.

of political participation and deterrence against the government's abuse of power. They would be a necessary guarantee of the freedom of expression as well as the foundation for the survival and development of existing political groups.

By the end of 1988, it appeared that the Chinese authorities would insist on the nomination and election of the chief executive by an electoral college at least for the initial two or three terms. As expected, they wanted to retain a measure of control on the election of the powerful chief executive, and would not allow the unpredictable and uncontrollable method of direct election. This was not acceptable to the pro-democracy movement, and no compromise was in sight.[20] There was every indication, however, that the Chinese authorities would have their way, and they had successfully isolated the democracy movement through the skillful mobilization of various groups and sophisticated exploitation of the mass media. The pro-democracy movement was also much handicapped by the growing apathy of the community. Then, in the spring of 1989 came the student demonstrations in Beijing, culminating in the tragic power struggles in China. These obviously provided a major boost for the morale of the pro-democracy movement in Hong Kong, which had reached a low point in the early months of the year. Suddenly, the arguments for democracy appeared irrefutable, and the community agreed that freedom and human rights could only be guaranteed by a system of representative government.

After the imposition of martial law in parts of Beijing, the movement established the Hong Kong Alliance in Support of the Patriotic Democratic Movement in China. The alliance was able to organize three rallies on three consecutive Sundays with over one million participants each time. This was exactly the kind of people's power that the movement had longed for. Members of the Legislative and Executive councils also reached a consensus that all seats of the HKSAR legislature should be directly elected by 2003, and that the chief executive should also be directly elected by universal franchise in the same year. Nevertheless, the Business and Professional Group of members of the BLCC still adopted a wait-and-see attitude.

---

[20] *Ibid.*, November 13, 1988.

In the struggle for a democratic political system with proper checks and balances as articulated in this chapter, the difficulties ahead would be formidable once the initial emotional reactions began to cool down. With an accelerating exodus of the middle class, the pro-democracy movement or its political parties would find it difficult to sustain its appeal, especially to the talented middle-class professionals to secure their time and resources for the cause of democracy in Hong Kong. If the hardline leaders who were responsible for the military crackdown on the Beijing students managed to stay in power (and initial indicators were that this would be so), then it would be very difficult to overcome the sense of political impotence in the people of Hong Kong.

A powerful chief executive and a weak legislature approximate to authoritarianism. If Beijing insisted on the final say in the selection of this powerful chief executive, it would be a sure recipe for further erosion of confidence, and the current prosperity might only be perceived by those with the required assets and qualifications as a final opportunity to make more money before emigration. Discussions on the future political system of the HKSAR would be meaningful only when the following two conditions were met. The first was that there would be a clear consensus so as to strengthen the unity of the community and thus enable it to appeal to Beijing and, to a lesser extent, the international community. The second was that before 1997, there would be a credible and legitimate government in China that considers modernization the most important goal of the nation and valued Hong Kong's actual and potential contribution to China's modernization program. It was probable that these two conditions would be met, but there was no guarantee that they would be met soon so that the local community's confidence would be restored in time.

The second condition was certainly more important, but quite beyond Hong Kong people's control. A regime in Beijing that lacks legitimacy and is resented by the people of Hong Kong would obstruct meaningful consultation and consensus on the development of representative government. Many Hong Kong people considered it futile to be concerned with the issue of democracy under such circumstances and the community would be divided on whether or not to accommodate the demands of such a regime.

Acknowledgement

Originally published as Cheng, Joseph Y.S., "The Post-1997 Government in Hong Kong: Toward a Stronger Legislature", *Asian Survey*, Vol. 29, No. 8 (August 1989), pp. 731–748. Reproduced with kind permission from the publisher.

Chapter 6

Prospects for Democracy in Hong Kong After the Beijing Massacre

I Loss of Confidence After the Beijing Massacre

The promises made by the Chinese leadership on self-administration for Hong Kong people generated expectations, especially among the better-educated younger generation. In preparation for the elections to come, middle-class political groups were prompted to develop their organizations at the grassroots level and establish close ties with pressure groups. At the same time, they became concerned about social issues at the district level and took part in related campaigns for citizens' rights. This process contributed to the expansion of almost all political groups.

The mood of the Hong Kong people, however, dramatically changed during the tragic Tiananmen Incident and in its aftermath. An opinion survey in late May 1989 revealed that after the declaration of martial law in Beijing, only 52% of the respondents showed confidence in the future of Hong Kong, whereas the corresponding indicator had been 60% in April 1989, and 75% in January of the same year.[1]

---

[1] *South China Morning Post*, June 16, 1989. The survey was conducted by Survey Research Hong Kong for the newspaper on May 26 and 27, 1989, and a random sample of 1,000 Hong Kong citizens was interviewed.

In response to the developments in China then a marked increase in emigration-related enquiries was received by the consulates of countries like the United States (U.S.), Canada, and Australia in the summer of 1989. In an opinion poll that summer, 37% of the respondents said that they were actively preparing to emigrate, or had family members who either resided abroad or had secured the right of permanent residence in a foreign country.[2] The same series of surveys had reported earlier in January 1989 that only 29% of the respondents were in the above categories at that time. Among executives, professionals, and entrepreneurs, the survey in June 1989 demonstrated that 64% of them planned to leave Hong Kong, 18% more than in January 1989.

A survey by the Federation of Hong Kong Industries held three weeks after the Tiananmen crackdown also showed that 75% of the manufacturers polled were either planning or considering emigration, while the survey held before the incident indicated that only 40% were in such a category.[3] The poll by the Federation in late June 1989 also revealed that local manufacturers' confidence in the territory's future was directly affected by the changes in the Chinese political situation, and their investment horizons had become oriented more to the short-term.

Given the fears at that time, demands for the right of abode for the 3.25 million holders of British Dependent Territory Citizen (BDTC) passports had stepped up, while attempts were also made to seek some form of international guarantee for Hong Kong people's rights and freedoms beyond 1997. In their panic, the Hong Kong people also renewed such proposals as purchasing South Pacific Islands, placing Hong Kong under United Nations Trusteeship, independence, etc. According to a poll by the *South China Morning Post* in late June, 18% of the respondents indicated that the most ideal option for Hong Kong people would be complete independence, and 31% opted for being an independent country within the British Commonwealth. Only 15% considered that the ideal choice would be a SAR under Chinese sovereignty as originally planned.[4]

---

[2] *Ibid.*, July 4, 1989. The survey was conducted by Survey Research Hong Kong for the newspaper during June 22–30, 1989.

[3] See *Ming Pao*, July 6, 1989.

[4] See *South China Morning Post*, June 26, 1989. The survey was conducted by Inrasia Pacific Limited three weeks after the Beijing Massacre.

China did nothing to help put fears to rest. When superficial calm was restored in Beijing's political scene, the regime quickly turned its attention to Hong Kong. The initial reaction was criticism, by name, of Hong Kong's mass media by Beijing's *People's Daily* and other official media.[5] Chinese leaders in early June attacked attempts of using Hong Kong as a "counter-revolutionary base". Beijing's mayor, Chen Xitong, in his report to the Standing Committee of the National People's Congress on the suppression of the student demonstrations, included a detailed account of the news reports on the incident from Hong Kong's mass media as evidence of their collusion with foreign influences in a conspiracy to reduce China to an appendage of international monopolistic capital.

On July 11, 1989, when the new General Secretary of the Party, Jiang Zemin, met the leading figures of the BLDC and the Basic Law Consultative Committee (BLCC), he warned that Hong Kong should not interfere with China. Jiang considered that "according to the principle of 'one country, two systems', China practices socialism, Hong Kong practices capitalism; the well water should not interfere with the river water."[6] The statements of Jiang and those previously made by Chinese officials responsible for Hong Kong affairs were basically aimed at providing assurances for Hong Kong's stability and prosperity, and at warning the Hong Kong people to refrain from acts which would threaten the Chinese Communist regime.

Though the vast majority of Hong Kong people were unhappy with the existing Chinese regime and were willing to severely criticize the regime verbally or through the mass media last spring, they had no intention of taking further action against it. Jiang's statements on "one country, two systems", on the other hand, caused considerable anxiety among Hong Kong people, especially the intellectuals. Though some of them would agree with the analogy that "the well water should not interfere with the river water", they feared that, conversely, when the Chinese river flooded, Hong Kong's well water would be affected. For example, the Hong Kong society treasured the rule of law, which was an

---

[5] Lousie do Rosario, "Out of Reach", *Far Eastern Economic Review*, Vol. 145, No. 29, July 20, 1989, p. 19.
[6] See *South China Morning Post*, June 12, 1989.

important pillar supporting the stability and prosperity of the territory. If the Hong Kong people, apart from observing the local law, had to exercise various self-restraints in response to the Chinese leaders' guidance and statements, as Jiang indicated, then the rule of law would be much eroded, and people would find it difficult to maintain their existing lifestyles.

Hong Kong affected China mainly by its objective existence. Hong Kong's economic progress had certainly prompted the Chinese people in the Mainland to cast doubt on the superiority of socialism. Yet, as long as the Chinese leaders wanted to make use of the territory's resources, they had to accept the compromise of "one country, two systems". The Hong Kong people always treasured their freedom of speech and freedom of the mass media. Up till then, they were able to discuss freely the issues of Mainland China, and the local mass media were able to report frankly of developments in China and evaluate them objectively. Such reports and commentaries had a considerable impact on international public opinion, particularly public opinion in overseas Chinese communities.

At the same time, the coverage of world news by the local mass media had much affected the PRC's effective control of information directed towards its own people. Hong Kong's radio and television programs could be received in many parts of Guangdong, and the intelligentsia in many major cities in China had access to Hong Kong publications. As Deng Xiaoping had acknowledged Hong Kong's significance regarding information inputs for China, the Chinese leadership had to accept the price as well.

In June and July 1989, China's official mass media began to criticize the activities of the Hong Kong Alliance in Support of the Patriotic Democratic Movement in China. On July 21, a signed article of the *People's Daily* criticized by clear implication the leaders of the Alliance, Martin Lee and Szeto Wah.[7] These serious accusations caused much concern in Hong Kong. Pro-Beijing figures and leaders of the political establishment such as the senior unofficial Legislative Councillor Allen Lee made use of the opportunity and appealed to the Hong Kong

---

[7] Ai Zhong, "Sabotaging 'One Country, Two Systems' Will Not be Allowed", *People's Daily*, July 21, 1989. Regarding the responses of Martin Lee and Szeto Wah, see *Ming Pao*, July 22, 1989.

community to avoid confrontation with China. These accusations, conveyed through the local mass media, certainly created a deterrence effect among ordinary people, and resulted in a setback for the pro-democracy movement's plan to form a political party. However, the threat from Beijing simultaneously damaged the confidence of Hong Kong people in the territory's future.

II Consultation on the Basic Law

When the new Party General Secretary, Jiang Zemin, received the leaders of the Basic Law Drafting and Consultative Committees, he also indicated that the Basic Law would be promulgated as scheduled in spring 1990 at the third plenary session of the Seventh National People's Congress. The Standing Committee of the National People's Congress then decided to extend the period of consultation on the Basic Law by only three months till the end of October 1989. This considerably disappointed people in Hong Kong, because it implied that the Chinese authorities were reluctant to revise, in any significant way, the draft Basic Law released in February 1989.

This timetable ignored the fact that after the Beijing Massacre, serious cleavages emerged within the Hong Kong community concerning the territory's future. In the past, Hong Kong people had accepted the Sino-British Joint Declaration; they only worried that it would not be observed. However, to some people, the Tiananmen Incident had reduced the document to a piece of paper. An opinion poll published by the *South China Morning Post* on October 31, 1989, showed that 69% of the respondents were not very confident or even fairly confident that the Basic Law would ensure that the "one country, two systems" promise would be kept. Martin Lee went so far as to openly ask for a renegotiation of the Sino-British Joint Declaration. Obviously, a lot of people then felt that it was meaningless to talk about the Basic Law. Some community leaders, scholars, and others, particularly those who were involved in the pro-democracy movement, refused to maintain contact with Chinese organs in Hong Kong or engage in any formal exchanges. A considerable segment of the population also lost its trust in the British government, especially that at this point it rejected granting the right of abode to British Dependent Territory Citizen (BDTC) passport holders.

Yet the establishment of the local community, the business world, and some opinion leaders still believed that the Sino-British Joint Declaration must be upheld, that the Basic Law and related discussions must be treated seriously, that the British administration in the transitional period must be supported wholeheartedly, and that contacts with the Chinese authorities at all levels must be maintained. Such basic divisions of views created difficulties in attracting people to discuss the Basic Law and to reach a consensus that would bestow legitimacy on it.

After the Beijing Massacre, two of the 23 Hong Kong members of the BLDC, Louis Cha and Bishop Kwong, formally resigned, and Martin Lee and Szeto Wah were removed from the drafting committee by China's National People's Congress.[8] The representativeness of the remaining Hong Kong members had thus been much weakened; they certainly lacked the trust of most Hong Kong people.

To rekindle the Hong Kong community's interest in the Basic Law, the Chinese authorities had to reorganize the BLDC and enhance its representativeness, to promise to revise the Basic Law draft to meet the community's concerns after the political turmoil in China, to extend the consultative period and to delay the promulgation of the Basic Law. The proposal of a referendum on the document should also be considered. Admittedly, these were highly idealistic demands, and not in accordance with the political realities in China. However, Beijing's position then on the Basic Law certainly had not been conducive to the re-establishment of confidence in the community. The latter would respond to the consultation process and the actual promulgation of the Basic Law with apathy and indifference, and the legitimacy of the Basic Law would suffer as a result.

In these circumstances, there emerged a broad consensus favoring the acceleration of representative government in the territory in the transitional period before 1997. To minimize Britain's responsibility for the territory, London and the local British administration showed strong support for an acceleration of this democratization process. In May 1989, the Executive

---

[8] There were some withdrawals from the Basic Law Consultative Committee too, but as it had not been active in articulating the community's views, the withdrawals did not attract much attention. See *South China Morning Post*, July 25, 1989.

and Legislative Councils reached a consensus on the direct election by universal suffrage of the chief executive and all seats of the legislature by 2003; and on the election by the same means in 1997 of one-half of the seats in the legislature.[9] Senior Hong Kong government officials also reversed their position and indicated that the directly elected Legislative Council seats that would be introduced in 1991 would be increased from 10 to 20. The report of the British House of Commons Foreign Affairs Select Committee released in late June 1989 even boldly suggested that by 1991, half of the Legislative Council seats should be directly elected; and by 1995, all seats should be directly elected.[10] This proposal was endorsed by the Joint Committee for the Promotion of Democratic Government, an umbrella organization representing the various groups of Hong Kong's pro-democracy movement. The Joint Committee also demanded a "through train" arrangement which meant that the Legislative Councillors elected in 1995 should automatically become members of the first legislature of the Hong Kong SAR. As to the chief executive, the Joint Committee's position was consistent in demanding that the post be directly elected by universal suffrage.[11]

In 1988–1989, the future shape of the political system of the Hong Kong SAR was the major controversy between the pro-democracy movement and the conservative business community. The latter enjoyed Beijing's support, and the British administration had, since the end of 1985, succumbed to the pressure of the Chinese authorities and agreed that Hong Kong's political structure increasingly would "converge" with the Basic Law.[12] However, the Beijing Massacre changed the situation. While the community (as demonstrated by the opinion polls at that time) and London had endorsed an acceleration of the democratization process, the conservative business community was forced to keep a low profile from May to July 1989. Nevertheless, Beijing's position was still the crucial factor, and the Thatcher government understood this well. When the

---

[9] *Ibid.*, July 25, 1989
[10] The report was published in full in *ibid.*, July 1, 1989.
[11] *Ibid.*, July 21, 1989.
[12] See Joseph Y.S. Cheng, "The Pressure to Converge", *International Affairs* (London), Vol. 63, No. 2, Spring 1987, pp. 271–283.

Foreign Secretary Sir Geoffrey Howe visited Hong Kong in early July 1989, he avoided making any concrete promise regarding the accelerated pace of the development of a system of representative government, only mentioning the consensus of the local Legislative and Executive Councils and expressing his willingness to listen.[13]

In mid-July, after a meeting between Party General Secretary Jiang Zemin and leaders of the BLDC and the BLCC, local pro-Beijing political figures began to articulate the view that accelerating the democratization process might lead to greater confrontation with Beijing after 1997.[14] Meanwhile, the Legislative and Executive Councils on July 26, 1989, endorsed the British administration's position that 20 seats (one-third) of the Legislative Council should be directly elected by 1991.[15] This was contrary to the Basic Law draft released in February 1989, which allowed for only 27% of the seats of the first HKSAR legislature to be directly elected.[16] In response, pro-Beijing political figures had been hinting that demands for a political system more democratic than that in the Basic Law draft were "naïve", and they were stepping up publicity activities to counter-attack the demands for more democracy.[17]

In the drafting process of the Basic Law since 1985, it had been well demonstrated that the Chinese leaders demanded the final say on all vital issues.[18] Admittedly though, in the Basic Law draft released in February 1989, revisions were made regarding Article 18 on the application of national laws in the Hong Kong SAR, and Article 19 on an independent

---

[13] For details of Sir Geoffrey Howe's visit to Hong Kong, see Emily Lau, "Abide With Me", *Far Eastern Economic Review*, Vol. 145, No. 28, July 13, 1989, pp. 10–11.

[14] See *South China Morning Post*, July 21, 1989.

[15] *Ibid.*, July 27, 1989.

[16] See *The Basic Law of the Hong Kong Special Administrative Region of the People's Republic of China* (Draft), Hong Kong: Consultative Committee for the Basic Law, February 1989, Annex II, p. 50.

[17] See *South China Morning Post*, July 29, 1989.

[18] See Joseph Cheng, "The Draft Basic Law: Messages for Hong Kong People", in Hungdah Chiu (ed.), *The Draft Basic Law of Hong Kong: Analysis and Documents*, Baltimore: School of Law, University of Maryland. Occasional Papers/ Reprint Series in Contemporary Asian Studies, No.5 – 1988, pp. 7–48.

judicial power and that of final jurisdiction of the Hong Kong SAR. These revisions went a considerable way in meeting the community's demands at that time. However, after the Beijing Massacre Hong Kong people felt that the autonomy of the Hong Kong SAR as defined by Chapter Two of the Basic Law draft was inadequate.

In view of the role of the People's Liberation Army (PLA) in the Beijing Massacre, the community became quite sensitive towards the stationing of the PLA in the HKSAR. Naturally, the issue was largely symbolic because the PLA contingents stationed across the border would require less than an hour to reach the urban center of the territory. However, Beijing rejected the suggestion that it should avoid stationing the PLA in the Hong Kong SAR while retaining a sovereign right to do so in the Basic Law. Again, the Chinese leaders placed considerations of sovereignty above the sensitivities of the local community.

In response to martial law and the military crackdown in Beijing, the report of the British Parliamentary Foreign Affairs Select Committee specifically referred to the last paragraph of Article 18 of the draft Basic Law. It states: "In case the Standing Committee of the National People's Congress decides to declare a state of war or, by reason of turmoil within the Hong Kong Special Administrative Region which is beyond the control of the Region, decides that the Region is in a state of emergency, the State Council may decree the application of the relevant national laws in the Region".[19] The Select Committee's report expressed concern at the involvement of the central government in the maintenance of the public security of the Hong Kong SAR, and suggested that Article 18 should be amended.

The community's requests at that time for the right of abode in the United Kingdom (U.K.) and to turn Hong Kong into a United Nations trustee territory reflected its worry that the Sino-British Joint Declaration and the Basic Law would not provide sufficient assurance against interference from Beijing. Some form of international guarantee thus became an increasingly important issue, as the British government

---

[19] *The Basic Law of the Hong Kong Special Administrative Region of the People's Republic of China* (Draft), *op. cit.*, p. 6.

recognized then. Mrs. Thatcher's call on the Commonwealth heads of state to give a clear statement of support for Hong Kong during the summit in Malaysia in October was seen by China as a conspiracy to "internationalize" the issue of Hong Kong.

The Chinese authorities reaffirmed their welcome for foreign investment. As China's US$40 billion foreign debt became a serious burden, its need for foreign aid and foreign investment became more urgent.[20] Foreign investors had the right to demand from the Chinese government guarantees of a satisfactory investment environment. Hitherto, Beijing accepted such demands from the foreign investors or their governments and promised to satisfy them. Western countries including the U.S., Japan, the U.K., and West Germany were major trading partners of Hong Kong, where they also had substantial investments. What the Hong Kong people needed to ask of these countries then was that the definition of "an attractive economic environment and investment climate" should include the maintenance of the existing rule of law, freedoms, and human rights. On this basis, these governments, or at least their chambers of commerce in Hong Kong, could form a committee and send a delegation to Beijing every year and present a report on its monitoring of the local "economic environment and investment climate". Through the report, foreign investors could express their concerns and suggest measures for improvement.

If the Western governments could be persuaded to respond to the lobbying efforts on the part of the British government and the local groups, and promise to accept Hong Kong people should a violent crackdown take place in the territory, then some additional pressure could be brought to bear on China. These Western governments would then have all the more reason to be concerned with the rule of law, freedoms, and human rights in Hong Kong. The bill of rights that the British administration was then considering was a step in the right direction. Its impact would be limited, but it would attract the attention of the parties concerned.

---

[20] *China Daily* (Beijing) reported on July 16, 1989, that China's foreign debt amounted to US$42 billion at the end of March 1989.

III Sino-British Confrontation and Beijing's United Front Activities

In the 1980s, the Communist Party of China was stepping up its activities in the territory and seeking to establish itself as a dominant political force.[21] It began publicly building its community network and influence in 1985 when the local branch of the New China News Agency opened three district offices in Hong Kong Island, Kowloon, and the New Territories. They also began to organize grassroots neighborhood groups. These groups had considerable resources at their disposal from China to organize activities, and would constitute unfair competition in various elections.

Since the conclusion of the Sino-British Joint Declaration the local New China News Agency and pro-Beijing organizations had been in an all-embracing united front campaign to win the hearts of the Hong Kong people. There were numerous rounds of receptions, cocktail parties, and trips to China. To a certain extent, the Chinese organs in Hong Kong were successful in co-opting businessmen, professionals, fledgling politicians, and grassroots community leaders, who were flattered by the embrace of the Chinese motherland and, at the same time, afraid to reject it.

The Chinese authorities in Hong Kong were carefully cultivating the media too, and this policy paid dividends. Top officials of the local New China News Agency branch wined and dined with the Hong Kong media proprietors; middle- and lower-ranking executives as well as editors and reporters were important targets of the Chinese united front strategy. To be fair, the Chinese officials did not make any specific demands on local media proprietors, but the successful united front operation ensured that, with the exception of a limited number of newspapers and news monthlies, few harsh criticisms were aired against Chinese policies towards Hong Kong or against China in general. The television stations were especially friendly.

---

[21] Emily Lau, "Positioning for Power" and "Grasping the Grassroots", *Far Eastern Economic Review*, Vol. 137, No. 32, August 6, 1987, pp. 26–29; see also Loong Sin (pseudonym), *A Shadow Government of Hong Kong* (in Chinese), Hong Kong: Haishan Tushu Gongsi, no publication data given, probably 1986.

These hitherto successful united front activities encountered a major setback during the political turmoil in China at the end of the 1980s. A key element in the Chinese leaders' damage-control strategy in the aftermath of the Beijing Massacre was to portray it as having been necessary to suppress an anti-revolutionary rebellion. However, Hong Kong news reports, in Chinese and accessible to many in mainland China through their Hong Kong friends, had been seriously undermining the Chinese leaders' efforts to whitewash the massacre. This was why the Chinese authorities were publicly chiding the Hong Kong media for their treatment of Beijing's power struggles in the spring and summer of 1989.

Relations with the local media deteriorated sharply in May and June, but surprisingly united front activities started again in mid-June and achieved results. While reports of political suppression in China were still given prominent coverage in many newspapers in Hong Kong, they were also willing to carry publicity materials disseminated by the local New China News Agency and other Chinese organs. Emphasis on the maintenance of the stability and prosperity of the territory became conspicuous again, as the mass media followed closely the mood of the community. Self-censorship, as existed in the past two or three years prior to May–June 1989, gradually returned and was most prominent at the television stations. It was anticipated that self-censorship of the mass media would become more serious and a significant obstacle in the development of the local pro-democracy movement.

Beijing's united front strategy, however, was still considerably hampered by two factors. As pointed out by a former employee of a pro-Beijing organization in Hong Kong, since the Beijing Massacre and especially since the purge at *Wen Wei Po* (a local left-wing newspaper), "Hong Kong's Left has been ripped apart, with many of its stalwarts fleeing and many of its organizations in a state of crisis."[22] The continuing purge in pro-Beijing organizations in Hong Kong caused much subterranean bitterness and resentment among both mainland Chinese and the Hong Kong Chinese who worked for them. More important still, the purge

---

[22] K.H. Lau (pseudonym for a former employee of a left-swing organization in Hong Kong), "The Purge Next Door", *Far Eastern Economic Review*, Vol. 145, No. 36, September 7, 1989, p. 77.

resulted in the loss of many competent and enthusiastic local talents who joined these organizations in the mid-1970s. Many of them were holding upper-middle level jobs before the purge. Their departure would damage Beijing's united front work in the territory as well as the recruitment exercises of the pro-Beijing organizations.

A second factor was the Chinese leadership's reluctance to make concessions to salvage the loss of confidence in Hong Kong after the Beijing Massacre. Lu Ping, deputy director of the State Council's Hong Kong and Macau Affairs Office, stated in Macau on September 6, 1989: "They (the Hong Kong people) are just making unnecessary worries for themselves. The so-called confidence problem has been created by Hong Kong people, and should be solved by them because they are responsible for the problem".[23] As the incumbent Chinese leadership was responsible for the massacre and deemed it necessary and correct, it could admit that the political turmoil in China in 1989 had exacerbated the confidence crisis in the territory and that therefore something had to be done. Lu Ping understood Hong Kong too well to make such insensitive statements, but he had to toe the Party line.

Despite these two adverse factors, China's united front work remained formidable because its "unholy alliance" with the local conservative business community remained largely intact. The latter had been closely involved in business activities in China and was keen to maintain the economic status quo in the territory. It appreciated the Chinese leadership's maintenance of the open-door policy and was unwilling to accept the Hong Kong community's demand for an acceleration of democratic reforms, or London's support for those demands.

The Thatcher government, in its eagerness to demonstrate its "moral commitment" to the territory and enhance the legitimacy of the local British administration, attempted to bring pressure on China on such issues as the stationing of the PLA in the Hong Kong SAR, the political system of the Hong Kong SAR, and the relationship between the Hong Kong SAR and the central government. As the Chinese leaders refused to make concessions in response to the territory's confidence crisis, Sino-British "contradictions" sharpened after the Tiananmen massacre.

---

[23] *South China Morning Post*, September 7, 1989.

This confrontation was exposed to the public and escalated into a diplomatic confrontation when the Chinese authorities denounced a senior Hong Kong government official in charge of 1997 affairs for what they deemed to be gross violations of basic diplomatic rules.[24] Barrie Wiggham, Secretary for General Duties, made a speech entitled "Picking Up the Pieces" at a Rotary Club lunch meeting in mid-August 1989.[25] He listed several areas in the draft Basic Law that he said needed further examination, including the proposed arrangement for the stationing of the PLA in the Hong Kong SAR after 1997. In response to Wiggham's comments, the overseas edition of the *People's Daily* published a New China News Agency dispatch criticizing Wiggham for publicly interfering in the drafting of the Basic Law.[26] The decision on the PLA garrison in the Hong Kong SAR was closely associated with Deng Xiaoping personally, which meant that the Chinese officials responsible for Hong Kong affairs had to defend it vigorously. They too were angered by Wiggham's open raising of an issue that had been settled in the original negotiations leading to the Sino-British Joint Declaration — especially at a time when some in the local community were casting doubt on the document.

According to an opinion poll in July–August 1989, four out of five in the community favored speedier democratic reforms, even at the risk of confrontation with the Chinese government.[27] Moreover, 67% of the respondents supported the pace of reform as advocated for 1991 by the Legislative and Executive Councils. Another survey revealed that 64% of those interviewed favored the creation of political parties to contest direct elections to the Legislative Council, while only 17% were

---

[24] *Ibid.*, August 19, 1989.

[25] Barrie Wiggham's speech on August 14, 1989 was reported by all major Hong Kong newspapers the following day.

[26] *People's Daily* (overseas edition), August 18, 1989. The two local pro-China newspapers, *Wen Wei Po* and *Ta Kung Pao*, had earlier carried similar commentaries.

[27] See *South China Morning Post*, August 3, 1989. The survey was conducted by Inrasia Pacific Limited for the newspaper between July 28 and August 1, 1989, and a random sample of 619 respondents was interviewed.

against.[28] For the first time since the end of 1985, the British administration, the pro-democracy movement and public opinion were in accord.

Whereas the conservative business community kept a very low profile in May and early June 1989, in view of the emotional state of local opinion, when the Chinese media began to attack the anti-Beijing activities in the territory, the conservative business community became emboldened and launched a campaign for a political system in the Hong Kong SAR that would best guarantee its interests. The New Hong Kong Alliance, a group of businessmen and supporters of the Chinese government, proposed in early September 1989, a bicameral legislature for the Hong Kong SAR, with the second chamber made up of members from key functional constituencies, i.e., the business and financial community as well as the professionals.[29] Under the proposal, all legislation would require the approval of both chambers. The proposal was not well received, but it attracted much attention as many believed that Beijing was behind it.

Meanwhile, some self-proclaimed "middle-of-the-roaders" attempted to mediate between the pro-democracy movement and the conservative business community by proposing several compromise formulae. Similar attempts had been made in the second half of the 1980s, and many leading figures in this group had strong links to pro-Beijing organizations and business groups. The emergence of several such proposals on the political system of the Hong Kong SAR eroded the consensus behind the reform package advocated by the Legislative and Executive Councils, which in any case were not recognized by Beijing as representing the Hong Kong people. A Mainland member of the BLDC, Xiao Weiyun, indicated in early September 1989 that China would not consider the consensus model of the Legislative and Executive Councils for the development of Hong Kong's political structure. He stated: "How can we consider the opinion of the Executive Council, Legislative Council or other officials of Hong

---

[28] See *Sunday Morning Post*, August 20, 1989. The survey was conducted by Inrasia Pacific Limited for the newspaper between August 8 and August 14, 1989, and a random sample of 602 households was interviewed.

[29] See Emily Lau, "Red Herring", *Far Eastern Economic Review*, Vol. 145, No. 37, September 14, 1989, pp. 26–27.

Kong? The Sino-British Joint Declaration clearly states that the Basic Law is a Chinese internal affair. This is understood by China, Britain and Hong Kong".[30]

Under such circumstances, would the British government stand firm on its position then for a more democratic political system for Hong Kong and risk confrontation with the Chinese authorities? The answer to this question appeared to be negative. While London was obviously interested in doing something for Hong Kong in compensation for its rejection of the local population's demand for the right of abode in the U.K., in the longer term, it could fall back on the excuse that the pace of democratization had to be slowed in view of the opposition from Beijing and from the local conservative business community. After all, the Thatcher government wanted an honourable retreat from Hong Kong, and it was interested in continued cooperation with Beijing on Hong Kong as well as on other bilateral issues. Such a turnabout would be eased by the fact that the sense of political impotence on the part of Hong Kong people meant that they normally thought that it would be futile to exert pressure on either London or Beijing. At the same time, while they desired democracy, they did not attach much significance to it and were largely unwillingly to fight for it.

Nevertheless, if the Thatcher government backed down again on the issue of the pace of democratization, the legitimacy of the British administration in Hong Kong would be further eroded. And, as the pro-democracy movement failed to deliver, its leaders would lose credibility. The establishment leaders too would not be popular among the people as they had either failed to stand up to Beijing's pressure or, worse still, had been co-opted by Beijing's united front. The leadership vacuum in Hong Kong would become very serious.

The pro-democracy movement was not able to respond to Beijing's united front strategy effectively. Its major difficulty lay in the local community's renewed political apathy. If it could not demonstrate that its position was backed by the majority of the community, then its bargaining power would remain limited. It was expected that this political apathy would only become more widespread as 1997 approached. Members of

---

[30] *South China Morning Post*, September 7, 1989.

the middle-class political groups were absorbed with plans for emigration. They were largely professionals who had the means to do so, so their political sensitivity and strong feeling for personal freedom and democracy exacerbated their pessimism regarding the territory's future. The pro-democracy movement tended to be dominated by a small core of organizers and activists who performed well in electoral campaigns and mass rallies. However, without a broad base of successful middle-class professionals, the movement would have difficulty in winning the trust of the business groups and respectability within the community.

The pro-democracy movement had also failed in the late 1980s to mobilize sufficient numbers of competent writers and speakers to explain its position to the public via the mass media. On the other hand, the wealth of the conservative business community enabled it to employ prestigious public relations firms to manage its propaganda and image. A movement whose strength mainly lay in numbers at this stage found its effectiveness in exploiting the mass media and mobilizing the common people circumscribed by lack of resources. This was reflected in the failure of the three main political groups in the movement, namely, Meeting Point, the Hong Kong Affairs Society, and the Association for Democracy and People's Livelihood, to expand their memberships. The group most oriented to the middle-class, the Hong Kong Affairs Society, had been hardest hit.

The small group of intellectuals who backed the cause of democracy in the territory and who were influential in the local mass media gradually were losing enthusiasm for the cause. Some had dropped out because of their pessimism and their sense of helplessness in view of the pressure from Beijing. However, many of them planned to maintain their critical role from overseas, in the belief that freedom of speech and publication would become increasingly curtailed as Hong Kong approached 1997. They perceived their contribution as critics of China's developments, and they believed their strength lay in their ability to influence overseas Chinese opinion. The accelerating emigration of Hong Kong people to North America and the considerable number of scholars and students from China in the same continent created a potential readership which might be large enough to support publications. The *Nineties* and *Cheng Ming*, the two most influential news magazines in Hong Kong that were highly critical of China, managed to sell thousands of copies in North America at that time; and *Cheng Ming* even printed an American edition on the West Coast. Many newspapers in Hong Kong published overseas editions, and the anti-Communist ones might move overseas if they found it difficult to continue their operations in the territory. (Admittedly, none of the publications could yet survive on their overseas circulations alone.)

Internal unity within the pro-democracy movement was also a problem. Despite two or three years of negotiations among Meeting Point, the Hong Kong Affairs Society and the Association for Democracy and People's Livelihood failed to agree to form a united political party. Besides the normal mutual jealousies and competition for leadership, there was a major cleavage within the pro-democracy movement. Increasingly, the differences between those who were openly critical of China and those who were keen to maintain a dialogue with the Chinese authorities surfaced. In many ways, this was the major difference between those who were less optimistic about Hong Kong's future, more inclined to emigrate before 1997 and had no intention of seeking public offices and those who were less pessimistic regarding the territory's future, more likely to stay and more eager to seek public offices by electoral means.

Moreover, as the pro-democracy movement's leadership was then dominated by activists (many of whom held electoral offices), it lacked an overall view of the development of the movement and tended to respond to events as they emerged. This leadership was obviously much overburdened too. In sum, the pro-democracy movement had much to improve before it could withstand the formidable challenge of China's united front strategy.

IV Prognosis

Although news about the brain drain made headlines in Hong Kong so often in the late 1980s and early 1990s, those who could leave the territory between then and 1997 would be less than a million, probably around half a million. In other words, about five million people would have to stay in Hong Kong. From this local community's point of view, the Sino-British Joint Declaration had to be acknowledged as binding, the drafting of the Basic Law had to be taken seriously, the British administration in the transitional period had to be supported, and contacts with the Chinese authorities had to be maintained at all levels. A survey published in the *Ming Pao* on July 28, 1989, indicated that 55% of the respondents believed that local participation in the drafting of the Basic Law should be continued, while 44% considered that participation would not change the outcome.[31]

The Chinese leadership's policy line then was to maintain the open door policy and the reforms in the economic arena while pursuing a conservative Leninist line politically. The deteriorating economic situation in China and the shortage of foreign exchange would prompt the Chinese leadership to treat the maintenance of Hong Kong's stability and prosperity seriously. In many ways, their interests and those of the conservative business community were alike. So, if the territory's external environment did not change drastically, Hong Kong's economy would not be too adversely affected. However, obviously, too, the slow-down in the international economy and China's economic difficulties were likely to hurt Hong Kong's economic growth considerably.

At the same time, the sense of insecurity on the part of the Chinese Communist regime in the aftermath of China's mass protests, the three demonstrations in Hong Kong in May–June 1989 in which over one million people participated, the defections in May of the Chinese organs in Hong Kong,[32] and the impact of the local mass media inside China last spring would most likely cause Beijing to strengthen its control of and interference in Hong Kong. This implied that the freedoms that Hong Kong people would continue to enjoy would be those restricted to dancing and horse-racing. Hence, while Hong Kong people might have a reasonable chance of maintaining their existing living standards, their freedoms, human rights and the rule of law would probably be considerably eroded. The options were whether to acquiesce or emigrate. Unfortunately, almost five million people did not even have the choice.

---

[31] The survey was conducted by Survey Research Hong Kong for the newspaper in July 1989. A random sample of 540 citizens aged between 15 and 64 was interviewed.
[32] See Emily Lau, "Waiting for the Axe", *Far Eastern Economic Review*, Vol. 144, No. 25, July 22, 1989, p. 19.

The earlier analysis had not yet taken into consideration the future changes in the Chinese political scene. Most Hong Kong people expected a period of major chaos in China after Deng Xiaoping's death, and whether or not Hong Kong could survive this crisis was not known. Thus, at that time, a popular topic among concerned citizens was — what was the most appropriate timeframe for Deng's death, from the point of view of the territory's future?

It was a testing period for the pro-democracy movement. While it had to demonstrate leadership and provide guidance, developments in China were beyond its control. The movement would have to prepare for direct elections to the Legislative Council in 1991 and 1995, and it would have to perform on the bread-and-butter issues such as public housing, medical care, transport, and education. On the other hand, the political uncertainty of the territory's future and the anticipated economic difficulties in the territory following the political turmoil in China had seriously eroded the bargaining position of the advocates for more social services and greater redistribution of wealth.[33]

The pro-democracy movement would probably continue as the opposition both inside and outside the Legislative Council, but the resistance it encountered would become stronger, and sympathy from the mass media would be less forthcoming. While the movement's demand for more social services would remain popular, the danger was that it might have few achievements to boast of. As its members had little experience in policymaking, the movement's credibility as an alternative administration would be severely limited.[34] This limitation would be more clearly demonstrated when conservatives Stephen Cheong and T.S. Lo emerged with political groups which could claim to have the implicit

---

[33] According to a forecast by Business International, Hong Kong's economic growth would suffer over the next five years from China's Political turmoil and the slowing economies around the world. The territory's growth in real gross domestic product over the next five years would drop to an average of 4.3% per annum, compared with an average of 8.4 % per annum in the past five years. See *South China Morning Post*, September 6, 1989. The Hong Kong government also predicted that 42,000 people would emigrate from Hong Kong in 1989, and that the figure would rise to 55,000 in 1990; see *ibid.*, September 9, 1989.

[34] Margaret Ng, "Democratic Leaders Have Lost Direction", *ibid.*, December 6, 1988.

blessing of the Chinese authorities, the British administration and the business community. Their political groups would be able to claim they have ample experience in administering Hong Kong and could therefore maintain the continuity of the system. When people in Hong Kong were presented with a choice between the status quo and a radical change, they would most likely react in the same way as the electorates in Japan and Singapore, who tended to endorse the respective parties in power because of their contribution to the stability and prosperity of the two countries.[35]

In the long term, the pro-democracy movement would have to be prepared psychologically to remain in opposition for a decade and more, during which period it would have to strengthen its grassroots organization, demonstrate its commitment to Hong Kong's stability and prosperity, while fighting for social justice and a fairer distribution of wealth, and, above all, maintain its integrity under the pressure and temptations of China's united front strategy and the temptation of cooptation by the local political establishment. These were no easy tasks, but the prospects for democracy in Hong Kong were certainly no worse than they were in Taiwan and South Korea in the 1970s and early 1980s. Like its counterparts in almost all Third World countries, the movement would have to withstand a long period of severe tests. When the corrupt practices from China spread to Hong Kong, leaders of the movement might even be provided with an enhanced opportunity to reveal their superior moral fibre in the eyes of the community.

Discussions on the prospects for democracy in Hong Kong, however, would be meaningful only when the two following conditions were met. The first was that there must be a very clear consensus in favor of it, which would enable the local community to appeal to Beijing and, to a lesser extent, the international community. The second was that before 1997,

---

[35] In a survey conducted by Inrasia Pacific Limited for the *Sunday Morning Post* in August 1989 on the basis of a random sample of 602 respondents, it was discovered that the Hong Kong public was divided over three potential candidates for the post of the first chief executive of the Hong Kong SAR, with 27% of the respondents favoring Martin Lee, a leader of the pro-democracy movement, 24% supporting Lydia Dunn, appointed senior member of the Executive Council and 23% supporting Allen Lee, appointed senior member of the Legislative Council. The latter two establishment figures together obtained almost half of the "votes". See *Sunday Morning Post*, August 27, 1989.

there had to be a credible and legitimate government in China which considered modernization the most important goal and valued Hong Kong's actual and potential contribution to its modernization program. These two conditions might well be met in the end, but there was no guarantee that they would be met in sufficient time to restore the local community's confidence during the countdown to 1997.

Acknowledgement

Reproduced from Cheng, Joseph Y.S., "Prospects for Democracy in Hong Kong After the Beijing Massacre", *The Australian Journal of Chinese Affairs*, No. 23 (January 1990), pp. 161–185, ©1990 University of Chicago Press.

Chapter 7

The Basic Law: Messages for the Hong Kong People

I Introduction

The Sino-British Joint Declaration indicated that the People's Republic of China (PRC)'s basic policies regarding Hong Kong, as stated in the Joint Declaration and elaborated in its Annex I, "will be stipulated, in a Basic Law of the Hong Kong Special Administrative Region (HKSAR) of the People's Republic of China, by the National People's Congress (NPC) of the People's Republic of China, and they will remain unchanged for 50 years." The Joint Declaration further pointed out that the PRC's decision to establish a HKSAR was "in accordance with the provisions of Article 31 of the Constitution of the People's Republic of China."

Article 31 of the PRC Constitution states: "The state may establish special administrative regions when necessary. The systems to be instituted in special administrative regions shall be prescribed by law enacted by the National People's Congress in the light of specific conditions." In line with this, the Constitution grants the NPC the power "to decide on the establishment of special administrative regions and the systems to be instituted there."

The drafting of the Basic Law was therefore the PRC's domestic affair. It would be a "mini-constitution", defining the respective authorities of the Central Government in Beijing and the HKSAR government, the political system of the HKSAR and the rights and obligations of Chinese citizens in the HKSAR. Naturally, the people of Hong Kong were concerned as to whether their representatives would be involved in the drafting process and in which ways they would be consulted to make sure that the Basic Law would be acceptable to them before its formal promulgation.

As the PRC government could not hold elections in Hong Kong, it had to appoint representatives of the Hong Kong people to the Basic Law Drafting Committee (BLDC). The difficulty was how to select a respectable sample that would be trusted by the Hong Kong community and acceptable to the PRC authorities. The choice had to enhance the PRC's united front work in Hong Kong as well. This select group, however, had to avoid being perceived as a new centre of authority challenging the British administration in Hong Kong.

When membership of the BLDC was announced in July 1985, it was clear that the PRC government placed top priority on the stability and prosperity of the territory and that radical political reforms would be unlikely. There were 23 members from Kong 59-member committee, most of them were prominent businessmen and leading professionals. Interests of the establishment in Hong Kong apparently were assured, as the PRC authorities were keen to retain Hong Kong's attractiveness to investors. The most important function of the Hong Kong members in the BLDC was to provide legitimacy to the Basic Law. Their involvement in the drafting work and their endorsement of the final document were aimed at substantiating the claim that it was acceptable to the Hong Kong community. As BLDC held only two or three plenary sessions a year (nine sessions altogether), the actual drafting work was largely performed by a secretariat composed of experts from the PRC State Council's Hong Kong and Macau Affairs office and the relevant sections of the Ministry of Foreign Affairs. The role of the Hong Kong members was mainly advisory. After all, they were a minority in the BLDC and the Basic Law had to go through the NPC.

Though the Hong Kong members of the BLDC had been contacted and consulted by local New China News Agency officials, they were quite ignorant until their departure for Beijing of what their respective appointments were based on, to whom they were accountable, their terms of office, their powers and responsibilities, and even the agenda of their first meeting. Nor did they appear to be very concerned about these issues.

According to the speech of the Chairman of the BLDC, Ji Pengfei (also Director of the PRC State Council's Hong Kong and Macau Affairs Office), at the opening ceremony of the BLDC's first meeting:

> The Basic Law Drafting Committee is the working organ established by the National People's Congress for drafting the Basic Law of the Hong Kong Special Administrative Region; it is responsible to the National People's Congress, and when the National People's Congress is not in session, it is responsible to the Standing Committee of the National People's Congress.

In response to a small number of Hong Kong members of the BLDO, who articulated the local community's interests, the PRC authorities were forced to consider the moral responsibility that these members bore to the people of Hong Kong. Later, in a subgroup meeting, Ji Pengfei indicated that the Hong Kong members of the BLDC might consider issues from the point of view of "two systems" — yet they also should try to consider issues more from the point of view of "one country". In Ji's view, the Hong Kong members had to be accountable not only to their Hong Kong compatriots, but also to the entire Chinese nation, because they had been appointed by the Standing Committee of the NPC. Ji's explanation reflected the moral and political identity crisis of the Hong Kong members of the BLDC.

The first task of the Hong Kong members was to form a Basic Law Consultative Committee (BLCC). According to the constitution of the BLCC, its objective was "to engage in consultative activities in Hong Kong for the purpose of drafting the Basic Law of the Hong Kong Special Administrative Region in accordance with the will of the entire Chinese people including the Hong Kong compatriots." If the BLCC had to act "in accordance with the will of the entire Chinese people," then what weight should be attached to the will of the Hong Kong people?

In short, the organization and membership of the BLCC, the drafting of its constitution, and the associated controversy over the phrase "democratic consultations" in its draft constitution, and the authority of its executive committee and the procedures governing the revision of its constitution all demonstrated the PRC authorities' intention to control this supposedly unofficial, voluntary organization. The subsequent election of the Chairman, Vice-Chairmen, and Secretary-General of the BLCC's executive committee (based on a slate presented by a BLDC Vice-Chairman) caused an uproar, and Hong Kong became deeply suspicious of the PRC authorities intentions.

While the BLCC was being formed, some political groups and commentators indicated that the Hong Kong BLDC members should refrain from joining the BLCC, so as to ensure the independence of this unofficial and voluntary organization. Later, it also was suggested that, at the very least, the Hong Kong BLDC members should not serve on the BLCC's executive committee. The result, however, was that seven Hong Kong members of the BLDC joined the BLCC, and that six of them served on the BLCC's executive committee. Further, a BLDC Vice-Chairman served as the Chairman of the BLCC's executive committee and the Deputy Secretary-General of the BLDC served as the Secretary-General of the BLCC's executive committee (the latter was also concurrently Deputy Secretary-General of the Hong Kong branch of the New China News Agency). The control of the BLCC by the BLDC was considerable, despite the stipulation in its constitution that "the Consultative Committee and the Drafting Committee shall be independent of and not subordinate to each other."

The release of the *Draft Basic Law of the Hong Kong Special Administrative Region of the People's Republic of China* (for solicitation of opinions) (hereinafter the "draft Basic Law") on April 28, 1988, and the consultation process associated with it ideally should offer an important opportunity for inculcating a sense of belonging to the community. Further, they should consolidate support for the implementation of the ideal of "one country, two systems" through the establishment of the HKSAR. Unfortunately, traditional political apathy had already returned to Hong Kong by then. Survey results released in mid-May 1988 indicated that 56.7% of the respondents who had picked up copies of the draft Basic Law read the document, while 35% had read a small part of it. Among those who knew of the draft Basic Law, only 6.9% said they would comment on various articles of the draft, while 34.7% indicated that they had not yet decided and 58% were not prepared to give their views. Of those who were prepared to give their views, they did not seem to be aware of the channels offered by the BLCC. Ironically, 30.8% of them chose to rely on the District Boards and the District offices of the Hong Kong government.

When the Basic Law was formally enacted and promulgated by the NPC on April 4, 1990, there was hardly any interest in the document, and the event was treated in a low-key manner by the pro-Beijing organs in the territory. An opinion poll published by the *South China Morning Post* on October 31, 1989 showed that 69% of the respondents were not very confident nor even fairly confident that the Basic Law would ensure that the "one country, two systems" promise would be kept. The Hong Kong people at that time tended to believe that the sense of insecurity on the part of the Chinese Communist regime in the aftermath of China's mass protests in Tiananmen Square, the three demonstrations in Hong Kong in May–June 1989 in which over one million people participated, the defections in May 1989 of the personnel of the Chinese organs in Hong Kong, and the impact of the local mass media inside China in the spring of that fateful year would most likely cause Beijing to strengthen its control of and interference in Hong Kong. This implied that the freedoms the Hong Kong people would continue to enjoy would be those restricted to dancing and horse-racing. Hence, while the Hong Kong people might have a reasonable chance of maintaining their existing living standards, their freedoms, human rights, and the rule of law would probably be considerably eroded. The options were whether to acquiesce or emigrate. However, almost five million people would not even have the choice.

While intensely following the events in China, there emerged a conviction in the territory that if freedom, human rights, and democracy could not be guaranteed in China, they could not be well protected in Hong Kong after 1997. Most Hong Kong people also expected a period of major chaos in China after Deng Xiaoping's death, and whether or not Hong Kong could survive such a crisis was not known. A popular topic at that time among concerned citizens was — what would be the most appropriate time-frame for Deng's death, from the point of view of the territory's future?

II The Constitutional and Legal Status of the Basic Law and the HKSAR

In terms of the hierarchy of laws in the PRC, the Constitution "is the fundamental law of the state and has supreme legal authority." The basic laws, ordinary statutes, administrative rules, and regulations enacted by the State Council stand next in line. They are followed by the local regulations adopted by the people's congresses of provinces and municipalities directly under the central government and their standing committees. This hierarchy strictly defined, and laws of a lower level cannot contravene those of a higher level. The Basic Law of the HKSAR belongs to the category of "basic law"; a law similar to it in status is the Law on Regional Autonomy for Minority Nationalities of the PRC, which was adopted on May 31, 1984, by the NPC.

Ever since the ideas of "one country, two systems" and a Basic Law for the HKSAR were first raised by the PRC leaders, the relationship between the Basic Law and the PRC Constitution had been a serious concern of the Hong Kong community. The idea of "one country, two systems" was to allow Hong Kong's current social and economic systems to remain unchanged. This promise by the PRC leadership was embodied in Article 3(5) of the Sino-British Joint Declaration and has been stipulated in the Basic Law. The PRC Constitution, however, clearly states that "the Chinese people of all nationalities will continue to…follow the socialist road." A careful examination of the following articles of the Constitution obviously casts doubt on the ability of the Basic Law to provide for the continuance of the capitalist system in Hong Kong for 50 years after its return to the PRC in 1997. These constitutional provisions are:

> Article 1: "The People's Republic of China is a socialist state under the people's democratic dictatorship led by the working class and based on the alliance of workers and peasants."
>
> Article 5: "The state upholds the uniformity and dignity of the socialist legal system. No law or administrative or local rules and regulations shall contravene the Constitution."
>
> Article 6: "The basis of the socialist economic system of the People's Republic of China is socialist public ownership of the means of production, namely, ownership by the whole people and collective ownership by the working people."

Even before the initialing of the Sino-British Joint Declaration, various groups in Hong Kong indicated to the PRC officials responsible for Hong Kong affairs that the guarantee of a capitalist system in Hong Kong might be in violation of the PRC Constitution; and revision of Article 31 of the Constitution was suggested. The PRC authorities apparently were reluctant to discuss revision of the Constitution, but they were aware that some form of assurance was necessary.

The issue was raised repeatedly in the initial phase of the drafting of the Basic Law. Finally, Shao Tianren, co-convener of the Subgroup on the Relationship between the Central Government and the SAR of the BLDC and a legal expert of the PRC Ministry of Foreign Affairs, indicated after a May–June 1986 meeting of the Subgroup that the proposal to rewrite Article 31 of the PRC Constitution would not be accepted. Shao felt that the Constitution should not be altered too easily, and that the problem with previous Constitutions was that there had been too many changes. He, therefore, would like to solve the problem without having to amend the Constitution. Nonetheless, it was acknowledged that a consensus existed in the Subgroup on the need to clarify the relationship between the Basic Law and the PRC Constitution in order to assure the Hong Kong community that socialism as prescribed by the Constitution would not be practised in the territory. It was suggested that the PRC authorities' reluctance to amend the Constitution was largely related to the concept of "saving face" and the consideration that any amendment of Article 31 of the Constitution might imply that the very provisions of the Sino-British Joint Declaration were in violation of the Constitution as it stood in 1984.

The Hong Kong community's reaction was that these considerations should not be put above the rule of law. It also sensed a resentment against such a demand from PRC officials responsible for Hong Kong and Macau affairs, who felt that a small territory such as Hong Kong should not be involved with the highest level of state affairs like the revision of the Constitution. Incidentally, in April 1988, the Seventh NPC amended Article 10 of the Constitution, deleting the prohibition against leasing land and added the sentence: "Land-use rights according to legal regulation can be transferred."

In contrast to the PRC's national autonomous regions, the power of autonomy of the SARs is not guaranteed by the Constitution, but stipulated by basic laws promulgated by the NPC. (In the case of the HKSAR, the Sino-British Joint Declaration provides a further guarantee in its form an international agreement.) However, as the HKSAR's power of autonomy is to be defined by the Basic Law promulgated by the NPC, this power of autonomy, from a constitutional point of view, is of a lower order than that of the national autonomous regions embodied in the Constitution. In terms of the actual powers enjoyed by the HKSAR, as outlined by Annex I of the Sino-British Joint Declaration and the Basic Law, the HKSAR would enjoy a much higher degree of actual autonomy than the existing national autonomous regions of the PRC.

As a SAR under the sovereignty of the PRC, Hong Kong was warned against the tendencies of becoming an independent political entity. The Sino-British Joint Declaration states: "The HKSAR will enjoy a high degree of autonomy..." However, a high degree of autonomy also means limited autonomy. The PRC government obviously would not change the existing unitary systems into a federal one just for the reunification of Taiwan, Hong Kong and Macau. The idea of granting Hong Kong "residual power" which would allow the HKSAR full authority to handle its own affairs, except in foreign and defence affairs which are the responsibilities of the Central Government in Beijing, was raised by some groups in the Hong Kong community. The suggestion, had it been accepted, certainly would have affected the absolute authority of the Central Government.

In a unitary system, the authority of a local government comes entirely from the central government, and this authority, at least theoretically, may be changed or withdrawn at will by the central government. In contrast, the central government and the local governments in a federal system have their respective authorities well defined in a constitution which cannot be amended without the consent of a majority of the constituent units of the federation. Thus, when the PRC government promised in the Sino-British Joint Declaration that it would enact a Basic law "in accordance with the Constitution of the People's Republic of China, stipulating that after the establishment of the Hong Kong Special Administrative Region...Hong Kong's previous capitalist system and lifestyle shall remain unchanged for 50 years," it implied that in these 50 years, a federal relationship would exist to a certain extent. Since the Sino-British Joint Declaration and the Basic Law were approved by the NPC, and the Basic Law also has a limited time span of 50 years, the arrangement should not be considered an infringement of the PRC's unitary system of government. The arrangement certainly has implications for Taiwan too. It was on this premise that Hong Kong people had raised the legitimate demand that the Basic Law should stipulate clearly that except in foreign and defence affairs, the HKSAR had the sole authority to handle its domestic affairs.

This demand was not accepted by the PRC authorities. According to Wu Jianfan, member of the BLDC and Director of the China Law Society, the BLDC in its second plenary session adopted the view that there was no question of residual power as to the HKSAR, and Basic Law should the not include any provisions on this point. Wu justified the decision as follows:

> It [the question of residual powers] implicates China's state system, especially the nature and status of special administrative regions, and the origins of power, as well as a whole series of other critical issues. Therefore, we must adopt a prudent attitude toward this issue. The question of residual powers usually exists in countries with a federal system...China's situation is different. China does not have a federal system, but has a unitary system. A locality's powers are not inherent in themselves, but are conferred by the state. Neither before nor after the establishment of the Hong Kong Special Administrative Region does it possess independent sovereignty. The Hong Kong Special Administrative Region's high degree of autonomy is conferred by the state through the Basic Law, and it cannot enjoy powers that were never conferred. So how can there be any residual power? If one insists that there are residual powers, then these powers can only belong to the Central Government and not to the Hong Kong Special Administrative Region.

The "high degree of autonomy" to be enjoyed by the HKSAR as interpreted by Zhang Youyu, member of the BLDC, Deputy Chairman of the NPC Legal Committee and a leading legal expert of the PRC, was even more threatening. Zhang stated that:

> The high level of autonomy it [the HKSAR] will enjoy is conferred on it by the central organs of state power, and this high level of autonomy is not without limits. When exercising its high level of autonomy, Hong Kong will not proceed entirely without guidance, and even necessary intervention, from the central government. However, China's national sovereignty may not be damaged by Hong Kong's enjoyment of its high level of autonomy.

In line with the demand for "residual power" for the HKSAR, various groups in Hong Kong also demanded that the power to propose to amend the Basic Law be vested in the HKSAR government. A local political group, Meeting Point, suggested that the power to propose to amend the Basic Law should be vested in the HKSAR legislature; proposals of amendments should first be adopted by a two-thirds majority of the legislature, and then approved by the Standing Committee of the NPC. Since the Central Government could not formally initiate amendments, this proposal would be in accord with the promise that "Hong Kong's previous capitalist system and life-style shall remain unchanged for 50 years." The arrangement would provide for the necessary revisions of the Basic Law. In addition, since all amendments would have to be approved by the Standing Committee of the NPC, the PRC's sovereignty would not be compromised, and Hong Kong would be prevented from becoming an "independent political entity."

Article 159 of the Basic Law, however, states:

The power of amendment of this Law shall be in the National People's Congress.

The power to propose bills for amendments to this Law shall be vested in the Standing Committee of the National People's Congress, the State Council and the Hong Kong Special Administrative Region...

Before a bill for amendment to this Law is put on the agenda of the National People's Congress, the Committee for the Basic Law of the Hong Kong Special Administrative Region shall study it and submit its views.

No amendment to this Law shall contravene the established basic policies of the People's Republic of China regarding Hong Kong.

According to Article 159, the Central Government of the PRC would have full control of the amendment process. Similar to the issue of revising the Constitution, the controversies concerning "residual power" and the amendment of the Basic Law receded into the background and apparently the Hong Kong community conceded quietly to the position of the PRC authorities.

After the release of the draft Basic Law in April 1988, critics in Hong Kong, especially the legal profession, paid much attention to Articles 16, 17, 18, and 169 regarding the relationship between the Central Government and the HKSAR. Draft Article 16 states:

The Hong Kong Special Administrative Region is vested with legislative power.

If the Standing Committee of the National People's Congress, after consulting its Committee for the Basic Law of the Hong Kong Special Administrative Region, considers that any laws of the Region is [*sic*] not in conformity with this Law or legal procedures, it may return the law in question for reconsideration or revoke it, but it shall not amend it. Any law returned for reconsideration or revoked by the Standing Committee of the National People's Congress shall immediately cease to have force. The cessation shall not have retroactive effect.

As Section II of Annex I to the Sino-British Joint Declaration already stipulates that "the legislative power of the Hong Kong Special Administrative Region shall be vested in the legislature of the Hong Kong Special Administrative Region," it has been suggested that the first paragraph of Article 16 should be amended as follows: "The legislative power of the Hong Kong Special Administrative Region shall be vested in the legislature of the Hong Kong Special Administrative Region." This proposal, however, was not accepted.

More important still, the Hong Kong community was concerned that power on the Standing Committee 16 would compromise the autonomy of the HKSAR and the legislative power of the HKSAR legislature. Some groups therefore suggested that the third paragraph of draft Article 16 should be amended as follows: "If the Standing Committee of the National People's Congress it may return the question for reconsideration by the legislature of the Hong Kong Special Region." The legal profession in Hong Kong, on the other hand, argued that, in a common law system, all the laws passed by the legislature are to be construed by the courts and not by the executive or the legislature, whereas in the PRC, the Standing Committee of the NPC has the power to interpret all the laws and the Constitution. It therefore proposed that the constitutionality of the laws passed by the HKSAR legislature should be the Court of Final Appeal of the HKSAR, following the example of the U.S. Supreme Court in construing the U.S. Constitution.

The BLDC was responsive to such arguments, and an amendment was adopted. When the second draft of the Law was released in February 1989, the paragraph in question (third paragraph, Article 17) reads:

If the Standing Committee of the National People's Congress, after consulting its Committee for the Basic Law of the Hong Kong Special Administrative Region, considers that any law enacted by the legislature of the Region is not in conformity with the provisions of this Law regarding affairs within the responsibility of the Central Authorities or the relationship between the Central Authorities and the

Region, it may return the law in question but it shall not amend it. Any law returned by the Standing Committee of the National People's Congress shall immediately cease to have force. This cessation shall not have retroactive effect, unless otherwise provided for in the laws of the Hong Kong Special Administrative Region.

Draft Article 17 of the April 1988 version caused considerable concern. It states:

Laws, enacted by the National People's Congress or its Standing Committee, which relate to defence and foreign affairs as well as other laws which give expression to national unity and territorial integrity and which, in accordance with the provisions of this Law, are outside the limits of the high degree of autonomy of the Hong Kong Special Administrative Region, shall be applied locally by the government of the Hong Kong Special Region by way of is the legislation on the directives of the State Council, whenever there need to apply any of such laws in the Region.

Except in cases of emergency, the State Council shall consult the Committee for the Basic Law of the Hong Kong Special Administrative Region before issuing the above-mentioned directives.

If the government of the Hong Kong Special Administrative Region fails to act in compliance with the directives given by the State Council, the State Council may decree the application of the above-mentioned law in the Hong Kong Special Administrative Region.

The possibility that laws enacted by the NPC or its Standing Committee might be applied locally by way of promulgation on the directives of State Council was quite threatening. The scope of "other laws which give expression to national unity and territorial integrity and which, in accordance with the provisions of this Law, are outside the limits of the high degree of autonomy of the Hong Kong Special Administrative Region" was equally disturbing. Most comments focusing on this article after the release of the draft Basic Law tended to support the view that the laws concerning defence and foreign affairs should be applied by way of legislation by the HKSAR legislature at the request of the Standing Committee of the NPC. Further, apart from the laws concerning defence and foreign affairs, the nationwide laws which gave expression to national unity and territorial integrity and which would be applicable to the HKSAR should be listed in an annex to the Basic Law.

Again, the BLDC was willing to accept the above arguments, and amendments were adopted. In the second draft of the Basic Law published in February 1989, the paragraphs in question (second, third and last paragraphs of Article 18) read:

> National laws shall not be applied in the Hong Kong Special Administrative Region except for those listed in Annex III to this Law. The laws listed in Annex III to this Law shall be applied locally in the Region by way of promulgation or legislation.
>
> The Standing Committee of the National People's Congress may make additions to or deletions from the list of laws in Annex III after consulting its Committee for the Basic Law of the Hong Kong Special Administrative Region and the government of the Region. Laws listed in Annex III to this Law shall be confined to those relating to defence and foreign affairs as well as other laws outside the limits of the autonomy of the Region as specified by this Law In case the Standing Committee of the National People's Congress decides to declare a state of war or, by reason of turmoil within the Hong Kong Special Administrative Region which is beyond the control of the Region, decides that the Region is in a state of emergency, the State Council may decree the application of the relevant national laws in the Region.

Paragraphs 3 and 4 of draft Article 18 of the April 1988 version, which caused considerable controversy, are as follows:

> Courts of the Hong Kong Special Administrative Region shall have no jurisdiction over cases relating to defence and foreign affairs, which are the responsibility of the Central People's Government, and cases relating to the executive acts of the Central People's Government. Courts of the Hong Kong Special Administrative Region shall seek the advice of the Chief Executive whenever questions concerning defence, foreign affairs or the executive acts of the Central People's Government arise in any legal proceeding. A statement issued by the Chief Executive regarding such questions shall be binding on the courts. Before issuing such a statement, the Chief Executive shall obtain a certificate from the Standing Committee of the National People's Congress or the State Council.

The community's concern was mainly with the broad definition of "the executive acts of the Central People's Government." Because a party who wanted to adopt delaying tactics might try to claim that the case in dispute involved questions concerning defence, foreign affairs, or the executive acts of the Central People's Government, the efficiency and authority of the HKSAR courts would be considerably hampered in any legal proceedings. Hence, it was suggested that the above two paragraphs should be deleted and that the retention of paragraph 2 of Article 18 should be sufficient to safeguard the sovereignty of the PRC. Paragraph 2 states: "Courts of the Hong Kong Special Administrative Region shall have jurisdiction over all cases in the Region, except that the restrictions of their jurisdiction imposed by Hong Kong's previous legal system shall be maintained."

Although the BLDC was responsive to the territory's concern with the broad definition of "the executive acts of the Central People's Government," the necessary amendment could not be secured before the release of the February 1989 draft, and one had to wait for the final version of the Basic Law for those amendments which were more satisfactory to the Hong Kong community. In place of the controversial paragraphs, the compromise version (third paragraph, Article 19) then reads:

> The courts of the Hong Kong Special Administrative Region shall have no jurisdiction over acts of state such as defence and foreign affairs. The courts of the Region shall obtain a certificate from the Chief Executive on questions of fact concerning acts of state such as defence and foreign affairs whenever such questions arise in the adjudication of cases. This certificate shall be binding on the courts. Before issuing such a certificate, the Chief Executive shall obtain a certifying document from the Central People's Government.

Finally, draft Article 169 of the April 1988 version, which dealt with the interpretation of the Basic Law, was criticized by the local legal profession as paralyzing the whole judicial system of the HKSAR. It states:

> The power of the interpretation of this Law is vested in the Standing Committee of the National People's Congress.
>
> When the Standing Committee of the National People's Congress makes an interpretation of a provision of this Law, the courts of the Hong Kong Special Administrative Region, in applying that provision, shall follow the interpretation of the Standing Committee. However, judgments previously rendered shall not be affected.
>
> The courts of the Hong Kong Special Administrative Region may interpret the provisions of this Law in adjudicating cases before them. If a case involves an interpretation of the provision of this Law concerning defence, foreign affairs and other affairs which are the responsibility of the Central People's Government, the courts of the Region, before making their final judgment on the case, shall seek an interpretation of the relevant provisions from the Standing Committee of the National People's Congress.

> The Standing Committee of the National People's Congress shall consult its Committee for the Basic Law of the Hong Kong Special Administrative Region before giving an interpretation of this Law.

The concerned public in Hong Kong requested that the Standing Committee of the NPC would delegate irrevocably to the HKSAR courts its power to interpret those articles of the Basic Law which were within the scope of the HKSAR's autonomy in adjudicating cases. Regarding the other articles which fell outside the scope of the HKSAR's autonomy, the Standing Committee of the NPC might, if necessary, interpret such articles, provided that its interpretation should not affect cases that were being adjudicated, or that already had been decided by the HKSAR courts.

These controversies largely demonstrated the difficulties encountered in the actual implementation of "one country, two systems". They also reflected the PRC authorities' intention to retain the final say in almost every significant area. By 1988, the community had already largely acceded to the PRC authorities' position on the revision of the Constitution and the amendment of the Basic Law, while the concerned public and the legal profession were concentrating on the preservation of the independence of the HKSAR's judicial system.

The amendments adopted by the BLDC before the release of the second draft of the Basic Law in February 1989 went a considerable way in meeting the request of the territory's concerned public. The final version did not make any significant change, and the article on the interpretation of the Basic Law (Article 158) then states:

> The power of interpretation of this Law shall be vested in the Standing Committee of the National People's Congress.
>
> The Standing Committee of the National People's Congress shall authorize the courts of the Hong Kong Special Administrative Region to interpret on their own, in adjudicating cases, the provisions of this Law which are within the limits of the autonomy of the Region.
>
> The courts of the Hong Kong Special Administrative Region may also interpret other provisions of this Law in adjudicating cases. However, if the courts of the Region, in adjudicating cases, need to interpret the provisions of this Law concerning affairs which are the responsibility of the Central People's Government, or concerning the relationship between the Central Authorities and the Region, and if such interpretation will affect the judgments on the cases, the courts of the Region

shall, before making their final judgment's which are not seek an interpretation of the relevant provisions from the Standing committee of National People's Congress through the Court of Final the Region. When the Committee makes an interpretation of the provisions the Region, applying those provisions, shall follow the interpretation of the Standing Committee. However, judgments previously rendered shall not be affected.

The Standing Committee of the National People's Congress shall consult its Committee for the Basic Law of the Hong Kong Special Administrative Region before giving an interpretation of this Law.

In view of the amendment made to Articles 16, 17, 18, and 169 of the draft Basic Law released in April 1988, it appeared that the Chinese authorities were willing to make concessions for the sake of maintaining Hong Kong's stability and prosperity. In contrast to the demand for democracy, the requests for amendments regarding the above articles were supported by the business community as well which also considered it important to uphold the rule of law and the existing legal system. The Chinese authorities were willing to respond only when they believed that the sovereignty issue had not been compromised.

While discussing the relationship between the Central Government and the HKSAR in an American law journal in early 1988, Wu Jianfan, a leading legal scholar from Beijing on the BLDC, refuted the claim originally held by many in the Hong Kong community that the affairs managed by the Central People's Government would be limited strictly to foreign affairs and national defence, and that all other affairs would be within the scope of the HKSAR's high degree of autonomy. He referred to such a claim as a "misinterpretation of the [Sino-British] Joint Declaration." The claim was based previously on Article 3(2) of the Joint Declaration. That provision stipulates: "The Hong Kong Special Administrative Region will enjoy a high degree of autonomy, except in foreign and defence affairs which are the responsibilities of the Central People's Government." This claim was also based on numerous verbal assurances to that effect made by PRC officials responsible for Hong Kong and Macau affairs to various groups in Hong Kong during the Sino-British negotiations in 1982–1984. Wu Jianfan, however, pointed out that Article 3(2) of the Sino-British Joint Declaration only states that foreign and defence affairs would be the responsibilities of the Central People's

Government. Article 3(2) does not say that the affairs managed by the Central People's Government would be limited to foreign and defence affairs. After all, Article 3(4) of the Joint Declaration clearly provided for the appointments of the Chief Executive and the principal officials of the HKSAR by the Central People's Government.

III The Political System of the HKSAR

The political system of the HKSAR was probably the most controversial issue in the drafting of the Basic Law, partly because, while the Sino-British Joint Declaration promised that Hong Kong's "capitalist system and life-style shall remain unchanged for 50 years," the colonial political system obviously had to be replaced. Moreover, the Sino-British Joint Declaration and its annexes do not provide for a political system for the HKSAR.

Article 3(4) of the Sino-British Joint Declaration states:

> The Government of the Hong Kong Special Administrative Region will be composed of local inhabitants. The chief appointed by the Central People's Government on the basis of the results of elections or consultations to be held locally. Principal officials will be nominated by the chief executive of the Hong Kong Special Administrative Region for appointments by the central People's Government.

The third paragraph of Section I of Annex I further elaborates: "The legislature of the Hong Kong Special Administrative Region shall be constituted by elections. The executive authorities shall abide by the law and shall be accountable to the legislature." As Beijing and London had never informed the Hong Kong community in a formal manner their interpretation of the above key paragraphs, controversies regarding the meaning of the executive authorities' accountability to the legislature and other issues often emerged in the process of drafting the Basic Law.

While the issue of direct elections, political parties, and the like remained controversial in Hong Kong, a consensus on certain basic principles nevertheless existed soon after the initialling of the Sino-British Joint Declaration. In the first place, almost everyone agreed that the political system of the HKSAR should be designed to achieve a high degree of stability. A presidential system, for example, gives the chief executive security of tenure and is therefore a relatively stable political system. An electoral system based on proportional representation, on the other hand, encourages a multiparty system; if this was combined with a parliamentary system, Hong Kong might well encounter the situation in Italy and some Western European countries where shifting coalitions of political parties result in frequent falls of government and general elections, Hong Kong could ill afford such a scenario, and it might well lead to an early termination of whatever autonomy the territory might have been enjoying.

Second, the future HKSAR government was intended to be an efficient one. Overemphasis on separation of powers as well as checks and balances might lead to deadlock and confrontation between different branches of the government, resulting in political crisis and paralyzing the government. Nevertheless, the HKSAR government must be subject to effective democratic supervision to prevent any abuse of power. "Power corrupts, absolute power corrupts absolutely" (Lord Acton). Effective democratic supervision guarantees liberty and the rule of law, and also provides opportunities for political participation.

On the basis of this consensus, a modified presidential system appears to suit Hong Kong's need best. To ensure the stability of the HKSAR government, security of tenure for the Chief Executive, whose term may be limited to four or five years, is an important condition. Hence, as long as the Chief Executive does not violate the law and abuse his power, his tenure should not be threatened.

The legislature's ability to check and balance the executive mainly lies in its authority to appropriate money, to legislate and to approve government appointments, To ensure the effective supervision of the executive by the legislature, the Basic Law should provide the legislature with the power to question, investigate and impeach the principal officials of the executive, including the Chief Executive. In the event of a violation of the law or serious neglect of duty, the Central Government might remove any principal official or the Chief Executive from office, acting on an impeachment resolution passed by the local legislature.

Article 45 of the Basic Law reaffirms what is stipulated in the Sino-British Joint Declaration: "The Chief Executive of the Hong Kong Special

Administrative Region shall be selected by election or through consultations held locally and be appointed by the Central People's Government." It had been anticipated that this appointment would be a mere formality to demonstrate China's sovereignty over Hong Kong. Chinese officials responsible for Hong Kong affairs, however, indicated that the power of appointment would be a "substantial" one, implying a veto power in the hands of the Central Government.

To be in line with the above method of selection, the Chief Executive "shall be accountable to the Central People's Government and the Hong Kong Special Administrative Region in accordance with the provisions of this Law" (Article 43). The entire section on the Chief Executive does not mention that the Chief Executive has to be accountable or responsible to the Legislative Council. Yet, Article 64 of the following section on the executive authorities stipulates: "The Government of the Hong Kong Special Administrative Region must abide by the law and be accountable to the Legislative Council of the Region … It appears therefore that the Chief Executive does not have to be accountable to the Legislative Council, while only the executive authorities (treated in a separate section of Chapter IV Political Structure of Basic Law) have to be accountable to the Legislative Council. This certainly was not in accord with the general understanding of the Hong Kong community concerning the promise in the Sino-British Joint Declaration that "the executive authorities shall abide by the law and shall be accountable to the legislature." On the other hand, Article 59 states that "the Government of the Hong Kong Special Administrative Region shall be the executive authorities of the Region," and Article 60 states that "the head of the Government of the Hong Kong Special Administrative Region shall be the Chief Executive of the Region." This may be interpreted to mean that the Chief Executive is part of the executive authorities and therefore has to be accountable to the Legislative Council.

Obviously, ambiguity had to be removed. In fact, Li Hou, Deputy Director of the PRC State Council's Hong Kong and Macau Affairs Office, told a visiting delegation of the Hong Kong Christian Industrial Committee in Beijing on July 6, 1988, that it would be more appropriate for the Chief Executive to be accountable to the HKSAR than to the Legislative Council, as "this accountability is much broader than the scope of the legislature."

Article 43 also raises the following issue — although the Chief Executive's accountability to the Central People's Government can be well-defined, since the Central People's Government is a concrete entity and controls his appointment, the Chief Executive's accountability to the HKSAR is largely symbolic and has not been defined by the Basic Law. Article 48.8 further states that the Chief Executive has to "implement the directives issued by the Central People's Government in respect of the relevant matters provided for in this Law." The PRC Constitution promulgated in 1982 clearly stipulates that the State Council is "the highest organ of state administration" (Article 85) and it has the power

> [...] to exercise unified leadership over the work of local organs of state administration at different levels throughout the country, and to lay down the detailed division of functions and powers between the Central Government and the organs of state administration of provinces, autonomous regions and municipalities directly under the Central Government. (Article 89.4)

It is not sufficiently clear in what way and to what extent the HKSAR differs from the provinces, autonomous regions, and municipalities in its accountability to the Central Government. Is the HKSAR government also one of the "local organs of state administration", as defined by the PRC Constitution? Moreover, the State Council is one of the three parties that have been empowered by the Basic Law to propose amendments to the Basic Law. With the consent of the National People's Congress, it can seek to expand its power *vis-à-vis* the HKSAR government (Article 159). Article 1 of Annex 1 of the Sino-British Joint Declaration is equally unclear. On one hand, it states that "the Hong Kong Special Administrative Region shall be directly under the authority of the Central People's Government"; on the other hand, it stipulates that 'the executive authorities shall abide by the law and shall be accountable to the legislature."

It is significant to note that the Chief Executive's power of appointing and dismissing the principal officials of the HKSAR government is quite limited. He may nominate them and report such nominations to the Central People's Government for appointment and may propose to the Central People's Government the removal of the principal officials (Article 48.5). The Basic Law does not specify the criteria according to which the Central People's Government will approve the Chief Executive's nominations and his proposals for dismissing the principal officials. If the Central People's Government refuses to approve the Chief Executive's proposal to remove some of the principal officials, it would cause substantial difficulties within the HKSAR government. The lack of well-defined power of dismissal of the principal officials would affect the Chief Executive's status as head of government.

According to the Constitution of the PRC, local people's congresses, at their respective levels, "elect, and have the power to recall, governors and deputy governors, or mayors and deputy mayors, or heads and deputy heads of counties, districts, townships and towns." The Constitution further provides that "the standing committee of a local people's congress at and above the county level... decides on the appointment and removal of functionaries of state organs within the limits of its authority as prescribed by law." According to Article 9 of the Organic Law of the Local People's Congresses and the Local People's Government of the PRC, revised by the Fifth Session of the Fifth NPC in 1982, the local people's congresses have the power to remove members of the local people's governments at their respective levels. Article 28.8 further provides the standing committee of a local people's congress at or above the county level with the power to decide on the appointment and removal of the secretary-general, agency heads, bureau directors, and the like of its corresponding local people's government. Such appointments and dismissals have to be reported only to the local people's government at a higher level for recording purpose. Similar provisions exist for the organs of self-government of national autonomous areas.

In the PRC's history, the appointment of the chief executive and the principal officials of a local government by the Central Government only occurred under extraordinary circumstances. In 1950, the Political Council (*Zhengwuyuan*, the predecessor of the State Council) adopted the "General Principles on the Organization of Provincial People's Government." Article 2 of the document stipulated that appointees to provincial governments would be nominated by the Political Council and approved by the Central People's Government Committee; the article explained that the purpose of the arrangement was to establish rapidly the revolutionary order during the early stage of the liberation. The document was superseded by the formal promulgation of the first Constitution of the

PRC in 1954; it therefore remained valid only before the Constitution came into existence. The second example is the "Brief Outline of the organization of the Preparatory Committee for the Tibetan Autonomous Region." The preparatory committee was equivalent to a temporary local people's government. Article 5 of the outline stipulated that the appointment, removal and replacement of committee members were to be based on consultations among the parties concerned, which would then be approved by the State Council. The State Council would formally appoint the chairman, deputy chairman and members of the preparatory committee. The outline further stipulated that the appointment of heads and deputy heads of the various agencies and bureaus under the preparatory committee should be based on nominations through consultations to be approved by the State Council. It is believed the validity of the document lasted until the rebellion broke out in 1959.

In these two examples, the Central Government had an even larger measure of control over the local governments' personnel than is stipulated by the Basic Law. However, Hong Kong is certainly far more stable than either the various provinces immediately after liberation in 1949 or Tibet in 1956. The situation in Tibet in 1956, nonetheless, had some relevance for Hong Kong; and the appointment of local government personnel in Tibet by the Central Government had two important implications for Hong Kong. First, the Central Government might, if necessary, help to establish a consensus among the diverse local interests, while allowing a certain measure of autonomy for such interests. This occurred in Tibet. Second, the autonomy promised to Tibet was not yet constitutional, and the Central Government was eager to retain ultimate control. Appointment in this context also symbolized such control and the PRC sovereignty over the territory.

Above all, in actual practice, the Communist Party of China (CPC) controls the appointment of local government personnel at all levels, without regard for the constitutional powers granted to the local people's congresses. When control of the local Party organs is not yet secure as in the three aforementioned cases, then the Central Government would have to assume that ultimate control.

The HKSAR political system as outlined in the Basic Law enables the Chief Executive to be a very strong leader within the local government.

The Chief Executive has powers and functions similar to the U.S. President, though the former probably has even larger powers *vis-à-vis* the legislature. According to Articles 48 to 52, bills passes by the Legislative Council have to be signed by the Chief Executive before being promulgated as laws (Article 48.3). If the Chief Executive considers that a bill passed by the Legislative Council is not compatible with the overall interests of the HKSAR, he may return it to the Legislative Council within three months for reconsideration. If the Legislative Council passes the original bill again by no less than a two-thirds majority, the Chief Executive must sign and promulgate it within one month (Article 49). The Chief Executive, however, has one further option that is not available to the U.S. President — he may still refuse to sign it and can dissolve the Legislative Council instead. He may also dissolve the Legislative Council when the latter refuses to pass the budget or other important bills and consensus cannot be reached after consultations (Article 50).

The strength of the Chief Executive and the weakness of the Legislative Council are further demonstrated by the Chief Executive's power "to approve the introduction of motions regarding revenues or expenditure to the Legislative Council" (Article 48.10) and "to decide, in the light of security and vital public interests, whether government officials or other personnel in charge of government affairs should testify or give evidence before the Legislative Council or its committees" (Article 48.11). If the Chief Executive can, without having to give reasons, reject any motion presented to the Legislative Council regarding revenues and expenditure, then basically the Legislature Council can only respond to the Chief Executive's proposals regarding revenues and expenditure. It is not sufficiently clear whether the Legislative Council can reject certain items of the budget, though it does not appear likely. It has subsequently been established as the practice. If the Legislative Council can only accept or reject the budget as a whole and the refusal to pass the budget will lead to its dissolution, the Legislative Council's power over government revenues and expenditure would be quite limited indeed. Under such circumstances, the Legislative Council may have to rely largely on the pressure of public opinion to persuade the Chief Executive and the executive authorities in the process of consultation between the two branches of government. This is the actual situation today.

The Chief Executive's power to exempt government officials or other personnel in charge of government affairs from testifying or giving evidence before the Legislative Council or its committees would severely hamper the latter's function as a watchdog of the Chief Executive and the executive authorities. Considerations of security and vital public interests are not sufficient reasons for preventing the Legislative Council from calling government officials or other personnel in charge of government affairs to testify or give evidence. The testimony or the giving of evidence can obviously take place in closed sessions. In the U.S., the Chairman of the Joint Chiefs of Staff and the Director of the Central Intelligence Agency also have to testify and give evidence before the Congress. The provision in the Basic Law assumes that the Chief Executive has a greater concern for security and vital public interests than members of the Legislative Council. Such an assumption is obviously subject to dispute.

Further, regarding bills relating to government policies, members of the Legislative Council may only introduce them with the prior written consent of the Chief Executive (Article 74). There obviously would be a danger that "government policies" may be defined so broadly as to render members of the Legislative Council almost powerless to introduce bills.

The section on the legislature in the Basic Law has not touched upon the power of the legislature to impeach members of the executive authorities and the Executive Council. Neither has it any power over the appointment of the principal officials and members of the Executive Council of the HKSAR.

In sum, the political system outlined in Chapter IV of the Basic Law presents an "executive dominant" system in which the Chief Executive would have powers similar to those of the previous British Governor. The Legislative Council would only have limited powers. As the Chief Executive has to be accountable to the Central People's Government but not to the Legislative Council of the HKSAR, and the appointment as well as removal of the Chief Executive and principal officials have to be approved by the Central People's Government, the autonomy of the HKSAR would certainly be affected.

A careful study of Article 56 of the Basic Law provides a hint. It states:

Except for the appointment, removal and disciplining of officials and the adoption of measures in emergencies, the Chief Executive shall consult the Executive Council before making important policy decisions, introducing bills to the Legislative Council, making subordinate legislation, or dissolving the Legislative Council.

If the Chief Executive does not accept a majority opinion of the Executive Council, he or she shall put the specific reasons on record.

This is a superficial and largely meaningless replication of the previous colonial system. In the previous British administration, appointments to the Executive Council were to be made by the British Crown, i.e., the Secretary of state for Foreign and Commonwealth Affairs; and the Commander of the British Forces, the Chief Secretary, the Financial Secretary, and the Attorney General were *ex-officio* members of the Executive Council. The appointments of these senior government officials also had to be approved by the Secretary of State according to the *Civil Service Regulations*. In this way, the need for the Governor to consult the Executive Council on all important matters of policy constituted a means of checks and balances, which was especially significant in view of the almost dictatorial powers of the Governor. In the case of the Chief Executive of the HKSAR, he has full authority to appoint and dismiss members of the Executive Council, and it is difficult to see how the need to consult the Executive Council will similarly constitute a means of checks and balances. It should be noted, however, that an earlier draft of the Basic Law stipulated that members of the Executive Council should be nominated by the Chief Executive and appointed by the Central People's Government and that if the Chief Executive did not adopt a majority opinion of the Executive Council, he should register his specific reasons and report them to the Central People's Government for record purposes.

There was obviously an attempt to retain the political structure of the previous colonial government as both Beijing and the conservative business community accepted it as part of the foundation of Hong Kong's economic success and political stability. A statement by the former Chairman of the Hong Kong Stock Exchange, Ronald Li, at an international investment conference in June 1987, perhaps reflected the conservative business community's attitude. Li declared: "Hong Kong is a colony. It is a dictatorship, although a benevolent one. It is and has been a British colony, and it's going to be a Chinese colony, and as such it will prosper. We do not need free elections here." The colonial government in Hong Kong was certainly a benevolent one; there was ample liberty in the territory and the rule of law was observed. This colonial government, however, had to be accountable ultimately to a democratic government willing to defend freedom and the rule of law. This was the guarantee of its benevolence.

IV Consultations in 1989–1990 and the Electoral System

When the second draft of the Basic Law was released in February 1989 people in Hong Kong were already exhausted with discussions on the Basic Law. With the exception of the electoral system and the formation of the first government of the HKSAR, the community did not expect major changes of the Basic Law before its promulgation. Those who were concerned with the development of representative government in Hong Kong were especially disappointed because what appeared in the second draft regarding the electoral system was not exactly based on the alternatives listed in the first draft. This made a mockery of the heated debates on the issue in 1988 among the political groups in the territory.

The political turmoil in Beijing in the spring and summer 1989, however, did much to promote the appreciation of democracy among Hong Kong people. To minimize Britain's commitment to the territory, London and the local British administration showed strong support for an acceleration of the democratization process. In May 1989, the Executive and Legislative Councils reached a consensus on the direct election by universal suffrage of the Chief Executive and all seats of the legislature by 2003; and that one half of the seats of the legislature should be directly elected by universal suffrage in 1997. Senior Hong Kong government officials also reversed their position and indicated that the directly elected Legislative Council seats to be introduced in 1991 would be increased from 10 to 20. The report of the British House of Commons Foreign Affairs Select Committee released in late June 1989 even boldly suggested that by 1991, half of the Legislative Council seats should be directly elected and by 1995, all seats should be directly elected. This proposal was endorsed by the Joint Committee for the Promotion of Democratic Government, an umbrella organization representing the various groups of the pro-democracy movement in Hong Kong. The Joint Committee also demanded a "through train arrangement which meant that the Legislative Councillors elected in 1995 should automatically become members of the first legislature of the HKSAR. As to the Chief Executive, the Joint Committee's position was unchanged, and demanded that the post be directly elected by universal suffrage.

Beijing's position, nevertheless, was still the crucial factor, and the Thatcher government understood this well. When the former Foreign Secretary Sir Geoffrey Howe visited Hong Kong in early July 1989, he avoided making any concrete promise regarding the accelerated pace of the development of a system of representative government. He only mentioned the consensus of the local Legislative and Executive Councils, and expressed his willingness to listen.

When superficial calm was restored in Beijing's political scene after the Tiananmen Incident, the regime turned its attention to Hong Kong and attempted to regain the initiative. When the new General Secretary of the Party, Jiang Zemin, met the leaders of the BLDC and the BLCC on July 11, 1989, he indicated that the Basic Law would be promulgated as scheduled in spring 1990 at the third plenary session of the Seventh NPC. The Standing Committee of the NPC then decided to extend the period of consultation on the Basic Law by three months until the end of October 1989. This was quite disappointing to the Hong Kong people, because it implied that the Chinese authorities were reluctant to revise in any significant way the draft Basic Law released in February 1989.

After the Tiananmen Incident, two of the 23 Hong Kong members of the BLDC, Louis Cha and Bishop Kwong, formally resigned, and Martin Lee and Szeto Wah indicated that they would terminate their participation until the existing Chinese leadership changed. The representativeness of the remaining Hong Kong members was thus much weakened and they certainly lacked the trust of the community. There were some withdrawals from the BLCC too. However, since the BLCC had not been active in articulating the community's views, the withdrawals did not attract much attention.

To counter the political model endorsed by the Legislative and Executive Councils, whose legitimacy and representativeness were not recognized by Beijing, the New Hong Kong Alliance, a pro-Beijing group of businessmen and professionals, proposed a bicameral system for the HKSAR legislature, in which only one-quarter of the legislature would be elected by universal suffrage. The latter proposal attracted little support from the community, but it enabled Beijing to reject the claim of the Legislative and Executive Councils that their proposal represented the consensus of the territory, and the Chinese authorities could then use the pretext that the community was divided and dictate the terms. It was also significant that most political groups considered the political model of the Legislative and Executive Councils "tainted" because it had been suggested by colonial institutions, and they tried to agree on a third model on which the two Councils had little influence. Such divisions opened up fertile ground for Beijing's united front strategy.

Under such circumstances, few people in Hong Kong expected that the Chinese leaders would make concessions and allow the HKSAR to have a more democratic political system and that the British government would stand firm on its position for a more democratic political system for Hong Kong and risk confrontation with the Chinese authorities. The Chinese mass media were severely criticizing the pro-democracy movement in Hong Kong, and the emphasis of Beijing's united front strategy was clearly on the conservative business community. In view of the increasing political apathy of the community, the Chinese leaders had little reason to concede. On the other hand, London was obviously interested in doing something for Hong Kong in compensation for its rejection of the local population's demand for the right of abode in the U.K. However, the demand could not be long sustained; and when the heat was over, there was always the excuse that the pace of democratization had to be slowed down in view of the opposition from Beijing and the local conservative business community. After all, the Thatcher government wanted an honorable retreat from Hong Kong, and it was interested in continued cooperation with Beijing on Hong Kong as well as other bilateral issues. The sense of political impotence on the part of Hong Kong people was revealed in that they naturally thought that it would be futile to exert pressure on Beijing. At the same time, while they desired democracy, they did not attach much significance to it and were largely unwilling to fight for it. In the end, just as the 1984 Sino-British Joint Declaration on Hong Kong's future was the product of secret negotiations between Beijing and London, the final decision on the territory's future political system was also settled directly between the two governments. The Sino-British decision emerged on February 15, 1990, and is presented in Table 7.1:

Table 7.1. Hong Kong Legislature Towards 1997 and Beyond

	1995–1999	1999–2003	2003–2007
Functional constituencies	30	30	30
Direct election	20	24	30
Indirect election by an election committee	10	6	0
Total number of seats	60	60	60

The decision was approved without further ado the next day by the BLDC. Even before this formality, the British Foreign Secretary Douglas Hurd had unveiled the decision to the British Parliament, indicating that the deal cleared the way for the introduction of eighteen directly elected seats to the territory's Legislative Council in 1991. While conceding that the pace of political reform, as reflected in the Basic Law, was not as fast as many Hong Kong people or the British government would like, Hurd argued that the agreement was "in the interest of continuity" and "makes good sense for Hong Kong." Both Hurd and the Hong Kong government maintained that they would press Beijing for more rapid democratization of the territory in the transitional period up to 1997 and beyond. However, Chinese officials insisted that the Basic Law would not be amended before 1997.

The Basic Law also stipulates that the Chief Executive shall be elected by an Election Committee of 800 members with 200 from the industrial commercial and financial sectors; 200 from the professions; 200 from labor, social services, religious, and other sectors; and 200 from members of the Legislative Council, representatives of district-based organizations, Hong Kong deputies to the NPC, and representatives of Hong Kong members of the National Committee of the Chinese People's Political

Consultative Conference. This system would facilitate the domination of conservative political forces. It would also offer a better guarantee that the Chief Executive would be someone acceptable to Beijing as its lobbying work would not be too difficult.

Three more points may be made regarding the electoral system. In the first place, amendments to the method for the selection of the Chief Executive would freeze for the terms prior to the year 2007. For the terms after that, "such amendments must be made with the endorsement of a two-thirds majority of all the members of the Legislative Council and the consent of the Chief Executive, and they shall be reported to the Standing Committee of the NPC for approval" (Article 7 of Annex I). Amendments to the method for the formation of the Legislative Council were governed by the same rules, except that they should only be required to be reported to the Standing Committee of the NPC for the record (Article III of Annex II). It was obvious how easily such amendment proposals could be blocked.

The Election Committee arrangement figured prominently in the electoral system. Indirect election tended to favor conservative political forces. In the context of the HKSAR, the Election Committee had additional advantages from Beijing's point of view: it facilitated lobbying it enabled highly unpopular candidates favoured by Beijing to be elected, and it offered rewards in support of Beijing's united front work. After all, membership of the Election Committee would be considered prestigious by many, as membership of the BLCC demonstrated.

Finally, many details of the electoral law had yet to be defined. Political scientists appreciate that electoral arrangements may have a significant impact on the political system. It was feared that the later the electoral law was discussed and promulgated, the less impact the community could make.

When the first draft of the Basic Law was published in April 1988, the method for the formation of the first government and the first Legislative Council of the HKSAR was dealt with by Annex III. It reflected the PRC's position first revealed by Lu Ping, Deputy Secretary-General of the BLDC, in October 1987. It was significant that Annex III did not include the alternatives proposed by individual members of the BLDC from Hong Kong, but only registered them in "A Collection of

Opinions and Suggestions of Some Members in Regard to the Articles Drafted by Their Respective Special Subject Subgroups" attached to the draft Basic Law.

The gist of Annex III basically became the decision of the Seventh NPC adopted at its third session on April 4, 1990. According to the decision, the NPC should, in 1996, establish a Preparatory Committee for the HKSAR composed of Mainland members and Hong Kong members who should constitute no less than 50% of its membership. Its chairman and members should be appointed by the Standing Committee of the NPC. This Preparatory Committee should in turn be responsible for the establishment of the Selection Committee for the First Government of the HKSAR. The Selection Committee of 400 members should be composed entirely of permanent residents of Hong Kong with 25% from the industrial, commercial and financial sectors; 25% from the professions; 25% from labor, grassroots, religious, and other sectors; and 25% from among former political figures, Hong Kong deputies to the NPC and representatives of Hong Kong members of the National Committee of the Chinese People's Political Consultative Conference. The Selection Committee should recommend the candidate for the first Chief Executive through local consultations or through nomination and election after consultations, and report the recommended candidate to the Central People's Government for appointment. The term of office of the first Chief Executive should be the same as the regular term.

Regarding the first Legislative Council of the HKSAR, the Chinese authorities accepted the "through train" arrangement. The NPC decided that if the composition of the last Hong Kong Legislative Council before the establishment of the HKSAR was in conformity with the Basic Law, those of its members who upheld the Law of HKSAR of the PRC and pledged allegiance to the HKSAR of the PRC, and who met the requirements set forth in the Basic Law of the Region might, upon confirmation by the Preparatory Committee, become members of the first Legislative Council of the Region. The term of office of members of the first Legislative Council should be two years.

Obviously, the Chinese authorities wanted to have a considerable measure of control over the formation of the first government and the first Legislative Council of the HKSAR. Articles of the Basic Law, like any constitution, can only provide the bare skeleton of a political system that also involves numerous precedents, conventions, practices and regulations to be established through the actual implementation of the Basic Law. The first two or three years after 1997 therefore could be crucial.

V Conclusion

To a political scientist, the study of the PRC Constitution is of limited value, because the role and function of the CPC are largely omitted from the document. Similarly, an attempt to analyze the Basic Law had serious limitations without a good understanding of the future role of the CPC in the HKSAR, which, unfortunately, was a matter of sheer speculation at best before 1997.

Local organs of state administration in the PRC are involved in two systems of accountability. For example, the Bureau of Commerce of a province has to be accountable to the provincial people's government. In turn, the provincial people's government has to be accountable to the provincial people's congress. The bureau, however, has to be accountable to the Ministry of Commerce at the State Council level too. Parallel to the system of state administration is the hierarchy of CPC organs. The provincial Party committee normally has an office (And a deputy secretary) in charge of finance and economics, which has jurisdiction over the Bureau of Commerce. The provincial Party committee is accountable to the Central Committee and the Political Bureau of the CPC. In addition to this complicated nexus of ties, there are Party groups within organs of state administration. For example, Party members among the senior officials of the Bureau of Commerce form a Party group of the bureau which is accountable to the provincial Party committee.

This complicated system probably would not be borrowed by the HKSAR government. What needs to be highlighted here is that, within the PRC, problems that arise from the dual accountability on the part of a local organ of state administration are normally resolved by the Party committee at the corresponding or higher level. It is not clear what would happen if conflicts arise between the HKSAR Chief Executive's accountability to the Central People's Government and his accountability to the local legislature or to the HKSAR as a whole. It is now assumed that the Party leadership in Beijing makes the final decisions.

The Hong Kong Work Committee probably has a role to play in resolving such conflicts. Its views would likely be sought by the State Council or the Secretariat of the Party Central Committee, which will facilitate the top Party leadership to make the final decisions. The Hong Kong Work Committee is the CPC organ in Hong Kong, and its status is equivalent to that of a provincial Party committee. Ever since the 1950s, the Director of the Hong Kong branch of the New China News Agency had also served as the secretary of the committee. Xu Jiatun, the former Director of the Hong Kong branch of the New China News Agency, was first secretary of the Jiangsu Provincial Party Committee and a member of the CPC Central Committee before he took up his post in Hong Kong. It was considered that, given the presence of a considerable number of senior PRC cadres in Hong Kong working in places like the Bank of China's Hong Kong branch, a cadre with Central Committee membership would be required to coordinate the various lines of activities of the Party and the state administration in Hong Kong.

The Basic Law has not prescribed the role of the CPC in the HKSAR. Xu Jiatun, however, indicated to a group of Hong Kong journalists at an off-the-record briefing in June 1987 that the future role of the CPC in Hong Kong would be "to assist the Special Administrative Region government."

According to the Basic Law, a Committee for the Basic Law of the HKSAR would be set up under the Standing Committee of the NPC. At this stage, the process whereby Hong Kong deputies to the NPC were chosen was unknown to the Hong Kong community. An educated guess was that they were selected through consultations among the CPC and the PRC organs in Hong Kong, with the Hong Kong Work Committee and the Hong Kong branch of the New China News Agency both playing a key role. How the Hong Kong deputies to the NPC would be elected after 1997 when the PRC authorities can hold elections in the HKSAR is not covered by the Basic Law. This remains the prerogative of the Organic Law of the NPC of the PRC. The extent to which this Committee for the Basic Law of the HKSAR should be consulted by the HKSAR government, and the degree of influence it will have on the HKSAR government, are similarly left to speculation. It was not unnatural for the Hong Kong deputies to the NPC to demand a role in the HKSAR government. If they are elected by methods similar to those by which members of the HKSAR legislature are elected, then they certainly have a legitimate claim to represent the people of the HKSAR also.

Meanwhile, in the transitional period, the PRC authorities were stepping up their activities in the territory and seeking to establish themselves as an important political force. They began publicly building their Hong Kong community network and influence in 1985 when the Hong Kong branch of the New China News Agency opened three district offices in the Hong Kong Island, Kowloon, and the New Territories. Pro-Beijing political forces mounted a campaign to block the introduction of direct elections to the Legislative Council in 1988. They also mobilized their supporters, identified candidates, and isolated political opponents in the district board elections in March 1988.

The above discussions have highlighted the political factors, as well as the limitations, relating to an analysis of the Basic Law. The PRC's increasing involvement in the Hong Kong economy would have a significant impact too, an important subject which is not dealt with in this chapter.

The PRC leaders' sincerity in maintaining Hong Kong's stability and prosperity in the transitional period and after 1997 was beyond doubt otherwise they would not have taken the trouble to hammer out the Sino-British Joint Declaration and the Basic Law for the HKSAR. The concern with maintaining the prosperity of the territory, however, clearly took precedence over the promises of "a high degree of autonomy" and "self-administration" for the HKSAR.

The refusal to revise the PRC Constitution meant that the problems concerning the constitutional and legal status of the Basic Law and the HKSAR raised in an early part of this chapter would remain unsolved. This might not pose too serious a problem if the prevalent policy orientation of the PRC leadership was maintained; after all, the reformers in the PRC had also encountered difficulties in finding a convincing ideological foundation to support their reforms. The "primary stage of socialism" argument was obviously not satisfactory. In the event of political conflicts in Beijing leading to uncertainties concerning existing policies, programs or even major redefinitions of them, the shock for

Hong Kong would be considerable — the theoretical and constitutional bases of the "one country, two system" policy would be in doubt.

In the course of drafting the Basic Law, it became clear that the Central People's Government of the PRC often wanted to retain final control, especially in matters relating to the autonomy of the political system. The decisions on the concept of "residual power", the amendment, and the interpretation of the Basic Law were significant examples. The result appears to be that the Basic Law would offer very limited guarantees for the political autonomy of the HKSAR. The instinct of the CPC regime in following the Leninist principles of democratic centralism for maintaining control might well be at work here — when the control of the CPC is not secure in the HKSAR, the ultimate control of the Central People's Government has to be defined even more clearly in legal terms. Suspicions over Hong Kong becoming an "independent political entity" (and after the Tiananmen Incident, "an anti-communist base') were articulated openly by PRC officials in charge of Hong Kong affairs. They, as well as the PRC leadership, were constantly aware of the example that the HKSAR set for the rest of the PRC. The PRC leaders were unwilling to dilute the unitary system of the state to accommodate Hong Kong or even Taiwan. Any concessions made were likely to be of a temporary, ad hoc, and tactical nature.

Within the HKSAR political system, the appointments by the Central People's Government of the Chief Executive and the principal officials imply that their accountability is to the Central People's Government. This has been reaffirmed by Article 43 of the Basic Law, stipulating that the Chief Executive shall be "accountable to the Central People's Government and the Hong Kong Special Administrative Region." The people in Hong Kong gradually realized that the Chief Executive would have to be someone acceptable to the PRC authorities. This, in return, reinforced the general perception in the community that Beijing had the final say on all important issues and dampened the community's interest in political participation and eroded the legitimacy of the development of representative government.

The increasing presence and participation of the PRC authorities in the Hong Kong economy and society, together with the stepping up of the united front activities of the local Party and state organs, would probably create a dominant political force in the HKSAR which could be mobilized at will on the order of the Central People's Government. These developments certainly did not augur well for the political autonomy of the HKSAR, nor for the development of a democratic political system there.

In the final analysis, the Hong Kong community might have to count not so much on the Basic Law but on the following domestic and international factors to ensure that the PRC leadership would live up to its promises made to the Hong Kong people during the Sino-British negotiations for the Joint Declaration. In the first place, the PRC leadership had been assuring the international community that its open-door policy would remain unchanged. Its policy towards Hong Kong was also looked upon as a litmus test of its open-door policy. Any violation of the spirit and the terms of its promises to Hong Kong would hurt the world's confidence in the PRC. Second, as a SAR under the PRC's sovereignty, Hong Kong would set a significant example for Taiwan. Third, a change in the PRC's policy towards Hong Kong might have a signaling effect on its domestic reforms too. Various liberal economic policies in the special economic zones and the coastal cities would most likely be affected. Finally, as long as the PRC leadership valued Hong Kong's contributions to its modernization program, this capitalist enclave might continue to be tolerated. All these factors, however, did not constitute an absolute guarantee that Hong Kong would remain unchanged up to the year 2047. Moreover, these factors might be more effective in ensuring "that Hong Kong's previous capitalist system and life-style shall remain unchanged for 50 years" than in guaranteeing the "high degree of autonomy" and "self-administration" promised.

Acknowledgement

Originally published as Cheng Joseph Y.S., "The Basic Law: Messages for Hong Kong People", *in The Other Hong Kong Report 1990*, ed. Richard Y.C. Wong and Joseph Y.S. Cheng. Hong Kong: Chinese University Press, 1990, pp. 29–63. Reproduced with kind permission from the publisher.

Chapter 8

Values and Attitudes of the Hong Kong Community

Hong Kong developed so rapidly that even local people often found it difficult to catch up with the changed. Their values also change. Despite sharp fluctuations in attitudes regarding certain issues, their values tended to follow some recognizable trends. The publication of the index to the first four volumes of *The Other Hong Kong Report* provided an opportunity to examine the values of the community.

I Political Attitudes and Values

(i) *Hong Kong's Future*

Telephone opinion polls conducted by the City and New Territories Administration (CNTA) queried local residents if they had confidence that Hong Kong would continue to be prosperous and stable. The percentage of those who said that they had the confidence decreased gradually from 61% in July 1990 to 54% in January 1991. It increased to 64% in September 1991 and stayed at 60% in March 1992. In another survey conducted in the summer of 1988 by the social scientists of local tertiary institutions, slightly more than half of the respondents (55.5%) expressed confidence in Hong Kong's future while only 26.1% held the opposite view.[1]

---

[1] See Lau Siu-kai, Kuan Hsin-chi and Wan Po-san, "Political Attitudes," in *Indicators of Social Development: Hong Kong 1988*, edited by Lau Siu-kai, Lee Ming-kwan, Wan Po-san

That public opinions on the confidence in the territory's future fluctuated considerably was a well-established fact. The respondents' confidence appeared to be closely related to their trust in the Hong Kong government and the Chinese government. Those who claimed a "Chinese" identity and expressed satisfaction with the Hong Kong government were more likely to have confidence in the territory's future. In addition, the more they trusted the Hong Kong government and the Chinese government, the more likely they were to report a higher level of confidence in the territory's future.

Despite the relatively high level of confidence in the territory's future, the confidence problem remained one of the most-mentioned responses in local opinion surveys. In the late 1980s and early 1990s, the percentage of respondents in CNTA polls who mentioned "Hong Kong future" and "Hong Kong political system" as a problem decreased steadily (68% in November 1989, 54 percent in March 1990, 49% in September 1990, 29% in March 1991, 34% in September 1991 and 21% in March 1992). In the summer 1988 survey mentioned above, 47.7% of the respondents indicated that they were worried about political instability before 1997 while 45.7% were not.[2] In the 1988 survey, a pessimistic perception of the territory's future could be seen in the respondents' anticipation of several possible socioeconomic changes after 1997. A total of 75.5% of the respondents thought that it was likely or very likely that after the return of Hong Kong to China, civil rights would be curtailed. Another 73.2% anticipated a reduction of individual freedom, 66.9% expected stagnation or even deterioration in living standards, and 61.1% envisaged the deterioration of the legal system. Only 42.4% thought that the status quo could remain unchanged for 50 years, and a mere 25.7% were optimistic that the lives of Hong Kong people would be better and happier after 1997. A comparison with relevant findings in the 1986 survey in the same series seemed to indicate a gloomier attitude to the future.[3]

---

and Wong Siu-lun, Hong Kong: Hong Kong Institute of Asia-Pacific Studies, The Chinese University of Hong Kong, 1991, p. 175.

[2] *Ibid.*

[3] *Ibid.*, pp. 176–177.

The Commission on Youth conducted a territory-wide survey in January 1991 among young people aged between 15 and 24 years old. Their attitudes regarding the territory's future seemed to be slightly more pessimistic than the community as a whole. A total of 48% of the respondents revealed a lack of confidence in the territory's future, while 42% indicated confidence. The 1997 question would have an adverse impact on their future, according to 44% of the respondents. A total of 23% of the respondents believed that it would mean unemployment, 17% economic recession and 12% less freedom.

Lack of confidence in the Chinese authorities' promises appeared to be the root cause of this worry. A survey conducted in the last week of June 1991 by Asian Commercial Research and published in the *Sunday Morning Post* on June 30, 1991 best illustrated this lack of confidence (see illustration below).

In fact, opinion surveys in 1986–1992 consistently yielded the same results. In contrast, the business community demonstrated a remarkable bullishness on investments in Hong Kong and the Pearl River Delta.

The apparent contradictions in Hong Kong people's attitudes towards the future could be explained in terms of their options, opportunity costs and their assessments of future developments in Hong Kong and in China. Younger and richer people were much more worried about 1997 than those who had no options other than to stay. In the *Sunday Morning Post* survey mentioned above, while 65% of the people aged between 18 and 24 expected their freedoms to diminish after 1997, only 49% of those over 45 were as gloomy. Similarly, although two-thirds of those in households earning more than $20,000 a month did not think Beijing would stick to its "one country, two systems" promise, only one-half of the lower-income earners had such doubts. Many of those doubting China's promises were still cheerful about the territory's prospects, with 58% saying they were confident about Hong Kong's future, compared with 36% who were not. It was significant that 42% of those who did not trust China to keep the "one country, two systems" promise still had confidence in the territory's future.

It seemed that those who had the option to emigrate tended to do so in order to secure an "insurance policy". Afterwards, they could afford to have a realistic assessment of China's policy towards Hong Kong.

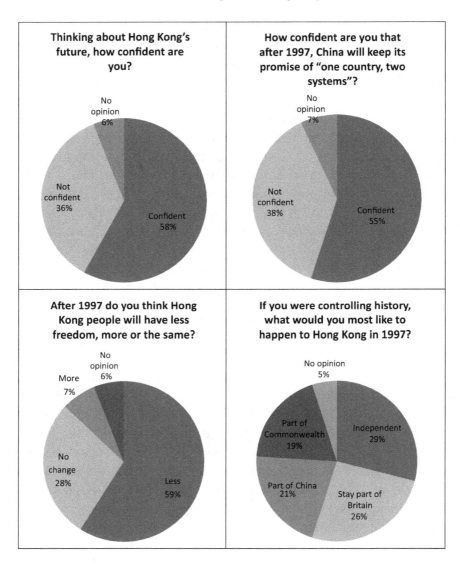

Whether they chose to leave the territory or not would depend on their opportunity costs. For the businessmen, the opportunity costs were generally too high; they normally preferred to secure their insurance policy and stay in Hong Kong to develop their business. Businessmen who migrated and stayed abroad for good usually had lower opportunity costs because they did not run major business concerns, or because they were approaching retirement. The territory had been losing many nurses exactly because their opportunity costs for emigration were low.

Most Hong Kong people believed that democracy had very limited prospects in the territory, and that freedoms would be curtailed after 1997. Their living standards too would probably decline a little. But they had been encouraged by the developments in the Pearl River Delta after the Tiananmen incident. Most Hong Kong people preferred Shenzhen to Edmonton in Canada. Even if Hong Kong were to become like Shenzhen in terms of freedom, human rights, legal system, etc., they thought this tolerable. Hence Hong Kong people had confidence in the territory's future and at the same time worried about it.

In the wake of the Tiananmen Incident, surveys indicated that about one-third of the territory's 1.55 million households were planning to emigrate.[4] In the two or three years since then, the percentage of people saying that they had actual plans or had taken action to emigrate to other countries had decreased gradually. The proportion of people who were undecided also declined. An opinion survey conducted by a group of academics from the Hong Kong Baptist College and the City Polytechnic of Hong Kong in November 1991 indicated that 7% of respondents stated that they would not stay in Hong Kong after 1997, and another 15.7% said that they were undecided.[5] This was the result of their realistic appraisals of the options and opportunity costs of emigration. The opportunity costs had further risen in view of the economic difficulties in Canada, Australia, the U.S., New Zealand, and the U.K. A survey published by the *South China Morning Post* on October 31, 1991, indicated that 19% of households with members abroad had, or expected to have, relatives coming back to work in Hong Kong that year. The rate surpassed the 7% recorded in 1988 and 6% in 1989 and 1990. In the early 1990s, Hong Kong people appeared to be much less interested in discussing the 1997 issue and their emigration plans with their friends. They probably had made up their minds then and they considered themselves politically

---

[4] *South China Morning Post*, July 4, 1989. The survey was conducted by Survey Research Hong Kong for the newspaper during June 22–30, 1989.

[5] *Ming Pao*, May 30, 1992.

impotent. Sales of all serious political magazines in Chinese dropped, while fortune-telling and geomancy retained their popularity.

(ii) *Relations with the Chinese Government*

The lack of confidence in the Chinese leadership's promises concerning Hong Kong meant that the Hong Kong people did not trust the Chinese government. In the abovementioned survey conducted by the local tertiary institutions in the summer and winter of 1990, only 10% of the respondents said that they trusted the Chinese government. In comparison, 20% of the respondents indicated their trust for the British government, while 42.9% expressed their trust for the Hong Kong government. Fifteen percent of the respondents said that they did not trust the Hong Kong government. The same survey also showed that distrust of the Chinese government generated a popular perception of conflict of interest between China and Hong Kong. The common interests of the two societies were largely under-estimated. The evidence was that one-half of the respondents agreed with the view that the interests of China and Hong Kong were in conflict, while only 30% took the opposite view.[6]

The business community, on the other hand, fully recognized the common interests between China and Hong Kong, and it especially appreciates the economic development in Guangdong's Pearl River Delta. In a survey of members of the local American Chamber of Commerce published in the *South China Morning Post* on June 10, 1992, only 7% of the respondents indicated that the five-year investment outlook for China was not favourable, compared with 31% in the previous survey just a year ago. Sixty-three percent and 30% of the respondents, respectively said that the investment outlook for China was "favorable" and "very favorable." The figures were 62% and 8% respectively in the previous poll. Regarding Hong Kong, 11% of the respondents considered that the investment climate for the next five years as "unfavorable," compared with 22% in the last survey. Sixty-four percent and 25% of the respondents believed that the investment climate in the territory for the next five years

---

[6] See Lau Siu-kai, "Social Irrelevance of Politics: Hong Kong Chinese Attitudes Toward Political Leadership," *Pacific Affairs*, Vol. 65, No. 2, Summer, 1992, pp. 236–237.

would be "favorable" and "very favorable" respectively, compared with 69% and 9% respectively in the earlier poll.

The Legislative Council elections in September 1991 also reflected the community's distrust of the Chinese government. Pro-democracy candidates who adopted a very critical stand against the Chinese government won a landslide victory, while the pro-Beijing candidates were all defeated. Over 100,000 people participated in major activities in memory of the Tiananmen incident in 1991. The number maintained at the 60,000 level in 1992. Given the appropriate opportunity, many Hong Kong people wanted to show their anger against the Chinese government which was seen to be responsible for the 1997 worries. At the same time, confrontation with Beijing was not considered the preferred way of relating to China. In the above survey, 75.1% of the respondents were against confrontation with China, and only 11.3% of the respondents were for it.[7] The community's clear support for the Sino-British Memorandum of Understanding on the Port and Airport Development Strategy (PADS) was a significant indicator of Hong Kong people's desire to avoid confrontation with Beijing. A majority of 61.9% of the respondents approved of the Sino-British accord which enabled Hong Kong to go ahead with its plan for a new airport, according to a *South China Morning Post* survey published on July 8, 1991. Only 8% of those interviewed disapproved of the agreement.

Hong Kong people, however, were hard to please. Some were suspicious of a Sino-British conspiracy to rip off the territory. Some were unhappy that Hong Kong people had been denied a role in the confidential bilateral negotiations. As a result, only slightly more than a quarter of the respondents said that their confidence in the Hong Kong government had been enhanced by the Memorandum of Understanding, while 21% thought the opposite. Similarly, politicians who advocated for better relations with China tended to be distrusted by the community. A *Sunday Morning Post* survey published on December 29, 1991, indicated that more than half of the respondents believed that the Legislative Council had the right to take on the Chinese authorities regarding disputes over the Court of Final Appeal, the committee system in the Legislative Council, etc. While Hong Kong people often applauded for political groups which

---

[7] *Ibid.*

were critical of the Chinese leaders, they certainly did not welcome confrontation with Beijing. They feared that would have a serious adverse impact on the stability and prosperity of the territory.

Despite emotions against the Chinese government, Hong Kong people understood that they had to accommodate with it and adapt to the changes in 1997. Senior civil servants too recognized this need for adaptation. The Hong Kong government was ahead of public opinion in advocating for "an harmonious and effective partnership with counterparts at all levels in China." This statement in Governor Wilson's policy speech in October 1991 attracted a lot of attention. Not many people applauded, but there was no strong criticism either. Hong Kong people desired a "smooth and successful transfer of sovereignty in 1997" and they assumed this to be the responsibility of the British administration. They remained reluctant to voice their strong support for this goal though. The change, however, might come quickly. In a territory-wide poll conducted by Professor S.K. Lau of The Chinese University of Hong Kong in the summer and autumn of 1991, 76.6% of the respondents believed that it was unavoidable that China would increasingly participate in Hong Kong affairs. A total of 51.1% of the respondents believed that it was unavoidable that China should increase its participation in the territory's affairs in the second half of the transitional period, while only 17.4% disapproved. More significantly still, 23.4% of the respondents considered that China's increasing participation in Hong Kong affairs would be advantageous for the territory, while 15.7% considered it disadvantageous; another 38.7% thought that it would not make much difference.[8] A poll published by Sunday Morning Post on June 21, 1992, indicated that 39% of the respondents thought that the British government was the most to blame for the current row on PADS, while only 19% believed that the Chinese government was the most to blame.

(iii) *Evaluation of the Hong Kong Government*

In the recent CNTA poll conducted in March 1992, 41% of the respondents said that they were satisfied with the overall performance of the Hong

---

[8] The author is most grateful for the data supplied by Professor S.K. Lau.

Kong government, compared with 37% who were dissatisfied. In the survey conducted by the social scientists of local tertiary institutions in the summer and winter of 1990, slightly over half of the respondents (52.6%) rated the Hong Kong government's performance as about average; 15.1% thought it was poor; and 22.8% considered it good.[9] In the same survey, 45.1% of the respondents expressed satisfaction with the existing political conditions, as against 28.5% who did not. Similarly, even though 59% of the respondents found the existing political system acceptable, 25.9% of them did not fully endorse it.

Hong Kong people were almost evenly split in their attitudes towards political reform. A total of 43.1% of the respondents in the above survey wanted to maintain the existing political system, but 38.5% thought it should be reformed. As far as the pace of democratic reforms was concerned, a preponderant majority (74.4%) of the respondents preferred a gradualist approach. Only a small minority of them desired a rapid (6.2%) or a slow (5.4%) pace of democratization. In any case, the community was not sanguine about the prospect of establishing a democratic political system because only 33.1% of the respondents considered the chance of successful democratization to be good. In response to the Legislative Council elections in September 1991, 47% of the respondents in a survey published in the *South China Morning Post* on October 31, 1991, said that the direct elections of liberals to the legislature did not affect their perception of the territory. Of the remaining 53%, less than half felt that the electoral outcome had raised their confidence. Only 10% of those who believed that the elections influenced their attitude to Hong Kong said that they were disturbed by the results. Those who felt encouraged by the elections tended to be professionals and people with higher incomes and education. However, doubts about the Legislative Council elections were also stronger among this group.

In sum, while the majority of Hong Kong people was satisfied with the performance of the Hong Kong government, the minority who was dissatisfied was expanding. The latter grew in times of high tension between Beijing and Hong Kong, and during economic difficulties.

---

[9] See Lau Siu-kai, "Social Irrelevance of Politics, Hong Kong Chinese Attitudes Toward Political Leadership," *op.cit.*, pp. 237–238.

Table 8.1: Evaluation of the Hong Kong Government's Performance (%)

	1986 (N = 359)	1988 (N = 396)	1990 (N = 803)
Very bad	0.6	0.3	1.5
Bad	8.9	6.3	13.8
Average	46.6	46.5	53.4
Good	37.3	41.2	22.0
Very Good	0.0	0.8	1.1
Don't know/No answer	6.7	5.0	8.1

Table 8.2: Trust in the Hong Kong Government (%)

	1986 (N = 359)	1988 (N = 396)	1990 (N = 803)
Very distrustful	0.0	0.9	0.5
Distrustful	20.6	17.3	15.8
Average	—	27.5	38.4
Trustful	65.5	45.1	37.9
Very Trustful	1.3	3.4	2.0
Don't know/No answer	12.6	5.7	5.5

According to the CNTA polls, more and more Hong Kong people: considered the civil service inefficient; regarded civil servants' working attitudes bad; severely criticized the Hong Kong government's lack of transparency; believed that the Hong Kong government was indifferent about public opinion; and criticized it for not taking into account public opinion when deciding on policies and actions. A series of territory-wide social indicators surveys conducted by the social scientists of local tertiary institutions revealed similar phenomena (see Table 8.1 and Table 8.2).[10]

Several factors contributed to this trend. The approach to 1997 enhanced the perception of the Hong Kong government as a lame-duck government. The development of representative government helped to expose the mistakes of the Hong Kong government more effectively.

---

[10] See Wan Po-san, "The Quality of Life," in *The Other Hong Kong Report 1991*, edited by Sung Yun-wing, and Lee Ming-kwan, Hong Kong: The Chinese University Press, 1991, pp. 432–433.

Political groups then took pride in challenging the administration. The media were spreading messages that the civil service suffered from low morale and lack of direction. Hong Kong people worrying about the uncertainties of the future tended to blame the British administration more. The latter, preoccupied with economy measures, was in a more difficult position to please the community.

Hong Kong people demonstrated a general preference for democracy over authoritarianism. This explained why all political groups in the territory claimed to support democracy. The abovementioned survey published by *Sunday Morning Post* on June 21, 1992, showed that 66% of the respondents thought that the Governor should introduce more democracy, even if it meant confronting China; while 23% considered that the Governor should not. Further, 63% of the respondents supported the increase of directly elected seats in the Legislative Council to thirty in 1995, while only 11% opposed. However, the community did not expect full democracy by 1997 and beyond. Demand for significant steps towards further democratization in the transitional period was not backed by action and a willingness to sacrifice. The United Democrats of Hong Kong and other pro-democracy groups were popular because they were courageous in criticizing the Hong Kong government and the Chinese leaders on behalf of Hong Kong people. They were considered honest and uncontaminated by special interests. They were therefore relied upon to generate some form of checks and balances *vis-à-vis* the Hong Kong government, the business community, and, to a lesser extent, the Chinese authorities.

The Hong Kong government's authority was widely perceived as an important factor in the maintenance of political stability and effectiveness. In a survey conducted by the social scientists of local tertiary institutions in the summer of 1988, a substantial proportion of the respondents (54.3%) believed that the authority of the Hong Kong government had been eroded in the past three years, 28.3% did not think so and 17.5% gave no definite answer on this matter.[11] The majority of the respondents (64.9%) considered that the erosion of the Hong Kong government's

---

[11] See Lau Siu-kai, Kuan Hsin-chi and Wan Po-san, "Political Attitudes," in *Indicators of Social Development: Hong Kong 1988*, pp. 188–189.

authority would endanger the territory's prosperity and stability. Only 23.5% did not think so and 11.7% had no definite answer. Respondents who were worried about the occurrence of political instability before 1997, and those who distrusted the Chinese government, showed a greater tendency to affirm the detrimental effects of the erosion of the British administration's authority on Hong Kong's prosperity and stability.

In examining the respondents' perceptions of the reasons for the erosion of the Hong Kong government's authority, two possible causes were raised. The Chinese government was regarded as the first cause of the erosion of the Hong Kong government's authority by a great majority (76.7%) of the respondents. As to the second cause, 35.8% agreed that the erosion had been caused by the pro-democracy groups. However, about half of the respondents (48.4%) disagreed that the activities of the pro-democracy groups had eroded the authority of the British administration.

Hong Kong people recognized the danger of eroding the Hong Kong government's authority, and they would rally to support the Hong Kong government whenever they perceived that its authority being unduly challenged. Public opinion normally condemned the Chinese authorities for intervening in the territory's affairs. The public also severely criticized the demand of the United Democrats of Hong Kong that the Governor should appoint Legislative Councillors from the political group's list. The disputes among political groups within the legislature did not contribute to the development of representative government. Hong Kong people would probably become more apathetic and politically cynical. Since they did not seem to be prepared to involve themselves in the conflicts initiated by the political elites, the scale of political conflicts in Hong Kong was constrained. It would be impossible for competing political elites to divide and mobilize the masses. At the same time, political leaders and groups would be deprived of the opportunity to earn the trust of the people.[12] A survey in March 1992 showed that support for the United Democrats of Hong Kong dropped 4% to 60.7% compared with that half a year ago.[13]

---

[12] See Lau Siu-kai, "Social Irrelevance of Politics: Hong Kong Chinese Attitudes Toward Political Leadership", *op. cit.*, pp. 239–242.

[13] *Ming Pao*, May 31, 1992.

(iv) *Political Participation*

Hong Kong people in general adopted an instrumental and pragmatic approach to politics. They calculated the value of politics or political participation in terms of the concrete benefits that could be secured. If conflicts among political leaders and groups were not seen to be relevant to their social and economic interests, public trust invested in these leaders and groups would be low. Even though the Hong Kong people were still reasonably satisfied with the existing conditions, attitudinal differences among them on a variety of issues were widening. Thus, there was a growing reservoir of social and economic issues which could be exploited by political leaders and groups. However, in the eyes of the people, political leaders and groups so far largely neglected to address these emerging conflicts effectively in their competition with each other. Accordingly, they saw no strong reason to trust and support them. As conflicts among political elites were conducted frequently in political terms devoid of social and economic implications, these conflicts were mostly seen as personal and rhetorical, thus fostering the unattractive image of playing a power game among the politically ambitious. Consequently, Hong Kong people maintained their detached view of politics, and this was obviously not conducive to public trust in political leaders and groups.

Exit polls conducted by the two television stations on the day of the territory's first Legislative Council elections revealed that two thirds of the voters cast their votes to fulfill a civic obligation and support the development of democracy, other factors were insignificant. Influenced by publicity campaigns, the community had high — almost unrealistic — expectations of the Legislative Councillors in September 1991. In a *Sunday Morning Post* survey conducted in the week before the elections, when asked "After the election, who will best look after your interests?", 46% of the respondents said the new directly elected Legislative Councillors, 12% said the Hong Kong government, 10% said the Legislative Councillors returned by functional constituencies, and 10% said the Legislative Council. When asked "After the election, who will have the most power to govern Hong Kong?", 28% of the respondents said the Legislative Council, 23% said the Governor, 12% said the Executive Council, 11% the British government, and 6% the Chinese government.

A survey of teachers' political attitudes and political participation, published in the local newspaper at the end of 1991, revealed that 38% of the respondents planned to emigrate. Among those who opted to stay in Hong Kong, 29.9% showed no confidence in the territory's future. One-sixth and 16.4% respectively chose to stay because they had confidence and because they had a sense of mission. Among the teachers polled, 35.4% regularly participated in elections; 6.4% frequently took part in public affairs; 25.6% had never voted; and 57.7% had never participated in public affairs. One-fifth did not even bother to read newspapers. The findings were not very encouraging, but observers believed that they reflected the reality.

(v) *Identity and Sense of Belonging*

The disparity of development between Hong Kong and Mainland China in the past decades caused Hong Kong, as a social entity, to drift quite far from its Motherland. A distinctive Hong Kong identity, hinging upon the demarcation between "Hongkongese" and "Chinese", had developed gradually among Hong Kong Chinese. This new identity had a considerable impact on their political values. In the survey conducted in the summer of 1988 by the social scientists of local tertiary institutions, the majority of the respondents (63.6%), when asked to choose between "Hongkongese" and "Chinese" as their primary identity, identified themselves as the former while 28.8% still considered themselves as "Chinese".[14] It was quite natural that the "Chinese" identity was predominately adopted by the older respondents, particularly those who were not born in Hong Kong, or who had experienced a different socialization process. For example, 53.9% of those over 54 years old considered themselves "Chinese", whereas only 21.4% of those below 30 claimed that identity.

In addition to claiming Hong Kong identity, which defined Hong Kong Chinese as a distinctive group of Chinese, a substantial proportion of respondents also distinctive group of Chinese, a substantial proportion of respondents also indicated a strong sense of attachment to the society

---

[14] See Lau Siu-kai, Kuan Hsin-chi and Wan Po-san, "Political Attitudes," in *Indicators of Social Development: Hong Kong 1988*, pp. 177–178.

of Hong Kong. A total of 63.5% of the respondents declared that they had a very strong or strong sense of belonging to Hong Kong while a mere 8.9% expressed very little or little sense of belonging. Ironically, although younger and the better-educated respondents were more likely to claim a "Hong Kong identity", the "sense of belonging" to Hong Kong was stronger among the less-educated than other educational groups. Hence, claiming a Hong Kong identity was not tantamount to having a strong sense of belonging to Hong Kong. The younger and the better-educated had a better chance of leaving Hong Kong. Since emigration was an option on their mind, their sense of belonging to the territory was correspondingly weaker.

In the remaining years of the transitional period, Hong Kong people would become more confused regarding their identity. Those who had acquired foreign passports would seek to protect their rights if they chose to stay in Hong Kong. The pro-Beijing united front would continue to step up its appeal to nationalism and patriotism. Contradictions between the Hong Kong people and the colonial administration would also be exploited. Within the community, the contradictions between those who had the option to emigrate and those who did not would be sharpened. Resentment against the recent immigrants of Chinese cadres in the territory would increase. These newcomers in town would likely become targets of the frustration caused by worries over the uncertainty of the future. The use of Cantonese might well become a controversial issue.

II Economic Attitudes and Values

As Hong Kong people approached 1997, there was considerable worry regarding the limited time horizon of the community. In the late 1980s and early 1990s, the medical and law faculties of the tertiary institutions encountered difficulties in recruiting top students. The loss of attraction of these once highly popular faculties was mainly caused by the consideration that students entering these faculties could only start their lucrative careers after 1997.

Similar to the U.S. in the second half of the 1980s, the financial sector was most attractive to new graduates. On the other hand, some professions, like engineering, noted with concern the declining proportion of graduates who were willing to go through professional training after graduation. A significant and expanding percentage of graduates in the engineering and computer science fields opted for jobs in the financial sector, or in the marketing field, instead of trainee posts in engineering or manufacturing industries.

The Census and Statistics Department's General Household Survey during the second quarter of 1988 estimated that the number of persons participating in part-time courses was 100,700, representing 2.3% of the population aged 15 and over. The decline was very serious. Perhaps the rapid expansion of the tertiary institutions contributed to the decline. However, there was also speculation that young people had become reluctant to engage in long-term planning and long-term investment in improving their qualifications because of 1997.

(i) *Young Employees*

Employers at this stage often complained about the work ethics of young employees. Their complaints normally related to unrealistic expectations of promotion, lack of long-term commitment to the organization, frequent turnover (often without sufficient prior notice or explanation), and lack of respect for the employers and senior colleagues. As the younger employees often did not have any family financial burden (their parents did not expect them to contribute to the family expenditure), they could afford to give up jobs or change jobs. Some young people might save while working and then gave up their jobs to travel. The demand for leisure, job satisfaction, and the pursuit of individual interests was strengthening as the society became more affluent.

There was a view that children of the increasingly affluent middle class would find it difficult to attain a sense of achievement. In general, the post-war generation in Hong Kong had a hard time in its childhood. Members of this generation often suffered various economic hardships before completing their education. However, their career development and Hong Kong's economic growth brought them much satisfaction through job advancement and improvement in living standards. On the other hand, young people from middle-class families in the 1990s would probably have to endure a decline in living standards when they became independent, and they would have to work for many years before they could catch up with their parents. To them, a sense of satisfaction and achievement would more difficult to come by.

Hong Kong's work force has been maintaining its efficiency and high spirits very well. Though the territory's employees were highly mobile, they were very dedicated to their work and they secured considerable job satisfaction besides financial rewards. Undeniably, the exodus of talents and frequent turnovers had their adverse impact, but the yuppies still gave their employers value for money.

Despite the maturation of the economy and the increasing advantage of the economy of scale, the entrepreneurial spirit among Hong Kong people remained strong, especially among the young generation. Their relatively light family burden might be an important factor. From 1981 to 1991, the number of employers increased from about 90,000 to 153,000, according to the 1991 Population Census.

(ii) *Ethics and Disparity*

Professional ethics, however, appeared to be one of the casualties of the uncertainty of the future. Hong Kong people's trust for professionals was in decline. When advised by a doctor to have an operation, very often there was strong suspicion that the advice was based on greed rather than medical grounds. Young professionals were over eager to establish their own practices before building an adequate clientele. They were therefore under pressure to relax their professional standards and engage in work in the "grey areas" or even illegal activities.

According to a survey of young adults from urban households by the Sociology Department of the University of Hong Kong published in 1973, 62.7% of the young adults interviewed agreed that "Hong Kong is truly a land of opportunity and people get pretty much what they deserve here."[15] Despite the considerable gap between the rich and poor, and the

---

[15] A total of 31.2% of the young adults interviewed disagreed with the statement, while 6.1% did not reply or indicated that they did not know. See D.C. Chaney and D.B.L. Podmore, *Young Adults in Hong Kong: Attitudes in a Modernising Society*, Hong Kong: Centre of Asian Studies, University of Hong Kong, 1973, p. 60.

juxtaposition of luxurious apartments and squatter huts, young adults still held such a view. This certainly helped to explain why Hong Kong remained politically stable and demand for political participation low.

The perception of the community in the early 1990s, however, was that the gap between the rich and poor was widening. This perception was probably generated by rampant speculative activities in the economy. It was also supported by the changes in the Gini coefficient which rose from 0.43 in 1971 and 1976 to 0.45 in 1981 and 0.48 in 1991. Such perception exacerbated class consciousness and class contradictions in the territory. The pro-Beijing united front was poised to exploit this perception.

The spread of speculative activities and years of double-digit inflation had a considerable impact on the community's savings, investment and consumption habits. As interest rates offered by banks were substantially lower than inflation rates, Hong Kong people had to look for ways to protect their savings. Foreign currency deposits offered options to many elderly people. However, a significant segment of Hong Kong people had not been successful in securing returns for their savings to cover inflation. Young people also found it extremely difficult to save up to buy a flat. These phenomena would certainly generate dissatisfaction, and would induce unsophisticated investors to engage in speculative activities they did not fully understand.

On the other hand, the fact that most families in the territory were still willing to work very hard, to make all sorts of sacrifices to provide for their children's education, and to acquire their own accommodation, was most assuring. These values would certainly continue to contribute to the growth of the territory's economy.

(iii) *Mobility and Socioeconomic Status*

The willingness to sacrifice for the education of one's children was related to Hong Kong people's belief that their society was open, fluid, and providing ample opportunities. They also believed that personal endeavours would bear fruit eventually. Such optimism also pertained to their view of their children's future. In the survey in the summer of 1988 conducted by the social scientists of local tertiary institutions, nearly 80% of the respondents thought that their children would be in the middle (54%) or the upper-middle (25%) socioeconomic stratum.[16] The optimism did not seem to wane too much even when the future meant 1997 and beyond. The majority were of the view that the socioeconomic status of their children would be better than their own both before and after 1997. The working class (i.e., the manufacturing workers) was, on the whole, more optimistic than the middle-class with respect to this question. It is interesting to note that 30% of middle-class respondents thought that their children's socioeconomic status would worsen after 1997.

In the same survey, the respondents were asked to which class they felt they belonged. A total of 65% answered "working class", 23% "middle class," and 6% "capitalist class." The rest chose "don't know" or did not answer. On the other hand, when asked to which social stratum they belonged, more than 70% felt that they belonged to the middle strata, including lower-middle (32%), middle (36%), and upper-middle (4%). Those claiming membership of the upper social stratum were insignificant in terms of percentage. On the other hand, 23% of the respondents considered that they belonged to the lower social stratum.[17]

The same survey confirmed the general perception that Hong Kong was a place full of opportunities with a high degree of social openness. When asked what criteria would determine one's social status, 40% of the respondents indicated wealth, 26% education, 11% "contribution to society", 8% family background, and 8% power. It was also significant that 83% of the respondents believed that employees could become bosses.[18]

When asked about the chances of developing their own careers in the next ten years, respondents in the 1988 survey were on the whole more cautious and realistic. A total of 20% and 15% of the respondents respectively indicated "very little chance" and "little chance." A total of 36% of the respondents believed that their chances would be average; while

---

[16] See Thomas W. P. Wong, "Inequality, Stratification and Mobility," in *Indicators of Social Development: Hong Kong 1988*, p. 168.
[17] *Ibid.*, p. 148.
[18] *Ibid.*, pp. 158–159.

22% and 7% respectively considered that their chances would be "great" and "very great."[19] With respect to the perceived best upward-mobility route, two observations emerged from the survey. In the first place, it was quite that both "acquiring professional qualification" and "starting one's own business" were most favoured, chosen by 39% and 41% of the respondents respectively. The second observation was that acquiring a job with good promotion prospects, the third best upward-mobility route, was favoured by only 9% of the respondents.

III Social Attitudes and Values

Despite living in a cosmopolitan city fully exposed to Western cultural influences, Hong Kong people were quite conservative in their social attitudes and values. Traditional Confucian values went through decades of slow erosion, but they remained a predominant influence on the behavioural patterns of local people. Compared with Western societies, Hong Kong still had distinctively lower divorce rates despite a significant increase in the past decade (divorced and separated females in 1991 were 150% more than 1981). People's attitudes towards sex appeared conservative event in the East Asian context. A survey revealed that only 2.4% of a sample of new students at the local tertiary institutions had premarital sex experience.[20]

Apparently any explicit attempt by the Hong Kong government to influence the community's values would generate much suspicion. But at the same time the community would make demands on the administration based on traditional values. Opposition to the decriminalization of homosexuality, the establishment of off-course betting centres by the Royal Hong Kong Jockey Club, the sale of Mark-Six lottery tickets in supermarkets, etc., were obvious examples. Politicians too believe that the demands for more services for the elderly and stricter control of pornography would be popular.

---

[19] *Ibid.*, pp. 163–164.
[20] *Ta Kung Pao*, December 12, 1991.

Table 8.3: The Most Important Ingredients for a Happy Life (%)

	1986 (N = 517)	1988 (N = 1,598)	1990 (N = 786)
Health	57.4	39.9	36.5
Money	8.9	12.5	16.3
Peace of mind	—	6.3	12.7
Filial piety	7.0	6.4	8.5
Freedom	—	10.5	8.1
Career	6.0	3.9	6.9
Love and marriage	13.2	9.4	4.5
Material enjoyment	0.0	0.6	1.3
Social services	0.4	0.6	0.5
Others	7.1	9.8	4.7

A series of territory-wide social indicator surveys conducted by the social scientists of local tertiary institutions offered a preliminary analysis of Hong Kong peoples' perception of the quality of life.[21]

As shown in Table 8.3, Hong Kong people had a relatively broad consensus on the idea of a happy life. They desired both non-materialistic satisfaction and materialistic gratification. Their perception of happiness was very personal and individualistic. Good health was always the most cherished value. Money came second. Nevertheless, in these surveys people were not quite explicit about their materialistic orientation. Very few of them identified material enjoyment as the most important ingredient of happiness. The emphasis placed on certain Confucian values, such as filial piety and peace of mind, might reflect the lingering influence of traditional Chinese culture. It was interesting to note that, despite the importance of the family in Chinese societies, love and marriage were often given a relatively low significance. These findings in the second half of the 1980s seemed to indicate (1) the

---

[21] See Wong Siu-lun and Shirley Yue, "Satisfaction in Various Life Domains," in *Indicators of Social Development: Hong Kong 1988*, p. 15; see also Wan Po-san, "The Quality of Life," in *The Other Hong Kong Report 1991*, pp. 426–427.

declining importance of health, love and marriage, and (2) the growing significance of money and peace of mind, as the most important sources of happiness. Although Hong Kong people were often praised for their hardwork, the importance of career in a happy life was low. The community was certainly generous in its donations for charitable causes, but social services were definitely not regarded as important for personal wellbeing.

A comparison with the findings of an earlier survey held in June 1982 and sponsored by the Hong Kong Observers was interesting.[22] The findings showed that the aspirations of the Hong Kong community then were similar to those of other peoples in developing countries. In that survey money was not the most important thing in life. Money was said to be important to 79% of the respondents, but more to the 25 to 44 age group and people with less education (primary or below). The "opportunity to make money" was a little more important (82%). Its importance however, was almost equal to that of freedom of speech (83%), but outranked by comfortable living environment (85%) and freedom of choice (86%). "A meaningful life" (77%) came close to the importance of money. Good food was more important (65%) than "other material comforts" (36%). Good clothing was important to 21% of the respondents. The younger and better-educated placed greater importance on intangibles like "a meaningful life" while material comforts were more important to the less-educated and lower-income groups.

The 1990 survey attempted to assess Hong Kong people's degree of satisfaction with personal life. The results of the survey are summarized in Table 8.4.[23]

---

[22] "The Hongkong Observers poll" in Pressure Points, edited by the Hong Kong Observers (updated edition); Hong Kong: Summerson (HK) Educational Research Center, 1983, pp. 196–202.
[23] See Wan Po-san, "The Quality of Life," in *The Other Hong Kong Report 1991*, pp. 433–436.

Table 8.4: Degree of Satisfaction with Personal Life

	\multicolumn{6}{c}{Degree of Satisfaction (%)}
	1	2	3	4	5	Mean
Overall	1.3	7.8	34.0	52.2	4.7	3.512
Specific						
Family life	0.6	4.6	24.6	64.8	5.4	3.699
Friend	0.5	2.0	31.4	60.9	5.1	3.681
Relatives	0.9	5.6	37.9	50.5	5.1	3.532
Health condition	1.0	10.3	28.0	56.3	4.4	3.528
Leisure	0.1	7.8	47.8	41.7	2.6	3.389
Work	1.2	12.0	36.7	49.4	0.8	3.367
Housing conditions	2.0	17.8	31.5	44.8	3.9	3.308
Financial situation	2.4	15.5	45.9	34.4	1.8	3.177
Educational attainment	3.6	36.7	33.3	24.6	1.7	2.840

Note: 1 = very dissatisfied, 2 = dissatisfied, 3 = average, 4 = satisfied, 5 = very satisfied.

(i) *Family and Marriage*

Despite the growing incidence of family conflicts and the rise in family dissolutions, all surveys showed that Hong Kong people's highest satisfaction level was found in the domain of family life, followed by other personal social ties such as relationships with friends and relatives. Seven out of 10 respondents in the 1990 survey said that they were satisfied with their family life, and only 5.4% were not. This profile of satisfaction — high satisfaction with one's personal social network and low satisfaction with one's education and economic status — was similar to that found in many other countries. If one disregarded measurement biases in these studies (for example, people were less likely to admit that their marriages were in trouble than having a difficult boss), then the most likely reasons for this profile of satisfaction were two. In the first place, the nature of people's relationship with their family members, friends, and relatives were more intimate, all-encompassing, less competitive, and thus were more intrinsically rewarding. Secondly, people's quality of life and sense of satisfaction are based on comparison with others. While there were always external and objective criteria for people to assess their social standing (for example, educational attainment and economic status), there was no commonly accepted standard whereby people could evaluate their intimate life. At any rate, it was encouraging to find that, living in a competitive and fast-changing world, Hong Kong people were still able to maintain the integrity of their private life and found comfort in it.

Hong Kong people seemed to be satisfied with their marriages. A survey conducted by Professor S.K. Lau in Kwun Tong in the third quarter of 1987 showed that 72.9% of the respondents expressed satisfaction in their marriages, and only 2% indicated dissatisfaction. Those who were better-educated seemed to be more satisfied with their marriages.[24] In their daily conversations, many Hong Kong people expressed their concern on extramarital relationships, reflecting their conservative Confucian attitudes and the importance they attached to marriage and family.

In the 1988 survey of the series of territory-wide social indicators surveys conducted by the social scientists of local tertiary institutions, the respondents were asked to indicate their attitudes towards eight types of unconventional sexual relationships. The findings indicated that, on the whole and across the spectrum, Hong Kong people were conservative in their attitudes towards sex. Such conservatism protected marriage and family life. With perhaps the exception of divorce, the majority of the respondents could not accept any one of the following unconventional sexual relationships.[25]

The case of divorce perhaps reflected a pragmatic attitude. About half (47.1%) of the respondents could not accept divorce. However, there were more who would either reserve making a judgement (30.9%) or simply accept it (21.3%). Attitudes towards premarital cohabitation and pregnancy were similar. Respondents were relatively more lenient towards these two types of behavior than the other types. Though the majority of the respondents could not accept premarital cohabitation and pregnancy, as

---

[24] See Lau Siu-kai and Wan Po-san, *Preliminary Report on Research on Indicators of Hong Kong's Social Development* (in Chinese), Hong Kong: Centre for Hong Kong studies, The Chinese University of Hong Kong, September 1987, p. 29.

[25] See Lee Ming-kwan, "Family and Social Life," in *Indicators of Social Development: Hong Kong 1988*, pp. 54–55.

Table 8.5: Attitudes Towards Sexual Norms (%)

	Very Much Against Accepting	Against Accepting	It Depends	Accept	Very Much Accept
Cohabitation marriage	9.4	48.8	15.1	26.0	0.7
Pregnancy before marriage	8.9	51.1	12.5	27.1	0.5
Sex with casual partner	18.0	70.1	7.5	4.4	0.0
Men having extra-marital relations	20.8	64.3	7.8	7.1	0.0
Women having extra marital relations	25.7	64.6	5.9	3.8	0.0
Prostitution	20.0	56.4	16.4	6.7	0.5
Divorce	7.4	39.7	30.9	21.3	0.7
Homosexuality	38.7	53.9	3.8	3.6	0.0

many as 26.7% and 27.6% respectively would be sympathetic. It would seem then that there was some degrees of normative flexibility here. Such flexibility was not applicable to the other five unconventional categories. Fewer than one-tenth of the respondents could accept casual sexual relations, affairs by married men or women, prostitution, and homosexuality. They were, however, slightly less indignant when these acts were committed by men than when they were committed by women.

The above findings highlighted that the changing family system was obviously the most crucial factor affecting the community's social attitudes and values. The 1991 Population Census reaffirmed the obvious trend towards smaller households. The average size of domestic households was 3.4 persons in 1991, compared with 3.9 in 1981. It was particularly noted that the proportion of households with 6 persons or more dropped drastically from 23% to 11% over the past decade. More domestic households consisted of one unextended nuclear family; their share increased from 54% in 1981 to 62% in 1991. The proportion of extended families decreased from 16% to 13% in the same period.

(ii) *Demand on Social Services*

The above trends, together with the rapid increase in the population of elderly people and their extended life expectancy, contributed to demands for services for the elderly provided by the Hong Kong government.

Admittedly, relations between elderly people and their children remained close in general; but such relations were suffering an inevitable erosion.

The small size of the households meant that children at this stage got a lot of attention from their parents, and lots of money to spend. But their parents were often confused as to how to teach them. Their parents were not too sure whether they should insist on traditional Confucian values, or they should encourage their children to adapt to the demands of the highly competitive and materialistic society. Concerned middle-class parents could normally count on their own efforts to handle the problems, but parents who were not well-educated believed that they needed help.

Hong Kong people realized that the family and the school were the most significant sources of values in the socialization process. So it was natural that they either chose to rely on their own efforts or to make demands on (as well as to blame) the education system. Hong Kong people often referred to the education system in their discussion of the community's social ethics and values. Those who severely criticized the education system tended to blame the media as well. Small nuclear families, especially those with working mothers and single-parents families, were carrying heavier burden alone. Social workers were advocating mutual aid as one solution. This might well be the development of new types of non-political neighbourhood groups.

(iii) Satisfaction in Other Domains

While Hong Kong people in general enjoyed their family life, they had shown ambivalent attitudes towards the general social situation. In the 1990 survey of the series of territory-wide social indicators surveys conducted by the social scientist of local tertiary institutions, an attempt was made to assess the community's degree of satisfaction with different social conditions. The results are summarized in Table 8.6.[26]

In the 1988 survey of the same series, the respondents were asked which aspect of their family life they were most keen to improve. The first priority appeared to be their living environment, with 37.2% of them

---

[26] See Wan Po-san, "The Quality of Life," in *The Other Hong Kong Report 1991*, pp. 430–432.

Table 8.6: Hong Kong People's Degree of Satisfaction with Different Social Conditions

	\multicolumn{7}{c	}{Degree of Satisfaction (%)}
	1	2	3	4	5	DK/NA	Mean
Political situation	4.0	28.5	28.5	14.4	0.5	24.1	2.723
Law and order	4.6	36.4	33.5	22.5	0.6	2.4	2.777
Transport	3.7	24.8	37.5	19.9	1.1	12.9	2.884
Housing	2.9	28.5	35.0	27.0	1.4	5.2	2.953
Medical services	2.6	23.7	40.2	28.3	1.0	4.2	3.014
Education	2.2	20.4	30.6	38.4	1.9	6.5	3.184
Economic situation	1.1	19.6	28.6	39.1	1.5	10.1	3.226
Employment	0.9	11.8	35.2	42.1	1.4	8.7	3.341
Recreation	0.7	10.2	31.4	44.8	1.9	10.9	3.414

Note: 1 = very dissatisfied, 2 = dissatisfied, 3 = average, 4 = satisfied, 5 = very satisfied, DK/NA = Don't know/No answer

highlighting it. The second priority was their financial situation, which was emphasized by 19.5%. Lower down the list of priorities were family relations with 9%, children's education with 8.6%, and other aspects with 4.3%. A total of 8.3% of the respondents seemed to be contented with their existing family life and saw no need for specific improvements.[27]

Since June 1986, CNTA surveys had tried to identify the problems of most concern to Hong Kong people (see Table 8.7).

These and other surveys indicated a relatively high public consciousness of social problems. Admittedly, public perceptions of social problems often changed from time to time. The most common causes of these changes were the shift in values, the solution of old problems and the emergence of new ones. The problems of the Vietnamese boat people and "brain drain" causes considerable worry in 1989 and 1990, but their significance then sharply declined. In Table 8.7, concern for housing-related problems went up significantly since the latter half of 1991, and the same applied to economy-related problems since 1991. Hong Kong people also appeared to be much more worried about crime-related

---

[27] See Wong Siu-lun and Shirley Yue, "Satisfaction in Various Life Domains," in *Indicators of Social Development: Hong Kong 1988*, pp. 19–20.

234   *Political Development in Hong Kong*

Table 8.7: Problems of Most Concern to Hong Kong People, 1986–1992 (First Quarter)

Problems of Most Concern to Hong Kong People	6/86 %	12/86 %	6/87 %	12/87 %	6/88 %	12/88 %	5-6/89 %	8/89 %	9/89 %	11/89 %	1/90 %	3/90 %	5/90 %	7/90 %	9/90 %	11/90 %	1/91 %	3/91 %	5/91 %	7/91 %	9/91 %	11/91 %	1/92 %	3/92 %
Housing-related	24	24	19	20	13	16	6	5	4	5	5	7	6	9	9	8	8	12	12	11	20	24	13	16
Transport-related	6	7	8	11	16	18	5	3	5	7	6	6	4	6	7	5	3	9	5	5	5	3	3	2
Crime-related	8	6	6	6	3	4	1	1	1	1	*	1	2	2	11	7	18	10	6	9	8	8	8	16
Economy-related	11	6	8	11	6	7	1	2	1	2	3	10	11	6	11	13	14	18	29	26	19	23	28	21
Education-related	6	7	4	3	3	3	1	1	1	1	2	1	1	1	2	2	1	3	1	1	1	1	1	1
Hong Kong future	22	28	28	20	28	26	46	44	52	62	58	48	49	52	43	40	40	24	24	24	27	18	23	15
Hong Kong political system	1	3	6	6	1	4	1	*	1	*	*	1	1	1	1	1	1	1	1	*	1	1	1	1
Medical services	2	1	1	1	1	1	*	*	1	1	1	1	2	1	1	1	1	1	1	*	1	1	1	1
Social welfare-related	1	3	3	4	2	2	1	*	1	1	1	2	2	2	1	2	2	3	2	3	2	2	2	3
Youth	2	2	1	1	1	1	*	*	*	1	*	*	*	1	—	1	*	*	1	1	1	*	1	—
Illegal immigrants	—	*	*	*	—	—	—	—	—	—	—	—	—	*	*	*	—	—	—	*	—	—	*	—
Environmental protection-related	1	2	3	2	4	3	1	2	2	1	2	2	2	3	2	3	2	2	2	2	1	*	1	*
Refugees	NA	NA	NA	*	13	2	31	38	30	14	13	8	11	6	3	6	2	3	4	3	4	6	1	2
Labour	NA	NA	NA	1	1	1	1	1	*	1	1	1	1	3	3	3	1	1	2	4	3	6	10	9
Taxation	NA	NA	NA	*	*	*	*	*	—	—	*	3	1	—	*	1	—	8	5	1	1	*	*	9

Notes: (1) NA — Not available. (2) * — less than 0.5%.

problems in early 1992. On the other hand, confidence in the territory's future obviously improved since the Tiananmen incident.

(iv) Work and Worries

Employees in the territory usually had a very heavy workload. In the early 1990s, Hong Kong people became more conscious of their health and diet. More and more people were on diet and pay more attention to exercises. The yuppies phenomenon was spreading to the older generations. The General Household Survey held in the last quarter of 1988 discovered that 12.7% of the respondents aged 15 and over had visited country parks in the past three months. The proportion rose to 23.4% among those with a post-secondary education. Tai Chi and Qigong were very popular among intellectuals and professionals whose work pressure is considerable. General Household Surveys also showed that the proportion of daily smokers in the population aged 15 and over steadily dropped from 23.3% in the first quarter of 1982 to 16.8% in July 1988.

The territory's work pressure and pace of life were conducive to mental distress. As a result, worries, anxieties, and negative mental experiences were common indicators of Hong Kong people's ill-being. For example, about 30% of the respondents could be classified as suffering from mental illness as measured by D. Goldberg's General Health Questionnaire in his 1988 survey. In the 1990 survey by the social scientists of local tertiary institutions, when asked whether they had any worries in the past six months, 41.3% of the respondents replied that they had sometimes been troubled by problems and 14.9% said that they had frequent worries.[28]

Over time, there seemed to be a significant change in the source of people's worries. In the 1960s, financial problems were the most frequent scourge. It was identified by nearly half of the respondents (46.5%) as the major cause of worry.[29] In the late 1980s and early 1990s, people's worries were diversified yet stable. Notwithstanding their perception of economy-

---

[28] See Wong Po-san, "The Quality of Life," in *The Other Hong Kong Report 1991*, pp. 436–437.

[29] See "Family Life in Urban Hong Kong Codebook" (unpublished material), Hong Kong: Social Research Centre, The Chinese University of Hong Kong, 1967.

related issues as serious social problems and their strong desire to improve the personal financial conditions, less than one quarter (23.6%) of the respondents in the 1990 survey who had occasional or frequent worries were troubled by money matters. Only 14.8% complained that their income was insufficient to cope with their daily expenses. Problems concerning work and study were reported by a substantial number of respondents (24.1%) as the major source of worry. Other sources of worry include family matter (children's problems: 11.9%; family problems: 6.6%); health conditions: 10.7%; personal future: 10.2%; and the territory's future: 8.6%.

(v) *Leisure and Escapes*

In step with the increasing affluence of the community, Hong Kong people, especially the younger generations, placed more and more emphasis on leisure activities. The willingness to save up for foreign travels was impressive. The amounts of money spent on leisure activities and conspicuous consumption, especially by the teenagers, were equally spectacular. Exposure to fine arts apparently was increasing. Western classical music in compact discs was easily available. More and more music-lovers made use of public libraries too. However, in the General Household Survey in the first quarter of 1988, only 21.1% of the respondents aged 15 and above claimed to have an interest in cultural performances (excluding pop concerts), and less than three-tenths of them had attended cultural performances in the past twelve months.

On the other hand, comics offered a popular form of escapism for Hong Kong people.[30] According to *Capital* monthly, as at March 1990, local publishers produced 27 comics with a total monthly turnover of HK$12.87 million. One distinguishing feature of local comics was their fantastical quality and the remoteness of their contents from real life. Among the bestsellers, four-fifths of them were *kung-fu* or other fighting stories, in which masculine virility and prowess were celebrated. Words

---

[30] See Choi Po-king, "Popular Culture," in *The Other Hong Kong Report 1990*, edited by Richard Y.C. Wong and Joseph Y.S. Cheng, Hong Kong: The Chinese University Press, 1990, pp. 559–563.

were inserted in the cartoons, but it was not the words, but the sense of violence and force carried in the pictures that constituted the major attraction. No survey of the readership of comics was done. The general observation was that their readers were mostly, though not exclusively, from the lower socioeconomic strata: those who received not much formal education and who held blue-collar jobs, as well as secondary school students. Readership was predominantly male, especially for the fighting genre, though women of the streets were also said to be avid readers. Comics, therefore, constituted a cultural product mostly for consumption at the grassroots level, while the market for popular songs, films and books either spanned the whole social spectrum, or, as in the case of popular books, more skewed towards the middle class. In the late 1980s and early 1990s, however, there were signs that comics publishers were attempting to go upmarket.

(vi) *Greening and Subcultures*

It was too early to predict that Hong Kong yuppies would follow the example of their counterparts in the U.S. — becoming less materialistic, placing more emphasis on family life and leisure, less attracted to conspicuous consumption, more concerned with the environment, and more committed to religion. However, Hong Kong yuppies were obviously more conscious of environmental protection. Prominent figures in the local green movement such as Chow Shiu-cheung and Chan Koon-chung contributed to the emergence of new social values among the middle class.

The rise of subcultures would make it more difficult to understand the community's values and attitudes as a whole. Hong Kong people believed that a generation meant ten years or so. Teenagers' subcultures change very quickly in particular. Since the 1980s, new immigrants had found it difficult to adapt and they became more isolated. In turn, their children often became over protected and alienated too.

On the whole, Hong Kong people's perceptions of social ethics and values were reassuring. There was no fear of a vacuum. Confucianism still provides a solid foundation while new challenges stimulated constructive responses.

Acknowledgement

Originally published as Cheng Joseph Y.S., "Value and Attitudes of the Hong Kong Community", *in Hong Kong Trends 1989–1992: Index to Other Hong Kong Reports*, ed. Paul Chu Kuen Kwong. Hong Kong: Chinese University Press, 1992, pp. 62–80. Reproduced with kind permission from the publisher.

Chapter 9

Political Participation in Hong Kong: Trends in the Mid-1990s[1]

In this chapter, "political participation" refers to any act on the part of the people of Hong Kong to influence policy making in the territory. The author conducted a series of in-depth interviews in the second half of 1995. The 100 or so interviewees included senior government officials; political party leaders; members of the Legislative Council, Urban/Regional Council, and District Boards; leaders of various types of interest groups and grassroots organizations; some members of the Preliminary Working Committee (PWC) of the Preparatory Committee for the Hong Kong Special Administrative Region (HKSAR), Hong Kong Affairs Advisors, and District Affairs Advisors; executives and journalists of the territory's media; and a few academics interested in the subject. A follow-up series of in-depth interviews was conducted in the third quarter of 1996 to update the information and analysis. It covered about one quarter of those interviewed earlier.

The purpose of this research project was to study the political mood of the people of Hong Kong, including how they attempted to articulate their interests, how they assessed the performance of the British administration, the political parties, interest groups, and grassroots organizations, and how they defined and exercised their options in

---

[1] This chapter is an adaptation of a paper with the same title presented at the Conference on the 1995 Legislative Council Election, May 17–18, 1996, organized by the Hong Kong Institute of Asia-Pacific Studies, The Chinese University of Hong Kong.

protecting and promoting their interests. No attempt was made to quantify the findings of the interviews, although quantitative analysis would be the likely objective in a later stage of the project. Wherever it was possible and relevant, available opinion surveys were used. Since the vast majority of the people of Hong Kong were politically quiescent, surveys helped to find those who would otherwise be inactive. Admittedly, the views articulated were not very strong and clear.[2] At this stage, the author was satisfied with the detection and identification of the prevalent trends of political participation in the territory, as well as preliminary attempts to explain such trends.

In the first half of the 1980s, political participation in the territory picked up momentum significantly, spurred by the Sino-British negotiations on Hong Kong's future and the Chinese authorities' promise of *gangren zhigang* (self-administration) to the people of Hong Kong.[3] In the mid-1990s, a number of conflicting indicators appeared, making the work of identifying the trends of political participation much more complicated and fascinating.

I The Political and Economic Environment

With the approach of 1997, the Chinese authorities' influence on Hong Kong became increasingly significant. At the end of December 1995, membership of the Preparatory Committee for the HKSAR was announced, and it had a formal office in the territory. According to Chen Zhiying, deputy head of the State Council's Hong Kong and Macau Affairs Office, the recovery of China's sovereignty over Hong Kong had entered the stage of concrete work.[4] In December 1996, the first Chief Executive, Mr. C.H. Tung, was nominated by the Selection Committee for the First Government of the HKSAR established by the Preparatory Committee for

---

[2] Sidney Verba, "The Citizen as Respondent: Sample Surveys and American Democracy," *American Political Science Review*, Vol. 90, No. 1, March 1996, pp. 1–7.

[3] Joseph Y. S. Cheng, "Hong Kong: The Pressure to Converge," *International Affairs* (London), Vol. 63, No. 2, Spring 1987, pp. 271–283.

[4] *Ming Pao* (a Chinese newspaper in Hong Kong), June 25, 1995.

the HKSAR.[5] Later in the month, the Selection Committee also elected the provisional legislature. In February 1997, the team of top civil servants would be announced. Both the Chief Executive and the provisional legislature would start working after their elections.

It was significant that the people of Hong Kong had no input in these processes. Moreover, the community did not appear to be concerned about their exclusion. Few people were interested in the issues, and the media merely speculated on the chances of the potential candidates to fill the post of the first Chief Executive. In September and October of 1996, the media offered many profiles of the declared candidates. The media's orientation meant that the pro-democracy camp did not have many opportunities to criticize the Chinese authorities. Indeed, the pro-democracy political groups did not treat such issues as an important part of their political platforms in the Legislative Council elections in September 1995.

The people of Hong Kong were predictably more dissatisfied with the British administration, and Governor Chris Patten became their target. According to opinion surveys, the community's support for the Governor's annual policy speeches dropped steadily from 67.82% in 1992, to 61.40% in 1993, to 57.48% in 1994, to 52.06% in 1995.[6] In response to Chris Patten's final policy speech, delivered on October 2, 1996, a survey indicated that 30.2% of the respondents thought that the territory had declined as a result of his years as Governor, 24.9% thought that it had gained in stature, and 42.2% thought that it had maintained its stature. The same survey population gave Chris Patten a score of 56.9% for increasing democracy in Hong Kong, 55.1% for improving social welfare, 41% for enforcing the Basic Law, and 36.8% for forging good relations between Hong Kong and China. Significantly, only 15.2% of the respondents

---

[5] See "Decision of the National People's Congress on the Method for the Formation of the First Government and the First Legislative Council of the Hong Kong Special Administrative Region," adopted by the Seventh National People's Congress at its third session on April 4, 1990, in The Basic Law of the Hong Kang Special Administrative Region of the People's Republic of China, Hong Kong: One Country Two Systems Economic Research Institute Ltd., 1992, pp. 67–69.

[6] *Ming Pao*, October 12, 1995.

believed that the Governor's popularity would increase during that month, and 37.6% thought that his popularity would decrease.[7]

Another series of polls likewise indicated that the people's evaluations of Chris Patten were becoming increasingly negative. Approval ratings for his competence fell from 68.77% in July 1992 to 60.36% in June 1996; approval ratings for his trustworthiness declined from 64.69% to 54.40% over the same period.[8] More damaging still, in an opinion survey taken in May 1995, 48% of the respondents said that the territory would be better served if the Governor were to leave two years early and be replaced by a council of local people.[9] It appeared that the Governor had absorbed the blame for the deterioration in Sino-British relations over Hong Kong. In a series of opinion polls on the replacement of the Governor, the proportion of respondents favouring his departure reached a peak of 26.3% in January 1994, decreasing to 18.5% in July 1995, when Sino-British relations improved somewhat as a result of an agreement on the Court of Final Appeal.[10]

While the Hong Kong community expressed its increasing frustration with the British administration, its assessment of the Chinese authorities was only slightly better. The community's evaluations of Zhou Nan and Zhang Junsheng, leading officials at the local branch of New China News Agency, had been relatively stable at a low level. Approval ratings for their competence improved from 52.45% in July 1992 to 54.32% in June 1996; approval ratings for their trustworthiness increased slightly from 46.34% to 47.52% in the same period.[11] Zhou Nan and Zhang Junsheng trailed the Governor, but the gap was narrowing.

By mid-1995, the Hong Kong community's confidence in the "one country, two systems" arrangement seemed to have risen slightly. An opinion survey in mid-July showed that 44% of the respondents indicated confidence in "one country, two systems"; with an increase of three

---

[7] *South China Morning Post* (an English newspaper in Hong Kong), October 7, 1996.
[8] Ming Pao, July 8, 1996.
[9] *South China Morning Post*, May 29, 1995.
[10] *Ming Pao*, July 10, 1995. For the Sino-British agreement on the Court of Final Appeal, see *Hong Kong Economic Journal* (a Chinese newspaper in Hong Kong), June 10, 1995.
[11] *Ming Pao*, July 8, 1996.

percentage points, it reached the level recorded in early 1993. At the same time, 38% of the respondents revealed no confidence in "one country, two systems."[12] There remained a reluctance to accept the eventual return of Hong Kong to China, but it seemed to be in decline as July 1997 approached. A survey in mid-1995 indicated that 52% of the respondents still preferred independence or remaining under the British administration to becoming a Special Administrative Region under Chinese sovereignty. This proportion did not differ significantly from that in early 1993, when about 42% to 44% of the respondents hoped to see the return of Hong Kong to China.[13] In February 1996, another poll in the same series showed that 46% of the respondents wanted Hong Kong to become part of China; the proportion of those who wanted Hong Kong to be independent fell from 25% in 1993 to 14% in early 1996.[14]

The trend became more significant later in the year. In May 1996, a survey showed that 55% of the respondents indicated confidence in the future of Hong Kong, while only 15.3% indicated a lack of confidence. This was the first time that over half of the respondents in an opinion poll demonstrated confidence in the territory's future.[15] Similarly, 59% of the respondents in a survey in November 1996 said that they would feel happy at midnight on June 30, 1997, while 20% said that they would feel sad at the critical moment.[16]

In the second half of 1995, the people of Hong Kong expressed their frustration with the territory's political, economic, and social environment. An opinion survey revealed that 36.8% of the respondents believed that the political environment had deteriorated when compared with that of 1992; only 24.2% believed that it had improved. Similarly, 69.3% thought that the economic environment had worsened, while only 17.2% thought it had improved; 46.4% considered that the social environment had deteriorated, while 29.4% considered that it had improved.[17] In assessing

---

[12] *Ming Pao*, August 3, 1995.
[13] *Ming Pao*, July 15, 1995.
[14] *South China Morning Post*, February 17, 1996.
[15] *Ming Pao*, May 28, 1996.
[16] *South China Morning Post*, November 25, 1996.
[17] *Ming Pao*, August 10, 1995.

the future, the same survey showed considerable pessimism: 32.5% of the respondents believed that the political environment would worsen in the coming three years, while 14.9% believed that it would improve. Similarly, 35.5% thought that the economic environment would decline further, while 19.7% thought that it would gain strength; 34.6% expected the social environment to deteriorate, while 19.4% expected to see improvement. The approach of 1997 has brought about a vague sense of unease.

More specifically, Hong Kong residents were concerned with the spread of corruption. About 72% of the respondents in a poll taken in October 1995 believed that the 1997 changeover would lead to an increase in corruption.[18] In March 1996, the commissioner of the Independent Commission Against Corruption (ICAC) noted that the number of police officers convicted of corruption had increased from 23 in 1994 to 58 in 1995. He acknowledged that the uncertainty surrounding 1997 prompted many people to make "quick money."[19] Journalists, as expected, were disturbed by the phenomenon of self-censorship. A series of surveys of the profession from the end of 1993 to 1995 revealed that about 90% of the respondents assumed that self-censorship existed. About 60% indicated that self-censorship existed where they worked, and over 50% said self-censorship came from pressure from their superiors.[20] Less than 10% of those surveyed expected to work until retirement. In June 1996, it was reported that about 60% of the staff of Radio Television Hong Kong worried that they would lose their editorial independence after 1997.[21]

Reports from various sectors showed that senior police officers, senior staff members of the ICAC, and teachers were the professions hit hardest by emigration. A study conducted by the Royal Hong Kong Police reported that 18% of those who held the rank of police inspector and above planned to leave; of this percentage, 40% were chief superintendents and senior

---

[18] *Ming Pao*, October 14, 1995.
[19] *Ming Pao*, March 16, 1996.
[20] *Ming Pao*, August 5, 1995.
[21] *Ming Pao*, June 13, 1996.

superintendents.[22] It was confirmed in June 1996 that 44 local police officers, with ranks ranging from senior superintendent to senior assistant commissioner of police, had asked to leave by July of 1997.[23] Similarly, the ICAC determined that, among its fourteen directorate-grade officials, about one half would depart before the end of 1996. Some legislative councillors expressed serious concern that Hong Kong's ability to combat corruption might be adversely affected by such trends.[24] In the education sector, the Education Department released a survey of teachers in March 1995 showing that more than 1,100 teachers and principals had emigrated from 1992 to 1994.[25] This emigration flow was expected to peak in 1996. The main reason for this trend appeared to have been that teachers and principals in the primary and secondary schools were worried about their superannuation funds, and therefore opted for early retirement to claim payments before 1997. (Middle-class teachers between 40 and 50 years old were qualified to emigrate to Canada, Australia, and New Zealand.)

The most striking feature of the public mood since the summer of 1995 had been the "feel bad factor." An editorial in the *South China Morning Post* made the following observation: "One of the year's most curious phenomena has been how growing pessimism about Hong Kong's economy, among all sectors of society, has remained so sharply at odds with official statistics — which continue to predict healthy growth."[26] The economy grew by 4.6% in 1995. Unemployment was at a 10-year high; however, it reached only 3.5% in the third quarter of the year. Exports were strong, and massive infrastructure projects continued to stimulate the economy. However, a survey in October 1995 indicated that about 30% of employees were concerned about losing their jobs; 8% of them were very worried.[27] Employees could still vividly remember that in the early 1990s, employers were quick to offer improvements in remuneration and

---

[22] *Ming Pao*, July 29, 1995.
[23] *South China Morning Post*, June 6, 1996.
[24] *Ming Pao*, July 13, 1995.
[25] *Ibid.*
[26] "Feel Bad Factor," editorial, *South China Morning Post*, August 9, 1995.
[27] *Ibid.*; *Ming Pao*, October 22, 1995.

promotions to retain staff. At the same time, private consumption had been declining.[28]

Most analysts concluded that this "feel bad factor" was largely psychological and related to the approach of 1997. The rise in unemployment was primarily due to long-term structural changes in the economy. As labor costs rose, manufacturers in the territory moved their operations to the Pearl River Delta in China and Southeast Asia. The process began in the early 1980s and picked up momentum in the second half of the decade. Until the mid-1990s, the rapid expansion of the service sector was able to absorb the surplus labour while maintaining the wage level. Since then, growth rates began to decline, and even some labour-intensive service industries had moved to China to cut costs — data-processing was a prime example. Under these circumstances, the unemployment rate climbed slowly. Admittedly, some jobs — for example, in the construction industry — could not attract enough local labourers.

Private consumption has been declining among employees in the low-income brackets as a consequence of stagnation in wages. In the mid-1990s, restraint spread to the middle class; their propensity to spend had been eroded by the retreat in the real estate and stock markets since early 1994. Many middle-class families had the extra financial burden of supporting family members living abroad; a high proportion of them also sent their children to study overseas. With the approach of 1997, there emerged a deliberate attempt to enhance savings in preparation for the uncertainty ahead. Apparently, the real estate companies and the airlines had absorbed much middle-class consumption power at the expense of restaurants and department stores.

By mid-1996, the economic situation seemed to have improved; the economic confidence indicator recovered after two years of continuous decline. It rose from 73 points to 76 points in January 1996, and further

---

[28] In the second quarter of 1995, private consumption grew by only 1.4% on an annual basis. In the following November, retailers were warning that consumer demand was still weak, with the latest monthly figures registering the seventh month of successive decline. Car sales had dropped by 20%, while people continued to shun costly consumer durables. See *South China Morning Post*, November 7, 1995.

increased to 84 points in April and 87 points in October.[29] Then the unemployment rate gradually dropped to 2.8% in June to August 1996.[30] Both the stock market and the real estate market performed well too.

Trade unions and labourers were not impressed, however. The Hong Kong Confederation of Trade Unions complained that 1.5 million employees suffered a decline in real wages in 1996, as was the case in 1995.[31] Trade unions also refused to accept the explanation that the fall in unemployment rate represented an upturn in Hong Kong's economy, as some workers had been forced to accept considerable cuts in wages after being unemployed for a certain period of time. A survey of labourers in September 1996 revealed that 51.3% of the respondents believed that wage levels would deteriorate after 1997, and only 8.3% believed that they would improve; 52% thought that the unemployment situation would deteriorate after 1997, and only 18.6% thought that it would improve; further, 45.6% of the respondents believed that social welfare would deteriorate after 1997, and only 8.3% believed that it would improve.[32] Middle-class families too revealed some concern about the decline in real income and the job situation, especially employment opportunities for their children. Notably, in late August of 1996, the Hong Kong government reduced its forecast for economic growth for 1996 from 5% to 4.7%.[33]

II Elections and the Development of Political Parties

With the development of the representative system of government, elections became an increasingly important factor in the political process in the territory. Since the Legislative Council elections in September 1991, the British administration could no longer be assured of stable majority support in the legislature. Endorsement of its legislative programmes and

---

[29] *Ming Pao*, April 29, 1996; *South China Morning Post*, October 28, 1996.
[30] *Ming Pao*, September 17, 1996.
[31] *Ming Pao*, September 12, 1996.
[32] *Ming Pao*, September 15, 1996.
[33] *South China Morning Post*, August 31, 1996.

requests for appropriations depended on strenuous lobbying of the legislators by senior government officials, who had also attempt to secure public support. With the removal of the remaining three official members and eighteen appointed members in the new Legislative Council in October 1995, the British administration found it even more difficult to lobby for majority support in the wholly elected legislature.[34]

The Chinese authorities, too, recognized that they had a serious stake in the elections despite the rejection of "through train" arrangements for the District Boards. Urban/Regional Council, and Legislative Council in 1997. They would like to prevent the pro-democracy groups from winning a majority in the legislature, and they would like to secure a majority which would at least respect China's vital interests. The Democratic Alliance for the Betterment of Hong Kong (DAB), the key pro-Beijing political group, would be responsible for coordination within this majority. Since the Sino-British negotiations on the territory's future, the Chinese authorities had been expending considerable resources in establishing a pro-Beijing united front. Certainly, this united front had to demonstrate its mobilization power in the 1995 Legislative Council elections. From an orthodox ideological point of view, it had to develop itself and expand through campaigns while testing the calibre and loyalty of its supporters. From an organizational point of view, it had to cultivate candidates, consolidate and expand its grassroots networks, and refine its campaign strategies and tactics.

The conservative political groups finally came to realize that they had to prove themselves in elections; otherwise, they risked losing their clout and ceasing to be a significant political force. The creation of nine new functional constituencies and the electoral college provided them with important opportunities too. On the other hand, the pro-democracy groups certainly wanted to maintain the lead they had achieved in the 1991

---

[34]The composition of the new Legislative Council after the 1995 elections was as follows: 30 seats elected by functional constituencies, 10 elected by an electoral college, and 20 directly elected. For background information, see the author's "Hong Kong's Legislative Council Elections: Review of 1991 and Planning for 1995," in Benjamin K.P. Leung & Teresa Y.C. Wong (eds.), 25 Years of Social and Economic Development in Hong Kong, Hong Kong: Centre of Asian Studies, the University of Hong Kong, 1994, pp. 291–313.

elections, when they did not encounter serious opposition in electoral contests.

It is not the intention of this chapter to analyze the results of the 1995 Legislative Council elections. This section focusses only on the features believed to be significant in terms of political participation and the development of political parties.

Over 920,000 voters participated in the 1995 Legislative Council elections, surpassing by about 170,000 the turnout seen in 1991. The voter turnout rate, however, was 35.79%, more than three percentage points lower than in 1991.[35] The number of registered voters increased from 1.9 million in 1991 to 2.57 million in 1995; therefore, it would have been unrealistic to expect an improvement in the voter turnout rate. In general, with the exception of young voters who had recently qualified to vote, those who registered in later rounds were less enthusiastic political participants than those who had registered in the initial rounds. Rough estimates indicated that registered voters constituted 60% of the qualified voters, which meant that actual voters consisted of only 21 or 22% of those qualified.

The voter turnout rate reflected the community's political apathy. The people of Hong Kong realized that most major decisions were made by Beijing or on the basis of Sino-British agreements; such perceptions reinforced their sense of political impotence. They too understood that the Legislative Council elections would have a limited impact on the livelihood issues which most concerned them, especially economic growth and unemployment. Admittedly, many Hong Kong residents had not established a habit of participating in elections. Most of them voted in order to fulfil a civic obligation, rather than to exercise their political right to elect a government. The increase in the number of voters was partially due to the mobilization power of pro-Beijing groups and the lowering of the voting age from 21 to 18. These factors suggested that it would be increasingly difficult to improve voter turnout.

Given the Sino-British quarrels over the elections, the low voter turnout rate easily prompted claims that the elections lacked representativeness. An electoral system, however, gives the people the

---

[35] See all major newspapers in Hong Kong on September 18, 1995.

right to elect their own representatives, and it requires those representatives to be accountable to the electorate. As long as the elections are genuinely open and fair, low turnout rates can be attributed to the political culture; it cannot be assumed that elections with low turnouts are unrepresentative.

The most noteworthy result of the Hong Kong elections in 1995 was the outstanding performance by pro-democracy groups. According to various estimates — based on assessments of the political inclinations of some independents and the Hong Kong Association for Democracy and People's Livelihood (HKADPL) — such groups and their allies controlled 27 to 31 seats in the legislature. On issues ranging from the further development of representative government and Sino-British negotiations on Hong Kong, to the expansion of social services, the pro-democracy alliance commanded majority and could therefore oppose positions taken by Beijing, by London, or by the two regimes jointly.

The electoral victory of the pro-democracy groups was obviously embarrassing for the Chinese authorities: Voters had supported Beijing's critics. It was natural for the electorate to expect that criticisms and strict monitoring would create checks and balances on those in power, and their feeling was that Beijing's power over Hong Kong exceeded that of the British administration. This should not be interpreted to mean that Hong Kong people wanted to confront the Chinese authorities. In the elections in the 1980s, the electorate similarly supported harsh critics of the territory's British administration; even so, most people at that time trusted the Hong Kong government and were satisfied with its performance.

A vast majority of the people of Hong Kong would like to give the "one country, two systems" arrangement the benefit of the doubt; nonetheless, they had some vague fears and worries concerning 1997. It was generally believed that if the Chinese authorities' policy toward Hong Kong had become more tolerant and flexible, the pro-Beijing groups would have been able to secure more electoral support, and vice versa. On the eve of the elections, incidents such as the behaviour of the Chinese public security personnel in the Fourth World Women's Conference, the denial of labour activist Han Dongfang's return to China by the local New China News Agency, and the latter's reaffirmation that there would be no "through train" arrangement for the Legislative Council in 1997 damaged the chances of pro-Beijing candidates.

Some surveys taken before the elections indicated that people were most concerned with the economy and with unemployment and public housing issues. The candidates' attitudes toward China as well as their positions on the Tiananmen incident had become less significant. One possible explanation was that, although voters paid the closest attention to issues affecting their livelihood, candidates had not responded to these concerns. Rather, they presented similar platforms, with the result that voters did not expect the elections to have much impact on issues of concern to them.[36]

The development of political parties in Hong Kong had been highly dependent on the evolution of the electoral system. Indeed, similar to their Western counterparts, local political parties existed largely to provide the machinery for winning elections; reflecting this, their electoral performance provided an accurate indicator of their growth and strength.

Despite their spectacular electoral victories in 1991, the pro-democracy groups failed to expand their membership significantly. The Democratic Party (DP) probably did not have more than 200 to 300 active members, nor did it plan to develop into a mass party — hence, its heavy dependence on the media to maintain an attractive image in the community. Image-building usually dominated the tactical considerations of DP leadership. The DP had been successful in establishing itself as a staunch critic of both the Chinese authorities and the British administration, and as the most important group fighting for the freedoms and rights of the people of Hong Kong. Its efforts had been rewarded at the elections.

The DP, however, encountered severe challenges that it had not been able to overcome. In the first place, its concern for publicity often alienated it from grassroots pressure groups. Such groups were issue-oriented; they want concrete solutions to problems. The DP could certainly help by raising issues espoused by grassroots groups in the Legislative Council or with senior government officials, thus exerting pressure on the British administration to come up with solutions. However, the party's high profile and hunger for publicity often resulted in failure

---

[36] See the author's analysis of the Legislative Council elections in September 1995 in "A Relaxed and Tolerant Policy is the Only Way to Ensure a Stable Transition (in Chinese)," *Ming Pao*, September 26, 1995.

to compromise and delay in achieving settlements. Many grassroots pressure groups worried about being used in this way and therefore preferred to act without the involvement of political parties.

To attract the media's attention, the DP legislators usually dramatized their gestures and statements. A harsh criticism of Beijing obviously has a better chance of making newspaper headlines than a balanced statement. The DP's success with the media, however, made it very difficult for its leaders to establish a dialogue of mutual trust with senior civil servants. This success also provided Chinese officials with a convenient excuse for rejecting any contact with the party. Such political posturing also had a negative impact on party support among the intelligentsia. However, as July 1997 approached, the middle class in the territory was overly willing to compromise.

Chinese authorities regarded the Hong Kong Alliance in Support of the Patriotic Democratic Movement in China, which emerged in the wake of the Tiananmen Incident, as a "subversive" organization. Most of the leaders of the alliance were also leading members of the DP. The Chinese authorities officially ruled out contact with the DP not only on that basis, but also on the basis of the DP's refusal to support the Basic Law and its opposition to the provisional legislature.

In 1996, however, the Chinese authorities began to soften their stance. When Lu Ping, director of the State Council's Hong Kong and Macau Affairs Office, visited the territory in April 1996 to consult with the local community on the work of the Preparatory Committee, attempts were made to invite leaders of the Hong Kong Professional Teachers' Union (PTU) to take part in the consultative sessions. Two important leaders of the PTU, Szeto Wah and Cheung Man-kwong, were also DP leaders and Legislative Councillors. A formal dialogue between Lu Ping and the PTU leaders therefore could be interpreted as a breakthrough. Subsequently, the PTU leaders made some uncompromising statements, and their invitations were withdrawn. It was generally assumed that different views existed among the Chinese authorities on the resumption of a dialogue with the pro-democracy groups in Hong Kong.

In the following August, Vice-Premier Qian Qichen, head of the Preparatory Committee, indicated in its fourth plenary session in Beijing that the Chinese authorities were willing to discuss Hong Kong-related issues with people who held varying views on democracy. This was seen as an olive branch from Beijing to the DP, perhaps with a view to involve the DP in the Selection Committee soon to be established. The DP refused to alter its stance, and again, Beijing's gesture did not lead to a breakthrough. It was significant that opinion surveys run by several local newspapers, as well as a DP poll of its own membership, uniformly indicated majority support for DP members' participation in the Selection Committee, and for DP's changing its stand on the provisional legislature in return for a dialogue with Beijing.[37]

The DP leadership believed that participation in the Selection Committee would give it no influence in the process of setting up the first HKSAR government. It was concerned with the united front offensive from Beijing and its divisive tactics. It also feared that softening its position would lead to severe challenges from The Frontier, a new political group founded by radical legislators such as Emily Lau, Lau Chin-shek, and Lee Cheuk-yan. The general public obviously welcomed a dialogue between Beijing and the DP, as it would contribute to the territory's political stability. The author also believed that it would be beneficial for the DP to alter its relationship with the Chinese authorities from one of conflict to one of civil discourse. Securing official recognition to engage in legitimate political struggles would be an important achievement, given the differing views among the Chinese authorities. The DP should try to operate both within and outside the establishment.

From the DP's point of view, it had to map out its strategy for the post-1997 era. At this stage, it has no choice but to prepare to survive as the opposition in the political wilderness. Its impact on the HKSAR government's decision-making process would be limited, and its influence would very much depend on the extent of freedom enjoyed by the mass media. This new position will require considerable adjustment on the part of the DP leaders. Their electoral successes in 1991 and especially 1995 enabled them to play a key role in the legislature. In many ways they had become part of the political establishment, and their influence was felt through constitutional channels. Would the post-1997 era demand a return to the pressure-group role of the late 1970s? Would some DP legislators

---

[37] *South China Morning Post*, August 21, 1996.

opt to stay within the formal political structure, and, if so, would they be absorbed by the pro-Beijing united front?

Meanwhile, the formation of The Frontier meant that at least three prodemocracy groups would compete among themselves.[38] The Frontier adopted a staunchly anti-Communist stand, while the HKADPL would be keen to maintain a dialogue with Beijing and to operate within the establishment. The Frontier was founded in anticipation of the transformation of the electoral system into one of proportional representation in direct elections. The radical independents had to group together in order to carve their share of the votes from the DP. There is speculation that the Chinese authorities were pleased with the emergence of The Frontier.[39]

The pro-Beijing groups did not perform well in the 1995 Legislative Council elections in terms of seats won. However, they secured 34% of the vote, and their mobilizing power was impressive in a number of ways. In the Hong Kong Island East constituency, a relatively unknown candidate representing the pro-Beijing Hong Kong Progressive Alliance competed against Martin Lee, leader of the DP, and received almost 30% of the vote. This performance indicated the power of the grassroots network underlying the pro-Beijing organizations. Most significantly, public opinion revealed great sympathy for the DAB leaders who lost to the candidates of the pro-democracy groups. Many Hong Kong residents felt that the former had been doing a good job in serving the public, and their presence in the legislature would have contributed to the well-being of the community and the development of representative government. If the existing simple majority, single-seat constituency system was replaced by a proportional representation system or the single-vote, medium-size, multi-seat constituency system recently abandoned by Japan, the DAB and its allies would be able to secure six or seven seats out of twenty in the direct elections on the basis of their share of the votes in 1995. The indications were that the Chinese authorities would likely change the electoral system after 1997, and the Hong Kong community might not be strongly against that change.

---

[38] For a brief introduction to The Frontier, see *South China Morning Post*, July 30, 1996.
[39] *Ming Pao*, August 27, 1996.

The DAB's performance in the elections showed that in the long run, the community service offered by the pro-Beijing groups would be rewarded. Given their financial resources, they would be able to expand their grassroots network gradually. Moreover, the pro-Beijing united front could also reward its supporters with honours such as memberships in the National People's Congress, the Chinese People's Political Consultative Conference, and the provincial counterparts of these two bodies, as well as appointments to the Preparatory Committee for the HKSAR, Hong Kong Affairs Advisors, and District Affairs Advisors. By the mid-1990s, the Chinese authorities had established their system of honours for the Hong Kong community. Such efforts and resources have laid a strong foundation for pro-Beijing political groups. With a more favourable electoral system and the support of the pro-business groups, the Chinese authorities can hope to secure reliable majority support in the legislature after 1997. Willingness to accept elections will support the Chinese authorities' attempts to seek legitimacy for the HKSAR government and encourage them to be responsive to public opinion in the territory.

The DAB also demonstrated, however, that in order to win elections, it could not afford to toe the Beijing line closely at all times. The Chinese leaders' insecurity regarding Hong Kong since the Tiananmen incident and the Sino-British confrontation did not allow the DAB much room to manoeuvre. Signs of disagreements between the DAB and the Chinese officials responsible for Hong Kong were apparent. In the appointments to the Preparatory Committee for the HKSAR announced at the end of 1995, the DAB received four seats, while other pro-Beijing groups — which had been far less effective in elections but which had been faithful in supporting the Beijing line — were more handsomely rewarded.

In contrast to the Legislative Council elections in 1991, the Liberal Party had to fight for its survival in 1995. Its leader, Allen Lee, won a seat in the New Territories Northeast constituency, and it did well in the old functional constituencies and in the nine newly created functional constituencies. Anticipated changes to the electoral system after 1997 would favour the Liberal Party, which would likely remain a formidable force in the legislature. The development of representative government had convinced some business leaders that competing in elections would safeguard their business interests.

In the District Board elections in September 1994, the Urban/Regional Council elections in March 1995, and the Legislative Council elections in September 1995, the major political groups all demonstrated sophisticated campaign strategies and skills.[40] With perhaps the exception of the DAB and the Hong Kong Federation of Trade Unions, most political groups were severely limited by their relatively small work force and shortage of funds. Consequently, they had to deploy their resources very efficiently. All political groups had been skilful in attracting media attention and in using opinion surveys. The pro-democracy groups no longer had the edge they enjoyed in the previous decade.

By the standard of developing democracies, Hong Kong's elections had been remarkably clean. One could argue that the interests at stake were limited, but the political culture obviously detested "money politics," and the purchase of votes was unthinkable. Minor violations of electoral rules were common: they usually took the form of disobeying the regulations concerning the display of publicity materials, under-reporting of campaign expenditures, and so forth. Violence was virtually non-existent.[41]

III The Chinese Authorities' Position on the Representative Government

In the course of drafting the Basic Law, it became clear that the Chinese authorities often wanted to retain final control, especially in matters relating to the autonomy of the political system.[42] Their decisions regarding the concept of "residual power" and the amendment and interpretation of the Basic Law were significant examples. Within the HKSAR political system, the fact that the Central People's Government appoints the Chief Executive and the principal officials implies that they

---

[40] See Chi-keung Choi, Sai-leung Lau, & Pak-kwan Chow, *Politics of Elections and Legislature* (in Chinese), Hong Kong: Hong Kong Humanities Press, November 1995.

[41] The discussions above are based on my interviews of leaders of political parties, political scientists following the elections, and journalists in the two weeks before and after the Legislative Council elections in September 1995.

[42] See Joseph Y.S. Cheng, "The Basic Law: Messages for Hong Kong People," in Richard Y.C. Wong and Joseph Y.S. Cheng (eds.), *The Other Hong Kong Report 1990*, Hong Kong: The Chinese University Press, 1990, pp. 29–63.

are accountable to the Central People's Government. Hong Kong residents realized that the Chief Executive needed to be someone acceptable to the Chinese authorities; in the mid 1990s, this criterion apparently also applied to the principal officials.

The gist of Chris Patten's political reform proposals announced in October 1992 was that the pro-democracy groups would have a chance to secure a majority in the Legislative Council and thus control the legislature. This was certainly antithetical to the original plan of the Chinese authorities to ensure a majority in the legislature that was acceptable to Beijing.[43] It was expected that in the Legislative Council elections in 1998, the nine new functional constituencies would be redefined and the composition of the Election Committee, which would return 10 legislators, would strictly follow the Basic Law. In short, the Chinese authorities wanted an electoral system which would guarantee reliable majority support for their Hong Kong policy and the HKSAR government.

Since the conclusion of the Sino-British Joint Declaration in 1984, the Chinese leaders had been according a top priority to the cultivation of the business community in the territory. Their rationale was simple and straightforward. Hong Kong must remain attractive to investors. If investors stay, the stability and prosperity of the territory will be maintained. In both the Basic Law Drafting Committee and the Preparatory Committee for the HKSAR, business leaders dominate the memberships.[44] The business community in return had been firmly supporting the Chinese government in the Sino-British conflict. It had confidence in China's economic reforms and its openness to the outside world. Such momentum picked up soon after the Tiananmen crackdown. Business people believed that the trend would be irreversible; consequently, they had been bullish about the economic future of China and Hong Kong's role in China's development.[45]

---

[43] See Joseph Y. S. Cheng, "Sino-British Negotiations on Hong Kong During Chris Patten's Governorship," *Australian Journal of International Affairs*, Vol. 48, No. 2, November 1994, pp. 233–234.

[44] For an analysis of the membership list of the Preparatory Committee for the HKSAR, see *Ming Pao*, December 27–28, 1995.

[45] See, for example, Bruce Gilley, "Red Flag Over Hong Kong," *Far Eastern Economic Review*, Vol. 158, No. 49, December 7, 1995, pp. 72–78.

Seen in this context, the Sino-British confrontation was a temporary phenomenon which would become increasingly irrelevant as July 1997 approached. Such business confidence explained the continuing boom in the real estate and stock markets in the years just before 1997, though mild adjustments had taken place in the property market since the second quarter of 1994 and in the stock market since the beginning of the year. Undeniably, a great deal of money flowed from China into the markets too. It was not surprising that the business community was most critical of Chris Patten's China policy.

In terms of political participation, local business leaders enjoyed access to the very top Chinese leaders. When the latter visited Guangdong, they typically arranged to see the richest dozen or so of Hong Kong's tycoons. Local business leaders believed that the future HKSAR government would respect their interests, and they considered that the best way to articulate those interests was to cultivate and maintain good relations with the Chinese leadership. The most effective means of achieving this end appeared to be major investments in China and generous donations. Local business leaders tended to believe that support for pro-business political parties was unimportant; in fact, it might even be troublesome. They preferred instead to donate to the Better Hong Kong Foundation or similar projects, which, they thought, were apolitical.

The existing political system, despite the implementation of Chris Patten's political reform proposals, continued to favour the business community. The functional constituencies provided more than a dozen seats for business interests in the legislature, and business people dominated the major advisory committees. Most important, the political philosophy of the British administration was in accord with that of the business interests. However, local business leaders do opposed the Governor's handling of relations with Beijing and his political reforms.

A group of second-generation business leaders felt compelled to mobilize in order to counter the labour groups in the 1995 Legislative Council elections. They were the leaders of the Liberal Party, and they worked hard to win seats in the nine new functional constituencies.[46] After the 1995 elections, the pro-democracy groups plus the pro-Beijing labour

---

[46] See Chi-keung Choi, Sai-leung Lau, & Pak-kwan Chow, *op. cit.*, pp. 211–222.

unions commanded a clear majority in the legislature. Their positions on issues such as labour importation schemes and a mandatory pension fund were not acceptable to the business community, yet the government had to meet their demands. The business community has expressed its uneasiness with the situation; however, it was relatively powerless. Business leaders seemed resigned to the fact that the existing legislature would be replaced by a provisional legislature by 1997, elected by the Selection Committee for the First Government of the HKSAR, established by the Preparatory Committee for the HKSAR.

An important task of the Preparatory Committee was to form a 400-member Selection Committee, whose membership was announced in early November 1996. The first Chief Executive and the provisional legislature were chosen by the Selection Committee in December. The most significant functions of the Preparatory Committee were to serve Beijing's "united front" strategy and to legitimize the formation of the first government of the HKSAR. Establishment of the Selection Committee was another major offensive in Beijing's united front strategy following the appointments to the Preliminary Working Committee and the Preparatory Committee, and those of Hong Kong Affairs Advisors and District Affairs Advisors. Besides individual community leaders, the targets included the important interest groups in the territory such as business organizations, professional associations, political parties, and grassroots groups.

In 1985, when the Basic Law Consultative Committee was formed, the Chinese authorities invited most of the important groups in Hong Kong to recommend members, and their recommendations were respected. However, the Chinese authorities ensured their own safe majority within the Basic Law Consultative Committee by appointing a proportion of the members.[47] It appeared that the tasks of selecting the first Chief Executive and the provisional legislature of the HKSAR were more significant than the consultative work relating to the Basic Law, and that, because of the deterioration of Sino-British relations in the past

---

[47] See Kit-fung Cheung, Kin-hing Yeung, Wing-hung Lo, & Lo-sai Chan, *No Change, 50 Years? — The Sino-British Hong Kong Contest Concerning the Basic Law* (in Chinese), Hong Kong: Long Chiu Publisher, 1991, Chapter 3, pp. 45–53, 73–83.

eleven years, the Chinese officials concerned could not allow more than a modicum of error. From the beginning, the Preparatory Committee adopted the principles of confidentiality and collective responsibility. Those who had hoped to see a larger share of democracy and transparency in Preparatory Committee operations relative to those of the Preliminary Working Committee were sorely disappointed.

An opinion survey taken in June 1996 showed that 56.3% of the respondents had no confidence in the Preparatory Committee; 26.9% and 11.7% of the respondents had, respectively, "extremely low" and "low" confidence in the Preparatory Committee.[48] This level of confidence was even lower than that expressed in the Preliminary Working Committee. Professor Lau Siu-kai, a member of both committees, admitted that people were disappointed when the Preparatory Committee failed to consult the people of Hong Kong actively.[49]

On the basis of the Preparatory Committee's membership, it seemed that the Chinese authorities planed to cultivate a number of pro-Beijing groups and avoid dependence on one single political organization. One Country Two Systems Economic Research Institute received eight seats, New Hong Kong Alliance seven, Hong Kong Progressive Alliance five, and Liberal Democratic Federation five.[50] These political groups did not have much popular support, and their performance in recent elections was far from satisfactory. In comparison, the DAB secured only four seats, despite the fact that it has established a solid grassroots network and was able to pose a serious challenge to the DP in the elections that took place in 1994 to 1995. This might well be a sign that the Chinese officials responsible for Hong Kong wanted to strengthen control of the united front, and to prevent the emergence of possible checks and balances as well as the further development of political parties with strong mass support.

In both the election of the first Chief Executive and that of the provisional legislature, the Chinese authorities wanted to ensure that nothing could go wrong. The formation of the Selection Committee had

---

[48] *South China Morning Post*, June 24, 1996.
[49] *Ibid.*
[50] See footnote 43.

been critical, and the process well demonstrated the style of "election with Chinese characteristics." The Preparatory Committee rejected the proposal that various important interest groups in the territory be allowed to nominate a number of representatives to the Selection Committee. Instead, people who wanted to join the Selection Committee would take part on an individual basis; therefore, they would not be accountable to the organizations to which they belonged. In drawing up the final list of candidates, the Preparatory Committee's presidium had ample discretionary power. Finally, in the voting process, it was assumed that the fifty-six mainland China members of the Preparatory Committee voted alike, influencing decisively the outcome of the elections.

The Chinese authorities therefore expected no surprises from the Selection Committee, and the question of whether the Chinese leadership had designated a candidate for the post of the first Chief Executive was insignificant. Similarly, in the election of the provisional legislature, when Qian Qichen appealed for support for those candidates with experience in legislative affairs, the Selection Committee understood and returned 33 incumbent Legislative Councillors plus eight former Legislative Councillors. Among the 60 members of the provisional legislature, 51 were members of the Selection Committee; 33 were members of both the Selection Committee and pro-Beijing political groups. Only six were neither members of the Selection Committee nor pro-Beijing. Lau Siu-kai, a Preparatory Committee member heavily involved in designing the political system of the HKSAR, observed that the Chinese authorities were satisfied with the outcome of the provisional legislature election. He noted that since no political party could dominate the provisional legislature, the Chief Executive would not be restrained by the provisional legislature.

As a result of the Sino-British confrontation, the British administration found it increasingly difficult to co-opt respectable community leaders into the consultative system. This weakened the appeal of the administration. At the same time, senior civil servants have been tempted to appoint more compliant figures on their advisory committees. This made their jobs easier, as they had to spend more time on the Legislative Council and the media. Members of many advisory committees also complained about an absence of important papers to discuss, reflecting the lack of initiatives and the difficulties of the senior civil servants at the final stage of the transition. Serious members — who were often severe critics — in some advisory committees might feel that they had little to contribute, and a few resigned in frustration. To a large extent, advisory committees could not compete with the Legislative Council for the limelight.

The British administration had an earlier strategy: to choose a group of prominent non-politicians — business people, professionals, and academics — to fill the advisory committees so that they could offer the civil servants valuable advice and support. Apparently, the emphasis had been too much on support. As a result, while the system of advisory committees had not been problematic for the Hong Kong government, it gradually lost its important function. It was likely that the first HKSAR government will place an equal emphasis on support, given the pattern of Beijing's united front strategy. Further, community leaders at this stage already displayed an over eagerness to please the Chinese authorities, which resulted in severe criticism.

Since members of the Preparatory Committee were largely business leaders, they did not have much time for the work of the Preparatory Committee. As in the case of the drafting of the Basic Law, the secretariat of the Preparatory Committee assumed a heavy responsibility. The secretariat was based in Beijing and relied on cadres located there. Participation by Hong Kong experts was limited. One Country Two Systems Economic Research Institute, a think tank funded by a group of important Preparatory Committee members, also might play a role in policy research. Another think tank of a similar nature, Hong Kong Policy Research Institute, had become active since the mid-1990s. How these institutes would develop and what role they would assume after 1997 was worth monitoring.

IV Development of Interest Groups

With the approach of July 1997, different interest groups had to respond to the new challenges and devise strategies to ensure their effective articulation. For instance, the Hong Kong General Chamber of Commerce had to shed its image of enjoying special status under the British administration, its leadership having been dominated by the British *hongs*.

In the mid-1990s, the chamber had elected leaders who could communicate well with the Chinese authorities, and their recognition has been affirmed by appointments to the Preliminary Working Committee and Preparatory Committee. In 1995, for the first time, the chamber joined other established business groups in the celebration of the National Day of the People's Republic of China.

Similar changes took place within a number of important professional associations. Access to Chinese authorities was considered an important factor in their competition among the leaders of these associations, while expatriates, voluntarily or involuntarily, were adopting lower profiles. Most professional associations would like to persuade the Chinese authorities to allow them to retain their role in determining their respective professional qualifications in the territory. With the rapid expansion of economic exchanges between Hong Kong and China since the late 1970s, professional firms with an early start in the China market tended to do well, their status and influence rising correspondingly. Heads of these firms often received appointments and honours from the Chinese authorities, which obviously gave them a vested interest in maintaining good relations with Beijing.

The Chinese united front's emphasis on individuals, however, complicated the decision-making process for business and professional groups. An even more significant challenge was the development of representative government in the territory. Ever since the British administration lost its safe majority in the Legislative Council in 1991, business and professional groups had to lobby the legislature as well as the Hong Kong government. Their relationship with the legislature was frustrating. While they could normally count on the support of the pro-business Liberal Party and the legislators from their own functional constituencies, these groups often needed to secure the votes of legislators from the pro-democracy parties to ensure majority support from the Legislative Council.

In general, the dialogue between business groups and the pro-democracy political parties in the 1990s was not fruitful. Rather, it served to expose the discrepancy in values between the two camps. There was little incentive on both sides to engage in a give-and-take bargaining process. Usually, the pro-democracy parties were only too eager to champion the causes of the lower social strata, and they feared that compromises with business groups would be perceived as betrayals of their supporters and violations of their party platforms. The business groups did not have much to offer to induce the pro-democracy parties to cooperate, and they could not effectively challenge the pro-democracy parties in elections. They therefore chose to concentrate on lobbying the government.

As the Hong Kong government increasingly had to play a balancing role in the legislature, it could not afford to endorse the policy positions of the pro-establishment interest groups consistently, even when it shared their concerns and values. Such groups, in their frustration, believed that it might be more rewarding to lobby the Chinese authorities, at least with regard to post-1997 scenarios. The Chinese authorities respected business interests and were keen to maintain an executive-led system of government after 1997, which would diminish the legislature's role in the policy-making process.[51] In the mid-1990s, political parties had become much more skilful in parliamentary tactics. Given the number of votes it controlled, the pro-democracy camp became quite effective in extracting concessions from the Hong Kong government.[52] It remained to be seen how the provisional legislature and its successor would revamp the parliamentary procedures and conventions established in the early-1990s in anticipation of the need to re-adjust the balance between the executive and legislature after 1997. Ideology aside, both business and professional groups demanded efficient government, and they refused to accept the price of democracy in the form of time-consuming debates and delays. For example, none of the eighteen proposals put forward by the Legislative Councillors in 1995 came to fruition in January 1996, and only one had a date set for its first reading.[53]

Despite the development of representative government, a significant segment of the Hong Kong community and grassroots pressure groups treated political parties and politicians with suspicion, and were of the

---

[51] See Joseph Y. S. Cheng, "The Political System," in Peter Wesley-Smith & Albert Chen (eds.), *The Bask Law and Hong Kong's Future*, Hong Kong: Butterworths, 1988, pp. 141–171.

[52] See Section 2 of Chi-keung Choi, Sai-leung Lau, & Pak-kwan Chow, *op. cit.*

[53] *Sunday Morning Post*, January 7, 1996.

opinion that they were interested only in publicity. Grassroots pressure groups were usually issue-oriented; their supporters were interested in concrete results. Consequently, they were often reluctant to enlist the support of political parties, including those from the pro-democracy camp. They appreciated the publicity secured by political parties, as well as the opportunities this afforded to raise their concerns with top government officials and legislators; however, they feared that this publicity might over politicize their issues, thus reducing the chances of exacting prompt concessions from the government departments concerned.

Due to its limited resources and its concentration on parliamentary work in the mid-1990s, the DP neglected the cultivation of grassroots pressure groups, thus further alienating some groups. This neglect sparked initiatives among groups of radical social workers. Some social workers and grassroots activists were disappointed with the lack of progress in the democratization process. Consequently, they became confrontational, resulting in further polarization. In the middle of the decade, many small radical groups emerged to protest against the Chinese authorities.

Many interest groups outside the establishment were wrestling with the divisive issue of how to prepare for the approach of July 1997. For example, in mid-1996 arguments and differences of viewpoint became apparent in the territory's Christian community.[54] The Catholic Church wanted to serve as "the conscience of society," but it ran a large number of schools, hospitals, and charities which depended very heavily on government funding; Catholic Church leaders appreciated the need to maintain a good relationship with the incoming HKSAR government. Other Christian groups quarrelled over the issue of church commemoration of China's National Day. Apparently, the Lutherans and Methodists were most amenable to cooperating with the Chinese authorities. Some of their leaders argued that "Hong Kong is returning not only to China but to the People's Republic of China." On the other hand, local evangelical churches, which had strong links to China's secret "house churches," began moving underground.[55]

---

[54] See Melana K. Zyla, "Devil of a Dilemma — Churches Ponder How Close to Get to Beijing," *Far Eastern Economic Review*, Vol. 159, No. 31, August 1, 1996, p. 17.

[55] *Ibid.*; *Hong Kong Economic Journal*, June 15, 1996.

The Chinese authorities began publicly building their community network and influence in the territory in 1985, when the local New China News Agency opened three district offices in Hong Kong Island, Kowloon, and the New Territories. Pro-Beijing political forces mounted a campaign to block the introduction of direct elections to the Legislative Council in 1988. They mobilized their supporters, identified candidates for support, and attacked political opponents in subsequent elections. The local New China News Agency had been active in cultivating district-based community leaders, voluntary bodies, and interest groups. It normally sent high-ranking officials to attend the latter's functions, most of whom were experts in united front tactics.

The Hong Kong government apparently did not see this as a threat; it reduced funding for the Home Affairs Branch (previously known as the City and New Territories Administration) in the early 1990s. Since the latter half of the 1980s, people often complained about District Officers as well — that they were too young and immature, that they were unable to speak Cantonese well, and that they were insensitive to local traditions and customs. Because they remained in their posts for only two to three years, they did not have time to establish strong ties with community leaders in their respective districts.

In the 1991 Legislative Council elections, many district-based pro-Beijing groups emerged. Their development was hindered by the Tiananmen incident, but it was regaining momentum with the approach of July 1997. Examples of such groups were the Kwun Tong Manchung Friendship Promotion Association and Hong Kong Eastern District Community Association. While they did not seem to be very active, their names appeared increasingly in advertisements and posters supporting the work of the Preparatory Committee. Funding for these groups came mainly from pro-Beijing business people, and their leaders and activists were often honoured with appointments by the Chinese authorities. At this stage, such groups tended to concentrate on social activities. From the united front's point of view, however, they should develop into organizations with effective mobilization power and the ability to reach ordinary people at the neighbourhood level.

The mobilization power of pro-Beijing groups was mixed at best, despite the financial and political resources at their disposal. In the 1995

Legislative Council elections, Choy So-yuk of the Hong Kong Progressive Alliance challenged Martin Lee, leader of the DP, in the Hong Kong Island East constituency. Few voters had heard of Choy, who had no significant service record at the district level. Yet she won almost 30% of the votes. In contrast, Fung Chi-kin of the DAB competed in the Financing, Insurance, Real Estate and Business Services functional constituency and lost badly to the DP candidate, Cheng Kar-foo. Fung was assumed to have the firm endorsement of all the Chinese enterprises and their friends in these sectors; his failure indicated that many employees of Chinese enterprises refused to deliver the votes as directed by their superiors.

V Conclusion

By early 1997, both Chinese leaders and the people of Hong Kong exhibited more confidence in the notion of a stable transfer of power compared with, say, seven years ago. Even the leadership succession of Beijing did not seem to pose a threat, as people accepted that the post-Deng era had already begun. This improvement in confidence stemmed from a number of causes. Hong Kong residents realized that Chinese leaders valued the territory, and had been working hard to retain investors — an important indicator being the composition of the Preparatory Committee. It was obvious that China's economic reforms and openness to the outside world would be irreversible.

Given the choice of being unemployed in Canada or Australia, or obtaining a job comparable to their own in Shenzhen, most Hong Kong professionals would opt for the latter. Worry over 1997 was much reduced by the realization that there were no greener pastures outside the territory. The return flow of former emigrants has indeed been expanding as Hong Kong approached July 1997. It was reported that for every 100 emigrants leaving Hong Kong in 1995, 60 former emigrants returned to the territory from overseas. The corresponding proportions in previous years were 27.9% in 1994, 29.1% in 1993, 16.2% in 1992, 7.7% in 1991, and 7.2% in 1990.[56] The people of Hong Kong, however, also lowered their expectations of the future. Few supported a high degree of autonomy for

---

[56] *Ming Pao*, September 11, 1996.

the HKSAR. They accepted the stationing of the People's Liberation Army in the urban areas. They no longer demanded a say in the selection of the first Chief Executive. In sum, they accepted stability and prosperity as the substitute for democracy and autonomy. Slackening economic growth and unemployment were then the Hong Kong community's foremost concerns.

Increasingly, Hong Kong residents came to believe that since Hong Kong had become the focus of much international media attention, and given Chinese leaders' concern about their image, all would go well in 1997. These might, however, be pragmatic rationalizations to suppress fears for the time being. They indicated that worries of a major upheaval occurring by 1997 had been diluted to concerns that the rule of law, the freedoms then enjoyed, and, indeed, the way of life in Hong Kong would slowly erode. These rationalizations also meant that the Chinese authorities had gained time. They were given the benefit of the doubt to make "one country, two systems" work. They were also given a vote of confidence by local and international investors. Less reassuringly, however, a study at that time estimated that 700,000 members of the local population held foreign passports, and that probably another 500,000 possessed the right of abode in a foreign country.[57] It was believed that they were largely well-educated, middle-class families who had adopted a "wait-and-see" attitude.

Respect for the rule of law and freedom of the media was perhaps the best way to win the hearts of the Hong Kong community. Operations of the Preparatory Committee were the most significant starting point. While the people of Hong Kong understood that the Preparatory Committee was not accountable to them, they would closely monitor its performance to assess whether it justified their benefit of the doubt. The needs for transparency and due process could not be over-emphasized, and shortcomings would not escape notice.

---

[57] See a report prepared by Hong Kong Policy Research Institute; a version of this report appears as Jane C.Y. Lee & Ng Chi-sum, "The Nationality and Right of Abode Policy for Hong Kong Residents — Political or Pragmatic Consideration?" *Hong Kong Journal of Social Sciences* (in Chinese), No. 7, April 1996, pp. 192–211.

The author's interviews with Preparatory Committee members in early October 1996 revealed that the Chinese authorities were largely satisfied with the situation. They were especially encouraged by the fact that approximately 6,000 people had applied to join the 400-seat Selection Committee. With the exception of the pro-democracy camp, applicants represented the elites from all sectors of the community. Many retired politicians and former senior civil servants also applied, apparently in an attempt to show their support for the Chinese authorities. In the competition for the post of Chief Executive of the first HKSAR government, a small number of candidates considered acceptable to the Hong Kong community competed vigorously. In an opinion survey in early October 1996, the two front runners, Sir Ti-liang Yang and Che-hwa Tung, received approval ratings of 73% and 56% respectively; their disapproval ratings were 14.1% and 26.9% respectively.[58] The competition reduced the suspicion that the Chinese authorities completely controlled the process. In general, the election of the first Chief Executive went smoothly; however, election of the provisional legislature did not.

The Chinese authorities were particularly pleased with the pragmatism of Hong Kong residents, who typically preferred to avoid confrontation with Beijing. In his final policy speech, Governor Chris Patten strongly defended his political reform package and argued for non-cooperation with the provisional legislature.[59] An opinion survey held soon afterward revealed that 78.1% of the respondents believed that the Hong Kong government should help the provisional legislature if it operated from early 1997; even among those who did not support the provisional legislature, the percentage was as high as 71.1%.[60]

Various opinion surveys gauged the public selection of the first Chief Executive. The incumbent Chief Secretary, Anson Chan Fang On-sang, was consistently the most popular choice; she consistently secured 50% to 60% of the respondents' support. As her chances declined in the autumn of 1996, however, support among respondents also dropped to 39.6% in

---

[58] *Sunday Morning Post*, October 6, 1996.

[59] For the text of the policy speech, see all major newspapers in Hong Kong on October 3, 1996.

[60] *South China Morning Post*, October 8, 1996.

October. Martin Lee, leader of the DP, did not appear to be a popular choice. He received the support of 16.2% of the respondents in December 1995, a level that gradually decreased to 4.8% in October 1996.[61] The people of Hong Kong apparently preferred to see a senior civil servant assume this post; this would represent continuity and maintenance of the administration by civil servants. They did not believe that pro-democracy leaders would be ideal candidates, since they wanted to avoid confrontation with Beijing. However, they did want pro-democracy leaders to remain in the legislature as critics of Beijing and the local government; pro-democracy leaders remained very popular among the Hong Kong populace.

Political development in the post-war era in Hong Kong had been a process of promoting citizens' demands and rights, or those of a segment of the community, through the combination of public opinion, legal means, and pressure group activities within the existing political system.[62] Inherent to this process was an implicit negation of the "winners take all" model, with all parties accepting that political strategies should consist of long-term negotiation, bargaining, cooperation, and conflict resolution.[63] Such a system was most likely an important model for China at this stage of its political development.

The spirit of bargaining and negation of "winners take all" permeated every level of Hong Kong politics. At the highest level, before the Sino-British Joint Declaration in 1984, neither the colonial government nor the Hong Kong community desired a fundamental change of the political system as it might attract interference from Beijing. Since 1984, the people of Hong Kong understood that their option was either to accept the "one country, two systems" arrangement or to emigrate. At the grassroots level, petitions and protest rallies in the territory were usually peaceful and orderly; protesters and the police were willing to cooperate to avoid

---

[61] *Sunday Morning Post*, October 6, 1996.
[62] See Joseph Y.S. Cheng, "Political Modernization in Hong Kong," *The Journal of Common-wealth and Comparative Politics*, Vol. 27, No. 3, November 1989, pp. 294–320.
[63] See Tsou Tang, Twentieth Century Chinese Politics (in Chinese), Hong Kong: Oxford University Press, 1994.

clashes. Hong Kong residents generally shunned confrontation and violence.

In the process of drafting the Basic Law, for example, political groups and the concerned public seriously debated every controversial clause in the document. Though many in Hong Kong had doubts concerning the binding power of the Basic Law on the Chinese authorities, there was general acceptance that securing a Basic Law acceptable to the community was almost the only option available. The hope was also expressed that the serious debates would have an educational effect on all parties concerned.

The people of Hong Kong adopted a utilitarian attitude toward democracy: They viewed it as a means to realize practical, concrete objectives. Few actually practiced democracy as a way of life. For example, many voted in elections in order to fulfil a civic obligation. Many voted for the candidates of the pro-democracy camp who were severe critics of the Hong Kong government and the Chinese authorities because they hoped to achieve a certain degree of checks and balances. They neither expected nor desire the pro-democracy camp to capture the government. Since the Hong Kong community treated democracy as a means to an end, they were prudent in the calculation of the cost of political participation. While they perceived democracy as an important means to guarantee their freedoms, their lifestyles, and their living standards, they also considered that their own individual efforts were more significant — more liable to improve their own lives. Such attitudes and orientations continue to define political participation in Hong Kong in the mid-1990s.

Acknowledgement

Originally published as Cheng Joseph Y.S., "Political Participation in Hong Kong: Trends in the Mid-1990s", in *Hong Kong under Chinese Rule: The Economic and Political Implications of Reversion*, ed. Warren I. Cohen and Li Zhao, Cambridge, Eng.: Cambridge University Press, 1997, pp. 155–183. Reproduced with permission of the Licensor through PLSclear.

Chapter 10

Political Changes Since the Establishment of the Hong Kong Special Administrative Region, 1997-1999

Before Hong Kong's return to China, local people still had considerable fears and uncertainties concerning the Hong Kong Special Administrative Region (HKSAR)'s future. In 1996 and the first half of 1997, however, the international business community and the people of Hong Kong were somewhat bullish regarding the HKSAR's economic prospects, as reflected by the booming stock market and the real estate market. By the beginning of 1999, the mood of Hong Kong people had almost completely reversed. They were generally satisfied with Beijing's limited interference in Hong Kong, and they had developed some trust in the Chinese leadership. They also noted that Hong Kong was more dependent on China than the other way around, and this dependence would only strengthen in the future. However, Hong Kong people also had become more aware of the structural weaknesses of their economy, and they were pessimistic regarding the prospects of a substantial recovery and continued respectable growth.

    This chapter intends to examine the significant changes in the territory's political environment between the handover and mid-1999, and the responses to the changes from various social strata, interests groups, political parties, etc. Attempts will be made to identify the emerging political trends, as well as to analyze the underlying causes for them and their future evolution.

I Trust in China and Identification with China

In 1997, only 30,900 Hong Kong people emigrated, compared with just over 40,000 people in 1996, and an average of about 60,000 per annum in the 1989–1994 period.[1] In the same year, Hong Kong registered a 3% increase in population, the highest since 1979. About 86% of the population growth was contributed to a net inflow of 167,700 people.[2] Since the inflow from China had been limited to about 63,875 per annum (175 per day), the number of returning emigrants should have been about 130,000, after balancing the new emigrants with the returning emigrants from abroad. The huge inflow of returning emigrants reflected that many had left simply to seek foreign passports as an insurance policy, and that most of them had serious difficulty finding comparable employment abroad. Nevertheless, the return flow of emigrants and the decline in the number of people leaving obviously demonstrated enhanced confidence in the HKSAR.

This rise in confidence coincided with a strengthening identification with China. A survey by the Department of Journalism and Communication of the Chinese University of Hong Kong in September 1997 indicated that 32.1% of the respondents identified themselves as "Chinese," compared with 25.7% in an earlier survey in August 1996; 23.2% of the respondents identified themselves as "Hongkongese," compared with 25.2% in the earlier survey. Those who claimed to be "Hongkongese as well as Chinese" decreased slightly from 32.9% to 31.8%, while those who considered themselves to be "Chinese as well as Hongkongese" also dropped from 14.7% to 11.6%.[3] In a survey conducted in the summer of 1988 by the social scientists of local tertiary institutions, 63.6% of the respondents chose "Hongkongese" as their primary identity, while only 28.8% considered themselves to be "Chinese."[4]

---

[1] *South China Morning Post* (a Hong Kong English language newspaper), January 1, 1998.
[2] *Ibid.*, February 14, 1998
[3] *Ming Pao* (A Hong Kong Chinese Newspaper), February 4, 1998.
[4] See the author's "Values and Attitudes of the Hong Kong community," in Paul C.K. Kwong, *Hong Kong Trends, 1989–92*. Hong Kong: The Chinese University Press, 1992, pp. 28–29.

The same surveys by the Department of Journalism and Communication of the Chinese University of Hong Kong revealed that Hong Kong people felt more comfortable with the People's Liberation Army (PLA) and the public security personnel in China since the handover. In the survey in August 1996, 30.3% and 38.9% of the respondents felt uncomfortable with the PLA and the public security personnel respectively; and in the survey in September 1997, the corresponding proportions dropped substantially to 10.9% and 24.8%.

While identification with China strengthened, Hong Kong young people's knowledge of China was still unsatisfactory, though improving slightly. In September 1998, a youth group conducted a survey among people in the age group of 18–40 years old. The results indicated that 15% of the respondents could not identify Jiang Zemin as President of the People's Republic of China (PRC), 45% could not name Zhu Rongji as Premier, and 81% could not identify Li Peng as Chairman of the Standing Committee of the National People's Congress (NPC).[5] Understanding China requires strenuous efforts which can only be maintained by a keen interest and firm dedication; these elements apparently were lacking among Hong Kong people then, who were very much preoccupied with their daily livelihood concerns.

Since the handover, Chinese leaders had demonstrated to the local and international communities that they intended to follow a strict hands-off policy towards Hong Kong. To demonstrate its respect for the HKSAR's autonomy, the Chinese Ministry of Foreign Affairs politely turned down requests by foreign dignitaries to arrange their Hong Kong visits and asked them to approach the HKSAR government directly. Commenting on the first anniversary of the handover, the U.S. Consul-General in Hong Kong, Richard Boucher, praised the success of the HKSAR government. In response to a question on the Chinese government's interferences in the territory, Boucher declared that the doubts which had existed in the previous year were no longer mentioned because the answer was amply clear. Nonetheless, Boucher criticized the inadequate representativeness of the local legislature, and reiterated the U.S. concern for Hong Kong's

---

[5] *Ming Pao*, October 1, 1998

democratic development and the rule of law.[6] Similarly, Alan Paul, the British senior representative to the Sino-British Joint Liaison Group, described the performance of the HKSAR government in its first year as "positive and healthy." He expressed satisfaction that the Sino-British Joint Declaration had been faithfully implemented, that the spirit of a high degree of autonomy for Hong Kong had been respected by China, and that the operation of the HKSAR government had also realized the principle of Hong Kong people governing Hong Kong.[7]

At the beginning of 1999, the European Commission, in its first annual report on the HKSAR, acknowledged that "basic rights, freedoms and autonomy have been broadly upheld." The report welcomed steps towards broader suffrage in the legislative elections in May 1998, and appealed that the HKSAR government should announce soon a clear commitment to full democracy and fix a "reasonably early" date for its full implementation. It also noted that there had been regular demonstrations, unbridled press criticism, and no detentions or harassment of political opponents or human rights activists.[8] Such assessments were obviously shared by the local community. Radical pro-democracy groups, as expected, disagreed. Frontier legislator, Emily Lau, for example, responded to the European Commission report as follows: "They have their own agenda and standards. Their expectations are low. As there was no democracy in the colonial days, they don't see it as an erosion of democracy if we don't have it now."[9]

In the relationship between the HKSAR on the one hand, and the central ministries and local governments in China on the other, the Hong Kong and Macau Affairs Office (HKMAO) assumed the role of gatekeeper. It handled the exchanges between the two sides, and visitors from the mainland had to be cleared by the HKMAO. The latter was strict in the performance of this task, so much so that many officials and academics in the mainland often complained that it was more difficult to go to Hong Kong than to the U.S. In a discussion paper prepared for the legislature,

---

[6] *Ibid.*, July 1, 1998
[7] *Ibid.*
[8] *Sunday Morning Post*, January 10, 1999
[9] *Ibid.*

the HKSAR government indicated in October 1998 that, with the assistance of the Chinese Foreign Affairs Ministry Office in the territory, the HKSAR had concluded 21 bilateral agreements with foreign countries, and had been authorized to sign an additional 23. HKSAR government officials had participated as members of PRC de delegations in over sixty international conferences and had taken part in about nine hundred international conferences as members of delegations from "Hong Kong, China."[10] Hong Kong officials believed that they had been given better treatment and status as members of PRC delegations compared with colonial days when they were part of British delegations.[11]

The relationship between Hong Kong and China was not without problems. The HKSAR government introduced the Adaptation of Laws (Interpretative Provisions) Bill to the provisional legislature, which passed it in April 1998, and made the law retroactive to July 1, 1997. The law changes colonial definitions in all the laws of the HKSAR, replacing phrases such as "the Crown" with "the state". Article 22 of the Basic Law states: "All offices set up in the Hong Kong Special Administrative Region by departments of the Central Government, or by provinces, autonomous regions, or municipalities directly under the Central Government, and the personnel of these offices shall abide by the laws of the Region."[12] The pro-democracy groups therefore argued that the law was a breach of the Basic Law and that it gave up considerable jurisdiction unjustifiably by exempting the New China News Agency (NCNA) and other mainland bodies from some laws.[13] Moreover, the HKSAR government refused to provide a definition of "the state,"[14] or a list of mainland organs in Hong Kong which come under the definition of "the state". The pro-democracy groups had asked the government to postpone the introduction of the bill until after the first legislature had been elected.

---

[10] *Hong Kong Economic Journal* (a Hong Kong Chinese newspaper), October 17, 1998.
[11] *Ming Pao*, June 22, 1998
[12] *The Basic Law of the Hong Kong Special Administrative Region of the People's Republic of China*, Hong Kong: Basic Law Consultative Committee, 1990, p.13.
[13] *Sunday Morning Post*, March 29, 1998.
[14] *Ming Pao*, April 8, 1998

In December 1997, the Selection Committee which had earlier selected the first Chief Executive and members of the provisional legislature, selected 36 deputies to represent the HKSAR in the NPC. Thirty-five deputies were members of the Selection Committee and the only non-member returned was Jiang Enzhu, head of the Hong Kong branch of the NCNA. Following the normal practice in mainland China, Jiang, the most senior Chinese official in Hong Kong, was a natural choice to represent the territory in the NPC. However, many Hong Kong people believed that Jiang would certainly toe the central government line rather than articulate local interest. Their view, therefore, was that Jiang should be returned to the NPC as a senior cadre in the State Council. The local pro-Beijing circles and media strongly defended Jiang's candidacy, and Jiang received the highest number of votes in the selection process.[15]

In the colonial era, the British administration avoided any special ties with Guangdong, and maintained a policy of treating all provinces and central ministries on an equal footing. However, it could not be denied that, in view of the close economic integration between Hong Kong and Guangdong, special channels of communication and co-ordination had to be created. In March 1998, the Hong Kong–Guangdong Cooperation Joint Conference was inaugurated and was scheduled to meet twice a year in Hong Kong and Guangzhou alternatively. HKMAO Director Liao Hui was present at e inauguration ceremony, and he indicated that he would continue to play the role of the agent of communications and service provider.[16]

Lu Ruihua, governor of Guangdong, said the co-operation would emphasize three areas: a) trade and economic cooperation, including infrastructure and information industry; b) exchanges in the fields of education, technology, and professions; and c) checkpoint establishment and management, including a smooth flow of passengers vehicles, and freight. Guangdong officials were eager to promote cooperation with Hong Kong; however, they felt constrained because their proposals had to go through the central government which tended to be cautious. They therefore hoped that the HKSAR government would take the initiative.

---

[15] See all major newspaper in Hong Kong on December 9, 1997

[16] *Ming Pao*, March 30, 1998 and *South China Morning Post*, March 31, 1998.

There was a view within local pro-Beijing circles that Hong Kong government officials were not enthusiastic regarding co-operation with China, and that they still often looked down on developments in China. Many in these circles were quite critical of Anson Chan, the Chief Secretary for Administration, and they believed that the Hong Kong-Guangdong Co-operation Joint Conference was inadequate.[17]

At the same time, the HKSAR government found it confusing and difficult to handle the aggressive and uncoordinated approaches to the territory by local governments in Guangdong. The Lingdingyang Crossing project was a good example. This 27-kilometer, six-lane crossing from the Zhuhai Special Economic Zone to Tuen Mun in Hong Kong was given low priority in the latter's blueprint for the next century, but it was much advertized by Zhuhai. Hong Kong believes that related issues such as immigration control, traffic volume, and the impact on existing transport operators had yet to be studied.[18]

There were also occasions when successful compromises were reached. A water supply contract was concluded in 1989 between the Hong Kong government and the Guangdong provincial government. However, it grossly overestimated the territory's demand for water because the impact of Hong Kong industries' moving to the Pearl River Delta had not been adequately assessed. Since 1995, Hong Kong had been requesting to reduce the amount of water transferred to the territory, but Guangdong insisted on full payments. In early 1998, a compromise was reached: Hong Kong would provide an interest-free loan of HK$2.364 billion in the next four years to build a 83-kilometer closed water transport system to Hong Kong, thus reducing pollution and improving water quality. Hong Kong would lose HK$2 billion in interest payments but would save HK$2.24 billion in the next seven years by giving up unwanted water without charge.[19]

The greatest challenge to the relationship between the central authorities and the HKSAR did not arrive until February 1999, when the Court of Final Appeal (CFA) delivered its landmark ruling on the cases of

---

[17] *Ming Pao*, August 13, 1998.
[18] *Hong Kong Standard* (a Hong Kong English-language newspaper), February 1, 1998.
[19] *Ming Pao*, March 31, 1998.

illegal migrant children. The CFA claimed that the courts of the HKSAR have the jurisdiction to examine whether legislative acts of the NPC or its Standing Committee are consistent with the Basic Law and to declare them to be invalid if found to be inconsistent. This decision was regarded by four legal experts in mainland China as a violation of the Basic Law. They argued that NPC is the organ of supreme state power in China, and that no organization can challenge the laws promulgated by it or its decisions. They also asserted that the authority to interpret the Basic Law rests with the Standing Committee of the NPC; and the CFA's ruling willfully expanded its rights to partially interpret the Basic Law.[20]

These legal experts further indicated that the Preparatory Committee for the HKSAR attempted to prevent a rapid population increase in Hong Kong which would exert pressure on all sectors, hence it held certain views on the implementation of the second clause of Article 24 of the Basic Law.[21] These legal experts implicitly criticized the CFA's ruling for facilitating a huge influx of people into Hong Kong, thereby creating a negative impact on Hong Kong society. The harsh criticisms of the CFA were then endorsed by the head of the State Councils Information Office, Zhao Qizheng. The HKSAR government subsequently sent it Secretary for Justice, Elsie Leung, to Beijing to seek the central authorities' understanding. The Chinese authorities' reaction to the CFA's ruling also caused a diplomatic row between Beijing and London. In response to the British media's criticisms, the Chinese Foreign Ministry released a statement suggesting that Britain had no right to comment on the CFA's ruling. A spokesman for the British prime minister Tony Blair responded by insisting that Britain had the right to comment on developments in Hong Kong because of its role in the Sino-British Joint Declaration.[22]

Differences in the interpretation of the Basic Law between the HKSAR and the central authorities in Beijing are natural and almost

---

[20] *China Daily* (a Beijing English-language newspaper), February 8, 1999. These four legal experts were closely involved in the drafting of the Basic Law. As their opinions reported prominently in the official media, they were considered to reflect the official view.

[21] The second clause of Article 24 of the Basic Law defines the qualifications for permanent residents of the HKSAR. See the *Basic Law of the Hong Kong Special Administrative Region of the People's Republic of China*, p. 14.

[22] *South China Morning Post*, February 13, 1999.

inevitable. In the first 50 years of American history, the U.S. Supreme Court attempted to expand its jurisdiction and some of its rulings were controversial. The CFA naturally wanted to define its judicial independence and the HKSAR's high degree of autonomy to the fullest extent possible, and, in doing so, might well be challenged by the central authorities. Procedure wise, before its final judgement (which is not appealable), the CFA should seek an interpretation from the Standing Committee of the NPC concerning provisions of the Basic Law covering affairs which are the responsibility of the Central People's Government or involve the relationship between the central authorities and the HKSAR. There is no guarantee that the CFA will refer to the Standing Committee of the NPC for an interpretation in every case which the latter considers necessary.[23]

The Chinese authorities obviously did not want to damage the good image regarding Hong Kong's high degree of autonomy and their non-interference in the territory. However, they believed that the challenges to the NPC and its Standing Committee posed by the CFA's ruling had to be rectified.[24] Under such circumstances, considerable adverse reaction was inevitable. In an opinion poll in February 1990, 70% of the respondents indicated that a constitutional crisis would emerge if the CFA's ruling was overturned; 72% of the respondents believed that the HKSA government should explain the ruling to the central government in Beijing and seek to uphold the CFA's independence; only 11% of the respondents believed that Hong Kong should follow Beijing's instructions.[25]

It was widely believed that the Chief Executive Tung Chee-hwa had engaged in intensive lobbying of the Chinese authorities to minimize damage. At the request of the HKSAR government, the CFA took the unprecedented step of clarifying its ruling on the cases of the illegal migrant children. The five judges released a brief, unanimous statement which stated that its earlier ruling "did not question the authority of the Standing Committee [of the National People's Congress] to make an interpretation under Article 158 [of the Basic Law] which would have to

---

[23] Article 158 of the Basic Law. See the *Basic Law of the Hong Kong Special Administrative Region of the People's Republic of China*, p. 54.
[24] *Ming Pao*. February 9, 1999.
[25] *Sunday Morning Post*, February 14, 1999.

be followed by the courts of the region." The CFA indicated that "it cannot question that authority"; and that it "accepts that it cannot question the authority of the National People's Congress or the Standing Committee to do any act which is in accordance with the provisions of the Basic Law and the procedure therein."[26]

The local Bar Association and many in the territory's legal community believed that the CFA's response would undermine the rule of law by giving the impression that it had bowed to political pressure.[27] The local Law Society, however, endorsed the CFA's action. Within days, the Chinese authorities indicated that the CFA had taken the "necessary step" to clarify its controversial ruling, and the constitutional crisis seemed to have ended.[28] This was a considerable relief for Hong Kong people who wanted to avoid further troubles in times of economic hardship. The controversy well demonstrated the discrepancies in the legal doctrines of the two legal systems, and that the maintenance of judicial independence and a high degree of autonomy in the HKSAR within the "one country, two systems" framework was a constant challenge.

II Decline of the Civil Service and Its Reforms

Since the handover, one troubling question frequently posed in the local media and in Hong Kong people's conversations had been — what had gone wrong with Hong Kong's civil servants? From the bird flu, to the opening of the new airport, to the Sally Aw case, Hong Kong's top civil servants had committed one blunder after another. Their incompetent performance was magnified by two factors: (1) they could not blame nature for the latter fiascos, and (2) their reluctance to apologize and accept responsibility made Hong Kong people only angrier.

In the final years of the transitional period, Hong Kong civil servants were praised as the best in the world. The local community had found the performance of its civil service satisfactory and was eager to maintain continuity and avoid neutral senior civil servants being replaced by

---

[26] *South China Morning Post*, February 27, 1999
[27] *Ibid.*
[28] *Sunday Morning Post*, February 28, 1999.

pro-Beijing figures. However, the Hong Kong people were reminded even then that, if their civil servants were so outstanding, why was it that they were never recruited as consultants by Britain and other advanced countries? While many criticisms of the civil service undoubtedly were justified, one had to take note that the economic difficulties since the handover had made Hong Kong people much more critical of their senior civil servants, and the latter had been conveniently blamed for the territory's current troubles.

Nevertheless, there were long-term structural questions that haw to be examined. Hong Kong's civil service system was of course, modelled after that of the U.K. However, in contrast to their counterparts in Whitehall, top civil servants in Hong Kong made policies and attempted to secure acceptance of their policies by the public. In this regard, they were politicians and far from neutral. Yet, they did not have to be accountable to the people in the sense that they had to resign should their policies fail. This difference tended to be ignored when the government's performance proved to be satisfactory; in times of economic difficulties and civil service blunders, however, people were dissatisfied that no senior civil servants had been sanctioned for serious policy or administrative mistakes.

While the British and Japanese civil service systems are very similar, they differ in one important aspect: the Japanese administrative officers are highly specialized. They join one ministry after appointment upon graduation, and normally stay there until retirement. This means that they have much time to develop their policy expertise. In Hong Kong, following the British practice, administrative officers move from one department/ policy branch to they are supposed to be generalists. Whether generalists could manage to lead in policy areas which increasingly demanded expertise, and which were highly complicated became doubtful. When speculators attacked the Hong Kong dollar, some of the senior civil servants were clearly perceived to be inadequate because they lacked experience in the money and currency markets. They therefore could not inspire confidence and respect in the financial community.

Most of the top local civil servants studied literature and history as university students, and in the last decade, experienced frequent transfers and promotions because of the departure of expatriates and the shrinking pool of talents in the administrative officer grade. This, in turn, was related to the inadequate localization before the Sino-British Joint Declaration, when half of the administrative officers and police inspectors were recruited overseas. During the transition period, a few senior civil servants emigrated and some left for the private sector. At the same time, the civil service expanded considerably because of economic development and improvements in social services provided by a more prosperous government. This resulted in rapid promotions for administrative officers so much so that a considerable proportion of the HKSAR's senior civil servants did not have sufficient experience behind them and did not have enough time to cultivate the expertise necessary for their current positions. Obviously, this situation was not a simple question of what had happened since the departure of the British.

More questions should be raised concerning the system itself. Would it be wise and fair to recruit administrative officers on the basis of one examination normally taken shortly before university graduation? Would there be sufficient tests and reviews to weed out those administrative officers who were not qualified for senior positions? Administrative officer examinations emphasized English-language skills which tended to favour liberal arts graduates. Would there be a need to recruit persons with more diverse backgrounds, including those with degrees in engineering and information technology? Grooming of administrative officers for senior positions generated resentment among civil servants of professional grades who believed their talents and experiences were overlooked. They found it difficult to accept leadership from administrative officers who lacked the necessary professional qualifications and policy expertise.

At the middle and junior levels, the quality of Hong Kong's civil servants suffered as standards of local university graduates declined. This decline was not limited to proficiency in English, Chinese and creativity; more importantly, there was a deterioration in students' sense of responsibility and commitment. This might help to explain why water supplies stopped and telephones did not work when the new airport opened.

Hong Kong's civil service system had been slow to come up with an effective incentive system. Civil servants could only be promoted and transferred. They enjoyed an "iron rice-bowl"; yet opportunities for promotion (except for the administrative officers) had become more limited because the civil service as a whole, was becoming younger while it was expanding more slowly. Starting salaries were considerably higher than those in the private sector, and seniority remained the most important factor in determining promotions. Such a system could not reward outstanding performers and it could not weed out those who do not deliver. If the above problems were not resolved satisfactorily, it would be difficult to improve the quality of the civil service.

One option was the introduction of a ministerial system. Another option for managing the civil service, which could be introduced at this stage without encountering substantial opposition, would be to offer contracts to top civil servants following the Australian model. Top civil servants believed that they were underpaid compared with their counterparts in the private sector. The contract system could offer them substantially higher salaries, while breaking the "iron rice-bowl," i.e., contracts might not be renewed. Top civil servants would be given the option to hold onto their tenure or to opt for contracts, and, therefore, they would not have grounds for complaint. Those who were fifty-five years of age or above would not lose much by opting for initial contracts of three to five years. Hopefully, such arrangements would change the culture, at least at the top echelons of the civil service, and further justify the gradual implementation of the contract system throughout the civil service. Top civil servants would be more accountable, and the Chief Executive would have a better chance of forming his own team.

There were many rumors that the Chief Executive did not get along with the Chief Secretary for Administration, Anson Chan. At the very least, it did not bolster public confidence that the two often had to tell the mass media that, indeed, they cooperated well. There were perhaps structural factors which helped to explain the difficulties in the relationship between Tung Chee-hwa and the top civil servants. In the first place, Tung and the pro-Beijing circles might be concerned that the team of top civil servants was cultivated by Chris Patten and were forced upon the HKSAR government, which accepted them for the sake of continuity. There were many in the pro-Beijing camp who believed that previously discrimination was leveled against them by senior civil servants in the colonial era, and believed that these persons had to change their attitudes. However, the civil service of the colonial era had developed its own conventions and mode of operation, and senior civil servants, viewing them as assets, were keen to preserve them. In the eyes of the pro-Beijing political elite, these were but colonial legacies and their adjustment and replacement were only natural and inevitable.

In contrast to British governors, Tung Chee-hwa believed that he understood Hong Kong well, while the former felt obliged to consult the senior civil servants in order to have a good grasp of the values and attitudes of the community. Further, in the transitional era, British governors were mainly absorbed by negotiations with Beijing, and, therefore, left daily administration largely to top civil servants. Since the handover, the HKSAR government had been preoccupied with Hong Kong's financial crisis and with the long-term planning of social services, including housing, education, etc. Tung Chee-hwa was well-known for his long working hours and his hands-on approach of doing things, hence the top civil servants might feel more constrained.

III Relationship Between the Executive and the Legislature

In the July 1984 Government Green Paper entitled "The Further Development of Representative Government in Hong Kong," it was proposed that a majority of appointed unofficial members of the Executive Council should be replaced progressively by members elected by the unofficial members of the Legislative Council.[29] This proposal was abandoned because the Basic Law drafters, the majority of whom were sympathetic to Beijing policies, rejected the Westminster model and favoured a presidential system for the HKSAR to ensure ample power for the executive branch of government.

The current constitutional arrangement, however, did not guarantee the Chief Executive a safe majority support in the legislature. Constitutionally, the Basic Law drafters reduced the power of the legislature to ensure that there would be an "executive-led" system of

---

[29] *Green Paper: The Further Development of Representative Government in Hong Kong*, Hong Kong: Government Printer, July 1984.

government.[30] The strength of the Chief Executive and the weakness of the legislature were well illustrated by the following arrangements. In contrast to the U.S. Congress, the legislature has no power over the appointment of principal officials and members of the Executive Council nor is there provision for the legislature to impeach them.

Further, the Chief Executive has the power "to approve the introduction of motions regarding revenues or expenditure to the Legislative Council" and "to decide, in the light of security and vital public interests, whether Government officials or other personnel in charge of Government affairs should testify or give evidence before the Legislative Council or its committees."[31] If the Chief Executive can, without having to give reasons, reject any motion presented to the Legislative Council regarding revenues or expenditure, then the Legislative Council can only respond to the Chief Executive's proposals. The Chief Executive's power to exempt government officials or other personnel in charge of government affairs from testifying or giving evidence before the Legislative Council or its committees would severely hamper the latter's function as a watchdog of the Chief Executive and the executive authorities. Considerations of security and vital public interests would not be legitimate reasons for preventing the Legislative Council from calling government officials or other personnel in charge of governmental affairs to testify or give evidence.

Further, regarding bills relating to government policies, members of the Legislative Council may only introduce them with the prior written consent of the Chief Executive.[32] There is obviously a danger that "Government policies" may be defined so broadly as to render members of the Legislative Council almost powerless to introduce bills. Finally, the passage of motions, bills, or amendments to government bills introduced by individual members of the Legislative Council required a simple majority vote of each of the two groups of members present: members returned by functional constituencies, and those returned by geographical

---

[30] See the author's "The Political System", in Peter Wesley-Smith and Albert Chen (eds.), *The Basic Law and Hong Kong's Future*, Hong Kong: Butterworths, 1988, pp. 141–171.
[31] Article 48.10 and 48.11 of the Basic Law. See *The Basic Law of the Hong Kong Special Administration Region of the People's Republic of China*, p. 21.
[32] Article 74 of the Basic Law, *ibid.*, p. 29.

constituencies through direct elections and by the Election Committee.[33] This meant that, with the support of over half of the members returned by functional constituencies (16 seats out of 60), the Tung administration could forestall any initiative from the legislature against the executive branch.

The electoral system, at the same time, ensured that there would be a safe majority in the legislature in support of China's policy towards Hong Kong and the policy programs of the executive branch. Functional constituencies and the Election Committee together returned 40 seats in the 60-seat legislature. These 40 seats were dominated by the business community and professional bodies sharing its political views. A multi-seat constituency, single vote system was introduced to return twenty seats in geographical constituencies through direct elections. This system ensured that the pro-Beijing political groups would win at least a quarter of the seats (one seat in each of the five geographic constituencies) and prevent the pro-democracy political parties from securing a clean sweep, as was possible under the single-seat constituency, simple-majority system. As expected, in the first legislative elections of the HKSAR held in May 1998, the Democratic Party won 42.87% of the vote in the direct elections, but secured only thirteen seats.[34]

Article 55 of the Basic Law states that members of the Executive Council shall be appointed by the Chief Executive from among the principal officials of the executive authorities, members of the Legislative Council, and public figures. The official interpretation of the article seemed to be that there must be members of the Legislative Council in the Executive Council, rather than that it is possible for Legislative Councillors to concurrently serve in the Executive Council. The first interpretation might not be correct, and clarification was essential. If the latter interpretation was adopted, then a separation between the Executive

---

[33] Annex II to the Basic Law: Method for the Formation of the Legislative Council of the Hong Kong Special Administrative Region and Its Voting Procedures. *Ibid.*, p. 60.

[34] For a brief report on the elections, see Frank Ching, "Are Hong Kong People Ruling Hong Kong? Implementation of the Sino-British Joint Declaration, 1997–1998," in Larry Chuen-ho Chow and Yiu-kwan Fan (eds.), *The Other Hong Kong Report 1998*, Hong Kong: The Chinese University Press, 1999, pp. 20–21.

and Legislative Councils could be introduced again, as was the case when Chris Patten arrived. It would then be easier for the Executive Council to serve as an organ for assisting the Chief Executive in policymaking, as stipulated by Article 54 of the Basic Law.[35] Incidentally, an important reason for Chris Patten to separate the Executive and Legislative Councils in 1992 was to meet the Chinese authorities' demand not to appoint Democratic Party members to the Executive Council.

If the existing interpretation was to be maintained, then certain principles had to be established, in part, to prepare for the further democratization of the Legislative Council. One model was to introduce a ministerial system. Members of the Executive Council would mainly come from a coalition of political parties commanding a majority in the Legislative Council. In this way, decisions of the Executive Council would be backed by a majority in the Legislative Council, and this would guarantee smooth passage of policies made by the Executive Council through the Legislative Council.

Besides the apparent reluctance of Beijing and the Chief Executive to implement a ministerial system at this time, the model would encounter three further difficulties. In the first place, senior civil servants might not accept the leadership of the Executive Council. They still might want to compete for the Chief Executive's ears and retain their initiatives in policymaking. Secondly, political parties might be reluctant to be part of a governing coalition, as this would have limited appeal to the electorate. They might be reluctant to have their leaders serving in the Executive Council — too, as they would then be bound by the rules of collective responsibility and confidentiality. Finally, the parties willing to form a governing coalition might not be able to cooperate and maintain a stable coalition.

If the existing arrangement was to stay, then who would be responsible for lobbying the Legislative Council to ensure that government policies would secure majority support in the Legislative Council? Senior civil

---

[35] Article 54 seats: The Executive Council of the Hong Kong Special Administrative Region shall be an organ for assisting the Chief Executive in policymaking. See *The Basic Law of the Hong Kong Special Administrative Region of the People's Republic of China*, p. 23.

servants could certainly continue performing this role, and the Chief Executive could be a very effective lobbyist. He could, like the U.S. president, invite legislators for breakfast and luncheon meetings before crucial votes on controversial issues. Legislative councilors serving in the Executive Council, however, could do better than senior civil servants in lobbying legislative councilors because, ultimately, it was a matter of bargaining between political parties and the government's executive branch. Choosing legislative councilors to serve in the Executive Council then should be based on the same criteria used in choosing public figures.

The real change would come in the longer term when directly-elected members constitute half or over half of the legislature. Under such circumstances, the Chief Executive will be like a U.S. president facing a hostile majority in the Congress. In the short term, as demonstrated by experience since July 1997, the problem seemed to be that members of the Executive Council had been very quiet in defence of government policies, and that the Chief Executive had become very exposed. At the same time, there were rumors of friction between the Executive Council and senior civil servants. The Chief Executive also appeared very keen to create high-profile advisory committees, such as the Commission on Strategic Development. In times of economic difficulties, when the government had to face many criticisms, one got the impression that the government did not have its act together.

Nevertheless, Hong Kong people still expected leadership from the government. This was natural because they largely accepted an "executive-led" system of government. Even in democracies, policy initiatives come from the executive branch of the government because it has the resources and is best equipped for policy-planning. However, the HKSAR government's policy research capability and consultative mechanisms apparently had not been strengthened to catch up with the increasing demands of the community. The blunders of the civil service often revealed its lack of a good understanding of the feelings, grievances, and expectations at the grassroots level.

For example, to enhance information technology education in the schools, the government provided many computers in 1998. The complaints from school administrators included that their schools had no room to properly install the computers; some (or many) teachers lacked the required skills; there was no money to employ technicians to manage and maintain the computers; etc. The policy of designating schools allowed to teach in English also generated much controversy, and it reflected a lack of understanding of the parents' aspirations for their children. Schools which succeeded in the screening process were perceived to be elite schools, and parents obviously wanted their children to go to the prestigious schools, thus defeating the government's objective of encouraging education in the mother tongue.

Many senior civil servants believed that criticisms from the legislature were often unfair and unnecessarily harsh. Hence, they were under pressure to better explain their policies to the public and show that they had consulted the people. Senior government officials were making considerable efforts to explain government policies to the community. However, they had to realize that there was very strong competition from some political parties whose leaders understood that had to maintain good relations with the public. Quite often, government officials were still perceived as arrogant and lacking sympathy for ordinary people; in improving relations with the community, civil servants had much to learn from the politicians.

The purpose of Hong Kong's advisory committee system was to generate useful information to improve the policymaking process. Since the introduction of direct elections to the legislature in 1991, senior civil servants had to spend probably a third of their time lobbying legislators, answering their queries, etc. They therefore tended to neglect the advisory committees. Instead of ensuring that the representative and concerned interest groups had adequate opportunities to articulate their views and challenge government policies in the drafting stage, the emphasis at this stage tended to avoid controversy.

Since advisory committee members were selected by senior civil servants, the appointments since the early 1990s had been aiming at creating consensus and avoiding controversies. After the handover, the HKSAR government obviously had to reward the pro-Beijing united front. Appointments based on this consideration further weakened the advisory committee system. A small group of trusted community leaders, each sitting on many advisory committees, would help to limit challenges to the government, but there would be very little meaningful consultation.

Investigations into the blunders concerning the opening of the new airport in July 1998 showed that the boards of directors of the Airport Authority and the Airport Authority and the Airport Consultative Committee had not been playing a very active role as representatives of the community in monitoring the airport project.[36] It appeared that the members of these two bodies had devoted only limited time to the task, that many of them did not have the relevant expertise, and that too many board members treated their memberships not as an important duty, but largely as an honour.

Hong Kong's advisory committee system must be reinvigorated by enlisting more participation from the grassroots. Members of advisory committees should be people respected by the respective policy groups dedicated to serving the territory, and their obligations should include a readiness to explain government policies to the public. If residents of Hong Kong did not believe that they had been involved in the policymaking process and that their ideas had been duly considered, naturally they would be reluctant to openly voice their endorsement of government policies. In this regard, the Housing Authority did a good job in the 1980s. In the late 1990s, its Estate Management Advisory Committee Scheme served as a model for absorbing public opinion and explaining government policies at the grassroots level.

In response to the 1966–1967 riots, the British administration started the City District Officer Scheme in 196 to enable the government's consultative network to reach the grassroots. In 1972, each City District Office set up area committees within its jurisdiction. In the following year, the government encouraged the formation of mutual aid committees in support of its Fight Crime Campaign and Clean Hong Kong Campaign. Earlier, the government had also persuaded the owners of private housing to organize owners' corporations to promote better building management and security.

---

[36] The Select Committee of the Legislative Council released its report on the investigation into the opening of the new airport on January 27, 1998. For summaries of the report and responses to it, see all major newspapers in Hong Kong on January 28, 1999. See also the *Office of the Ombudsman, Hong Kong, China, Executive Summary of the Report of the Investigation into the Commissioning and Operation of the New Airport at Chek Lap Kok*, Hong Kong: Government Printer, January 1999.

In the 1990s, the above grassroots network was much neglected by the British administration. Funding for the Home Affairs Branch (previously known as the City and New Territories Administration) was in decline. The results of this decline were amply clear — the Chief Executive admitted that Hong Kong had become dirtier and a few disastrous fires demonstrated the appalling neglect of building management.

Similar to other major cities, economic development and work pressure had exacerbated local people's sense of loneliness and alienation. In the mid-1990s, Japanese society was shocked by a story of two people who had died in their apartment, partly because they could not reach help. Their deaths were not discovered until sometime afterward. In Hong Kong, the community was shocked no more. The Social Welfare Department installed an alarm system for old people living alone.

There was obviously a considerable potential for the emergence of a new type of neighbourhood group to satisfy the acute need for emotional support in a highly competitive society. Retirees, young people who were well-educated and ready for some voluntary work, etc., formed a substantial pool of potential members ready to come together in service of their respective neighborhoods. These people were distinct from members of existing grassroots groups because they were financially better off and did not plan to seek help directly from the government. They did not intend to take an active part in politics, but they wanted meaningful interaction with the community through which they sought mutual help, emotional support, and satisfaction through service. At this time, religious organizations came closest to satisfying this demand, but there was much room for similar secular groups to develop. Most Hong Kong people believed that improvement of their living standards was their most important concern, and they relied on their own efforts to achieve that objective. However, more and more people needed emotion support outside the family, and at least some people were willing to help. It should be the government's responsibility to take the lead to help the community become organized.

The Chief Executive probably still wanted to depoliticize society and cultivate traditional values. At a practical level, Hong Kong people had to organize to manage their buildings better and maintain a clean environment. These efforts required a grassroots organizational network so that people could participate. In view of the economic difficulties and the community's grievances, the government should welcome channels through which it could have a better understanding of the mood of the community. In this way, the network could serve as an early-warning system. A more ambitious objective would be to use this organizational network to collect constructive views from the grassroots to enhance the government's policy-making process. Then there would be an alternative option for people who at this time just rang up the media criticize the government.

IV Political Parties and Political Participation

On May 24, 1998, 53.29 % of Hong Kong's registered voters, 1.49 million people, took part in the first legislative elections of the HKSAR.[37] It seemed that as usual, Hong Kong people went to vote to fulfill a civic obligation, and to choose their representatives to monitor the work of the government and to maintain the territory's checks and balances mechanisms. The government's expensive publicity campaign and the mobilization of the political parties certainly helped. Together they overcame adverse factors such as bad weather and the complexity of the electoral system.

The legislative elections were not expected to change the political landscape much because, as explained above, the electoral system was designed to provide a safe majority in support of Beijing's policy towards Hong Kong and the Chief Executive's policy programs. Further, public opinion surveys showed that voters did not believe that the elections would have much impact on the livelihood matters of most concern to them, including the economy, employment, housing and education.[38]

---

[37] For analyses of the elections, see all major newspapers in Hong Kong on May 25, 1998.
[38] Ma Ngok and Ivan Chi-keung Choy observed that economic policy issues failed to distinguish different candidates and parties. Reducing interest rates, reducing rents and public service fees, tax reduction, expanding public expenditure to create jobs, etc., were common themes of candidates from different political parties. However, few proposals aroused much debate among candidates. See Ma Ngok and Ivan CSK. Choy, "Party Competition Pattern Under the New Electoral System: A Comparison of the 1995 and 1998 Campaigns," paper presented at the Conference on Electoral Systems and the Development of Democracy, Case Studies of China, Taiwan and Hong Kong, held at the City University of Hong Kong on January 8–9, 1999, pp. 26–27.

The return of the Democratic Party and its allies to the legislature did not change the fact that they could have very little impact on the government's policy-making process. As the Tung Chee-hwa administration enjoyed the backing of a safe majority in the legislature, it did not have to lobby for the approval of the pro-democracy groups which were treated as the opposition. The Democratic Party was complaining that, as the largest political party in the legislature, there had been little meaningful consultation between the party and the government. It gradually lost interest in its regular meetings with the Chief Executive; for example, a number of Democratic Party legislators refused to participate in the meeting with Tung Chee-hwa in January 1999, as a way of demonstrating their dissatisfaction.[39]

The political situation was different from that in the Patten era. Chris Patten treated all political parties alike and formed shifting majorities in the legislature in support of his administration's various policy programs. Regarding negotiations with Beijing on the territory's future, democratic reforms, and human rights issues, Patten could count on the approval of the pro-democracy groups. Concerning general economic policies, Patten had to turn to the Liberal Party and other pro-business legislators from the functional constituencies. The current sense of political impotence on the part of the Democratic Party and the pro-democracy groups was exacerbated by Hong Kong people's improved trust in China. In general, the pro-democracy politicians were still most trusted by that segment of the Hong Kong community which found the democrats' criticisms of the Chinese authorities and the HKSAR government an important part of the checks and balances mechanisms. That was why the democrats still won handsomely in the May 1998 legislative elections. But attacking the Chinese authorities' infringements of the community's freedoms and human rights had become less attractive to voters as before. The most important concerns of Hong Kong people were obviously the economy and unemployment, and the Democratic Party as well as other pro-democracy groups were not perceived to have much to offer.[40]

---

[39] *Ming Pao*, January 11, 1999.

[40] The results of an opinion survey among young people (16–25 years of age) released in late June 1998 indicated that 61.6% of the respondents considered the economy to be the priority of the elected legislature, and 36% of the respondents considered employment to be the most pressing matter. Moreover, about 70% of the respondents did not trust the legislators. *Ibid.*, June 29, 1998.

Under such circumstances, the "young Turks" of the Democratic Party felt frustrated and attempted to challenge the leadership in December 1998. It appeared that intra-party differences were concentrated on three issues: (1) the party's relationship with the Chinese authorities and the HKSAR government; (2) whether the party should attempt to aggregate class interests or to articulate more distinctively labour interests; and (3) whether the party should try to secure change by working within the legislative system, or resort to mass movements outside the political establishment.[41] The "young Turks" and the non-mainstream factions were opposed to efforts to improve relations with the Chinese authorities by means such as presenting candidates to compete for seats in China's National People's Congress. They were not interested in a better relationship with the HKSAR government and publicly called for the resignation of Tung Chee-hwa. Regarding the party's policy platform, they warned the party leadership against opportunism in attempting to represent the interests of all classes. In turn, they were accused of trying to turn the party into a labour party and adopting a populist approach. Above all else, the "young Turks" and the non-mainstream factions appealed for a return to the grassroots to mobilize the masses instead of engaging in futile parliamentary politics. Naturally, there was some dissatisfaction with the over-concentration of power in the leadership and the inadequate attention paid to the interests of the younger generation of politicians who were about to be directly affected by the government's plan to abolish the elected Urban and Regional Councils.

The challenge was launched in the elections of the Democratic Party leadership in mid-December 1998. The "young Turks" and the non-mainstream factions won nine seats in the twenty-five-seat central committee, an increase of seven. They also supported Lau Chin-shek's election as a new party vice-chairman, who defeated the incumbent, Anthony Cheung Bing-leung.[42] Differences within the party were subsequently patched over and a split was avoided.

---

[41] See Ivan Chi-keung Choy, "Shuangyue Zhengbian — Minzhudang Feizhuliupai de Fanpu (A Coup in the Frosty Month — Counter-attact by the non-mainstream Factions of the Democratic Party)", *ibid.*, December 16, 1998.

[42] Ibid., December 14, 1998.

The episode, nonetheless, highlighted many important issues in the development of political parties in Hong Kong. Despite its spectacular electoral victories, the Democratic Party failed to expand its membership in a significant way. It probably did not have more than six hundred members, of whom about one-third remained active. In view of its limited resources, it was preoccupied with parliamentary politics and elections, and it had not made much progress in institutionalization. The party's systems and procedures were not well established, and because of the work pressure, a small number of parliamentary leaders had to make decisions within a short period of time. Hence, accountability to the general membership, internal transparency, and internal democracy had not been well developed.

Since the handover, the Chinese authorities were largely perceived by Hong Kong's public to have been observing a strict non-interference policy towards the region. Consequently, Sino-British confrontation and the contradictions between Beijing and Hong Kong had lost considerable significance. Naturally, Beijing's tolerance and non-interference policies were based on the fact that it was in full control of the situation. In his first policy speech, the Chief Executive indicated that housing, education, and services for the elderly were his policy priorities. It seemed that these were the policy priorities of the community too. However, the Democratic Party was not in a position to respond, and it had not shown significant initiatives in presenting Hong Kong people with well-researched policy alternatives. In sum, it failed to demonstrate, from the perspective of policy platform, how it could perform the role of an effective and constructive opposition. The alternative advocated by the "young Turks" and the non-mainstream factions probably was not viable. Hong Kong people desired stability and they feared mobilization in the form of protests and demonstrations.

To attract the media's attention, Democratic Party legislators usually had to dramatize their gestures and statements. A harsh criticism of Beijing obviously had a better chance of making headlines in the newspapers than a balanced statement. The party's success with the media, however, made it very difficult for its leaders to establish a dialogue of mutual trust with senior civil servants. It also offered convenient excuses to the Chinese officials for rejecting any contact with the party. Such political posturing often had a negative impact on the intelligentsia's support for the party.

The Democratic Party at this time encountered difficulties too in its relationship with grassroots community organizations which emerged and developed in the late 1960s and 1970s and which had been supporting the pro-democracy political groups. The Democratic Party certainly could help to raise issues of importance to grassroots community organizations in the legislature or with senior government officials, thus exerting pressure on the administration to develop solutions. But, the party's high profile and eagerness for publicity often resulted in failures to compromise and delays in achieving settlements. Many grassroots community organizations worried that they might be taken for a ride, and they often preferred to act without the involvement of political parties. After all, grassroots community organizations were issue-oriented; they wanted concrete solutions to their problems. Further, the introduction of proportional representation in the direct elections to the legislature in 1998 and the split in the pro-democracy camp exerted pressure grassroots community organizations camp had exerted pressure on grassroots community organizations to take sides. They were eagerly courted by the pro-Beijing political groups. The Democratic Party understood the problems, but its options were limited.

The Hong Kong Association for Democracy and People's Livelihood failed to secure any seats in the legislative elections in May 1998; in contrast, The Frontier won three seats. The electoral results appeared to indicate that staunch critics of Beijing and the HKSAR government maintained a strong appeal to the electorate. With the dissolution of the Urban and Regional Councils, it was difficult for the Hong Kong Association for Democracy and People's Livelihood to secure enough resources to function as an effective political group. Meanwhile, The Frontier attempted to transform itself into a formal political party in January 1999, but its members did not show enthusiastic support.[43] Similar to the Democratic Party, electoral success had not led to significant expansion in membership.

---

[43] *South China Morning Post*, January 18, 1999.

Two of the three political groups in support of the Tung Chee-hwa administration in the legislature, i.e., the Liberal and the Hong Kong Progressive Alliance, failed to win any seats in the direct elections in 1998. This cast doubt on what could be achieved in the review of the legislature's electoral system in 2007. The community anticipated that the review would lead to a higher proportion of directly elected seats, and the pro-democracy groups would demand that the entire legislature be elected by universal suffrage. However, there was a catch — changing the electoral system would require the endorsement of two-thirds of all legislators and the consent of the Chief Executive.[44]

It was difficult to imagine why members returned by functional constituencies would support an increase in directly-elected seats at the expense of functional-constituency seats. If the legislature maintained its existing size, which functional constituencies would be abolished, and according to what criteria? A less controversial way to increase the proportion of directly-elected seats in the review in 2007 would be to expand the size of the legislature to 90 seats, and increase the number of directly-elected seats to sixty. Political parties would find it easier to agree on this, and a two-thirds majority in the legislature to support the change would be possible. The pro-democracy groups would have to wait for the next review to achieve their objective of having the entire legislature elected by direct elections. In view of the conservatism of the business community in the territory, the above scenario was probably too idealistic.

Immediately after the legislative elections in May 1998, the Democratic Party and The Frontier, taking advantage of the unexpectedly high voter turnout rate and the pro-democracy camp's electoral success, demanded direct elections of the entire legislature and the Chief Executive in the near future.[45] However, the demand failed to attract support and attention, and it quietly faded away in a matter of two to three days. This reluctance on the part of Hong Kong people to demand democratic reforms and to struggle hard to realize such a goal remained the most formidable obstacle to further democratization.

---

[44] See Annex II to the Basic Law.

[45] See all major newspapers in Hong Kong on May 25 and 26, 1998.

V Conclusion

Hong Kong people's perception of the observance of a policy of non-interference by the Chinese authorities and the sharp deterioration of the Hong Kong economy had altered the community's priorities. Most people were less concerned with political issues, and the mass media also devoted fewer resources to in-depth political reporting as they had become predominantly profit-oriented. The high voter turnout rate in the May 1998 legislative elections was a mere pleasant surprise.

The executive-led system of government and the electoral arrangements further restricted the pro-democracy political parties. They did not respond to the new challenges effectively; and in the new political environment, differences suppressed during the transitional period had re-emerged and assumed greater significance. While being reduced to opposition parties, the pro-democracy parties had been behaving remarkably well in the legislature, and they had shunned the kinds of tactics adopted by the opposition parties in Japan, South Korea, and Taiwan when faced with a governing party or governing coalition controlling a safe majority in the legislature. While the new political system, as defined by the Basic Law, had begun to function since the handover, the legislature and the political parties had been ineffective and reluctant to exploit opportunities to establish new precedents and conventions to expand the legislature's role and enhance the check and balance mechanisms *vis-à-vis* executive branch of government. The political culture which shuns confrontation and accords priority to stability and prosperity had been an important limiting factor.

While the HKSAR government had not been seriously challenged by the opposition parties which were severely handicapped by the constitutional arrangements and the electoral system, its legitimacy and its prestige had been in decline since the territory's return to China. The economic difficulties had been an important factor, and the community was dissatisfied with the lack of leadership in handling Hong Kong's economic problems. The series of blunders committed by the civil service naturally damaged the public's confidence too. According to an opinion survey in a series released after Tung Chee-hwa's second policy speech in October 1998, Hong Kong people's political confidence fell to a low of 83 points, only one point higher than the low level reached during the Tiananmen Incident. About 50% of the respondents believed that the proposals presented in the policy speech were "entirely ineffective" or "largely ineffective" in resolving the territory's economic problems. In another poll held at the same time, the HKSAR government only scored 4.6 out of 10 in an assessment of its administrative competence.[46] A similar survey in the same period showed that 24.5% of the respondents were satisfied with the performance of the HKSAR government, while 32.8% were dissatisfied. Regarding Tung Chee-hwa, the same survey revealed that 23.4% of the respondents were satisfied with his performance, and 34% were dissatisfied. Tung's scores were far behind those of Zhu Rongji and Jiang Zemin, and were only ahead of those of Li Peng.[47]

Since October 1998, Hong Kong's economy had improved and so had people's political and economic confidence and their assessments of the HKSAR government and Tung Chee-hwa. But the media and many academics still spoke of a crisis in the administration. When the Singaporean government considerably reduced the wage level of the labour force in the island republic at the end of 1998, many people in Hong Kong lamented that the Tung Chee-hwa administration would not have the political support and political will to do so.

The expanding gap between people's expectations of leadership from the government and their disappointment with its performance exacerbated their dissatisfaction. Meanwhile, the economic difficulties, the restructuring of the economy, and the widening gap between the rich and poor exerted further pressure on the government. There was considerable concern that rising unemployment and the widening gap between the rich and poor would become sources of social unrest. Hong Kong's unemployment rate rose to 6% in the December 1998–February 1999 quarter, and many economists expected that it would probably

---

[46] *Ming Pao.* October 19, 1998.

[47] In comparison, 66.5%, 50.4%, and 10.3% of the respondents were satisfied with the respective performances of Zhu Rongji, Jiang Zemin, and Li Peng; 3.3%, 8.5%, and 42.9% of the respondents were dissatisfied with the respective performances of Zhu, Jiang and Li. See *ibid.*, October 22, 1998.

reach 7% or so before it would come down slowly.[48] According to a study by the United Nations and the World Bank, Hong Kong ranked 79th among 93 countries or regions in efforts to eliminate the disparities between the rich and poor. In 1996, the Gini coefficient of Hong Kong reached 0.518, which was higher than that of Malaysia, Thailand, the Philippines, and China. The economic difficulties in 1997–1998 probably had exacerbated the situation. The territory's adult illiteracy rate was 8%, which reflected that Hong Kong's uneducated and unskilled labor force remained substantial and increasingly find it difficult to secure employment.[49]

The situation was not yet an explosive one. Hong Kong people understood that it was important to maintain social stability so that the territory would continue to attract investors. However, many people were unhappy and frustrated, and they easily blamed the Government for their problems. On its part, the HKSAR government should intervene more in the economy because of the recession and should define long-term social service strategies which had long been neglected. It, therefore, badly needed strong support from the community, but its task had become all the more difficult because of the people's declining trust and respect for it. All parties concerned realized that an effective HKSAR Government was a prerequisite for Beijing to maintain its non-interference policy concerning Hong Kong.

Acknowledgement

Originally appeared as Cheng, Joseph Y.S., "Political Changes since the Establishment of Hong Kong Special Administrative Region, 1997–1999", *American Asian Review*, Vol. XVII, No. 4, Winter, 1999, pp. 77–113. Ceased publication.

---

[48] *Ibid.*, March 16, 1999.
[49] *Ibid.*, October 17, 1998.

Chapter 11

Administrative Performance and the 2000 LegCo Elections

I The Emergence of Discontent

According to an official survey released in late July 2000, only one in five Hong Kong residents were happy with the performance of the Hong Kong Special Administrative Region (HKSAR) government. Three-fifths of the respondents were dissatisfied with the government, while the remaining one-fifth had no opinion.[1] With an economic growth rate of over 14 % in the first quarter of the year, it was at first sight difficult to explain this record high level of dissatisfaction with the government.

To be fair to the C.H. Tung administration, since 1982 or so, the colonial government had been preoccupied with negotiation with Beijing, and it had lost the political will to push for necessary domestic reforms. The abandonment of the central provident fund in the early 1990s was a significant example. This naturally meant that, after the handover, major reforms were needed in almost every important policy area.

The globalization process and the information technology age had broadened the gap between the rich and poor. The lower socioeconomic strata had been suffering from a decline in real incomes because of a surplus of unskilled labor, and middle-class professionals for the first time in their life often encountered the threat of unemployment. Even if they

---

[1] The poll was one of the series carried out every two months by the Home Affairs Department; see: *South China Morning Post,* July 29, 2000.

did not, they might have to worry about their children. Many of them also felt the pressure of coping with the challenges of the times. Most Hong Kong people already worked very long hours; the drive by the turn of the century to enhance efficiency might well mean a workload too heavy for them. Surveys revealed that many people did not have enough time for their children. The threat of downsizing and the associated deterioration in office politics contributed to the "feel bad" factor too.

Despite the talk of economic recovery on the part of the government, many people had not felt its benefits yet, and they tended to blame the government for the lack of strategy to ensure Hong Kong's prosperity in the future. The above-mentioned survey also revealed that 39% of the respondents indicated that they had little confidence that the HKSAR would continue to be prosperous and stable, the highest figure since 1996. At the same time, the Hong Kong Council of Social Service stated in its annual submission to the Chief Executive that in the past four years the income of the lowest-earning 20% of the population had decreased by 27.7%, while that of the highest-earning 20% had increased by 4.2%. The Council's director, Hui Yin-fat, warned that the worsening income disparity would generate social instability.[2]

The government, however, could not escape responsibility for not managing its reforms well. Each set of reforms appeared logical and necessary; but each set of reforms also challenged a group of vested interests, for example in the civil service and in the teaching profession. When many reform programs were implemented simultaneously in many sectors, cumulative grievances might be too much for the government to handle. It also appeared that the broad programmes of reform in the civil service, in education, etc., were initially supported by the community, but when it came to concrete policy proposals, resistance gradually grew. In this connection, the officials involved might not have done sufficient preparatory work.

With respect to language tests for teachers, for example, there was obviously inadequate consultation with the teachers concerned as well as with their trade unions, and the teachers did not consider that the officials had a good understanding of the issues. Under such circumstances,

---

[2] *Ibid*, July 20, 2000.

officials who did not enjoy the trust and respect of their clients would only find their work all the more difficult. Unfortunately, this became an increasingly common phenomenon.

II Problems with the Civil Service

In view of the many civil service blunders since the handover, from the handling of the chicken-flu crisis and the chaos at the opening of the new airport at Chek Lap Kok, to the series of public housing construction scandals, many Hong Kong people were asking where their civil service had gone wrong. The community was aware that it had basically the same civil servants at the time as before the handover, and so it found it difficult to understand why their performance had deteriorated so sharply.

To some extent, the deterioration was exacerbated by a change of mood. Before the handover, Hong Kong people wanted continuity and morale to be maintained in the civil service to ensure a smooth transfer of power. At that time, the community was eager to agree with the former Governor Chris Patten that Hong Kong's civil servants were among the best in the world. However, at this stage, people were more inclined to blame them for the HKSAR's problems and to demand punishment for those civil servants who had failed to achieve results.

Instead of focusing on individuals, a review of the entire civil services system was necessary. Changes regularly took place in the U.S. civil service and the advantage of this was that talented people were constantly recruited from various sectors. In Hong Kong, the civil service was a closed system, where administrative officers were generalists who joined the civil service after graduation. As the policymaking process became more complicated and demanded more expertise, it was doubtful whether a team of generalists could lead competently and generated confidence. Many in the financial sector were not impressed by the senior civil servants' handling of the Asian financial crisis, and some senior civil servants obviously displayed a lack of competence. It was also suggested that an expert should have been recruited from outside the civil service to head the relatively new Information Technology and Broadcasting Branch.

Despite many similarities, not least of which was their common sense of professionalism, Hong Kong's civil services differed from Japan's in one important way. An administrative officer in Japan was assigned to a ministry and stayed there for his entire career. This ensured that administrative officers knew their policy areas well, but it also created close ties between senior civil servants and their clients. There was no need for Hong Kong to imitate Japan in this respect, but the rapid transfer of senior civil servants did not contribute to credibility. Senior civil servants needed time to become familiar with their portfolios, and to establish ties with their clients. The departure of expatriates and some senior civil servants shortly before 1997 made transfers more frequent than desirable. Perhaps it should be decided that senior civil servants stayed in their posts for at least three years.

Although Hong Kong's civil servants tried to remain neutral, this could sometimes be difficult. Their working style normally allowed few opportunities for them to interact closely with different sectors of the society. This was appropriate in the United Kingdom (U.K.) because policies were made by the ruling political party. Accountability was assured because political parties had face elections. In Hong Kong, it was difficult to enforce the accountability of the civil service to the public. Senior civil servants were not neutral politically because they made policies. One of the questions raised by the international media in the wake of the air cargo crisis at Chek Lap Kok was why no senior civil servants accepted responsibility and resigned. They noted that in Japan, South Korea, and Taiwan, concerned officials had resigned after serious air traffic accidents. Gradually, Hong Kong people also raised similar questions, and the political parties in the legislature finally passed a no-confidence motion on the chairperson of the Hong Kong Housing Authority, Rosanna Wong Yick-ming, and the head of the Housing Department, Tony Miller, on June 28, 2000, regarding the then public housing construction scandals.[3] Anticipating the voting outcome, Rosanna Wong had earlier resigned.

III A Ministerial System for Hong Kong?

Dissatisfaction with the civil service attracted some discussion on the possible introduction of a ministerial system. Theoretically, if a political

---

[3] See all major newspaper in Hong Kong on June 29, 2000.

party or coalition of political parties can control a majority in the legislature, it can dictate policies to the executive branch of government and can demand to control the appointments of at least some senior civil service positions. This concept of government, however, was against the principle of "executive-led government" advocated by the Chinese leadership.

Hence the pro-China and pro-HKSAR government political parties, i.e., the Liberal Party, the Democratic Alliance for the Betterment of Hong Kong (DAB) and the Hong Kong Progressive Alliance, as well as the independents of similar political orientation, who together constitute a safe majority in the legislature in support of the Chief Executive, had no intention of demanding a ministerial system because it was not favoured by C.H. Tung nor by the top civil servants. The pro-democracy political groups were not paying much attention to the issue at this stage because they understood that, without substantial electoral reforms, they would not be in a position to secure a majority of seats in the legislature.

If by a ministerial system, one simply referred to the recruitment of talents from outside the civil service to fill positions at the secretary level, then C.H. Tung had already appointed Elsie Leung as Secretary for Justice, Edgar Cheng as head of the Central Policy Unit, and Dr. Yeoh Eng-kiong as Secretary for Health and Welfare. There were precedents for such appointments in the British administration, where appointing a small number of senior civil servants from the private sector was an established practice. The crucial issue was a matter of scale.

At the same time, rumours circulated that the Chief Executive did not trust his senior civil servants and that the community wanted the resignation of a few civil servants at the secretary level. Indeed, a vote of no confidence against the Secretary for Justice was defeated only narrowly in March 1999 after intense lobbying by the Chief Executive. Replacing a number of top officials with outsiders might be controversial and damaging to the morale of the civil service. Nonetheless, there was considerable support for such a move because it would enhance the accountability of senior civil servants, weed out a small number of them who was incompetent or unpopular in the eyes of the public, improve the image of C.H. Tung as a decisive and strong leader, and ensure that he had his own team in the government instead of inheriting some administrators who were groomed by Chris Patten.

Soon after his election as Chief Executive and his appointment of his future Executive Council, C.H. Ting informed the public that three of the Executive Councillors, Antony Leung, Leung Chun-ying and Tam yiu-chung, would be given special policy responsibilities in education, housing and services for the elderly, three policy areas which Tung later identified as his priorities in his first policy speech.[4] There was considerable speculation then on the relationship between the three Executive Councillors and the respective policy secretaries, and whether all Executive Councillors would eventually be given policy portfolios covering all the policy branches in the government. Within a year or so of the handover, it had become clear that Executive Councillors had not become super-secretaries; in fact, no more Executive Councillors were given specific policy portfolios.

The very heavy responsibilities of the three Executive Councillors outside the Council meant that they were in a highly handicapped position to compete with the respective policy secretaries for control of the policy-making process. Policy secretaries enjoyed the full backing of the civil service which controlled access to information and other resources essential to policy-making. The three Executive Councillors apparently had to count on their own resources. Indeed, since the handover, Executive Councillors were often criticized for adopting too low a profile, and for rarely being available to defend government policies. In sum, they were not perceived to be very influential or to have contributed much to the HKSAR government's handling of its many challenges. However, constitutionally, the Chief Executive could strengthen the role of his Executive Council and transform it into his cabinet, like that of the U.S. President.

Another option for managing the civil service, which could be introduced at the stage without encountering substantial opposition, would be to offer contracts to top civil servants following the Australian model. Civil servants believed that they were underpaid compared with their counterparts in the private sector. The contract system could offer them substantially higher salaries, while breaking the "iron rice-bowl", i.e., contracts might not be renewed. Top civil servants would be given the

---

[4] For the text of C.H. Tung's first policy speech, see all major newspapers in Hong Kong on October 9, 1997.

option to hold on to their tenure or to opt for contracts; therefore, they would not have grounds for complaint. Those who were 55 years of age or above would not lose much by opting for initial contracts of three to five years. Such arrangements, it could be hoped, would change the culture, at least at the top echelons of the civil service, and further justify the gradual implementation of the contract system throughout the civil service. Top civil servants would be more accountable, and the Chief Executive would have a better chance of forming his own team.

In the first days of the millennium, DAB chairman Tsang Yok-sing warned Hong Kong people that the government would gradually fall into the hands of mediocre people in the absence of political reforms. Tsang appealed to the Chief Executive to reform the relationship between the executive and legislative branches of the government, and he proposed that the major parties in the legislature should form a coalition to nominate the candidate for the Chief Executive. At the same time, he advocated a ministerial system involving political parties, i.e., the Chief Executive would recruit his principal officials from the political parties supporting him. Tsang, however, admitted that his proposals could not be implemented in the foreseeable future.[5]

The general speculation was that Tsang's proposal was an attempt to articulate the DAB's frustration generated by its difficult position. The HKSAR government expected the party to support its policy programmes, but the party did not feel that it had been fully consulted or had adequate inputs in the policymaking process. Sometimes support for the government's policies could be quite unpopular and costly in terms of voters' support. The DAB was acutely aware that its criticisms of the government, accompanied by consistent delivery of its votes in support of the Ting administration in the legislature, was eroding its credibility in the eyes of the electorate. The local political culture expected political parties to assume the role of the opposition constituting part of the checks and balances mechanisms. Political parties therefore dared not identify too closely with the government. The limited role of the pro-democracy groups and the pro-government parties in the political process meant that all political parties had serious difficulties in political recruitment.

---

[5] *Ming Pao*, January 3, 2000.

At the same time, senior government officials increasingly found their position untenable, and were tempted to leave for more lucrative positions in public sector corporations or in the private sector. Since there was no government party, they had to lobby hard for legislators' support, and they had to bear with severe criticisms in the legislature from opposition as well as pro-government legislator who were eager to secure media attention. They often felt humiliated, not only because they had to be polite to most legislators, despite their sometimes unreasonable criticisms, so as to retain their goodwill to facilitate future lobbying efforts. That was why Tsang Yok-sing lamented that talented people in Hong Kong would not find senior positions in the civil service nor seats in the legislature attractive.

It was not likely, however, that the Chinese leadership would allow the political parties to usurp the power of appointing principal officials from the Chief Executive, as this was perceived to be a violation of the principle of an "executive-led" system of government. While there was considerable frustration on the part of senior government officials and the pro-government political parties, the HKSAR government still enjoyed a safe majority support in the legislature and there was no danger of a constitutional or political crisis. So those who held power had no incentive to reform.

In theory, the C.H. Tung administration could allow the pro-government political parties to introduce important bills in the legislature, so that they could win credit for supporting the government and could claim to have delivered to the electorate. This was less a challenge to the "executive-led" system of government because the Chief Executive had full power to control the introduction of bills by members of the legislature. Introducing a contract system for principal government officials might serve to enhance their accountability to the legislature and the public, because the Chief Executive could refuse to renew their contracts or even terminate their contracts early if their performance were unsatisfactory. It would also strengthen the Chief Executive's hand over the senior civil servants. But admittedly these measures would not solve the basic problems in the existing system. Meanwhile, C.H. Tung had clearly stated that he would not consider the adoption of a "ministerial system" at this stage.

As explained earlier, the relationship between the administration and the legislature was unsatisfactory, and resulted in frustration and dissatisfaction among senior civil servants, legislature was unsatisfactory, and resulted in frustration and dissatisfaction among senior civil servants, legislators and the general public. On the eve of the legislative elections in September 2000, some journalists secretly hoped that the two radical candidates, Tsang Kin-shing (Independent, Hong Kong Island) and Leung Kowk-hung (April 5 Action, New Territories East), would win, as they had pledged to shock the legislature with physical action.

It was suggested that "the administration has power but no votes, and the parties/legislators have votes but no power". This was a political myth far from reality. The Chief Executive belonged to no political party, and no legislator had an obligation to support the administration. Tam Yiu-chung, who was appointed to the Executive Council, was perhaps the only exception. Yet the administration enjoyed a safe majority support in the legislature. The administration's supporters in the legislature accepted Beijing's policy towards Hong Kong, the "executive-led" system of government and the Chief Executive's policy programmes. Theoretically, the administration, had to arrive at an agreement with this loose majority coalition in the legislature, spelling out the privileges and obligations of the latter. It seemed, however, that these legislators were willing to support the administration without demanding much in return.

DAB chairman Tsang Yok-sing's complaints about the executive-legislature relationship mentioned above were both significant and puzzling. Since the Tung administration could not function without a safe majority support in the legislature, the DAB, together with the Hong Kong Progressive Alliance and the Liberal Party, could almost dictate their policies to the administration and even had a strong say on the appointment of the principal officials. Even if an adequate consensus did not exist among the three parties, DAB alone still carried a lot of weight. If it threatened to withdraw its support for the Tung administration and switch to the opposition, it would certainly manage to extract important concessions. So, obviously it was not true that legislators had votes but no power. The truth was that the safe majority in the legislature backing the Ting administration did not have the political will to challenge the "executive-led" system of government because it did not dare to antagonize Beijing.

IV Preparing Public Opinion

The record turnout of 53% of voters in the 1998 legislative elections was probably a pleasant surprise to all.[6] Experts had earlier predicted a voter turnout rate of 30%–35%. Based on past experience, most Hong Kong voters went to vote to fulfill their civic obligation and to choose a critic to monitor the work of the government, but the legislature formed a most important part of the checks and balances mechanisms in the territory. Despite the fact that the Basic Law provided for a strong executive-led system of government and limited the legislature's powers,[7] the government could not get new laws passed and could not get money to implement its policy programmes without the consent of the legislature. These are the two most important powers of all legislatures in democratic countries, and the HKSAR's legislature has such powers at its disposal. A useful function of the legislature is to focus on policy issues. A small, dedicated opposition can effectively influence the government's agenda if it succeeds in securing the community's attention and the support of public opinion.

In the past, many Hong Kong people voted for staunch critics of Beijing and the Hong Kong government. They also supported an acceleration of the pace of democratization. Such values favoured the pro-democracy camp. By the turn of the century, it seemed that the community had been reasonably assured of Beijing's non-interference policy; and it realized that it would be difficult to push for democratic reforms before 2007. To generate support for electoral reforms, political parties in the territory had to demonstrate that they were ready to govern, and not just limit themselves to the roles of opposition and critic. Yet, in the 1998 election campaign, the community perceived that Hong Kong's political parties had similar platforms in elections. Moreover, they tended to make promises of service rather present concrete policy proposals. The two major parties in Hong Kong, the Democratic Party and the DAB, had a

---

[6] For a brief analysis of the 1998 legislative elections, see Ma Ngok and Chou Chi-keung, "The evolution of the electoral system and party politics in Hong Kong", *Issues and Studies*, Vol. 3, No.1, January/February 1999, pp. 188–193.

[7] See Joseph Y.S. Cheng, "The Basic Law: Messages for Hong Kong people", in *The Other Hong Kong Report*, edited by Richard Y.C. Wong and Joseph Y.S. Cheng, *1990*, Hong Kong; The Chinese University Press, pp. 29–63.

considerable number of teachers among their members and some of them had become members of the Legislative Council and District Councils. Obviously, education was an issue of major concern to the public, yet neither party seemed to have a comprehensive policy proposal on education to offer, leaving the concerned public unaware of their stance on the territory's education policy.

Hong Kong people were most concerned with employment and the economy, but the understood that they could not expect much from the political parties in these areas. While the community was unhappy with the performance of the Tung administration, public opinions surveys showed that such dissatisfaction had spread to cover almost all political parties too. Hence some radical candidates perceived an opportunity in exploiting anti-establishment sentiment and offered themselves as candidates. It appeared that such anti-establishment sentiment also existed in the normally conservative functional constituencies. Incumbents with long years of service and excellent connections with the government were challenged by candidates who tend to be more critical of the government. Some of these candidates had taken part in the earlier Election Committee elections, and had secured satisfactory levels of support.[8]

In general, the electoral system was designed to ensure a majority support in the legislature for the executive branch of the government. It was therefore not expected that there would be significant changes in the balance of political forces after the September 2000 elections. Political observers, for example, had predicted the Democratic Party to lose one seat and the DAB to win two more seats before the latter became tainted by the conflict-of-interest scandal of its vice-chairman, Gary Cheng. In the direct elections, because of the proportional representation system based on party slates of candidates, competition was largely focused on the last one or two seats in each constituency. But because of the following factors, there was keener competition in the direct elections. In the first place, the increase in the number of directly-elected seats from 20 to 24 attracted a considerable number of new candidates, including those who wanted to exploit the anti-establishment sentiment. The Hong Kong

---

[8] For an analysis of the Election Committee elections, see all major newspapers in Hong Kong on July 10 and 11, 2000.

Island and New Territories East constituencies were good examples, and radical candidates eroded the support for the Democratic Party to some extent. The abolition of the Municipal Councils led a few of their former members to join the Legislative Council race. The Democratic Party was in a difficult position, with some members departing to contest as independents. In order to maximize e number of seats won, the Democratic Party presented more than one list of in the two Territories constituencies. It was a test of party loyalty and party organization to arrange optimal electoral support for separate lists of candidates, and there was a danger that a decline in electoral support coupled with bad organization might lead to unexpected losses.

Again, it was not expected that the Liberal Party could win a seat in the direct elections. Two incumbent legislators from the Hong Kong Progressive Alliance contested the direct elections under the banner of other political groups. Paradoxically, while the prospects of the Hong Kong Progressive Alliance as a viable political party in the legislature were in doubt, its performance was the best among all political parties in the July 2000 Election Committee elections.[9] If the two major political parties in the coalition which provided the majority support in the legislature for the Tung administration could not prove themselves in direct elections, would they support democratic reforms after 2007? After all, the proposed changes to the electoral system then would require a two-thirds majority endorsement by the legislature and the consent of the Chief Executive.

V The Legislative Elections of September 2000

It was estimated that about 4.5 million people in Hong Kong would be qualified voters in the 2000 elections: of these, 67% of 3.05 million were registered.[10] The voter turnout rate in the legislative elections in 2000 was

---

[9] The Hong Kong Progressive Alliance won 64 seats in the Election Committee elections. See *Ming Pao*, July 11, 2000.

[10] This information was based on interviews and discussions by the author with academics and journalists engaged respectively in research and reporting on the September 2000 elections.

43.6 %, 9.7% lower than in the 1998 legislative elections. But it was still higher than 35.8 % in 1995 and 39% in 1991.[11] It might be that the voter turnout rate was exceptionally high in 1998. They were the first to be held since the handover, and there was substantial community resentment against the Provisional Legislative Council. In the September 2000 elections, some people might have been put off because souvenirs were offered to voters, and bad weather might have kept people at home in 2000 watching television. These factors might all have contributed to lower voter turnout than in 1998. Most analysts attributed the decline in the voter turnout rate in 2000 to disappointment with the "powerless" legislature, dissatisfaction with the performance of the political parties and politicians, and the smear campaign tactics in the elections.

The design of the electoral system was such that the major parties were not expected to win or lose more than two seats over their 1998 performance. In the end, the Democratic Party won 13 seats (one less than in 1998), the DAB secured 11 seats (one more than 1998), the Liberal Party eight, and the Hong Kong Progressive Alliance four, losing two seats and one seat respectively. A number of small political groups also managed to win seats — the Frontier two, the Confederation of Trade Unions two, and one seat each went to the Association for Democracy and People's Livelihood, the Neighbourhood and Workers' Service Centre, the Federation of Trade Unions, the Federation of Hong Kong and Kowloon Labour Unions, and New Century Forum. The remaining 16 seats went to independents.

There were not many faces returned by the 30 functional constituencies; in fact nine incumbents were re-elected with no challenge. Among incumbents seeking re-election, only Fung Chi-kin (Financial Services) and Edward Ho Sing-tin (Architectural, Surveying and Planning) lost. Keen competition took place in the Medical and Health Services functional constituencies because the departure of the incumbents attracted a number of candidates of comparable strength. At the same time, the DAB worked hard to win more seats in the functional constituencies. Its success was limited as it won only one extra seat in the

---

[11] For an analysis of the legislative elections on September 10, 2000, see all major newspapers in Hong Kong on September 11 and 12, 2000.

newly-created District Council functional constituency, but the attempted would likely be repeated in the future as the party would continue to strive to become the largest party in the legislature and eventually the governing party in the HKSAR. Similarly, in the Election Committee six incumbents were returned out of the ten elected in 1998.

Just before the election, it was revealed that Gary Cheng, a vice-chairman of the DAB, was alleged to have passed on a classified document obtained from the government in his capacity as a legislator to a public-relations firm, and that he might have involved in cases of conflict of interest while operating two consultancy firms engaged in advising major business corporations on their public-relations strategies. The scandal was a major blow to the DAB, and initial opinion surveys indicated a sharp decline in support for the party. As shown in Table 11.1, however, the

Table 11.1: Votes Won by the Democratic Party (DP) and the Democratic Alliance for the Betterment of Hong Kong (DAB) in the 1998 and 2000 Legislative Elections (by Geographical Constituencies)

DP	No. of Votes Won in 1998	No. of Votes Won in 2000	Comparing the 2000 Results with those in 1998 (in no. of votes)	Comparing the 2000 Results with those in 1998 (in percent of votes)
Hong Kong Island	143,843	92,074	−51,769	−36.0
Kowloon West	113,079	73,540	−39,539	−35.0
Kowloon East	145,986	103,863	−42,123	−28.9
New Territories West	147,098	117,733	−29,365	−20.0
New Territories East	84,629	75,213	−9,416	−11.1
Total	634,635	462,423	−172,212	−27.1
DAB				
Hong Kong Island	90,182	72,617	−17,565	−19.5
Kowloon West	44,632	41,942	−2,690	−6.0
Kowloon East	109,296	108,587	−709	−0.6
New Territories West	98,492*	101,629	+3,137	+3.2
New Territories East	56,731	66,943	+10,212	+18.0
Total	399,333	391,718	−7,615	−2.0

Note: * DAB votes plus rural votes.
Source: *Ming Pao* (a Hong Kong Chinses newspaper), September 14, 2000

DAB in fact did remarkably well in the elections despite the scandal. While the voter turnout rate declined from 53.3% in 1998 to 43.6% in 2000, the number of votes secured by the DAB dropped by only 2%.

The DAB's satisfactory performance reflected the success of its services at the grassroots level. It was the strongest party in terms of financial and manpower resources, and it deployed its resources effectively to establish an extensive grassroots network of support. Its supporters responded to the party's mobilization because they were grateful for the services it provided, and because they identified with its emphasis on stability and prosperity. Since the handover, its pro-Beijing stand had not been a political liability. Indeed, its close relationship with Beijing and the HKSAR government enabled it to reward its supporters with honours and important appointments. The decline in the voter turnout rate and the dispersal of votes among independents also increased the relative weight of the DAB's committed supporters in the vote count.

On the other hand, the Democratic Party lost 27.1% of the votes it won in 1998. Its stance, critical of the Chinese leadership, was losing its appeal as the community was no longer worried about interference from Beijing. The local People's Liberation Army garrison was well received Hong Kong people.[12] Moreover, its strong advocacy of democracy was less because most Hong Kong people did not expect major political reforms or further democratization before 2007. The party was also troubled by internal disagreements. The "young Turks" criticized the party leadership for concentrating too much on parliamentary work and neglecting the mobilization of the masses. Although their earlier challenges had failed, they were proven correct to some extent this time by the election results. Further, some of them left the party and stood as independents, thus eroding support for the Democratic Party.

The Party's relationship with other pro-democracy groups was not amicable either. Above all, the party failed in its policy research, and was not able to offer constructive policy alternatives to the policy initiatives of the government. The community, especially the well-educated, gradually

---

[12] Glenn Schloss and Chow Chung-yan, "Long march to the community", *South China Morning Post*, September 22, 2000, p. 17.

lost respect for a party which constantly criticized the government's policy proposals without offering alternatives.

The Democratic Party's initial response to its electoral setbacks was not well received. Party leaders tended to criticize the voters and the mass media, and to place the blame on the party's lack of resources. They subsequently altered their position and were more willing to engage in self-criticism. A panel was formed to study the cause for the weakening of electoral support for the party. At the same time, some suggested uniting the pro-democracy forces into an opposition alliance, but commentators were not optimistic.[13]

It appeared that Hong Kong people's dissatisfaction with the government had spread to the major political parties, as many independents emerged during the direct elections, and some did reasonably well. The media were particularly interested in the two radical independents, "the Bull" Tsang Kin-shing and "Long Hair" Leung Kwok-hung; the considerable support for them (9,896 votes and 18,235 votes respectively) was commonly perceived as in indicator of frustration and disappointment with the legislature. Another sign was the increase in the number of blank votes in the elections. A week before the elections, a group of social senior government officials and the Electoral Affairs Commission felt it necessary to make a counter-appeal. In the end, there were 8,483 blank votes in the direct elections, an increase of 90% over 1998, and in the functional constituencies there were 950, 749 and 452 blank votes respectively in the Health Services, Education and Social Welfare constituencies.[14]

The C.H. Tung administration realized that it would continue to enjoy safe majority support in the legislature, and the Chief Executive indicated soon after the elections that he had no intention of reshuffling the Executive Council. It was true that the balance of forces within the legislature was not altered, and the next elections would only take place in 2004, but the pressure on the Tung administration in the legislature was expected to increase for the following reasons.

---

[13] *South China Morning Post*, September 18, 2000.
[14] *Ming Pao*, September 12, 2000.

In the first place, the political parties which supported the Tung administration were more eager to exert pressure on the government to reward them for their support, and this eagerness was strengthened by their perception that the Tung administration was vulnerable and unpopular. This pressure would further increase when the election of the next Chief Executive approached. The Liberal Party would be looking for prestigious and influential appointment to various important statutory bodies and advisory committees. As Liberal Party legislators came mainly from functional constituencies, they would also be pressing for concessions from the government to satisfy their respective constituencies. The Tung administration would find it more difficult to satisfy the demands of the DAB which was the only political party seriously preparing itself to become the governing party of the future. The DAB was acutely aware of its difficult role in the legislature. It had both criticize the performance of the government to satisfy the electorate, and support the government subsequently in the voting process. The Tung administration would have to consider measures to allow political parties supporting it to play a more active role in the policy-making process, such as allowing them to introduce popular measures in the legislature so that they could claim to have "delivered" to the electorate, and consulting them over important appointments to statutory bodies and advisory committees. Moreover, in the immediate future, the government might encounter proposals supported by a majority in the legislature to promote employment and to bridge the widening gap between the rich and poor. Some of these proposals might go against the government's philosophy, but legislators from the DAB and the Federation of Trade Unions would find it difficult to toe the government line on these issues.[15]

VI Concluding Observations

The community was looking for leadership to meet the challenges of the new century. In contrast with previous decades, Hong Kong people were more dependent on their government. There were expectations that government would assume a more significant role in the development of

---

[15] *South China Morning Post,* September 22, 2000.

high-tech industries, in facilitating foreign investment, such as the Disney project, in mitigating the expanding gap between rich and poor, in providing quality education and manpower training programmes to reduce unemployment, and in other areas. While they were much less concerned with interference from Beijing, they were worried about the general deterioration of the territory into an ordinary metropolis within China. This worry reflected and was exacerbated by the unsatisfactory performance of the HKSAR government. This widening gap between the rising expectations of the government and the perception of its deteriorating performance partly explained the symptoms of political disillusionment as revealed in the legislative elections in 2000. Above all, it indicated the huge challenge faced by the HKSAR government in the years ahead.

Soon after the legislative elections in September 2000, C.H. Tung indicated that he planned no changes for the Executive Council. A major reshuffle of the top civil service and the Executive Council would be a strong signal from the Ting administration that it was taking serious steps to tackle its problems. Refusal to change conveyed the message that the Tung administration apparently felt satisfied that no major changes were weened to improve its performance. This would not help restore the community's confidence in the government. In his first three policy speeches, Tung did not touch on political reform. Moreover, there was little to offer in this area in his fourth policy speech delivered on October 11, 2000.

The HKSAR government had, however, already promised to study electoral reform after the Legislative Council elections in September 2000. It was not expected that it would propose radical changes, and hence, it was likely that its proposals would attract many domestic and international criticisms. Logically, the legislature's electoral system beyond 2007 would have a higher proportion of directly-elected seats, even to the extent that the entire legislature might be elected by universal suffrage. It was difficult to imagine why members returned by functional constituencies would support an increase in directly-elected seats at the expense of functional constituency seats. If the legislature maintained its existing size, then which functional constituencies would be abolished, and according to what criteria?

A less controversial way to increase the proportion of directly-elected seats in the review in 2007 would be to expand the size of the legislature to 90 seats, and increase the number of directly-elected seats to 60. Political parties would find it much easier to agree on this, and a two-third majority in the legislature to support the change might become possible. If the Tung administration and the legislature could agree on the date and conditions of the next review, then directly-elected members might be able to secure the necessary majority in the legislature to abolish functional constituency seats eventually and have all sears directly-elected. It was clear, though, that this compromise formula would still be perceived by Beijing, the Tung administration and the local business community as too radical.

Since the legislative elections of September 2000, the pro-democracy camp had not even raised the issue of democratization and political reform. The community as a whole had yet to demonstrate its firm commitment to demand democracy. Under such circumstances, the Tung administration and the business community might hope that the improvement of the economic situation would largely erode Hong Kong people's discount on this and other matters.

Acknowledgement

Originally published as: Cheng, Joseph Yu Shek, "Administrative performance and the 2000 LegCo Elections" in *Hong Kong in Transition: One Country, Two Systems*, ed. Robert Ash *et al.*, London: Routledge Curzon, c2003, pp. 111–124. Reproduced with permission of The Licensor through PLSclear.

Chapter 12

Elections and Political Parties in Hong Kong's Political Development

I Introduction

The Sino-British negotiations on the territory's future generated expectations of autonomy and democracy. In September 1984, after two years of arduous negotiations, the Chinese and British governments initialled the Sino-British Joint Declaration on the Future of Hong Kong. From then till June 1997, Hong Kong entered a stage of transition.

During the negotiations which led to the initialling of the Sino-British Joint Declaration, the Chinese government offered "self-administration" (*gang ren zhigang*) to Hong Kong people. In July 1984, the British administration published a Green Paper on the Further Development of Representative Government in Hong Kong. The Green Paper had three aims, the first of which was "to develop progressively a system of government the authority for which is firmly rooted in Hong Kong, which is able to represent authoritatively the views of the people of Hong Kong, and which is more directly accountable to the people of Hong Kong." The positions thus taken by both governments were a great boost to the morale of those who supported political reform and the democratization of government in Hong Kong. Even ordinary citizens without any strong interest in political participation realized that as colonial rule was to be terminated in 1997, and none of the parties concerned wanted the future

Hong Kong Special Administrative Region (HKSAR) to be directly administered by Beijing, the establishment of a HKSAR government with a high degree of autonomy, as stipulated in the Sino-British Joint Declaration, would be a natural development. Such a government would also help to guarantee the maintenance of the status quo in Hong Kong for a period of 50 years after 1997.

Since then, however, political reform had become a source of controversy not only between Beijing and London but also within the Hong Kong community itself. After the release of the Green Paper, some business leaders openly opposed direct elections to the Legislative Council which the Green Paper had proposed. In January 1986, when Lu Ping, secretary-general of the Chinese State Council's Hong Kong and Macau Affairs Office, visited Hong Kong and consulted the Basic Law Consultative Committee, these businessmen voiced similar opinions on the committee.

These businessmen probably made the logical choice to protect their interests. They believed in the Chinese leadership's sincerity and determination to maintain stability and prosperity. They were therefore confident that Chinese leaders would respect and promote their interests. An elected government, accountable to the electorate and hoping to win the next election, would find it difficult to resist the pressure to improve social services, which would in turn hurt business interests.

Further, it was thought that a Hong Kong government appointed by Beijing would be more stable and predictable than an elected one. Many business leaders believed that they had the experience and ability to deal with Beijing's appointees, but lacked the confidence to bargain with an elected government. They harboured deep suspicions of the leaders of grassroots pressure groups, and felt that they had no values in common with them. Finally, these businessmen felt that a government nominated by Beijing would be able to maintain a direct dialogue with Chinese leaders and would therefore be in a better position to withstand pressures from cadres of Chinese organs in Hong Kong, from the Guangdong provincial government or from the relevant ministries in Beijing.[1]

---

[1] See the author's "Hong Kong: The Pressure to Converge," *International Affairs* (London), Vol. 63, No. 2, Spring 1987, pp. 271–283.

When membership of the Basic Law Drafting Committee was announced in July 1985, it was clear that the Chinese government placed top priority on the stability and prosperity of the territory and that radical political reforms would be unlikely. There were twenty-three members from Hong Kong, most of them were prominent businessmen and leading professionals, on the committee of fifty-nine members. The interests of the establishment in Hong Kong apparently were assured, as the Chinese authorities were keen to retain Hong Kong's attractiveness to investors.

By the spring of 1988, it was clearly revealed that the mainstream view within the Basic Law Drafting Committee favoured an "executive-led" system of government for the future HKSAR with power concentrated in the hands of the Chief Executive.[2] No major change had been introduced between the release of the draft Basic Law in April 1988 and its formal promulgation in April 1990.

The Chinese authorities' demand to have the final say was reflected in the powers of interpreting and amending the Basic Law (Articles 158 and 159). Regarding the political system, both the Sino-British Joint Declaration (Annex I, Article 1) and the Basic Law (Articles 45 and 48.5) provide the Central People's Government with the power to appoint the Chief Executive and the principal officials of the HKSAR government. It had been anticipated that such appointments would be a mere formality to demonstrate China's sovereignty over Hong Kong. Chinese officials responsible for Hong Kong affairs, however, indicated that the power of appointments would be a "substantial" one, implying a veto power in the hands of the Central People's Government.

The HKSAR political system, as outlined in the Basic Law, enables the Chief Executive to be a very strong leader within the local government. The Chief Executive has powers and functions similar to the U.S. President, though the former probably has even larger powers *vis-a-vis* the legislature. For example, the Chief Executive may dissolve the Legislative Council when the latter refuses to pass the budget or other important bills and consensus cannot be reached after consultation (Article 50).

---

[2] See the Drafting Committee for the Basic Law, *The Draft Basic Law of the Hong Kong Special Administrative Region of the People's Republic of China (for solicitation of opinions)*, Hong Kong, April 1988.

The strength of the Chief Executive and the weakness of the Legislative Council are further demonstrated by the Chief Executive's power "to approve the introduction of motions regarding revenues or expenditure of the Legislative Council" (Article 48.10) and "to decide, in the light of security and vital public interests, whether government officials or other personnel in charge of government affairs should testify or give evidence before the Legislative Council or its committees" (Article 48.11). If the Chief Executive can, without having to give reasons, reject any motion presented to the Legislative Council regarding revenues and expenditure, then basically the Legislative Council can only respond to the Chief Executive's proposals regarding revenues and expenditure. The Chief Executive's power to exempt government officials or other personnel in charge of government affairs from testifying or giving evidence before the Legislative Council or its committees will severely hamper the latter's function as a watchdog of the Chief Executive and the executive authorities.

Further, regarding bills relating to government policies, members of the Legislative Council may only introduce them with the prior written consent of the Chief Executive (Article 74). There obviously is a danger that "government policies" may be defined so broadly as to render members of the Legislative Council almost powerless to introduce bills. The Legislative Council also has no powers over the appointments of the principal officials and members of the Executive Council of the HKSAR.

In sum, the political system outlined in Chapter IV of the Basic Law presents an "executive dominant" system in which the Chief Executive enjoys powers similar to those of the former British governor. The Legislative Council has only limited powers. In April 2000, Christine Loh, a member of the Legislative Council, decided to quit elective politics because she was frustrated by the fact that the role of elected representatives in the HKSAR's political process remained limited.[3]

Further, the Chinese authorities wanted to ensure that the Chief Executive would have a safe majority support in the legislature. Let us examine the preferred scenario of the Chinese authorities before Chris

---

[3] *South China Morning Post* (a Hong Kong English newspaper), April 12, 2000.

Patten's political reform proposals.[4] In the 60-seat legislature in 1995, there were 30 seats for functional constituencies, an expansion of nine compared with the 21 seats in the 1991 elections. The Chinese authorities had hoped that candidates acceptable to Beijing would pick up 70%, or 21 of the 30 seats. Functional constituencies favoured the Establishment, which preferred not to confront the Chinese authorities and disturb the stability and prosperity of Hong Kong. After the 1991 elections, the pro-democracy camp could best count on the support of about one-third of the legislators returned by the functional constituencies. The Chinese authorities expected that they would have a say in the identification of the nine new functional constituencies for the 1995 elections, and thus would be assured that about two-thirds of the legislators returned by functional constituencies would pose no challenge to Beijing. They had also hoped that pro-Beijing political groups would win at least three or four seats in the direct elections. The Election Committee, which returned ten seats to the legislature would thus have been crucial. The Election Committee, according to the Basic law, would have been composed of members in the following proportion: one-quarter from the industrial, commercial, and financial sectors, one-quarter from the professions, one-quarter from the labor, grassroots, religious, and other sectors, and the remaining quarter from former political figures, in addition to Hong Kong deputies to the National People's Congress and representatives of Hong Kong delegates to the National Committee of the Chinese People's Political Consultative Conference. The Chinese authorities certainly had planned to capture a

---

[4] See Decision of the National People's Congress on the Method for the Formation of the First Government and the First Legislative Council of the Hong Kong Special Administrative Region, adopted at the Third Session of the Seventh National People's Congress on April 4, 1990, in *The Basic Law of the Hong Kong Special Administrative Region of the People's Republic of China*, Hong Kong: The Consultative Committee for the Basic Law of the Hong Kong Special Administrative Region, April 1991, pp. 65–67. It was stipulated in the Decision that if the composition of the last Hong Kong Legislative Council before the establishment of the HKSAR had been in conformity with the relevant provisions of the Decision, then its members would have become members of the first Legislative Council of the HKSAR, provided certain other conditions had been fulfilled. Hence, it had expected that the 1995 elections would have been held in accordance with the relevant provisions of the Decision so as to achieve a "through train" arrangement.

vast majority in the Election Committee through their united-front work, and thus return ten legislators acceptable to Beijing.

Chris Patten's political reform proposals allowed the pro-democracy groups a chance to secure a majority of seats in the legislature, and were therefore unacceptable to the Chinese authorities. Despite the implementation of the reforms for the 1995 Legislative Council elections, the Chinese authorities decided to dissolve the duly-elected Legislative Council and to replace it with a provisional legislature in July 1997. For the Legislative Council elections in 1998, the old model as envisaged by the Basic Law in 1990 was adopted. Further, regarding the twenty seats for direct elections, the single-seat constituency, simple majority system was replaced by a medium-sized, multi-seat constituency, single-vote system, similar to that in Japan before its electoral reforms in the late 1990s. This change limited the chance of a sweeping victory in the direct elections for the pro-democracy groups with the support of around 60% of the voters. The electoral system also forced the pro-democracy groups to compete against each other.

II Elections and the Initial Development of Political Parties

In response to the Sino-British Joint Declaration, the British administration began to prepare for elections to the Legislative Council, as outlined in its White Paper on the Further Development of Representative Government in Hong Kong released in November 1984. Political activists in various social strata began to organize in order to meet the challenge of democratization and political reform. The Hong Kong People's Association and the Association for Democracy and Justice were founded in the spring of 1984 around the time of the visit of Sir Geoffrey Howe, the British Foreign Secretary, in April. Though their supporters and platforms differed markedly, they had in common the objective of forming a pseudo-political party in preparation for the coming elections for various positions in public office. Then in the following summer, the Progressive Hong Kong Society initiated its groundwork. The scale of this society, the resources at its disposal and the respectable figures from various fields and social strata that it had enrolled seemed to indicate that the political development in Hong Kong had entered a new stage. This was the first time that core members of the political establishment had cooperated with the business groups controlled by the major families rooted in Hong Kong to form a political group. Its impact was felt by all who were involved in Hong Kong politics.

In the spring of 1985 there were three forces which seemed capable of forming a political group comparable to the Progressive Hong Kong Society: an elite group, with Legislative Councillor Allen Lee and the members of his 1983 delegation to Beijing as the core, backed up by the local Shanghainese business community; a possible coalition of middle-class groups, including the Hong Kong Observers, the Hong Kong Affairs Society and the Hong Kong People's Association, which was organizing a joint committee with other political groups to discuss the Basic Law and other issues in an attempt to strengthen cooperation among them; and a coalition of grassroots pressure groups, with the Association for Democracy and Justice and a number of young, recently elected District Board members providing the foundation. It appeared that the latter two coalitions still needed considerable time to materialize, and that the resources available to them would be quite limited in the initial stage. It should be recognized that it was sometimes difficult to distinguish between middle-class and grassroots coalitions, as both tended to have some groups from each social stratum.

At the time of Margaret Thatcher's visit to China in September 1982, many Hong Kong people wanted a leader like Prime Minister Lee Kuan Yew of Singapore. Two years later, concerned citizens were raising a more sophisticated question — could a strong political party emerge which was accepted by the Chinese authorities, the British administration in Hong Kong and the local business community? The hope was that this party could encompass respected figures from all social strata and therefore be in a position to win the community's confidence, emerge victorious in all major elections, and then form a government capable of maintaining the territory's stability and prosperity.

In the District Board elections in March 1985, many types of intra-district and inter-district coalitions appeared. Almost every political group supported a small number of candidates. And most of them achieved satisfactory results. Successful candidates came from a broad spectrum of the community, and the number of professionals, social workers and educators showed a remarkable increase. The average age of the elected District Board members also showed a significant decline. What merited special attention was the political culture and the degree of political mobilization introduced by the elections. The number of voters in the District Board elections reached a record high of 476,500, a milestone in Hong Kong's political development. Assuming that each of the 501 candidates had recruited 100 friends to campaign for him, the number of activists participating in the elections would have been 50,000. These figures reflected a considerable degree of politicization of the community.[5]

The September 1985 elections to the Legislative Council were based on the electoral college, comprising members of the District Boards, the Urban Council and the Provisional Regional Council, and the functional constituencies.[6] Qualified voters therefore only numbered about 70,000 and those who actually voted amounted to about 25,000. The scale of political mobilization was limited as many people were unaware of the elections, but they were nevertheless a significant step in Hong Kong's political development. Twenty-four of the 56 Legislative Councillors had to be accountable to their respective constituencies, unlike the appointed unofficial members, who were accountable to the Governor of Hong Kong (who made the appointments). Even the oath of allegiance was changed — it could then be directed to the citizens of Hong Kong or to the Queen. In fact, most of the newly elected unofficial members opted for the former.

These elections facilitated the development of political groups in Hong Kong. Middle-class political groups were prompted to develop their organizations at the grassroots level and establish close ties with the

---

[5] See the author's "The 1985 District Board Elections in Hong Kong," in his edited work, *Hong Kong In Transition*, Hong Kong: Oxford University Press, 1986, pp. 67–87.

[6] The electoral college elected 12 unofficial members of the Legislative Council. Eighteen District Boards were organized into ten groups, and the Urban Council as well as the Provisional Regional Council constituted one group each. Each group returned a Legislative Councillor. The nine functional constituencies returning 12 unofficial members comprised the commercial, industrial, financial, labor, social services, educational, legal, medical, and engineering, and associated professions. See *White Paper: The Further Development of Representative Government in Hong Kong*, Hong Kong: Government Printer, November 1984, p. 17.

grassroots pressure groups. At the same time, they became concerned with the social issues at the district level and took part in the related campaigns for citizens' rights. This process contributed to the expansion of almost all political groups.

This process also represented a significant improvement over political participation in the previous decade. In the 1970s, political participation and campaigns developed at two levels. Regarding issues with a direct impact on their daily life, people from the lower socioeconomic strata gradually learned to organize themselves to appeal to public opinion, to petition and to engage in various forms of protest activities to protect and promote their interests. Social workers from voluntary agencies funded by Western churches and student activists from the tertiary educational institutions also began to take part in these campaigns. The most obvious example of these *ad hoe* campaigns were the protests and petitions organized by the affected residents in the clearances of illegal squatter huts by the government. In the late-1970s, the development of grassroots pressure groups reached the stage when territory-wide campaigns for citizens' rights could be organized. Classical examples were campaigns against the raising of bus fares and those demanding citizen supervision of the monopolistic electric power companies.

The problem for such grassroots pressure groups was that people were as yet reluctant or unable to fight for their interests from a macro point of view instead of a micro one. Great difficulties existed in mobilizing people to become concerned with and to supervise the government's major policies. This showed that ordinary people were only willing to fight for immediate interests directly related to their daily life, and they were not concerned about the government's decision-making process.

At the same time, student movements developed in the tertiary educational institutions. They played an important role in the campaign for Chinese as an official language.[7] However, their ideals and concern for

---

[7] See Chan King-cheung, "Hong Kong's Student Movement" (in Chinese), in the author's edited work in Chinese, *The Political System and Politics of Hong Kong*, Hong Kong: Cosmos Bookstore Ltd., 1987 pp. 289–314; and Hong Kong Federation of Students (ed.), *Review of Hong Kong's Student Movement* (in Chinese), Hong Kong: Wide Angle Press Ltd., 1983.

global developments and their understanding of the Motherland (the People's Republic of China) obviously could not appeal to the grassroots pressure groups. Elections and the development of pseudo-political parties in the 1980s facilitated these two levels of political participation to accommodate with each other and even merge together.

Elections to the Legislative Council based on the electoral college, as well as the elections of District Board chairmen and committee chairmen within the District Boards, exposed the limitations of the elected members operating on an individual basis and encouraged various forms of coalitions within the District Boards. The British administration, through the appointment of one third of the District Board members, exercised considerable influence in the above elections. In fact, the grassroots pressure groups and the middle-class political groups had limited success in the elections of District Board chairmen and the following elections to the Legislative Council based on the Electoral College. In all the elections in 1985, both Maria Tam, a member of the Executive and Legislative Councils and leader of the Progressive Hong Kong Society, and Allen Lee, who was then attempting to organize a political party, were in active support of many candidates. In fact, some of the candidates took the initiative of enlisting their support. Such campaign activities naturally played a role in extending party politics into the new Legislative Council.

In sum, in the mid-1980s, the introduction of elections to the legislature, as part of the arrangements to prepare Hong Kong for its return to China, provided significant momentum for the development of political participation and political parties.

For participation theorists, democracy means that a vast majority of the people are regularly, actively and intensively involved in the making and implementation of public policies. They usually identify four fundamental objectives to realized.[8] First, popular participation is the best way both for leaders and for the people themselves to discover what the people want. Second, widespread participation will guarantee that all concerned interests are taken into consideration. Third, participation may increase the legitimacy, acceptance, and enforceability of policies, partly

---

[8] See, for example, Richard S. Katz. *Democracy and Elections*, Oxford and New York: Oxford University Press, 1997, pp. 67–68.

because decisions made in the context of popular participation should be more in line with the people's desires. Finally, democracy, with mass participation in political life, is supported primarily because "such involvement is an essential means to the full development of individual capacities,"[9] which is regarded as the central aim of government and society.

These objectives, however, did not appear to be the major concerns of the British administration and the Hong Kong community when democratization was introduced in 1984. Political reforms were an important part of the British political tradition in the twilight of the colonial era. Further, the British government in London wanted to achieve an honourable retreat from Hong Kong; and democratization was perceived as an important means by which Britain could enhance Hong Kong's autonomy *vis-à-vis* China after 1997. Finally, another objective of democratization was to strengthen the confidence and the sense of belonging of the community, including the reduction of emigration from the territory.[10]

III Political Mobilization in Response to Elections

In the first District Board elections in 1982, the British administration shouldered the burden of the publicity campaigns almost all by itself to encourage qualified residents to register and to vote, and in some instances senior government officials even encouraged community leaders to stand as candidates. The British administration then indicated that such involvement would not be repeated in the following elections, and voter registration as well as voting would have to rely on voluntary efforts of the citizenry. The British administration, however, was again substantially involved in the 1985 elections. Such involvement was generally accepted, and even perceived as necessary in view of the community's general political apathy and the absence of well-organized political groups. The British administration also considered that it should help prepare the

---

[9] Peter Bachrach, *The Theory of Democratic Elitism*, Boston: Little & Brown, 1967, p. 4.
[10] Lo Shiu-hing, *The Politics of Democratization in Hong Kong*, Basingstoke and London: Macmillan Press Ltd., 1997, pp. 86–89.

foundation for the development of representative government in the territory after the conclusion of the Sino-British Joint Declaration. This time the mass media and various newly-formed political groups were very active in promoting voter registration and encouraging voters to vote.

The British administration's efforts tended to be more low-key in the District Board elections in 1988. While routine programs were run as before to promote voter registration by the City and New Territories Administration, Radio Television Hong Kong and other government agencies, as well as senior government officials generally avoided the subject. By then, the British administration had abandoned taking the initiative to shape political reforms in Hong Kong, and the community was involved in heated debates on the introduction of direct elections to the Legislative Council in 1988. In the month before the District Board elections, governmental publicity programs on the District Board elections were smaller in scale and the mass media in general appeared to be less interested. In response to this lack of interest, the British administration stepped up its efforts in the last week or so, and the Secretary for District Administration, Donald Liao, was much relieved when the voter turnout rate finally passed the 30% mark which he had earlier predicted. It was said that community workers were sent to districts like Mong Kok where turnout was particularly low to mobilize voters to vote in the evening of the polling day.[11] The initiative was probably taken by the District Officers concerned.

In the three District Board elections, it was clearly established that the rural areas had higher voter turnouts than urban areas; and in urban areas, districts with a greater proportion of public housing residents usually achieved higher voter turnout rates. This was mainly because face-to-face contacts by grassroots neighborhood groups remained the most effective channel to mobilize voters to vote. In the rural districts like Sai Kung, North and Islands, there existed a traditional system of electing village representatives and the residents knew each other and the candidates well, hence voters could easily be reached by the candidates and the peer group pressure to vote was high. In Yuen Long and Tai Po, where a number of public housing estates had been built since the early 1980s, the voter

---

[11] *Ming Pao* (a Hong Kong Chinese newspaper), March 11, 1988.

turnout rates showed an above average decline in the last two elections combined. The oldest new town in the New Territories, Tsuen Wan, Kwai Chung and Tsing Yi, consistently registered the lowest turnout rates in the New Territories which were only slightly above the territory-wide averages. The new towns of the 1980s, Sha Tin and Tuen Mun, had voter turnout rates higher than those of Tsuen Wan, Kwai Chung, and Tsing Yi, but lower than those of the other more rural districts of the New Territories.

Grassroots neighborhood groups, mainly mutual aid committees of public housing estate blocks and various district-level groups with such names as "Concerned Group for the People's Livelihood of X District," were more active in the new towns and public housing estates. In the former, there was often a need to get organized to solve the problems of community building and to redress the grievances caused by the inadequacies of town planning. Similarly the mutual aid committees in most public housing estates had been active in various "Clean Hong Kong Campaigns" and "Fight Violent Crime Campaigns" and enjoyed good access to the residents. This was why new towns and urban districts with a higher proportion of public housing residents usually achieved higher voter turnout rates than old urban districts where such grassroots neighbourhood groups were not well developed. As expected, Kwun Tong, Wong Tai Sin, Sham Shui Po, and Southern (where there is located the traditional fishing port of Aberdeen) consistently attained higher than average voter turnout rates.[12]

In line with the above, voters in the lower socio-economic strata tended to be more enthusiastic in District Board elections. In comparison with middle-class voters, they had a greater need for District Board members who were expected to articulate their interests, help to redress their grievances, explain to them government policies and show them the proper channels to obtain the necessary services from relevant government departments. This utilitarian element of participation in District Board elections not only partially explained the motivation to vote but also helped to answer why voter turnout rates were usually lower in middle-class urban districts.

---

[12] See Janet L. Scott, *Local Level Election Behaviour in an Urban Area*, Hong Kong: Centre for Hong Kong Studies, The Chinese University of Hong Kong, January 1985.

The liberal pro-democracy camp attached much significance to the District Board elections. As it had failed to secure direct elections to the Legislative Council in 1988, the District Board elections in March 1988 and the Legislative Council elections in the following September were the only opportunities for them to demonstrate their political prowess. Due to the decline of political expectations and confidence in the second half of the 1980s, the three major political groups in the pro-democracy camp (the Hong Kong Affairs Society, Meeting Point, and the Association for Democracy and People's Livelihood) largely failed to make much headway in expanding their organizations. The District Board elections were vital to new recruitment and a boost of morale which had suffered in the series of political setbacks.

Under such circumstances, the groups could not afford to be too selective in endorsing candidates. They basically welcomed all candidates who were willing to join them, offering the candidates the general blessing of the pro-democracy camp, limited financial assistance and the endorsement of their leading figures like Legislative Councillors Martin Lee, Szeto Wah and working-class champions like Lau Chin-shek, director of the Christian Industrial Committee. Candidates of the pro-democracy camp usually lacked social status and financial resources, but they had excellent support from effective grassroots groups. They managed to recruit well-educated campaign workers from the tertiary educational institutions, and their key campaign managers were the most experienced in the territory. Obviously, their youth, academic, and professional qualifications, and the campaign efforts of Martin Lee and company were valuable assets. The three groups reached an agreement to co-ordinate nominations so as to avoid clashes among their candidates, but they stopped short of poolling resources.

Opposing the pro-democracy camp was the conservative camp which in the District Board elections was largely represented by the traditional community leaders of the kaifongs (traditional, conservative community groups at the district level) in the urban areas and the Heung Yee Kuk (the Rural Consultative Council, the statutory body representing rural interests) and rural committees in the New Territories. They were usually better off economically and conservative in political outlook. Naturally, they were favoured by the British administration and were cultivated by the officials of the local District Offices. They tended to be appointed to the local area committees and other committees and played a supportive role in activities and campaigns initiated or sponsored by the British administration. Many of these traditional community leaders were businessmen and above 40 years of age. Among this group, however, there was an increasing number of school principals, lawyers, business executives and other professionals who were similarly conservative in political outlook, and they were actively coopted by government officials.

The conservative cause's main champions were Legislative Councillors Maria Tarn, Allen Lee, Selina Chow, and Stephen Cheong. Maria Tam was head of the Progressive Hong Kong Society, formed in 1985 and had the foundation of a conservative political party. It then adopted a very low political profile when Beijing made it clear that it objected to the rapid development of representative government and the emergence of political parties in the territory. Like the political groups in the pro-democracy camp, the Progressive Hong Kong Society could not afford to abandon active participation in the District Board elections. It supported 49 candidates (another report indicated that it supported about 70 candidates), and actively campaigned for them, enlisting the help of beauty queens and television stars.[13] The conservative camp also vastly improved its campaign strategies by 1988, imitating many of the effective tactics earlier adopted by the pro-democracy camp. With much more financial resources at its disposal, it presented a formidable threat to the pro-democracy political groups.

The Chinese authorities began publicly building their Hong Kong community network and influence in 1985 when the Hong Kong branch of the New China News Agency opened three district offices on Hong Kong Island and in Kowloon and the New Territories. Pro-Beijing political forces mounted a campaign to block the introduction of direct elections to the Legislative Council in 1988. They also mobilized their supporters, identified candidates and isolated political opponents in the District Board elections in March 1988.

Participation on a considerable scale by pro-Beijing organizations was an interesting phenomenon in the 1988 District Board elections. In many

---

[13] Emily Lau, "One Point for Democracy," *Far Eastern Economic Review*, Vol. 139, No. 12, March 24, 1988, p. 26; see also *South China Morning Post*, March 16, 1988.

cases, pro-Beijing candidates, who included bankers and other professionals, camouflaged their backgrounds, stressing their credentials as local residents who only wanted to serve the community. In the rural areas in the New Territories, pro-Beijing candidates were bolder and publicly admitted to being linked with China. The pro-Beijing Hong Kong Federation of Trade Unions indicated that 12 of its members stood for the elections (compared with 10 in the 1985 elections), but it revealed only two names. Presumably these two were very strong candidates and they did get elected.

In some cases, prominent conservative political leaders endorsed candidates from the pro-Beijing camp, which was also against rapid development of representative government in Hong Kong. In return, pro-Beijing organizations, in their letters to members, instructed them to vote for candidates from the conservative camp as well. Participation by pro-Beijing organizations became a cause of concern because the Communist Party of China had been seen to be stepping up its activities in the territory and seeking to establish itself as the dominant political force.[14] Earlier they began to organize grassroots neighborhood groups in districts like Kwun Tong and Wong Tai Sin. These groups would have considerable resources from China at their disposal and would constitute unfair competition in various elections. In some constituencies in Hong Kong Island, China Resources (Holdings) Co., Ltd. and China Merchants Steam Navigation Co., Ltd. provided transport to support the pro-Beijing candidates on election day. These two were major Chinese corporations in Hong Kong and were directly accountable to the then Chinese Ministry of Foreign Economic Relations and Trade and the Ministry of Communications respectively.

As observed by Lo Shiu-hing, the dynamics of democratization in Hong Kong were almost unique, because there was no cleavage between conservative or reactionary hard-liners and liberal, reformist soft-liners in the political establishment. In the absence of any clear-cut elite division, Hong Kong's democratization between 1984 and 1988 was the product of opposing Sino-British plans on whether Hong Kong's polity remaining colonial in its run-up to 1997.[15] Besides the political reform proposals

---

[14] Emily Lau, "Positioning for Power" and "Grasping the Grassroots," *Far Eastern Economic Review*. Vol. 137, No. 32, August 6, 1987, pp. 26–29.

[15] Lo Shiu-hing, *op.cit.*, p. 94.

formally presented by the British administration, it also contributed much to the democratization process by encouraging community leaders at all levels to take part in politics, usually through initial appointments to governmental advisory bodies. To facilitate the emergence of politicians and political parties, the British administration offered very generous remuneration for members of elected bodies including District Boards, the Urban Council and the Regional Council, as well as the Legislative Council. Political groups in the pro-democracy camp had largely been relying on contributions from their elected members for their activities and development. Arguably, the British administration was attempting to cultivate a political elite which would help London to retain its influence in the HKSAR after 1997.

In the analysis of the global wave of democratization in the 1970s and 1980s, Guillermo O'Donnell and Philippe Schmitter observe that usually a democratic opening allows or facilitates the emergence of social groups spearheaded by intellectuals, who "press for more explicit democratization or even revolution."[16] At the same time, privileged groups including industrialists, merchants, bankers and landowners begin to act like a *de facto* opposition, and they are concerned that the democratic transition "will not stop at a point compatible with the contractual freedoms of the market or the cozy relationship they enjoy with the state apparatus."[17] In the case of Hong Kong, the privileged groups were gradually absorbed by Beijing's united front since 1984, and they remained in the evolving new political Establishment.

Hong Kong's younger generation and intelligentsia indeed were the main forces fighting for democratization, but their demands were mild. They argued that only an elected administration could effectively maintain the territory's international status and promote the interests of its citizens. After 1997, substantial coordination between the central government in Beijing and the HKSAR government would become essential. In handling this relationship, the people of Hong Kong would need a government

---

[16] Guillermo O'Donnell and Philippe C. Schmitter, *Transitions from Authoritarian Rule: Tentative Conclusions about Uncertain Democracies*, Baltimore: Johns Hopkins University Press, 1986, p. 49.

[17] *Ibid.*, p. 50.

directly accountable to them. Further, the territory's economic development depended on the maintenance of its existing international status and identity. In order to maintain this status and be able to negotiate with other governments on economic and trade issues, Hong Kong, as a SAR under Chinese sovereignty, had to be recognized and accepted by the international community. An elected government would be best placed to win this recognition and acceptance, and be able to safeguard and promote Hong Kong's interests in non-political international negotiations unrelated to China's sovereignty. Most important of all, self-administration was what attracted them most in the return of the territory to China.

In the 1980s, the development of social services provided by the public sector entered a stage of consolidation. The rapid economic growth in the 1970s and the ambitious programs of the MacLehose administration (1971–1982) largely satisfied the community's basic demand for social services. Anticipating slower economic growth in the future, and in view of the natural expansion of the existing programs, the British administration had to reconsider its various social service commitments. The increase in the ratio of Home Ownership Scheme flats to rental public housing flats, the doubling of rents for public-housing tenants whose incomes exceeded the income limits for applicants and who had been residing in public housing for more than 10 years, the establishment of an independent Hospital Authority to manage public hospitals, etc., all demonstrated the government's intention to limit its social service commitments. Due to the uncertainty over Hong Kong's future, Beijing and all parties concerned wanted to maintain the territory's attraction to investors, and thus much weakened the demand for more social services and a greater degree of income redistribution. A good example was the British administration's plain rejection of the proposal for a central provident fund scheme.

The conservative business leaders' attacks on "free lunches" (social service programs of the public sector) resulted in considerable self-restraint among the pressure groups within the pro-democracy camp. In the second half of the 1980s, the British administration offered no new major social welfare programs, nor had the community made any specific demand. The proposed central provident fund scheme involved no direct financial burden on the part of the British administration. The local community was aware of Beijing's demand for balanced budgets; and at the end of the 1980s, the Governor and the Financial Secretary indicated that the expenditure of the sector should be kept at the level of about 16% of the territory's gross domestic product.

Besides the above factors, Hong Kong's traditional political culture encouraged self-reliance, and the past spectacular economic growth as well as the anxiety over the future lowered the community's expectations of social services from the British administration. Hence, the contraction of the public sector and the reduction in the growth of social services did not cause much dissatisfaction in the community, and there were no indications that people had been prompted to satisfy their demand for social services through political participation.

IV The Impact of the Tiananmen Incident

In the spring and summer of 1989, the Hong Kong people established a very strong identity with their compatriots in China while intensely following the tragic events. There emerged a conviction that as long as freedom, human rights, and democracy could not be guaranteed in China, they could not be protected in Hong Kong after 1997. When over one million Hong Kong people marched for democracy and freedom in China and against the suppression of the student movement on May 21, 1989, a vast majority of the participants were marching for the first time in their lives. They were motivated by anger and shock at what was happening in China, and at the same time struck by a sense of despair and insecurity regarding their own future. Most of them marched again on the following two Sundays.[18]

The emotions of the Hong Kong community and the direct elections to the Legislative Council in 1991 much facilitated the development of the pro-democracy political groups and their unity. The rallies and marches during the Tiananmen Incident led to the formation of the Hong Kong Alliance in Support of the Patriotic Democratic Movement in China, an umbrella group embracing about two hundred grassroots organizations associated with the pro-democracy camp. In December 1989, the United

---

[18] See the author's "Prospects for Democracy in Hong Kong," in George Hicks (ed.). *The Broken Mirror: China After Tiananmen*, Essex, United Kingdom: Longman Group, 1990, pp. 278–295.

Democrats of Hong Kong was established; it was intended to be the political party of the pro-democracy camp combining the three leading pro-democracy political groups, i.e., the Association for Democracy and People's Livelihood, Meeting Point and the Hong Kong Affairs Society. However, some leading members of the former two refused to join and preferred to maintain their separate identities. Despite the fact that over a million people marched during the Tiananmen Incident, the United Democrats of Hong Kong had an initial membership of only about 220. At the same time, a small group of liberal businessmen and professionals formed the Hong Kong Democratic Foundation in June 1990.

The failure of the pro-democracy camp to form a single, united party mainly reflected differences on two important issues — relationship with the Chinese Communist regime and the balance of class interests in Hong Kong. Most members of Meeting Point, for example, did not want to engage in confrontation with the Chinese leadership; they had a strong "nationalist" orientation, they were very concerned with developments in China and were keen to contribute to China's modernization. In contrast, many leaders of the United Democrats of Hong Kong had deep distrust for the Chinese leadership, and were eager to exploit the Hong Kong people's fear of communism and future Chinese interferences in the territory for electoral purposes. At the same time, the leaders of the Association for Democracy and People's Livelihood wanted to demonstrate a strong commitment to grassroots interests and was suspicious of the United Democrats of Hong Kong's efforts to reach a compromise between the interests of the grassroots and those of the middle class. The Hong Kong Democratic Foundation, on the other hand, attempted to promote the "enlightened" interests of the upper socioeconomic strata while trying to support the democratization process.

In the 1991 Legislative Council elections, more than 750,000 voters voted (39.15% of the eligible voters). A considerable proportion of the 1:9 million registered voters did not register voluntarily,[19] and probably over

---

[19] The British administration spent considerable efforts contacting Hong Kong people and encouraging them to register as voters. Those who qualified normally could find no excuse to refuse registration. But some of them obviously had no intention to register as voters and to vote.

one million of them had never actually voted since 1982. It was not surprising that the significance of the Legislative Council elections and its associated publicity had failed to mobilize a majority of them. The fact that 330,000 more voters came out to vote in the Legislative Council elections than in the previous District Board elections was a moderate success already.

In view of the spectacular victory of the pro-democracy camp, it appeared that the more politically active segments of the community (the voters) supported the cause of democracy.[20] The pro-democracy camp could not claim to have the support of the entire community; but it could certainly claim to have the backing of the politically active who desired further democratization. Regarding those voters who stayed away and those who even refused to register, they were certainly apathetic to some extent. But it could also be interpreted that they were satisfied with the status quo and did not desire to change it by political means, or that they could see no way to change the status quo and had little faith in the development of representative government.

The Tiananmen Incident, for a short while, did much to promote the appreciation of democracy among Hong Kong's political establishment. To minimize Britain's responsibility for the territory, London and the British administration supported an acceleration of the democratization process. In May 1989, the Executive and Legislative Councils reached a consensus on the direct election by universal suffrage of the Chief Executive and all seats of the legislature by 2003; and on the election by the same means in 1997 of one-half of the seats of the legislature.[21] Senior British administration officials also reversed their position and indicated that the directly elected Legislative Council seats to be introduced in 1991 would be increased from 10 to 20. The report of the British House of Commons Foreign Affairs Select Committee released in late June 1989 even boldly suggested that by 1991, half of the Legislative Council seats should be directly elected; and by 1995, all seats should be directly elected.[22]

---

[20] Only 18 seats out of 60 were directly elected in 1991, and the pro-democracy camp won IS. A prodemocracy independent also secured an additional seat.
[21] *South China Morning Post*, July 25, 1989.
[22] The report was published in full in *ibid.*, July 1, 1989.

In response to the demand for accelerating the democratization process, local pro-Beijing political figures articulated the view that such a demand was "naive" and might lead to greater confrontation with Beijing after 1997.[23] They also stepped up publicity activities to counter-attack the demands for more democracy.[24] It was therefore not surprising that in January 1990, the political system sub-group of the Basic Law Drafting Committee endorsed a snail's pace for democratic reforms. It agreed during its final session to adhere to its earlier decision to limit the number of directly elected seats in the legislature in 1997 to 18. Of the remaining 42 seats, 30 would be elected by functional constituencies, while the other 12 would be chosen by an election committee. Beginning from the second legislature in 1999, the number of directly elected seats would be increased to 24. By the third legislature in 2003, the legislature would be constituted by an equal number of directly elected and functional group representatives. At this point, the British government was willing to accept the proposal with minor revisions.

The conservative business sector realized that it had to organize itself to articulate its interests. There had been a coalition of 89 businessmen and professionals in the Basic Law Drafting Committee and the Basic Law Consultative Committee representing conservative business interests. After the promulgation of the Basic Law, some of them formed the Business and Professional Federation in June 1991 which actively lobbied the Chinese leaders in Beijing for the interests of the conservatives. Others formed a Liberal Democratic Federation, with the objective of supporting candidates to run for the 1991 elections. In general, the conservative business and professional groups were reluctant to get involved in electoral politics, but preferred to exercise their informal influence through lobbying important British administration and/or Beijing officials. They therefore remained vacillating in their attitude towards party politics in Hong Kong.

This lack of commitment almost proved to be fatal. The Liberal Democratic Federation was totally ineffective in the direct elections despite the fact that it had secured three seats in the functional constituencies. The Business and Professional Federation was also totally impotent in the direct elections and it lacked a base to improve as well. The hard-liners in the

---

[23] *Ibid.*, July 21, 1989.
[24] *Ibid.*, July 28, 1989.

pro-Beijing united front had previously attacked the leader of the Business and Professional Federation for promising the Chinese authorities to mobilize the business community to fight in the Legislative Council elections in 1991 in return for a more liberal version of the political system in the Basic Law. He was subsequently accused for failing to keep his promise.

The pro-China groups suffered severe setbacks in the Tiananmen Incident; they were forced to keep a very low profile for some months. The New Hong Kong Alliance, for example, was established in mid-1989 by some leading pro-China businessmen and professionals, who formulated a political model to prevent the pro-democracy camp from dominating the future legislature. Other pro-China figures who at one stage openly condemned China's suppression of the student leaders in Beijing soon also re-aligned themselves to mobilize support in the elections in 1991. The pro-China groups were certainly disappointed with the loss of all three candidates in the direct elections to the Legislative Council in 1991, but there was obviously a basis for a formidable comeback in future years. They demonstrated their effective organization and mobilization power in the campaigns. Their candidates, however, had not been given sufficient time to cultivate a good image and appeal to the voters. The local New China News Agency admitted that it had been reluctant to promote political stars, and it had to change immediately. The pro-Beijing united front also blamed the developments in the Soviet Union just before the elections and the mass media's emphasis on the pro-Beijing background of their candidates as important reasons for their failure.

V The Final Years of the Transition

The British administration's situation in the legislature became increasingly difficult since the 1991 elections. It mainly counted on the support of three official members and a majority of the eighteen appointed unofficials. Then it formed shifting majorities with either the pro-democracy groups or the conservative Liberal Party,[25] depending on the issues at stake.

---

[25] The conservative or pro-business legislators formed a loose group known as the Co-operative Resources Centre soon after 1991 elections. It then consolidated into a political party, the Liberal Party.

The small number of elected independents were prime targets of the British administration's lobbying efforts too. Senior civil servants complained that they spent up to one-third of their time in the Legislative Council, trying to explain the British administration's policy positions and lobbying for support. This called not only for commitment and dedication, but also an enthusiasm to adapt to the changing political environment and cultivate new political skills.

The situation worsened after the 1995 elections when there were no more appointed seats in the legislature. Beijing's direct and indirect influence in the legislature, especially on the conservative legislators, was certainly on the ascent. In the crucial votes on the political reform packages in late June 1994, it was reported that Beijing officials had contacted a few legislators who were also Hong Kong Affairs Advisors appointed by the Chinese authorities in an attempt to influence their voting behavior.

The British administration, like any democratic government, required a stable majority support in the Legislative Council in order to function smoothly. After the 1995 elections, on issues concerning relations with China and the pace of political reforms, the British administration had to count on the support of the pro-democracy parties and their sympathizers as the pro-business legislators were most reluctant to antagonize Beijing. Under such circumstances, the danger was that the British administration might be forced into a more radical position than appropriate, and that this in turn reinforced the Chinese authorities' suspicion of collusion between the British administration and the pro-democracy parties to confront Beijing in the final years of the transition. On social service issues, the British administration encountered considerable pressure from the pro-democracy parties so much so that its basic political philosophy was sometimes threatened. Its position became more untenable because of the reluctance of the pro-business legislators to compromise. The latter were eager to establish their credentials in the eyes of Beijing, and were unwilling to engage in serious bargaining with the British administration and the pro-democracy parties because the Chinese leaders were only too eager to discredit them.

As the British administration no longer enjoyed a complete control over the legislature, the bargaining power and the room of manoeuvre for all political parties were strengthened. The pro-democracy parties and the pro-Beijing groups obviously wanted to establish their clear political identities and often clashed with the British administration; even the conservative pro-business Liberal Party did not want to be closely associated with the British administration. The business community often believed that the direct lobbying of Chinese leaders in Beijing would be the best way to articulate their interests; but its political party, the Liberal Party, realized that it had to take part in elections, including direct elections, to enhance its credentials in the eyes of the British administration and Beijing.

In July 1992, a pro-Beijing grassroots political party, the Democratic Alliance for the Betterment of Hong Kong (DAB), was formally established. It symbolized the recognition of the legitimacy of the electoral system by the pro-Beijing united front, and its preparation for electoral competition with the pro-democracy camp. The united front would like to prevent the pro-democracy parties from winning a majority in the legislature, and they would like to secure a majority which would at least respect China's vital interests. The DAB would be responsible for co-ordination within this majority. Since the Sino-British negotiations on the territory's future, the Chinese authorities had been spending considerable resources in establishing a pro-Beijing united front. Certainly, this united front had to demonstrate its mobilization power in the 1995 Legislative Council elections. From an orthodox ideological point of view, it had to develop itself and expand through campaigns while testing the calibre and loyalty of its supporters. From an organizational point of view, it had to cultivate candidates, consolidate and expand its grassroots networks, and refine its campaign strategies and tactics.

Over 920,000 voters participated in the 1995 Legislative Council elections, surpassing by about 170,000 the turnout in 1991. The voter turnout rate, however, was 35.79%, more than three percentage points lower than in 1991.[26] The number of registered voters increased from 1.9 million in 1991 to 2.57 million in 1995; therefore, it would have been unrealistic to expect an improvement in the voter turnout rate. Nonetheless, the voter turnout rate reflected the community's political apathy. The people of Hong

---

[26] See all major newspapers in Hong Kong on September 18, 1995.

Kong realized that most major decisions were made by Beijing or on the basis of Sino-British agreements; such perceptions reinforced their sense of political impotence. They too understood that the Legislative Council elections would have a limited impact on the livelihood issues which most concerned them, especially economic growth and unemployment. Admittedly, many Hong Kong residents had not established a habit of participating in elections. Most of them voted in order to fulfill a civic obligation, rather than to exercise their political right to elect a government. The increase in the number of voters was partially due to the mobilization power of the pro-Beijing groups and the lowering of the voting age from 21 to 18.

The most noteworthy result of the Legislative Council elections in 1995 was the outstanding performance of the pro-democracy parties. According to various estimates, based on assessments of the political inclinations of some independents and the Association for Democracy and People's Livelihood, such parties and their allies controlled twenty-seven to thirty-one seats in the legislature. On issues ranging from the further development of representative government and Sino-British negotiations on Hong Kong to the expansion of social services, the pro-democracy alliance commanded a majority and could therefore oppose positions taken by Beijing, by London, or by the two regimes jointly.

The electoral victory of the pro-democracy parties was obviously embarrassing for the Chinese authorities: voters had supported Beijing's critics. It was natural for the electorate to expect that criticisms and strict monitoring would create checks and balances *vis-a-vis* those in power, and their feeling was that Beijing's power over Hong Kong exceeded that of the British administration. This should not be interpreted to mean that Hong Kong people wanted to confront the Chinese authorities. In the elections in the 1980s, the electorate similarly supported harsh critics of the territory's British administration; even so, most people at that time trusted the Hong Kong government and were satisfied with its performance. Under such circumstances, there was obviously no incentive for the Chinese leadership to accept further democratization of Hong Kong.

Though the pro-Beijing groups did not perform well in the 1995 Legislative Council elections in terms of seats won, however, they secured 34% of the vote, and their mobilizing power was impressive in a number of ways. In the Hong Kong Island East constituency, a relatively unknown candidate representing the pro-Beijing Hong Kong Progressive Alliance competed against Martin Lee, leader of the Democratic Party, and received almost 30% of the vote. This performance indicated the power of the grassroots network of the pro-Beijing organizations. Most significantly, public opinion revealed considerable sympathy for the leaders of the DAB who lost to the candidates of the pro-democracy parties. Many Hong Kong residents felt that the former had been doing a good job in serving the public, and their presence in the legislature would have contributed to the well-being of the community and the development of representative government. If the existing simple majority, single-seat constituency system had been replaced by a proportional representation system in medium-sized, multi-seat constituencies, the DAB and its allies would have been able to secure at least five seats out of twenty in the direct elections on the basis of their share of the votes in 1995. Such a change was indeed adopted for the 1998 Legislative Council elections.

The performance of the DAB in the 1995 elections showed that in the long run, the community services offered by the pro-Beijing parties would be rewarded. Given their financial resources, they would be able to expand their grassroots network gradually. Moreover, the pro-Beijing united front could also reward its supporters with honors such as memberships in the National People's Congress, the Chinese People's Political Consultative Conference, and the provincial counterparts of these two bodies, as well as appointments to the Preparatory Committee for the HKSAR, as Hong Kong Affairs Advisors, and as District Affairs Advisors. By the mid-1990s, the Chinese authorities had established their system of honours for the Hong Kong community. Such efforts and resources laid a strong foundation for the pro-Beijing political parties. With a more favourable electoral system and the support of the pro-business groups, the Chinese authorities could hope to secure a reliable majority support in the legislature after 1997. Willingness to accept elections would support the Chinese authorities' attempts to seek legitimacy for the HKSAR government and encourage them to be responsive to public opinion in the territory.

The DAB of Hong Kong also demonstrated that in order to win elections, it could not afford to toe the Beijing line closely at all times. The

Chinese leaders' sense of insecurity regarding Hong Kong since the Tiananmen Incident and the Sino-British confrontation, however, had not allowed the political party much room to manoeuvre. Signs of disagreements between the party and the Chinese officials responsible for Hong Kong were sometimes obvious.

In the District Board elections in September 1994, the Urban/Regional Council elections in March 1995, and the Legislative Council elections in September 1995, the major political groups all demonstrated sophisticated campaign strategies and skills.[27] With perhaps the exceptions of the Democratic Alliance for the Betterment of Hong Kong and the Hong Kong Federation of Trade Unions, most political groups were severely limited by their relatively small work force and shortage of funds. Consequently, they had to deploy their resources very efficiently. All political groups had been skillful in attracting media attention and in using opinion surveys. The pro-democracy political parties no longer had the edge they enjoyed in the previous decade.

By the standard of developing democracies, Hong Kong's elections were remarkably clean. One could argue that the interests at stake were limited, but the political culture obviously detested "money politics," and the purchase of votes was unthinkable. Minor violations of electoral rules were common: they usually took the form of disobeying the regulations concerning the display of publicity materials, under-reporting of campaign expenditures, and so forth. Violence was virtually non-existent.[28]

VI Elections and Political Parties in the HKSAR

Since the establishment of the HKSAR, the Chinese authorities and the HKSAR government carefully implemented the political design outlined in the Basic Law as analyzed in the first section of this chapter. In view of the political reforms carried out by Chris Patten in disregard of the

---

[27] See Chi-keung Choi, Sai-leung Lau and Pak-kwan Chow, *Politics of Elections and Legislature* (in Chinese), Hong Kong: Hong Kong Humanities Press, November 1995.

[28] See the author's "Political Participation in Hong Kong — Trends in the Mid-1990s," in Warren I. Cohen and Li Zhao (eds.), *Hong Kong Under Chinese Rule*, Cambridge: Cambridge University Press, 1997, p. 170.

Chinese authorities' opposition, the latter abolished the "through train" arrangement and established a provisional legislature elected by the same Election Committee which elected the Chief Executive. The first legislative elections in the HKSAR had to wait till May 1998.

By then, Hong Kong people's political expectations had been much lowered. Many opinion polls before the elections showed that a very small proportion of the community understood the electoral system. One of the surveys indicated that only 18% of the respondents could give the correct number of seats in the legislature to be directly elected.[29] However, one should not under-estimate the intelligence of Hong Kong people. Mothers carefully studied the scheme of entering secondary schools for their children. Public housing tenants meticulously weighed the pros and cons of purchasing the flats they occupied. These were difficult choices, and yet even those without much formal education came to sensible decisions through enquiries, informal consultation and careful deliberation.

The real question was: did Hong Kong people think that the voting exercise was worth their efforts? Apparently, many did not think so. The legislature elections would not change the political landscape much because it was expected that there would be a safe majority in support of Beijing's policy towards Hong Kong and the Chief Executive's policy programs. Further, voters did not believe that the elections would have much impact on their most concerned livelihood issues such as the economy, employment, housing, education, etc. Based on past experiences, most Hong Kong voters went to vote to fulfill their civic obligation and to choose a critic to monitor the work of the government. In the 1998 legislature elections, Hong Kong people realized that they were not voting for a government. They were voting for an opposition which they hoped would monitor the work of the government. The legislature formed part of their checks and balances mechanisms.

Hence Hong Kong people welcomed staunch critics of Beijing and the HKSAR government. Martin Lee, Emily Lau and Lau Chin-shek were among the territory's most popular politicians. Before C.H Tung emerged as the hot favourite for the post of the first HKSAR Chief Executive, Hong

---

[29] See the author's "It will be tough to get HK to vote," *The Straits Times* (a Singapore English newspaper), May 20, 1998.

Kong media conducted a number of opinion surveys oil the community's choice for the position. Anson Chan, the then Chief Secretary, topped the polls every time, and she often secured more than 60% endorsement among the respondents. Martin Lee, on the other hand, only won 5%–15% of support. Other leaders of political parties did not receive much attention at all. The Hong Kong people's political sophistication was obvious. They favoured continuity and they had confidence in the civil service. They only hoped that their politicians would serve as critics, and they did not have high expectations that they would lead.

Despite the fact that the Basic Law provides for a strong executive-led system of government and limits the legislature's powers, the government cannot get new laws passed and cannot get money to implement its policy programs without the consent of the legislature. These are the two most important powers of all legislatures in democratic countries, and Hong Kong's legislature has such powers at its disposal. A useful function of the legislature is to focus on issues. A small, dedicated opposition can effectively influence the government's agenda if it succeeds in securing the community's attention and support of public opinion. However, most observers noticed that the 1998 legislature elections were not about issues. Political parties and politicians mainly counted on their images as staunch critics of the government, as well as their ability and track record in articulating the grievances of the people. To attract voters, political parties interested in direct elections concentrated on constituency services and handling cases of complaint. Such services were laudable, but there was no shortage of effective channels for complaints offered by the government.

The total memberships of Hong Kong's four major political parties numbered less than 2,300 people. The small memberships of the political parties well demonstrated that they had failed to offer meaningful political participation to those not interested in running for public offices. In general, Hong Kong's political parties had failed to consult the public and come out with well-researched policy platforms. Almost everyone in Hong Kong felt that they had something to say on education and housing. However, they did not seem to have been much consulted so that their ideas became the policy platforms of the political parties they supported. The Democratic Party and the DAB often asked the government to do more for the lower socioeconomic strata, but they did not have a comprehensive strategy to assist them. They were vastly helped by the government's substantial budget surpluses and huge financial reserves, because they did not normally have to explain where the money should come from in order to support their policy proposals.

The record turnout of 53% of voters in the 1998 legislative elections was a pleasant surprise to all. It did not have to be interpreted as a vote against the HKSAR government, but it certainly showed people's enthusiastic support for direct elections. The surge in the community's political participation reflected a dissatisfaction with the provisional legislature. The voter turnout and the voters' preferences indicated the community's support for the kind of legislature it had in 1995–1997.

As expected, the HKSAR government did not warmly receive the message that people wanted democracy, and take the initiative to seek Beijing's approval to quicken the pace of democratization. Its immediate challenge was how to treat the return of a vocal opposition to the legislature which rightly considered it had won a moral victory. Normally, the HKSAR government was able to count on the support of a safe majority in the new legislature, consisting of the DAB, the Liberal Party, and the Hong Kong Progressive Alliance. A dozen or more independents returned by the Election Committee and functional constituencies shared pro-establishment values and usually supported the government too.

The relationship between the administration and legislature as a whole, however, was unsatisfactory, and it resulted in frustration and dissatisfaction among senior civil servants, legislators and the general public. It was suggested that "the administration has power but no votes, and the parties/legislators have votes but no power." This was a political myth far from reality.

The Chief Executive belonged to no political party, and no legislator had an obligation to support the administration. Tam Yiu-chung, who was appointed to the Executive Council, was perhaps the only exception. Yet, a safe majority of the legislators supported the administration because they accepted Beijing's policy towards Hong Kong, the Chief Executive's policy programs and the "executive-led" system of government. Theoretically, the administration had to arrive at an agreement with this majority coalition in the legislature, spelling out the privileges and obligations of the latter. It seemed, however, that these legislators had been willing to support the administration without demanding much in return.

In a way, the complaints of Tsang Yok-sing, chairman of the DAB, by the turn of the century about the executive-legislature relationship were both significant and puzzling.[30] Since the Tung administration could not function without a safe majority support in the legislature, Tsang's party, together with the Hong Kong Progressive Alliance and the Liberal Party, could almost dictate their policies to the administration and even had a strong say on the appointments of the principal officials. Even if an adequate consensus did not exist among the three parties, the DAB alone still carried a lot of weight. If it threatened to withdraw its support for the Tung administration and switch to the opposition, it would certainly manage to extract important concessions. So obviously it was not true that legislators had votes but no power. The truth was that the safe majority in the legislature backing the Tung administration did not have the political will to challenge the "executive-led" system of government.

Meanwhile, the DAB was acutely aware that its criticisms of the government accompanied by consistent delivery of its votes in support of the Tung administration in the legislature had been eroding its credibility in the eyes of the electorate. The local political culture expected political parties to assume the role of the opposition constituting part of the checks and balances mechanisms. Political parties therefore dared not identify too closely with the government. On the other hand, as the pro-democracy political parties commanded no more than one-third of the votes in the legislature, they could not exert much pressure on the government and contribute to its policy-making process, and the government did not have to make concessions to cultivate the support of the opposition.

While there was considerable frustration on the part of senior government officials, there was no danger of a constitutional or political crisis yet. So those who held power had no incentive to reform; and they were reluctant to accept further democratization of the electoral system. In the coming years, the Tung administration could allow the pro-government political parties to introduce important bills in the legislature, so that they could win credit for supporting the government and could

---

[30] *Ming Pao*, January 3, 2000.

claim to have delivered to the electorate. This was less a challenge to the "executive-led" system of government because the Chief Executive, according to the Basic Law, had full power to control the introduction of bills by members of the legislature.

Introducing a contract system for principal government officials might serve to enhance their accountability to the legislature and the public, because the Chief Executive could refuse to renew their contracts or even terminate their contracts early if their performance was unsatisfactory. It would also strengthen the Chief Executive's hand over the senior civil servants. However, admittedly these measures would not solve the basic problems in the existing system. Meanwhile, Tung Chee-hwa has clearly stated that he would not consider the adoption of a "ministerial system" at this stage.

Annex II of the Basic Law implicitly promised a review of the electoral system of the legislature in 2007. The promise was made when the Basic Law was about to be promulgated in the wake of the Tiananmen Incident. At that time, demand for a quicker pace of democracy was at its peak. Logically, a review of the legislature's electoral system in 2007 would lead to a higher proportion of directly elected seats, even to the extent that the entire legislature would be elected by universal suffrage. But there was a catch here: changing the electoral system then would require the endorsement of a two-thirds majority of all legislators and the consent of the Chief Executive. It was difficult to imagine why members returned by functional constituencies would support an increase in directly elected seats at the expense of functional constituency seats. If the legislature maintained its existing size, then which functional constituencies would be abolished, and according to what criteria?

The HKSAR government had already promised to study electoral reform after the Legislative Council elections in September 2000. It was not expected that it would propose radical changes, and its proposals would then attract much domestic and international criticism. A less controversial way to increase the proportion of directly elected seats in the review in 2007 would be to expand the size of the legislature to 90 seats, and increase the number of directly elected seats to 60. Political parties would find it much easier to agree on this, and a two-thirds majority in the legislature to support the change might become possible.

If the Tung administration and the legislature could agree on the date and conditions of the next review, then directly elected members might be able to secure the necessary majority in the legislature to abolish functional constituency seats eventually and have all seats directly elected. It had to be admitted that the above compromise formula would still be perceived by Beijing, the Tung administration and the local business community as too radical.

To generate support for electoral reforms, political parties in the territory had to demonstrate that they were ready to govern, and not just limit themselves to the roles of opposition and critics. Yet, the community perceived that Hong Kong's political parties had similar platforms in elections. Moreover, they tended to make promises of services rather than present concrete policy proposals. The two major parties in Hong Kong, the DAB, had a considerable number of teachers among their members, and a few of these had become members of the Legislative Council and District Councils (formerly District Boards). Obviously, education was an issue of major concern to the public, yet neither party seemed to have a comprehensive policy proposal on education to offer, leaving the concerned public unaware of their respective positions on the HKSAR's education policy.

Political parties in Hong Kong had limited resources and it was difficult to expect them to prepare detailed policy studies in competition with the civil service. However, Christine Loh Kung-wai's Citizen's Party prepared its annual policy addresses and budget speeches, and was also productive in the field of environmental protection. Yet, the manpower resources of the Citizen's Party were much smaller than those of the Democratic Party and the DAB. This suggested that it was not a matter of resources, but a question of priorities. Political parties in the pro-democracy camp seemed to believe that resources were better spent on building support in constituencies by providing services, and consider policy research to be less important.

In general, political parties in the HKSAR relied heavily on the media for publicity, and they blamed the media for taking no interest in serious policy research. Most legislators still believed that a clever soundbite was what the media wanted. This short-sightedness was already exacting its toll on the pro-democracy camp. Policies such as opposition to Beijing and fighting for democracy were at this stage of diminishing appeal to most Hong Kong people. They were more concerned with the economy and employment, and they also understood that they could not expect too much from local political parties in these areas. However, people expected advice from political parties on such issues as housing, education, mandatory provident fund and medical insurance. When government proposals were severely criticized, people wanted to know what the alternatives were. The poor performance of the pro-democracy camp in the area of policy studies also eroded its support among intellectuals. Many grassroots pressure groups, such as the Society for Community Organization, were critical of the Democratic Party for its lack of solid work on policy studies and over-eagerness in seeking publicity. Moreover, its failure to undertake much policy research meant that the Democratic Party was also neglecting an important channel to attract members and expand its base of support. Serious discussions of issues such as education and housing policy would enable the Democratic Party to reach out to the public.

After the handover, community organizations had found their influence enhanced by competition for their support from both pro-Beijing political groups and the pro-democracy groups. This trend, which had been in evidence since 1992, was heightened in the run-up to the Legislative Council elections in 1998 and 2000. The split of the pro-democracy camp and the introduction of proportional representation were relatively new factors. As explained above, the pro-democracy parties have been in the political wilderness since 1997, with limited influence over the HKSAR government's policymaking process. The pro-Beijing political groups, on the other hand, constituted the core of the majority support for the HKSAR government in the legislature. Moreover, the pro-Beijing groups could, through their recommendations to the HKSAR government and the Chinese authorities, offer appointments and honours to their supporters. Hence, they had a strong appeal to community organizations and had made some progress in absorbing them into their supporting networks.

Meanwhile, the worsening differences among the pro-democracy groups, the introduction of proportional representation in the 1998 and 2000 direct elections to the legislature and the considerably fewer seats available for competition meant that compromises cannot be reached.

They have to engage in all-out competition, including competition for community organizations' support. The contest between the Democratic Party and the Association for Democracy and People's Livelihood has been especially fierce.

Increasingly funding became a pressing problem for Hong Kong's grassroots community organizations. Financial support from United Nations-related agencies and from Western churches declined, mainly because prosperous Hong Kong was reckoned to be able to fund its own groups — especially after the smooth handover of sovereignty. Incidents involving radical social workers, meanwhile, heightened the caution and reservation of church groups.

The most important challenge for community organizations at this stage was to focus on livelihood issues and facilitate people at grassroots level to articulate their concerns and to enable them to influence the policymaking process. The organizations had to show that they could continue to serve as an effective bridge between ordinary people and the government as well as between ordinary people and political parties, and thus offer meaningful political participation.

VII Conclusion

Elections offer the most important channel of political participation because they allow ordinary people to choose their own representatives. The fact that there are representatives means that the political system has a certain autonomy and follows its own logic. The government needs not respond immediately and to all demands; rather, the relationship between societal demands and governmental actions is mediated by elected representatives who normally form political parties. Political parties, sooner or later, assume a key role in the representation process.[31] This was exactly what happened in Hong Kong when elections and universal suffrage were first introduced in 1982 at the District Board level by the British administration, which had no plan of introducing full parliamentary democracy to the territory.

---

[31] Hans-Dieter Klingemann, Richard I. Hofferbert and Ian Budge, *Parties Policies, and Democracy*, Boulder and Oxford: Westview Press, 1994, pp. 1–19.

With the Sino-British agreement on the return of Hong Kong to China, a new constitution (the Basic Law) and new political institutions had to be introduced in the 1980s and 1990s. Elections to the legislature were implemented in 1985, partly to fulfill the Chinese authorities' promise of self-administration for the people of Hong Kong, and partly to provide legitimacy for the future HKSAR government. As argued by March and Olsen, "preferences and meanings develop in politics, as in the rest of life, through a combination of education, indoctrination, and experience." Institutions then affect the distribution of resources and impact upon the power of political actors who go on to remould political institutions to their own ends.[32]

The introduction of elections and new political institutions, in turn encouraged interest articulation and political participation, and political parties emerged and developed. The same process also facilitated the development of community organizations. However, the Chinese authorities only allowed limited democracy for Hong Kong, and the establishment of new political institutions had not been a process of institutionalization of democracy. Elections on the basis of universal suffrage could not change the government, and could not even change the majority in support of the government in the legislature. The prospects for further democratization remained uncertain too.

Under such circumstances, the purpose of political parties and political participation had to adjust to the political restrictions, and people had to lower their expectations. Elections were largely perceived as a means of checks and balances through which people elected their representatives to monitor the work of the government, and political parties in the pro-democracy camp realized that they had to remain in the opposition for a long time.

A vast majority of Hong Kong people did not appreciate political participation as a way of life providing satisfaction and meaning. They perceived see it largely as the fulfillment of civic obligations, or as an instrument to realize practical political objectives, such as the articulation

---

[32] James March and Johan Olsen, "The New Institutionalism: Organizational Factors in Political Life," *American Political Science Review*, Vol. 78, No. 3, September 1984, pp. 734–749, especially p. 739.

of grievances and the monitoring of the work of the government. This utilitarian approach implied that Hong Kong people constantly engaged in a cost-benefit analysis in their political activities.[33] The Sino-British negotiations on the territory's future in 1982–1984 and the Tiananmen Incident in 1989 were exceptional periods of intense emotions, and the events proved to be significant catalysts in Hong Kong's political development. However, as emotions faded, political apathy to some extent returned. At the same time, emigration remained an option to a considerable segment of the population. It reached a peak in the immediate years after the Tiananmen Incident; and it again emerged as an option at this stage when people were dissatisfied with the performance of the Tung administration and worried about the territory's economic future.

Acknowledgement

Originally published as Joseph Y.S. Cheng, "Elections and Political Parties in Hong Kong's Political Development", *Journal of Contemporary Asia*, Vol. 31, No. 3 (2010), pp. 346–374. Reproduced with kind permission from the publisher.

---

[33] See Anthony Downs, *An Economic Theory of Democracy*, New York: Harper& Row, 1957.

Chapter 13

Hong Kong: Democratization at a Critical Stage

1 Causes of the Hong Kong People's Grievances

On July 1, 2003, more than half a million people took to the streets to protest against the Article 23 legislation[1] and demand democracy. People who took part in the rally felt that they made history, and were proud of the peace and order among the protesters. They felt that the rally showed the Hong Kong people at their best. This protest rally differed from the three major protest rallies in May–June 1989 during the Tiananmen

---

[1] Article 23 of the Basic Law (Hong Kong's constitution) states: "The Hong Kong Special Administrative Region shall enact laws on its own to prohibit any act of treason, secession, sedition, subversion against the Central People's Government, or theft of state secrets, to prohibit foreign political organizations or bodies from conducting political activities in the Region, and to prohibit political organizations or bodies of the Region from establishing ties with foreign political organizations or bodies." This article was written into the draft Basic Law after the massive protest rallies in Hong Kong during the Tiananmen Incident in 1989; obviously, the Chinese authorities were concerned with a repetition of such activities.

The Tung administration was wise enough not to initiate the controversial legislative process in his first term. In response to the open prompting of the Chinese authorities, a paper addressing the implementation of Article 23 of the Basic Law was finally unveiled for public consultation in September 2002. As expected, the proposals stirred fears of a crackdown on human rights groups and Falun Gong. The pro-democracy camp in the territory also perceived the proposals a threat to civil liberties. See *South China Morning Post*, September 25, 2002.

Incident in two ways. This time, the Hong Kong people marched for Hong Kong issues. Further, during the Tiananmen Incident, there was no opposition to the demonstrators, the pro-Beijing united front kept very quiet; but with regard to the Article 23 legislation and the issue of democratization, the pro-Beijing united front had been fully mobilized in support of the Tung administration.

The Tung administration and its supporters blamed the economy for the grievances of the community. The implication was that when the economy improved, people's dissatisfaction with the government would evaporate. If this was the case, there should be more tolerance for the government, because many external variables were beyond Hong Kong's control, and the small territory's economic performance was bound to be much affected by the global and regional economic cycles. No doubt the sharp deterioration in the territory's economic performance since 1997 had caused much misery and dissatisfaction among the Hong Kong people. The average annual rate of per capita GDP growth fell from 4.5% in the period 1983–1997 to 1.9% in 1997–2001. Almost full employment was maintained from 1985 to mid-1997, as the unemployment rate ranged from 1.3% to a peak of only 3.5%. Since Hong Kong's return to China, the unemployment rate had been climbing from 2.1% in mid-1997 to a record high of 8.7% in mid-2003.[2] It was not expected that the unemployment rate would decline substantially in the near future even when the economy gradually improved, as much of the unemployment was structural; 47.8% of the population had less than nine years of formal education; and in view of the territory's wage structure and its transformation into a modern service economy, the surplus of unskilled labor would remain.

The impact of uncontrollable external variables was perhaps best illustrated by the Asian financial crisis, whose curtain raiser was the devaluation of the Thai baht which took place on the following day of

---

[2] See Sung Yun-wing, "Hong Kong Economy in Crisis", in *The First Tung Chee-hwa Administration*, edited by Siu-kai Lau, Hong Kong: The Chinese University Press, 2002, p. 123. In the quarter of October–December 2003, the unemployment rate was reduced to 7.3%, the November 2003–January 2004 quarter remained the same; see *South China Morning Post*, February 20, 2004.

Hong Kong's return to the Motherland. Hong Kong's unique position as the gateway to China was gradually eroded by the development of China's coastal cities too; and in the early years of the new century, Hong Kong people were acutely aware of the pressure of competition from north of the border, especially from Shanghai.

In the initial years of his administration, the Hong Kong people found Tung a sincere man with his heart in the right place. His inclinations to depart from the hitherto followed *laissez-faire* philosophy (euphemistically known as positive non-interventionism) caused some concern even in the business community. Even before his assumption of office, he already indicated that his priorities were housing, education, and services for the elderly. His plan of expanding housing supply to 85,000 units per annum was highly controversial and attracted much criticism. Tung's plan was to curb speculative activities which had driven housing prices to irrational heights so as to lower the cost structure in the territory to enhance its competitiveness. Implicitly, he had hoped that lower housing prices would lead to lower wages and lower prices in general, which would then strengthen Hong Kong's international competitiveness. However, unfortunately, Tung's plan coincided with the Asian financial crisis. The bubble in the real estate market burst and the government's plan to expand housing supply much exacerbated the fall in housing prices. Given the significance of the housing sector in the territory's economy, the dramatic downward adjustment in housing prices (up to 65% from the peak in the summer of 1997) was naturally blamed for the decline in consumer demand and the associated deflation, etc. The housing problem also created a new group of middle-class flat owners whose properties had become liabilities instead of assets because of the sharp drop in real estate prices.[3]

To be fair to Tung, when he announced his housing plan, it was favorably received. His fault was his inability to adjust his policy to the new situation. In addition to being considered incompetent, most people

---

[3] According to a local leading real estate agency, property-owners suffering from negative assets numbered 177,468 in July 2003, and the number declined to 161,958 in the following September; see *Ming Pao* (a Chinese newspaper in Hong Kong), September 23, 2003.

believed that Tung did not have a strong personal base of support. He could not trust the senior civil servants (for example, he did not get along with the previous Chief Secretary for Administration, Anson Chan Fang On-sang), he only consulted a narrow circle of friends and aides dominated by the rich families in the territory, he refused to maintain a dialogue with the opposition camp, and he found it difficult to make hard decisions and tended to procrastinate. It was said that the former Chinese Premier Zhu Rongji once criticized Tung for "discussing without decisions, making decisions without execution". This subsequently became a most popular line of criticism against Tung.

In order to strengthen control over his administration, Tung introduced an accountability system (ministerial system) in his second term, making all of his policy secretaries political appointees and members of the Executive Council. They were no longer civil servants and had to be accountable to Tung himself. Although few people believed Tung's claim that the system would make the top government officials more accountable to the public, the community accepted that Tung should have his own team of ministers.

However, quite a number of his ministers soon got into trouble. Frederick Ma Si-hang, Secretary for Financial Services and the Treasury, first came under severe criticism for his proposal to de-list the penny stocks;[4] then Financial Secretary Antony Leung Kam-chung was accused of dishonesty for buying a car just before his sharp increase of the first vehicle registration tax; and of course, Yeoh Eng-kiong, Secretary for Health, Welfare and Food, was called upon to resign because of his ill-handling of the Severe Acute Respiratory Syndrome (SARS) crisis. In all these cases, Tung chose to defend his ministers and they were allowed to keep their positions. Tung therefore had to pay the political price of absorbing the public's wrath.

It was in the context of these developments that Tung introduced the Article 23 legislation. Admittedly, most people in Hong Kong did not have the time and expertise to go through the bill in detail. However, they certainly became concerned and worried when the legal profession, the social workers, the journalists, the librarians, the bankers, the Catholic

---

[4] *South China Morning Post*, August 12, September 11, 12, 15 and 16, 2003.

Church, and the Christian churches, etc., came out to articulate their opposition. The resentment rapidly escalated because of the arrogance of Regina Ip Lau Suk-yee, Secretary for Security, who was responsible for "selling" the bill to the public. In the beginning of 2003, the Tung administration decided against the introduction of a "white bill" for further consultation of the public. With the benefit of hindsight, this was probably the fatal decision. If the government had been willing to spend more time consulting the public in the form of a "white bill", and had offered the three important amendments it announced later on July 5, the legislation most probably would have been able to go through the legislature. The rejection of the "white bill" approach was seen as further evidence of the lack of concern for public opinion on the part of the Tung administration, and that it was determined to complete the legislative process to fulfill its commitment to Beijing.

Meanwhile, the SARS outbreak that resulted in about 300 deaths in Hong Kong generated more dissatisfaction and frustration with the Tung administration. Naturally, it was accused of poor coordination in fighting the epidemic, and SARS also dealt a severe blow to the economy. All kinds of grievances prompted various groups to march in protest against the Tung administration on July 1, 2003.

Tung Chee-hwa, however, did not seem to have received the message. On the following Saturday, he announced that the government would introduce three major amendments to the draft bill, but the second and third readings would proceed as scheduled on July 9. It was the withdrawal of support by the Liberal Party for the legislative timetable announced on the following day that finally forced the government to shelve the bill for the time being. There were further demonstrations and gatherings organized by the pro-democracy camp on July 9 and the following Sunday, that were attended by about 50,000 and 20,000 people respectively.

These events attracted much international media attention. The Hong Kong crisis became an important issue high on the agenda of the Chinese leadership. How the new leaders, especially President Hu Jintao and Premier Wen Jiabao, handled the crisis would shape their international image, and affect how Western leaders and how the international community would assess them. Further, the crisis in Hong Kong might well have a demonstration effect on China. It was significant enough that the Chinese authorities censored all reports on the protests in Hong Kong, though obviously, they were soon known to the educated public in China who had access to the Internet and other sources of information.

The incompetence and unpopularity of the Tung administration could no longer be covered up. It was obvious that a majority of the Hong Kong people wanted him to step down. His situation was made worse by his inept handling of the crisis. The head of the Central Policy Unit (the government think-tank), Professor Lau Siu-kai, told the media earlier that he expected a maximum turnout of 30,000 people at the rally, and that the challenge to the HKSAR government would be limited. After the rally, the Central Policy Unit came out to defend itself and indicated that it had been closely monitoring the situation all the time; and in the week just before the rally, its opinion survey revealed that the turnout could be as high as a million people.[5] If the Central Policy Unit had been correct in its forecast, then the Tung administration should have been better prepared for the protest rally. Instead, it had to wait for six days before its presentation of the amendments to the bill.

When the Tung administration announced on July 5 that the legislative process regarding the Article 23 legislation would proceed as scheduled, the community believed that Tung had studied the situation and had enlisted the support of a majority of legislators. However, on the very next day, the Liberal Party withdrew its support and Tung's plan collapsed. Obviously, Tung did not have much understanding and control of his own "ruling coalition". At the same time, support for the Tung administration in the pro-Beijing camp also seemed to have been shaken. The head of the pro-Beijing party, Democratic Alliance for the Betterment of Hong Kong (DAB), Tsang Yok-shing, indicated that he had to consider whether or not to resign from the Executive Council, following the example of James Tien, the leader of the Liberal Party. Then, three Hong Kong deputies to the National People's Congress (NPC) publicly appealed to Tung to consider stepping down. There was considerable speculation that some leaders in Beijing were only lukewarm in their support of Tung Chee-hwa, and that it was likely that Tung would resign soon.

---

[5] *Ming Pao*, July 5 and 12, 2003.

Beijing's support was therefore critical for Tung's political survival, and Chinese leaders understood this well. Tung was invited to report to Chinese leaders in Beijing on July 19, and he met with President Hu Jintao, Vice-President Zeng Qinghong, Premier Wen Jiabao, etc. Apparently, the Chinese leaders wanted to show that they were united in their support for Tung. Three days earlier, two important officials who had incurred the wrath of the community, Secretary for Security Regina Ip Lau Suk-yee and Financial Secretary Antony Leung Kam-chung, offered to resign from the government; and their resignations helped to ease the people's anger toward the Tung administration. On September 5, contrary to expectations, the Tung administration announced the withdrawal of the draft bill indefinitely. There were some signs of economic recovery; the rises in the stock market and real estate market improved the community's sentiments.

II China's Support for the Tung Administration

Apparently, the Chinese leadership had been aware of Tung's incompetence and unpopularity even before his re-election in the spring of 2002. Visitors to Mainland China discussing Hong Kong affairs with junior cadres who had no responsibilities for Hong Kong could easily detect awareness among them that the Tung administration did not perform well. It was also rumored in 2001 or so that the Central Liaison Office (the central government's representative office) in Hong Kong tried to dissuade visitors to Beijing from complaining against Tung in front of the top Chinese leaders. These visitors were leaders of the pro-Beijing united front and the territory's very rich tycoons because only they, and not the ordinary people, enjoyed access to the Chinese leadership. The latter, however, decided to support Tung's re-election probably because of the following reasons.

In the first place, China's official propaganda line had been that Hong Kong was doing very well since its return to the Motherland. Replacing Tung would go against this propaganda line. Further, there had been an eagerness among Chinese leaders to show the world that the local Chinese could govern Hong Kong better than the British. Replacing Tung again would shatter this claim. Finally, to find a successor for Tung required a consultation exercise as well as a mobilization exercise to generate support for the candidate. These exercises could not be conducted in secrecy and would immediately reduce the Tung administration into a lame-duck government. This would be costly in terms of the territory's political stability and economic development.

Concern for Tung's unpopularity prompted the Chinese authorities to alter the electoral arrangements so as to deter challenges to Tung's re-election. Nominations were to be open; and as Beijing's support for Tung was so obvious, members of the Election Committee felt the pressure to show their support for the Chinese leadership's candidate. As a result, more than 700 out of the 800 members of the Election Committee openly indicated their nomination of Tung. There could not be another candidate because nomination by at least 100 members was required. Tung was therefore elected on an *ipso facto* basis.

Chinese leaders understood that they had to soften the opposition to Tung within the pro-Beijing united front and the business community. They therefore chose to help Hong Kong solve its economic problems. Assistance included a sharp increase in the number of tourists allowed to visit Hong Kong, a Closer Economic Partnership Arrangement (CEPA) giving Hong Kong better access to the China market,[6] and political pressure on Guangdong to improve cooperation with the territory. The Hong Kong people appreciated the economic support from the central government, and they in general had a very good impression of the new leaders in China, namely, Hu Jintao and Wen Jiabao. When Wen visited Hong Kong in late-June and early-July 2003, he was well received by the local community. Wen basically reiterated the central government's support for Tung, promised the territory economic help, and reassured Hong Kong people that the Article 23 legislation would not compromise their freedoms and human rights.[7] It was significant that Wen did not have a single word of praise for Tung during his visit.

The new Chinese leaders had been following the dictum of "stability takes precedence over everything else" in the handling of Hong Kong's

---

[6] For the details of CEPA, see all major newspapers in Hong Kong on September 30, 2003.
[7] For Wen Jiabao's message to Hong Kong, see all major newspapers in Hong Kong on July 2, 2003.

political crisis. They probably believed that they had no other option except to continue to support Tung. Replacing him would generate more instability, as Beijing was concerned with Hong Kong's demonstration effect on China and raising the expectations of the pro-democracy camp in the territory. The massive protest rally in Hong Kong attracted much attention in Taiwan too, and it was seized upon by the pro-independence movement there to discredit the "one country, two systems" arrangement and the opposition parties, i.e., the Kuomintang and the People First Party, which were more moderate in dealing with Beijing.

The Chinese leadership's clear support for Tung naturally meant deterrence against open criticisms of the Tung administration by the local pro-Beijing united front and the business community. In the following August and September, the Chinese authorities invited a host of delegations to visit Beijing, and they were received by Chinese leaders and senior officials. These meetings helped to further stabilize the situation in Hong Kong, as the united front exercise accorded political recognition and status to members of the establishment in the territory. They were given opportunities to articulate their grievances as well as their suggestions to help solve Hong Kong's problems; and they were told to support the Tung administration.

While the Hong Kong people were grateful for the central government's economic support, they also felt embarrassed by the fact that people enjoying a per capita annual GDP of over US$24,000 had to seek assistance from people with a per capita annual GDP of about US$1,000. Actually, the Hong Kong community should have been contributing to the poverty-alleviation programs and the development of China's poor interior provinces.[8] More important still, the heavy involvement of Chinese leaders in Hong Kong affairs further weakened the legitimacy and effectiveness of the Tung administration. Business leaders probably felt that if they needed anything, they should lobby Beijing. Vice-President Zeng Qinghong also received delegations from the three pro-Beijing parties, namely, the DAB, the Hong Kong Progressive Alliance, and the Liberal Party, in a high-profile manner and praised them for their contributions to Hong Kong. This was unprecedented and might be

---

[8] See the author's "Shame on us", *South China Morning Post*, September 1, 2003.

interpreted as political intervention in support of the pro-Beijing political parties, as the Chinese authorities have been refusing any contact with the territory's pro-democracy camp since the Tiananmen Incident. Further, the DAB soon visited the Guangdong and Shanghai authorities; and with the help of the latter, it could claim to serve Hong Kong by reflecting the community's views and demands to the provincial governments, a service which obviously could not be delivered by the pro-democracy camp.

The Chinese authorities had been sending many agents to the HKSAR to collect information after the massive protest rally as their confidence in the Central Liaison Office, the State Council's Hong Kong and Macau Affairs Office, and the Tung administration had been badly shaken. It was said that all three had informed the Chinese leaders that they expected a turnout of about 30,000 to 40,000 people for the July 1 protest rally, the actual turnout therefore showed that they did not have a good understanding of the situation, and that they probably had been sending unrealistically favorable reports on the territory to the Chinese leadership. Some leaders in the pro-democracy camp had been contacted too; but when these contacts were reported by the media, they were denied. It seemed that the Chinese authorities were ready to listen to all walks of life in Hong Kong so as to better understand the situation, but they were yet reluctant to grant the pro-democracy camp the official recognition by engaging in a dialogue with it.

III The Pro-democracy Movement

The pro-democracy movement was in a difficult state in the year before the massive protest rally. There was considerable frustration with the lack of progress as no one expected any breakthrough before 2007. Even the political parties in the pro-democracy camp did not believe that democratization was an issue with much political appeal. The Democratic Party (i.e., the party with the most seats in the legislature) and its allies could make very little impact on the government's policymaking process. As the Tung administration enjoyed the backing of a safe majority in the legislature, it did not have to lobby for the approval of the pro-democracy groups which were treated as the opposition. In fact, there had been little meaningful consultation between the pro-democracy groups and the government.

While the Tung administration failed to show the Hong Kong people the way ahead, the Democratic Party and other pro-democracy groups had not been able to demonstrate significant initiatives in presenting the Hong Kong people with well-researched policy alternatives. They failed to perform the role of an effective and constructive opposition from the perspective of policy platform. According to Lau Siu-kai's survey in 2001, 63.6% of the respondents indicated that the Chief Executive could not represent their respective views, and only 12.1% of the respondents said he could. Similarly, 51.7% of the respondents revealed that the HKSAR government could not represent their respective views, and only 15.2% said it could. However, the Democratic Party was not much better — 46% of the respondents indicated that it could not represent their respective views, and only 13.4% said it could. The public affairs concern groups were considered most representative — only 22.1% of the respondents said that they could not represent their respective views, and 38.6% indicated that they could.[9]

The pro-democracy political parties were encountering difficulties in their relationship with grassroots community organizations, which emerged and developed in the late-1960s and 1970s and which had been supporting pro-democracy political groups. The parties could certainly help to raise issues of importance to grassroots community organizations in the legislature or with senior government officials, thus exerting pressure on the Tung administration to provide solutions. However, their high profile and eagerness for publicity often resulted in failures to compromise and also in delays in achieving settlements. Many grassroots community organizations worried that they might be taken for a ride, and they often preferred to act without the involvement of political parties.

It was in this context that new groups such as Power for Democracy, Hong Kong Democratic Development Network, and Civil Human Rights Front emerged in early-2002. They planned to concentrate on the cause of democracy and human rights, and wanted to offer an alternative to

---

[9] See Lau Siu-kai, "Socio-economic Discontent and Political Attitudes", in *Indicators of Social Development: Hong Kong 2001*, edited by Lau Siu-kai, Lee Ming-kwan, Wan Po-san and Wong Siu-lun, Hong Kong: Hong Kong Institute of Asia-Pacific Studies, Chinese University of Hong Kong, p. 69.

political parties in political participation. Their emergence and development reflected the disappointment with political parties in the pro-democracy camp and the suspicions against its politicians. It is significant that these new groups were dominated by church activists and academics who were generally seen as having no political ambitions. At this stage, these groups attempted to bring together various types of organizations in support of democracy and human rights because of the decline in appeal of the pro-democracy political parties, the suspicions against them, and the in-fighting among them and that between them and the grassroots community organizations. This was not a healthy phenomenon as political parties had the resources and the most important role to play in the push for democracy in the territory.

Nevertheless, the pro-democracy camp managed to present a united platform in the District Council elections in November 2003. More than 200 candidates from all pro-democracy groups supported: (a) direct election of the Chief Executive by universal suffrage by 2007; (b) direct elections of all seats of the legislature by universal suffrage by 2008; (c) initiation of public consultations on political reforms by the government before the end of 2003; and (d) abolition of all appointed seats to the District Councils after the November 2003 elections. The pro-democracy camp understood that it could not mobilize hundreds of thousands of people to march on the streets all the time; and it therefore hoped to use the elections to send a message to the Tung administration, to Beijing, and to the world that the Hong Kong people had not forgotten the demand for democratization.

The record voter turnout rate (44.1%) was the most important feature of the District Council elections. While the pro-Beijing united front had tried to explain the participation in the 2003 protest rally as a reflection of the current economic difficulties, and that people had various types of grievances, the record voter turnout rate was a clear indication that people remained dissatisfied with the Tung administration, even though Beijing strongly backed Tung and provided economic assistance for Hong Kong. Further, candidates from the pro-democracy camp won handsomely, while the pro-government DAB suffered a serious defeat.

The victory in the District Council elections and the prospect of securing half of the seats in the Legislative Council elections in September

2004 symbolized the revival of the pro-democracy movement. The expectations, at the same time, also generated considerable pressure. Various pro-democracy groups had to remain united, and they had much to catch up in presenting themselves as an alternate government, and not just engaging in opposition for the sake of opposition. Cooperation among the pro-democracy political groups in the Legislative Council elections would be much more difficult than in the District Council elections. The latter adopted a single-member constituency, simple majority system, and the pro-democracy camp did not have enough candidates to run in the 400 constituencies. Cases of direct confrontation among the pro-democracy candidates in more than 20 constituencies were tolerated as the undesirable outcomes (competition between pro-democracy candidates in the same constituency benefitting the pro-government candidate) were insignificant. Legislative Council candidates, on the other hand, compete in medium-sized multi-member constituencies, and voters can only vote for one slate of candidates. Pro-democracy political groups competed against each other in the past two elections in 1998 and 2000. In order to maximize the number of seats won in September 2004, they had to work together closely and present to the Hong Kong people a list of candidates endorsed by the entire pro-democracy camp.

Meanwhile, two developments had an important bearing on the progress of democracy in the territory — the relations across the Taiwan Straits and the pace of political reforms in China. As Taiwan President Chen Shui-bian won his second term in March 2004, tension might well escalate across the Taiwan Straits; under such circumstances, Beijing would be more conservative on democratization in Hong Kong. Further, if the Chinese leadership secured enough political will and support for political reforms in China, democratization in Hong Kong might have brighter prospects. However, both of these would be beyond the control of the Hong Kong people.

IV Pressures from China and the Political Implications

Since Tung's visit to Beijing in early December 2003, the Chinese authorities' strategy regarding political reforms in the territory had become quite clear. In the first place, through formal and informal channels, Beijing was telling the Hong Kong people that the Chinese authorities had full control over the entire reform process, and that they had considerable reservations on democratization. In this way, Beijing was trying to lower people's expectations. Further, the Chinese authorities also adopted delaying tactics, demanding to define various issues of principles and processes, thus avoiding the consultation of the public on options of political reforms in the beginning of 2004, as had been promised by the Tung administration.

Then the Chinese authorities fully mobilized the territory's united front and the business leaders to articulate support for the central government's position. Not only did they have to show support for the Chinese authorities, but they also had to criticize the pro-democracy camp this time. The pro-Beijing united front then launched a propaganda campaign against leaders of the pro-democracy movement like Martin Lee and Emily Lau. The campaign was aimed at reducing the Hong Kong people's support for the pro-democracy movement, and to justify the Chinese leaders' worries about democratization in Hong Kong.

Finally, in late April 2004, the Standing Committee of the National People's Congress ruled against the introduction of universal suffrage and extensive changes to the elections of the Chief Executive and legislature in 2007 and 2008 respectively. It did not release any timetable for future reform and instead argued that "Hong Kong has been enjoying unprecedented democratic rights".

The above strategy had been effective within a matter of months. Opinion polls showed that the community's support for the direct election of the Chief Executive by universal suffrage in 2007, and the direct elections of all seats of the legislature by universal suffrage in 2008, dropped from a peak of about 80% in the second half of 2003 to below 60% in mid-2004. Even before the formal decision of the Standing Committee of the National People's Congress, the Hong Kong people already realized that the chances of achieving the above objectives were low.

The initiative of controlling the entire political reform process was in the hands of the Chinese authorities. The latter accepted the handling of this hot potato because they did not consider that the Tung administration could be relied upon to prevent the pro-democracy camp from winning half of the seats of the legislature in the September elections. Even if the opposition groups could secure 28 seats or so, they would be able to exert a lot of pressure on the Tung administration.

The Chinese leadership, however, paid a substantial price too. It had to continue to support Hong Kong economically; various gifts to the territory would generate considerable dissatisfaction among China's local leaders. The high-handed strategy on the part of Beijing to contain the community's demand for democratization badly damaged its reputation of self-restraint won through the patient efforts of the past years.

The pro-democracy movement was still willing to engage in a dialogue with the Chinese authorities. However, this dialogue had to avoid adversely affecting the solidarity of the movement. A firm position maintaining unity at worst might result in the missing of some limited opportunities. A wavering position would lose the support of the Hong Kong people, the very foundation of engaging in a dialogue with the central authorities.

Another important challenge for the pro-democracy movement was to present a rational policy platform in the September Legislative Council elections, so that the Hong Kong people could understand that the pro-democracy groups were in support of stability and prosperity too. Fighting for democracy in Hong Kong was an arduous long-term process. A rational, principled stand was the only way to maintain the people's support and the momentum of the pro-democracy movement.

The pro-democracy movement in the territory and the Hong Kong people in general understood that the chances for the Chinese leadership to meet their demands for democracy were low. The business community in Hong Kong remained conservative and had substantial reservations regarding democratization. It was unhappy with the Tung administration as most businessmen had lost a part of their fortunes since Tung has assumed power. However, they did not trust the pro-democracy camp, and believed that their privileges and interests would be threatened if full democracy was to be implemented in the territory. Further, they considered that their interests had been well respected by the Chinese leadership, and they therefore preferred lobbying Beijing than engaging in the democratic process, like their counterparts in the Western world.

The British colonial administration secured its legitimacy by results; the Tung administration and its successor had no results to boast of, they had no legitimacy in the eyes of the Hong Kong people. Take the example of the government's budget deficit which amounted to about HK$40.1 billion in fiscal year 2003–2004 (ending on March 31, 2004). The Tung administration was under considerable pressure to cut expenditure and raise revenues, but these were bound to be unpopular measures, and it did not have the mandate or the political appeal to ask the people to tighten their belts to tide over the difficult years. Any group adversely affected by these measures would very likely protest strongly, and the Tung administration was too weak to absorb the political cost.

Meanwhile, unemployment would remain at a high level. Also, the gap between the rich and the poor had been widening. The Gini coefficient in the territory climbed from 0.476 in 1991, to 0.518 in 1996, and 0.525 in 2001. The population has been aging too; the proportion of the population aged 65 and over gradually rose from 8.7% in 1991, to 10.1% in 1996, and 11.1% in 2001. These socioeconomic problems would force the government to redefine its social service commitments. At the same time, Tung had indicated that he wanted a more active role for the government in the economy, but he had yet to define this role.

The only way to forge a consensus on all these important policy issues was for a candidate running for the Chief Executive position to declare his platform, and win the election and the mandate to implement his policy programs. A weak government like the Tung administration at this stage could not be bold enough to introduce the necessary "bitter medicine" to implement economic reforms, it would continue to avoid controversies while Hong Kong's economy slowly deteriorated. This was exactly the Hong Kong people's fear, that the two terms of the Tung administration would be an era of economic stagnation like the "lost decade" of Japan in the 1990s.

Delaying tactics, lowering the community's political expectations, dampening the appeal of the pro-democracy camp, etc., might succeed in maintaining a political system which allows the Chinese authorities to control the situation for some time, but they would also prolong the Hong Kong people's dissatisfaction and grievances in a period of slow economic growth and deteriorating social contradictions. Even the traditional pro-Beijing united front leaders were angry because the Tung administration was perceived to be over-dependent on the major business tycoons. There was a danger that Hong Kong would be transformed into an economic and political liability of the Chinese authorities, and this could hardly be described as a satisfactory state of the "one country, two systems" model.

V Conclusion

As the development of representative government was not expected to make any significant progress in the foreseeable future, maintenance of the rule of law and freedom of the media in Hong Kong was perhaps more important. It was essential to enlist the business community, at least its enlightened segment, to support such an objective; and the best way to secure this support was to demonstrate that it would be in the interests of the business community to do so.

At this stage, the Hong Kong people had to strengthen their consensus based on the highest common factor of enlightened self-interests in persuading Chinese leaders to maintain the territory as it was. Securing democracy in Hong Kong would be a long-term arduous process. It ultimately would depend on political developments in China, but the prevention of further deterioration in the development of a system of representative government and the preservation of the existing freedoms would have to rely on the efforts of the community as a whole.

Acknowledgement

Originally published as Cheng, Joseph Y.S., "Hong Kong: Democratization at a Critical Stage", [*Views and Policies: Taiwan Forum*], Vol. 1, No. 1, September 1, 2004, pp. 29–53. Reproduced with kind permission from the publisher.

Chapter 14

Hong Kong Since Its Return to China: A Lost Decade?

I The Economy: Had We Been Doing Better?

Chinese leaders, being orthodox Marxist-Leninists, believed that a strong economy was the key to political stability. The Hong Kong Special Administrative Region (HKSAR) government naturally toed the Beijing line. When more than half a million people took to the streets to protest against the Article 23 legislation[1] and demanded democracy on July 1, 2003, the Tung Chee-hwa administration and its supporters blamed the

---

[1] Article 23 of the Basic Law (Hong Kong's constitution) states: "The Hong Kong Special Administrative Region shall enact laws on its own to prohibit any act of treason, secession, sedition, subversion against the Central People's Government, or theft of state secrets, to prohibit foreign political organizations or bodies from conducting political activities in the Region, and to prohibit political organizations or bodies of the Region from establishing ties with foreign political organizations or bodies." This article was written into the draft Basic Law after the massive protest rallies in Hong Kong during the Tiananmen Incident in 1989; obviously, the Chinese authorities were concerned with a repetition of such activities.

The Tung administration was wise enough not to initiate the controversial legislative process in his first term. In response to the open prompting of the Chinese authorities, a paper addressing the implementation of Article 23 of the Basic Law was finally unveiled for public consultation in September 2002. As expected, the proposals stirred fears of a crackdown on human rights groups and the Falun Gong. The pro-democracy camp in the territory also perceived the proposals as a threat to civil liberties. See *South China Morning Post* (an English language newspaper in Hong Kong), September 25, 2002.

economy for the grievances of the community. The Chinese authorities responded to the political crises by offering strong economic support for the territory. The rationale was simple — if the economy improved, the people would largely be satisfied, and they would be much less interested in democracy. Political stability would no longer be challenged.

When Donald Tsang, Tung's successor, visited Beijing on his duty trip in December 2006, he told the central government that "Hong Kong's economy is the best it has been in almost twenty years."[2] The message was clear — the economy was in good shape, there should be no severe political challenges, and the Chinese leadership should be satisfied with his administration. His re-election thus was reassured, as perceived by all the Hong Kong people. Tsang apparently had the statistics behind him, as demonstrated by Tables 14.1, 14.2, 14.3, and 14.4.

Many Hong Kong people, however, disagreed. On the basis of the views expressed in various phone-in programs, they did not feel that they had benefited from economic growth since 1997, nor in the middle of the first decade in the new century.

A study by the Bauhinia Foundation, a think-tank close to Donald Tsang, revealed that the median household income in 2005 was still 15.8% lower than that in the previous peak year of 1997. More serious still, between 1996 and 2005, the number of households with a monthly income below HK$8,000 rose by 76.5%, to more than 500,000; and their proportion of the total number of households rose from 13% to 22%.[3]

Obviously, the Chief Executive felt the pressure to respond. Speaking in a question-and-answer session in the Legislative Council in January 2007, Donald Tsang admitted that some low-income households had failed to benefit from the stronger economy, but the most important thing was to create jobs through a stronger economy. He indicated that at least wage levels had stopped declining; in the last quarter of 2005, those earning HK$15,000 or more per month accounted for more than one-third of the labor force, compared with one-quarter during the same period a decade ago. Further, the proportion of workers earning less than HK$9,000 per month had also

---

[2] *South China Morning Post*, December 28, 2006.
[3] *Ibid.*, January 10, 2007; and *Ming Pao* (a Chinese language newspaper in Hong Kong), January 10, 2007.

Table 14.1: Gross Domestic Product (GDP) of Hong Kong, 1997–2006

Year	GDP At Current Market Prices HK$ Million	% Change	At Constant (2000) Market Prices HK$ Million	% Change	Implicit Price Deflator of GDP (2000=100)	% Change	Per capita GDP At current market prices HK$	% Change	At Constant (2000) Market Prices HK$	% Change
1997	1,365,024	11.0	1,216,102	5.1	112.2	5.6	210,350	10.1	187,401	4.2
1998	1,292,764	-5.3	1,149,662	-5.5	112.4	0.2	197,559	-6.1	175,690	-6.2
1999	1,266,702	-2.0	1,195,624	4.0	105.9	-5.8	191,738	-2.9	180,977	3.0
2000	1,314,789	3.8	1,314,789	10.0	100.0	-5.6	197,268	2.9	197,268	9.0
2001	1,298,813	-1.2	1,323,167	0.6	98.2	-1.8	193,135	-2.1	196,756	-0.3
2002	1,276,757	-1.7	1,347,495	1.8	94.8	-3.5	188,118	-2.6	198,541	0.9
2003	1,233,983	-3.4	1,390,495	3.2	88.7	-6.4	181,385	-3.6	204,408	3.0
2004	1,291,425	4.7	1,509,915	8.6	85.5	-3.6	190,377	3.8	222,586	7.7
2005	1,382,675	7.1	1,623,479	7.5	85.2	-0.4	202,941	6.6	238,284	7.1
2006	1,472,291	6.5	1,734,280	6.8	84.9	-0.4	214,710	5.8	252,917	6.1

Notes: (1) Figures in this table are the latest data released on 28 February 2007. (2) # indicates that figures are subject to revision later on as more data become available.

Source: Census and Statistics Department, The Government of the Hong Kong Special Administrative Region, "Hong Kong Statistics — Statistical Tables." http://www.censtatd.gov.hk/hong_kong_statistics/statistical_tables/index.jsp?charsetID=1&subjectID=12&tableID=030. Accessed on 28 March 2007.

Table 14.2: External Merchandize Trade Aggregate Figures of Hong Kong, 1997–2006

Year	Imports HK$ Million	% Change	Domestic Exports HK$ Million	% Change	Re-Exports HK$ Million	% Change	Total Exports HK$ Million	% Change	Merchandize Trade Balance (HK$ Million)
1997	1,615,090	5.2	211,410	-0.4	1,244,539	5.0	1,455,949	4.2	-159,141
1998	1,429,092	-11.5	188,454	-10.9	1,159,195	-6.9	1,347,649	-7.4	-81,443
1999	1,392,718	-2.5	170,600	-9.5	1,178,400	1.7	1,349,000	0.1	-43,718
2000	1,657,962	19.0	180,967	6.1	1,391,722	18.1	1,572,689	16.6	-85,273
2001	1,568,194	-5.4	153,520	-15.2	1,327,467	-4.6	1,480,987	-5.7	-87,208
2002	1,619,419	3.3	130,926	-14.7	1,429,590	7.7	1,560,517	5.4	-58,903
2003	1,805,770	11.5	121,687	-7.1	1,620,749	13.4	1,742,436	11.7	-63,334
2004	2,111,123	16.9	125,982	3.5	1,898,132	16.8	2,019,114	15.9	-92,009
2005	2,329,469	10.3	136,030	8.0	2,114,143	11.7	2,250,174	11.4	-79,295
2006	2,599,804	11.6	134,527	-1.1	2,326,500	10.0	2,461,027	9.4	-138,777

Notes: (1) Figures in this table are last revised on November 26, 2018. (2) Hong Kong's external trade statistics are compiled based on information contained in import/export declarations. The Hong Kong Special Administrative Region is a separate customs territory, as stated in "The Basic Law of the Hong Kong Special Administrative Region of the People's Republic of China," Import/export declaration is also required of Hong Kong's trade with Mainland China, and statistics relating to this are included in Hong Kong's external trade statistics.

Source: Census and Statistics Department, The Government of the Hong Kong Special Administrative Region, "Hong Kong Statistics — Statistical Tables." http://www.censtatd.gov.hk/hong_kong_statistics/statistical_tables/index.jsp?charsetID=1&subjectID=3&tableID=055.

Table 14.3: Hong Kong's Trade with Mainland China and the United States, 1997–2006 (HK$ million)

Year	Imports China	Imports US	Domestic Exports China	Domestic Exports US	Re-Exports China	Re-Exports US	Total Trade China	Total Trade US
1997	608,372	125,381	63,867	55,073	443,878	261,372	1,116,117	441,826
1998	580,614	106,537	56,066	54,842	407,366	259,856	1,044,045	421,236
1999	607,546	98,572	50,414	51,358	399,188	269,444	1,057,149	419,374
2000	714,987	112,801	54,158	54,438	488,823	311,047	1,257,968	478,286
2001	681,980	104,941	49,547	47,589	496,574	282,189	1,228,101	434,720
2002	717,074	91,478	41,374	41,908	571,870	291,043	1,330,317	424,729
2003	785,624	98,730	36,757	39,130	705,787	285,084	1,528,169	422,945
2004	918,275	111,994	37,898	38,636	850,645	302,964	1,806,818	453,594
2005	1,049,335	119,252	44,643	37,767	967,923	322,872	2,061,900	479,892
2006	1,192,952	123,569	40,268	33,159	1,115,941	337,971	2,349,162	494,699

Note: Figures in this table are last revised on November 26, 2018.

Source: Census and Statistics Department, The Government of the Hong Kong Special Administrative Region, "Hong Kong Statistics — Statistical Tables." http://www.censtatd.gov.hk/hong_kong_statistics/statistical_tables/index.jsp?charsetID=1&subjectID=3&tableID=057; http://www.censtatd.gov.hk/hong_kong_statistics/statistical_tables/index.jsp?charsetID=1&subjectID=3&tableID=058; http://www.censtatd.gov.hk/hong_kong_statistics/statistical_tables/index.jsp?charsetID=1&subjectID=3&tableID=059; and http://www.censtatd.gov.hk/hong_kong_statistics/statistical_tables/index.jsp?charsetID=1&subjectID=3&tableID=060.

dropped from 42% in 1996 to 36% in 2005; while the lowest income group, earning less than HK$5,000 per month, represented only 5% of the working population. The Chief Executive also pointed to the falling unemployment rate, which stood at 4.4% at the end of 2005 (see Table 14.4).[4]

Dr. Kenichi Ohmae's book, *The Impact of Rising Lower-Middle Class Population in Japan: What Can We Do About It?*, was a bestseller in Japan, and had generated much discussion in Taiwan as well.[5] Dr. Ohmae considered that a vast majority of Japanese would fall into the lower-middle class socioeconomic group because globalization would lead to further

---

[4] *South China Morning Post*, January 12, 2007.
[5] See Ohmae Kenichi, *The Impact of Rising Lower-middle Class Population in Japan: What Can We Do About It?* (in Japanese), Tokyo: Kodansha, 2006.

Table 14.4: Statistics on Labour Force, Unemployment and Underemployment in Hong Kong, 1997–2006

Year	Labour Force No. (Thousand)	% Change	Unemployed (Thousand)	Unemployment Rate (%)	Under-Employed (Thousand)	Under-Employment Rate (%)
1997	3 234.8	2.3	71.2	2.2	37.1	1.1
1998	3 276.1	1.3	154.1	4.7	81.8	2.5
1999	3 319.6	1.3	207.5	6.2	96.9	2.9
2000	3 374.2	1.6	166.9	4.9	93.5	2.8
2001	3 427.3	1.6	174.3	5.1	84.8	2.5
2002	3 472.6	1.3	254.2	7.3	104.4	3
2003	3 465.8	–0.2	275.2	7.9	121.9	3.5
2004	3 512.8	1.4	239.2	6.8	114.3	3.3
2005	3 534.2	0.6	197.6	5.6	96.3	2.7
2006	3 571.8	1.1	171.1	4.8	86.3	2.4

Note: Figures in this table are the latest data released on November 26, 2018.

Source: Census and Statistics Department, The Government of the Hong Kong Special Administrative Region, "Hong Kong Statistics — Statistical Tables". http://www.censtatd.gov.hk/hong_kong_statistics/statistical_tables/index.jsp?charsetID=1&subjectID=12&tableID=006.

widening of the gap between the rich and the poor, and exacerbate social polarization.

Perhaps Hong Kong's new graduates could most easily associate with Dr. Ohmae's arguments. A sociology professor of a local university told the author this true story early in 2014, when Hong Kong's economy had hit rock-bottom in the wake of the SARS epidemic. He was talking to some new graduates, and when he addressed them as the young middle class, one student said he did not feel like they belonged to the middle class. The economy at this stage was of course, better. However, the median monthly salary of new graduates was between HK$10,000 and HK$11,000; many also owed the government HK$200,000 or so in student loans. Unless they could depend on their parents for food and accommodation, they would hardly be able to maintain a middle class lifestyle. Neither could they expect steady promotions and salary increases.

The post-war generation in Hong Kong enjoyed satisfactory salary increases on the basis of hard work. Dr. Ohmae argued that this could not be expected in Japan at this stage, where employees' salaries would probably peak when they hit 40. Further rises would be difficult, and Hong Kong's situation was probably similar. Dr. Ohmae suggested that the Japanese should adjust their lifestyles, since not everyone would join the middle class. They might have to forget about owning cars or houses in the suburbs, or paying expensive tuition fees to prepare their children for top universities.

Further, in an ageing society with a sharply falling fertility rate, the financial burden of social services would increase. Taxation would rise in the absence of administrative reforms. At this stage, Hong Kong's Mandatory Provident Fund was inadequate to provide for the community's retirement, and the Hong Kong people had yet to tackle the long-term financing of their hospital services.

Hong Kong's international competitiveness had been in decline, triggered off by the Asia-Pacific financial crisis in 1997–1998. The Hong Kong people were acutely aware that both the Tung and the Tsang administrations had offered no convincing plans to reverse the trend. This inaction on the part of the government eroded the community's confidence which did not compare favorably with that of the people of Singapore and Taiwan, though in terms of economic statistics, Hong Kong had been doing better.

Arguably, the weakening of the Hong Kong economy began much earlier. Real per capita gross domestic product (GDP) growth in Hong Kong fell from an annual average of 5.2% in the 1980s to 3.5% in 1990–1996; and per worker GDP annual growth fell from 4.7% to 3.3%.[6] Further, a group of economists at the Chinese University of Hong Kong observed that the total factor productivity in the manufacturing sector had been declining from 1984 to 1993; its study showed that "the manufacturing sector could produce in 1993 only 87% of the output in 1984.[7]" Access to cheap labor in the Pearl River Delta and the huge profits it generated had weakened the local manufacturing sector's incentive to invest to raise its technological level, in contrast to the other three "little dragons of Asia". The "economic bubble" in the run-up to 1997 generated by dramatic rises

---

[6] Tsang Shu-ki, "Changing Structure of Hong Kong's Economy," in Gungwu Wang and John Wong (eds.), *Hong Kong in China: The Challenges of Transition*, Singapore: Times Academic Press, 1999, p. 108.

[7] Kwong Kai-sun, Lawerence J. Lau and Lin Tzong-biau, *The Impact of Relocation on Total Factor Productivity of Hong Kong Manufacturing, Mimeograph*, Hong Kong: Department of Economics, The Chinese University of Hong Kong, August 1997.

in prices in the real estate market and stock market also made the economic adjustment process much more painful.

The values of the Hong Kong people had been changing gradually. Before 1997, unemployment was not a concern. The community believed that anyone who was willing to work should have no difficulty finding a job. In the early years of the new century, it had to accept that the territory's unemployment rate was higher than those in the United States (U.S.) and the United Kingdom (U.K.), and this would remain the trend in the near future. Hence, even those who were gainfully employed worried about the employment of their next generation.

The unemployment issue was compounded by the widening gap between the rich and the poor. While Donald Tsang said that "Hong Kong's economy is the best it has been in almost twenty years," it was reported that the Hong Kong people had the highest individual net worth in the world, amounting to US$202,000. According to a global study by the United Nations' World Institute for Development Economics Research in 2006, Hong Kong was ahead of Luxembourg, Switzerland, and the U.S., which ranked second, third, and fourth respectively, while Japan ranked ninth and Singapore 12th.[8] From 1981 to 2001, Hong Kong's Gini coefficient steadily rose from 0.451 to 0.525 (see Table 14.5a); in terms of this measurement of income distribution, Hong Kong compared rather unfavorably with the developed countries, and was in a situation similar to those of Argentina and Zambia (see Table 14.5b).

The Regional Economic Outlook in Asia and Pacific released by the International Monetary Fund (IMF) in September 2006 observed that income inequality had worsened "dramatically" in Asia in the past decade.

Table 14.5a: Gini Coefficient of Hong Kong

	1981	1986	1991	1996	2001
Gini coefficient	0.451	0.453	0.476	0.518	0.525

Sources: Census and Statistics Department of the Hong Kong Government, *1991 Population Census Main Report*, Hong Kong: Government Printer, 1992; and Census and Statistics Department of the Hong Kong Special Administrative Region, *Population Census 2001 Main Report — Volume I*, Hong Kong: Government Printer, 2002).

---

[8] *South China Morning Post*, December 7, 2006.

Table 14.5b: Gini Coefficients of Hong Kong and Selected Developed Economies

Region/Country	Gini Coefficient	Survey Year
South Africa	0.593	1995
Brazil	0.591	1998
Zambia	0.526	1998
Hong Kong, China	0.525	2001
Argentina	0.522	2001
Singapore	0.425	1998
United States	0.408	2000
United Kingdom	0.360	1999
Australia	0.352	1994–1998
Canada	0.331	1995
France	0.327	2000
Taiwan	0.326	1998
South Korea	0.316	2000
Germany	0.283	2000
Sweden	0.250	1993
Japan	0.249	

Source: Fact Sheet on Gini Coefficient released by Research and Library Services Division, Legislative Council Secretariat, Hong Kong on December 6, 2004. The Fact Sheet quotes sources from The World Bank, 2004 World Development Indicators, Washington, D.C.: The World Bank, 2004; Census and Statistics Department of the Hong Kong Special Administrative Region, *Population Census 2001 Main Report — Volume I,* Hong Kong: Government Printer, 2002); *and Distribution of Income in Taiwan.* http://www.gio.gov.tw/info/taiwan-story/economy/edown/table/table-10.1.htm. Accessed November 29, 2004.

Thirteen out of 18 Asian countries experienced increases in income inequality, as measured by the Gini coefficient. A common assumption was that globalization led to a widening of the gap between the rich and the poor, but the IMF report disagreed.[9] It argued that no link existed

---

[9] Craig Meer and Jonathan Adams, "Specter of Inequality Haunts Taiwan," *Far Eastern Economic Review*, Vol. 169, No. 10, December 2006, pp. 38–39.

between free trade and income inequality, and net foreign direct investment flows had no impact on income equality too. Instead, it considered that technological change was a more probable cause, as "skill-biased technological progress represented a shift in the production technology that favoured skilled over unskilled labour."

Up to one-third of Hong Kong's labor force had only nine years of formal education or less; naturally, they would find it difficult to benefit from the territory's economic growth. The surplus of unskilled labor in the territory was vividly reflected by the hourly wage of its McDonald's outlets. Exacerbating income inequality easily led to a sense of grievances and possibly social instability. An opinion survey conducted in late 2006 by the Democratic Party based on a sample of middle-class respondents revealed that 22.5% of them thought that Donald Tsang mainly considered the interests of major business groups, 22.4% those of the central government, 13% those of the citizenry, 5.5% those of the middle-class, and 2.1% those of the grassroots, while 43.3% thought that their life remained more or less the same under the Donald Tsang administration, and 38% thought that probably there would be no major change if Tsang got re-elected.[10]

Since the Beijing visit of Margaret Thatcher, the then British Prime Minister, in 1982, the British administration had been almost totally absorbed in the Sino-British negotiations on the territory's future and the associated diplomatic confrontations. As a result, it took no major initiatives in economic reforms and social services in the transitional period before 1997. This meant that when the Tung administration took over, it really had its hands full in tackling the accumulated problems in almost every major policy sector. Tung himself had conveniently come up with a "conspiracy theory," i.e., he had to spend tremendous efforts removing the "land-mines" left by the British administration.

This "land-mines" thesis, however, had not enhanced the community's sympathy for the Tung administration by the summer of 2003. Most people considered that the Tung administration might have needed some time to tackle the "land-mines"; but after six years or so, it should at least be able to show the community the way forward. This dissatisfaction with C.H. Tung was reflected by his popularity rating (see Table 14.6).

---

[10] *Ming Pao*, November 27, 2006.

Table 14.6: Rating of Former Chief Executive C.H. Tung — Half-yearly Average, 1997–2005

Survey question:
Please use a scale of 0–100 to rate your extent of support to the Chief Executive Tung Chee-hwa, with 0 indicating absolutely not supportive, 100 indicating absolutely supportive and 50 indicating half-half. How would you rate the Chief Executive Tung Chee-hwa? (half-yearly average)

Month of the Survey	Total Sample (Half-Yearly Average)	Supporting Rating (Half-Yearly Average)	Recognition Rate (Half-Yearly Average)
Jan–Jun 2005	7,146	47.4	96.5%
Jul–Dec 2004	12,227	48.2	96.5%
Jan–Jun 2004	15,397	44.2	96.5%
Jul–Dec 2003	14,466	42.3	95.6%
Jan–Jun 2003	16,908	44.1	95.1%
Jul–Dec 2002	12,490	48.4	94.3%
Jan–Jun 2002	14,745	54.1	93.0%
Jul–Dec 2001	14,736	50.7	92.9%
Jan–Jun 2001	12,619	53.9	92.9%
Jul–Dec 2000	14,854	51.3	91.8%
Jan–Jun 2000	8,523	53.7	95.1%
Jul–Dec 1999	7,281	53.9	95.0%
Jan–Jun 1999	6,867	57.6	95.4%
Jul–Dec 1998	8,868	56.5	94.9%
Jan–Jun 1998	7,440	58.8	92.7%
Jul–Dec 1997	11,007	64.8	91.7%
Jan–Jun 1997	9,133	59.5	80.5%

Note: Tung Chee-hwa was the Chief Executive of the Government of Hong Kong Special Administrative Region from 1 July 1997 to March 12, 2005. He was elected on December 11, 1996.

Source: The web site of the Public Opinion Programme of The University of Hong Kong, "POP Polls: Rating of Chief Executive Tung Chee-hwa — half-yearly average." http://hkupop.hku.hk/english/popexpress/ceall/cerq/halfyr/datatables1.html. Accessed December 1, 2006.

In comparison with Macau, the Hong Kong people noted that despite the immense problems inherited from the Portuguese administration, Edmund Ho Hau Wah's government apparently had been doing very well and enjoyed much support from the community. Finally, the political skills of

Table 14.7: People's Satisfaction with the HKSAR Government — Half-yearly Average, 1997–2006

Survey question:
Are you satisfied with the overall performance of the HKSAR government? (half-yearly average)

Month of Survey	Total Sample	Very Satisfied	Quite Satisfied	Half-Half	Not Quite Satisfied	Very Dissatisfied	Don't Know/ Hard to Say
Jul–Dec 2006	6,076	4.2%	37.8%	47.7%	11.4%	3.7%	1.1%
Jan–Jun 2006	7,113	5.8%	45.7%	36.5%	8.5%	2.4%	1.1%
Jul–Dec 2005	6,097	5.2%	44.0%	35.7%	9.5%	3.1%	2.4%
Jan–Jun 2005	6,109	2.9%	26.2%	37.9%	20.2%	8.6%	4.3%
Jul–Dec 2004	6,148	2.7%	17.5%	35.3%	27.6%	14.2%	2.8%
Jan–Jun 2004	6,207	1.9%	13.0%	33.1%	30.6%	18.1%	3.5%
Jul–Dec 2003	7,364	1.5%	12.2%	26.9%	35.3%	21.3%	3.0%
Jan–Jun 2003	6,293	1.1%	14.3%	25.6%	36.9%	18.6%	3.6%
Jul–Dec 2002	6,260	1.0%	17.0%	28.1%	37.9%	11.3%	4.8%
Jan–Jun 2002	6,217	1.3%	23.7%	31.3%	32.8%	6.1%	4.9%
Jul–Dec 2001	6,321	1.0%	19.2%	30.9%	33.4%	10.5%	5.0%
Jan–Jun 2001	6,348	1.3%	25.3%	35.0%	26.7%	6.5%	5.2%
Jul–Dec 2000	6,324	1.5%	19.9%	31.3%	32.1%	9.6%	5.7%
Jan–Jun 2000	4,240	1.6%	22.4%	39.1%	22.9%	9.0%	5.1%
Jul–Dec 1999	3,205	1.4%	22.8%	39.2%	23.6%	8.0%	5.0%
Jan–Jun 1999	4,213	0.7%	24.5%	39.9%	26.3%	5.4%	3.2%
Jul–Dec 1998	4,755	1.0%	21.7%	35.8%	29.0%	8.0%	4.6%
Jan–Jun 1998	3,744	0.8%	27.4%	38.7%	23.0%	4.6%	5.5%
Jul–Dec 1997	3,181	1.9%	40.7%	32.7%	13.6%	1.9%	9.3%

Source: The web site of the Public Opinion Programme of The University of Hong Kong, "POP Polls: People's Satisfaction with the HKSAR Government — half-yearly average." http://hkupop.hku.hk/english/popexpress/sargperf/sarg/halfyr/datatables.html. Accessed March 28, 2007.

Chris Patten, the last British governor of Hong Kong, overshadowed the performance of Tung. In general, the Hong Kong people's attitude towards the government was more moderate (see Table 14.7); and opposition parties tended to do well (see Table 14.8).

Table 14.8: Satisfaction and Dissatisfaction with the Performance of Various Political Parties, September 2004, November 2005, and March 2006.

Political Party	September 2004 Dissatisfied with performance	September 2004 Satisfied with performance	September 2004 Difference	November 2005 Dissatisfied with performance	November 2005 Satisfied with performance	November 2005 Difference	March 2006 Dissatisfied with performance	March 2006 Satisfied with performance	March 2006 Difference
DAB	79	21	−58	58	42	−16	55	45	−10
FTU	62	38	−24	36	64	+28	37	63	+26
Liberal Party	49	51	+2	51	49	−2	47	53	+6
Democratic Party	48	52	+4	59	41	−18	68	32	−36
The Frontier	47	53	+6	54	46	−8	52	48	−4
The Alliance	—	—	—	54	46	−8	54	46	−8
HKCTU	34	66	+32	32	68	+36	39	61	+22
ADPL	28	72	+44	29	71	+42	37	63	+26
Article 45 Concern Group	24	76	+52	27	73	+46	31	69	+38

Note: DAB = Democratic Alliance for the Betterment and Progress of Hong Kong, FTU = Federation of Trade Unions, The Alliance = The Hong Kong Alliance in Support of Patriotic Democratic Movements of China, HKCTU = Hong Kong Confederation of Trade Unions, ADPL = Hong Kong Association for Democracy and People's Livelihood.

Source: Parties, Policies and Political Reform in Hong Kong, a report written by The Hong Kong Transition Project and commissioned by National Democratic Institute for International Affairs (May 2006), pp. 76–78.

Globalization meant that it would be more difficult to maintain Hong Kong's international competitiveness. Like Singapore, the territory was handicapped by its high cost structure, as every Hong Kong citizen realized that the wages across the border in Shenzhen were only one-fifth of those in Hong Kong. From the very first policy address of C.H. Tung to the Action Agenda on "China's 11th Five-Year Plan and the Development of Hong Kong" of the Donald Tsang administration in January 2007,[11] the HKSAR government had been trying hard to maintain the territory's international competitiveness and respectable economic growth rate.

Hong Kong would continue to function as an international financial centre and business services centre. Though the territory's unique position in the China market would decline, the China market was expected to maintain its impressive growth in the foreseeable future. Hence, the absolute size of a declining share of an expanding pie (i.e., the China market) might still expand. The territory would have to work hard to improve its productivity and competitiveness so that the share of the pie would not shrink too much. This also meant that Hong Kong had to remain a cosmopolitan metropolis and avoid becoming just another coastal city in China. Such a consideration would help to preserve the freedoms and the rule of law in Hong Kong as it was in the interest of every party to do so.

Hong Kong would continue to seek new niches to prosper, which had been its typical mode of operation. An increasing share of the accumulated wealth of the major business groups in the territory would go to Mainland China; this partly explained why while Hong Kong's GDP continued to grow, the lower socioeconomic strata did not experience an improvement in living standards. There had to be more investment in education and human resources development; the major challenge was to ensure that the education system would encourage creativity and innovation.

The development of high-tech industries in Hong Kong had not made much progress, in contrast to the other three "little dragons of Asia". Meanwhile, the re-allocation of manufacturing industries to the Pearl River Delta in southern China and beyond had almost been completed.

---

[11] For the contents of the Action Agenda and the initial responses to it, see all major newspapers in Hong Kong on January 15, 2007.

The employment situation would remain tight because the service industries would continue to adopt automation and other cost-cutting measures to maintain their competitiveness and profit margins.

In the first decade of the HKSAR, there was a suggestion that high-tech industries might be developed in the territory with Hong Kong's capital, marketing skills, and international network, as well as the scientific and technological talents from Mainland China and its advanced industrial base. Unfortunately, nothing much had been achieved so far. Hong Kong's only connection with high-tech industries was its financial institutions which served to raise venture capital supporting their development.

In the aftermath of the Asia-Pacific financial crisis, Singapore mobilized the entire nation to deliberate on how to face the challenges of globalization. As a result, it had a grand strategy well understood by the people. The Hong Kong government was still restrained by its traditional *laissez-faire* philosophy. The Tung administration attempted to take a more active approach in promoting economic development, but the results were mixed. The Disneyland theme park was in general welcomed, but the Cyberport project was often perceived as an example of collusion with big business. The administration of Donald Tsang was under considerable pressure to demonstrate major initiatives to guide the territory's economic development, as the business community and the Hong Kong people in general expected the government to assume a more active role.

Hong Kong's search for new niches exploiting its entrepreneurship and pragmatism might well bring fortunes to some business groups, but it might not be adequate to maintain a healthy economic growth rate for the territory as a whole in the long term. According to a study by the China Institute of City Competitiveness released at the end of 2006, Hong Kong remained the most competitive city in Greater China, ahead of Shanghai, Beijing, Shenzhen, Taipei, Guangzhou, Macau, Tianjin, Hangzhou, and Nanjing (in that order). However, in terms of growth potential, Hong Kong was ranked number four, behind Shenzhen, Macau, and Beijing. In the previous annual survey, Hong Kong was second after Shenzhen.[12]

---

[12] *South China Morning Post*, December 29, 2006.

II Economic Integration with China

The Hong Kong people at this stage realized that the territory's economy was highly dependent on that in Mainland China; they had lost their pride in the territory which served as a valuable window for China's opening up to the external world in the late 1970s and 1980s. In the early years of China's economic reforms, Hong Kong concentrated on business and financial services while its manufacturing industries moved northward. Guangdong, the province bordering Hong Kong, welcomed this arrangement of the Pearl River Delta as the workshop, while Hong Kong served as the shopfront. Guangdong was seeking a more balanced division of labor at this stage, but Hong Kong was not able to respond effectively.

Shortly before 1997, leaders of Guangdong approached Hong Kong for close cooperation, with the intention of exploiting the territory's capital, advanced business and marketing services, and international networks. In the first two or three years after Hong Kong's return to China, the HKSAR government was lukewarm in its response to the initiatives from its neighbor. Hong Kong's civil service, led by Anson Chan Fang On-sang, did not know Guangdong well; and it also wanted to maintain a certain distance between Hong Kong and Mainland China so as to better preserve the "one country, two systems" arrangement.

Later, when the HKSAR government better appreciated the significance of economic integration with China, its bargaining position had much weakened. Guangdong was much more interested in upgrading its industrial structure, absorbing advanced technology and management, as well as establishing international wholesale and retail networks. Major corporations in the province therefore accorded priority to joint ventures with multinational corporations in the Fortune 500 list. Investment from Hong Kong was still welcomed, but Guangdong was no longer short of investment funds. The provincial authorities much resented Hong Kong's earlier cool response to their initiatives, and perceived that Hong Kong turned to its northern neighbor only when it encountered difficulties.

Hong Kong's economic problems adversely affected its political and social stability. Even before the massive protest rallies in 2003 and 2004, the Chinese leadership was aware of the plight of the Tung administration. Economic assistance was seen as the most effective support for the territory and the Tung administration, and economic cooperation became a political responsibility for Guangdong and other coastal provinces. Unfortunately, the HKSAR government compounded its earlier mistake by often taking its requests to Beijing instead of engaging in patient negotiations with Guangdong and other provincial governments. Obviously, the latter had no choice but to make concessions in view of the national policy to ensure Hong Kong's political stability, but this pressure from Beijing was not conducive to the maintenance of a cordial, cooperative relationship between Hong Kong and its neighbor in the long term.

At this stage, Guangdong had experienced more than two decades of impressive economic growth and it anticipated a per capita GDP of US$7,000 by 2010. Guangdong's economy grew 12.5% in 2005, and its GDP reached 2.17 trillion yuan (US$264.84 billion), outpacing those of Hong Kong (US$165.5 billion) and Singapore (US$111.45 billion). In fact, in terms of GDP, Guangdong had overtaken Singapore and Hong Kong since 1997 and 2002, respectively. Guangdong's expansion continued to be mainly fuelled by increases in investment and exports. Exports from the province accounted for about one-third of the country's total, and amounted to US$238.2 billion in 2005, a rise of 24.3% over that of the previous year.[13] In 2006, Guangdong's GDP was expected to exceed 2.5 trillion yuan (US$305.1 billion), with an annual growth rate of 15.2%;[14] and its foreign trade topped US$500 billion in the same year, up 20% over that of the previous year.[15] To the average Hong Kong citizen, the most vivid sign was the value of the yuan rising above that of the Hong Kong dollar in the beginning of 2007, so much so that when they went to Shenzhen to have a good time, some shops and restaurants refused to take Hong Kong dollar. Guangdong leaders were acutely aware that the challenge of globalization, symbolized by China's entry into the WTO, would mean keener competition. The province would not only encounter fierce competition from abroad, it would also have to contend with domestic competition, especially from the Yangtze River Delta region

---

[13] *Ibid.* January 27, 2006.
[14] *Ibid.*, November 29, 2006.
[15] *Ibid.*, January 8, 2007.

with Shanghai as its centre. Innovation and restructuring focused on improving quality and efficiency would be needed to maintain economic growth in the years ahead.

The Guangdong leadership planned to promote regional economic integration to expand the province's hinterland. The Pan-Pearl River Delta (PRD) economic cooperation involving nine provinces as well as Hong Kong and Macau was approved by the Beijing leadership, and the Framework Agreement on Pan-PRD Regional Co-operation was signed in June 2004. The implementation of the Framework Agreement would lead to the emergence of the largest economic region in China. Guangdong hoped to exploit the resources and markets of the interior provinces through the Pan-PRD economic cooperation; and Hong Kong was eager to offer its international financial and business services to the interior provinces too.

Some critics in Guangdong believed that the Pan-PRD economic cooperation was far too ambitious. They were concerned that the other provinces all had their hidden agendas and that they lacked sufficient commitment to the common good. They considered that Guangdong should better concentrate on the province alone. Hong Kong welcomed an organizational framework to approach the interior provinces, but it was not adequately involved to influence the process. So far, it remained aloof from the rivalries among the local governments in Mainland China.

The HKSAR enjoyed provincial status, and therefore mainly relied on its dialogue with the Guangdong authorities. Shenzhen, on the other hand, felt neglected. It had an economic plan independent of Guangdong and directly accountable to the State Council. It was therefore in competition with the province.

To overcome the issues of protocol, the Hong Kong government should secure the services of business groups such as the Hong Kong General Chamber of Commerce and the Chinese General Chamber of Commerce. They were not bound by considerations of government hierarchy, and should have more room of maneuver in exploring new ideas.

Mobility of professional talents between Hong Kong and Mainland China would continue to improve. Multinational corporations in Hong Kong would have good opportunities to recruit Mainland talents to be trained and to serve in Hong Kong first, and then sent back to Mainland China to expand their networks of services. This development, however, might further exacerbate competition among local professionals. The gap in remuneration between that for the best and the mediocre would further widen.

In mid-January 2007, the Donald Tsang administration released its Action Agenda on "China's 11th Five-year Plan and the Development of Hong Kong." The Action Agenda was significant in two important aspects. In the first place, it revealed the extent of economic integration between Hong Kong and Mainland China. Similar to other provincial governments, the HKSAR government had to lobby and influence the central government to advance the territory's interests. Naturally, it had much to learn regarding the related research as well as lobbying strategies and techniques. Further, it showed that the HKSAR government intended to assume an important role in the territory's economic development. Earlier in September 2006, Donald Tsang denied that its administration had made "positive non-interventionism" a blueprint for its economic development strategy, but instead it would adhere to the principle of "big market, small government.[16]" The Chief Executive's statement attracted criticism from Nobel Prize-winning economist Milton Friedman who once lauded Hong Kong as the perfect model of a free market economy. Dr. Friedman called it a "mistake" for the HKSAR government to shift from the policy of "positive non-interventionism" to a policy of "big market, small government".[17]

Despite Milton Friedman's criticism, Hong Kong retained its top ranking for the 13th year straight as the world's freest economy, according to The Heritage Foundation, a Washington-based think-tank which compiled the Index of Economic Freedom with The Wall Street Journal.[18] According to the Fraser Institute in Vancouver, Canada, Hong Kong had also been ranked the freest economy in the world since 1970 by its Economic Freedom of the World annual report (see Table 14.9). However,

---

[16] *Ibid.*, September 12, 2006.

[17] *Ibid.*, September 27, 2006. See also Milton Friedman, "Hong Kong wrong," *The Wall Street Journal* (Eastern edition, New York), October 6, 2006, p. A14.

[18] *South China Morning Post*, January 17, 2007.

Table 14.9: The Chain-Linked Summary Economic Freedom Index, 1970–2004

	1970	1975	1980	1985	1990	1995	2000	2001	2002	2003	2004
Hong Kong	8.2 (1)	8.3 (1)	8.5 (1)	8.2 (1)	8.5 (1)	9.1 (1)	8.8 (1)	8.7 (1)	8.1 (1)	8.7 (17.5)	8.7 (1)
Japan	6.2	5.9	6.4	6.5	7.1	6.9	7.3	7.0	6.9	7.47.2	7.5
Luxembourg	6.9	6.9	6.8	7.2	7.4	7.6	7.8	7.7	7.6	7.7	7.9
New Zealand	6.0	5.4	6.1	5.9	7.3	8.5	8.4	8.2	8.2	8.2	8.2
Russia	—	—	—	—	—	3.7	4.9	4.9	5.1	5.2	5.6
Singapore	7.5	7.3	7.5	7.9	8.5	8.9	8.5	8.5	8.5	8.5	8.5
South Korea	5.4	5.4	5.7	5.7	6.3	6.7	6.6	7.0	6.9	6.9	7.1
Sweden	5.3	5.2	5.6	6.2	6.6	7.1	7.4	7.2	7.3	7.5	7.3
Taiwan	6.6	5.8	6.7	6.9	7.1	7.3	7.2	7.1	7.2	7.2	7.3
Thailand	5.7	5.6	5.9	5.9	6.8	7.2	6.7	6.7	6.6	6.6	6.6

Notes: (1) Numbers in brackets represent the rankings of Hong Kong. Hong Kong has been ranked the freest economy in the world in the index published annually in Economic Freedom of the World since 1970 to 2004. (2) The chain-linked summary economic freedom index is based on the 2000 rating as the base year. Changes to the index going backward (and forward) in time are then based only on changes in components that were present in adjacent years.

Source: James Gwartney and Robert Lawson with William Easterly, *Economic Freedom of the World: 2006 Annual Report*, Vancouver: The Fraser Institute, 2006, pp. 19–21.

Tim Kane, director of The Heritage Foundation's Centre for International Trade and Economics, warned that a minimum wage and other policies that imposed price controls were threatening Hong Kong's position as the world's freest economy. Hong Kong's score in the Fraser Institute's Summary Economic Freedom Index also declined from a peak of 9.1 (10 being the full mark) in 1995 to 8.7 in 2004.

Obviously, the community accepted that the government would assume a more proactive role in promoting the territory's economic development; and in its economic integration with Mainland China, the Hong Kong people and the business community expected that the government would effectively articulate the territory's interests and try to influence the central government's policy in the territory's favor. Hence, the Tsang administration had to define its role clearly, and seek to arrive at a consensus through community-wide discussion. Making occasional odd statements like the above would only confuse the public and the international community.

The Action Agenda was the result of an economic summit held in the previous year on the same subject. It offered 207 concrete proposals on the development of financial services; trade and business; maritime, logistics and infrastructure; and innovation, tourism, and professional services; i.e., the four pillars of the Hong Kong economy. This was also considered a major publicity program promoting Hong Kong after the Brand Hong Kong program with its dragon symbol launched in May 2001 in the wake of the Asia-Pacific financial crisis.[19] The Action Agenda was released two months before the election of the Chief Executive, so it was perceived as Donald Tsang's campaign platform in a way. As the economic summit involved almost all the territory's business leaders, the Chief Executive probably felt compelled to involve all their proposals. As a result, a major criticism against the Action Agenda was its lack of identification of priorities.

Hong Kong's economic summit was different from those held in Taiwan and Singapore by the turn of the century to formulate economic development strategies for the years ahead. There was no serious attempt to involve representatives from various socioeconomic strata, nor allow the opposition to articulate its views. It was no accident that the Action

---

[19] See the web site of Brand Hong Kong, www.brandhk.gov.hk. See also *Ming Pao*, January 16, 2007.

Agenda included a proposal to employ truck drivers from the Mainland to reduce the costs of the logistics sector, which led to a small-scale protest by the trade unionists concerned. There was no systematic consultation with the academic community too, which was in sharp contrast to the practice of Chinese governments at all levels.

The feasibility of the 207 policy proposals remained controversial. In an earlier question-and-answer session in the Legislative Council, Donald Tsang criticized the pro-democracy legislators for only being able to offer visions, but his administration would ensure the concrete implementation of its policy programs.[20] Donald Tsang therefore emphasized the feasibility of all the proposals in the Action Agenda. However, even Joseph Yam, Chief Executive of the Hong Kong Monetary Authority, openly admitted that some of the proposals were "subjective wishes" and might not be realized.[21] The Tsang administration also stressed that the proposals in the Action Agenda would bring a win-win situation to Mainland China and Hong Kong. To ensure their feasibility and the win-win situation, it seemed that this could not be achieved through unilaterally making the proposals; certainly detailed negotiations among the bureaucracies and business communities concerned were required. However, at this stage, such negotiations had yet to begin.

Actually, 2007 was the second year of the 11th Five-Year Economic and Social Development Programme. Hong Kong seemed to be a bit late in raising its proposals when the media in Mainland China were already concentrating on evaluating the program's performance in its initial year. Perhaps, the HKSAR government should seriously consider at this stage how to articulate its next series of policy proposals so as to facilitate its incorporation into China's 12th Five-Year Programme.

III Governance, Democracy, and Legitimacy

Hong Kong has never enjoyed a fully democratic system. After its return to China, it was obvious that the Chief Executive had to be someone trusted by the Chinese leadership and accepted by the local business

---

[20] *Ibid.*, January 12, 2007.
[21] *Ibid.*, January 17, 2007.

community. In the executive-led system of government, the Chief Executive enjoyed very substantial powers. The electoral system of the legislature was also designed in such a way so as to prevent the pro-democracy camp from securing a majority.[22] In many ways, the political system of the HKSAR was even less democratic than that in the final years of the British administration which secured its legitimacy by results. The Hong Kong people accepted the colonial administration because it was able to deliver the goods, i.e., it maintained law and order well, guaranteed the freedoms that the Hong Kong people treasured, and brought economic development and prosperity to the community. In the opinion surveys in the decade or more before 1997, the Hong Kong people consistently showed substantially more trust and support for the colonial administration than for London and Beijing, while the latter usually trailed behind London by a relatively small margin.

The earlier discussion in section I of chapter 13 obviously shows that the Tung administration gradually lost its legitimacy, and this loss was clearly demonstrated in his popular ratings (see Tables 14.6 and 14.7) and by the demand for him to step down from the participants in the protest rallies in 2003 and 2004. In the first place, many people experienced a fall in living standards (see Table 14.1); and a substantial segment of the middle-class families suffered from negative assets which meant that a substantial part of their life savings evaporated. Further, most people did not believe that the Tung administration could offer the leadership to revive Hong Kong's economy. They also perceived that there was increasing collusion between the Tung administration and the major local business leaders, a perception generated and reinforced by several business deals such as the Cyberport project as well as the widening gap between the rich and the poor. Article 23 legislation was probably the last straw on the camel's back because the Tung administration was seen to be willing to sacrifice the Hong Kong people's freedoms to please Beijing.

Democratization came into the picture because people were angry that they had no part in selecting C.H. Tung as the Chief Executive; and when

---

[22] See Joseph Y.S. Cheng, The Basic Law: messages for Hong Kong people," in Richard Y.C. Wong and Joseph Y.S. Cheng (eds.), *The Other Hong Kong Report 1990*, Hong Kong: The Chinese University Press, 1990, pp. 29–63.

he performed badly and caused them misery, there was no way to get rid of him. Various arguments against the premature introduction of full democracy, i.e., universal suffrage as articulated by the pro-Beijing united front, fell flat because the community in the final years of the Tung administration believed that any candidate would be better.

The Chinese leadership was acutely aware of this decline in legitimacy on the part of the Tung administration, and it was eager to help to maintain the territory's political and social stability.

Chinese leaders understood that they had to soften the opposition to Tung at least within the pro-Beijing united front and the business community. They therefore chose to help Hong Kong solve its economic problems. Assistance included a sharp increase in the number of tourists allowed to visit Hong Kong (the Individual Visit Scheme), the Closer Economic Partnership Arrangement (CEPA) which gives Hong Kong better access to the China market,[23] and political pressure on Guangdong to improve cooperation with the territory. The Hong Kong people appreciated the economic support from the central government, and they in general had a very good impression of the new leaders in China, namely, Hu Jintao and Wen Jiabao (see Table 14.10). When Wen visited Hong Kong in late-June and early-July 2003, he was well received by the local community.

The new Chinese leaders followed the dictum of "stability takes precedence over everything else" in the handling of Hong Kong's political crisis, and they were willing to pay the economic price. While the Hong Kong people were grateful for the central government's economic support, they also felt embarrassed by the fact that people enjoying a per capita annual GDP of over US$24,000 had to seek assistance from the Mainland, where people had a per capita annual GDP of about US$1,000 (2003 figures for both Hong Kong and Mainland China).

The Chinese authorities had been sending many agents to the HKSAR to collect information after the massive protest rally on July 1, 2003, as their confidence in the Central Liaison Office, the State Council's Hong Kong and Macau Affairs Office, and the Tung administration was badly shaken. It was said that all three had informed the Chinese leaders that they expected a turnout of about 30,000 to 40,000 people for the protest

---

[23] For details of CEPA, see all major newspapers in Hong Kong on September 30, 2003.

Table 14.10: People's Trust in the Beijing Central Government — Half-yearly Average, 1992–2006

Survey question:
On the whole, do you trust the Beijing Central Government? (half-yearly average)

Month of Survey	Very Trust	Quite Trust	Half-Half	Quite Distrust	Very Distrust	Don't know/ Hard to Say
Jul–Dec 2006	11.7%	32.9%	31.4%	13.6%	6.1%	4.3%
Jan–Jun 2006	12.5%	36.0%	28.2%	13.1%	5.6%	4.6%
Jul–Dec 2005	13.5%	33.3%	23.8%	15.9%	8.5%	5.0%
Jan–Jun 2005	10.5%	32.7%	25.3%	16.3%	8.4%	6.9%
Jul–Dec 2004	13.1%	33.9%	25.5%	14.0%	6.9%	6.6%
Jan–Jun 2004	9.6%	30.4%	26.2%	16.9%	8.7%	8.2%
Jul–Dec 2003	8.4%	37.3%	24.6%	15.0%	5.6%	9.1%
Jan–Jun 2003	5.5%	32.1%	21.9%	22.3%	7.1%	11.1%
Jul–Dec 2002	4.2%	36.8%	21.8%	21.1%	5.1%	11.0%
Jan–Jun 2002	5.7%	42.9%	21.5%	17.5%	3.1%	9.2%
Jul–Dec 2001	5.0%	38.9%	24.0%	17.3%	4.8%	9.9%
Jan–Jun 2001	4.3%	29.5%	24.9%	23.3%	7.8%	10.3%
Jul–Dec 2000	4.6%	27.0%	22.8%	22.7%	8.3%	14.7%
Jan–Jun 2000	4.9%	27.0%	27.1%	20.7%	6.6%	13.7%
Jul–Dec 1999	5.0%	24.3%	27.4%	22.3%	7.4%	13.6%
Jan–Jun 1999	3.2%	24.1%	30.0%	22.1%	5.3%	15.3%
Jul–Dec 1998	3.2%	27.3%	28.4%	24.4%	6.3%	10.2%
Jan–Jun 1998	3.3%	25.4%	28.5%	24.5%	5.6%	12.7%
Jul–Dec 1997	3.8%	28.6%	24.0%	24.5%	5.4%	13.8%
Jan–Jun 1997	3.3%	25.7%	21.0%	33.0%	8.6%	8.3%
Jul–Dec 1996	2.6%	24.4%	23.7%	32.7%	8.3%	8.4%
Jan–Jun 1996	2.2%	20.2%	23.9%	33.5%	12.0%	8.4%
Jul–Dec 1995	2.3%	20.4%	19.5%	34.9%	12.1%	10.8%
Jan–Jun 1995	2.8%	17.8%	19.2%	38.4%	12.9%	8.9%
Jul–Dec 1994	1.5%	16.4%	21.9%	38.6%	13.6%	8.1%
Jan–Jun 1994	3.0%	17.6%	21.2%	35.3%	14.2%	8.8%
Jul–Dec 1993	2.3	21.0%	16.7%	36.4%	13.9%	9.7%
Jan–Jun 1993	3.2	21.4%	17.9%	32.7%	14.9%	10.0%
Jul–Dec 1992	1.9	17.0%	20.7%	34.8%	18.8%	6.8%

Source: The web site of the Public Opinion Programme of The University of Hong Kong, "POP Polis: People's Trust in the Beijing Central Government — half yearly average." http://hkupop.hku.hk/ english/opexpress/ trust/trustchigov/halfyr/datatables.html. Accessed December 1, 2006.

rally. The actual turnout of more than half a million people therefore showed that they did not have a good understanding of the situation, and that they probably had been sending unrealistically favorable reports on the territory to the Chinese leadership.

The victory of the pro-democracy camp in the District Council elections in November 2003 and its being perceived to have a small chance of securing half of the seats in the Legislative Council elections in September 2004 symbolized the revival of the pro-democracy movement, as well as the extent of public dissatisfaction with the Tung administration threatening Beijing's fundamental policy towards Hong Kong.

The Chinese authorities therefore had to be involved to ensure that the pro-Establishment candidates would be able to retain a solid majority in the Legislative Council elections in 2004. Support from Beijing included some shadowy activities too. It was reported in the media that the Hong Kong people doing business and working in the Pearl River Delta were contacted by cadres advising them to vote for pro-China candidates and not to support the pro-democracy candidates. Town and township heads in China also rang up their acquaintances in Hong Kong repeating the same message. The successive resignations of three popular radio talk-show hosts before the protest rally on July 1, 2004, were widely believed to have been caused by pressure from the pro-Beijing united front, if not from the Chinese authorities. Finally, there was a prostitution case involving a Democratic Party candidate in Dongguan in the Pearl River Delta just before the Legislative Council elections, and apparently the public security organ in Dongguan was involved in propaganda activities discrediting the pro-democracy camp. In sum, the pro-democracy camp felt that they were fighting against a powerful state machinery in the elections.

The heavy involvement of Chinese leaders in Hong Kong affairs further weakened the legitimacy and effectiveness of the Tung administration and, in fact, the HKSAR government. Business leaders probably felt that if they needed anything, they should lobby Beijing. Soon after the July 1, 2003 protest rally, Vice-President Zeng Qinghong received delegations from the three pro-Beijing parties, namely, the Democratic Alliance for the Betterment of Hong Kong (DAB), the Hong Kong Progressive Alliance, and the Liberal Party, in a high-profile manner and praised them for their contributions to Hong Kong. This was unprecedented and might be interpreted as political intervention in support of the pro-Beijing political parties, as the Chinese authorities had been refusing any contact with the territory's pro-democracy camp since the Tiananmen Incident. Further, the DAB visited the Guangdong and Shanghai authorities roughly at the same time; and with the help of the latter, it could claim to serve Hong Kong by reflecting the community's views and demands to the provincial governments, a service which obviously could not be delivered by the pro-democracy camp.

Despite the political stability after the Legislative Council elections in September 2004, Tung Chee-hwa did not seem to be able to capitalize on the situation. His administration was still plagued by the mishandling of the issue of the Link REIT, the West Kowloon Cultural District development project, and the sale of the Hunghom Peninsula Home Ownership Scheme flats to a private developer who planned to tear the buildings down. It was under such circumstances that Tung offered to resign on March 10, 2005, for health reasons. It came as a surprise to all parties concerned, including the local pro-Beijing united front; and the Hong Kong community believed that he had been asked to step down by Beijing.

Chinese leaders probably realized that Tung had become too much a political liability. Replacing him with Donald Tsang, a more competent and more popular career civil servant serving as the Chief Secretary for Administration then, would help to restore Hong Kong people's confidence in the HKSAR government (see Tables 14.11 and 14.7). Moreover, the economy was recovering. This change of leadership therefore was perceived by Beijing as conducive to maintaining political stability and dampening Hong Kong people's demand for democracy.

In mid-2005, visitors from Mainland China's think-tanks on Hong Kong emphasized the "new thinking" of the Chinese leadership's policy towards the HKSAR. They indicated that Chinese leaders had adopted a new approach not only in dealing with Taiwan, but also with Hong Kong. They pointed to the resignation of Tung Chee-hwa, his replacement by Donald Tsang, and the new contacts with the pro-democracy camp as concrete evidence of this "new thinking". Given the past failures resulting in successive political crises, a new approach was most welcome. The

Table 14.11: Rating of Donald Tsang Yam-kuen as Financial Secretary, Chief Secretary for Administration, and Chief Executive — Half-yearly Average, 1997–2006

Survey question:
Please use a scale of 0–100 to rate your extent of support to the Chief Executive Donald Tsang Yam-kuen, with 0 indicating absolutely not supportive, 100 indicating absolutely supportive and 50 indicating half-half. How would you rate the Chief Executive Donald Tsang Yam-kuen? (half-yearly average)

Month of Survey	Total Sample (Half-Yearly Average)	Support Rating (Half-Yearly Average)	Recognition Rate (Half-Yearly Average)
Jul–Dec 2006	13,180	62.9	98.0%
Jan–Jun 2006	13,253	67.3	90.9%
Jul–Dec 2005	13,083	67.4	96.0%
Jan–Jun 2005	10,197	68.0	94.2%
Jul–Dec 2004	6,079	61.3	96.3%
Jan–Jun 2004	8,165	62.3	95.4%
Jul–Dec 2003	6,178	62.0	95.4%
Jan–Jun 2003	8,306	59.6	93.6%
Jul–Dec 2002	6,230	61.8	92.0%
Jan–Jun 2002	9,595	65.3	89.0%
Jul–Dec 2001	2,108	64.8	86.6%
Jan–Jun 2001	3,627	69.8	92.6%
Jul–Dec 2000	1,038	70.0	86.0%
Jan–Jun 2000	535	64.7	92.1%
Jul–Dec 1999	1,035	63.8	87.0%
Jan–Jun 1999	1,049	70.0	91.7%
Jul–Dec 1998	1,608	61.4	89.9%
Jan–Jun 1998	538	61.7	86.6%
Jul–Dec 1997	1,077	62.6	76.0%
Jan–Jun 1997	525	61.3	74.4%

Note: Donald Tsang Yam-kuen became the Financial Secretary under British rule in September 1995; he continued to serve as the Financial Secretary of the Government of Hong Kong Special Administrative Region from July 1, 1997 onwards; was promoted to be the Chief Secretary for Administration on May 1, 2001; appointed as the Acting Chief Executive on March 12, 2005; and formally elected as the Chief Executive on June 21, 2005.

Source: The web site of the Public Opinion Programme of The University of Hong Kong, "POP Polls: Rating of Chief Executive Donald Tsang Yam-kuen — half-yearly average." http://hkupop.hku.hk/english/popexpress/ce2005/donald_new/hyear/datatables.html. Accessed March 31, 2007.

focus of this "new thinking", however, seemed to be on the improvement of governance, maintenance of political stability, and dampening of the community's demand for democracy.

In view of the political fatigue on the part of the Hong Kong people, such a more progressive and more tolerant approach proved effective at this stage. The community welcomed Donald Tsang as the Chief Executive for a change, and the economic upturn also removed considerable dissatisfaction (see Tables 14.1, 14.2, 14.3, and 14.4). The absence of a positive response to the community's demand for democracy, however, would only be avoiding the issue. As a mature economy, Hong Kong's economic growth rates, in the longer term, would bound to slow down. It had to face the same set of problems facing the advanced Western countries, Japan, and Singapore. They included — an ageing population, high structural unemployment, budget difficulties leading to re-definition of the government's commitments in the provision of social services, etc. Competition for the resources of the public sector would become fiercer. The debates on small-class teaching, social security for single parents, and charges for hospital services, etc., indicated that many more similar controversies would follow. Only by strengthening its legitimacy and accountability would the government be in a better position to resolve the competition. Otherwise, it would either choose to avoid the problems or become terribly worn down through involving in a long series of controversies.

Regarding the former, Donald Tsang's policy address in October 2006 was a classic example, as the government still lacked a strategy and a timetable on important issues such as the long-term financing for hospital services. His administration chose to shelve the goods and services tax proposal too. Despite the economic boom and the careful management of the community's expectations, Donald Tsang's strategy of avoiding controversial issues until after his re-election apparently backfired. According to a public opinion survey by the University of Hong Kong's Public Opinion Programme, the average score for the 2006–2007 policy address among the respondents was 55.8 out of 100, 10.6 lower than that for Tsang's first policy address, and 0.5 lower than that for Tung's last policy address; while 34% of the respondents found the policy address satisfactory, 25% found it unsatisfactory; with regard to Tsang's first policy address, 48% of the respondents found it satisfactory, and only 9% found it unsatisfactory.[24]

Jacob Hacker, a political scientist from Yale University, warned in 2006 of a pervasive feeling of permanent insecurity among Americans in his new book, *The Great Risk Shift*. He believed that Americans increasingly realized that they had to rely on their own efforts to pay for their healthcare and retirement plans instead of depending on their employers and the government. Hacker argued that this creeping doubt could lead to big shifts in the political landscape.[25] Apparently, this feeling of insecurity was shared by the Hong Kong people, and they realized that time lost at this stage would make a significant impact in the future decades.

The competence of the Chief Executive was therefore not the key; but institutions were the foundation. The Singaporean model had a lot of appeal to the neo-conservatives in Beijing. However, the Singaporean governance was obviously more than strongman politics; it had a highly efficient mass governing party. The People's Action Party (PAP) had to face the test of open elections, and it had to count on electoral victories to consolidate its political legitimacy.

The Chinese leadership at this stage assumed an increasingly significant role regarding the maintenance of legitimacy for the HKSAR government. It had to take up responsibility for the choice of the Chief Executive. The perception of its decisive role was certainly much reinforced by the resignation of Tung Chee-hwa and his replacement by Donald Tsang. The Hong Kong people also realized that the decisions on the territory's democratization were made in Beijing, and not by the HKSAR government. Their sense of political impotence had been exacerbated because they were often afraid to exert pressure on the Chinese leadership, and they understood that the territory's prosperity was increasingly dependent on Beijing's good will. The Chinese leadership's responsibility reduced the pressure on the Chief Executive and his administration. Their legitimacy deficit was made up by strong support

---

[24] *Ming Pao*, October 13, 2006.
[25] See Jane Bryant Quinn, "The economic perception gap", *Newsweek*, Vol. CXLVIII, No. 21, November 20, 2006, p. 39.

from the Chinese leadership, but it would also be much more difficult for them to secure their legitimacy through efforts of their own.

IV The Pro-democracy Movement

The pro-democracy movement was in a difficult state in the years before the massive protest rally on July 1, 2003. There was frustration with the lack of progress as no one expected any breakthrough before 2007. Even the political parties in the pro-democracy camp did not believe that democratization was an issue with much political appeal. The Democratic Party, the party with the most seats in the legislature until September 2004, and its allies could make very little impact on the government's policymaking process. As the Tung administration enjoyed the backing of a safe majority in the legislature, it did not have to lobby for the approval of the pro-democracy groups which were treated as the opposition. In fact, there had been little meaningful consultation between the pro-democracy groups and the government.

The sense of political impotence on the part of the pro-democracy groups was exacerbated by the Hong Kong people's strengthening trust in China (See Table 14.10). Attacking the Chinese authorities' infringements of the community's freedoms and human rights had become less attractive to voters than before. The most important concerns of the Hong Kong people were obviously the economy and unemployment (Table 14.12), and the pro-democracy groups were not perceived to have much to offer.

The challenge of the "young Turks" in the Democratic Party against its leadership in December 1998 highlighted many important issues in the pro-democracy movement in Hong Kong. Before Hong Kong's return to China, there was substantial moral and public opinion pressure to maintain unity within the pro-democracy camp. Such pressure soon evaporated after July 1997. In the frustration in the political wilderness, differences in political orientations were exacerbated and could no longer be contained. The above differences remained controversial among pro-democracy groups at this stage.

Initially, some of the "young Turks" left the Democratic Party and joined more radical groups such as The Frontier, and the differences existed both at the intra-party and inter-party levels. There were several

Table 14.12: Perceived Problems in Hong Kong Most Mentioned by Respondents in Telephone Opinion Surveys Conducted by the Government, 1997–2003

Time of Survey/ Problem	Jan 1997	Mar 1997	May 1997	July 1997	Sept 1997	Nov 1997	Jan 1998	Mar 1998	May 1998	July 1998	Sept 1998	Nov 1998	Jan 1999	Mar 1999	May 1999	July 1999	Sept 1999	Nov 1999	Jan 2000
Labor-related	27%	25%	19%	18%	19%	24%	33%	41%	54%	48%	49%	50%	46%	49%	47%	45%	38%	47%	51%
Economy-related	18%	12%	7%	9%	12%	29%	52%	44%	48%	66%	60%	57%	61%	54%	38%	43%	51%	42%	42%
Governance of HK Government-related	—	—	—	—	—	—	—	—	—	—	—	—	—	—	—	—	—	—	—
Politics and HK future-related	—	—	—	—	4%	5%	5%	5%	3%	3%	—	—	—	—	—	—	4%	2%	2%
Education-related	13%	11%	18%	15%	19%	14%	9%	10%	11%	8%	9%	9%	7%	12%	12%	11%	17%	13%	13%
Housing related	68%	66%	60%	69%	63%	62%	44%	46%	30%	20%	29%	24%	17%	16%	20%	15%	22%	20%	21%
Social welfare-related	25%	25%	21%	17%	26%	20%	14%	14%	8%	6%	8%	9%	12%	10%	6%	7%	10%	7%	7%
Transport-related	15%	13%	13%	15%	19%	12%	8%	9%	4%	3%	—	—	5%	4%	3%	6%	6%	6%	—
Environment protection-related	—	—	—	—	—	—	—	—	4%	2%	2%	5%	3%	6%	4%	5%	9%	14%	11%
Medical and health-relate	6%	4%	6%	4%	11%	6%	—	—	—	—	—	—	—	—	—	—	—	—	—
New arrivals from mainland-related	—	—	—	—	—	—	—	—	2%	—	1%	1%	2%	14%	—	—	—	—	—
(Base: No. of respondents)	1,040	1,045	1,017	1,099	1,033	1,033	1,144	1,099	1,185	1,272	1,233	1,296	1,350	1,219	1,350	1,219	1,101	1,237	1,292

(Continued)

Table 14.12: (Continued)

Time of Survey/Problem	Mar 2000	May 2000	July 2000	Sept 2000	Nov 2000	Jan 2000	Jan 1998	Mar 1998	May 1998	July 1998	Sept 1998	Nov 1998	Jan 1999	Mar 1999	May 1999	July 1999	Sept 1999	Nov 1999	Jan 2000
Labor-related	45%	39%	45%	50%	46%	47%	33%	41%	54%	48%	49%	50%	46%	49%	47%	45%	38%	47%	51%
Economy-related	40%	34%	38%	48%	42%	46%	52%	44%	48%	66%	60%	57%	61%	54%	38%	43%	51%	42%	42%
Governance of HK Government-related	—	—	—	—	—	—	—	—	—	—	—	—	—	—	—	—	—	—	—
Politics and HK future-related	1%	3%	4%	—	—	—	5%	5%	3%	3%	—	—	—	—	—	—	4%	2%	2%
Education-related	18%	19%	17%	16%	14%	16%	9%	10%	11%	8%	9%	9%	7%	12%	12%	11%	17%	13%	13%
Housing related	17%	20%	32%	18%	17%	19%	44%	46%	30%	20%	29%	24%	17%	16%	20%	15%	22%	20%	21%
Social welfare-related	11%	10%	4%	6%	7%	7%	14%	14%	8%	6%	8%	9%	12%	10%	6%	7%	10%	7%	7%
Transport-related	15%	13%	13%	15%	19%	12%	8%	9%	4%	3%	—	—	5%	4%	3%	6%	6%	6%	—
Environment protection-related	—	—	—	—	4%	4%	—	—	4%	2%	2%	5%	3%	6%	4%	5%	9%	14%	11%
Medical and health-relate	9%	26%	9%	6%	10%	10%	—	—	—	—	—	—	—	—	—	—	—	—	—
New arrivals from mainland-related	—	−10%	3%	3%	2%	6%	—	—	2%	—	1%	1%	2%	14%	—	—	—	—	—
(Base: No. of respondents)	1,278	1,268	1,253	1,154	1,107	1,118	1,144	1,099	1,185	1,272	1,233	1,296	1,350	1,219	1,350	1,219	1,101	1,237	1,292

Source: The telephone opinion surveys were conducted by the Home Affairs Bureau of the Hong Kong Special Administrative Region Government (formerly the Home Affairs Branch of the Hong Kong Government) since January 1983 until August 2003 to monitor public opinion trends in respect of perceived problems in Hong Kong. Government's overall performance and expectations about the general situation of Hong Kong. The data were provided by the Home Affairs Bureau upon request.

waves of such departures from the Democratic Party, resulting in considerable damages to its image. The frustrations of the "young Turks" were exacerbated by bottlenecks in their political careers. The two municipal councils were abolished in 2000; and there were very limited chances of getting elected to the Legislative Council as the "old guards" held on to their seats. Hence, they had to serve as District Councilors for many years, and the remuneration was insufficient to support full-time political careers.

It was only natural that splittism bred more wildly in political wilderness. Politicians in the pro-democracy movement believed that the Chinese authorities had no intention of allowing genuine democracy in the territory in the near future; there was therefore no chance for the pro-democracy groups to form a government. Further, in contrast to the colonial administration in its final years, the HKSAR government was not interested in consulting the opposition when it was normally assured of a safe majority support in the legislature on important issues on which the Chinese authorities had clear positions. The pro-democracy groups had almost no influence on the government's policy-making process. Under such circumstances, unity and discipline had less and less appeal to the politicians in the pro-democracy camp. Moreover, the multi-member, single-vote geographical constituencies in the Legislative Council elections exacerbated splittism. In the largest constituency, i.e., New Territories West, which returned eight legislators, a candidate could secure a seat with 8%–9% of the votes. Hence, moving towards a more radical position might contribute to a sharp image with a strong appeal to a sufficient minority of the electorate. Emily Lau adopted this approach successfully, and she was followed by "Long Hair" Leung Kwok-hung. At the other end of the pro-democracy political spectrum, the Hong Kong Association for Democracy and People's Livelihood avoided controversial political issues and concentrated on district work in Sham Shui Po. Their different political orientations made the maintenance of solidarity within the pro-democracy camp more problematic.

There were other types of problems as well. Despite its electoral victories, the Democratic Party failed to expand its membership in a significant way. It probably had less than 600 members, of whom about one-third remained active. In view of its limited resources, it was preoccupied with parliamentary politics and elections, and had not made much progress in institutionalization. The party's systems and procedures were not well established, and because of the work pressure, a small number of parliamentary leaders had to make decisions within a short period of time. Hence, accountability to the general membership, internal transparency, and intra-party democracy were not well developed. In the first half of the first decade of the new century, the Democracy Party was plagued by internal quarrels, and leadership changes, from Martin Lee to Yeung Sum, Lee Wing-tat, and then Albert Ho, had not brought significant improvements. These internal disputes damaged the party's appeal to supporters of democracy in the territory and adversely affected its political will and ability to provide leadership to the pro-democracy movement.

While the Tung administration failed to show the Hong Kong people the way ahead, the Democratic Party and other pro-democracy groups were not able to demonstrate significant initiatives in presenting the Hong Kong people with well-researched policy alternatives. They failed to perform the role of an effective and constructive opposition from the perspective of policy platform. According to Lau Siu-kai's survey in 2001, 63.6% of the respondents indicated that the Chief Executive could not represent their respective views, and only 12.1% of the respondents said he could. Similarly, 51.7% of the respondents revealed that the HKSAR government could not represent their respective views, and only 15.2% said it could. However, the Democratic Party was not much better — 46% of the respondents indicated that it could not represent their respective views, and only 13.4% said it could. The public affairs concern groups were considered most representative — only 22.1% of the respondents said that they could not represent their respective views, and 38.6% indicated that they could.[26]

To attract the media's attention, legislators from the pro-democracy political parties usually had to dramatize their gestures and statements. A harsh criticism of Beijing obviously had a better chance of making headlines in the newspapers than a balanced statement. Their success with

---

[26] See Lau Siu-kai, "Socio-economic Discontent and Political Attitudes," in Lau Siu-kai, Lee Ming kwan, Wan Po-san and Wong Siu-lun (eds.), *Indicators of Social Development: Hong Kong 2001, op. cit.*, p. 69.

the media, however, made it very difficult for their leaders to establish a dialogue of mutual trust with senior civil servants. It also offered convenient excuses to the Chinese officials for rejecting any contact with them. Such political posturing often had a negative impact on the intelligentsia's support for the pro-democracy political parties.

In early-2002, new political groups emerged within the pro-democracy movement. Power for Democracy and the Hong Kong Democratic Development Network were handicapped by limitations in resources. There were small groups whose influence came mainly from their moral appeal, and were often politely ignored by the pro-democracy political parties. The Civil Human Rights Front remained extremely suspicious of the pro-democracy political parties which were perceived to be mainly interested in elections for the benefits of their leaders. The more active of the groups belonging to this front organization tended to concentrate on the empowerment of the under-privileged groups. Their strong support for the homosexual community often created difficulty in their relations with the church groups.

The dissatisfaction with the Tung administration produced the massive protest rally on July 1, 2003. It was a major boost for the morale of Hong Kong's pro-democracy movement. The opposition to the Article 23 legislation was linked to the demand for democracy, and the anger with the Tung administration also highlighted the significance of democracy. The pro-democracy camp managed to present a united platform in the District Council elections in November 2003. More than 200 candidates from all pro-democracy groups supported: (1) the direct election of the Chief Executive by universal suffrage by 2007; (2) direct elections of all seats of the legislature by universal suffrage by 2008; (3) the initiation of public consultations on political reforms by the government before the end of 2003; and (4) the abolition of all appointed seats to the District Councils after the November 2003 elections.

The record voter turnout rate (44.1%) was the most important feature of the 2003 District Council elections. After the July 1, 2003 massive protest rally, Hong Kong came out to vote in the local elections to express their dissatisfaction with the government and their demand for democratization again. While the pro-Beijing united front had tried to explain the participation in the protest rally on July 1, 2003 as a reflection of the economic difficulties then, and that people had various types of grievances, the record voter turnout rate was a clear indication that people remained dissatisfied with the Tung administration, even though Beijing strongly backed Tung and provided economic assistance to Hong Kong. Further, candidates from the pro-democracy camp won handsomely, while the pro-government DAB suffered a serious defeat.[27] In early 2003, it was widely expected that the DAB would do well in the coming District Council elections because of its huge resources spent in district work in the past years as well as the difficulties within the pro-democracy movement discussed above. In sum, the victory in the District Council elections and the prospect of securing half of the seats in the Legislative Council elections in September 2004 symbolized the revival of the pro-democracy movement.

Subsequently, in the 2004 Legislative Council elections, the pro-democracy camp secured 18 seats in the geographical constituencies — two more than in 2000, and seven in the functional constituencies — two more than in 2000. The result could have been better. In terms of the share of votes won, the pro-democracy camp increased its proportion from 58.2% in 2000 to 60.5% in 2004.[28] The Chinese authorities should feel relieved with the election results though, as the pro-democracy camp failed to capture half of the seats of the legislature. The Chinese authorities had clearly indicated their opposition to universal suffrage by 2007 and 2008, and this position had weathered the anger and protest of the community. They expected no severe challenges in the immediate future.

It was in this context that the HKSAR government introduced its political reform plan in October 2005 for consultation.[29] Basically, the existing mode of the Election Committee would remain unchanged, although the membership would be expanded from 800 to 1,200. The inclusion of all the District Council members in the Election Committee would facilitate the claim that all voters in Hong Kong would be involved

---

[27] See Joseph Y.S. Cheng, "The 2003 District Council elections in Hong Kong," *Asian Survey*, Vol. 44, No. 5, September/ October 2004, pp. 734–754.

[28] See Joseph Y.S. Cheng, "Hong Kong's Democrats Stumble," *Journal of Democracy*, Vol. 16, No. 1, January 2005, pp. 138–152.

[29] See all major newspapers in Hong Kong on October 20, 2005.

in a limited way in the election of the Chief Executive, and that the representativeness of the Election Committee would then be strengthened. There would be five more directly elected seats in the legislature in 2008, plus another five to be elected among all the District Councillors. The reform package did not respond to the pro-democracy camp's demand for a timetable for the introduction of universal suffrage as well as a roadmap showing how the final goal would be achieved. The Chinese authorities and the Tsang administration worked very hard to persuade at least six legislators (out of 25) in the pro-democracy camp to defect so as to secure a two-thirds majority in the legislature to endorse the political reform proposal. They failed; the pro-democracy legislators remained united and defeated the Donald Tsang administration's political reform package.

The political reform package demonstrated the respective political dilemmas on both sides. The Chinese leadership wanted to show Hong Kong, Taiwan, and the world that democratization was making progress in the territory, and that it was fulfilling its pledge that universal suffrage would ultimately be realized. A moderate political reform package endorsed by the required two-thirds majority in the legislature would enhance the legitimacy of the political system. The defeat of the package damaged the legitimacy of the Tsang administration and the political system as the pro-democracy camp had just won 60.5% of the popular votes in the elections in 2004.

The pro-democracy movement was in a difficult position too. It considered that it could not retreat from the political platforms in the earlier District Council elections and Legislative Council elections demanding universal suffrage for the coming Chief Executive election and the elections of the entire legislature. While a consistent majority of the Hong Kong people favored the implementation of universal suffrage at the earliest possible date (from slightly over 50% to almost 80% in various opinion surveys in the early years of the new century), there was also a majority support for the Tsang administration's political reform package. Rejection of the package would mean no progress in democratization at least until 2012; and the younger-generation leaders in various pro-democracy groups believed that the increase in the number of seats in the legislature would offer them significant opportunities. The Tsang administration did not seem eager to negotiate with the pro-democracy movement; the latter did not have the solidarity and consensus to formulate a strategy to negotiate with and to exert pressure on the Tsang administration. There was just enough unity to hold on to the common line of demanding universal suffrage in the 2007 and 2008 elections. The only victory won by the pro-democracy movement was that it succeeded in foiling the Tsang administration's attempt to divide and rule, and to win over the Tsang administration's targeted six pro-democracy legislators.

The political reform issue then went to the Commission on Strategic Development, a high-level consultative body appointed by the Chief Executive. The same competition for legitimacy would likely be reported, as the political will to engage in negotiation between the HKSAR government and the pro-democracy movement was lacking on both sides. In the end, the latter would continue to severely criticize the former for lack of sincerity as there were still no timetable and roadmap, and the latter's inflexibility would be blamed for the lack of progress in democratization by the establishment.

In the Chief Executive election by 2007, the pro-democracy movement was able to secure more than 100 seats in the Election Committee to ensure the official nomination of its candidate, Alan Leong. This small breakthrough demonstrated that the Hong Kong people, and in this specific case, the professional groups, valued competition, accountability, and checks and balances. Though it was clearly understood that Donald Tsang would be able to secure his re-election easily, opinion surveys revealed that up to 70% of the respondents wanted to see competition in the Chief Executive election.

The pro-democracy camp would face an uphill battle in the District Council elections in 2007 and the Legislative Council elections in 2008. In the District Council elections in 2003, the pro-democracy camp candidates much benefitted from the poor performance of the Tung administration and the grievances of the community as reflected in the huge turnout in the previous July 1 protest rally. This advantage would no longer be available in 2007, and the hard work backed by the impressive resources of the pro-Beijing united front was expected to pay dividends. A District Councilor from the pro-democracy camp normally had to deliver 10% of his/her salary and allowances to his/her political group to pay for its expenditure. A District Councilor of the pro-Beijing united front, on the other hand, could expect HK$30,000 or so per month (a bit more than the amount of a District Councilor's salary and allowances) from his/her political group to support his/her services for the constituents. Further, these pro-Beijing District Councilors would have better access to government resources such as the use of community hall facilities, small-scale funding for cultural and educational activities, etc. They too could expect various types of honors and appointments from the HKSAR government and the Chinese authorities; the format would certainly be more helpful in support of these District Councilors including the redressing of grievances of their electorates.

Undeniably, the pro-Beijing political groups were able to attract dedicated candidates, offer them good training, and adopt highly sophisticated campaign strategies. In contrast, the pro-democracy camp candidates were much weaker in resources, and were divided among themselves. The electorate in support of the pro-democracy camp was divided too. In short, the pro-democracy camp would likely suffer a setback in the District Council elections in 2007, and would be considered lucky to retain all its seats in the Legislative Council elections in the following year.

V Conclusion

In the first decade of the HKSAR, the territory encountered similar challenges facing Japan and the other three "little dragons of Asia". The territory entered a period of mature development with considerably lower economic growth rates. At the same time, its delivery of social services was hard pressed by more limited supply due to financial difficulties resulting from slower economic growth, as well as by greater demand because of higher expectations from the community and an ageing population. Redefinition of priorities meant hard choices, and was often costly in terms of political support for and legitimacy of the government.

Economic development alone was no longer sufficient to ensure legitimacy by results. In this sense, the HKSAR government faced severer challenges than the British colonial administration. The economic summit held in 2006 to exploit the opportunities offered by China's 11th Five-Year Economic and Social Development Programme (2006–2010) was a significant example. The summit involved almost all important business leaders, but labor groups were not represented. The Tsang administration was not prepared to consult the experts and the political opposition either. In the end, the community had no sense of ownership concerning the development blueprint.

The Chinese leadership considered that economic growth remained the key to the territory's social and political stability; but would not guarantee a harmonious society. Beijing's "new thinking" is discussed above. This "new thinking" stayed within a united front framework without the intention of introducing genuine democracy. Since the status quo was still satisfactory to the community which had no intention to challenge the Chinese authorities, moderate economic growth was adequate to dampen grievances to maintain stability. However, the government lacked the legitimacy to redefine the priorities even in the economic and social services field. In view of Beijing's perception of threat from the pro-democracy movement, it was unlikely that it would release a timetable and a roadmap to implement genuine democracy.

Apparently, value change in the Hong Kong society was a subject much neglected by all parties concerned. The experiences in the first decade of the HKSAR taught the Hong Kong people to lower their expectations concerning promotions and salary increases. Many young families did not want children; they therefore had less pressure to work hard to increase their incomes. Naturally, they paid more attention to issues relating to the quality of life, health, the environment, the protection of the Victoria Harbor, and the preservation of historic buildings, etc.

Ten years after the territory's return to China, there had been no further progress in democracy. In fact, interference from Beijing had increased after July 2003 when compared with the initial three years after 1997. The dogmatic insistence on an "executive-led" system of government meant that the systemic difficulties in the executive-legislature relationship had not been tackled. Meanwhile, the absence of serious civil service reforms resulted in declining performance of the system as well as accumulating frustration.

The economy demonstrated its resilience. However, relative international competitiveness had been in decline; and the community's confidence in future development had been eroded. While values were changing, the government's policy program did not show such awareness. In sum, this might not have been a decade lost, but it was obviously a crucial era in which there was not much to show off.

The lesson was people sought satisfaction in their daily life; they hoped to secure meaning in it. After meeting their basic needs, they wanted to make a contribution to society. If the Chinese leadership and the HKSAR government continued to think that when the economy improved, political stability would not be challenged, then they had not been able to catch up with the times.

Acknowledgement

This chapter is originally published in *The Hong Kong Special Administrative Region in Its First Decade,* ed. Joseph Y.S. Cheng, pp. 1–48, © 2007 City University of Hong Kong. Used by permission of City University of Hong Kong Press. All rights reserved.

Chapter 15

The Pro-Democracy Movement: A Lost Decade?

I Introduction

In 2007, the pro-democracy movement in Hong Kong was not in good shape. It did not appear that universal suffrage would be implemented even in 2012. There had been no formal dialogue with the Chinese authorities since the establishment of the Hong Kong Special Administrative Region (HKSAR) in 1997. The sense of insecurity on the part of the Chinese leadership had been much exacerbated by the massive protest rally on July 1, 2003, and the subsequent political turmoil;[1] as a result, the Chinese authorities had become more active in containing the influence of the pro-democracy movement. In the crucial Legislative Council elections in September 2004, for example, the pro-democracy parties believed that they were competing with the state machinery directed by Beijing.[2]

Nevertheless, the Hong Kong people still valued the maintenance of checks and balances, and they considered that support for the pro-democracy camp in elections constituted an important means of limiting the power of the HKSAR government. It was interesting to note that in the election of the Chief Executive in 2007, opinion surveys consistently

---

[1] See the author's edited work, *The July 1 Protest Rally: Interpreting a Historic Event*, Hong Kong: City University of Hong Kong Press, 2005.
[2] See the author's "Hong Kong's Democrats Stumble," *Journal of Democracy*, Vol. 16, No. 1, November 2005, pp. 138–152.

showed that about two-thirds of the people in Hong Kong wanted to see competition in the election, even though everyone expected Donald Tsang to win and the level of support for Alan Leong, the pro-democracy movement candidate, stayed at around 20%. Support for the movement in the Election Committee elections in December 2006 even surpassed its expectations.[3]

The values the Hong Kong people had had been changing. Experiences during the decade since the territory's return to the Motherland had probably lowered their expectations concerning economic growth, career development, and increases in incomes. They expected the government to assume a more significant role in the economy. They began to pay more attention to family issues, environmental protection, preservation of the territory's historic sites, and so on. Apparently, neither the government nor the major political parties were able to grasp this value change; this in turn meant that people's satisfaction with the respective performances of the government and political parties had been in decline (see Tables 15.1 and 15.2).

This chapter attempts to analyze and assess the pro-democracy movement in the decade 1997–2007 from the perspectives of people's expectations, the movement's internal dynamics, the community's value change, and its problems and challenges ahead.

II People's Expectations

According to Thomas W.P. Wong, in 1997, in selecting the most important values from the four choices of economic prosperity, social stability, personal freedom, and political democracy, more than half (56%) of the respondents chose social stability, 24.7% economic prosperity, 11.1% political democracy, and 8.2% personal freedom.[4] In times of political

---

[3] See all the major newspapers in Hong Kong, December 11 and 12, 2006.

[4] Thomas W. P. Wong, "Core Values: Revelations from Research in Hong Kong's Social Indicators (1988–2001)," in Siu-kai Lau et al. (eds), *Trends and Challenges in Social Development: Experiences of Hong Kong and Taiwan (in Chinese)*, Hong Kong: Hong Kong Institute of Asia-Pacific Studies, The Chinese University of Hong Kong, 2006, p. 108.

Table 15.1: People's Satisfaction with the HKSAR Government — Half-yearly Average, 1997–2006

Survey question:
Are you satisfied with the overall performance of the HKSAR Government? (half-yearly average)

Month of Survey	Total Sample	Very Satisfied	Quite Satisfied	Half-half	Not quite Satisfied	Very Dissatisfied	Don't know/ Hard to say
July–Dec 2006	6,076	4.2%	37.8%	41.7%	11.4%	3.7%	1.1%
Jan–June 2006	7,113	5.8%	45.7%	36.5%	8.5%	2.4%	1.1%
July–Dec 2005	6,097	5.2%	44.0%	35.7%	9.5%	3.1%	2.4%
Jan–June 2005	6,109	2.9%	26.2%	37.9%	20.2%	8.6%	4.3%
July–Dec 2004	6,148	2.7%	17.5%	35.3%	27.6%	14.2%	2.8%
Jan–June 2004	6,207	1.9%	13.0%	33.1%	30.6%	18.1%	3.5%
July–Dec 2003	7,364	1.5%	12.2%	26.9%	35.3%	21.3%	3.0%
Jan–June 2003	6,293	1.1%	14.3%	25.6%	36.9%	18.6%	3.6%
July–Dec 2002	6,260	1.0%	17.0%	28.1%	37.9%	11.3%	4.8%
Jan–June 2002	6,217	1.3%	23.7%	31.3%	32.8%	6.1%	4.9%
July–Dec 2001	6,321	1.0%	19.2%	30.9%	33.4%	10.5%	5.0%
Jan–June 2001	6,348	1.3%	25.3%	35.0%	26.7%	6.5%	5.2%
July–Dec 2000	6,324	1.5%	19.9%	31.3%	32.1%	9.6%	5.7%
Jan–June 2000	4,240	1.6%	22.4%	39.1%	22.9%	9.0%	5.1%
July–Dec 1999	3,205	1.4%	22.8%	39.2%	23.6%	8.0%	5.0%
Jan–June 1999	4,213	0.7%	24.5%	39.9%	26.3%	5.4%	3.2%
July–Dec 1998	4,755	1.0%	21.7%	35.8%	29.0%	8.0%	4.6%
Jan–June 1998	3,744	0.8%	27.4%	38.7%	23.0%	4.6%	5.5%
July–Dec 1997	3,181	1.9%	40.7%	32.7%	13.6%	1.9%	9.3%

Source: The web site of the Public Opinion Programme of The University of Hong Kong, *POP Polls: People's Satisfaction with the HKSAR Government — half-yearly average*. Retrieved from: http://hkupop.hku.hk/english/popexpress/sargperf/sarg/halfyr/datatables.html, accessed on March 28, 2007.

uncertainty, it was natural that people opted for stability first. Perhaps, people were already aware that Hong Kong was a mature economy and one could no longer expect rapid economic growth. However, what constituted the foundation of social stability was still not clear; and it was also likely that the perceptions of the major ingredients of social stability

Table 15.2: Ratings of Major Political Groups, 1998–2006
Survey question:
Please use a scale of 0–100 to rate your extent of support to XXX, with 0 indicating absolutely not supportive, 100 indicating absolutely supportive and 50 indicating half-half. How would you rate XXX?

Name of Political Group	1998	1999	2000	2001	2002	2003	2004	2005	2006
HKFTU	57.2	55.6	56.6	57.8	57.9	52.0	50.8	52.1	53.3
A45 Concern Group/ Civic Party*	—	—	—	—	—	—	53.4	53.8	51.8
HKCTU	—	52.2	54.2	56.7	56.7	52.8	52.3	51.3	51.2
ADPL	—	48.6	50.8	53.8	55.3	50.1	49.7	48.6	49.8
DAB	51.6	50.5	50.7	53.3	53.7	45.3	42.9	47.0	49.7
Liberal Party	50.2	48.5	48.3	50.5	51.7	49.7	49.1	48.7	49.3
Democratic Party	56.3	52.3	51.3	52.6	51.5	50.2	51.1	47.9	47.0
The Frontier	53.7	50.0	50.4	50.8	50.9	48.0	47.1	45.8	45.6
HKASPDMC	—	49.2	48.4	49.5	48.4	46.4	45.9	45.6	43.1
AFA	—	—	37.5	39.8	39.0	36.8	37.6	36.6	35.8

Notes: 1. *The A45 Concern Group disbanded in March 2006 to form The Civic Party.
2. HKFTU = Hong Kong Federation of Trade Unions
HKCTU = Hong Kong Confederation of Trade Unions
ADPL = Hong Kong Association for Democracy and People's Livelihood
DAB = Democratic Alliance for the Betterment of Hong Kong (currently Democratic Alliance for the Betterment and Progress of Hong Kong since 2005)
HKASPDMC = Hong Kong Alliance in Support of Patriotic Democratic Movements of China
AFA = April Fifth Action
Source: Yearly averages calculated from figures at the web site of the Public Opinion Programme of The University of Hong Kong, *POP Polls: Rating of Top Ten Political Groups*. Retrieved from: http://hkupop.hku.hk/english/popexpress/pgrating/topten1.html, accessed on February 28, 2007.

changed in accordance with the prevailing conditions. For example, when the economy was in bad shape and the unemployment rate was very high, people were more concerned with the economy and the job market (see Table 15.3). In the months before July 2003, people were obviously angry with the proposed Article 23 legislation and the performance of the Tung administration (see Table 15.1).

Table 15.3: Perceived Problems in Hong Kong most mentioned by respondents in telephone opinion surveys conducted by the government, 1997–2003

Problem \ Time of Survey	Jan 1997	Mar 1997	May 1997	July 1997	Sept 1997	Nov 1997	Jan 1998	Mar 1998	May 1998	July 1998	Sept 1998	Nov 1998	Jan 1999	Mar 1999	May 1999	July 1999	Sept 1999	Nov 1999	Jan 2000
Labor-related	27%	25%	19%	18%	19%	24%	33%	41%	54%	48%	49%	50%	46%	49%	47%	45%	38%	47%	51%
Economy-related	18%	12%	7%	9%	12%	29%	52%	44%	48%	66%	60%	57%	61%	54%	38%	43%	51%	42%	42%
Governance of HK Government-related	—	—	—	—	—	—	—	—	—	—	—	—	—	—	—	—	—	—	—
Politics and HK future-related	—	—	—	—	4%	5%	5%	5%	3%	3%	—	—	—	—	—	—	4%	2%	2%
Education-related	13%	11%	18%	15%	19%	14%	9%	10%	11%	8%	9%	9%	7%	12%	12%	11%	17%	13%	13%
Housing-related	68%	66%	60%	69%	63%	62%	44%	46%	30%	20%	29%	24%	17%	16%	20%	15%	22%	20%	21%
Social welfare-related	25%	25%	21%	17%	26%	20%	14%	14%	8%	6%	8%	9%	12%	10%	6%	7%	10%	7%	7%
Transport-related	15%	13%	13%	15%	19%	12%	8%	9%	4%	3%	—	—	5%	4%	3%	6%	6%	6%	—
Environmental protection-related	—	—	—	—	—	—	—	—	4%	2%	2%	5%	3%	6%	4%	5%	9%	14%	11%
Medical and health-related	6%	4%	6%	4%	11%	6%	—	—	—	—	—	—	—	—	—	—	—	—	—
New arrivals from mainland-related	—	—	—	—	—	—	—	—	2%	—	1%	1%	2%	14%	—	—	—	—	—
(Base: No. of respondents)	1,040	1,045	1,017	1,099	1,033	1,033	1,144	1,099	1,185	1,272	1,233	1,296	1,301	1,247	1,350	1,219	1,101	1,237	1,292

(*Continued*)

Table 15.3: *(Continued)*

Time of Survey Problem	Mar 2000	May 2000	July 2000	Sept 2000	Nov 2000	Jan 2001	Mar 2001	May 2001	Jul 2001	Sept 2001	Nov 2001	Jan 2002	Mar 2002	May 2002	Jul 2002	Oct 2002	Jan 2003	May 2003	Aug 2003
Labor-related	45%	39%	45%	50%	46%	47%	49%	42%	49%	52%	54%	55%	57%	58%	70%	60%	51%	42%	49%
Economy-related	40%	34%	38%	38%	42%	46%	42%	47%	44%	55%	52%	48%	52%	44%	43%	36%	40%	46%	41%
Governance of HK Government-related	—	—	—	—	—	—	—	—	—	—	2%	2%	3%	3%	2%	5%	11%	22%	14%
Politics and HK future-related	1%	3%	4%	—	—	—	—	—	—	—	2%	2%	2%	3%	3%	7%	6%	4%	8%
Education-related	18%	19%	17%	16%	14%	16%	18%	21%	19%	20%	16%	13%	15%	14%	14%	11%	8%	5%	8%
Housing-related	17%	20%	32%	18%	17%	19%	20%	16%	15%	21%	13%	10%	11%	11%	8%	9%	7%	4%	7%
Social welfare-related	11%	10%	4%	6%	7%	7%	6%	6%	4%	4%	4%	5%	6%	8%	5%	5%	7%	4%	2%
Transport-related	—	—	—	—	—	4%	4%	3%	4%	2%	4%	2%	3%	2%	3%	5%	—	—	—
Environmental protection-related	9%	26%	9%	6%	10%	10%	7%	9%	8%	4%	3%	4%	4%	4%	3%	—	—	—	—
Medical and health-related	—	10%	3%	3%	2%	6%	4%	—	—	—	—	—	—	—	—	—	—	—	—
(Base: No. of respondents)	1,278	1,268	1,253	1,154	1,107	1,118	1,149	1,157	1,158	1,128	1,181	1,152	1,236	1,237	1,317	1,424	1,359	1,447	1,292

Source: The telephone opinion surveys were conducted by the Home Affairs Bureau of the Hong Kong Special Administrative Region (formerly the Home Affairs Branch of the Hong Kong Government) since January 1983 until August 2003 to monitor public opinion trends in respect of perceived problems in Hong Kong, Government's overall performance and expectations about the general situation of Hog Kong. The data were provided by the Home Affairs Bureau under request of the author.

In his very first policy address, C.H. Tung indicated that his administration intended to be more proactive.[5] He was obviously concerned with the territory's declining international competitiveness. His housing policy of providing 85,000 units per annum was an attempt to lower the prices of accommodation, which had become increasingly unaffordable for ordinary Hong Kong people, but he also perceived high real estate prices as a significant factor in pushing up Hong Kong's cost structure, making its goods and services more costly and less competitive. Tung placed a high priority on education as a means, again, to improve Hong Kong's international competitiveness in the long run; while his emphasis on services for the elderly reflected his concern for the demands of an ageing population and the community's rising expectations for improvements in social services.

Undeniably, the sharp deterioration in the territory's economic performance since 1997 had caused much misery and dissatisfaction among the Hong Kong people. The average annual rate of growth in per capita gross domestic product (GDP) fell from 4.5% in the period 1983–1997 to 1.9% in 1997–2001. Almost full employment was maintained from 1985 to mid-1997 as the unemployment rate ranged from 1.3% to a peak of only 3.5%. Since Hong Kong's return to China, the unemployment rate climbed from 2.1% in mid-1997 to a record high of 8.7% in mid-2003.[6]

Though the Tung administration failed to solve Hong Kong's economic problems, the pro-democracy movement did not have much to offer in terms of the territory's economic development strategy either. It was not able to demonstrate significant initiatives in presenting the Hong Kong people with well-researched policy alternatives. It failed to perform the role of an effective and constructive opposition from the perspective of a policy platform.

In terms of the community's value change and social policies, both the government and the political parties had not been responsive. It did not

---

[5] For Tung's first policy address, see http://www.policyaddress.gov.hk/pa97/english/paindex.htm, retrieved on February 28, 2007.
[6] Sung Yun-wing, "Hong Kong Economy in Crisis," in Siu-kai Lau (ed), *The First Tung Chee-hwa Administration*, Hong Kong: The Chinese University Press, 2002, p. 123.

appear that they had been trying hard to understand the issues. In the final years of the Tung administration and before the re-election of Donald Tsang, the HKSAR government did not have the political will or the initiative. However, the pro-democracy movement had not been effective in the policy areas of education, health insurance, youth work, community-building, and so on. Globalization had led to a widening of the gap between the rich and the poor; even young university graduates became uncertain of their middle-class status. The slowing down of economic growth, the downsizing of the civil service and most public sector organizations, the streamlining of enterprises to enhance their profit rates, and so on, meant that the younger generations of middle-class professionals and executives encounter more limited opportunities,[7] and they probably would have to seek new sources of satisfaction. This trend might promote the further development of civil society, or might exacerbate the community's dissatisfaction and lead to protests.

Taiwan offered an interesting example. The democratization process since the late 1980s had been accompanied by an impressive development of civic groups. Many of them engage in large-scale philanthropic activities attracting voluntary worked and donations. In a few cases of natural disaster relief campaigns, their voluntary workers reached the sites ahead of government personnel. Despite the disillusionment at this stage with the political parties, the development of civic groups in Taiwan had not been adversely affected. Apparently, neither the political parties nor the existing civic groups in Hong Kong had been able to exploit this potential. In contrast to the 1980s, the appeal of the pro-democracy political parties for the student unions of the territory's tertiary sector had been in decline.

At the same time, the keen interest of the community in the protection of Victoria Harbor and the preservation of some historical sites including the Star Ferry Pier in Central Hong Kong at this stage had caught the government and all political parties by surprise. They underestimated the significance of these issues. The government was complacent in view of the improved economic conditions — unemployment rate gradually

---

[7] Ohmae Kenichi, *The Impact of Rising Lower-middle Class Population in Japan: What Can We Do About It? (in Japanese)*, Tokyo: Kodansha, 2006.

declined to 5% in mid-2006, and economic growth rate rose from 1.8% in 2002 to 3.2% in 2003, 8.6% in 2004 and 7.3% in 2005.[8] The pro-democracy political parties, on the other hand, had been perceived as insensitive to changes in the community's value.

III Elections and Political Reforms

Apparently, most Hong Kong people still adopted a utilitarian attitude towards democracy. They perceived democracy as a means to realize practical, concrete objectives. Few of the Hong Kong people really practiced democracy as a way of life. Since the Hong Kong people treated democracy as a means to an end, they are prudent in the calculation of the costs of political participation. While they perceived democracy as an important means to guarantee their freedom, their lifestyles, and their living standards which they treasured, they also considered that one's own efforts were probably more significant and more reliable to improve one's life.[9] In view of the broad trends of economic globalization, they were probably less confident in the first decade of the new century of their individual hard work, and expected the government to play a more significant role.

Upon the return of the territory to the Motherland, the vast majority of the Hong Kong people had, to some extent, accepted the substitution of stability and prosperity for democracy. They lowered their expectations of democracy because they realized that this was not a realistic goal and they valued the high standards of living that the territory had been offering them. When such calculations were altered, however, the mood of the community could change dramatically. The massive demonstrations in response to the Tiananmen Incident in 1989 were a vivid example. On July 1, 2003, more than half a million people took to the streets to protest against the Article 23 legislation and demand democracy. People who took part in the rally felt that they had made history, and were proud of the

---

[8] Hong Kong Statistics: *Understanding the Present, Planning the Future*, poster released by the Census and Statistics Department, HKSAR Government, early July 2006.
[9] See the author's edited work, *Political Participation in Hong Kong — Theoretical Issues and Historical Legacy*, Hong Kong: City University of Hong Kong Press, 1999.

peace and order among the protesters. The crisis attracted much international media attention, and it also became an issue high on the agenda of the Chinese leadership.

The massive protest rally on July 1, 2003 was a major boost to the morale of Hong Kong's pro-democracy movement. The opposition to the Article 23 legislation was linked to the demand for democracy, and the anger with the Tung administration also highlighted the significance of democracy. People realized that they had no part in the re-election of Tung, and while his performance was terrible, the community could not force him to step down. The pro-democracy camp understood that it could not mobilize hundreds of thousands of people to march on the streets all the time; it therefore hoped to use the elections to send a message to the Tung administration, Beijing and the world that Hong Kong people had not forgotten the demand for democratization.

The record voter turnout rate (44.1%) was the most important feature of the November 2003 District Council elections. After the July 1, 2003 protest rally, the Hong Kong people came out to vote in local elections to express their dissatisfaction with the government and their demand for democratization again. In the beginning of 2003, most observers had agreed that the pro-government Democratic Alliance for the Betterment of Hong Kong (DAB) should be able to secure a major victory in the upcoming District Council elections. The party's confidence was reflected by the 206 candidates it fielded. However, the DAB's support for the Tung administration and its position on the Article 23 legislation became conspicuous political liabilities. The other pro-government parties, the Liberal Party and the Hong Kong Progressive Alliance, suffered only minor losses.

The Democratic Party reversed its decline in recent years and in 2003 gained nine more seats to reach 95, compared with 86 in 1999. The party certainly benefitted from the public's dissatisfaction with the Tung administration, the associated anger with the DAB, and the upsurge in demand for democracy in the community, symbolized by the July 1 protest rally. The Democratic Party fielded 120 candidates, in comparison with DAB's 206, demonstrating its earlier appreciation of the need to consolidate. The relatively large number of district councillors was an important asset of the Democratic Party in terms of financial and human resources and grassroots networks. The party remained the largest and the most powerful organization within the pro-democracy camp. Meanwhile, the other pro-democracy groups, such as, The Frontier and the Hong Kong Association for Democracy and People's Livelihood (ADPL), also performed well in the District Council elections.

Although the pro-democracy camp was seen to have won in the 2003 District Council elections and the DAB to have suffered a serious setback, in terms of actual distribution of political force in the 18 District Councils, the pro-democracy camp enjoyed a majority in only seven councils, while pro-government members held the majority in 10, with a balanced situation in Kowloon City. This scenario further deteriorated as a result of the appointment system which gave the Tung administration the opportunity to reward its supporters and tip the respective political balances in favor of the government in several District Councils. After the appointments, the pro-democracy camp enjoyed a majority only in two District Councils. The pro-government majorities in the 16 District Councils meant that their resources would largely be denied to the pro-democracy camp. The victory for democracy therefore should be seen largely in terms of the political messages sent by the voters.

An important weakness of the pro-democracy camp was revealed by the number of candidates it fielded, about 200 altogether in 400 constituencies. The relatively low number of candidates was a sign of difficulties in political recruitment. Further, the strengths of the DAB discussed above remained, and again, it was expected to do well in the 2007 District Council elections, an appropriate reward for its impressive services at the grassroots level.

The momentum of the pro-democracy movement was only partly maintained in the September 2004 Legislative Council elections. The voter turnout reached a new high of 55.6%, up from a staggering 12% from that in 2000. About 1.78 million Hong Kong people cast their votes. In terms of the number of seats won, the pro-democracy camp did not do very well. It secured 18 seats in the geographical constituencies — two more than in 2000, and seven in the functional constituencies — two more than in 2000. The results could have been better.[10]

---

[10] See the author's "Hong Kong's Democrats Stumble," *op. cit.*, pp. 138–152.

The pro-democracy camp was probably adversely affected by scandals, hostile media, and backward campaign strategies. In terms of the share of votes won, the pro-democracy camp increased its share from 58.2% in 2000 to 60.5% in 2004. However, this was still slightly lower than its share of 63.2% in 1998.[11] In the context of a record voter turnout rate and the impressive turnout for the two protest rallies on July 1, 2003, and July 1, 2004, this was slightly disappointing because the pro-government legislators managed to retain their majority in the legislature and thus the pro-democracy groups remained in the opposition, with little impact on the legislative process. However, this was exactly the intent of the design of the electoral system, which served to deny the pro-democracy groups a majority in the legislature despite their absolute majority support in direct elections. The Legislative Council elections in 2004 also failed to generate meaningful discussions on the significance of the elections and related important policy issues.

The Donald Tsang administration then offered its political reform package, which suggested adding five directly-elected seats and five functional constituency seats to the Legislative Council in 2008. The latter would be returned by district councillors, implying that the pro-democracy groups could hope to win two or three seats from such additional functional constituency seats.[12] The pro-democracy movement insisted on a timetable and a roadmap for the implementation of universal suffrage for the elections of the Chief Executive and the entire legislature. It refused to accept the government package as a compromise interim measure. According to the Basic Law, there should be a review of the systems for elections after 2007, hence the reform package from the Tsang administration. Any proposals for reform, however, had first to secure a two-thirds majority support in the legislature, and this provision gave the pro-democracy legislators a veto power. They were encouraged by the

---

[11] These percentages vary a little depending on who are counted as members of the pro-democracy camp. Experts differ to a small extent regarding the exact categorization of one or two marginal/controversial candidates.

[12] For the political reform package, see the website of the Constitutional Reform Bureau of the HKSAR government at http://www.cab.gov.hk/cd/eng/past/index.htm, retrieved on 28 February 2007. See also all major newspapers on 22 December 2005.

impressive turnout at a protest rally (250,000 according to the organizers, and 63,000 according to the police) on December 4, 2004, rejecting the reform package,[13] and managed to maintain their solidarity against the Tsang administration's attempts to win over six of them to secure the required two-thirds majority support in the legislature.

The rejection of the political reform package by 24 votes was widely seen as a major setback for the Tsang administration.[14] It was hardly a victory for the pro-democracy movement, however, because public opinion was in favour of supporting the reform package. The Chinese authorities perceived this adamant position as confrontational and terminated their more friendly approach towards the pro-democracy groups that had been initiated after the September 2004 Legislative Council elections, and the latter had to face the lack of electoral reforms in the foreseeable future, a considerable disappointment to their second-tier leaders. By then, in the absence of any realistic chance of achieving breakthroughs, the pro-democracy movement had lost its momentum.

IV Problems and Challenges Ahead

During the past decade and more, the pro-democracy movement had proved to be effective in its electoral campaigns. In the direct elections to the legislature, it normally secured about 60% of the electorate's support. This was mainly due to the political wisdom of a majority of Hong Kong voters, who wanted to maintain effective checks and balances by returning pro-democracy candidates to the legislature to avoid the government enjoying unlimited powers. Without democratic reforms, it was difficult to imagine how the pro-democracy camp could win a majority of seats in the legislature within the existing electoral system. Hence, the pro-democracy camp was not perceived as a credible alternative government, and it had not made much effort to achieve such an objective. It was not able, for example, to present a shadow cabinet. Alan Leong's candidacy in the 2007 Chief Executive election represented an attempt on the part of the

---

[13] *South China Morning Post*, 5 and 6 December 2005.
[14] *Ibid.*, 22 December 2005.

movement to offer a comprehensive policy platform, but the debates on it were limited.

Most Hong Kong people accepted that the issue of political reforms in the territory would be determined by the Chinese leadership, and they were reluctant to engage in confrontation with the Chinese authorities. They appreciated that if there was no democracy in China, it would be difficult to expect genuine democracy in Hong Kong. In its second term, the Hu Jintao administration was tightening control of the media, Internet information services, dissidents, non-governmental organizations, etc., and the prospects of political reforms in China were not promising. In the longer term, however, there was perhaps greater optimism based on the belief that economic reforms and liberties would ultimately introduce democratic reforms.

Meanwhile, the Chinese authorities refused to engage in a formal dialogue with the pro-democracy groups, partly as a sanction against their role in the Tiananmen Incident and their subsequent demand to reverse the official verdict on the issue, and partly as an element of the Chinese authorities' general campaign to discredit the pro-democracy groups. There was no lack of informal contact, however, with the purpose of collecting information from the activists and engaging in the usual united front tactics of winning over those who could be won over. The pro-democracy groups were not ready for a dialogue either, and there was inadequate solidarity, trust, and coordination among them to formulate a strategy for negotiations. The groups were notorious for not being able to keep secrets, and they failed miserably in avoiding leakage of confidential information to the media. Hence, the easy way out was to stick to the bottom line inflexibly, while flexibility or tactical concessions might be easily labelled as betrayal. The responses to the Donald Tsang administration's political reform package were a typical example.

Given their strong position, the Chinese authorities had no intention to negotiate. They treated the pro-democracy groups within a united front framework; in fact, they probably treated all groups in the territory within such a framework. Their basic policy was to induce the pro-democracy groups to accept their fundamental policy position regarding Hong Kong. This acceptance would be rewarded, probably along the lines of the treatment given the "democratic parties" in China. However, this was political suicide, even for the pro-Beijing political groups in the territory. The ADPL chose to stay in the unelected provisional legislature in 1997 instead of boycotting it like other pro-democracy groups; in the 1998 legislative elections, it lost all four seats in the Legislative Council. The passive toeing of the Beijing line by the Hong Kong Progressive Alliance finally led to its demise in 2004; it lost all four seats in the Legislative Council elections and was forced to merge with the DAB in the following year.

Following the logic of the united front strategy, the pro-democracy groups opposing the Beijing line most strongly were singled out for severe sanctions, a clear demonstration of Beijing's intentions. The Civic Party, formally launched in March 2006 and based on the Article 45 Concern Group, rejected Donald Tsang's political reform package, and the business community was secretly warned against giving donations to the new party. The pro-Beijing mass media also concentrated their criticisms against the group, so much so that the Democratic Party felt less pressure.

Beijing's united front strategy largely failed to divide the pro-democracy groups in any significant manner, but solidarity among them was nonetheless severely threatened. Before Hong Kong's return to China, there was substantial moral and public opinion pressure to maintain unity within the pro-democracy camp. Such pressure soon evaporated after July 1997. In the frustration of the political wilderness, differences in political orientations were exacerbated and could no longer be contained. The differences were initially concentrated on three issues: (a) the relationships with the Chinese authorities and the HKSAR government; (b) whether to aggregate class interests or to articulate more distinctively labour and grassroots interests; and (c) whether priority should be given to effect changes by working within the legislature, or by resorting to mass movements outside the political establishment.

At this stage, The Frontier still adopted the puritanical position of refusing to take part in the functional constituency elections to the Legislative Council. In the 2007 Chief Executive election, Alan Leong's campaign was supported mainly by the Civic Party and the Democratic Party. The Frontier, the Hong Kong Confederation of Trade Unions, and the Neighbourhood and Worker's Service Centre all refused to take part in this "small circle" election; and the newly-formed League of Social Democrats even actively opposed Alan Leong's campaign.

These differences in political orientation were even more serious within the Democratic Party, as it was easier for the pro-democracy groups to ignore their inter-group differences. The frustrations of the "young Turks" of the Democratic Party led to their challenge of the party leadership in December 1998.[15] The "young Turks" and the non-mainstream factions were opposed to efforts to improve relations with the Chinese authorities by such means as presenting candidates to compete for seats in China's National People's Congress. They were not interested in a better relationship with the HKSAR government and publicly called for the resignation of C.H. Tung. Regarding the party's policy platform, they warned the party leadership against opportunism in attempting to represent the interests of all classes. In turn, they were accused of trying to turn the party into a labor party and adopting a populist approach. Above all else, the "young Turks" and the non-mainstream factions appealed for a return to the grassroots to mobilize the masses instead of engaging in futile parliamentary politics.

The differences within the Democratic Party led to several waves of departure from the party on the part of the more radical members. These movements tarnished the image of the party. At the same time, the pro-democracy political parties encountered difficulties too in their relationship with grassroots community organizations that emerged and developed in the late 1960s and 1970s, and had been supporting pro-democracy political groups. The pro-democracy political parties certainly could help to raise issues of importance to grassroots community organizations in the legislature or with senior government officials, thus exerting pressure on the C.H. Tung and Donald Tsang administrations to provide solutions. However, their high profile and eagerness for publicity often resulted in a failure to compromise and in delays in achieving settlements. Many grassroots community organizations worried that they might be taken for a ride, and they often preferred to act without the involvement of political parties. After all, these organizations were issue-oriented; they wanted concrete solutions to their problems. A few cases of unpleasant experiences

---

[15] Ivan Chi-keung Choy, "A Coup in the Frosty Month — Counter-attack by the Non-mainstream Factions of the Democratic Party (in Chinese)," *Ming Pao* (a Chinese language newspaper in Hong Kong), 16 December 1998.

had resulted in their alienation from the pro-democracy political parties. At the same time, they were eagerly courted by the pro-Beijing political groups, which apparently were making progress in their united front work.

In the past decade, a new generation of political activists had emerged, assuming leadership in many small grassroots community organizations. These activists were less interested in the pursuit of democracy in the territory and were more focused on environmental protection, community-building, homosexual rights, labor grievances, services for the under-privileged groups, and so on. They adopted more radical positions, and perceived the pro-democracy political parties as part of the political establishment. They resented the latter's concentration on parliamentary work, and criticized many pro-democracy leaders as politicians only interested in their own political careers. Their promotion of homosexual rights and those of prostitutes sometimes created difficulties for the participation of conservative religious groups.

The differences among pro-democracy political parties, within the Democratic Party, and between pro-democracy political parties and grassroots community organizations were complicated and sometimes petty as well as personal. However, they attracted considerable media attention, and resulted in damage to the reputation of all parties concerned. Moreover, these quarrels also caused disappointment among ordinary supporters of the pro-democracy movement.

It was in this context that new groups such as Power for Democracy, Hong Kong Democratic Development Network, and Civil Human Rights Front emerged in early 2002. They planned to concentrate on the cause of democracy and human rights, and wanted to offer an alternative to political parties in political participation. Their emergence and development reflected the disappointment with political parties in the pro-democracy camp and the suspicious attitude towards its politicians. It was significant that these new groups were dominated by church activists and academics who were generally seen as having no political ambitions. At the time of the movement against the Article 23 legislation, these groups attempted to bring together various types of organizations in support of democracy and human rights because of the decline in appeal of the pro-democracy political parties, the suspicions against them, and the in-fighting among them and between them, and the grassroots community organizations.

This was not a healthy phenomenon, as political parties had the resources and the most important role to play in the push for democracy in the territory. Moreover, these new groups had very limited resources, and the pro-democracy parties were reluctant to follow their lead. Over time, the Civil Human Rights Front became dominated by the new generation of political activists, and its relationship with the pro-democracy political parties was now problematic. Power for Democracy still assumed a useful role in the co-ordination of the pro-democracy camp's electoral campaigns in the 2003 District Council elections, the 2004 Legislative Council elections, and the 2007 District Council elections.

The pro-democracy movement at this stage and in the near future would be handicapped by three serious constraints. In comparison with the DAB and even the Liberal Party, the pro-democracy parties had not been successful in political recruitment. Businessmen and business executives were reluctant to be seen to be associated with them because of their increasingly close business ties with Mainland China. The problem was more serious in terms of the generation gap. It was expected that most of pro-democracy leaders would retire in the coming decade because of age. Yet, the talents among the second-tier leadership were not promising. Inadequate efforts and commitment had been accorded to the cultivation of successors.

In general, pro-democracy political parties including the Civic Party, had financial problems. The Taiwan model, in which enterprises offered donations to all political parties according to their relative strengths, was the envy of the pro-democracy camp in Hong Kong. District councillors affiliated to the pro-democracy political parties in Hong Kong normally had to contribute one-tenth of their salaries and allowances to pay for the functioning of their respective party headquarters, while district councillors of the DAB were said to receive a monthly subsidy of about US$4,000 each in support of their constituency work. This disparity illustrated the financial plight of the political opposition and explained the impressive grassroots services of the DAB.

As political parties in Hong Kong were cadre parties, they were very dependent on the media for image building and projection to maintain their appeal to the community. Hence, the self-censorship of the local media was probably the most common complaint among pro-democracy legislators. Most media were in the hands of major business groups which, almost without exception, had substantial business activities in Mainland China. Hence, media operators did not want to antagonize Beijing. Worse still, some owners of media even used them as a tool to cultivate business ties with the Chinese authorities. After all, the latter fully appreciated the significance of the media in containing the pro-democracy movement; most media operators were granted the honor of membership of the National Committee of the Chinese People's Political Consultative Conference.

Self-censorship was obviously not a problem with the international media. However, after 1997, Hong Kong as a special administrative region could not expect to attract much international media attention. In view of the importance of business ties and good relations with China, fewer and fewer Western governments were willing to articulate their support for democracy in Hong Kong. Pro-democracy groups in the territory were very careful and were reserved in their ties with Taiwan and the U.S.

V Conclusion

Upon Hong Kong's return to the Motherland, the community's expectations of democracy was lowered and the pro-democracy movement's development was limited by the more hostile environment in contrast to the encouragement given by the British colonial administration in its final years. The failure of the Tung administration and the provocative Article 23 legislation process brought the pro-democracy movement a high tide once again. With the benefit of hindsight, the high tide revealed the restrictions imposed by the design of the electoral system, and it also showed that the Chinese authorities were ready to intervene to defend their fundamental interests in and position on Hong Kong. The dilemma for the pro-democracy movement was this — while trying to secure the acceptance of the Chinese authorities would be political suicide, posing a genuine challenge would provoke a substantially higher degree of intervention. However, the choice was obvious, that is, to maintain the integrity of the movement in anticipation of democracy in China.

The survival of the pro-democracy movement, fortunately, was guaranteed by two factors. All parties concerned realized the importance of the maintenance of the rule of law and the freedom of information flow in the territory in ensuring its functioning as an international financial centre and international business services centre. A majority of Hong Kong voters also wanted to guarantee a minimum of checks and balances by returning pro-democracy candidates in Legislative Council elections. Despite all the limitations in financial resources and media self-censorship, the very existence of the pro-democracy movement in the territory would not be threatened in the foreseeable future.

The immediate prospects were not promising in that genuine universal suffrage would likely not be implemented by 2012; and the Chinese authorities' efforts to contain the pro-democracy movement and support the Donald Tsang administration would continue. In the absence of unexpected morale booster such as the protest rally on July 1, 2003, the pro-democracy groups could not realistically expect to secure substantial gains in the 2007 District Council elections nor could they in the 2008 Legislative Council elections.

Better coordination among the pro-democracy groups and more serious contributions to policy studies in areas such as education and health insurance were the immediate challenges of the pro-democracy political parties, and they would be judged on this basis by their supporters and the media. Their past record was obviously not impressive, but there was no reason to be unduly pessimistic either.

Acknowledgement

Originally published as Cheng, Joseph Y.S., "The Pro-democracy Movement: A Lost Decade?", *European View*, Vol. 7, Issue 1, 2008, pp. 53–66. © 2008. Reproduced with kind permission from the publisher.

Chapter 16

Hong Kong District Councils: Political Development and Community Building

I Simple Theoretical Framework of Political Development

The definition of political development is usually based on a comparison between modern political systems and traditional political systems. Using the concepts of Max Weber, political development involves the rationalization of authority, traditional authority, and the charismatic authority of political leaders being replaced by legal-bureaucratic authority.[1] In history, political development normally follows the establishment of the modern state, the sovereignty of which is recognized by the international community and is realized domestically through the organization of a government with ultimate authority. To meet the demands of political development, the organization of government becomes complicated and hierarchical. Political development certainly involves increases in political participation on the part of the individual and the community. A high level of political participation strengthens society's supervision of the states; but in authoritarian countries, this may

---

[1] See Max Weber, *The Theory of Social and Economic Organization*, trans. edited by A.M. Henderson and Talcott Parsons, with an introduction by Talcott Parsons, New York: Free Press, 1964, Section III, pp. 324–407.

well enhance the state's control of society. In all modern states, citizens cannot avoid being involved in public affairs and affected by government policies.

Political participation is a simple and basic concept in political science. It may be defined as the actions of private citizens seeking to influence or support government and politics.[2] This is a relatively broad definition in that it also includes ceremonial and support activities. In discussions on political participation, political scientists often try to explain human behavior as it relates to the political system. They also recognize that the political system and political culture have a significant impact on individual political behavior.[3] Yet, many social scientists believe that at the basic level, human beings follow the same behavioral laws irrespective of the culture they live in.

Political participation may be seen as a means or an end in itself. It is looked upon as an instrument to realize self-rule or to secure self-protection; but it is also considered as a process of self-realization. Those who treat political participation as an instrument believe that it is a better way of defending individual or group interests than entrusting such interests to political leaders. They probably share the distrust of rulers of James Mill and John Stuart Mill who considered that rulers had a "natural tendency...to misuse their power."[4] According to Peter Bachrach, self-protection has two consequences: (1) protection against tyranny, and (2) protection of self-interest.[5] The fundamental assumptions behind this instrumental view of political participation are as follows — the individual is the best judge of his/her own interests, and an individual should be

---

[2] Lester W. Milbrath and M.L. Goel, *Political Participation*, Lanham, Maryland: United Press of America, 1977, (2nd edition), p. 2.

[3] See, for example, Gabriel A. Almond and Sidney Verba, *The Civic Culture*, Princeton, N.J.: Princeton University Press, 1963.

[4] Graeme Duncan and Steven Lakes, "The New Democracy," *Political Studies* XI, No. 2, June 1963, p. 164.

[5] Peter Bachrach, "Interest, Participation and Democratic Theory," in *Participation in Politics*, edited by J.R. Pennock and J. Chapman, New York: Lieber-Atherton, 1975; discussed in Peter Ronald de Souza, "Leadership, Participation and Democratic Theory", Ph.D. diss., University of Sussex, December 1986), p. 26.

given a say in matters which affect him/her. Governments which deny their citizens this natural right of participation are therefore illegitimate.

When considered as a process of self-realization, it is assumed that the fullest potential of human capacities can only be realized through participation in politics. The latter is an activity through which individuals develop as full, creative, sensitive, and productive members of a community. Taking part in the making of decisions which affect others as well as oneself improves the individual's character and gives him/her a sense of responsibility. Political participation is a moral education in that it requires the individual to consider interests other than his/her own, and to manage conflicts of interest by applying general rules. It develops understanding, helps to develop the quality of sympathy, and gives the individual a sense of efficacy, a feeling that he/she is participating more fully in affairs which are of concern to him/her. It creates a sense of involvement in, and identification with, the political system.[6]

II District Councils: Historical Background

After the extension of the British administration to the New Territories in 1898 based on its lease to the British Empire by the Qing Dynasty, a District Office system was adopted. This was based on a real principle of organization with the District Officer acting as a semi-omnipotent viceroy in his region. He would maintain law and order, arbitrate in civil disputes, and pass judgments on criminal affairs.

Traditionally, the New Territories Administration with its District Officers was designed to maintain the status quo in a rural setting. With the development of new towns in the 1970s, District Officers had to be responsible for town planning, public works, supervision and monitoring of private developers, provision of urban services, and the promotion of commerce and industry. To perform such tasks, a responsive machinery capable of making swift and interim arrangements was badly needed; and the District Officer as an administrative coordinator was handicapped by the fact that central departments were far from adequately represented in his/her district to ensure quick responses to local problems.

---

[6] *Ibid.*, pp. 27–28.

The British administration was then reluctant to accept the recommendations of the Working Party on Local Administration reporting in November 1966 to establish democratically elected local administrations[7] nor the Heung Yee Kuk's request to establish a Political Board for the New Territories.[8] Instead, only piecemeal measures were adopted.

In the late 1960s, District Officers were entrusted with the overall responsibility for coordinating the development process in their respective districts. In Tsuen Wan, the very first new town in the New Territories that could trace its development to the early 1960s, a Town Manager was appointed in early 1976 to oversee the implementation of the development programs, with a special responsibility to promote new community organizations such as Mutual Aid Committees, and to develop community relations. At the same time, a Town Centre Advisory Committee was appointed to provide opportunities for a broad spectrum of the new town residents to participate in development administration. In association with this, many other machineries for public participation were subsequently organized, a good example being the City Amenities and Recreational Committee. This experiment was considered successful by the government, and it became the model for the District Advisory Boards established in November 1977.[9]

A new system thus gradually took shape — each district in the New Territories was headed by a District Officer (a Town Manager in the case of Tsuen Wan), who was responsible, in close liaison with the project manager, for the overall coordination of the development process, and with a special responsibility for developing the social and organizational fabric of the new community. The major government departments,

---

[7] See *Report of the Working Party on Local Administration*, Hong Kong: Government Printer, 1966.

[8] See, for example, *Striving for Justifiable Rights for the People of the New Territories*, Vols. I and II (Vol. II in Chinese only), Hong Kong: Heung Yee Kuk, 1964; and *The New Territories Community of Hong Kong under Colonial Administration*, Hong Kong: Heung Yee Kuk, 1977.

[9] Hsin-chi Kuan and Siu-kai Lau, *Planned Development and Political Adaptability in Rural Hong Kong*, Occasional Paper No. 88, Hong Kong: Social Research Centre, The Chinese University of Hong Kong, January 1980, pp. 21–22.

including Public Works, Education, Medical and Health, Transport, Housing Authority, Urban Services, Fire Services, Royal Hong Kong Police, Social Welfare and Labour, were all represented on a District Management Committee chaired by the District Officer. Alongside the traditional system of rural representation, a new consultative machinery was provided by the District Advisory Boards.

For the new residents in a new town, the District Advisory Board was an unqualified improvement. It provided them with the opportunity to participate in an important governmental consultative organ in their own district, and they had longed for this right. Initially, the District Advisory Boards were not meant to be representative assemblies based on electoral principles, but rather a mirror of public opinion and a training ground for the future local elites. Their future development then was still an open question. The compositions and sizes of the District Advisory Boards varied from district to district, reflecting the different make-ups of the local communities. However, in general terms, a District Advisory Board was comprised of a balance of unofficial representatives appointed from the local community, the Rural Committee chairmen of the district as ex-officio members, and senior government officers of the district with the District Officer assuming the chairmanship. The unofficial representatives were all appointed by the government at the advice of the Secretary for the New Territories. They generally represented all walks of life, and had demonstrated a commitment to serve the community through serving in a number of voluntary organizations. Many of them were respected for their achievement in their respective professions too. The major weakness, however, was that they were appointed by the government and were therefore accountable only to the government, and not to their respective local communities. Further, a vast majority of them did not have any grassroots support at all.

Meanwhile, similar developments took place in the urban area as well as on a territory-wide basis. The British administration had learned a lesson from the riots in 1966 and 1967 and became more responsive to public opinion. It even claimed to be a "government by consultation." The system of advisory committees following the British tradition was further developed to involve community leaders of the upper socioeconomic strata, and such "administrative absorption" was used to strengthen the colonial government's representativeness.[10]

The City District Officer Scheme, which started in 1968 as a response to the 1966–1967 riots, was expanded in the 1970s. This enabled the government's consultative network to reach the grassroots and facilitated the absorption of the activists at the grassroots level into its system of advisory committees.[11] In 1972, each City District Office set up within the district a number of area committees whose members were community leaders nominated by the City District Officer. In the following year, the government encouraged residents of public housing estates and private residential blocks to form mutual aid committees in support of its Fight Crime Campaign and Clean Hong Kong Campaign. Earlier, the government also persuaded the owners of private housing to organize owners' corporations to promote better building management and security.[12]

Although democratization was not entertained by the British administration at this stage, it was obvious that the development process in the territory demanded the introduction of broader political participation and the expansion of the government's consultative process. The colonial government was aware of its lack of legitimacy in the absence of democratic elections, but it was ready to earn it through good performance. The latter had to be supplemented by responsiveness to the local population's demands and involvement of the community in the policymaking process. A pseudo-representative and consultative mechanism at the district level became a key component in the political development process. Community building was perceived to facilitate

---

[10] See Ambrose Yeo-chi King, "The Administrative Absorption of Politics in Hong Kong," *Asian Survey* 15, No. 5 (May 1975): 422–439.

[11] *The City District Officer Scheme, A Report by the Secretary for Chinese Affairs*, Hong Kong: Government Printer, January 1969.

[12] See Cho-bun Leung, "Community Participation: The Decline of Residents' Organizations," in *Hong Kong in Transition*, edited by Joseph Y.S. Cheng, Hong Kong: Oxford University Press, 1986, pp. 354–371; see also David K.K. Chan, "Local Administration in Hong Kong," in *Hong Kong Society — A Reader*, edited by Alex Y.H. Kwan and David K.K. Chan, Hong Kong: Writers' & Publishers' Cooperative, 1986, pp. 111–135.

government access to the people and contribute to social and political stability.

III District Board Elections, the Future of Hong Kong Issue and the Development of Political Groups

The official visit to Beijing in March 1979 of the Hong Kong Governor, Sir Murray MacLehose, meant that the issue of the territory's future had become an important agenda item of the British administration with the benefit of hindsight. Its presentation of the district administration scheme in June 1980 with the proposed introduction of universal suffrage and the elections of district boards was related to the British administration's preparation for decolonization. It also encouraged existing political groups such as the Hong Kong Observers to take part in the first district board elections, promising that a number of elected district board members would be appointed to the Legislative Council. Further, generous allowances were given to district board members to facilitate them serving their respective electorates and establishing community networks.

In 1982–1985, concern for the future of the territory and the challenge posed by the development of representative government contributed to the organization and development of many political groups and grassroots pressure groups.

In the district board elections in March 1985, the number of voters reached a record high of 476,500, a milestone in Hong Kong's political development. Assuming that each of the 501 candidates had recruited 100 friends to campaign for him or her, the number of activists participating in the elections would have been 50,000. These figures reflected a considerable degree of politicization of the community.[13]

The September 1985 elections to the Legislative Council were based on the electoral college, comprising members of the district boards, the Urban Council and the Provisional Regional Council, and the functional

---

[13] See Joseph Y.S. Cheng, "The 1985 District Board Elections in Hong Kong," in *Hong Kong in Transition, op. cit.*, pp. 67–87.

constituencies.[14] These elections facilitated the development of political groups in Hong Kong. Middle-class political groups were prompted to develop their organizations at the grassroots level and establish close ties with the grassroots pressure groups. At the same time, they became concerned with the social issues at the district level and took part in the related campaigns for citizens' rights. This process contributed to the expansion of almost all political groups.

Elections to the Legislative Council based on the electoral college, as well as the elections of district board chairmen and committee chairmen within the district boards, exposed the limitations of the elected members operating on an individual basis and encouraged various forms of coalitions within the district boards. The government, through the appointment of one-third of the district board members, exercised considerable influence in the above elections. In fact, the grassroots pressure groups and the middle-class political groups had limited success in the elections of district board chairmen and the following elections to the Legislative Council based on the electoral college. In all the elections in 1985, both Maria Tam, leader of the Progressive Hong Kong Society, and Allen Lee, who was then organizing a political party, were in active support of many candidates. In fact, some of the candidates took the initiative of enlisting their support. Such campaign activities naturally played a role in extending party politics into the new Legislative Council.

District boards in this initial stage of the development of pseudo-parties assumed a significant role. They provided an important training ground for politicians and facilitated the task of political recruitment by political parties. Elected district board members were given resources by the government which in turn became assets of political parties. The latter were aware of the importance of the cultivation of community networks, and their work in this area contributed to community building. District boards as newly-formed political bodies were soon engaged in lobbying

---

[14] The nine functional constituencies returning 12 unofficial members comprised the commercial, industrial, financial, labour, social services, educational, legal, medical, and engineering and associated professions. See *White Paper: The Further Development of Representative Government in Hong Kong*, Hong Kong: Government Printer, November 1984, p. 17.

the government for more resources to satisfy demands for public services at the district level. This also contributed to community building and improved the government's relations with community groups at the district level.

After the introduction of the legislative elections in 1985, the attention of the government and the mass media turned from the district boards to the legislature; and even more so after the direct elections to the legislature in 1991. The priority accorded to the legislature was only natural given the urgency to secure its consent to legislation and requests for appropriations. However, the neglect of grassroots pressure groups had been part of the cause for the decline of public support for the British administration in its final years.

Since the latter half of the 1980s, there were considerable complaints against the District Officers. They were often criticized for being too young, immature, unable to speak good Cantonese, and were insensitive to traditions and customs. They stayed in their posts for two to three years only, and did not have sufficient time to establish strong ties with the community leaders of their respective districts. In contrast, the local New China News Agency was active in cultivating the district-based community leaders, voluntary bodies and interest groups. The British administration apparently did not see this as a threat and had been reducing funding for the Home Affairs Department (previously known as the City and New Territories Administration) since the early 1990s.

IV Voter Turnout Rate, Political Culture, and Community Building

With the exception of 2003, voter turnout rates in district board/council elections stayed in the range of 30.3% and 38.1%. Such a range was not too disappointing for elections to local advisory bodies which have no control over issues of top priority in the voters' minds such as housing, education, transport and taxation. The turnout rate compared favourably with similar local elections in Western democratic countries, especially the U.S. The turnout rate of 44.1% in 2003 was probably influenced by the highly charged political atmosphere following the massive protest rally on July 1, 2003 (see Table 16.1).

Table 16.1: Voters and Voter Turnout Rates in District Council Elections, 1982–2003

	No. of District Board/Council Constituencies*	No. of Seats to be Elected	No. of Registered Voters	No. of Actual Voters**	Voter Turnout Rate** (%)
2003	400	400	2,973,612	1,065,363	44.1%
1999	390	390	2,832,524	816,503	35.8%
1994	346	346	2,450,372	693,215	33.1%
1991	209	272	1,840,413	423,923	32.5%
1988	157	264	1,610,998	424,201	30.3%
1985	145	237	1,421,391	476,558	37.5%
1982	122	132	899,559	342,764	38.1%

*District Councils were known as District Boards before 1997; in the elections in 1991 and before, some constituencies returned two members each.

**Since some candidates were elected unopposed, some registered voters did not have to vote; the voter turnout rates were adjusted accordingly.

Sources: Author's data collection based on government data.

The turnout rates and voters' attitudes also reflected the lack of a participatory political culture in Hong Kong;[15] demonstrating that interest in politics and knowledge of the political system remained weak. A survey conducted by the Student Union of the Chinese University of Hong Kong on the polling day of the second district board elections in 1985 (March 7) indicated that 22% of the voters were not clear about the work of district boards and another 37% were not aware of what the district boards had done.[16] As the voters were the politically more active citizens, the general level of knowledge of the district boards among ordinary citizens might even be lower. Other polls, mostly conducted by student groups of local tertiary institutions, also revealed that about 50% of the respondents could not name even one district board member from their own district.[17]

---

[15] Gabriel A. Almond and Sidney Verba, *The Civic Culture*, Princeton: Princeton University Press, 1960.

[16] See *Ming Pao* (a Hong Kong Chinese newspaper), March 12, 1985.

[17] Most of these polls were small in scale and not very vigorous in methodology. For a summary of them, see Cheung Lok-chung, "Behind the Voting — A Preliminary Study of the Voters' Political Attitudes (in Chinese)," *Pai Shing Semi-Monthly*, No. 92, March 16, 1985, p. 58.

In the district board elections in the 1980s and early 1990s, it was clearly established that the rural areas had higher voter turnouts than the urban areas; and in the urban areas, districts with a greater proportion of public housing residents usually achieved higher voter turnout rates. This was mainly because face-to-face contacts by grassroots neighborhood groups remained the most effective channel to mobilize voters to vote. In the rural districts like Sai Kung, North and Islands, there existed a traditional system of electing village representatives and the residents knew each other and the candidates well; hence, voters could easily be reached by the candidates and the peer group pressure to vote was high. In Yuen Long and Tai Po, where a number of public housing estates had been built in the 1980s, the voter turnout rates showed an above average decline in the late 1980s. The oldest new towns in the New Territories, including Tsuen Wan, Kwai Chung, and Tsing Yi, consistently registered the lowest turnout rates in the New Territories which were only slightly above the territory-wide averages. The new towns developed in the 1980s, Sha Tin and Tuen Mun, had voter turnout rates higher than those of Tsuen Wan, Kwai Chung, and Tsing Yi, but lower than those of the other more rural districts of the New Territories.

Grassroots neighborhood groups, mainly mutual aid committees of public housing estate blocks and various district-level groups with such names as "Concerned Group for the People's Livelihood of X District" were more active in the new towns and public housing estates in the 1980s. In the former, there was often a need to get organized to solve the problems of community building and redress the grievances caused by the inadequacies of town planning. Similarly, the mutual aid committees in most public housing estates were active in various "Clean Hong Kong Campaigns" and "Fight Crime Campaigns", and had good access to the residents. This was why new towns and urban districts with a greater proportion of public housing residents usually achieved higher voter turnout rates than old urban districts where such grassroots neighbourhood groups were not well developed. As expected, Kwun Tong, Wong Tai Sin, Sham Shui Po, and Southern Districts (where there was located the traditional fishing port of Aberdeen) consistently attained higher than average voter turnout rates.[18]

---

[18] See Janet L. Scott, *Local Level Election Behavior in an Urban Area*, Hong Kong: Centre for Hong Kong Studies, The Chinese University of Hong Kong, January 1985.

In line with the above, voters in the lower socioeconomic strata tended to be more enthusiastic in district board elections. In comparison with middle-class voters, they had a greater need for district board members who were expected to articulate their interests, help to redress their grievances, explain to them government policies, and show them the proper channels to obtain the necessary services from relevant government departments. The lower socioeconomic strata also had greater expectations from the district boards concerning cultural and recreational services. This utilitarian element of participation in district board elections not only partially explained the motivation to vote but also helped to answer why voter turnout rates were usually lower in middle-class urban districts.

The relatively stagnant voter turnout rates were certainly related to the expansion of the electorate. Through substantial efforts of the government, the number of registered voters steadily increased, and the number of actual voters also rose correspondingly (see Table 16.1). In the district board elections in the 1980s, the British administration usually made an effort to mobilize voters to vote, and to avoid the voter turnout rate falling below 30%. In the 1988 district board elections, it was said that community workers were sent to districts like Mong Kok, where the turnout was particularly low to mobilize voters to vote in the evening of the polling day.[19] The initiative was probably taken by the District Officers concerned.

In the 1990s, political parties rapidly developed in the territory after the Tiananmen Incident in 1989 and in response to the introduction of direct elections to the legislature in 1991. As in other democracies, political parties in Hong Kong performed their important functions of (a) political recruitment; (b) interest articulation and aggregation; (c) provision of services; and (d) serving as a channel of political communication and political mobilization. Political parties supported political stars, who in turn attracted political followers to political parties. Hong Kong people gradually lost their worry about ties with political parties, and they recognized and identified with political parties largely through their respective leaders.

Apart from depending on their leaders' charisma and political appeal, political parties had to establish their grassroots networks to mobilize

---

[19] *Ming Pao*, March 11, 1988.

voters. District board members were the natural coordinators of such networks at the district level. They delivered services within their districts, and were supported by their respective parties' legislators who were in better positions to exert pressure on the government. District board members relied on the appeal of their party leaders to attract voters' support in the district board elections; they in turn mobilized voters to support the legislators in the Legislative Council elections through the networks they had established. District board election candidacy therefore often became the initial step of a political career, and in this way, district board elections contributed to political parties' recruitment of activists and second-tier leaders.

The British administration also offered respectable allowances and remuneration for district board members in support of their political careers. These financial resources became assets of political parties because they could then rely on the district board members to build the parties' grassroots networks; and some pro-democracy political parties even demanded their district board members to deliver a portion (usually 10%) of their remuneration to help maintain the party operations. In these ways, the district board systems contributed to the development of political parties in Hong Kong.

As political parties gradually dominated the district boards in the 1990s, the British administration's support for them declined slowly as it was absorbed by the negotiations and confrontations with the Chinese authorities over the territory's future in its final years. The mass media also lost interest in the work of the district boards which was then seldom reported. However, district boards became increasingly skilful in exerting pressure on the government for more resources in support of their work and that of their individual members. Meanwhile, the pro-business Liberal Party and the pro-Beijing Democratic Alliance for the Betterment of Hong Kong (DAB) made great efforts to catch up with the grassroots services offered by the pro-democracy groups; and they brought substantial resources through their fundraising capabilities.

In the 1990s, there was less and less room left for genuine independents and small neighbourhood grassroots groups in the district board/council elections (see Tables 16.2 and 16.4). District board members affiliated to the major political parties enjoyed the support of the latter and their

Table 16.2: Performance of Major Political Parties in District Board/Council Elections, 1994–2003

	Number of Candidates in 2003	Number of Seats Won in 2003	Percentage of Contested Seats Won in 2003*	Number of Seats Won in 1999	Number of Seats Won in 1994
Democratic Party	120	95	79.2	86	75
DAB	206	62	30.1	83	37
ADPL	37	25	67.6	19	29
Liberal Party	25	13	52.0	15	18
The Frontier	13	6	46.1	4	0
Hong Kong Progressive Alliance	38	20	52.6	21	2

*Percentage of contested seats won includes seats won unopposed.
Notes: DAB Democratic Alliance for the Betterment of Hong Kong
ADPL Hong Kong Association for Democracy and People's Livelihood
Sources: Author's data collection based on government data and those from local newspapers.

respective legislators. Political parties also took a keen interest in district work in their development. In some cases, however, candidates in the district board/council elections still presented themselves as independents though they had close ties with political parties, reflecting the lingering suspicions against the latter.

Meanwhile, the pro-democracy political parties encountered difficulties too in their relationship with grassroots community organizations which emerged and developed in the late 1960s and 1970s, and had been supporting pro-democracy political groups. The prodemocracy political parties certainly could help to raise issues of importance to grassroots community organizations in the legislature or with senior government officials, thus exerting pressure on the government to provide solutions. However, their high profile and eagerness for publicity often resulted in failures to compromise and in delays in achieving settlements. Many grassroots community organizations worried that they might be taken for a ride, and they often preferred to act without the involvement of political parties. After all, grassroots community organizations were issue-oriented; they wanted concrete solutions to their problems. A few cases of unpleasant experiences subsequently resulted in their alienation from the pro-democracy political parties. On the other hand, they had been eagerly courted by the pro-Beijing political groups which apparently had been making progress in their united front work.

Since the turn of the century, a new generation of political activists had emerged, and it gradually assumed leadership in many small grassroots community organizations. These activists were less interested in the pursuit of democracy in the territory, and were more focussed on environmental protection, community-building, homosexual rights, labor grievances, services for the under-privileged groups, etc. They adopted more radical positions, and perceived the pro-democracy political parties as part of the political establishment. They resented the latter's concentration on parliamentary work, and criticized many pro-democracy leaders as politicians only interested in their own political careers. Their promotion of homosexual rights and those of prostitutes sometimes created difficulties for the participation of conservative religious groups.

In the initial stage of the district board/council elections, the pro-democracy groups were pioneers in the development of campaign strategies and techniques which proved to be effective. These strategies and techniques were then quickly followed by other political parties. They were also models for the campaigns in Urban/Regional Council elections and Legislative Council elections. In the second half of the 1990s, however, the pro-democracy parties no longer enjoyed any edge in campaign strategies and techniques; instead, their lack of resources became a severe handicap.

V District Councils in the Hong Kong Special Administrative Region (HKSAR)

Besides reintroducing the appointed members and changing the name of district boards to district councils, institutional changes at the district level were limited. Hong Kong is now divided into 18 districts, and each is served by a district council. The council remains a consultative organ, and it advises the HKSAR government on the following: (a) matters affecting the well-being of people in the district; (b) the provision and use of public facilities and services within the district; (c) the adequacy and priorities of government programs for the district; and (d) the use of public funds allocated to the district for local public works and community activities. Each district council is also given limited funding to engage in: (a) environmental improvements; (b) the promotion of recreational and cultural activities; and (c) community activities. Until the end of 2015, a district council was composed of elected members, appointed members, and in the case of a district council in the rural areas, the chairpersons of rural committees as ex-officio members.

A political party or a coalition of parties securing a majority in a district council can exploit the funding available for community, recreational, and cultural activities to its advantage. Facilities such as community halls, which are at the disposal of the district councils, may also be similarly exploited.

An interesting phenomenon in the 2003 district council elections in terms of political recruitment was that an increasing number of candidates were full-time politicians, i.e., they were either full-time politicians serving as Legislative Councilors and/or district councillors, assistants to Legislative Councilors, or staff members of political parties (see Table 16.3). Difficulties in finding jobs at that time reduced the opportunity cost for young people taking up political careers, and political parties eager to enhance their appeal by recruiting young talents, to demonstrate that their candidates were younger and better educated than previous

Table 16.3: Number of Candidates Who Were Full-time Politicians in the District Council Elections in 1999 and 2003

Political Party	2003	1999
Democratic Party	65 (54%)	50 (29%)
DAB	106 (51%)	58 (33%)
ADPL	22 (59%)	13 (41%)
Liberal Party	6 (26%)	5 (11%)
The Frontier	9 (69%)	3 (33%)

Note: Figures in parentheses show the percentages of full-time politicians among the total number of candidates from the corresponding political parties.

Source: Ivan Choy Chi-keung, "*Canzheng Yicheng Zhuanye* (Running for Elections Has Been Professionalized)," *Ming Pao* (a Hong Kong Chinese newspaper), October 20, 2003.

candidates. This high percentage of full-time politicians among candidates also revealed that district councillors' work was becoming more and more demanding, and those who could not devote full time to the job would find it very difficult to meet constituents' expectations. This was an indicator of political development and the resources offered by political parties in support of community building.

District council elections, like local elections in most countries, were normally not very exciting or significant in Hong Kong. However, in the wake of the massive protest rally on July 1, 2003, in which more than half a million people marched in the streets to protest the legislation on Article 23 of the territory's Basic Law concerning subversion, theft of state secrets, etc., the 2003 district council elections attracted considerable attention from the Chinese leadership and the international media.

An opinion survey conducted by The University of Hong Kong in mid-September 2003 on the coming district council elections indicated that 77% of the respondents considered that a candidate's position on livelihood issues would be their major consideration, the same as in 1999. Candidates' performances and platforms were still considered very important, but the ratio of respondents who attached more importance to platforms rose from 24.3% in 1999 to 35.2% in 2003, while those who attached more importance to job performance slipped from 41.9% to 37.9%. Meanwhile, those who accorded more significance to a candidate's political orientation increased from 2.2% to 4%, and to his or her political affiliation from 6.2% to 10.2%.[20] These figures showed the impact of the politicization of local elections because of the political protests; the impact became considerably more significant two months afterwards in the actual elections.

An exit poll conducted by the University of Hong Kong on the day of the 2003 district council elections produced some interesting data on their politicization. As expected, 62% of the respondents indicated that they had voted because of fulfillment of civic duty, 13% out of habit and only 13% hoped to make use of the elections to improve society, community and people's livelihood, while 2% wanted to show their support for the cause of democracy. It was obvious that the Hong Kong people normally

---

[20] *South China Morning Post* (a Hong Kong English newspaper), October 20, 2003.

did not expect much from local elections. In terms of voters' political orientations, 81% of the respondents supported direct election of the Chief Executive by 2007, and 84% supported direct elections of all seats of the legislature by 2008. Thirty-five percent said that the July 1, 2003 rally enhanced their motivation to vote, while 65% indicated that there was no impact. Twenty-nine percent of the respondents, however, actually took part in the rally.

Regarding the basis of the voters' choice, 54% of the respondents revealed that their choices were mainly based on support for individual candidates and 28% on support for political parties. Sixty percent of the respondents indicated that the candidates' most important attraction was their past performance; 5%, their political background or party affiliation; and 15%, their political platforms and views.[21] Relative to similar surveys on past elections, more voters accorded priority to the candidates' party affiliations and political platforms.

In view of the record voter turnout rate and the voters' expressed political values, it was hardly surprising that the pro-democracy groups won handsomely. The interesting question was whether this politicization of district council elections would become a significant trend, or the 2003 district council elections were just an exception to the rule. It appeared that the latter would likely be the case, though politicization would continue to increase in a very small way as political parties' domination of the elections would continue to strengthen.

Keen competition among political parties generated substantial non-governmental resources for community building. The pro-government parties enjoyed considerable fund-raising capabilities, and they therefore could afford ample financial resources in support of their district projects, which attracted participation at the grassroots level. "Snake banquets" held by the DAB already became popular events. Other activities, such as seafood tours to the New Territories at weekends and holiday packages to the Mainland, certainly became very attractive to cost-conscious consumers. Again, pro-government parties were in a much better position to attract sponsorships for their district projects from the business

---

[21] The author is most grateful for the data offered by Robert Chung Ting-yiu, director of the Public Opinion Program, The University of Hong Kong.

community. For example, when they held a Mid-Autumn Festival carnival, they should be able to get donations of mooncakes quite easily.

In contrast, pro-democracy district councillors still often had to spend about 10% of their remuneration in support of their groups. Their counterparts did not have any financial obligations to their parties; and, instead, they received substantial subsidies from their political groups to finance their district work. Very often, these subsidies amounted to twice the sum of their official remuneration. Under such circumstances, they should be able to deliver satisfactory report cards with relative ease. This was unfair competition as delivery of services was an important function of political parties, and this in turn depended on political parties' resources.

Pro-democracy district councillors, however, often complained that government officials treated their requests and proposals with a lower priority than those accorded to their counterparts from the pro-government parties. Moreover, the latter could normally expect favourable treatment in applications for funding support from various government departments. The HKSAR government must maintain its fairness and neutrality at the district level. Otherwise, civil servants involved in district work might lose their respect and would find themselves in a difficult position in case of conflicts among political parties.

A more challenging and long-term question was the implications of the government ceding community building to political parties. Since the turn of the century, the Home Affairs Bureau had been given much less resources for community building, and it could not compete with the political parties which now have far more manpower and money. Hence, it would be very costly to regain the initiative. Inertia, however, might mean problems when community building on the part of political parties became more politicized and when polarization among political parties further deteriorated.

VI The Issue of Appointed Members and Other Reforms

In the final years of the British administration, the Chris Patten government abolished the system of appointed seats on district boards. The Tung administration, however, restored the practice in 1999, appointing 102 district councillors. The two reasons given by the Tung administration were: (a) the appointed system would enhance the representativeness of district councils, because some local community leaders would decline participate in elections and the appointment system would facilitate their inclusion; and (b) the appointment system would enable the government to recruit professionals and other talents to join the district councils to strengthen their work.

These arguments, as expected, were severely rebutted by the pro-democracy political groups. They believed that since direct elections to district councils were part of the democratic process, restoration of the appointment system was a serious step backward in terms of political development. If professionals and other talents had to be recruited to improve the performance of district councils, they could be appointed as advisors or in other appropriate capacities instead. According to an occupational analysis of appointed district councillors in 1999–2003 conducted by Ma Ngok, business persons or company directors took up 41 seats and professionals (accountants, medical doctors, lawyers, academics, etc.) occupied 21 seats. These proportions were roughly equivalent to those among elected members, i.e., about 40% were from business and 17.5% were professionals.[22] Hence, the Tung administration's rationale for appointing district councillors was not observed in actual practice.

The appointment system was a kind of pork-and-barrel politics that allowed the HKSAR government to reward its supporters. After the 1999 district council elections, the Hong Kong Progressive Alliance received 12 appointed seats, the DAB 11, and the Liberal Party nine.[23] Altogether, more than 30% of the appointed seats went to political parties within Tung's governing coalition. As expected, the pro-democracy political groups received no appointments (they had earlier indicated that they would not accept such appointments).

---

[22] Ma Ngok, "*Quyihui Weirenzhi Pianbang Zhengdang* (District Councils' Appointment System Favors Political Parties)," *Apple Daily* (a Hong Kong Chinese newspaper), October 30, 2003.

[23] *Sing Tao Daily* (a Hong Kong Chinese newspaper), December 18, 2003.

The appointment system further strengthened the pro-government forces in the district councils. The elections of chairpersons were a good indicator of this. After the 1999 elections, the pro-democracy political groups could only secure two chairmanships out of 18. This meant that with the help of the appointed seats, pro-government members controlled a majority in 16 district councils. They therefore managed to allocate the resources of the district councils largely in accordance with their preferences, from chairmanships and vice-chairmanships of committees and working groups to financial resources for minor construction projects, cultural, entertainment and sports activities, etc. These privileges were normally reinforced by appointments to territory-wide advisory committees and other honors bestowed by the Tung administration. The appointment system is, therefore, widely perceived as an unfair way of twisting the allocation of political resources against the pro-democracy camp.

Abolition of the system was included as one of the four major demands in the united political platform of the pro-democracy candidates in the 2003 district council elections. Buoyed by their success in the elections and determined to continue to exert pressure on the Tung administration, the pro-democracy political groups formed an ad hoc alliance against the appointment system to organize meetings, signature campaigns, and protest activities to appeal for the abolition.

The administration, however, rejected such an appeal and in December 2003 appointed 102 district council members, the same number as in 1999. Among the pro-government political groups, the Liberal Party received 8 appointments (one less than in 1999), the DAB six (five fewer), the Hong Kong Progressive Alliance six (six fewer), and the New Century Forum one. In response to the community's criticisms, the number of appointees with political party affiliations was reduced from 39 in 1999 to 21 this time.[24] The HKSAR government was eager to maximize its control of the district councils to try to demonstrate that government policies had the Hong Kong people's support. The government had used the support of a majority of district councils as evidence of the community's endorsement of its controversial policies, such as soccer gambling, and it was unwilling to abandon this important base of support.

---

[24] See all major newspapers in Hong Kong on December 18, 2003.

Before the appointments in 2003, the pro-democracy camp enjoyed an edge in seven district councils, namely, Central and Western, Wan Chai, Kwun Tong, Yau Tsim Mong, Sham Shui Po, North, and Kwai Tsing. The camp also captured half of the seats in Kowloon City (see Table 16.4). However, after the appointments, the pro-democracy camp only enjoyed a majority in two district councils. It could certainly claim that the appointment system devalued people's votes and twisted their expressed choices. The Liberal Party and the Hong Kong Progressive Alliance nonetheless openly stated that reducing political party-affiliated appointees was unfair, as this would discourage people who are eager to serve the

Table 16.4: Distribution of Political Forces in the 18 District Councils, 2004–2007

Name of District Council	Total Number of Elected Members	Pro-democracy Camp	Pro-Beijing United Front	Liberal Party or Neutral
Central and Western	15	9	1	5
Eastern	37	12	20	5
Wan Chai	11	6	2	3
Southern	17	2	5	10
Yau Tsim Mong	16	9	4	3
Sham Shui Po	21	16	2	3
Wong Tai Sin	25	12	11	2
Kowloon City	22	11	7	4
Kwun Tong	34	19	13	2
Tsuen Wan	17	7	4	6
Tuen Mun	29	13	10	6
Yuen Long	29	7	11	11
North	16	10	6	0
Tai Po	19	6	9	4
Sai Kung	20	7	11	2
Sha Tin	36	14	18	4
Kwai Tsing	28	19	3	6
Islands	8	0	4	4

Source: Ming Pao, November 25, 2003.

public from joining political parties.[25] In subsequent elections of district council chairpersons, the pro-democracy camp won in two councils, independents won in two, and the rest went to pro-establishment district councillors. The pro-democracy camp did slightly better in the elections of vice-chairpersons by winning in five district councils, but the pro-establishment forces won in the rest.

Facilitating fair political competition is a very important task on the part of the government. A political party or coalition of political parties which captures a majority in a district council naturally seeks an edge in the allocation of political and other substantial resources. This is legitimate as long as the competition is seen to be fair among the parties involved. Allowing the majority group in a district council more resources and more responsibility is a step forward in political development. However, if the rules of competition are seen to be unfair, the distribution of resources and responsibilities will be considered illegitimate, and the neutrality of the civil servants involved in district work will be compromised. The situation will deteriorate when political polarization among political parties is further exacerbated at the territory-wide and/or district level.

Power for Democracy, an umbrella platform including almost all major pro-democracy groups in Hong Kong, released two documents on the reform of district councils in February and July 2006 respectively. In the latter document, *Reform Proposals on the Powers and Responsibilities, Structure and Composition of District Councils*, it proposed the abolition of appointed and ex-officio membership. It also brought back the old proposal of combining the existing eighteen district councils into five municipal councils with similar powers enjoyed by the former Urban/Regional Council. Before this more thorough reform, it proposed the delegation of the responsibilities and resources of the former Urban/Regional Council to the eighteen district councils so that the latter would have decision-making and management powers on culture, recreation, and municipal administration. An innovative proposal was the direct elections of 18 district commissioners to be responsible for district administration, absorbing the responsibilities given to district officers then.

---

[25] *Ming Pao*, December 18, 2003.

It was not expected that these proposals would receive the government's serious attention, but they reflected the eagerness of the more ambitious district councillors to fight for a more important role in the district councils. At this stage, the government seemed to be ready to give more money to district councils for minor construction projects and cultural and recreational activities because of its enviable financial position, but it had no plan for more thorough reforms. However, in the longer term, district councils had to be granted more responsibilities in order to recruit and cultivate political talents.

VII Conclusion

Apparently, value change in the Hong Kong society has been a subject much neglected by all parties concerned. The experiences in the past decade have taught Hong Kong people to lower their expectations concerning promotions and salary increases. Many young families do not want children; they therefore have less pressure to work harder to increase their incomes. Naturally, they pay more attention to issues relating to the quality of life, health, the environment, the protection of the Victoria Harbor, and the preservation of historic buildings, etc.

Twenty years after the territory's return to China, there was no further progress towards democracy. In fact, interference from Beijing has increased after the July 1, 2003 protest rally when compared with the initial three years after 1997. The dogmatic insistence on an "executive-led" system of government means that the systemic difficulties in the executive-legislature relationship have not been tackled. Meanwhile, the absence of serious civil service reforms has resulted in declining performance of the system as well as accumulating frustration.

The lesson is — people seek satisfaction in their daily life; they hope to secure meaning in it. After meeting their basic needs, they want to make a contribution. Political participation at the district level offers many opportunities to secure meaning in life and make a contribution to the community. So far, the potential of the district councils has not been fully tapped; the enthusiasm to involve ordinary people in district affairs, which was at its peak in the early 1980s has actually been in decline. While district councillors have been able to build strong links with the legislature through political parties and grassroots networks for political mobilization — admittedly a progress in political development, insufficient efforts have been made in autonomous community building, i.e., community ties not involving mobilization by political parties. This is probably where the government should regain its initiative with the major objective of enabling people to secure satisfaction through participation in community work, and thus strengthening social stability.

Acknowledgement

Originally published as Cheng, Joseph Y.S., "Hong Kong District Councils: Political Development and Community Building", *Journal of Comparative Asian Development*, Vol. 8, No. 1, 2009, pp. 207–230. Reproduced with kind permission of the publisher.

Chapter 17

Challenge to the Pro-democracy Movement in Hong Kong: Political Reforms, Internal Splits, and the Legitimacy Deficit of the Government

The Hong Kong Special Administrative Region (HKSAR) government released the document "Methods for Selecting the Chief Executive and for Forming the Legislative Council in 2012" (henceforward referred to as the "Political Reform Proposals") in November 2009. It did not, as demanded by the territory's pro-democracy movement, provide a concrete timetable and roadmap for the election by universal suffrage of the Chief Executive in 2017 and of all seats in the Legislative Council in 2020. This was very disappointing from the movement's perspective.

The contents of the Political Reform Proposals were nevertheless not at all surprising. Rather, the divisions within the pro-democracy movement overall suggested that a permanent split within the movement had become inevitable.[1] Further, in the eyes of the Hong Kong people, the Chinese leadership and the HKSAR government were not interested in the

---

[1] See, for example, the column by Lee Sin-Chi entitled "*Jianzhipai dali zaoshi, fanmin fenlie cheng dingju*" (The establishment strenuously building a favorable environment, the pan-democratic camp destined to split)", *Ming Pao*, December 21, 2009, p. A4.

promotion of genuine democracy, and its implementation had become uncertain.

A political movement that had been in opposition since its birth in the 1980s and that had no prospect of securing political power inevitably became divided in strategy and tactics, with one segment acting in moderation and pursuing negotiations with the authorities, and another segment opting for radicalism. This split reflected increasing polarization in the Hong Kong society as well, as the majority became more and more apathetic, and a significant minority demonstrated rising frustration and anger, not only over the stagnation in the democratization process, but also over the widening gap between the rich and the poor.

This chapter intends to examine the challenges facing the pro-democracy movement in Hong Kong at this stage, as well as the general political and social situation in the territory. It argues that the deterioration and divisions within the pro-democracy movement might not be political gains for the pro-Beijing united front, as political and social polarization posed serious problems for effective governance as well. An administration threatened by legitimacy deficit would encounter increasing difficulty in its provision of economic development and social services, thus forcing itself into a vicious circle as unsatisfactory performance further worsened its legitimacy deficit.

I The Progress or Lack of Progress in Electoral Reforms

The attempt to introduce Article 23 legislation[2] and the difficult economic situation caused by the Severe and Acute Respiratory Syndrome (SARS)

---

[2] Article 23 of the Basic Law (Hong Kong's constitution) states: "The Hong Kong Special Administrative Region shall enact laws on its own to prohibit any act of treason, secession, sedition, subversion against the Central People's Government, or theft of state secretes, to prohibit foreign political organizations or bodies from conducting political activities in the Region, and to prohibit political organizations or bodies of the Region from establishing ties with foreign political organizations or bodies." This article was written into the draft Basic Law after the massive protest rallies in Hong Kong during the Tiananmen Incident in 1989, obviously, the Chinese authorities were concerned about a repetition of such activities. The Tung administration was wise enough not to initiate the controversial

epidemic prompted more than half a million people to take to the streets in protests, demanding democracy.[3] In response, the HKSAR government established the Constitutional Development Task Force in January 2004. It also decided to initiate the mechanism for amending the electoral methods for the Chief Executive and the Legislative Council in accordance with the National People's Congress Standing Committee (NPCSC)'s interpretation of April 2004, in an attempt to strengthen the democratic elements of the Chief Executive election in 2007 and the Legislative Council elections in 2008.

In October 2005, the HKSAR government announced a package of proposals to reform the electoral systems starting in 2007/2008. The package suggested including all District Council members in the Election Committee for the election of the Chief Executive,[4] and expanding the Legislative Council from 60 to 70 members, with one additional seat for each of the five geographical constituencies, and another five to be elected from among the District Council members. Later, in November 2005, the Chief Executive also initiated discussions on the models, roadmap, and timetable for implementing universal suffrage through the appointed Commission on Strategic Development.

In the following month, pro-democracy legislators vetoed the electoral reform package. They could not accept that both the central government and the HKSAR government had refused to provide a concrete roadmap and timetable for the implementation of universal suffrage for the election of the Chief Executive and the entire legislature. They were also against the retention of appointed and ex-officio members in the District Councils.

---

legislative process during his first term. In response to the open promotion of the Chinese authorities, a paper addressing the implementation of Article 23 of the Basic Law was finally unveiled for public consultation in September 2002. As expected, the proposals stirred fears of a crackdown on human rights groups and the Falun Gong. The territory's pro-democracy camp also perceived the proposals as a threat to civil liberties. See *South China Morning Post*, September 25, 2002.

[3] See Joseph, Y.S. Cheng (ed.), *The July 1 Protest Rally — Interpreting a Historic Event*, Hong Kong, City University of Hong Kong Press, 2005.

[4] At that time, Hong Kong was divided into 18 districts, with District Councils serving as local advisory bodies. There were about 400 members elected by small single-member constituencies, and more than 100 appointed members and ex-officio members who were chairmen of Rural Committees.

The defeat of the HKSAR government's electoral reform package meant that the existing electoral methods would continue to apply. The pro-democracy movement believed that Beijing and the HKSAR government had no sincere intentions to implement genuine democracy in Hong Kong, while the pro-Beijing united front attacked the pro-democracy groups for blocking progress in electoral reforms and delaying the democratization process. Meanwhile, from the end of 2005 to mid-2007, the Commission on Strategic Development continued its task.

The HKSAR government released the Green Paper on Constitutional Development on July 11, 2007, to consult the public on the options, roadmap, and timetable for implementing universal suffrage for the elections of the Chief Executive and the Legislative Council. On December 12, 2007, Donald Tsang submitted a report to the NPCSC. Meanwhile, opinion surveys in Hong Kong in the past decade or so had consistently shown that around 60% of the population supported the prompt implementation of universal suffrage for the elections of the Chief Executive and the entire legislature (referred to as "dual universal suffrage"). The pro-democracy groups that had been demanding immediate implementation of "dual universal suffrage" also succeeded in securing about 60% of the votes in the direct elections to the Legislative Council (they won even more votes in earlier elections). Hence, in its report to the NPCSC, the Donald Tsang administration acknowledged that more than half of the public supported the implementation of "dual universal suffrage" in 2012, although it also pointed out that introducing universal suffrage to the Chief Executive election no later than 2017 would stand a better chance of acceptance by the majority of the Hong Kong community.

The NPCSC soon announced its "Decision on Issues Relating to the Methods for Selecting the Chief Executive of the HKSAR and for Forming the Legislative Council of the HKSAR in the Year 2012 and on Issues Relating to Universal Suffrage" on December 29, 2007. The decision stipulated: "The election of the fifth Chief Executive of the HKSAR in the year 2017 may be implemented by the method of universal suffrage; that after the Chief Executive is selected by universal suffrage, the election of the Legislative Council of the HKSAR may be implemented by the method of electing all the members by universal suffrage."

The Donald Tsang administration and the pro-Beijing united front had since been arguing that the timetable for the implementation of "dual universal suffrage" had been set. However, the pro-democracy movement was certainly right in criticizing this as far from a concrete timetable and firm commitment; they argued that the decision of the NPCSC might be interpreted as follows: "If the conditions are ripe, then the 'dual universal suffrage' may be implemented by 2017 and 2020 (the date of the Legislative Council elections following the Chief Executive election in 2017); and if the conditions are not yet mature, caution is advised and delay may be prudent."

Further, the nomination procedure of the Chief Executive election remained controversial. According to Article 45 of the Basic Law, the "ultimate aim is the election of the Chief Executive by universal suffrage upon nomination by a broadly representative nominating committee in accordance with democratic procedures." It was generally expected that the existing Election Committee electing the Chief Executive would then serve as the nominating committee; and according to Article 4 of Annex I to the Basic Law: "Candidates for the office of the Chief Executive may be nominated jointly by not less than 100 members of the Election Committee. Each member may nominate only one candidate." The Election Committee was expected to have 1,200 members in 2012, with 300 members elected from each of the following four sectors — industrial, commercial, and financial sectors; the professions; labor, social services, religious, and other sectors; members of the Legislative Council, representatives of district-based organizations, Hong Kong deputies to the NPC, and representatives of Hong Kong members of the National Committee of the Chinese People's Political Consultative Conference (CPPCC).

Since the elections to the Election Committee were heavily biased in favor of the establishment, the pro-democracy movement might not be able to win enough seats in the nominating committee to nominate its candidate, i.e., if the threshold for nomination was set too high, there would not be genuine competition, and the people of Hong Kong could only elect someone from a shortlist of candidates approved by the Chinese leadership.

The Hong Kong people well remembered that in the election of the Chief Executive in 2002, a change of procedures made the Election

Committee's nomination of candidates an open process. As a result, more than 700 members nominated C.H. Tung, and there were not enough votes left to nominate another candidate; Tung was elected for the second term on an *ipso facto* basis. Then, in the election of the third term Chief Executive in June 2005, the pro-democracy movement candidate, Democratic Party Chairman Lee Wing-tat, could not even secure the 100 votes necessary to qualify as an official candidate. In the fourth term Chief Executive election in 2007, the pro-democracy movement candidate, Alan Leong Kah-kit, managed to qualify as an official candidate and engaged in debates with Donald Tsang, who was seeking re-election. However, the pro-democracy movement only secured between 130 and 140 seats in the Election Committee, and it would have been extremely difficult for it to do better.

Proposals from pro-Beijing united front figures, including members of the Committee for the Basic Law of the HKSAR under the NPCSC, had alarmed the pro-democracy movement. These suggestions used the pretexts of orderly competition and ensuring the broad representativeness of the candidates to block the presentation of a candidate from the pro-democracy movement. Most of these proposals aimed to raise the nomination threshold; for example, nomination should require the endorsement of 200 (25%), instead of 100, members of the nomination committee; nomination should require the endorsement of a specific number of representatives from each the four sectors; and nomination should require the support of a number of Hong Kong deputies to the NPC. In response to these proposals, the pro-democracy movement demanded that the nomination threshold for candidates in the Chief Executive election should be no higher than the existing one.

Regarding the elections in 2012, the NPCSC decision in December 2007 stipulated that universal suffrage would, as before, apply to only half of the seats of the legislature. Further, half of the seats would still be returned by functional constituencies, and the procedures for voting on bills and motions in the Legislative Council would also remain unchanged. The latter actually meant that the majority of functional constituency seats would retain veto power over initiatives by pro-democracy legislators.

In the eyes of the Hong Kong community, if the scope of electoral reform was so limited for the elections in 2012, how could one expect significant progress in the years after 2012 and before 2017 and 2022? There were suspicions that the Chinese authorities had been adopting delay tactics, postponing the crucial issues of electoral reform until 2015 or 2016. Various statements made by key establishment figures soon after the release of the Political Reform Proposals raised strong doubts as to whether the Chinese authorities were really determined to abolish functional constituencies by 2020. On November 20, 2009, Maria Tam, a Hong Kong deputy to the NPC and a member of the Committee for the Basic Law of the HKSAR under the NPCSC, indicated to the media that if the Legislative Council seats returned by functional constituencies conformed to the principle of equality, they would qualify as election by universal suffrage; she further stated that universal suffrage would be defined by the central government in Beijing according to the Basic Law, and not in line with the International Covenant on Civil and Political Rights.[5] A day earlier, Chief Secretary Henry Tang Ying-yen (a leading contender for the Chief Executive post in 2012) declared that a system of "one man, two votes" would still be "fair and equal" if everyone had a chance to vote in the functional constituencies.[6] Hence, the abolition of functional constituencies became the most important theme in the existing campaign for genuine democracy.

In the electoral reform process at this stage, the autonomy of the HKSAR government appeared have been eroding. During Donald Tsang's campaign for re-election as Chief Executive in early 2007, he told journalists that he would "engage in a tough game" to settle the challenging issue of political reform. In his first policy address after re-election, he stressed that he had a constitutional duty to resolve the question of political reform in the territory. After the release of the Political Reform Proposals in late 2009, however, both central government officials and the Tsang administration indicated that Hong Kong did not have the authority to tackle political development beyond 2012 in the political reform package. So, when did the Donald Tsang administration lose the authority to handle political reform beyond 2012? When did the central government take back this authority from the HKSAR government? Both the central

---

[5] *Ming Pao*, November 21, 2009.
[6] *South China Morning Post*, November 20, 2009.

government and the HKSAR government still owed the Hong Kong people an explanation.

When the Hong Kong people studied the Basic Law, their understanding had always been that amendments to the method for selecting the Chief Executive after 2007 required the endorsement of a two-thirds majority of the full Legislative Council, the consent of the Chief Executive, and the approval of the NPCSC. Similarly, amendments to the method for forming the Legislative council could be made only with the endorsement of a two-thirds majority of the full Legislative Council and the consent of the Chief Executive; and it had to be reported to the NPCSC for record.

There were no stipulations in the Basic Law that the HKSAR government had to seek the authorization of the NPCSC before it could tackle the roadmap and timetable for political reforms beyond the present term.

During the drafting of the Basic Law, the Hong Kong people were not aware that there had been such discussions on the prerequisite of NPCSC authorization. Nonetheless, it was apparent the HKSAR government had to seek the NPCSC's authorization before it would seek to abolish functional constituencies in the Legislative Council by 2020.

Maria Tam's statement on universal suffrage in Hong Kong also raised serious questions. Was the HKSAR government consulted on this? If so, why did the Donald Tsang administration not consult the Hong Kong community, or at least inform it of the "new policy"? It was certainly inappropriate to have such a significant decision revealed to the Hong Kong people during a television talk-show.

There were rumors within local media circles in mid-2010 that some pro-Beijing legal experts in Hong Kong were working to produce a definition of "universal and equal representation" applicable to the territory's future political reform packages. There was no indication whether the Donald Tsang administration was involved in this work.

After meeting the Democratic Party delegation on the political reform issue, Li Gang, deputy director of the Central Liaison Office in Hong Kong, was at pains to explain to the media that his office was not a "second governing team" in the territory.[7] This was actually the first local

---

[7] *Ming Pao*, May 24, 2010.

press conference by the leadership of the Central Liaison Office; why should Li Gang consider the issue of the "second governing team" something to be clarified in this first press conference, when no reporter raised the issue? Certainly, he realized that many Hong Kong people had this perception; and it was more than the "personal comment" made by his former colleague Cao Erbao in an article published in the Study Times of the Central Party School in Beijing.[8]

When the central government authorized the Central Liaison Office to meet with the pro-democracy groups in Hong Kong, it should have carefully considered whether these groups should assume the role of receiving messages for the entire Hong Kong community, and serving as a bridge between Beijing and Hong Kong on the issue of political reform. If this was indeed the case, then it should have observed the principles of openness and high transparency, instead of selectively meeting some pro-democracy groups based on united front considerations.

II Beijing's Strong Influence

The Hong Kong people understood that the issue of electoral reform would be determined in Beijing and not by the HKSAR government. Symbolically, the protest rally for democracy held on January 1, 2010, abandoned the usual route and chose the Central Liaison Office, the representative of the central government in Hong Kong, as its destination. It was expected that more pro-democracy protest rallies would target the Central Liaison Office in the future.[9]

---

[8] Cao Erbao, "'*Yiguoliangzhi' tiaojianxia Xiang Gang de guanzhi liliang*" (The governance force of Hong Kong under the conditions of 'one country, two systems'), *Xuexi Shibao* (*Study Times*, a publication of the Central Party School in Beijing), January 29, 2008. Cao Erbao was a department head of the Central Liaison Office in Hong Kong. He argued in his article that Mainland cadres involved in Hong Kong work could serve as a force for the governance of Hong Kong when the Hong Kong community later learnt about the article, a controversy arose and generated considerable suspicion against Beijing's intervention in the territory.

[9] Protest rallies organized by the pro-democracy movement usually started from Victoria Park in Causeway Bay and ended at the government offices in Central. On January 1, 2010,

The community also realized that the Chinese leadership was reluctant to grant genuine democracy to the territory. Although a significant majority of Hong Kong people was in support of democracy, it was unwilling to confront Beijing. In view of the hardline position, most Hong Kong people tended to return to their traditional apathy. After all, the community was basically satisfied with the status quo of stability and prosperity, and was reluctant to sacrifice it in the pursuit of democracy.

When President Hu Jintao visited Macau in December 2009, he openly stated that the central government gave "a high rating" to the work of the outgoing Edmund Ho Hau-wah administration and its contribution to Macau and the nation.[10] When Hong Kong's Chief Executive, Donald Tsang Yam-kuen, made his duty visit to Beijing at the end of the month, he was told by Premier Wen Jiabao to resolve "some deep-rooted conflicts" in the Hong Kong society and was asked by President Hu to handle the territory's constitutional reforms "in an appropriate manner."[11] Premier Wen's remarks were broadly viewed as a public rebuke. Apparently, the central leadership was happy with the situation in Macau, but was dissatisfied with the political and social contradictions in Hong Kong.

What, then, was the political situation in Macau? There was only one candidate, Fernando Chui Sai-on, in the 2009 Chief Executive election, and therefore no competition and no public debate. Once Beijing indicated that it had a preferred candidate, the issue was settled. Much more shocking was the earlier election of the Election Committee — there were only 300 candidates to fill the same number of seats; hence, no competition, no campaigning, and no formal election.

The so-called Macau Street political culture was often described as follows — Macau was a small place, and nearly all community leaders of any standing were related to one another in some way. Electoral competition and controversy were to be avoided for the sake of future cooperation and maintaining harmony within the community. Organizations

---

the protest rally began in Central and ended at the Central Liaison Office in Sai Wan. See all major newspapers in Hong Kong on January 2, 2010.

[10] *South China Morning Post*, December 20, 2009.

[11] *Ibid*, December 29, 2009.

outside the establishment had secured only three seats in the legislature, and there was a limit to their political participation and mobilization.

The domination of the establishment and the lack of a developed civil society could be attributed to two factors. First, the local mass media were almost totally controlled by the establishment. Macau's media did not criticize its government or the Chinese government. Macau's people had ample access to Hong Kong newspapers, radio, and television — none of which carried much news about Macau. The only independent media to be found were in the Portuguese or English languages, serving the relatively small expatriate community. Second, almost every recognized civil group in Macau received generous financial support from the government, which in turn had been enjoying ample revenue from the casino industry at this stage. Even the powerful Catholic Church had to maintain good relations with the government in order to maintain its impressive social services. The only outlets for social grievances were occasional protest rallies, such as on May Day, which were usually confined to livelihood issues.

Hong Kong was still quite different. All parties concerned appreciated that rule of law and freedom of information were essential to the territory's functioning as an international financial and business services centre. If these two assets were severely eroded, Hong Kong would become just another Chinese city with no edge over Shanghai and other coastal cities. However, the lesson of Macau was clear — unless the Hong Kong people worked hard to protect their rights, civil society could degenerate. Some of the hallmarks of Macau politics were beginning to emerge in Hong Kong. Self-censorship in the media was becoming increasingly serious; rational, in-depth discussion of political issues was becoming much less frequent. The public was becoming more apathetic politically, expressing their grievances mainly through protest actions to make headlines.

In the long-term, the Hong Kong people realized that the territory's economy would be increasingly dependent on that of the mainland (see Table 17.1). This rising dependence had been accompanied by a relative decline in Hong Kong's international economic competitiveness. Over the past decade, the leaders of Shanghai no longer looked to the territory as a model for emulation; they had turned their eyes to New York and London. At the time of Hong Kong's return to China in 1997, the Guangdong authorities were eager to establish closer economic ties with the HKSAR,

Table 17.1: Trade, Investment, and Tourism between Mainland China and Hong Kong, 1978–2008

	Trade (US$ billion)			Entrepôt Trade			Investment (US$ billion)		Tourism (1,000 persons)	
Year	Exports from Mainland to HK	Imports of Mainland from HK	Total	Exports from Mainland to HK	Imports of Mainland from HK	Total	Investment from Mainland in HK	Investment from HK in Mainland	No. of Mainland Visitors to HK	No. of HK Visitors to Mainland***
1978	1.35 (—)	0.04 (—)	1.39 (—)	—	0.03	—	—	—	—	1,562
1981	3.78 (8.99)	1.41 (2.12)	5.19 (11.11)	—	1.03	—	—	—	15	7,053
1986	10.47 (9.78)	7.55 (5.61)	18.02 (15.39)	—	5.24	—	—	— (1.33)	44	21,269
1991	37.61 (32.14)	26.63 (17.46)	64.24 (49.60)	51.77*	19.66	71.43	—	— (2.58)	112	30,506
1996	73.13 (32.91)	61.46 (7.83)	134.59 (40.73)	87.63	53.56	141.19	2.59**	6.94** (20.87)	2,311	44,229
2001	87.43 (46.54)	70.02 (9.42)	157.45 (55.96)	103.64	63.66	167.30	4.94	8.50 (16.72)	4,449	74,345
2002	91.93 (58.46)	78.62 (10.73)	170.55 (69.19)	110.77	73.32	184.09	4.06	15.94 (17.86)	6,825	80,808
2003	100.72 (76.27)	95.20 (11.12)	195.92 (87.39)	123.99	90.49	214.48	4.87 (1.15)	7.68 (17.70)	8,467	77,527
2004	117.73 (100.87)	113.92 (11.80)	231.64 (112.67)	145.57	109.06	254.63	7.95 (2.63)	18.56 (19.00)	12,246	88,421

(Continued)

Table 17.1: (Continued)

Year	Trade (US$ billion)			Entrepôt Trade				Investment (US$ billion)		Tourism (1,000 persons)	
	Exports from Mainland to HK	Imports of Mainland from HK	Total	Exports from Mainland to HK	Imports of Mainland from HK	Total	Investment from Mainland in HK	Investment from HK in Mainland	No. of Mainland Visitors to HK	No. of HK Visitors to Mainland***
2005	134.53 (124.47)	129.82 (12.23)	264.35 (136.70)	168.36	124.09	292.45	9.35 (3.42)	16.71 (17.95)	12,541	95,928
2006	152.94 (155.31)	148.23 (10.78)	301.17 (166.09)	187.35	143.07	330.42	13.94 (6.93)	21.36 (20.23)	13,591	98,318
2007	170.47 (184.44)	167.74 (12.80)	338.20 (197.24)	204.84	162.53	367.73	13.36 (13.73)	36.40 (27.70)	15,486	101,136
2008	180.86 (190.73)	175.70 (12.92)	356.56 (203.64)	218.94	171.24	390.18	23.04 (38.64)	27.59 (41.04)	16,862	101,317
2009	160.83 (166.23)	3.44 (8.71)	164.27 (174.95)	—	—	159.18	—	— (46.08)	17,957	155,000

Notes: 1. Figures may not add up to the totals due to rounding up.
2. "—" indicates that the statistical data are unavailable, unknown or negligible.
3. Statistics from Mainland China sources are given in brackets.
4. Imports of Mainland from HK figures exclude HK's re-exports to China.
5. * Figure for 1992.
6. ** Figures for 1998.
7. *** No. of Hong Kong visitors to Mainland include visitors from Macau.

Sources: Census and Statistics Department, The Government of the Hong Kong Special Administrative Region, "Hong Kong Statistics", http://www.censtatd.gov.hk/hong_kong_statistics/index.jsp; *A Statistical Review of Tourism* (1981, 1986, 1991, and 1996 issues), Hong Kong: Research Department, Hong Kong Tourism Association, 1982, 1987, 1992 and 1997; Hong Kong Tourism Board, *Visitor Arrival Statistics* (published monthly), http://partnernet.hktourismboard.com; State Statistical Bureau, People's Republic of China (comp.), *China Statistical Yearbook* (1983, 1987, 1992, 1997, 2003, 2004, 2006, 2008, and 2009 issues), Beijing: China Statistics Press, 1983, 1987, 1992, 1997, 2003, 2004, 2006, 2008 and 2009; and Ministry of Commerce, National Bureau of Statistics and State Administration of Foreign Exchange, People's Republic of China, *2008 Niandu Zhongguo Duiwai Zhijie Touzi Tongji Gongbao (2008 Statistical Bulletin of China's Outward Foreign Direct Investment)*, September 2009, http://hzs.mofcom.gov.cn/accessory/200909/1253868856016.pdf.

but Hong Kong's top civil servants wanted to avoid a high degree of economic integration with the Mainland and were cool to Guangdong's overtures. At the end of the first decade of the new century, Guangdong was following in the footsteps of Shanghai, trying to attract investment from multinational corporations listed in the Fortune 500. The value of Hong Kong as an economic partner had thus been falling. In sum, dependence on the Mainland and the decline in relative bargaining power exacerbated Hong Kong people's willingness to accept Beijing's position on the territory's electoral reforms.

At the same time, the Hong Kong people's confidence in China's future continued to strengthen (Table 17.2). Apparently, this was related to their increasingly positive perception of Mainland China's international standing. A public opinion survey conducted by the New Youth Forum in March 2009 revealed that 86% of the respondents thought that China had considerable international influence; about 77% believed that China would definitely or possibly overtake the U.S. as a world superpower within 50 years; 80% felt that China was a peace-loving country; and 60% believed that China's development would not threaten the Asia-Pacific region.[12] The successful Beijing Olympics certainly helped; and most Hong Kong people believed that China, in contrast to the U.S., emerged from the global financial tsunami in 2008–2009 with its international status improved.

The economic difficulties and political controversies at the end of the first decade in the 21st century nevertheless undermined the Hong Kong community's trust in the central government and its confidence in "one country, two systems" (see Table 17.2). Given that the territory's economy was heavily dependent on the Mainland economy and the central government's policy support, and that the HKSAR Chief Executive was chosen by China's leaders, the Hong Kong people might have held the central government responsible for the performance of their economy and government. However, obviously the trends had been positive since 1997.

In the years around the Beijing Olympics, the Hong Kong people's trust in the central government had been considerably higher than its trust in the Hong Kong government, in contrast to the situation in the 1990s

---

[12] Ibid. March 30, 2009.

Table 17.2: Hong Kong People's Confidence in China and Trust for the Chinese Leadership as Reflected by Public Opinion Surveys, 1997–2009 (half-yearly average)

Date of Survey	Confidence in China's Future (A) Confident	Confidence in China's Future (A) Not Confident	Trust for the Central Government (B) Very Trust/ Quite Trust	Trust for the Central Government (B) Quite Distrust/ Very Distrust	Confidence in "One Country, Two Systems" (C) Confident	Confidence in "One Country, Two Systems" (C) Not Confident
7–12/2009	87.2%	8.5%	49.6%	18.8%	68.1%	26.0%
1–6/2009	88.2%	8.2%	52.6%	15.4%	72.5%	21.7%
7–12/2008	88.1%	7.9%	53.1%	14.4%	71.8%	21.6%
1–6/2008	87.9%	7.9%	54.9%	13.4%	74.6%	18.7%
7–12/2007	87.6%	7.8%	54.4%	15.6%	74.9%	18.8%
1–6/2007	87.5%	8.1%	49.9%	15.5%	72.9%	20.8%
7–12/2006	85.7%	9.3%	44.6%	19.7%	70.4%	23.6%
1–6/2006	85.0%	9.3%	48.5%	18.7%	69.4%	22.6%
7–12/2005	82.0%	11.0%	46.8%	24.4%	65.1%	25.3%
1–6/2005	79.0%	11.4%	43.2%	24.7%	57.2%	28.2%
7–12/2004	83.4%	9.2%	47.0%	20.9%	59.3%	28.4%
1–6/2004	82.6%	8.8%	40.0%	25.6%	51.7%	33.1%
7–12/2003	82.7%	8.3%	45.7%	20.6%	53.7%	30.9%
1–6/2003	79.1%	11.0%	37.6%	29.4%	49.2%	38.4%
7–12/2002	81.7%	9.6%	41.0%	26.2%	52.7%	34.3%
1–6/2002	81.1%	8.6%	48.6%	20.6%	58.7%	28.3%
7–12/2001	79.9%	10.0%	43.9%	22.1%	59.2%	27.3%
1–6/2001	—	—	33.8%	31.1%	56.7%	30.4%
7–12/2000	—	—	31.6%	31.0%	58.2%	27.5%
1–6/2000	—	—	31.9%	27.3%	62.0%	22.5%
7–12/1999	—	—	29.3%	29.7%	56.3%	29.6%
1–6/1999	78.6%	10.5%	27.3%	27.4%	57.7%	28.3%
7–12/1998	—	—	30.5%	30.7%	66.6%	21.9%
1–6/1998	71.0%	15.0%	28.7%	30.1%	64.5%	20.8%
7–12/1997	73.1%	11.8%	32.4%	29.9%	64.0%	18.7%

Notes: 1. Question asked for (A) — Do you have confidence in China's future? The other option was don't know/hard to say, which is not included in this table.

2. Question asked for (B) — On the whole, do you trust the Beijing Central Government? The other options were half-half and don't know/hard to say, which are not included in this table.

3. Question asked for (C) — On the whole, do you have confidence in "One Country, Two Systems"? The other option was don't know/hard to say, which is not included in this table.

Source: Public Opinion Programme, The University of Hong Kong, http://hkupop.hku.hk/, retrieved on January 25, 2010.

before the return of the territory to China. In a survey in December 2008 (one of the series recorded in Table 17.2), 56% of the respondents said they trusted the central government. By comparison, 42% of the respondents indicated that they trusted the HKSAR government, and 19% indicated that they distrusted it. The 14% gap between those who trusted the central government and those who trusted the HKSAR government was the greatest since the end of 2003.[13]

In early 1996, an opinion poll conducted by the Chinese University of Hong Kong revealed that 42% of the respondents trusted the British administration; those who trusted the British government amounted to less than 20%, while only 12% trusted the Chinese government.[14] A similar pattern emerged in various surveys on the same subject in the 1990s. Hence, the Chinese authorities should be satisfied with the achievements of its united front charm offensive in the territory. This trust in the central government and confidence in "one country, two systems" implied that the Hong Kong people were less inclined to demand democracy as a checks-and-balances mechanism against Beijing, in contrast to the mentality of "the exploitation of democracy as a bulwark against communism", which hit its peak in the wake of the Tiananmen Incident in June 1989.[15]

In terms of the Hong Kong People's identity, there had been positive changes in the long-term trends from Beijing's point of view, though the changes were more limited. As shown in Table 17.3, there had been a fairly steady decline in the Hong Kong people identifying themselves as "Hong Kong citizens", and a shift toward identifying themselves as "Chinese Hong Kong citizens", though there was a reversal of this trend in 2008 and 2009. Similarly, there had been a fairly steady rise in the Hong Kong people identifying themselves as "Chinese citizens" rather than "Hong Kong Chinese citizens"; again, there was a reversal of the trend from mid-2008 to mid-2009. A more perplexing phenomenon was

---

[13] Ibid, January 7, 2009.
[14] Sing Tao Evening Post, February 5, 1996.
[15] See Joseph Y.S. Cheng, "Prospects for Democracy in Hong Kong," in George Hicks (ed.), *The Broken Mirror: China After Tiananmen*, Harlow, Essex, United Kingdom: Longman Group U.K. Limited, 1990, pp. 278–295.

Table 17.3: Hong Kong People's Identity as Reflected by Public Opinion Surveys, 1997–2009 (half-yearly average)

	(A)				(B)	(C)
Date of Survey	Hong Kong Citizen	Chinese Hong Kong Citizen	Hong Kong Chinese Citizen	Chinese Citizen	Strength of Identity as a Hong Kong Citizen	Strength of Identity as a Chinese Citizen
7–12/2009	37.6%	23.9%	13.1%	24.2%	8.14	7.79
1–6/2009	24.7%	32.0%	13.3%	29.3%	7.83	7.72
7–12/2008	21.8%	29.6%	13.0%	34.4%	7.99	7.79
1–6/2008	18.1%	29.2%	13.3%	38.6%	7.80	8.02
7–12/2007	23.5%	31.5%	16.0%	27.2%	8.09	7.87
1–6/2007	23.4%	31.8%	16.7%	26.4%	8.00	7.66
7–12/2006	22.4%	24.3%	20.1%	31.8%	7.98	7.82
1–6/2006	24.8%	25.1%	14.9%	34.6%	7.79	7.68
7–12/2005	24.8%	26.5%	16.9%	30.7%	7.91	7.73
1–6/2005	24.0%	21.2%	14.7%	36.4%	7.77	7.56
7–12/2004	25.9%	23.1%	16.2%	31.6%	7.54	7.47
1–6/2004	28.0%	21.2%	14.3%	33.0%	7.54	7.48
7–12/2003	24.9%	23.4%	15.6%	32.5%	7.41	7.52
1–6/2003	32.6%	20.8%	13.5%	30.7%	—	7.54
7–12/2002	30.0%	21.7%	14.7%	31.1%	—	7.63
1–6/2002	29.9%	20.7%	15.5%	30.4%	—	7.76
7–12/2001	29.0%	24.2%	14.0%	28.7%	—	7.85
1–6/2001	33.8%	20.0%	14.7%	28.3%	—	7.78
7–12/2000	36.3%	23.0%	14.2%	21.3%	—	7.62
1–6/2000	37.5%	22.5%	15.9%	19.0%	—	7.50
7–12/1999	33.5%	22.6%	17.0%	23.6%	—	7.27
1–6/1999	41.4%	22.0%	13.2%	17.5%	—	7.02
7–12/1998	36.6%	23.5%	16.7%	19.9%	—	7.18
1–6/1998	32.2%	18.3%	17.4%	28.2%	—	7.10
7–12/1997	35.9%	23.6%	19.9%	18.0%	—	7.28

Notes: 1. Question asked for (A) — You would identify yourself as a Hong Kong Citizen/Chinese Citizen/Hong Kong Chinese Citizen/Chinese Hong Kong Citizen. The other options were other and don't know/hard to say, which are not included in this table.

2. Question asked for (B) — Please use a scale of 0–10 to rate your strength of identity as a Hong Kong citizen, with 10 indicating extremely strong, 0 indicating extremely weak, and 5 indicating half-half. How would you rate yourself?

3. Question asked for (C) — Please use a scale of 0–10 to rate your strength of identity as a Chinese citizen, with 10 indicating extremely strong, 0 indicating extremely weak, and 5 indicating half-half. How would you rate yourself?

Source: Public Opinion Programme, The University of Hong Kong, http://hkupop.hku.hk/english/popexpress/ethnic/index.html, retrieved on January 25, 2010.

that the strength of identity of the Hong Kong people as "Hong Kong citizens" and as "Chinese citizens" had both been rising, though the latter again showed a small decline from mid-2008 to mid-2009. Stronger identification as "Chinese Hong Kong citizens" and "Chinese citizens" on the part of the Hong Kong people might mean that they were more willing to accept reducing the differences between the territory and the Mainland.

The influence of the pro-Beijing united front had certainly been expanding rapidly since 1997. The resources at its disposal had been most impressive. The Chinese authorities and the HKSAR government could reward united front activists with decorations, honors, prestigious positions such as deputies and delegates to the Nation People's Congress (NPC) and the National Committee of the CPPCC as well as local counterparts, and appointments to various advisory committees of the HKSAR government. In many ways, the united front was becoming the most influential social club in the territory, where one could establish business ties and raise one's social profile. Deputies to the NPC and delegates to the National Committee of the CPPCC enjoy the privilege of meeting central government ministers and provincial heads at will; one can easily imagine how valuable this privilege can be for Hong Kong businessmen in China. Members of the advisory committee system of the HKSAR government likewise have good access to senior government officials. The large state-owned enterprises (SOEs) listed on the Stock Exchange of Hong Kong had been generous in supporting the united front's activities. Even grassroots leaders such as mutual aid committee chairmen of public housing estates were treated to visits to the Mainland, where they were pampered by local officials.

All of this easily explained why the pro-Beijing Democratic Alliance for the Betterment and Progress of Hong Kong (DAB) claimed a membership of well over 10,000, while the largest pro-democracy party, the Democratic Party (DP), had a membership of about 600, with only about one-third remaining active. It was also significant that the DP and the Civil Party (CP), another pro-democracy party with strong appeal to liberal middle-class professionals, did not have any mid-level executives of major corporations as their formal members. While almost all major enterprises in Hong Kong had significant business activities in Mainland China, their mid-level executives did not want to be associated with

Table 17.4: Gross Domestic Product (GDP) of Hong Kong, 1997–2009

Year	GDP At Current Market Prices HK$ Million	% Change	At Chained (2007) Dollars HK$ Million	% Change	Implicit Price Deflator of GDP (2007=100)	% Change	Per capita GDP At Current Market Prices HK$	% Change	At Chained (2007) Dollars HK$	% Change
1997	1,365,024	11.0	1,113,824	5.1	122.6	5.7	210,350	10.1	171,640	4.2
1998	1,292,764	-5.3	1,046,700	-6.0	123.5	0.8	197,559	-6.1	159,955	-6.8
1999	1,266,668	-2.0	1,073,453	2.6	118.0	-4.5	191,731	-3.0	162,484	1.6
2000	1,317,650	4.0	1,158,807	8.0	113.7	-3.6	197,697	3.1	173,865	7.0
2001	1,299,218	-1.4	1,164,568	0.5	111.6	-1.9	193,500	-2.1	173,446	-0.2
2002	1,277,314	-1.7	1,186,008	1.8	107.7	-3.5	189,397	-2.1	175,859	1.4
2003	1,234,761	-3.3	1,221,659	3.0	101.1	-6.2	183,449	-3.1	181,503	3.2
2004	1,291,923	4.6	1,325,091	8.5	97.5	-3.5	190,451	3.8	195,340	7.6
2005	1,382,590	7.0	1,418,935	7.1	97.4	-0.1	202,928	6.6	208,263	6.6
2006	1,475,357	6.7	1,518,541	7.0	97.2	-0.3	215,158	6.0	221,455	6.3
2007#	1,615,431	9.5	1,615,431	6.4	100.0	2.9	233,245	8.4	233,245	5.3
2008#	1,676,929	3.8	1,653,636	2.4	101.4	1.4	240,327	3.0	236,989	1.6
2009	1,632,284	-2.6	1,604,999	-2.8	101.7	0.2	233,060	-3.0	229,164	-3.2

Notes: (1) Figures in this table are the latest data released on November 13, 2009.
(2) # indicates that the figures will be finalized when data from all regular sources are incorporated.

Source: Census and Statistics Department, The Government of the Hong Kong Special Administrative Region, "Hong Kong Statistics – Statistical Tables". Retrieved from http://www.censtatd.gov.hk/hong_kong_statistics/statistical_tables/index.jsp?charsetID=1&subjectID=12&tableID=030 on January 22, 2010.

pro-democracy political parties that were critical of the Chinese authorities. As most of the media in Hong Kong were in the hands of the major business groups, self-censorship had been on the rise since the 1990s.

Since the mid-1980s, the pro-Beijing united front in Hong Kong had been gradually building an effective election machine in support of its candidates in various elections. Its mobilization power and sophisticated campaign strategies were well demonstrated in the Legislative Council elections in 2004 and 2008 as well as in the District Council elections in 2003 and 2007.[16]

The Chinese leadership was trapped in a fundamental dilemma. It had been trying hard to support Hong Kong economically in line with the ultimate objectives of ensuring political stability and demonstrating to the world that Beijing could administer the territory better than London. This active support and intervention had made the Hong Kong people aware of their dependence on the Mainland, but they were also concerned with maintaining checks-and-balances mechanisms through support for the pro-democracy movement. Since Chinese leaders understood that they lacked complete control over Hong Kong's political scene, they had been reluctant to allow genuine local democracy. They therefore had failed to win the hearts of those who still voted for the pro-democracy candidates in elections, and had to absorb part of the blame for the unsatisfactory performance of the local government.[17] As indicated above, it seemed that economic difficulties and the bad performance of the HKSAR government

---

[16] For some observations on the operation of this effective election machinery on the part of the pro-Beijing united front, see the author's "Introduction — Hong Kong Since Its Return to China: A Lost Decade?", in his edited volume, *The Hong Kong Special Administrative Region in its First Decade*, Hong Kong; City University of Hong Kong Press, 2007, pp. 43 and 46–47.

[17] Despite some signs of economic recovery, dissatisfaction with the Donald Tsang administration was on the rise at the end of 2009. According to the series of public opinion surveys conducted by the Public Opinion Programme of the University of Hong Kong, a poll at the end of October 2009 showed that 25.4% of the respondents were very satisfied/quite dissatisfied/very dissatisfied with his policy direction. In another survey during the same period, 34.6% of the respondents indicated that they would vote for Donald Tsang (if they had the right to vote and the election was to be held tomorrow), while 48.5% said that they would not. Information is available at http://hkupop.hku.hk/.

Table 17.5: Statistics on Labor Force, Unemployment, and Underemployment in Hong Kong, 1997–2009

	Labor Force					
Year	No. (Thousand)	% Change	Unemployed (Thousand)	Unemployment Rate (%)	Underemployed (Thousand)	Underemployment Rate (%)
1997	3,234.8	2.3	71.2	2.2	37.1	1.1
1998	3,276.1	1.3	154.1	4.7	81.8	2.5
1999	3,319.6	1.3	207.5	6.2	96.9	2.9
2000	3,374.2	1.6	166.9	4.9	93.5	2.8
2001	3,427.3	1.6	174.3	5.1	84.8	2.5
2002	3,472.6	1.3	254.2	7.3	104.4	3.0
2003	3,465.8	–0.2	275.2	7.9	121.9	3.5
2004	3,512.8	1.4	239.2	6.8	114.3	3.3
2005	3,534.2	0.6	197.6	5.6	96.3	2.7
2006	3,571.8	1.1	171.1	4.8	86.3	2.4
2007	3,629.6	1.6	145.7	4.0	79.2	2.2
2008	3,648.9	0.5	130.1	3.6	69.0	1.9
2009	3,676.6	0.8	196.7	5.4	86.4	2.3

Note: Figures in this table are the latest data released on August 19, 2010.

Source: Census and Statistics Department, The Government of the Hong Kong Special Administrative Region, "Hong Kong Statistics — Statistical Tables". Retrieved from http://www.censtatd.gov.hk/hong_kong_statistics/statistical_tables/index.jsp?charsetID=1&subjectID=12&tableID=006 on August 19, 2010.

had a spill-over effect on the community's trust in the central government and its confidence in "one country, two systems". More significant still, Chinese leaders' influence and intervention in Hong Kong had destroyed the appeal of the "one country, two systems" model for Taiwan.

III The HKSAR Government's Legitimacy Deficit

The British colonial administration won its legitimacy by performance.[18] Even at this stage, many Hong Kong people still compared it favorably with the C.H. Tung and Donald Tsang administrations. After 1993, the Chinese authorities responded to the political crises in the HKSAR by

---

[18] See Joseph Y.S. Cheng, "Political Modernization in Hong Kong," *The Journal of Commonwealth & Comparative Politics*, Vol. XXVII, No.3, November 1989, pp. 294–320.

offering strong economic support. Their rationale was simple — if the economy improved, the people would largely be satisfied, and they would be much less interested in democracy. Political stability would no longer be challenged.

When Donald Tsang visited Beijing on his duty trip in December 2006, he told the central government that "Hong Kong economy's is the best it has been in almost in twenty years."[19] Many Hong Kong people disagreed, however, even in the period of economic boom. Based on the views expressed in various radio phone-in programs, people did not feel they had benefitted from economic growth during the Donald Tsang administration.

A study by the Bauhinia Foundation, a think-tank close to Donald Tsang, revealed that the median household income in 2005 was still 15.8% lower than that in the previous peak year of 1997. More serious still, between 1996 and 2005, the number of households with a monthly income below HK$8,000 rose by 76.5%, to more than 500,000 and their proportion of the total number of households rose from 13% to 22%.[20]

According to the Census and Statistics Department, in June 2009, there were 0.3944 million workers earning less than HK$4,000 (about US$500) per month, compared with 0.3 million in 2001.[21] This low-income category, sometimes described by sociologists as the "working poor", mainly consisted of workers without skills and of low educational qualifications. As more than 90% of the territory's GDP came from the service sector, the decline in the manufacturing industries meant demand for unskilled workers had been falling fast. The hourly wage at MacDonald's outlets (around US$2.50) was a good indicator of the surplus of unskilled labor.

A research project at the Chinese University of Hong Kong revealed that its comprehensive quality of life index dropped 3.5% in 2008 compared with that in 2007, almost back to the level in 2003, when the territory was badly hit by the SARS epidemic. Between 2007 and 2008,

---

[19] *South China Morning Post*, December 28, 2006.
[20] *Ibid*, January 10, 2007; and Ming Pao, January 10, 2007.
[21] *Ibid.*, June 8, 2009.

the Hong Kong people's evaluation of the economy and of the affordability of their own accommodation likewise fell 30% and 33% respectively.[22]

Dr. Ohmae Kenichi believed that a vast majority of Japanese would fall into the lower-middle class socioeconomic group because globalization would widen the gap between the rich and the poor, and exacerbate social polarization.[23] Perhaps, Hong Kong's new graduates could most easily associate with Dr. Ohmae's arguments. The median monthly salary of new graduates was between HK$10,000 and HK$11,000; many also owed the government HK$200,000 or so in student loans. Unless they could depend on their parents for food and accommodation, they would have difficulty maintaining a middle-class lifestyle. Neither could they expect steady promotions or salary increases. Many still earned a monthly salary of HK$20,000 to HK$25,000 after more than a decade of employment and could not achieve meaningful breakthroughs in their careers.

Before 1997, unemployment was not a concern in Hong Kong. The community believed that anyone who was willing to work should have no difficulty finding a job. In the second half of the first decade of the new century, it had to accept an unemployment rate higher than those in the U.S. and U.K. Hence, even those who were gainfully employed worried about the employment of their next generation.

The unemployment issue was compounded by the widening gap between the rich and the poor. It was reported that the Hong Kong people had the highest individual net worth in the world, amounting to US$202,000. According to a global study by the United Nations' World Institute for Development Economics Research in 2006, Hong Kong was ahead of Luxembourg, Switzerland, and the U.S., which ranked second, third, and fourth respectively, while Japan ranked ninth and Singapore 12th.[24] From 1981 to 2001, Hong Kong's Gini coefficient steadily rose from 0.451 to 0.525 (see Table 17.7a); in terms of this measurement of income distribution, Hong Kong compared rather unfavorably with

---

[22] *Ibid.*, August 14, 2009.

[23] See Ohmae Kenichi, *The Impact of Rising Lower-middle Class Population in Japan: What Can We Do About It* (in Japanese), Tokyo: Kodansha, 2006.

[24] *South China Morning Post*, December 7, 2006.

Table 17.6: People's Satisfaction with the HKSAR Government — Half-yearly Average, 1997–2009

Survey question:
Are you satisfied with the overall performance of the HKSAR Government? (half-yearly average)

Month of Survey	Total Sample	Very Satisfied	Quite Satisfied	Half-half	Not Quite Satisfied	Very Dissatisfied	Don't Know/ Hard to Say
July–Dec 2009	6,033	3.4%	28.3%	35.8%	21.1%	10.9%	0.6%
Jan–June 2009	6,068	3.1%	24.9%	40.4%	20.5%	10.7%	0.4%
July–Dec 2008	6,213	2.7%	24.3%	41.9%	20.4%	9.6%	1.1%
Jan–June 2008	6,120	5.4%	42.2%	37.3%	10.2%	3.9%	1.0%
July–Dec 2007	6,072	5.2%	46.4%	35.1%	9.0%	3.2%	1.1%
Jan–June 2007	7,084	5.4%	42.0%	39.1%	9.3%	2.9%	1.2%
July–Dec 2006	6,076	4.2%	37.8%	41.7%	11.4%	3.7%	1.1%
Jan–June 2006	7,113	5.8%	45.7%	36.5%	8.5%	2.4%	1.1%
July–Dec 2005	6,097	5.2%	44.0%	35.7%	9.5%	3.1%	2.4%
Jan–June 2005	6,109	2.9%	26.2%	37.9%	20.2%	8.6%	4.3%
July–Dec 2004	6,148	2.7%	17.5%	35.3%	27.6%	14.2%	2.8%
Jan–June 2004	6,207	1.9%	13.0%	33.1%	30.6%	18.1%	3.5%
July–Dec 2003	7,364	1.5%	12.2%	26.9%	35.3%	21.3%	3.0%
Jan–June 2003	6,293	1.1%	14.3%	25.6%	36.9%	18.6%	3.6%
July–Dec 2002	6,260	1.0%	17.0%	28.1%	37.9%	11.3%	4.8%
Jan–June 2002	6,217	1.3%	23.7%	31.3%	32.8%	6.1%	4.9%
July–Dec 2001	6,321	1.0%	19.2%	30.9%	33.4%	10.5%	5.0%
Jan–June 2001	6,348	1.3%	25.3%	35.0%	26.7%	6.5%	5.2%
July–Dec 2000	6,324	1.5%	19.9%	31.3%	32.1%	9.6%	5.7%
Jan–June 2000	4,240	1.6%	22.4%	39.1%	22.9%	9.0%	5.1%
July–Dec 1999	3,205	1.4%	22.8%	39.2%	23.6%	8.0%	5.0%
Jan–June 1999	4,213	0.7%	24.5%	39.9%	26.3%	5.4%	3.2%
July–Dec 1998	4,755	1.0%	21.7%	35.8%	29.0%	8.0%	4.6%
Jan–June 1998	3,744	0.8%	27.4%	38.7%	23.0%	4.6%	5.5%
July–Dec 1997	3,181	1.9%	40.7%	32.7%	13.6%	1.9%	9.3%

Source: Public Opinion Programme, The University of Hong Kong, "People's Satisfaction with the HKSAR Government — half-yearly average". Retrieved from http://hkupop.hku.hk/english/popexpress/sargperf/sarg/halfyr/datatables.html on January 22, 2010.

Table 17.7(a): Gini Coefficient of Hong Kong

	1981	1986	1991	1996	2001	2006
Gini Coefficient	0.451	0.453	0.476	0.518	0.525	0.533

Sources: Census and Statistics Department of the Hong Kong Government, *1991 Population Census Main Report*, Hong Kong: Government Printer, 1992; Census and Statistics Department, The Government of the Hong Kong Special Administrative Region, *Population Census 2001 Main Report — Volume I*, Hong Kong: Printing Department, 2002; and Census and Statistics Department, The Government of the Hong Kong Special Administrative Region, *2006 Population By-census — Thematic Report: Household Income Distribution in Hong Kong*, retrieved from http://www.bycensus2006.gov.hk/FileManager/EN/Content_962/06bc_hhinc.pdf on January 22, 2010.

Table 17.7(b): Gini Coefficients of Hong Kong and Selected Developed Economies

Region/Country	Gini Coefficient	Survey Year
South Africa	0.578	2000
Brazil	0.550	2007
Hong Kong, China	0.533	2006
United Kingdom	0.510	2004/05
Canada	0.510	2004
Zambia	0.507	2004
Argentina	0.500	2005
Singapore	0.481	2000
United States	0.450	2005
Taiwan	0.340	2007
South Korea	0.316	1998
Germany	0.283	2000
Sweden	0.250	2000

Sources: The figures for Hong Kong, Canada, the United Kingdom, Singapore and the United States are from the Census and Statistics Department, The Government of the Hong Kong Special Administrative Region, *2006 Population By-census — Thematic Report: Household Income Distribution in Hong Kong*, retrieved from http://www.bycensus2006.gov.hk/FileManager/EN/Content_962/06bc_hhinc.pdf on January 22, 2010; the figure for Taiwan is from Council for Economic Planning and Development, Executive Yuan, Republic of China, *Taiwan Statistical Data Book 2009*, Taipei: Council for Economic Planning and Development, Executive Yuan, June 2009; and the remaining figures are from the database of The World Bank Group, *World Development Indicators (WDI) Online*.

developed countries, and was in a situation comparable to Argentina and Zambia (see Table 17.7b).

Up to one-third of Hong Kong's labor force had nine years of formal education or less; they would naturally find it difficult to benefit from the territory's economic growth. Exacerbated income inequality easily led to a sense of grievance and possibly also to social instability.

In the era of the British colonial administration, the free market led to the concentration of wealth and the unequal distribution of income. In the colonial political system, however, power was highly concentrated among the expatriate senior officials of the colonial government, who were perceived to be neutral, efficient, and largely free of corruption. This separation of political power and wealth in fact constituted a form of checks-and-balances. However, since the return of Hong Kong to China, most people perceive a rapid expansion of influence over the HKSAR government on the part of the major business groups. The latter had experienced rapid asset growth and had significant investment projects on the Mainland. They therefore enjoyed good access to China's top leaders, who were eager to attract external investment as well as maintain investor confidence in Hong Kong. Business leaders' assessment of the HKSAR government's performance apparently had considerable impact on Chinese leaders' evaluation of the Tung and Tsang administrations, which in turn had shown great respect for the interests of major local business groups.

During the Donald Tsang administration, critics of the HKSAR government often illustrated the collusion between the government and local business interests with the following examples. Middle-class families spent their life savings on their accommodation, while real estate developers refused to reveal the exact measurements of their flats. Working people made monthly contributions to their pension funds and various insurance schemes, but did not even know how much they were paying in commissions and management fees. Supermarkets provided false information on their discounts, and had not been sanctioned after media reports; worse still, consumers had no other options. These examples vividly reflected the oligopolistic control of the market by the territory's major business groups, while the government had been reluctant to introduce fair competition legislation to protect the interests of consumers and small investors.

The perception of government–business collusion had been exacerbated by the fact that many top government officials joined major corporations soon after their retirement with very attractive remuneration packages. At the same time, the official advisory committee system had been dominated by a small elite of 300 or 400 people, including the spouses and children of top business leaders. Worse still, some of them were so much favored by the government that they sat on more than 10 advisory committees, with their tenures extending beyond six years, in violation of established conventions.

From the very first policy address of C.H. Tung to the most recent one of the Tsang administration, the HKSAR government had been trying hard to maintain the territory's international competitiveness and a respectable economic growth rate. Obviously, they had not been successful. In his last policy address delivered on October 14, 2009, Donald Tsang identified six industries with a strategic edge, and indicated that the government would support then with land grants and various subsidies.[25] In contrast to Japan and the other "three little dragons of Asia", however, the HKSAR government did not control the banking and financial systems, nor did it possess state-owned investment funds and corporations to actively promote the development of strategic sectors. The Donald Tsang administration was therefore perceived as ineffective even by the business community and the pro-Beijing united front.

The legitimacy deficit of the HKSAR government largely explained why it had been trying to avoid controversial issues. In an ageing society with a sharply falling fertility rates, the financial burden of social services would increase. Taxation would rise in the absence of administrative reforms. At this stage, Hong Kong's Mandatory Provident Fund was inadequate to provide for the community's retirement, and the Hong Kong people had yet to tackle the long-term financing of their hospital services. Both the Tung and the Tsang administrations were reluctant to expand the taxation base and introduce a value-added tax and/or ask the Hong Kong people to increase their contribution to the Mandatory Provident Fund and pay for their own medical insurance. These were unpopular though essential policy programs that a government without an electoral mandate and which had not been performing well could easily postpone, with the burden ultimately falling on the people further down the road.

---

[25] For the contents of the policy address and the initial responses, see all major newspapers of Hong Kong on October 15, 2009.

IV The Challenges for the Pro-democracy Movement

The pro-democracy movement was in a difficult state. There was considerable frustration with the lack of progress, as no one expected any breakthrough soon. Even the political parties in the pro-democracy camp did not believe that democratization was an issue with much political appeal. They could make very little impact on the government's policymaking process because the Tung and Tsang administrations enjoyed the backing of a safe majority in the legislature; they did not have to lobby for the approval of the pro-democracy groups, which were treated as the opposition. In fact, there was little meaningful consultation between the pro-democracy groups and the government.

The sense of political impotence on the part of the pro-democracy groups was exacerbated by the Hong Kong people's growing trust in China (see Table 17.2). Attacking the Chinese authorities' infringement on the community's freedoms and human rights became less attractive to voters than before. The most important concerns of Hong Kong people were obviously the economy and unemployment, and the pro-democracy groups were not perceived as having much to offer.

Before Hong Kong's return to China, there was substantial moral and public opinion pressure to maintain unity within the pro-democracy camp. Such pressure evaporated soon after July 1997. In the frustration of the political wilderness, differences in political orientations were exacerbated and could no longer be contained. These differences were most evident in the responses to the recently released Political Reform Proposals. The Civic Party (CP) and the League of Social Democrats (LSD) proposed an implicit referendum on the Political Reform Proposals through the resignation of one pro-democracy legislator in each of the five geographical constituencies. By-elections would then have to be held, and the resigned pro-democracy legislators would seek re-election on a common single-issue political platform of rejecting the HKSAR government's Political Reform Proposals and demanding "dual universal suffrage" as soon as possible. The rationale for this proposal was that this was the only way to mobilize the entire electorate of the territory to indicate its stand on the issue of democracy and, hopefully, to demonstrate to the HKSAR government, the Chinese authorities, and the international community that the pro-democracy movement still enjoyed majority support among the Hong Kong population.

The Democratic Party (DP) and the other pro-democracy groups with representation in the legislature refused to support the "pseudo-referendum" plan, however. They asserted that it was too risky precisely because the electorate was apathetic regarding the issue of democratization, and any loss in the five geographical constituencies would tarnish the image of the pro-democracy movement. The DP and like-minded pro-democracy groups worried about the effective electoral machinery of the pro-Beijing united front, and openly stated the importance of retaining the veto in the legislature concerning the Political Reform Proposals.[26]

The voter turnout rate for the Legislative Council by-elections on May 16, 2020, was 17.1%, with about 580,000 voters coming out to vote. As expected, both sides had scripts prepared and offered well-anticipated interpretations.[27] The Tsang administration and the pro-Beijing united front emphasized the low turnout and hence the failure of the "de facto referendum". Naturally, they could report to the Chinese authorities that they had successfully discredited the campaign.

The crucial turning-point was Beijing's decision not to allow the pro-establishment parties to take part in the exercise. Chinese leaders obviously considered the "de facto referendum" a very sensitive precedent, and decided that the danger outweighed the potential of snatching one or two seats from the pro-democracy camp in the by-elections. In the end,

---

[26] According to Annex I to the Basic Law, amendment of the method for selecting the Chief Executive "must be made with the endorsement of a two-thirds majority of all the members of the Legislative Council and the consent of the Chief Executive, and they shall be reported to the Standing Committee of the NPC for approval." According to Annex II to the Basic Law, amendment of the method for forming the Legislative Council "must be made with the endorsement of a two-thirds majority of all the members of the (Legislative) Council and the consent of the Chief Executive, and they shall be reported to the Standing Committee of the NPC for the record." The provisions were initially intended to make changes to the electoral system difficult, with the final decision-making power in the hands of the Chinese authorities; but these provisions also offer veto power to the pro-democracy legislators regarding any electoral reform proposals initiated by the HKSAR government, as long as they control more than one third of the seats in the legislature. At that time, they held 23 seats in the Legislative Council, which were more than one-third.

[27] See all major Hong Kong newspapers on May 17 and 18, 2010.

the pro-establishment political parties refused to participate in the by-elections.

The Tsang administration was under pressure to do more to discredit the by-elections. Tsang's own decision not to vote certainly destroyed the neutrality of the executive branch in organizing the elections of the legislature. It also compromised the spirit of the rule of law. Even if the administration believed that the legislators or political parties had exploited a loophole in the existing legislation by treating the resignations and the by-elections as a "de facto referendum", the government should still have followed the law, organized the elections, carried out the usual publicity work to encourage people to vote, etc. It could then consider closing the loophole afterwards.

A voter turnout rate of 17.1% was not a satisfactory performance for a "de facto referendum", but as a protest campaign, mobilizing more than half a million people to say no to the Tsang administrations package of political reform proposals was quite an achievement, especially considering all the efforts to discredit the campaign by Chinese officials and the pro-Beijing united front. Meanwhile, Beijing continued to approach the democratization issue only within a united front framework. On the day following the by-elections, it was reported that central government officials would meet the Alliance for Universal Suffrage, an umbrella group led by the Democratic Party. It was subsequently revealed that the latter had indicated to the pro-Beijing united front earlier in December 2009 that it would be interested in a dialogue with the central government on the political reform issue. The dialogue surfaced after the Legislative Council byelections, and ultimately led to an agreement between the central government and the Democratic Party.

The central government accepted the Democratic Party's proposal that the five newly-created functional constituency seats for the District Councils would be voted for by the entire electorate except for those already enfranchised in the functional constituency elections. In this way, every voter in Hong Kong would have two votes in the Legislative Council elections in 2012. According to the Political Reform Proposals of the HKSAR government released in November 2009, there would be five more directly-elected Legislative Council seats, one for each of the five existing geographical constituencies; and five more functional constituency

Challenge to the Pro-democracy Movement in Hong Kong   497

Table 17.8: Hong Kong People's Support for the Political Parties, August 1997 to November 2009

Date of Survey	FTU	HKCTU	Civic Party	ADPL	DAB	DP	LP	LSD	HKASPDMC	Frontier	AFA	NWS
19–23/11/2009	51.7 (2)	51.3 (3)	50.2 (4)	50.1 (5)	48.9 (6)	48.4 (7)	44.9 (9)	40.6 (10)	46.6 (8)	—	—	51.8 (1)
18–25/8/2009	52.2 (1)	51.1 (2)	49.5 (5)	49.9 (3)	49.0 (6)	49.7 (4)	44.6 (8)	40.3 (9)	47.0 (7)	—	38.2 (10)	—
19–22/5/2009	52.6 (1)	51.7 (2)	51.3 (3)	49.9 (4)	48.7 (6)	48.8 (5)	44.9 (9)	39.6 (10)	48.0 (7)	47.6 (8)	—	—
16–18/2/2009	52.9 (1)	51.6 (2)	49.7 (4)	49.7 (5)	50.4 (3)	48.3 (6)	43.5 (9)	43.8 (8)	—	46.5 (7)	36.5 (10)	—
26–30/11/2008	53.4 (1)	52.3 (2)	51.1 (3)	50.7 (4)	48.5 (6)	49.5 (5)	41.0 (9)	45.4 (8)	—	46.6 (7)	36.5 (10)	—
18–20/8/2008	53.3 (1)	51.7 (3)	52.4 (2)	51.0 (4)	48.5 (5)	47.7 (6)	47.4 (7)	—	44.0 (9)	46.2 (8)	35.4 (10)	—
20–22/5/2008	55.7 (1)	52.1 (4)	53.1 (3)	51.1 (5)	53.6 (2)	48.7 (7)	49.8 (6)	—	46.4 (8)	45.9 (9)	35.7 (10)	—
18–20/2/2008	53.7 (1)	51.5 (4)	51.8 (2)	49.3 (5)	51.6 (3)	48.6 (7)	49.1 (6)	—	45.1 (9)	46.2 (8)	35.7 (10)	—
21–26/11/2007	52.3 (2)	50.0 (4)	51.9 (3)	48.9 (6)	52.6 (1)	47.0 (7)	46.4 (8)	—	—	45.3 (9)	33.0 (10)	49.7 (5)
13–16/8/2007	55.0 (1)	50.0 (6)	50.7 (4)	50.2 (5)	54.8 (2)	48.0 (7)	52.3 (3)	—	44.1 (9)	45.4 (8)	34.3 (10)	—
16–25/5/2007	53.5 (1)	50.4 (5)	51.7 (2)	51.3 (3)	49.6 (7)	49.8 (6)	51.2 (4)	—	46.9 (8)	46.1 (9)	35.7 (10)	—
12–14/2/2007	51.3 (3)	51.4 (2)	51.5 (1)	49.3 (5)	48.3 (6)	50.0 (4)	48.0 (7)	—	44.5 (9)	45.5 (8)	34.7 (10)	—
20–24/11/2006	53.2 (1)	51.5 (4)	51.9 (2)	50 (5)	49.2 (6)	48.4 (8)	49.1 (7)	—	—	47.3 (9)	36.9 (10)	51.6 (3)
11–15/8/2006	53.2 (1)	49.1 (3)	49.4 (2)	49.1 (4)	49.1 (5)	45.2 (7)	48.9 (6)	—	40.6 (9)	43.2 (8)	33.1 (10)	—
18–25/5/2006	54.2 (1)	52.6 (2)	52.2 (3)	50.5 (5)	51.1 (4)	47.4 (7)	50.2 (6)	—	44.8 (9)	46.6 (8)	37.6 (10)	—
9–14/2/2006	52.5 (2)	51.7 (3)	53.8 (1)	49.6 (4)	49.5 (5)	46.9 (7)	48.9 (6)	—	43.9 (9)	45.1 (8)	35.6 (10)	—

(Continued)

Table 17.8: (Continued)

Date of Survey	FTU	HKCTU	Civic Party	ADPL	DAB	DP	LP	LSD	HKASPDMC	Frontier	AFA	NWS
18–23/11/2005	52.7 (2)	51.7 (3)	53.8 (1)	48.0 (6)	47.5 (7)	48.2 (5)	49.7 (4)	—	45.7 (9)	46.5 (8)	37.5 (10)	—
22–25/8/2005	52.0 (2)	51.1 (3)	54.1 (1)	49.7 (5)	47.7 (6)	47.4 (7)	50.1 (4)	—	46.2 (8)	45.5 (9)	35.8 (10)	—
21–24/5/2005	52.2 (3)	52.5 (2)	54.0 (1)	48.3 (5)	46.5 (7)	49.0 (4)	47.4 (6)	—	45.2 (9)	46.4 (8)	36.3 (10)	—
17–20/2/2005	51.4 (2)	49.8 (3)	53.2 (1)	47.2 (5)	46.1 (7)	47.0 (6)	48.6 (4)	—	44.0 (9)	46.0 (8)	36.8 (10)	—
15–17/11/2004	50.8 (3)	52.1 (2)	54.1 (1)	49.2 (4)	45.0 (9)	49.0 (5)	48.6 (6)	—	46.3 (8)	47.6 (7)	37.9 (10)	—
21–28/8/2004	49.6 (4)	51.1 (3)	51.8 (1)	48.6 (5)	41.6 (9)	51.2 (2)	48.3 (6)	—	44.8 (8)	45.5 (7)	35.9 (10)	—
10–13/5/2004	51.6 (5)	53.7 (2)	54.3 (1)	51.8 (4)	42.5 (9)	53.2 (3)	49.9 (6)	—	47.4 (8)	48.3 (7)	39.4 (10)	—
20–23/2/2004	51.3 (2)	52.3 (1)	—	49.0 (6)	42.6 (9)	50.8 (3)	49.7 (5)	—	44.9 (8)	47.0 (7)	37.3 (10)	50.6 (4)
15–18/11/2003	50.7 (1)	50.1 (2)	—	47.7 (6)	42.1 (8)	49.0 (4)	49.3 (3)	—	—	45.2 (7)	35.7 (9)	48.4 (5)
18–20/8/2003	49.0 (4)	51.3 (1)	—	48.2 (6)	41.2 (9)	50.1 (3)	50.7 (2)	—	45.3 (8)	46.0 (7)	35.4 (10)	48.6 (5)
15–20/5/2003	54.1 (2)	54.4 (1)	—	52.4 (3)	47.9 (8)	49.8 (6)	49.3 (7)	—	47.5 (9)	50.6 (5)	39.1 (10)	52.3 (4)
14–18/2/2003	54.2 (2)	55.5 (1)	—	52.1 (4)	49.9 (7)	51.9 (5)	49.3 (8)	—	46.5 (9)	50.2 (6)	37.1 (10)	53.9 (3)
1–5/11/2002	—	55.8 (1)	—	54.4 (3)	53.3 (4)	51.8 (5)	50.3 (7)	—	47.6 (8)	51.3 (6)	37.7 (9)	54.7 (2)
14–19/8/2002	—	56.9 (1)	—	54.8 (2)	52.4 (5)	52.5 (4)	51.8 (6)	—	49.6 (8)	51.3 (7)	39.5 (9)	53.8 (3)
14–16/5/2002	58.8 (1)	57.9 (2)	—	56.0 (3)	55.1 (4)	51.2 (7)	52.5 (6)	—	47.9 (9)	50.5 (8)	40.0 (10)	54.0 (5)
18–21/2/2002	57.6 (1)	56.1 (2)	—	55.8 (3)	54.0 (4)	50.6 (7)	52.2 (6)	—	—	50.4 (8)	38.9 (9)	53.1 (5)
15–20/11/2001	57.0 (1)	56.1 (2)	—	54.9 (3)	52.7 (5)	51.7 (6)	50.3 (7)	—	48.1 (9)	49.3 (8)	38.6 (10)	53.0 (4)

(Continued)

Table 17.8: (Continued)

Date of Survey	FTU	HKCTU	Civic Party	ADPL	DAB	DP	LP	LSD	HKASPDMC	Frontier	AFA	NWS
17–24/8/2001	56.7 (1)	55.5 (2)	—	52.5 (4)	52.7 (3)	50.7 (6)	48.1 (9)	—	48.4 (8)	49.5 (7)	37.7 (10)	51.6 (5)
25–29/5/2001	57.5 (1)	54.6 (2)	—	51.9 (4)	52.4 (3)	50.6 (6)	50.2 (7)	—	46.2 (9)	50.0 (8)	36.6 (10)	50.7 (5)
19–21/2/2001	60.1 (2)	60.5 (1)	—	55.8 (5)	55.5 (6)	57.4 (4)	53.5 (9)	—	55.3 (7)	54.4 (8)	46.2 (10)	58.1 (3)
23–27/11/2000	56.4 (1)	55.6 (2)	—	52.6 (3)	51.1 (4)	50.5 (6)	48.3 (8)	—	—	48.4 (7)	37.5 (9)	51.0 (5)
25–30/8/2000	56.1 (1)	52.6 (2)	—	50.7 (5)	49.1 (7)	52.5 (3)	47.7 (8)	—	49.3 (6)	50.9 (4)	—	—
2–5/6/2000	58.7 (1)	54.8 (2)	—	51.1 (6)	51.9 (5)	52.7 (3)	49.1 (8)	—	50.2 (7)	52.3 (4)	—	—
3/4/2000	55.2 (1)	53.3 (2)	—	49.6 (6)	51.1 (5)	52.1 (3)	48.9 (7)	—	47.6 (8)	51.6 (4)	—	—
1–2/2/2000	56.6 (1)	54.5 (2)	—	50.0 (4)	50.3 (3)	48.5 (6)	47.7 (7)	—	46.7 (8)	48.6 (5)	—	—
6/12/1999	56.3 (1)	51.1 (2)	—	50.0 (4)	50.2 (3)	49.8 (5)	47.3 (8)	—	47.6 (7)	47.8 (6)	—	—
11–16/10/1999	53.1 (1)	51.1 (2)	—	45.7 (8)	48.6 (5)	50.4 (3)	47.3 (6)	—	48.9 (4)	46.9 (7)	—	—
2/8/1999	53.2 (1)	51.4 (3)	—	48.9 (5)	47.0 (7)	52.0 (2)	47.3 (6)	—	49.1 (4)	49.1 (4)	—	—
1/6/1999	56.8 (1)	55.2 (2)	—	49.8 (7)	51.9 (3)	51.6 (4)	49.0 (8)	—	51.3 (5)	50.8 (6)	—	—
9/4/1999	55.8 (1)	—	—	49.9 (5)	51.3 (4)	55.5 (2)	48.9 (7)	—	49.7 (6)	51.4 (3)	—	—
1/2/1999	58.5 (1)	—	—	52.6 (5)	53.7 (4)	54.7 (2)	50.9 (7)	—	51.1 (6)	54.0 (3)	—	—
1–2/12/1998	57.5 (1)	—	—	50.8 (6)	52.4 (4)	55.9 (2)	51.1 (5)	—	50.5 (7)	52.5 (3)	—	—
9/10/1998	56.4 (1)	—	—	50.8 (5)	49.9 (6)	55.6 (2)	48.2 (7)	—	50.9 (4)	53.7 (3)	—	—
4/8/1998	57.7 (1)	—	—	51.6 (6)	52.6 (4)	57.5 (2)	51.3 (7)	—	52.2 (5)	54.9 (3)	—	—

(Continued)

Table 17.8: (*Continued*)

Name of Political Party Date of Survey	FTU	HKCTU	Civic Party	ADPL	DAB	DP	LP	LSD	HKASPDMC	Frontier	AFA	NWS
3–4/6/1998	57.9 (2)	—	—	—	52.7 (4)	60.1 (1)	49.5 (5)	—	—	57.7 (3)	—	—
7/4/1998	58.7 (2)	—	—	54.6 (3)	54.4 (4)	59.0 (1)	53.0 (5)	—	—	—	—	—
2–3/2/1998	58.5 (1)	—	—	53.1 (4)	54.0 (3)	57.9 (2)	51.9 (5)	—	—	—	—	—
2–3/12/1997	60.1 (1)	—	—	—	53.7 (4)	58.5 (2)	50.1 (5)	—	53.8 (3)	—	—	—
3–4/10/1997	56.3 (1)	—	—	—	49.7 (4)	55.5 (2)	48.0 (5)	—	50.7 (3)	—	—	—
6/8/1997	61.4 (2)	—	—	—	57.2 (4)	63.8 (1)	56.0 (5)	—	59.9 (3)	—	—	—

Notes: (1) FTU = The Hong Kong Federation of Trade Unions; HKCTU = Hong Kong Confederation Trade Unions; ADPL = Hong Kong Association for Democracy and People's Livelihood; DAB = Democratic Alliance for the Betterment and Progress of Hong Kong; DP = The Democratic Party; LP = Liberal Party; LSD = League of Social Democrats; HKASPDMC = Hong Kong Alliance in Support of Patriotic Democratic Movements of China; AFA = April Fifth Action; NWS = Neighbourhood & Worker's Service Centre

(2) The Civic Party was established in March 2006; the data for the Article 45 Concern Group were used from May 2004 to February 2006. The League of Social Democrats was formed in October 2006. The Frontier merged with the Democratic Party in December 2008.

(3) The question in each survey was: Please use a scale of 0-100 to rate your extent of support to XXX, with 0 indicating absolutely not supportive, 100 indicating absolutely supportive and 50 indicating half-half. How would you rate XXX?

(4) The numbers in brackets indicate ranking in each of the surveys.

Source: Public Opinion Programme, the University of Hong Kong, "POP Polls: Rating of Top Ten Political Groups", from http:// http://hkupop.hku.hk.

seats to be elected with the District Council members as candidates on a universal suffrage basic, following the NPCSC stipulation that the two types of constituencies would remain equal in terms of numbers of seats. In return for the concession, the Democratic Party Legislators voted in support of the government's Political Reform Proposals, which were then endorsed by the legislature. Due to the change in position of the Democratic Party, the pro-democracy camp lost its veto power in the legislature this time. However, this veto power was expected to remain effective regarding the democratization issue in general.

The voting outcome in the Legislative Council on June 24 and 25, 2010 split the pro-democracy movement.[28] The Democratic Party and its supporters argued that the establishment of a dialogue with the central government following the Tiananmen Incident in 1989 was an important breakthrough, that the concession made by the central government was significant, and that they would continue to struggle for the ultimate realization of democracy in the territory. Those who voted against the government's Political Reform Proposals, including the Civic Party, the LSD, the Hong Kong Confederation of Trade Unions, etc., insisted on a roadmap and a timetable, and considered the so-called "concession" by the central government to have increased both the number and the legitimacy of functional constituencies. There was also suspicion that the Democratic Party had refused to support the "pseudo-referendum" earlier because it had wanted to establish trust with the Chinese authorities to facilitate negotiations on political reform.

The chasm between the radical and conservative wings of the pro-democracy movement then became very clear. Since the Chinese authorities had no intention of allowing genuine democracy in the territory in the near future, there was no chance for the pro-democracy groups to form a government. Further, as indicated above, they had almost no influence on the government's policymaking process. Under the circumstances, unity and discipline had decreasing appeal to politicians in the pro-democracy camp. Moreover, the multi-member, single-vote geographical constituencies in the Legislative Council elections exacerbated splittism. In the largest constituency, i.e., New Territories

---

[28] See all major newspapers of Hong Kong on June 24 and 25, 2010.

West, which returned eight legislators, a candidate could secure a seat with 8% to 9% of the votes cast. Hence, with the usual voter turnout rate at around 50%, a candidate could theoretically win a seat with the support of 4% or 5% of the constituency, as long as supporters could be motivated to come out and vote. Moving towards a more radical position might contribute to a sharp image appealing to a sufficient minority of the electorate. The LSD apparently had been very successful in following this type of strategy; it certainly had been attracting a lot of media attention. At the other end of the pro-democracy political spectrum, the Hong Kong Association for Democracy and People's Livelihood avoided controversial political issues and concentrated on district work in Sham Shui Po. Their different orientations made solidarity within the pro-democracy camp more problematic.

There were other types of problems as well. The frustrations of many "young Turks" in the radical wing of the pro-democracy movement were related to bottlenecks in their political careers. The two municipal councils were abolished in 2000, and there were very limited chances of getting elected to the Legislative Council as the "old guards" held on to their seats. Junior politicians therefore spent many years on the District Councils, where remuneration was insufficient to support full-time political careers.

These inter-party and intra-party differences within the pro-democracy movement became public over the "pseudo-referendum" issue. Mutual recriminations damaged the image of the entire pro-democracy movement while also discouraging its supporters. Worse still, the two founding elders of the DP, Martin Lee and Szeto Wah, had opposing views on the "pseudo-referendum". Szeto openly criticized Lee for his political immaturity, and accused youthful supporters of the "pseudo-referendum" of actually helping the Chinese Communist Party (CCP).[29]

When the pro-democracy movement organized a rally protesting against the Political Reform Proposals on New Year's Day 2010, the turnout was not expected to be impressive, with a general estimate that

---

[29] See, for example, *Ming Pao*, November 25, 2009 and December 14, 2009; Oriental Daily News, November 25, 2009 and November 29, 2009; and *Hong Kong Economic Journal*, December 14, 2009.

Table 17.9: Popularity Ranking of the Pro-democracy Legislators, February 1997 to October 2009

Date of Survey	Pro-Democracy Legislator As the Most Popular Legislators	No. of Pro-Democracy Legislators Among the Top Three in the Entire Legislature	No. of Pro-Democracy Legislators Among the Top Five Most Popular Legislators in the Entire Legislature	No. of Pro-Democracy Legislators Among the Top Ten Most Popular Legislators in the Entire Legislature
18–21/1/2010	Yes	3	5	8
15–19/10/2009	Yes	2	3	8
14–18/7/2009	Yes	2	4	7
21–23/4/2009	Yes	2	4	8
19–21/1/2009	Yes	3	4	8
22–24/10/2008	Yes	3	4	7
9–10/7/2008	No	2	3	6
16–18/4/2008	No	2	2	6
16–18/1/2008	No	1	2	6
22–25/10/2007	No	2	2	6
23–26/7/2007	No	1	2	6
17–20/4/2007	No	2	2	7
22–26/1/2007	No	1	2	6
23–27/10/2006	No	1	2	6
14–21/7/2006	No	1	2	6
18–21/4/2006	No	1	2	6
16–20/1/2006	No	1	1	6
9–13/11/2005	No	1	2	6
5–9/8/2005	No	0	2	6
9–12/5/2005	No	1	2	6
14–16/2/2005	No	1	2	6
8–11/11/2004	Yes	1	1	5
9–16/8/2004	Yes	1	2	6
3–7/5/2004	Yes	1	2	6
9–14/2/2004	Yes	1	2	5
10–12/11/2003	Yes	1	2	6
11–12/8/2003	Yes	1	2	5

(*Continued*)

Table 17.9: (Continued)

Date of Survey	Pro-Democracy Legislator As the Most Popular Legislators	No. of Pro-Democracy Legislators Among the Top Three in the Entire Legislature	No. of Pro-Democracy Legislators Among the Top Five Most Popular Legislators in the Entire Legislature	No. of Pro-Democracy Legislators Among the Top Ten Most Popular Legislators in the Entire Legislature
2–7/5/2003	No	1	2	5
4–7/2/2003	No	0	2	4
1–5/11/2002	Yes	2	3	5
2–7/8/2002	Yes	1	3	5
2–7/5/2002	No	1	2	5
4–6/2/2002	Yes	2	2	5
1–5/11/2001	Yes	2	2	5
1–3/8/2001	Yes	2	3	6
19–23/5/2001	No	2	2	5
5–13/2/2001	No	2	3	5
14–16/11/2000	No	2	2	5
8–12/8/2000	Yes	3	4	6
26–30/5/2000	Yes	3	4	6
13/3/2000	Yes	3	4	6
21–24/1/2000	No	1	2	4
24/11/1999	Yes	2	2	5
27/9/1999	Yes	2	4	7
26/7/1999	Yes	2	3	6
24/5/1999	Yes	3	3	6
25/3/1999	Yes	3	5	6
26/1/1999	Yes	3	5	6
25/11/1998	Yes	3	5	6
23–24/9/1998	Yes	3	5	6
28/7/1998	Yes	3	5	6
24/3/1998	Yes	1	1	1
23/1/1998	No	1	1	1
24–25/11/1997	No	1	1	1
15–18/9/1997	No	0	0	0

(Continued)

Table 17.9: (Continued)

Date of Survey	Pro-Democracy Legislator As the Most Popular Legislators	No. of Pro-Democracy Legislators Among the Top Three in the Entire Legislature	No. of Pro-Democracy Legislators Among the Top Five Most Popular Legislators in the Entire Legislature	No. of Pro-Democracy Legislators Among the Top Ten Most Popular Legislators in the Entire Legislature
22/7/1997	No	1	1	1
5–6/6/1997	Yes	3	5	7
19–20/5/1997	No	1	1	1
10–15/4/1997	Yes	3	5	7
17–18/3/1997	No	1	1	1
3–4/2/1997	Yes	3	5	6

Source: Public Opinion Programme, the University of Hong Kong, "POP Polls: Rating of Top Ten Legislative Councillors", from http://hkupop.hku.hk.

around 10,000 people would take part. The turnout actually reached 30,000, due in part to the heavy sentence imposed on Liu Xiaobo.[30] Another surprise was the enthusiastic opposition to the HKSAR government's costly plan for a highspeed railway from Kowloon linking to the high-speed railway system on the Mainland. The opposition came from young people referred to as the "post-1980s generation", who exhibited strong dissatisfaction with the establishment but had little respect and trust for the pro-democracy political parties.[31] There was also an unexpectedly high turnout of about 150,000[32] for the June 4 anniversary candlelight vigil in 2010, with many young people in attendance. The commemoration events in 2011 was similar; the organizers claimed that more than 150,000 people participated.

The frustrations and dissatisfaction of the "post-1980s generation" had attracted a lot of attention,[33] highlighting the exacerbating problems

---

[30] See all major Hong Kong newspapers on January 2, 2010.
[31] See all major Hong Kong newspapers on January 9, 2010.
[32] According to the figures announced by Szeto Wah, Chairman of the Hong Kong Alliance in Support of the Patriotic Democratic Movement of China, which organized the event. Different figures were claimed by different parties, nonetheless.
[33] See Michael E. DeGolyez, *Protest and Post-80s Youth, A Special Report on the Post-1980 Generation in Hong Kong*, Hong Kong. Transition Project, Hong Kong Baptist

of widening income disparity, declining opportunities for upward social mobility among young people and a perception of worsening social injustice as government policies were seen to favor major business groups. These problems certainly eroded the legitimacy of the HKSAR government, especially when the related grievances were sharply articulated by activists of the "post-1980s generation".

The expectations of the younger generation reflected the community's changing values and demands, and members of the "post-1980s generation" probably considered both the government and the pro-democracy parties to have failed them. While the Tung and Tsang administrations were lacklustre at best in their socioeconomic policy programs, the pro-democracy movement also felt the pressure of the perception that its concentration on political reform issues was inadequate and could attract the sustained support of the majority of the population.

V Conclusion

Most Hong Kong people understood that Chinese leaders had no intention of allowing genuine democracy in the territory, but they were unwilling to confront the Chinese authorities and were reluctant to sacrifice for the cause of democracy because the status quo was tolerable. Political apathy and the sense of political impotence in the community had therefore been growing in the first decade of the new century. The pro-democracy movement found increasingly difficult to mobilize the people, and frustration over the lack of progress exacerbated and publicized internal division. A major breakthrough in the foreseeable future seemed unlikely, while maintaining the momentum of the movement became a daunting challenge. These pressures, along with the resourcefulness and effectiveness of the pro-Beijing united front electoral machinery, were keenly felt when many leaders of the pro-democracy movement appealed

---

University, 2010. The Central Policy Unit of the HKSAR government and the Applied Socio-Economic Research Centre of the Hong Kong University of Science and Technology jointly organized a seminar on "Youth and Social Change" on December 17, 2010 to examine the issues of the territory's "post-1980s generation"; the papers are available at http://www.cpu.gov.hk/txttc/conference 20101217.htm

for caution and avoidance of risk in deciding against support for the "pseudo-referendum" proposal.

The difficulties of the pro-democracy movement had nevertheless not translated into advantages for the Tsang administration. Even the pro-Beijing united front was unhappy with the HKSAR government's performance, and blamed; its incompetence for the absence of an economic development strategy that would revive the territory's international competitiveness and relieve social polarization. The Chinese leadership's hardline position on political reform exacerbated the legitimacy deficit of the Tsang administration, which was perceived by people on both sides of the HKSAR border as dependent on support from the Chinese authorities. Tsang's position was probably salvaged by the fact that the Chinese leadership could hardly afford another forced resignation of a Chief Executive handpicked by Beijing.

Although the Hong Kong people's confidence in China and their trust in the Chinese leadership as well as their identification with the Mainland had been growing since the territory's return to China until the Beijing Olympics in 2008, the Chinese government's strong backing of the HKSAR had become a double-edged sword. The Hong Kong people realized that decisions on local political reform were made in Beijing, and they also partly blamed the Chinese authorities for the unsatisfactory performance of the HKSAR administration, which was chosen by and accountable to Beijing.

The lose-lose situation could only be reversed by the Chinese leadership becoming enlightened and secure enough to allow genuine democracy in the territory. This was unlikely, however, as Chinese leaders could still not accept erosion of the CCP's monopoly on political power, and the formula for political stability in China remained economic growth and an absence of democracy.

Acknowledgement

Originally published as Cheng, Joseph Y.S., "Challenge to the Pro-democracy Movement in Hong Kong: Political Reforms, Internal Splits and the Legitimacy Deficit of the Government", *China Perspectives*, 2011/2, pp. 44–60. Reproduced with kind permission from the publisher.

Chapter 18

Has He Got the Job Done: An Evaluation of Donald Tsang's Administration

I Why Donald Tsang?

When C.H. Tung was forming the first government of the Hong Kong Special Administrative Region (HKSAR), the political gossip reported in the media was that he would not wish to retain Donald Tsang, the colonial Financial Secretary, Peter Lai or Lam Woon-kwong in his cabinet. He was subsequently advised by Beijing that, for the sake of political stability, he should retain all the members of the previous British administration. When Donald Tsang formally became the Chief Executive on June 21, 2005, members of the pro-Beijing united front who were dissatisfied with him pointed out that, upon his departure as the last governor, Chris Patten had followed convention by asking that knighthoods be bestowed on his Chief Secretary and Financial Secretary, the latter accepted and the former declined. The message was that Donald Tsang had no expectations in the future HKSAR government while the Chief Secretary, Anson Chan, still entertained higher political aspirations.[1]

In 1999, Anson Chan was expected to step down upon reaching the retirement age. The pro-Beijing united front was about to celebrate her anticipated departure, while Michael Suen was expected to succeed Anson

---

[1] In July 1995, Anson Chan, Chief Secretary for Administration of the British administration, secretly visited Beijing.

Chan as the Chief Secretary for Administration. However, it was said that the Beijing officials responsible for Hong Kong affairs were not confident of C.H. Tung's political competence, and Anson Chan was specially invited stay to support the Tung administration.

The arrangement apparently did not work out. Stories of C.H. Tung and Anson Chan not getting along soon became an open secret in the territory's political circles. The open guidance given by the central leadership to Anson Chan to "better support" the work of the Tung administration during her visit to Beijing was perceived as evidence of the truth of this gossip. When Anson Chan finally retired in 2002, Donald Tsang was given the blessings of Beijing and C.H. Tung to succeed her.

During the crisis of the "Article 23" legislation, the central leadership strongly supported C.H. Tung.[2] Yet after the crisis, Tung's performance still proved to be unsatisfactory and he was forced to resign for health reasons. He was succeeded by Donald Tsang. According to the Standing Committee of the National People's Congress (NPCSC), the remaining years of Tung's second term would be Tsang's first term; hence he could only be re-elected one more time, and his administration would last for a maximum of seven years, not 12.

In his re-election campaign in 2007, Donald Tsang adopted the slogan "I will get the job done". Commentators observed that this probably reflected his mindset. Since he treated this as a job, naturally he would follow the demands of his superiors in Beijing, and one could not expect any mission or commitment on his part to fight for the rights and welfare of the people of Hong Kong.

In his earlier civil service career, Donald Tsang demonstrated well the loyalty of an employee. As a civil servant of the British administration, he was perceived as an arrogant colonial bureaucrat by members of the pro-Beijing united front who never had a good impression of him. This loyalty ultimately secured him the position of Financial Secretary in the final years of the British administration. With the C.H. Tung administration, despite the fact that Tung initially wanted to exclude him, he eventually

---

[2] See Joseph Y. S. Cheng, "Introduction: Causes and Implications of the July 1 Protest Rally in Hong Kong", in his edited volume, *The July 1 Protest Rally: Interpreting a Historic Event*, Hong Kong: City University of Hong Kong Press, 2005.

secured sufficient trust to be promoted to succeed Anson Chan as Chief Secretary for Administration.

It was often reported in the media that Liao Fei, head of the State Council's Hong Kong and Macau Affairs Office, had been Donald Tsang's most important supporter, despite the fact that the pro-Beijing united front in the territory disliked him. Obviously, after the return of Hong Kong to the Motherland, Tsang succeeded in winning the trust of the principal Beijing official responsible for Hong Kong. One had to admire Donald Tsang's skill in securing the trust and support of his superiors; and his assumption of the Chief Executive position again demonstrated the significant influence of Beijing in the HKSAR government's personnel decisions.

In the transitional period in the 1980s, the Chinese leadership originally planned the joint cultivation of the HKSAR government's first leaders with the British administration. However, after the Tiananmen Incident, Chris Patten as the last Governor pushed for further democratization in the territory. This angered Beijing which broke the co-operation and decided to "build another stove", i.e., it would cultivate Hong Kong's future leaders on its own.[3] According to the initial plan, the future leaders of the HKSAR government would mainly come from the civil service. The Sino-British confrontation over Hong Kong during Chris Patten's administration meant that Beijing could not accept the top civil servants groomed by Patten; its targets then switched to the business leaders and C.H. Tung was subsequently chosen. The failure of Tung prompted the Chinese leaders to look for his successors from among the top civil servants whose administrative competence and experience were treasured by Beijing. On this basis, Donald Tsang was selected.

II Donald Tsang's Philosophy of Governance

When Donald Tsang succeeded Tung, the territory's economy had already recovered from the recession caused by the Severe Acute

---

[3] Lo Chi-kin, "You zhitongche dao lingqi luzao" (From Through Train to Establishing Another Store) in Joseph Y.S. Cheng and Sonny Lo Shiu-hing (eds.), *Jiuqi guodu: Xianggang de tiaozhan* (In Transition to 1997: Hong Kong's Challenges), Hong Kong: Chinese University Press, 1997, pp. 37–46.

Respiratory Syndrome (SARS) epidemic. Hence he was under no pressure to "save" the economy and to introduce a stimulus package. At the end of 2004, Hong Kong's unemployment rate dropped to 6.7% from the peak of 8.6% in the previous year. The labour force actually expanded to a historical record of 3.3 million. Cases of negative equity, i.e. property owners whose down payments for their mortgages had been more than wiped out by the decline in the values of their properties, such that the values of their loans exceeded the values of their properties used to secure the loans had fallen from a peak of over 100,000 to about 25,000 in September 2004. This reflected a rebound in the property market, and that many middle-class families had been relieved from a significant financial burden.[4]

Donald Tsang's philosophy of governance was revealed, to a considerable extent, by his first policy address released in October 2005.[5] He indicated that his administration would pursue "excellent governance, a harmonious community and widespread economic growth". After the massive protest rallies in 2003 and 2004, as well as the shelving of "Article 23" legislation, Donald Tsang pledged "to secure a 'people-based' government", "strengthen co-operation between the Administration and the Legislative Council", and to "strengthen the role of District Officers to foster community spirit and to better solve local problems".

Regarding the pursuit of "excellent governance", Donald Tsang did not have many concrete proposals to offer. He suggested a reduction in the establishment of the civil service and improvement of its efficiency; but he also indicated that he planned to create "a small political cadre within the Administration to support the work of the Chief Executive and Principal Officials", i.e., more political appointments.

In the past, Donald Tsang had been skillful in managing expectations, especially while he was Financial Secretary. He stated that the number of

---

[4] See the final policy address delivered by C.H. Tung on January 12, 2005 entitled "Working Together for Economic Development and Social Harmony"; see *South China Morning Post, Apple Daily, Ming Pao, Hong Kong Economic Journal,* and all major local newspapers of the following day for commentaries.

[5] See the policy address delivered by Donald Tsang on October 12, 2005 entitled "Strong Governance for the People"; see all major local newspapers of the following day for commentaries.

policies and measures would not be significant. What was important was how many measures would be successfully implemented. The focus of his administration would be to help "the economy power ahead" under the principle of "big market, small government"; and its strategy would be to "leverage the Mainland and engage ourselves globally" as well as to "encourage entrepreneurship and fair competition". Apparently Donald Tsang wanted to avoid the impression of his predecessor having major plans in the economic arena, although he finally supported the Cyberport and Disneyland projects while he was Financial Secretary, and the West Kowloon cultural complex project while he was Chief Secretary for Administration.

In the initial years of the Tung administration, the civil service headed by Anson Chan was not enthusiastic about strengthening economic co-operation with the Mainland; and the Guangdong authorities were unhappy with this neglect. When Donald Tsang became Chief Executive, the entire territory was acutely aware of the significance of this co-operation. The Closer Economic Partnership Arrangement (CEPA) concluded in June 2003 was considered a "big gift" from the central leadership to Hong Kong to help maintain political stability through economic prosperity, as Chinese leaders believed that economic growth would reduce the discontent of Hong Kong people.

A new measure introduced by the Donald Tsang administration was to set up a Mainland Affairs Liaison Office in the Constitutional Affairs Bureau, to coordinate regional cooperation between Hong Kong and the Mainland, as well as the work of the Beijing office and other offices in Chinese cities, especially their liaison work with the central and local governments in the Mainland.

In the central government's Eleventh Five-Year National Economic and Social Development Programme (2006–2010) released in early 2006, Hong Kong was mentioned for the first time. Donald Tsang organized a summit meeting the following September as a discussion platform to facilitate the full exploration of the economic opportunities available in the Mainland to promote Hong Kong's development. Later, in July 2003, when the Guangdong Party Secretary Zhang Dejiang initiated the Pan-Pearl River Delta regional cooperation scheme, Hong Kong also actively responded.

Certainly it was too late to discuss how to better coordinate with the central government's economic plan after its release. Regarding the following Twelfth Five-Year Development Programme (2011–2015), the Tsang administration followed the practice of the provincial governments in the Mainland and engaged in lobbying of the central government in the very early drafting stage of the program to secure policies favourable for Hong Kong, especially in the field of *renminbi* business.

The central leadership accorded high priority to Hong Kong's economic prosperity, as it believed that political stability could be secured when people were stratified with their economic conditions; it was eager to maintain investors' confidence in the territory. But Hong Kong was already a mature economic entity; since its return to the Motherland its contribution to the Mainland's economic modernization had been in decline, and it was then perceived to be going to Beijing often to ask for favours. This was an embarrassment for the HKSAR government and Hong Kong people in general, especially when this point was raised by their counterparts in the Mainland.

The Donald Tsang administration was certainly more proactive in cooperation with Guangdong, but Hong Kong had probably missed the best opportunities. At this stage, the Guangdong authorities were eager to attract foreign direct investment from the leading multinational corporations which could offer high-tech, advanced management and overseas business networks for the province. Investment from Hong Kong was still welcome, but its value was less significant as the Guangdong authorities perceived that they were not short of capital investment.

Informally many leaders of the Guangdong authorities and the local governments below them resented the earlier arrogance of the HKSAR government and its neglect of them. Around 1997, they had enthusiastically tried to promote co-operation with Hong Kong but had been cold-shouldered. At this stage, Hong Kong was suffering from a decline in international competitiveness and had re-discovered the need for economic cooperation with Guangdong. The above perception on the part of Guangdong naturally meant that it was rather cool about Hong Kong's more active approach to regional cooperation in the middle of the first decade of the new century. Concerning the Pan-Pearl River Delta regional cooperation scheme, the other provinces tended to keep their options open and were reluctant to accept Guangdong's leadership. There were many conferences held, but actual progress was limited.

The focus of the business community regarding the HKSAR government's philosophy of governance centred on its attitude towards intervention in the economy. The C.H. Tung administration obviously behaved as if it had the green light to be more interventionist. The messages embodied in Tung's annual policy addresses were very much those of identifying business activities which were considered important, often significant enough to warrant governmental support in terms of public funding or land grants at below market prices. According to Tony Latter, Donald Tsang appeared to have supported Tung's interventionist orientations as his Financial Secretary.[6]

Conservative business leaders in Hong Kong subscribed to the doctrines of supply-side economics. They believed that the government should only concentrate on the maintenance of a favourable business environment, cultivate the talents needed through the education system, and ensure that the development of the infrastructure would meet the demands of the economy. They opposed the "picking of winners" by the government, i.e., identifying and supporting specific industrial sectors.

In his policy address in 2009, Donald Tsang identified six industries for support, namely, education services, medical services, testing and certification services, environmental industries, innovation and technology, and cultural and creative industries.[7] This was unprecedented; how this strategy and practice would affect the HKSAR government's role in the economy had yet to be observed. However, the government had no effective mechanisms to promote and support the development of these six industries; the entrepreneurs in these sectors criticized the government for the lack of coordinated measures; and Hong Kong people considered the government's strategy empty talk.

---

[6] Tony Latter, *Hands On or Hands Off? The Nature and Process of Economic Policy in Hong Kong*, Hong Kong: Hong Kong University Press, 2007, p. 36.

[7] See the policy address delivered by Donald Tsang on October 14, 2009 entitled "Breaking New Ground Together"; see all major local newspapers of the following day for commentaries.

In comparison, Japan and the other "three little dragons of Asia" had ample resources at the disposal of their governments in support of their strategic industries.[8] They enjoyed a strong influence on their respective domestic banking and financial systems, and were thus able to direct preferential loans to the strategic sectors. These governments had state-owned enterprises or government-linked corporations, and some of them had sovereign wealth funds too which could directly participate in the development of strategic industries.

Even if the community had endorsed the identification and support of strategic sectors on the part of the HKSAR government, the Donald Tsang administration obviously conveyed an impression of being over-ambitious and lacking careful planning. Given the handicaps of the HKSAR government in comparison with its counterparts in Japan and the other "three little dragons of Asia", it was hardly in a position to promote six strategic industries simultaneously; to say the least, there would be no economy of scale. In the case of education services, for example, the Tsang administration could only offer two small pieces of land in the urban areas to provide for four thousand student places; the tertiary education sector considered that far from sufficient to promote education services as an export of services following the Australian model.

Many cities in Mainland China and overseas metropolises had plans for university complexes or university towns to promote the development of education services, but these plans involved substantial resource inputs. There was a view that Hong Kong should perhaps concentrate on only one or two strategic sectors at every stage. For example, Singapore by the turn of the century was concentrating on its biotech industries with impressive results.

The lack of planning was mainly due to inadequate policy research resources. Again, in comparison with the other "three little dragons of Asia", Hong Kong had no major policy research think-tanks inside or outside the government. In the context of keen global competition, the development of a strategic industry demanded sophisticated research and planning. The proposal to develop the six strategic industries from the

---

[8] Chalmers Johnson, *MITI and the Japanese Miracle: the Growth of Industrial Policy, 1925–1975*, Stanford, CA: Stanford University Press, 1982.

Donald Tsang administration had not gone through any serious research and planning, and it was not much more than a slogan based on conventional wisdom.

The development of new strategic industries had to take into consideration the transformation of the territory's industrial structure, otherwise the major local business groups would remain focussed on real estate and infrastructure projects. Since the 1980s, there had been much discussion about the combination of Hong Kong's capital and overseas networks with the Mainland's research and development facilities to jointly develop high-tech industries, but no significant results had been seen. At this stage, major state-owned enterprises in the Mainland did not lack capital; the central government and various levels of local governments had all formulated their "going out" strategies.[9] Hong Kong therefore did not have much to offer.

When Donald Tsang delivered his policy address in October 2007, there was only one short paragraph on the six strategic industries. The Chief Executive merely stated that "we will continue to monitor the development of these six industries".[10] By then, those who were worried about an interventionist government might have their hearts at ease, at least for a while, because the Donald Tsang administration had less than two years to go.

In the summer of 2010, because of the widening gap between the rich and poor, there appeared some media discussions on the "hatred for the rich" among Hong Kong people. There was a suggestion from a business leader that the government should consider using its fiscal reserves to help the poor. As expected, there was no response from the Donald Tsang administration. Hong Kong's substantial fiscal reserves were a pride of the government and the people. In contrast to the U.S. and Japan, the HKSAR government had not gone into debt and it had ample fiscal reserves.

---

[9] See International Relations Department, Tsinghua University and Economic Diplomacy Research Centre, Tsinghua University (eds.), *China's Economic Diplomacy 2008*, Beijing: China Economic Publishing House, 2008.

[10] See the policy address delivered by Donald Tsang on October 13, 2010 entitled "Sharing Prosperity for a Caring Society"; see all major local newspapers of the following day for commentaries.

However, what level of fiscal reserves would be considered prudent? Besides ensuring a high degree of liquidity to meet the challenges of financial crises, what use did fiscal reserves have? On March 6, 2002, the then Financial Secretary, Antony Leung Kam-chung, indicated in his budget speech that "it should be sufficient to have fiscal reserves equivalent to around 12 months of government expenditure to meet operating and contingency requirements".[11]

At the beginning of the Tsang administration, i.e., in the early months of fiscal year 2007-08, the HKSAR government's fiscal reserves were adequate for nineteen months of its expenditure. However, when the then Financial Secretary John Tsang Chun-wah delivered his budget speech in February 2007, he suggested that a range of 30%–50% of GDP could be used as a "frame of reference", which was equivalent to 18 to 24 months of government expenditure. John Tsang further commented that an extra 18 months' worth of government expenditure might be required by 2030 as a cushion against the burden of an ageing population.[12]

When the Euro area was established, its member countries were asked to reduce their respective government debts to a safe and sustainable level; and it was agreed that debts up to 60% of GDP were considered safe. According to Tony Latter, applying this criterion to Hong Kong would allow government borrowing of up to about HK$850 billion in 2007. In view of the fact that the government enjoyed fiscal reserves of over HK$300 billion, this meant that theoretically it could issue government bonds and mobilize HK$1.2 trillion for various worthwhile causes, like building the community's social security net.[13]

The Tsang administration and its successor certainly would not do this, and there was no such demand from Hong Kong people. However, the above line of argument demonstrated that the government could afford to do much more to help prepare for the social security needs of an ageing population. In fact, in 2008 when the Tsang administration secured a budget surplus of HK$100 billion, Financial Secretary John Tsang decided to allocate HK$50 billion for a medical insurance programme

---

[11] See all major Hong Kong newspapers on March 7, 2002.
[12] See all major Hong Kong newspapers on March 1, 2007.
[13] Latter, *op. cit.*, pp. 51–52.

to be advocated later by the government. This was a significant example of how fiscal reserves could be used to finance the community's social security.[14]

Throughout the years of the Donald Tsang administration, there were no serious discussions on the government's fiscal reserves. Why was the range of 30–50% of GDP proposed by John Tsang a reasonable and appropriate level? How did he arrive at this "frame of reference"? If half of the government's budget surplus could be allocated for a future community-wide medical insurance plan, could budget surpluses in future years be appropriated for similar purposes? Should the annual earnings of the fiscal reserves be considered regular fiscal revenues which could be used to meet regular government expenditure? The government and Hong Kong people supported the general principle of keeping the wealth in the community, but how should this be implemented through concrete policies?

III The Widening Gap Between the Rich and Poor and Social Harmony

In 2001, the Gini coefficient in Hong Kong already reached 0.525; it is expected to be even higher in 2012. Normally, a level exceeding 0.4 deserved caution; and the territory's level was comparable to that in some Latin American countries. According to a document prepared by the local legislature, the Gini coefficient in Japan in 1993 was 0.249; that in Taiwan in 2000 was 0.326; that in South Korea in 1998 was 0.316; and that in Singapore in 1998 was 0.425.[15]

In September 2010, a survey of the Public Opinion Programme of the University of Hong Kong revealed that only 23% of the respondents were satisfied with the government's performance in "improvement of people's livelihood", a new low since the beginning of the Donald Tsang administration.[16] At that time, the latter was advertizing the recovery of

---

[14] See all major Hong Kong newspapers on February 28, 2008.
[15] The data come from Legislative Council Factsheet FS07/04-05, compiled by the Research and Library Services Division of the Legislative Council Secretariat.
[16] *Ming Pao* (a Hong Kong Chinese newspaper), September 29, 2010.

the economy, and it estimated that economic growth in the year would reach 5%–6%.

In the same month, Oxfam in Hong Kong published its report on poverty in the territory, which showed that the number of working poor families had been increasing, from around 172,600 in 2005 to about 192,500, a rise of 12%. The report also indicated that the incomes of the poorest one-fifth of families had shown no improvement in the past five-and-a-half years; and the median monthly incomes of the poorest one-tenth and one-fifth of families were HK$3,000 and HK$6,000 respectively.

In comparison, the median monthly income of the richest one-tenth of families had risen by 16% to HK$80,900, about 27 times that of the poorest one-tenth of families, reflecting that the gap between the rich and poor had been widening since 2004.[17]

In October 2010, the Hong Kong Council of Social Service released a research report, indicating that in the first half of the year the population of "poor families" in the territory reached 1.26 million, amounting to 18.1% of the population, a record high. The report also revealed that the median monthly income of the high-income household group had risen from HK$31,000 in the previous year to HK$32,950; while that of the low-income household group had basically remained unchanged at HK$9,000. The income gap between the two groups had been maintained at the ratio of 3.4:1 in the past four years; but in the first half of 2010, it rose to 3.7:1. Apparently, the income gap worsened in the economic recovery after the global financial tsunami in 2008.[18]

According to the Census and Statistics Department of the HKSAR government, in the quarter of September–November 2009, the number of households with a monthly income of HK$25,000 and above dropped

---

[17] *Ibid.* September 20, 2010. A working poor family is one which has at least one employed member; and its monthly income is less than half of the median monthly income of families in Hong Kong with the same number of members.

[18] *Ibid.*, October 4, 2010. Poor families in this research report were defined as those with incomes equal to or less than half of the median incomes of families in Hong Kong with the same number of members; for example, one-person families during the survey period each with monthly incomes of HK$3,275 or less, two-person families each with monthly incomes of HK$7,100 or less, three-person families each with monthly incomes of HK$10,000 or less, four-person families each with monthly incomes of HK$12,000 or less.

from that in the corresponding period of the previous year; while the number of households in various groups with a monthly income of below HK$10,000 had risen, with growth rates ranging from 2.4% to 9.7%.[19]

Earlier in August 2009, the Life Quality Research Centre of the Chinese University of Hong Kong released a set of statistical and survey data which demonstrated that the overall quality of life of Hong Kong people in the previous year had deteriorated to approximately the level in 2003, when the territory suffered severely from the Severe Acute Respiratory Syndrome (SARS) epidemic; and the overall index declined by 3.5% when compared with that in 2007. The community's evaluation of the economy and its ability to purchase accommodation through mortgage had dropped sharply, falling by 30% and 33% respectively; the index on satisfaction with the government's performance also dropped by 29%.[20]

Since most Hong Kong people accorded top priority to the economy when their living standards fell, their evaluation of the Donald Tsang administration would naturally be adversely affected; and it appeared that it had become an established trend. Before the territory's return to China, Hong Kong people rated the British administration highly. The colonial administration received a much better evaluation than that given to the British and Chinese governments; and the British government tended to secure a slightly better assessment than the Chinese government. Since Hong Kong's return to the Motherland, the situation had been reversed. In the end of the first decade and the beginning of the second decade in the new century, Hong Kong people have demonstrated a considerably higher degree of trust in the central government and a lower degree of satisfaction with the HKSAR government (see Table 18.1).

In the past, the gap between the rich and poor in Hong Kong had been substantial. At the beginning of the 1970s, the then Governor, Sir Murray MacLehose, made a substantial commitment in the public housing and education sectors, thus offering significant improvements in the quality of life at the grassroots level. However, neither the British administration nor the community were attracted to the "welfare society" model. Most important of all, before the Asia-Pacific financial crisis in 1997–1998,

---

[19] *Ibid.*, January 20, 2010.
[20] *Ibid.*, August 14, 2009.

Table 18.1: Hong Kong people's Evaluations of Donald Tsang (the Chief Executive), the HKSAR Government, and the Central People's Government, as Reflected by Public opinion Surveys, 2005–2010 (half-yearly averages)

Date of Survey	HK People's Rating of Donald Tsang (A) — Supporting Rate	HK People's Satisfaction with HKSAR Government (B) — Very Satisfied/ Quite Satisfied	HK People's Satisfaction with HKSAR Government (B) — Very Dissatisfied/ Not Quite Satisfied	HK People's Trust in Central Government (C) — Very Trust/ Quite Trust	HK People's Trust in Central Government (C) — Quite Distrust/Very Distrust
July–Dec 2010	53.10%	31.30%	35.30%	41.70%	22.10%
Jan–June 2010	51.40%	29%	38.70%	43.70%	30.40%
July–Dec 2009	52.90%	31.70%	32%	47.90%	16%
Jan–June 2009	53.90%	28%	31.20%	52.60%	15.40%
July–Dec 2008	53.20%	27%	30%	53.10%	14.40%
Jan–June 2008	63.50%	47.60%	31.20%	54.90%	13.40%
July–Dec 2007	64.90%	51.60%	29.60%	54.40%	15.60%
Jan–June 2007	66.10%	49.40%	14.10%	49.90%	15.50%
July–Dec 2006	62.90%	42%	15.10%	44.60%	19.70%
Jan–June 2006	67.30%	51.50%	10.90%	48.50%	18.70%
July–Dec 2005	67.40%	49.20%	12.60%	46.80%	24.40%
Jan–June 2005	68%	29.10%	28.80%	43.20%	24.70%

Notes:
1. Question asked for (A) — On the whole, do you support Donald Tsang? The other options were half-half and don't know/hard to say, which are not included in this table.
2. Question asked for (B) — Are you satisfied with the performance of the HKSAR Government? The other options were half-half and don't know/hard to say, which are not included in this table.
3. Question asked for (C) — On the whole, do you trust the Beijing Central Government? The other options were half-half and don't know/hard to say, which are not included in this table.

Source: Public Opinion Programme, The University of Hong Kong, http://hkupop.hku.hk/

Hong Kong people considered the territory a place full of opportunities, where individuals' efforts would be rewarded. Even those who lacked the educational qualifications and prospects for upward social mobility would still pin their hopes on their second generation, who hopefully would become professionals and business executives through tertiary education. The alleviation of inter-generational poverty became a social issue only by the end of the first decade in the twenty-first century.

In view of the globalization process, Hong Kong understood that it had to become a knowledge economy. Hence, the competitiveness of the low-education, low-skill labor force was in sharp decline; and the income gap of the labor force was widening. In the economic integration between Hong Kong and the Mainland, the former's labor-intensive industries moved to the Pearl River Delta in the early 1980s, and the labor-intensive services followed. Meanwhile, the inflow of immigrants from the Mainland expanded the supply of unskilled laborers with a low level of education, contributing to the phenomena of increased population of "working-poor" families, lack of improvement in incomes during the economic recovery after the global financial crisis in 2008, etc.

In September 2010, a survey revealed that among the fourth-generation Hong Kong people (born between 1976 and 1990) interviewed, 20% had experienced downward social mobility in the past five years, i.e., moving down the occupational ladder. This downward movement was more conspicuous among the strata of low-skilled and unskilled workers, which constituted 44% of the group of affected interviewees. Over half of the respondents admitted that they had no opportunities for upward social mobility because of low educational qualifications.

According to this survey, 51.9% of the fourth-generation Hong Kong people (assuming those who arrived at Hong Kong round about 1949 and before were the first generation) interviewed believed that they had failed to secure upward social mobility opportunities because of their "low educational qualifications"; 38.9% of the respondents blamed the Hong Kong economy; and 33.3% considered the fact that they had not worked hard enough and that faulty government policies were the root causes respectively.[21]

It was relatively easy to understand that those with "low educational qualifications" lacked upward social mobility opportunities; what about those with high educational qualifications? At the end of the 2000s and early 2010s, there was much media discussion on the frustrations and anger of the "post-1980s" generation, including university graduates who

---

[21] *Ibid.*, September 13, 2010. The survey was conducted by a consultancy firm commissioned by the Hong Kong Association of Professionals and Senior Executives in May–July 2010.

were regarded as social elite. Naturally, the supply of university graduates was increasing, and they had to adjust their expectations to avoid the scenario of "the higher the expectation, the bigger the disappointment".

In 2008-2009, the median monthly salary of a fresh university graduate was around HK$11,000. If the young person stayed with his or her parents, there was still some money to spend. The major grievance of young graduates is that, after working for ten years, their monthly salary might still stay at the level of below HK$30,000. Breakthroughs might occur during boom times, but their remuneration would often fall back to the usual level in economic difficulties. If, unfortunately, one became unemployed for more than half a year, there was a danger of being marginalized in the job market.

Ownership of residential property was often beyond young professionals and executives with satisfactory incomes. In the spring of 2010, a young couple complained in a radio phone-in program that as a doctor and a lawyer (the most enviable professions in the territory) respectively, they could not afford to buy a flat. Donald Tsang suggested that they should consider the northwestern districts in the New Territories. The episode became a hot talking-point in the community for a while. Obviously the younger generation was not optimistic about its future.

IV Social Cleavages and Collusion between the Government and Big Business

The pro-Beijing camp was generally unhappy with the performance of the Donald Tsang administration. Their major complaints were two: the Tsang administration failed to tackle the broad structural problems of the economy; and it has allowed dissatisfaction in the community to accumulate, exacerbating various types of confrontations. Local media observed that the central leadership appreciated the performance of the Edmund Ho administration in Macau more.

From an ideological point of view, the pro-Beijing camp did not insist on upholding the economic philosophy of "positive non-interventionism". It considered the China model a success, and believed that it was a good thing that the HKSAR government had the capability to engage in macro-economic adjustment and control. It looked for good results. At the same time, it was concerned with the gradual decline of the territory's international competitiveness, and that the Tsang administration was unable to turn the tide. The lack of achievements in the promotion of the six strategic industries and the limited success in economic co-operation with the Mainland were two of the foci of their criticisms.

These criticisms were widely shared by the people of Hong Kong. They considered that the maintenance of the rule of law and the reliability of the territory's financial system contributed to much reducing the potential damage of the Asia-Pacific financial crisis of 1997–1998 and the global financial tsunami in 2008–2009. However, Hong Kong had no significant new, innovative industries and services, and the greatest threat was a slow decline in its competitiveness.

In early 2010, a report on the development of provincial economic competitiveness in China in 2008–2009 published in Beijing indicated that Hong Kong's ranking declined from the first in 2007 to second in 2008, surpassed by Taiwan and also witnessed a narrowing of its lead over Beijing and Shanghai. It was Shanghai that secured the central leadership's endorsement to become an international financial centre in 2020, and Shanghai's ambition had an impact on Hong Kong too. The territory realized that it had to extend its lead in the years ahead and consolidate its status as an important international financial centre, otherwise its competitiveness would be weakened. But besides asking for Beijing's favourable policies in allowing Hong Kong to develop its *renminbi* business, the Donald Tsang administration did not have a credible response plan.[22]

The exacerbation of social cleavages was in violation of the broad objective of developing a harmonious society. During the Tsang administration, there was no repetition of the large-scale protest rallies of 2003 and 2004, but the community's evaluation of its performance was far from impressive. Donald Tsang declared that he did not think much of public opinion polls on his evaluation, but the resource allocation of his personal staff obviously showed that he cared for his image-building and the public responses to his policies.

In his second term, Donald Tsang did not have to worry about his re-election, and he had ample room to consider serious reforms and the

---

[22] *Ibid.*, March 1, 2010.

introduction of important policies. Political reforms had to be cleared with the central leadership; but the broadening of the tax base and the introduction of a value-added tax, a program for the provision of long-term finance for medical care etc., would all make significant contributions to the territory's development. The Donald Tsang administration, however, was avoiding controversial issues all the time; its low level of support was probably an important consideration, and the difficulty of arriving at a consensus in the community undoubtedly was a serious obstacle.

The latter was related to the exacerbation of various types of social cleavages, and they in turn were the result of the failure of the HKSAR government to mobilize the community for the long-term development of the territory. The widening of the gap between the rich and the poor was an increasingly serious structural problem, like that in Mainland China. However, there was one big difference between the two: people in the Mainland had enjoyed an impressive improvement in living standards in the past three decades and more, and they had confidence that tomorrow would even be better. In contrast, the majority of Hong Kong people consider that their quality of life had been in decline since the territory's return to the Motherland, and they were not optimistic regarding the prospects of an improvement of their living standards in the future. More important still, they did not believe that their government cared about their difficulties and demands.

Political reform was a significant bottleneck. The British administration was not an elected government, and its legitimacy was based on its performance.[23] Since Hong Kong's return to the Motherland, the performance of the HKSAR government had been disappointing, and the legitimacy accumulated before 1997 had been much eroded. Donald Tsang was obviously not a charismatic leader. As he was not interested in promoting democratic reforms, and he was not perceived to be performing well, his administration suffered from a legitimacy deficit. The only appeal of his administration was probably the support from the Chinese leadership.

---

[23] Joseph Y. S. Cheng, "Political Modernisation in Hong Kong", *The Journal of Commonwealth & Comparative Politics*, Vol. 27, No. 3, November 1989, pp. 294–320.

Since the design of the policy for securing the return of Hong Kong in the era of Deng Xiaoping, a very important consideration on the part of the Chinese leadership had been the maintenance of investors' confidence, hence their interests have been well protected.[24] A significant example was the stipulation in the Basic Law that legislators could not propose an increase in government expenditure, to ensure that the business community's taxation burden would not be made to rise too readily. As the local major business groups developed and expanded their investment in the Mainland, their influence on the Chinese leadership had correspondingly increased.

Top business leaders in Hong Kong had more contacts with Chinese leaders than the Chief Executive did; and they were the key group consulted by Beijing regarding the choice of the Chief Executive. In the early 2010s, there was a saying in the Mainland: previously tycoons courted senior officials, at this stage it was the other way round. The same applied to Hong Kong.

During British colonial rule, top civil servants made policies in a neutral manner without conflicts of interest; and the performance of the civil service government was appreciated by the community. After 1997, in the eyes of Hong Kong people, the HKSAR government increasingly favoured the major business groups at their expense. The lower social strata complain that they had not been able to enjoy the fruits of economic development; and the middle-class's sense of political impotence had grown.

The condition of the real estate market was probably most frustrating from the latter's point of view. Middle-class families often spent their life savings to buy their accommodation, and historically real estate developers refused to offer the exact measurements of their flats. Various phenomena of "inflated construction areas" were worsening. When prospective buyers went to see model units, they were often not allowed to take photographs or measurements. This arrogance of real estate tycoons gave rise to resentment against the rich which had become a media discussion topic in

---

[24] See Lu Ping's oral account compiled by Qian Yijiao, *Lu Ping's Oral Account on the Return of Hong Kong to China* (in Chinese), Hong Kong: Joint Publishing, 2009.

the early 2010s, and this emotion spread to cover the HKSAR government as well.

The "Lehman Brothers mini-bond issue" during the global financial tsunami caused many protests, and the protesters also severely criticized the inadequate supervision on the part of the government. In fact, the government had been catering to the interests of banks and other financial institutions; which had no obligation to inform their clients of the commissions charged by agents in the sales of their insurance and financial products. The supermarket business in the territory was a duopoly, even Carrefour failed to enter the market despite its success in the Mainland. Various real estate groups favoured their respective associated telecommunications firms in their housing projects so that the development of a territory-wide telecommunications platform had been handicapped. All these practices not only violated consumers' interests, they also adversely affected Hong Kong's long-term development.

In his Policy Address in October 2010, Donald Tsang finally indicated that his administration would tackle the issue of "inflated construction areas" by requiring real estate developers to provide exact measurements of their flats. But the HKSAR government then offered a "grace period" and stated that it would seek a consensus with real estate developers. In 2012, the community was still waiting to see if the Donald Tsang administration was serious in exerting pressure on them.[25]

During the tenure of the Tsang administration, there emerged more and more criticisms of collusion between the government and big business. An obvious indicator was the appointments to the government's advisory committees, for which the responsibility clearly fell on Donald Tsang and his top officials. Following the practice of his predecessor, membership of the government's advisory committee system was largely limited to between 400 and 600 people, who were mainly key members of the major business groups and their families as well as professionals associated with these business groups.

This situation was even less open than that in the 1970s and 1980s when the British administration was eager to involve some dissenting voices in the advisory committee system to ensure that a broader spectrum

---

[25] See footnote 9.

of views was heard and to demonstrate its liberal position. Further, the British administration established a convention that a community leader should not serve on more than six advisory committees nor serve on any committee for more than six years. During the Donald Tsang administration, this convention ceased to be observed. Media reports indicated that there were a few "kings of public offices" who served on dozens of government bodies; and there were members who served for more than six years in some advisory committees.

Moreover, many young members of the second and third generations of prominent business families often received appointments to important advisory committees. "Senior officials courting tycoons" was perceived as the only explanation. This situation has also discouraged many professionals who were eager to serve the government as a contribution to the community.

The legitimacy deficit of the Donald Tsang administration, the community's perception that it ignored Hong Kong people's interests, policies favouring major business groups, and the gradual blocking of consultation channels, all worked to exacerbate social divisions. The administration's response was the avoidance of controversial policy issues, reducing itself to a lame-duck government.

V Political Reforms and the Erosion of the HKSAR's Autonomy

During Donald Tsang's campaign for re-election as Chief Executive, he told journalists that he would "engage in a tough game" to settle the challenging issue of political reforms. In his first policy address after re-election, he stressed that he had a constitutional duty to resolve the question of political reforms in the territory.[26]

In spring 2010, however, both central government officials and the Donald Tsang administration indicated that the latter did not have the authority to tackle the political development of the territory beyond 2012

---

[26] See the policy address delivered by Donald Tsang on October 10, 2007 entitled "A New Direction for Hong Kong"; see all major local newspapers of the following day for commentaries.

in their promotion of the latter's political reform package. This begged the question: When did the Donald Tsang administration lose the authority to handle political reform beyond 2012? When did the central government take back this authority from the HKSAR government? Both the central government and the HKSAR government still owed Hong Kong people an explanation.

For the Hong Kong people, the general understanding of the Basic Law was that, for amendments of the method for selecting the Chief Executive for terms subsequent to the year 2007, the endorsement of a two-thirds majority of the full Legislative Council, the consent of the Chief Executive, and the approval of the NPCSC had to be secured. Similarly, amendments to the method for forming the Legislative Council could be made only if the endorsement of a two-thirds majority of the full Legislative Council and the consent of the Chief Executive were secured; and it had to be reported to the NPCSC for record.

There were no stipulations in the Basic Law that the HKSAR government had first to seek the authorization of the NPCSC before it could deal with the roadmap and the timetable of the political reforms beyond its present term. During the drafting of the Basic Law, Hong Kong people were not aware that there had been such discussions on the prerequisite of NPCSC authorization. Nonetheless, it was apparent that when the next HKSAR government intended to approach the abolition of function constituencies in the Legislative Council by 2020, it had to seek the NPCSC's authorization first.

When the Tsang administration announced its political reform package, Maria Tam Wai-chu, a Hong Kong member of the Committee for the Basic Law of the HKSAR under the NPCSC, revealed in a Radio Television Hong Kong (RTHK) television talk-show that "universal and equal representation" applied to the electoral right of Hong Kong people and it would be defined by the central authorities in Beijing, and not be based on any international human rights document. When did the central authorities arrive at this important decision? Had the HKSAR government been consulted on this? If so, why didn't the Tsang administration consult the Hong Kong community, or at least inform it of the "new policy"? It was certainly inappropriate for such a significant decision to be revealed to the Hong Kong people in a television talk-show.

There was gossip within local media circles in May–June 2010 that some pro-Beijing legal experts in Hong Kong were working to produce a definition of "universal and equal representation" applicable to the territory's future political reform packages. Was the Donald Tsang administration involved in this work? Certainly the incumbent HKSAR government had to be accountable to the Hong Kong public regarding Maria Tam's revelation. Further, it was obliged to ensure that Hong Kong people would be involved and consulted in this process. Regrettably we had not heard anything from the Tsang administration in this regard.

On May 24, 2010, after meeting the Democratic Party delegation on the political reform issue, Li Gang, Deputy Director of the Central Liaison Office in Hong Kong, was at pains in attempting to explain to the media that his office was not a "second governing team" in the territory. This was actually the first local press conference on the part of the leadership of the Central Liaison Office, and the "second governing team" was an important issue to be clarified. Why should Li Gang consider this something to be clarified in this first press conference, as no reporter raised this issue? Certainly he realized that many Hong Kong people had this perception; and it was much more than an idea floated in an article by his former colleague Cao Erbao published in *Study Times*, the official journal of the Central Party School in Beijing.[27]

When the central government authorized the Central Liaison Office to meet some pro-democracy groups in Hong Kong, it should have carefully considered whether the latter should assume the role of receiving messages from the entire Hong Kong community and serving as a bridge between Beijing and Hong Kong on the issue of political reforms. If this was the case, then it had to observe the principles of openness and transparency. If the Central Liaison Office had indeed assumed this role, then the Chinese leadership had to consider the impact on the HKSAR government and the HKSAR's autonomy. The Donald Tsang administration obviously had neglected its duty to safeguard the HKSAR's hitherto high degree of autonomy. In the early 2010s, more and

---

[27] See all major Hong Kong newspapers on May 25, 2010. They all referred to Cao Erbao, "Hong Kong's Governing Force under the Conditions of 'One Country, Two Systems'" (in Chinese), *Study Times*, a publication of the Central Party School in Beijing.

more protest rallies related to political reforms chose to approach the Central Liaison Office; this phenomenon was a good reflection that Hong Kong people realized that the Donald Tsang administration had no role in this regard.

In June 2010, when the Democratic Party released its political reform proposals, officials of the central government and Central Liaison Office, Rita Fan, Hong Kong deputy of the NPCSC, and Elsie Leung, deputy chairman of the Committee for the Basic Law of the HKSAR under the NPCSC, all went public to declare that the proposals contravened the related decisions of the NPCSC. But in less than a week's time, they all reversed their position: not only were the proposals said to be in line with the related decisions of the NPCSC, they also highly praised the proposals.

According to the Constitution of the People's Republic of China, the NPCSC has the authority to interpret the Constitution, like the Supreme Court of the U.S. and the Constitutional Courts of some European countries. The reversal of their previous positions on the part of the Chinese officials, Rita Fan and Elsie Leung on their assessment of the Democratic Party's political reform proposals seriously discredited the solemnity of the NPCSC's decisions.

The perception of the Hong Kong community was that as long as the central leadership had made the decision, the Chinese officials concerned would follow it to interpret the NPCSC's related decisions. Hence, they could only see the will of the leadership, and they failed to see a defence of the rule of law.

On June 21, 2010, the people of Hong Kong came to know that the Chinese authorities had endorsed the Democratic Party's political reform proposals; and on June 23, 2010 the Legislative Council had to vote on the revised political reform bill. There were significant differences between the original version of the HKSAR government's reform proposals and the revised version incorporating the amendments suggested by the Democratic Party. Regarding the former, there was a formal consultative document to facilitate discussions in the community; regarding the latter, the Hong Kong people only had a rough idea through media reports. The community was certainly confused by the conflicting statements made by the Chinese officials, Rita Fan and Elsie Leung on the proposals of the Democratic Party.

Through the intervention of the central government which succeeded in securing the support of the Democratic Party and the Hong Kong Association for Democracy and People's Livelihood, the Donald Tsang administration had enough votes in the Legislative Council to overrule proposals to delay voting on the political reform bill and to pass the revised political reform bill. However, due process required adequate time for Hong Kong people to deliberate on a very significant political issue. Though the Donald Tsang administration had to give way to the central government in the handling of political reforms, and it had no political will to defend the high degree of autonomy of the HKSAR, at least it should have the decency to respect due process in the passage of the political reform bill.

VI Differential Treatments and the Recruitment of Talents

The British administration was a civil service government. During the first term of the C.H. Tung administration, Tung did not get along well with his Chief Secretary for Administration, Anson Chan; and he had difficulty effectively exercising his command over the civil servants. In his second term beginning in 2002, Tung introduced the Principal Officials Accountability System (POAS), with the objective of forming his own political team. Donald Tsang went a step further to expand the political appointments to include a batch of deputy secretaries and political assistants. This generated new assets to reward the Chief Executive's supporters, thus facilitating the attraction of the community's elites to support the government.

Theoretically, the POAS served to recruit talents from the business community, the professions, academia etc. to help remedy the inadequacies of the existing civil service; more important still, it enabled the civil service to maintain its political neutrality. Regarding the former, apparently the C.H. Tung administration had failed to attract any heavyweights from the business community to join the government; and the situation continued to deteriorate during the Donald Tsang administration whose policy secretaries almost all came from the civil service. Under such circumstances, Hong Kong people naturally raised the question — if the political team was roughly the same batch of top civil servants, what was the point of introducing the POAS?

Difficulty in external recruitment was partly related to the absence of the American political culture where highly successful business leaders felt an obligation to accept public service with the associated political risks and sacrifices in income. Most local business leaders were not too concerned with the question of financial remuneration; they were discouraged mainly because they did not find the idea or opportunity attractive as they considered that as policy secretaries they might not be able to achieve much while attracting a lot of criticisms.

The appointments of deputy secretaries and political assistants on the part of Donald Tsang were quite controversial on issues such as their nationalities, the confidentiality of their salaries etc. These issues demonstrated a lack of careful consideration by the Donald Tsang administration; moreover, Hong Kong people did not seem to have a high evaluation of the appointees. After some years of service, they still did not seem to have won the community's support.

The Commission on Strategic Development deserved some attention. It was established by C.H. Tung in 1998; and at the beginning of the Donald Tsang administration it was considered the most important advisory body. In October 2005, in his first formal policy address, Donald Tsang declared that he would substantially expand its membership by inviting talents from different fields so that it might serve as a platform for all sectors of the community to explore with the government major issues pertaining to Hong Kong's long-term development, especially at the early stage of policy formulation. Four committees were then set up within the commission; and the commission and its four committees were served by a secretariat established within the Central Policy Unit, which provided both secretarial and research support. Despite the apparent priority accorded to the commission, the Hong Kong people hardly felt during the tenure of Donald Tsang its impact.[28]

In a democratic, pluralistic polity, the civil service has to maintain its neutrality, treating all political parties in the same manner. Since the introduction of the POAS, the defence of government policies should no

---

[28] Latter, *op. cit.*, pp. 115–119.

longer be the civil service's responsibility. But Donald Tsang stated that "there is a difference between those who are close to and those who are distant from the government"; and during his administration, in the District Councils and in many other areas, activists in the pro-democracy movement obviously did not feel that they had been given equal treatment by the civil service. In fact, not a few responsible persons of social service voluntary bodies and members of official advisory committees who had no political party affiliations considered that they were cold-shouldered by senior civil servants after openly articulating criticisms of the government.

These practices might create some deterrence effect against critics; but in the long term, Hong Kong people became more alienated from the government. On the other hand, the civil service's low morale was an open secret; the community's dissatisfaction with the Donald Tsang administration naturally affected its enthusiasm. Most political appointees under the POAS failed to win respect and support. Many civil servants lamented the fact that their superiors spent most of their time responding to media criticisms to the extent that they could not concentrate on their work. The low morale of the civil service in turn adversely affected the performance of the government, thus attracting more criticisms, and completed the vicious circle.

VII Conclusion

The economy of Hong Kong fortunately could still maintain stable growth. As its dependence on the Mainland economy increased and the latter achieved impressive growth, it naturally benefitted Hong Kong, which was already a mature economic entity, and the community understood that it could not expect very high growth rates. Middle-class households also realized that they enjoyed probably the highest living standards in Asia. In a society where the rule of law was respected and law and order well maintained, Hong Kong people felt secure. Despite the gradual decline of the territory's international competitiveness, the community was still proud of its achievements. All these were the foundation of Hong Kong's good governance. Though the Donald Tsang administration's performance was lacklustre, the government machinery on the whole ran effectively.

Dissatisfaction was accumulating in Hong Kong society, but most people's response was a sense of helplessness, not anger. Radical political actions symbolized by the protests of the League of Social Democrats, though far from radical by western European standards, could only attract the support of a minority, normally estimated to be around 10% of the public. Most Hong Kong people resented its protest activities. Their value orientations tended to be conservative, and they favoured the maintenance of the status quo. They selectively supported gradual reforms, and were worried that radical political campaigns might destabilize the society. The most popular political leaders attract the public's support by moderate images, and were perceived to have been articulating the voices of the silent majority. They were definitely not revolutionary leaders.[29]

In the eyes of the Hong Kong people, the widening of the gap between the rich and poor, the reduction in opportunities for upward social mobility and the decline in the territory's international competitiveness were broad trends; and they only hoped that through hard work they could be exceptions to the trends. Fortunately, a vast majority of Hong Kong people still believed that their efforts would be rewarded. In this context, the avoidance of controversial issues on the part of the Donald Tsang administration might not have been unwise, at least it could avoid confrontations and maintain stability.

A sense of helplessness usually did not lead to political confrontations. Most Hong Kong people perceived democracy as an ideal; but since the Chinese leadership was against it, the most they could do was to take part in protest rallies. They desired a better social security system too, but few would accept the Singaporean model of contributing a substantial portion of their incomes for a satisfactory pension scheme and a medical insurance program.

Perhaps among all people, C.H. Tung should be the most grateful to Donald Tsang. Comparing two Chief Executives who had not done much for them in terms of economic development, social services and political reforms, the Hong Kong people definitely favored an honest old man with

---

[29] Joseph Y. S. Cheng, "Hong Kong Since Its Return to China: A Lost Decade?", in his edited volume, *The Hong Kong Special Administrative Region in Its First Decade*, Hong Kong: City University of Hong Kong Press, 2007, pp. 35–47.

his heart in the right place than an arrogant leader who had little sympathy for the grassroots.

Acknowledgement

This chapter is originally published in *The Second Chief Executive of Hong Kong SAR: Evaluating the Tsang Years 2005–2012*, ed. Joseph Y.S. Cheng, pp. 1–30, © 2013 City University of Hong Kong. Used by permission of City University of Hong Kong Press. All rights reserved.

Chapter 19

The 2012 Chief Executive Election in Hong Kong and the Challenges for the Chinese Authorities

In recent years, Chinese leaders openly indicated that the Chief Executive of Hong Kong Special Administrative Region (HKSAR) has to be someone who loves the motherland and Hong Kong, has the competence to govern the territory effectively, and enjoys a high degree of trust and popularity among the local people. Few have argued against these qualifications; the pro-democracy movement instead has been concentrating on the universal rights of democracy and insisting that Hong Kong people should be given a choice. After all, selection of C. H. Tung as the first and Donald Tsang as the second Chief Executive had been disappointing. Both of their approval ratings were very low by the end of their tenures and most Hong Kong people considered their administrations unsatisfactory.

Up till mid-2011, the 2012 Chief Executive election was expected to be a smooth process with few surprises. Henry Tang was broadly perceived to be the candidate groomed by the Chinese authorities for more than a decade, holding consecutively the positions of Secretary for Commerce and Economic Development, Financial Secretary and Secretary for Administration in the first two HKSAR administrations. However, a challenger, C.Y. Leung, then emerged; apparently the Chinese authorities had to accept competition among the two pro-establishment candidates. It was said that Beijing had hoped to see a gentlemanly competition openly pledged by the two candidates too. Then scandals were exposed, initially with the extra-marital affairs of Tang, then the conflict of interest in the West Kowloon Cultural Complex project on the part of Leung, the illegal construction in Tang's residence, etc. The scandals not only attracted the community's attention, but also weakened the credibility of the two candidates, leading to the conclusion that the new Chief Executive would have a very difficult road ahead.

I The Community's Demands and Grievances

In February 2011, Financial Secretary John Tsang unveiled his budget proposals which included an offer of HK$6,000 to the Mandatory Provident Fund (MPF, pension) account of every citizen. At that time, the HKSAR government managed to deliver a rather impressive report card on the economy — 5.8% of economic growth in 2010, unemployment rate down to 3.8% and a budgetary surplus of over HK$40 billion from the previous fiscal year. The community's response however was unexpectedly critical, and the government quickly conceded by delivering the HK$6,000 directly and immediately to the people without looking into the details. It led to further controversies as to who should and should not be given the subsidy, i.e., the recent immigrants and Hong Kong citizens residing overseas, as well as procedural matters.

The dissatisfaction with the government including its economic performance was deep-seated and structural. The community, including the political elites and the pro-establishment groups, were concerned with the slow but steady decline in Hong Kong's international economic competitiveness, especially when compared with major coastal cities in China like Shanghai. The local business community at this stage closely monitored Shanghai's plan of establishing itself as an international financial centre in 2015 (ahead of the original schedule of 2020). The message from influential think-tanks in China was for Hong Kong to make good use of the remaining window of opportunity and the opportunities of offering offshore *renminbi* financial services. The other major common concern was the widening rich-poor gap and the resulting social and political polarization.

From the ordinary people's point of view, the widening rich–poor gap had become more significant in the globalization process, which in

Hong Kong meant closer economic integration with China. Hong Kong people in the past decades have not embraced economic equality or a "welfare society" along the Western and Northern European lines. At his stage the community was worried about the increasing influence of major business groups at their expense and the decline in upward social mobility opportunities especially for the young.

There was an increasing concern of a "collusion between top officials and the tycoons". After decades of consumers' demand, the real estate industry still failed to disclose the exact measurements of the flats they sold. Families who spent their life earnings on a property were given measurements of "construction areas", with actual usable space amounting to 65%–85% of the given "construction areas". The HKSAR government only issued guidelines which have only been implemented since the beginning of 2013 and not regulations for the industry. The arrogance of the industry was further demonstrated by its refusal to allow prospective buyers to take actual measurements and photographs of its model flats.

After years of charging excessive management fees to MPF contributors, the financial services industry finally agreed to reduce its charges by a small margin. There was obvious room for further reductions, but the government had not exerted pressure on the industry. Finally, in late-2011, small shopkeepers revealed that suppliers had threatened to cut off supplies if they sold a certain brand of quick noodles at prices below those of two major supermarket chains. Without an effective competition law, consumer rights were not safeguarded.

The Hong Kong people believe that many top government officials were eager to please tycoons to secure fat jobs for themselves upon retirement. A clear indicator was the appointment of the tycoons' family members to various important government advisory bodies. More importantly, major business leaders in Hong Kong enjoyed good access to Chinese leaders because of their investment activities in the Mainland. Top government officials understood that the former's assessments of their performance influenced the Chinese authorities' evaluations of their achievements.

The challenges facing Hong Kong were not unique. Taiwan and Singapore encountered similar problems. Despite an economic growth rate of slightly exceeding 10% in 2010, the ruling Kuomintang in Taiwan did not perform well in municipal elections in 2010. Similarly, despite an even more impressive economic growth rate of about 15% in 2010, the governing People's Action Party in Singapore only secured 60% of the electorate's support in the May 7, 2011, general election. Yet, Hong Kong differed from these two "little dragons of Asia" in terms of its strict *laissez-faire* economic philosophy and inadequate social security provisions supported by lower taxation.

As reflected by the academic analyses of China's major think-tanks, the Chinese authorities favoured a more interventionist approach to enhance the territory's international economic competitiveness. Donald Tsang in his policy address in October 2009 identified six strategic industries in which Hong Kong was considered to have an edge. However, without sovereign wealth funds, government-linked corporations and other instruments to promote their development, the Tsang administration could only offer small land grants and limited subsidies which were considered inadequate. Partly because of the low popular support, the Tsang administration lacked the political will to engage the community to deliberate on the broad changes required, and it was perceived as a lame-duck administration in its final years. The 2012 Chief Executive election therefore could have been a platform for meaningful policy discussions and debates especially in view of the competition.

Another important area for policy consultations and deliberations was social services. There was still no clear-cut consensus on the HKSAR government's future responsibilities and the associated burden of taxation. At this stage, the MPF was inadequate as a pension system for retirement. While the Hong Kong people were accustomed to relying on their savings, the improvement in life expectancy and the crises in the financial markets were causes for worry. Middle-class families were also concerned with the provision of hospital services in the public sector as their savings might not be adequate for long-term serious illnesses.

The Tsang administration did not offer any plans to strengthen the MPF scheme as additional payments from employers and employees were bound to be unpopular. Instead, it merely offered incentives to encourage people to acquire private sector health insurance. The proposal was not well received as people in general could not afford it and believe that public hospitals had to serve them. Middle-class families welcomed the limited incentives, but would rather the government assume the burden of serving as the insurer.

Public housing became a serious issue at this stage because of skyrocketing private housing prices which made private housing beyond the reach of the young. The Tsang administration stubbornly refused to revive the Home Ownership Scheme (HOS) until it was highlighted by Premier Wen Jiabao. This refusal to revive the HOS and expand the supply of public sector rental housing was broadly perceived as collusion with real estate developers.

In 1997, most people in Hong Kong desired the maintenance of the status quo; at this stage however they believed that reforms were seriously needed. The 2012 Chief Executive election had been disappointing as the media and the community concentrated on the scandals of the two pro-establishment candidates and not on policy platforms. It was easy for candidates to come up with policy proposals not substantiated by serious research and detailed consultations with the parties concerned.

II The Candidates and their Strategies

Until mid-2011, Tang was the favourite candidate to win. He was obviously groomed for the position and was believed to have the backing of Jiang Zemin. He enjoyed the support of the business community as he came from one of the Shanghai tycoon families; the business community believed that he would be status quo oriented and would not introduce major changes adversely affecting their interests. The civil service accepted him because he was perceived as incompetent and would therefore allow it a free hand.

Like the heir apparent in China's leadership succession process in the new century and before, Tang had been low-profile, avoided controversies or making enemies. Since the Hong Kong people did not know him well and had no say in the process, they did not have strong views. The political elites were well aware of his incompetence and concerned if he could handle a crisis like the Severe and Acute Respiratory Syndrome (SARS) epidemic in 2003 or the global financial tsunami in 2008–2009. However, this worry was irrelevant until a serious challenger emerged. Tang was over-confident and did not prepare well for the campaign. A Legislative

Councillor quipped of his mishandling of the scandals during his campaign: "Henry just prepared to assume the Chief Executive position; he never expected that he had to campaign hard for it."

Some political elites and seasoned journalists were well aware that C.Y. Leung had long been campaigning secretly for the Chief Executive position. However, they were not sure whether he would challenge Tang in 2012. Given Leung's age, he could wait till 2017; and there was of course the natural thinking that the Chinese authorities would handle the issue. In previous Chief Executive elections in Hong Kong and Macau, there were no precedents of keen, close competition and the outcomes were clear-cut before the voting processes. The reasons were obvious. The Chinese leadership wanted predictable outcomes in these elections and landslide victories for the winning candidates to establish and strengthen their respective authorities; keen competition could split up the pro-establishment camp and adversely affect its solidarity. Making too many electoral pledges by competing candidates in a close contest was considered unhealthy and in the case of Hong Kong, the pro-democracy Election Committee members should not be allowed to have an opportunity to decide on the election outcome if no candidate emerged as the winner with an absolute majority support in the first round of voting.

In the 2002 Chief Executive election, nominations were made open. Speculations had it that it was to ensure a smooth re-election for C.H. Tung whose performance was considered unsatisfactory by the general public and to avoid too many abstentions or even supporting votes for another candidate. In the end, since the Chinese authorities clearly endorsed Tung's re-election, more than 700 Election Committee members openly nominated him and there were simply not enough votes to nominate another candidate (100 votes needed in the then 800-member Election Committee). Tung was elected *ipso facto* as the only candidate. The open nomination process had become a very significant controlling mechanism for Beijing since most Election Committee members came from the establishment.

This was a serious challenge for C.Y. Leung. He needed to demonstrate that his candidacy had been endorsed by the Chinese authorities which accepted competition among pro-establishment candidates for the Chief Executive election. In the initial phase of the campaign and before the scandals of Henry Tang, there were strong doubts whether Leung could even secure the 150 votes needed for nomination. There was the obvious speculation that Beijing might not want to see keen competition between two pro-establishment candidates. This was why his key supporters reiterated that Leung had Beijing's endorsement.

Without the endorsement of the Chinese authorities, a pro-establishment aspirant could not even enter the race. This was exactly the case of Rita Fan and that of Regina Ip. Fan was a member of the Standing Committee of the National People's Congress and former chairperson of the Legislative Council. She indicated her intention to run rather early in the second half of 2011; she was a popular figure within the establishment. Her most significant advantage was her high approval ratings in public opinion polls; and if popular support was an important consideration of Chinese leaders, she might have been given a chance.

However, she hesitated for too long and gradually lost credibility. She finally announced that she would not run. Her candidacy aroused speculation that she was a potential backup candidate in Beijing's plan and she simply acted according to plan. There was also a suggestion that she was actually angling for a prestigious promotion to Vice Chairman of the National Committee of the Chinese People's Political Consultative Conference.

For Ip, no one doubted her political ambition. She was the Secretary for Security in 2002–2003 pushing hard for the unpopular Article 23 legislation. She subsequently resigned, went abroad for a brief period to study. She then ran for a seat in Legislative Council and became a very popular legislator. Her turnaround in terms of popularity was almost a miracle. However, she failed to secure votes for nomination because two pro-establishment candidates were already too many for the Chinese authorities. Her case demonstrated the controlling function of the open nomination process; in fact, she told the media that some Election Committee members had promised to vote for her (in the secret ballot process) pending her securing official nomination.

The story of Beijing's endorsement of C.Y. Leung was widely circulated in local political circles and in the media's gossip columns. Leung met Liu Yandong, then head of the Party Central United Front Department and member of the Political Bureau, as well as Liao Hui, former director of the Hong Kong and Macau Affairs Office of the State Council. Liao queried Leung on his intention to run and scolded him for not listening to the advice of Peng Qinghua, head of the Central Liaison Office in Hong Kong. Leung replied that Peng could not represent the central authorities and gave an account of his contributions on the return of Hong Kong to China as well as the development of the HKSAR after 1997. Liao warned that Leung might not even get the 150 Election Committee votes needed for his official nomination.

Apparently, the Chinese leadership allowed Leung to continue his campaign and did not deny that his candidacy was acceptable to Beijing. The position of the Chinese authorities was interesting; they accepted competition despite the potential undesirable effects explained earlier. They might believe that competition could generate a more liberal image and allowed them to keep their options open for a certain period of time for further study of the candidates and various parties' assessments of them. The idea of further study of the candidates naturally meant that public opinion would be a significant factor for consideration.

Hence Leung's strategy was to present himself as a candidate acceptable to the Chinese authorities and that he was a considerably more popular candidate in the eyes of the Hong Kong people for the Chinese leadership to endorse him, or at least allow an open competition between him and Tang. Leung was obviously a much more competent campaigner; he was successful in gradually narrowing the gap between him and Tang in public opinion polls and eventually establishing a lead over Tang after the latter's extramarital affairs went public.

Leung attempted to exploit the community's desire for changes and reforms, and its hope for an effective leader after the lacklustre performances of C.H. Tung and Donald Tsang. He was an excellent speaker in sharp contrast to Tang and worked hard to connect with people at the grassroots level. Tang was aware of his weaknesses and refused to debate with Leung and the pro-democracy candidate, Albert Ho before the formal nomination process. However, this avoidance only reinforced Tang's image that he was status quo oriented and would not introduce significant changes if elected. Worse still, his background naturally generated a linkage between him and the business community. Ordinary people did not know Leung well nor share the political elites' perception that he was aggressive and dangerous, thus improving his support level in public opinion polls. At the later stage, especially after the acknowledgement of his extramarital affairs, Tang became much more active in campaigning and even offered attractive policy proposals such as a HK$3,000 monthly allowance for the elderly.

For the pro-democracy camp, it was not very keen in participating in the 2012 Chief Executive election. The more radical wing believed that it should not participate in a "small circle election" as it would lend it credibility and legitimacy, or participate in an election that it could not win. In the last Chief Executive election, Alan Leong of the Civic Party, took part, secured enough Election Committee votes and was able to engage Donald Tsang in public debates as a formal candidate. This unprecedented progress had an element of novelty and demonstrated that the pro-democracy movement could do well in Election Committee elections among the professional categories. However, this time, there was already competition between Tang and Leung, and it was no longer a novelty.

The Democratic Party (DP) however decided to take part to make use of every election to spread its messages. It was also important to maintain the movement's support level in Election Committee elections to prepare for the 2017 Chief Executive election in which universal suffrage might be introduced. Most members of the pro-democracy movement still considered it a responsibility to present its demands and a comprehensive policy platform in the Chief Executive election to exert pressure on the HKSAR government.

The pro-democracy political groups did not do well in the District Council elections held in November 2011, but they did unexpectedly well in Election Committee elections in the following December especially in the functional constituencies of education, higher education, information technology, social welfare, and the legal profession. In the nursing, medical, engineering and accountancy functional constituencies, the groups achieved relatively satisfactory results. The initial objective was to secure at least 150 seats to ensure the official nomination of a pro-democracy candidate. The final result was 203 seats or so, much higher than the expected 170 to 180 seats, demonstrating the support of the professional middle-class.

Instead of consulting the political groups concerned, the pro-democracy movement started a primary election arrangement to elect a candidate. The primary election arrangement would be an acceptable way of electing the movement's candidate in the 2017 Chief Executive election when universal suffrage might be introduced. Competition was anticipated to be keen and it was important to have a primary election mechanism to ensure a legitimate contest while maintaining the movement's solidarity. The political parties in Taiwan learnt it the hard way in the first decade of this century.

The primary election arrangement was criticized by the local pro-Beijing media for involving only two candidates, Albert Ho of the DP and Frederick Fung of the Hong Kong Association for Democracy and People's Livelihood (HKADPL). It was based on a territory-wide public opinion survey (50% weighting) and actual voting by interested citizens on January 8, 2012 (50% weighting). Despite the crude facilities, about 34,000 Hong Kong people participated. Albert Ho won the primary election to represent the pro-democracy movement with 65% of the total weighted poll and voting.

The Election Committee elections and the primary election were achievements of the pro-democracy movement despite the odds. There were two drawbacks though. Two radical pro-democracy groups, the League of Social Democrats and People Power, protested against the primary election and the subsequent campaign activities of Albert Ho. They not only opposed the movement's participation in the Chief Executive election, but were strongly critical of the earlier endorsement of the Tsang administration's political reform proposal by the DP and the HKADPL as well as their engagement in negotiations with the Central Liaison Office in Hong Kong on the political reform package. These activities reinforced the public's perception of a divided pro-democracy movement, disappointing supporters.

Ho's campaign failed to attract much attention and his support level as reflected by public opinion surveys was low. The media was not interested in Ho's political platform as his chances of winning the election were slim and was therefore in no position to implement his policy proposals. It was overshadowed by the sensational pro-establishment candidates' scandals.

III More Scandals and Beijing's Dilemma

It was first reported in the media that Tang's residence in Kowloon Tong had a luxurious basement which was an illegal construction. The scandal itself was exacerbated by his mishandling which cast doubt on his integrity and competence in crisis management. Tang attempted to hide the embarrassing facts. Even when the details gradually emerged, he still did not come clean for a while. He finally apologized publicly, placing much of the blame on his wife. This caused an uproar in the community and many in opinion polls considered that he should abandon his campaign. He refused despite a sharp decline in his support level in opinion polls. Tang submitted his form with the open support of 379 Election Committee members, including the tycoons of the four major real estate groups and a representative sample of the richest business leaders.

It was speculated that the Chinese authorities continued to accept his candidacy, thus the support of the tycoons. This placed the Chinese authorities in a difficult position of being perceived as supporting an unpopular and incompetent candidate against the expressed will of the people. Public opinion therefore did not count in the eyes of the Chinese leadership which continued to defer to the interests of the business community. Business leaders were also ready to defy public opinion and embrace a highly discredited candidate to protect their own interests. There was probably a fear that since they had earlier indicated their support for Tang, the electoral victory of C.Y. Leung, who was somehow seen as a revengeful person, might hurt their business interests.

There was initially some speculation of a 'Plan B' on the part of the Chinese authorities. When Tang was seriously troubled by his illegal construction scandal, Regina Ip announced her renewed campaign to seek official nomination. However, she could only demonstrate the support of her own party leaders. Tsang Yok-sing, leader of the pro-Beijing Democratic Alliance for the Betterment and Progress of Hong Kong (DAB) and president of the Legislative Council, also stated publicly that he would consider entering the electoral race given that the DAB had enough Election Committee votes to support his official nomination. Tsang's consideration was interpreted as waiting for Beijing's endorsement, which did not come; and Tsang soon indicated that he would not run. Regina Ip, as expected, failed to secure enough support for her official nomination. Hence the Chinese authorities opted to maintain the status quo and rejected the execution of any plan B.

Introducing a 'Plan B' was probably feasible. If the Chinese authorities had insisted, Tsang Yuk-sing could have provided a viable alternative. However, introducing a 'Plan B' would have reinforced the perception that Chinese leaders were in full control and time was inadequate for serious preparation of another candidate. The community's perception that Tsang was a member of the Communist Party of China was also a serious handicap for his candidacy.

The Chinese leadership was apparently aware of the challenges ahead. The electoral process clearly showed that the Chief Executive election was a "small circle election" in which the Chinese authorities were in full control, and business leaders enjoyed significant influence. Worse still, not only did ordinary people not have the vote, public opinion did not seem to matter. Tang refused to abandon his campaign and the popular Regina Ip could not secure official nomination — Beijing was perceived to have a decisive role in these outcomes. As the campaign was dominated by scandals, there were no meaningful discussions of policy issues. The election could not bestow legitimacy for the new administration. The new Chief Executive, C.Y. Leung, has made some vague policy suggestions without thorough consultations and convincing policy research. The election probably had caused very damaging divisions within the pro-establishment camp weakening the administration.

Leung himself was soon involved in illegal construction scandals too, along with at least three members of his team (two ministers and an Executive Councillor) who were similarly plagued by other scandals. While the central leadership and Leung had appealed for a "grand reconciliation" within the establishment, it was overshadowed by the Legislative Council elections in September 2012 and the elections to the National People's Congress. There was no room for reconciliation before the elections. The Hong Kong people were worried about a deepening of the collusion between the administration and the business community as the new Chief Executive had lots of political debts to repay. He has found it difficult to attract respected community leaders to join his cabinet because of deep cleavages within the establishment and doubt in the ability and appeal of the new administration.

A series of opinion polls by the University of Hong Kong revealed that since 1997, the Hong Kong people identification with the Chinese nation as well as their trust of the Chinese authorities had been strengthening until 2008 or so when the trends reversed. It remained uncertain then whether the reversals were short-term or long-term. An explanation was the growing resentment towards increasingly obvious intervention by Chinese authorities and the Central Liaison Office in Hong Kong. It was significant that the DP entered into negotiations with the Central Liaison Office in 2010 regarding the political reform package.

In the eyes of the Hong Kong people, the Chinese leaders had thrice failed to pick good Chief Executives for the territory; giving the choice to the people could not be worse. The Chinese authorities should be responsible for the performance of the Chief Executive as they had made the selection. Meanwhile, Chinese leaders were offering preferential economic policies to the territory to support its economy in order to maintain social and political stability especially after the massive protest rallies in 2003 and 2004. This was expected to continue.

IV The Final Stage of the Election Campaign and the Election Result

When formal nomination closed on February 29, 2012, the status quo was maintained despite the scandals. However, after ten days or so, local media began to report that the Chinese leadership had decided to back Leung. The pro-Beijing DAB and the Hong Kong Federation of Trade Unions openly indicated support for Leung, who later chose to avoid a number of public electoral seminars and became more conservative and restrained in his policy statements. On the other hand, Tang worked considerably harder for his campaign and appeared more liberal in his policy pledges.

In a formal debate among the candidates on March 16, 2012, Tang revealed that in Executive Council meetings in 2003, Leung had proposed exerting pressure on Commercial Radio for allowing severe criticisms of the HKSAR government in its programs by shortening the licence period;

further, Leung suggested the use of the Police Tactical Unit and tear gas to deal with protesters against Article 23 legislation. The revelations violated the rule of confidentiality for Executive Council meetings; Tang was desperately trying to discredit Leung and erode his popularity.

In the final week of the campaign, it was reported that senior Chinese officials including Politburo member and State Councillor Liu Yandong stationed in Shenzhen crossed the border to ensure that Leung would secure an absolute majority in the election in the first ballot. This was essential to not only demonstrate that Leung enjoyed a reasonably high level of support, but also avoid the pro-democracy camp having a "kingmaker" role in a stalemate. As most pro-democracy Election Committee members publicly stated that they would not take part in the second ballot should their candidate be eliminated, there was the possibility of an aborted election, i.e., none of the candidates managed to secure an absolute majority of 601 votes. The Chinese authorities' efforts to ensure Leung's respectable electoral victory constituted gross interference in local politics which made a lot of Hong Kong people uncomfortable.

Most business leaders including Li Ka-shing openly stood by Henry Tang despite persuasion by Chinese leaders. It was rumored that Xi Jinping met Li but still failed to change his mind. This revealed business leaders' distrust of Leung, and their understanding that Tang was still an acceptable candidate for Beijing and their position would not attract the wrath of the Chinese leadership.

The Public Opinion Programme of the University of Hong Kong held a mock election for Hong Kong people on March 23 and 24, attracting the participation of 222,990 people. C.Y. Leung, Henry Tang, and Albert Ho received 17.8%, 16.3%, and 11.4% of the votes, respectively, while a good 54.6% cast blank votes, indicating their refusal to vote for any of the three candidates and implicitly supporting the appeal that an aborted election would be the preferred scenario. The pro-democracy Election Committee members also organized a protest rally on March 24, the day before the election, articulating their opposition to the Chinese authorities' blatant involvement in the Chief Executive election. Interestingly, Leung's popularity rating as reflected by public opinion surveys dropped by about 10% once the community learnt that he was endorsed by the Chinese leadership, while that of Henry Tang recovered somewhat.

The election result was predictable and offered no surprise. Leung received 689 votes, an absolute majority, in the first round of voting, while Tang and Ho received 285 votes and 76 votes respectively. There were 82 invalid votes and 61 Election Committee members were absent.

V Democratization: Significance for Hong Kong People and the Challenges Ahead

In principle, Hong Kong people supported democracy, a democracy that was quite different from that in the Western world. Some people might be satisfied with the administration for being responsive to their demands, while some might accept legitimacy of the administration based on performance. In the direct elections of the Legislative Council, the pro-democracy groups normally received 55%–60% of the votes because people appreciate the importance of checks and balances. In the 2012 Chief Executive election, according to opinion polls, only 1% of the respondents expected Ho to win; at best, slightly more than 10% of the respondents chose him as the Chief Executive. The community was realistic; it knew that a pro-democracy candidate was not acceptable to Beijing and could not secure stability and prosperity for the territory.

Hong Kong people understood that the local democratization process was determined by Beijing; pro-establishment candidates avoided pledges on this issue in their respective campaigns as they obviously felt impotent to confront Beijing or exert pressure on Beijing to accelerate the democratization process. Besides, most Hong Kong people were unwilling to sacrifice for the cause of democracy. They were also aware that the local economy was increasingly dependent on that of the Mainland and preferential policies from Chinese leaders were beneficial for the territory.

However, Hong Kong people were increasingly dissatisfied with the performance of the HKSAR government, nor were they happy with the 2012 Chief Executive election. On April 1, 2012, 15,000 Hong Kong people protested to articulate and express their anger and dissatisfaction. However, protests in Hong Kong were peaceful and orderly as the community cherishes stability; after all, the status quo was still largely acceptable because all parties concerned realize the importance of the rule of law and the freedom of information flow to the functioning of the international financial and business services centre.

The 2012 Chief Executive election, nonetheless, reinforced the community's pessimism for the future of the territory. The Leung administration lacked the political will and support to introduce significant reforms to restore and enhance Hong Kong's international economic competitiveness and narrow the rich–poor gap through improving the social security net.

People's grievances especially among the younger generation would continue to gather and protests would be frequent. Hong Kong people would protest and demonstrate to exert pressure on the local government and to send a message to Beijing and the international community.

The interferences from Beijing in the Chief Executive election, the scandals of the Leung administration and the accumulating grievances of the community resulted in the community's frustrations reaching a record high in early 2013. While their dissatisfaction was with the Leung administration, at this stage they were worried if their trusted civil service could remain neutral and effective. The involvement of the Buildings Department staff in the alleged cover-up of the Chief Executive's illegal construction was an obvious example.

The scandals and resignations of several members of the Leung team gave rise to gossips about quarrels at the top. The community naturally worried if the Leung administration could get anything done as it was so bogged down by internal divisions and scandals. Those who were in support of Leung's candidacy wanted reforms and improvements, which he evidently could not do so at his stage.

Even the strong discipline of the pro-Beijing united front seemed to have suffered erosion. The staunchly pro-Beijing monthly, *The Mirror*, severely criticized Rita Fan in its December 2012 issue for attacking the CE. Cheng Yiu-tong of the Hong Kong Federation of Trade Unions revealed that members withdrew because they were disappointed by the position of the popular legislator, Chan Yuen-han, on the proposed extra allowances for the elderly.

The pro-democracy camp continued to be plagued by internal arguments and distrust. Its supporters demanded the DP to acknowledge its mistake in reaching agreement with the Central Liaison Office on the political reform package as it had been proven wrong by the Legislative Council election results. The Civic Party had yet to deliver in internal democratization and had been losing members. In a District Council by-election in New Territories East in late 2012, competition between DP and the Neo Democrats delivered the seat to the pro-Beijing DAB candidate despite the pro-democracy camp securing over 60% of the votes.

As usual, it was the moderation and pragmatism of ordinary Hong Kong people who had been contributing to political stability by sanctioning through public opinion the parties which had gone out of line. But the community could not be optimistic that the territory could improve its international economic competitiveness and come up with effective solutions for its housing problem, etc.

The Chinese leadership would do well to take the lead in this dire situation by stopping the accusations of collusion among external forces, remnants of British colonialism and the opposition, and to treat contradictions within Hong Kong in an objective and flexible manner.

These gestures might generate the atmosphere of a meaningful dialogue between the Leung administration and the pro-democracy groups and the desire for political harmony in the territory. On the contrary, if the pro-Beijing united front further exerted pressure on the opposition, the confrontation would only exacerbate, especially in the coming consultations on the 2017 Chief Executive election.

Acknowledgement

Originally published as Cheng, Joseph Y.S., "The 2012 Chief Executive Election in Hong Kong and the Challenges for the Chinese Authorities", *East Asian Policy*, Volume 05, Issue 2, April & June 2013, pp. 91–103. Reproduced with kind permission from the publisher.

Chapter 20

Power, Transparency, and Control: The Hong Kong People's Adaptations to Life

I Introduction

Power is probably the most important concept in political science; transparency and control issues have generated much significant academic research in the recent decades. This chapter does not intend to contribute to the theoretical discourses, but instead it attempts to examine how the concepts of power, transparency and control were perceived in the life of ordinary Hong Kong people, and how the latter had been adapting to their perceptions and evaluations. The global financial tsunami of 2008 and its aftermath would likely have a serious impact on their values. People felt so powerless in the sudden economic difficulties; many felt frustrated that they had so little control over their own life despite a lot of hard work. Transparency in banking and financial services suddenly became a very important consideration.

Hong Kong is a modern city. Despite the absence of genuine democracy, people believed they enjoyed the rule of law and the freedom in life, including the freedom of information flow. All parties concerned cherished these two assets because they gave the territory an edge over China's coastal cities and help it maintain its international competitiveness. The Hong Kong people's experiences might in some ways represent those of modern men, especially those in East Asia.

II Power, Control and the Political Calculus

(a) *Power and Control in Everyday Life*

A widely accepted definition of power is "the capacity to change". As a social phenomenon, Denis H. Wrong defines it as "the capacity of some persons to produce intended and foreseen effects on others".[1] Power, or the exercise of power, is the production of any social effect. In this context, society is a system of power at both the macro-level of its major institutions and the micro-level of personal relations. The above definition of power is in line with Nietzschean and Foucauldian assertions that human being invariably seeks to dominate and impose their will on others.[2]

Individuals are unequal in power because some people have more money, property, status, etc. Hence, society is stratified; and Max Weber characterized "classes", "status groups" and "parties" as "phenomena of the distribution of power within a community". After Weber, Michael Foucault is probably the most influential recent writer on the subject of power. He advanced a general conception of power, as pervading all social relations in the form of a "micro-politics"; power is "something that is exercised from innumerable points, in the interplay of non-egalitarian and mobile relations". He argued that power "is everywhere, not because it embraces everything but because it comes from everywhere".[3] Foucault emphasized that power is not concentrated or centred in the state but is diffused through many non-political groups and organizations.

In his later writings, Foucault was especially concerned that the bodies of knowledge codified in the new human sciences have become the basis of new kinds of control and regulation of human beings by "experts", i.e., doctors, administrators, social workers and other professionals

---

[1] Dennis H. Wrong, *Power — Its Forms, Bases, and Uses*, New Brunswick and London: Transaction Publishers, 1995 edition, p. x.

[2] *Ibid.*, p. xiii; and Sallie Westwood, *Power and the Social*, London and New York: Routledge, 2002, pp. 19–22.

[3] Michel Foucault, *The History of Sexuality, Vol. I: An Introduction*, New York: Vintage Books, 1980, pp. 93–94.

exercising power that is legitimated by reference to certified and accredited formal knowledge. Foucault unmasked the most typical form of modern authority which appeals to reason, science, and self-interest — without any connotation of coercion and moral absolutism — as grounds for legitimization.

The authority of the expert, or competent authority according to Dennis H. Wrong, is a power relationship in which the subject obeys the guidance of the authority out of acceptance of the authority's superior competence or expertise to decide which actions will best serve the subject's interests and goals. Since the time of Socrates and Plato, the most common illustrations of competent authority have been the doctor–patient relationship and the responsibility of a helmsman for the navigation of a ship. During the Cultural Revolution in China, one of the titles for the charismatic leader Mao Zedong was the Great Helmsman.[4]

Moving from political science to critical social theory, John Oliga considers that the evolution of societies is reflected in a twin process of differentiation. The life-world becomes differentiated into three structural components: culture, society and personality; and action is coordinated via language as the medium of communication aiming at social integration. Society as a system becomes differentiated into two sub-systems — the economy and polity. Action coordination takes a delinguistified form — money in the sphere of economy and bureaucratic power in the sphere of politics. The objective here is system integration.[5]

Progress is defined as the continual development of the human potential for learning in the interest of having greater freedom (emancipation) in society. However, contemporary societies also suffer from pathologies which take two forms: (a) a colonization process via the medium of power (including the systemic media of money and bureaucratic power), leading to Weber's "loss of freedom"; and (b) a cultural impoverishment process via the medium of negative ideology, leading to Weber's "loss of meaning".

---

[4] Dennis H. Wrong, *op. cit.*, p. 53.
[5] John C. Oliga, *Power, Ideology, and Control*, New York: Plenum Press, 1996, pp. 291–293.

Control is exercised through power and ideology, leading to social domination. Hence the struggle for freedom (emancipation) requires educative enlightenment against ideology, empowerment processes against coercive forces of power, and transformative actions against dominative control.

(b) *The Case of Hong Kong*

In the case of Hong Kong, it was a British colony before 1997; and as a Special Administrative Region within the People's Republic of China (PRC), there is still no genuine democracy. The pro-democracy movement in the territory is still fighting for the direct election of the Chief Executive by universal suffrage, and the elections of all seats in the legislature by the same method. Under colonial rule, there was naturally a refugee mentality reflected by the feeling of living "in a borrowed place and a borrowed time".[6] This mentality dominated the local political culture until the postwar generation grew up in the 1970s. The refugee mentality is a kind of political alienation. This political alienation made ordinary Hong Kong people feel that they had no channel of political participation and that they could not influence government policy and administration. For political sociologists, the term "alienation" describes three different but related sets of attitudes, namely, the sense of powerlessness, the sense of meaninglessness and the sense of isolation.[7] Obviously, those who are frustrated and disappointed by the democratic systems in their own countries may feel alienated too.

The political system of the Hong Kong Special Administrative Region (HKSAR) apparently has not succeeded in removing this sense of political alienation. By the spring of 1988, it was clearly revealed that the mainstream view within the Basic Law Drafting Committee favoured an "executive-led" system of government for the future HKSAR, with power

---

[6] Richard Hughes, *Hong Kong: Borrowed Place, Borrowed Time*, London: Andre Deutsch, 1968.
[7] See Lewis Fener, "What is Alienation? The Career of a Concept", in *Sociology on Trial*, edited by Maurice Stein and Arthur Vidich, Englewood Cliffs, New Jersey: Prentice-Hall, 1963, pp. 127–147.

concentrated in the hands of the Chief Executive.[8] In accordance with the Sino-British Joint Declaration, the Central People's Government in Beijing would appoint the Chief Executive and the principal officials of the HKSAR government, and the exercise of the power of the appointments would be "substantial" rather than symbolic. The Chief Executive would be elected by a grand electoral college of about 600, dominated by the existing political establishment, i.e., business leaders and leading professionals sharing the values of the business community.

A leader of the local pro-democracy movement, Szeto Wah, attacked the system as "dictatorship of the grand electoral college", and he asked members of the pro-democracy movement to be prepared to remain in opposition for 20 years. On the other hand, Ronald Li, then chairman of the Hong Kong Stock Exchange, made a statement at an international investment conference which perhaps best reflected the conservative business community's attitude. Li declared: "Hong Kong is a colony. It is a dictatorship, although a benevolent one. It is and has been a British colony and it's going to be a Chinese colony, and as such it will prosper. We do not need free elections here."[9]

In the absence of democracy, both the British colonial administration and the HKSAR government needed to develop an ideology to ensure effective control. An ideology accepted by the community will facilitate the exercise of legitimate authority rather than coercive authority or even naked power.[10] The British colonial administration defended its denial of democracy to Hong Kong, in contrast to the other British colonies, by implicitly blaming Beijing; i.e., the British authorities did not want to

---

[8] See the Drafting Committee for the Basic Law, *The Draft Basic Law of the Hong Kong Special Administrative Region of the People's Republic of China (for solicitation of opinions)*, Hong Kong, April 1988. There were subsequently some minor amendments, but the basic political system designed then remains today. For an analysis of Basic Law, see the author's "The Basic Law: Messages for Hong Kong People", in *The Other Hong Kong Report 1990*, edited by Richard Y.C. Wong and Joseph Y.S. Cheng, Hong Kong: The Chinese University Press, 1990, pp. 29–63.

[9] *South China Morning Post* (Hong Kong), June 17, 1987.

[10] Bertrand Russell, *Power — A New Social Analysis*, London and New York: Routledge, 1938 (reprinted in 1995), Chapter 6, "Naked Power", pp. 57–71.

provoke the Chinese Communist regime by altering the status quo in a significant way.

The British administration secured its legitimacy by performance. Being refugees, most Hong Kong people would be satisfied as long as they could make a living, with the colonial government maintaining law and order. Colonial rule was an affront to national pride, but when compared with the rampant warlordism, chaos, corruption, and the abuse of power in China in the first half of the 20th century, it was quite acceptable. The colonial education system also played a significant role in providing an effective channel for upward social mobility in the territory. To the business community, the market economy of Hong Kong was probably the freest in the world (as certified by the U.S. Heritage Foundation) and experienced little interference from the government.

The free market economy led to the concentration of wealth and the unequal distribution of income; yet in a colonial political system, power had been highly concentrated in the senior officials of the colonial government and had not been affected by economic development until the Sino-British negotiations on the territory's future (unofficially since 1979 and officially started in 1982). This separation of political power and wealth in fact constituted a form of checks and balances.[11] More important still, the impressive economic growth in Hong Kong in its economic take-off stage since the 1950s improved the community's living standards significantly, and provided ample white-collar jobs and opportunities for emerging small businesses. Together with the vast expansion of the education system, all these made the people realize that they could solve their problems through their own efforts without having to exert pressure on the government by political participation. These factors contributed the basis of a political culture depicted by S.K. Lau as "utilitarian familism".[12]

Short of an ideal scenario in which people fight for democracy, i.e., securing political power through constitutional means and emancipating from political control through empowerment processes, Hong Kong

---

[11] See the author's "Political Modernisation in Hong Kong", *The Journal of Commonwealth & Comparative Politics*, Vol. XXVII, No. 3, November 1989, pp. 294–320.

[12] Siu-kai Lau, *Society and Politics in Hong Kong*, Hong Kong: The Chinese University Press, 1962.

people settled for limited political control guaranteed by checks and balances and economic freedom (emancipation) in pursuit of satisfaction in life. They defined their values guiding their pursuit which were compatible with the official ideology promoted by the colonial administration. "Utilitarian familism" might not be enlightenment, but obviously it was pragmatism which offered satisfaction and meaning replacing alienation. Political adaptation at the community level and striving for legitimacy by performance on the part of the colonial administration reflected pragmatism and a political cost-benefit calculus on both sides respectively. There was also an exit mechanism on both sides: emigration was always an option for Hong Kong people who wanted to seek greener pastures elsewhere; and the British colonial administration could also threaten to quit, as the Portuguese colonial administration did in Macau in 1967 and 1974.[13]

The British colonial administration had learned a lesson from the historic riots in 1966 and 1967, often referred as the Kowloon Disturbances. Essentially, in 1966, there were protests against a rise in ferry fares; and in 1967, there were months of pro-Beijing riots in response to the Cultural Revolution in Mainland China. The British administration was surprised by the dissatisfaction in the community despite the economic development and apparent improvement in living standards in the past year. Since then, the authorities became more responsive to the local public opinions. It even claimed to be a "government by consultation". The system of advisory committees following the British tradition was further developed to involve community leaders of the upper socioeconomic strata, and such "administrative absorption" was to strengthen the colonial government's representativeness.[14]

The British administration's pursuit of legitimacy by performance was an ideology of developmentalism. Apparently this ideology of developmentalism was embraced by the post-Mao leadership in China. When Deng Xiaoping and his supporters gained power in December 1978,

---

[13] Albert O. Hirschman, *Exit, Voice, and Loyalty: Responses to Decline in Firms, Organizations, and States*, Cambridge, Massachusetts: Harvard University Press, 1970.
[14] Ambrose Yeo-chi King, "The Administrative Absorption of Politics in Hong Kong", *Asian Survey*, Vol. 15, No. 5, May 1975, pp. 422–439.

they were aware that the Cultural Revolution had much eroded the people's support for the Communist regime. Instead there existed a crisis because of the prevalent lack of confidence in China's future, the absence of trust for the government and the Party, and the loss of conviction in the superiority of communism. The new leadership accepted that the legitimacy of the regime would henceforward have to depend on its ability to deliver the goods to improve people's living standards through the modernization of agriculture, industry, national defence, and science and technology. It also promised that there would be no more political campaigns like the Cultural Revolution; and attempts were made to strengthen socialist legalism. In fact, the first criminal law and criminal procedural law in the PRC only appeared in 1979.[15]

Economic growth alone is no longer adequate for the maintenance of the legitimacy of the Chinese Communist regime. At this stage, the basic strategy of the Chinese leadership to maintain the Party's monopoly of political power includes promoting economic growth, building a social security net for the under-privileged groups, and absorbing the elites of various sectors into the vested-interests strata. Chinese leaders are eager to pursue good governance if the measures concerned do not adversely affect the leadership of the Party. Chinese leaders today have an accurate assessment of the situation; they know how to exploit tools like opinion polls, "the Golden Shield Project" (for the control of the Internet), etc. to strengthen their control; the central government in possession of vast financial resources is in a better position to handle challenges; finally, the Chinese authorities understand their weaknesses, hence they try to defuse crises and avoid violent suppressions.

In the Sino-British negotiations over Hong Kong's future in the early 1980s, the Chinese leadership headed by Deng Xiaoping studied the Hong Kong situation in detail and it secured a good understanding of the factors behind the territory's economic success and social stability. This was not

---

[15] See the author's "Introduction — China's Modernization Programme in the 1980s", in his edited work, *China: Modernization in the 1980s*, Hong Kong: The Chinese University Press, 1989, p. ix.

to suggest that the Hong Kong model was then applied to China, rather the basic strategies to satisfy the people's demands and contain their dissatisfaction in the absence of democracy were similar. At this stage the "Beijing consensus"[16] has been able to compete effectively with the "Washington consensus"[17] in many Third World countries, demonstrating the attraction of China's development model.

Chinese leaders before Xi Jinping had not been actively promoting China's development model; they do not even use the term "Beijing consensus". Deng Xiaoping argued that there was no Chinese model to emulate; his advice was that each government should borrow and adapt to what would work best for its own people.[18] However, China does offer an example that development and sociopolitical stability can be achieved without democracy. What is significant, from the point of view of power considerations, is that the Chinese Communist regime refuses to give up its monopoly of political power and accept effective checks and balances. However, it also chooses to retreat from totalitarianism and allows sufficient room for the people, especially the emerging middle class, to enjoy the fruits of economic development.

The people then define their own political–economic cost-benefit calculus within the framework of the status quo. In the cases of both Hong Kong and China, there have been few direct challenges of the regimes' exercise of power, i.e., acceptance of their political control. The control has to be within limits so as not to provoke resistance and threaten the status quo. Hong Kong's first post-colonial Chief Executive administration's attempt to implement public security law under Article 23 of the Basic Law in 2003 during a period of severe economic difficulties is a good example that the control exceeded the

---

[16] Joshua Cooper Ramo, *The Beijing Consensus*, London: The Foreign Policy Centre, 2004, pp. 11–13.

[17] John Williamson, "What Washington Means by Policy Reform", in John Williamson (ed.), *Latin American Adjustment: How Much Has Happened?*, Washington, D.C.: Institute for International Economics, 1990, pp. 8–19.

[18] Edward Friedman, "How Economic Superpower China Could Transform Africa", *Journal of Chinese Political Science*, Vol. 14, No. 1, March 2009, pp. 6 and 10.

people's tolerable limits.[19] The people also want to have a good measure of control over their own life. They demand reasonable prospects to improve their economic well-being, hence education as an effective channel of upward social mobility is politically significant. This had also been vividly reflected by the Chinese leadership's pledge to maintain 8% of economic growth per annum at the end of the last century and in the beginning of the new century, and even in the wake of the global financial tsunami in 2008.

Marketization is an important element of the ideology of developmentalism. In the first place, it plays a key role in promoting economic growth. But the acceptance of market forces limits the control of the government and facilitates freedom and emancipation on the part of the individual. Marketization therefore serves to generate the impression that it restores the balance of control in favour of the individual. It is no accident that the Heritage Foundation in the U.S. consistently ranks the Hong Kong economy as the freest in the world.

The demand for democracy in Hong Kong has been much dampened by the arguments that the territory enjoys freedom and the rule of law, there is therefore no need for democracy. These two assets to a large extent have been guaranteed by market forces. All parties concerned appreciate that they are essential to the functioning of the territory as an international financial centre and business services centre; they also enable it to have a distinct edge over China's coastal cities including Shanghai.

Hence, the HKSAR government and especially the wealthy business leaders who argue against the introduction of genuine democracy in Hong Kong defend their position along the following lines. Hong Kong is an economic city; one should avoid turning it into a politicized community. Democracy can wait; the territory must proceed gradually and political reforms will be introduced when the conditions are ripe. Naturally, they

---

[19] Admittedly, most people in Hong Kong did not have the time and expertise to go through the bill in detail. However, they certainly became concerned and worried when the legal profession, social workers, journalists, librarians, bankers, the Catholic Church and Christian churches, etc. came out to articulate their opposition. See the author's "Introduction: Causes and Implications of the July 1 Protest Rally in Hong Kong", in the author's edited work, *The July 1 Protest Rally — Interpreting a Historic Event*, Hong Kong: City University of Hong Kong Press, 2005, pp. 1–26.

are clever enough not to specify what the conditions are and what standards are to be adopted to ascertain when the conditions are ripe. They sometimes will say that Hong Kong has the best of both worlds: it has all the advantages of a democracy, i.e., freedoms, human rights, and the rule of law, without its troubles. By troubles, they have the convenient example of Taiwan with its political polarization, corruption, degradation of the media, and slowing economic growth.

Most Hong Kong people understand that it will be most unlikely to realize full democracy in the territory in the foreseeable future. While they are sympathetic to the cause of democracy (usually 60% of the voters vote for pro-democracy candidates in the direct elections to the Legislative Council), they are reluctant to engage in a struggle for democracy. Instead they strive to improve their economic well-being so that they will have more control over their own life. This political orientation also explains the limited demand for social welfare in the community. In terms of their positions on the economy and social welfare, the Democratic Party and Civic Party in Hong Kong are similar to the Conservative and Liberal Parties in Western Europe. The HKSAR government also exercised considerable restraint in the promotion of "patriotic education" in the school system before the C.Y. Leung administration.

The above delicate balance of power and control in Hong Kong to some extent was reflected in the Legislative Council elections in September 2008.[20] Legislative Council elections are not expected to affect the administrative-led system of government in Hong Kong in any significant way because of the design of the Basic Law. The Chief Executive has ample powers to reduce the checks and balances impact of the legislature in terms of policy initiatives from the executive; and the electoral system has been formulated in such a way to make it almost impossible for the pro-democracy camp to win a majority of seats in the Legislative Council. In the Legislative Council elections in September 2008, given the adverse circumstances, the pro-democracy camp was satisfied that it accomplished its basic objective of retaining more than a third of the seats in the legislature so that it would still be able to veto the conservative political reform

---

[20] See the author's "Hong Kong's Legislative Council Elections in September 2008: Maintaining the Political Status Quo?", now under review by *Issues & Studies*.

proposals of the Donald Tsang administration. Despite the decline in the voter turnout rate by about 10%, the pro-democracy parties still captured almost 60% support in the direct elections. This support suggested that Hong Kong people would like to vote for the pro-democracy candidates to ensure the functioning of a minimal checks and balances system. This support did not suffer much even when the pro-Beijing united front had developed a very effective electoral machinery and when the pro-democracy parties did not perform well.

There were signs of spreading political apathy, especially evidenced by the substantial drop in voter participation. At the same time, there seemed to be rising resentment against the arrogance and incompetence of the Donald Tsang administration, as well as against the deepening collusion between the government and the major business groups. All parties concerned were aware that these grievances would become exacerbated when the economy deteriorated, and they could threaten social and political stability. Hence the Chinese leadership has been active in support of the territory's economy.

It is interesting to note that in explaining the "third wave" of democratization, Samuel P. Huntington identified that an important factor had been the dependence of the fallen authoritarian regimes on "performance legitimacy, and the undermining of that legitimacy by military defeats, economic failures, and the oil shocks of 1973–1974 and 1978–1979".[21] Hong Kong's political stability has been strongly backed by its economic stability; and at this stage the Chinese leadership understood that the global financial tsunami posed a serious threat to political and social stability in China.

III Transparency, Control and Power

(a) *Transparency and Control in Everyday Life*

The United Nations lends its support to freedom of information in its famous Resolution of the General Assembly of December 14, 1946:

---

[21] Samuel P. Huntington, *The Third Wave — Democratization in the Late Twentieth Century*, Norman and London: University of Oklahoma Press, 1993 (paperback edition), p. 45.

"Freedom of information is a fundamental human right and is the touchstone for all freedoms to which the United Nations is consecrated."[22] Article 19 of the Universal Declaration of Human Rights adopted by the United Nations General Assembly in 1948 gave "the right to seek, receive and impart information and ideas through any media and regardless of any frontiers". The right in question was rooted in a right to seek and pass on information rather than a right to government-held documents.[23]

Transparency is about access to information, but it is also about power. As knowledge is power, then transparency, by disseminating knowledge, empowers some groups but not others. This spread of information is not politically neutral; since when information changes hands, so too does influence. Moreover, the diffusion of power is not a one-way street. Transparency alters the balance of power as it can make the strong stronger as well as empowering the weak. Kristin Lord considers that five factors have led to the rise of global transparency — the spread of democratic governments, the development of the global media, the emergence of non-governmental organizations, the proliferation of international regimes demanding governments to release information, and the advance of information technologies.[24]

As democracy is a form of government that purports to treat all equally in terms of a right to equal and appropriate respect and consideration in the exercise of government power, so protection of human rights has become universally accepted by democratic governments. But, as indicated by Patrick Birkinshaw, statements of fundamental human rights seldom contain a right of access to information.[25] Freedom of information means access by individuals as a presumptive right to information held by public authorities. Though open processes and access

---

[22] United Nations, General Assembly Resolution 59(1) at 95 United Nations Documents A/64 (December 14, 1946).

[23] Cyril John Radcliffe, *Freedom of Information: A Human Right*, Glasgow: Jackson, Son and Co., 1953.

[24] Kristin M. Lord, *The Perils and Promise of Global Transparency*, Albany: State University of New York Press, 2006, pp. 4–5.

[25] Patrick Birkinshaw, "Transparency as a Human Right", in *Transparency — The Key to Better Governance?*, edited by Christopher Hood and David Heald, Oxford: Oxford University Press for The British Academy, 2006, pp. 49–50.

to information are readily acknowledged as essential to responsible and responsive government, there is also strong support for arguments used to oppose them among those in power, i.e., they undermine representative democracy and efficient and effective government by exposure to excessive criticism. Further, they would drive decision-making into ever more secret processes or expose individuals to unjustified invasion of privacy. Information overload corrupts wisdom and knowledge and descends to spin and spam. Openness involving too much access to information could endanger public and national security.

If one accepts participatory democracy as an ideal to be realized, then obviously the public requires the right of access to information to engage fully as citizens and to make participation meaningful. In the evolution of representative democracy, the struggle over the centuries was about legislatures being properly informed. Freedom of speech will be pointless if citizens are poorly informed. The argument for human rights is based on protection for individuals against inefficient and oppressive governments. Hence human rights and freedom of information are even more important in the absence of democracy; and in this context, censorship and self-censorship are significant issues.

David Heald discusses the optimal level of beneficial transparency which might be considered as the result of the trade-off between transparency and seven other objectives.[26] In terms of effectiveness, transparency about operational aspects of processes can affect behaviour in unintended and unanticipated ways. Policy formulation in public has become more difficult because of the inability and/or unwillingness of much of the media to analyze policy issues seriously. This has an adverse impact on rational and efficient policy-making by making the process vulnerable to interest groups over-simplifying complex issues and to opposition politicians jumping on populist bandwagons. Many top civil servants and heads of public institutions in Hong Kong would certainly agree to this; their responses, however, are not so much as to openly criticize the demands for transparency but to adapt to them for self-protection purposes. The public in turn tends to blame the popular media

---

[26] David Heald, "Transparency as an Instrumental Value", *ibid.*, pp. 61–68.

culture. The same problems are common in Taiwan where democracy flourishes.

Onora O'Neill in his Reith Lectures argued that increasing transparency "can produce a flood of unsorted information and misinformation that provides little but confusion unless it can be sorted and assessed.... Transparency can encourage people to be less honest, so increasing deception and reducing reasons for trust".[27] O'Neill was generally negative about transparency; and he proposed that, to enhance trust, the objective should be to reduce deception and lies rather than to promote transparency. O'Neill's views are relevant to the following discussion on competent authority and control.

Transparency is naturally related to accountability. Transparency in the public sector inevitably raises issues about the distribution of power and resources as well as the establishment of benchmarks and indicators. In the private sector, transparency is a more controversial issue. Audit developments after scandals in the United States such as Enron were supposed to have led to more rigorous and better enforced accounting standards. These developments, including the United States Sarbanes-Oxley Act with its international reach, had been perceived to have imposed "substantial transaction costs".[28] Obviously, the global financial tsunami in 2008–2009 had fully exposed the inadequacies of the safeguards, and the demands for stricter surveillance and greater transparency were so strong that the regulatory framework of the international financial service industries was bound to be overhauled.

Finally, transparency is often counterpoised with issues of confidentiality, privacy and anonymity. Limits to transparency are generally acknowledged, as they are required to contain resource consumption (both direct and compliance costs) and maintain a balance with the satisfaction of other objectives.

The pursuit of transparency, on the other hand, is still handicapped by the asymmetry of power between the powerful and resourceful who are reluctant to release the information and the powerless who also lack

---

[27] Onora O'Neill, *A Question of Trust — The BBC Reith Lectures*, Cambridge: Cambridge University Press, 2002, pp. 72–73.
[28] David Heald, *loc. cit.*, p. 64.

resources in seeking information. This asymmetry even exists in democracies, and it is reflected in various measures adopted by democratic governments to minimize the impact of freedom of information legislation. According to the analysis by Alasdair Roberts, these measures fall into two categories — (i) direct challenges to the right to information by amendment of the law or regulations; and (ii) informal administrative responses which, while maintaining a public pretence of conformity to the law, have the effect of limiting its significance in practice.[29]

Some governments have attempted to amend the legislation that creates a right to information. They may also attempt to restrict the meaning and the interpretation, if not the actual language, of the legislation. Informal administrative responses include changes in record-keeping. The right to information may be subverted by corrosion of the quality of records kept by government institutions. Obviously, a disclosure law cannot be effective if records are incomplete or non-existent. The demand for transparency often causes officials to become more reticent in recording potentially controversial information. Destruction or manipulation of government records is an uncommon but not unknown practice. Requests from journalists and opposition party researchers are usually tagged for sensitivity. If these practices are common in democratic governments, one can easily imagine what authoritarian regimes would do.

If knowledge is power, then competent authority is an important issue in the daily life of citizens in modern society. The professional, who possesses power based on knowledge, also possesses, according to Eliot Freidson, some of the attributes of power based on legally ratified status, and this status depends on the power of the collective organization of his fellow experts.[30] Freidson considers that the extraordinary prestige and high degree of organization of professionals in modern society carry the risk that "expertise is more and more in danger of being used as a mask for privilege and power rather than, as it claims, as a model of

---

[29] Alasdair Roberts, "Dashed Expectations: Governmental Adaptation to Transparency Rules", in Christopher Hood and David Heald (eds.), *op. cit.*, pp. 109–118.

[30] Eliot Freidson, "The Impurity of Professional Authority", in *Institutions and the Person*, edited by Howard S. Becker, Blanche Geer, David Riesman, and Robert S. Weiss, Chicago: Aldine, 1968, pp. 30–31.

advancing the public interest".[31] Freidson unavoidably has the medical profession in mind.

(b) *The Case of Hong Kong*

The Hong Kong people know very well the prestige, status and influence of the medical profession in the territory. The Hong Kong Medical Association has certainly been a very effective lobby. In the past decades, it has successfully lobbied for the limitation of the intakes of medical school students and the practice of doctors from advanced countries in Hong Kong. Obviously, the community would like to have more medical doctors to ensure better services and more competition. Another important example is the separation of the medical and pharmaceutical professions. Up till now, doctors in private practice in Hong Kong insist on directly providing their patients medicine, instead of giving them prescriptions so that they can buy from drug stores with pharmacists. This reduces checks and balances between the professions, and places patients in a disadvantageous position both from the point of view of patients and consumers as they suffer from lack of access to information on the medicine prescribed and the chances of buying the medicine from the drug stores offering the best prices.

This reveals the asymmetry in power between a prestigious, well-organized professional group and the unorganized consumers. In a democracy, there is at least a chance for some political parties to take up the cause of consumers, though the organized professional groups are usually much more sophisticated and successful in their lobbying efforts. An important factor in this asymmetry of power has been the effective defence of the professional bodies against the demands for transparency. In the first decade of the new century in Hong Kong, a few patients' rights groups have emerged, and they have attracted some media attention. A very important demand on their part is for access to information and transparency; but because of their limited resources, progress has been insignificant.

---

[31] Eliot Freidson, *Profession of Medicine*, New York: Dodd, Mead, 1972, p. 337.

This asymmetry in power sometimes spreads to the political arena. To ensure that the pro-democracy movement cannot capture an absolute majority of seats in the legislature despite its electoral support, the Chinese leadership still insists that half of the seats are to be returned by functional constituencies which are dominated by the business community and the professional groups. In the political confrontation in Thailand in 2008–2009 between the supporters of Thaksin Shinawatra and the elites in Bangkok (the People's Alliance for Democracy), the latter proposed an electoral formula which would allow the professional groups to elect their representatives to the legislature in order to balance against the former's electoral superiority.[32]

Compared with the handicaps encountered by ordinary people in their relations with competent authority, the asymmetry in power is much more serious in ordinary people's transactions with big businesses. Hong Kong middle-class families often spend their life's savings to buy their accommodation; yet real estate developers managed to refuse to offer the exact measurements of the properties they sold till the early 2010s. Next to real estate, Hong Kong people's other important investment outlets are probably life insurance and various types of investment funds. The insurance and financial service industries similarly succeeded in keeping their clients from having access to the information concerning the exact management fees they charged and the commissions they paid to their sales agents until the beginning of the second decade of the new century. Despite the good business sense of the Hong Kong middle class, they remained largely helpless.

Compared with housing ownership, life insurance and investment in financial instruments, oil prices may be less significant. But they are another significant illustration of the asymmetry in power between ordinary people and big businesses. It is an established fact that the international oil market is very much controlled by an oligopoly of major

---

[32] The People's Alliance for Democracy is mainly a coalition of the Democratic Party (with its base in Bangkok), the military, the crown and the civil service. One of its proposals was that popular representatives should be 70% nominated by certain occupational groups and 30% elected. See Ian Storey and Lee Poh Onn (eds.), *Regional Outlook — Southeast Asia 2009–2010*, Singapore: Institute of Southeast Asian Studies, 2009, p. 49.

companies. The Hong Kong market is in the hands of a very limited number of corporations too. Local people are in no position to judge if there is fair competition, and no implicit understanding exists among the local oil companies regarding their pricing policies, i.e., no cartel and anti-competition practices. But undeniably there is a common perception that local oil prices at the retail level rise rapidly and fall much more slowly in response to global oil price fluctuations.[33]

The global financial crisis in 2008–2009 certainly shocked the territory's small investors, i.e., the ordinary middle class. The lack of transparency and the unethical practices in the banking and financial service industries were probably no worse in Hong Kong than in other international financial centres, including those in democracies. However, the irony was that a vast majority of the Hong Kong people chose not to struggle for political power, but to work hard to secure a good measure of control over one's own life through an improvement of one's living standards.

IV Power Asymmetry, Exit and the Alternative

Democracy is premised on the ideal that life is meaningful through political participation in the community to which one belongs. An individual realizes his or her full potential only through this participation in running the community's affairs. In the political calculus of most Hong Kong people, this is too demanding an ideal for them and they instead opt for economic power at the micro-level to secure an optimal measure of control over the socioeconomic aspects of their own life. Even in democracies, for the less politically active, political participation remains a demanding ideal. The voter turnout rates at various levels of elections in the United States are good evidence of the less than enthusiastic response to the demands of political participation. Given the numerous decisions to be made for each ballot paper on voting day in the U.S., it can be safely assumed that only an extremely small proportion of the electorate has made the efforts to make intelligent and meaningful choices.

---

[33] See the author's "Consumers Losing Out in a 'Free Market'", *South China Morning Post* (Hong Kong), December 31, 2008.

At the same time, every individual would like to have a good measure of control over his or her own life. This objective has been proven extremely difficult to fulfill because of the asymmetry in power between the individual on one hand, and authoritarian regimes, big businesses, and organized interest groups on the other. This asymmetry in power is often reflected in the asymmetry in information held, which in turn is a result of the lack of transparency on the part of the powerful.

Exit is sometimes a viable option. In the years after the emergence of the question of the territory's future in the early 1980s, there was a steady outflow of emigrants to the English-speaking advanced democracies — the U.S., Canada, Australia, the U.K., and New Zealand. These emigrants were those who had the means to exercise the exit option in terms of wealth, professional competence, work experience and education level. A high proportion of them returned to Hong Kong before 1997 after securing their foreign passports. The HKSAR has not been able to offer democracy, and the Chinese leadership only pledged to largely maintain the status quo of the colonial era including the freedoms, the lifestyles and the market economy. Apparently, these conditions satisfied the émigrés' political calculus and were sufficient to induce their return.

In the new century, Hong Kong people gradually came to realize the extremely limited control they enjoyed over their own life. This realization had not prompted them to emigrate as they understood that the situations in democracies were not significantly better. The likely options were three:

(1) They might be more inclined to take part in protest activities to vent their anger and frustration. This is one type of response found under authoritarian regimes and in democracies.
(2) Some would raise their level of political participation and seek to redress the asymmetries in power through collective action. This is in line with the general theory of democratization.
(3) There might be a tendency to seek satisfaction from religious pursuits, voluntary work.

It was small wonder that the C.H. Tung administration attempted to appeal to Confucianism. More realistically, there might well emerge a new type of neighbourhood groups in Hong Kong. Given the acute need for emotional support in a highly competitive society where work pressure was substantial, a sense of loneliness and alienation was widespread. Single parents, retirees, and young people who were well educated and ready for some voluntary work, for instance, formed a substantial pool of potential members ready to group together in service of the neighbourhood. These people were distinct from members of the existing grassroots groups in that they were financially better off and did not plan to seek help directly from the government. They did not intend to take an active part in politics, but they wanted a meaningful interaction with the community in which they would seek mutual help, emotional support and satisfaction through service. At this stage, religious organizations come closest to satisfying this demand, but obviously there is much room for similar secular groups to develop. In Taiwan, the development of civil society had been impressive despite the people's disillusionment with the political parties. In China, it was still too early to detect distinct trends in the development of civil society, but there was no lack of small pockets of enthusiasts.

Acknowledgement

Originally published as Cheng, Joseph Y.S., "Power, Transparency and Control: Hong Kong People's Adaptations to Life", *International Journal for the Semiotics of Law*, Volume 24, Issue 2, pp 163–177. ©2011 Springer Science. Reproduced with kind permission from the publisher.

Chapter 21

New Trends of Political Participation in Hong Kong

I Introduction: Emergence of New Issues

The political system of Hong Kong is defined by the Basic Law. It promises the special administrative region "a high degree of autonomy" (Article 2). However, the Hong Kong people have often been reminded by Chinese officials that they have to think of "one country" more rather than "two systems", and that "a high degree of autonomy" means that it has limits.[1] As the central authorities have become increasingly dissatisfied with the situation in the territory, their intervention has become more frequent and obvious. In late-2013, Central Liaison Office officials and pro-Beijing media defended the former's lobbying of legislators as a routine which had to be accepted by the community.

Hong Kong's political system has often been described as "executive-led" because the Chief Executive enjoys strong presidential powers while the legislature's role is relatively limited. For example, it has no role in government personnel matters; it cannot seek to increase government revenues and expenditure; it cannot initiate public policy proposals without the approval of the Chief Executive; and the latter can refuse to

---

[1] Joseph Y.S. Cheng, *"The Basic Law: Messages for Hong Kong People"*, in Richard Y.C. Wong and Joseph Y.S. Cheng (eds.), The Other Hong Kong Report 1990, Hong Kong: The Chinese University Press, 1990, pp. 34–44.

allow government officials to testify before the Legislative Council because of security and public interests considerations.[2]

The Chief Executive till now is elected by an Election Committee dominated by the pro-establishment business and professional elites, while 30 seats in the 70-seat legislature are returned by functional constituencies again dominated by the establishment. The pro-democracy movement has been campaigning for the democratization of the electoral systems since the latter half of the 1980s; and the National People's Congress Standing Committee in Beijing agreed in 2010 that election of the Chief Executive by universal suffrage in 2017 and that of all seats in the legislature by the same method in 2020 might be implemented. Hence, political reform emerged as a significant political issue since early 2013.

Democratization had hardly made any progress in the territory of Hong Kong, yet there were many new trends and phenomena relating to political participation in the early-2010s that were deserving of attention. After all, Hong Kong was still a vibrant city.

This chapter attempts to study the basic factors affecting political participation in Hong Kong since its return to the Motherland and its new trends of political participation in this period; these factors included constitutional evolution and the political structure, as well as changes in the social structure and economic development. While offering observations of concrete phenomena, this chapter will also consider the relevant theoretical issues so as to achieve a better understanding of the territory's political development.

In terms of constitutional evolution and the political structure, differences within Hong Kong's pro-democracy movement had been fully exposed by the refusal of the central government of the People's Republic of China (PRC) to provide a clear roadmap for the elections of the Chief Executive and the entire legislature by universal suffrage, and the acceptance of the PRC government's slightly revised political reform package by the Democratic Party (DP) in 2010. There were elements in the pro-democracy movement who believed in a dialogue with both the

---

[2] *Ibid*, p. 44–52.

central government and the Hong Kong Special Administrative Region (HKSAR) government. The Civic Party (CP) and the Labour Party (LP) would probably continue to stand firm on the political reform issue, and maintain their moderate style. The original League of Social Democrats (LSD) group kept on splitting. Thus, there would be three rather distinct orientations. The establishment of the CP in 2006, and later the LP and the LSD, as well as the split of the Liberal Party soon after the Legislative Council elections in 2008, were significant developments in the pattern of political parties. Voters had more choices; in fact, they might become more confused. Government lobbying of the legislators became more complicated too.

More significant were the intermediate and long-term changes in the social structure. In the past, 60%–70% of the Hong Kong people considered that they belonged to the middle socioeconomic strata, they shared strong middle class values.[3] In the last two decades, however, Hong Kong increasingly developed into an "M-shaped" society, where many educated young people had doubts whether or not they belonged to the middle class.[4] As the gap between the rich and the poor widened, and opportunities for upward social mobility were reduced, dissatisfaction in society accumulated. These trends naturally affected the inducements and patterns of political participation.

There was a common concern among the Hong Kong people — would political participation continue to radicalize? Would a small minority, especially the young people, adopt more radical political actions in the context of rising political apathy among the majority? Naturally, what was considered radical in Hong Kong was still rather moderate when compared with political radicalization in European countries. Nevertheless, there was some media discussion on the "post-1980s

---

[3] See, for example, Lau Siu-kai, *Society and Politics in Hong Kong*. Hong Kong: The Chinese University Press, 1982; and Lau Siu-kai and Kuan Hsin-chi, *The Ethos of the Hong Kong Chinese*. Hong Kong: The Chinese University Press, 1988.

[4] Ohmae Kenichi, *M Xing Shehui: Zhongchan Jieji Xiaoshi de Weiji yu Shangji (M-shaped Society: The Crisis and Business Opportunities of the Vanishing of the Middle-Class)*, translated from Japanese by Liu Jinxiu and Jiang Yuzhen, Taipei: Shangzhou Chuban, 2006.

generation", and the Donald Tsang administration also felt the need to study the phenomenon.[5]

The performance of the HKSAR government obviously had an important impact on the mode of political participation in the territory. Although there were no very large-scale mass demonstrations between those in 2003–2004 and the Occupation Campaign in 2014, public opinion surveys revealed that there was substantial dissatisfaction with the performance of the C.H. Tung and Donald Tsang administrations. The latter understood its lack of popular appeal, and chose to avoid controversial policies. Regarding the confrontational political reform issue, the Hong Kong people realize that it is in the hands of the Chinese leadership. As perceived by the DP chairman, Albert Ho, the Chief Executive's role was "a bit dysfunctional".[6] The C.Y. Leung administration only got worse, as it had been plagued by scandals right from the beginning.

After the massive protest rally on July 1, 2003, the Chinese leadership was worried about the Hong Kong situation, and its intervention in Hong Kong politics had been much strengthened since then. The pro-Beijing united front therefore had more resources to mobilize the Hong Kong people and influence their political attitudes; the electoral machinery of the pro-Beijing political parties had become increasingly effective and sophisticated.[7] However, in the direct elections to the Legislative Council in 2008, the pro-democracy camp still secured almost 60% of the votes, demonstrating that the Hong Kong people valued effective checks and balances against the HKSAR government. In the following Legislative Council elections in 2012, its share of the vote fell to about 55%, reflecting

---

[5] See Michael E. DeGolyer, *Protest and Post-80s Youth, A Special Report on the Post-1980s Generation in Hong Kong,* Hong Kong Transition Project. Hong Kong: Hong Kong Baptist University, 2010. On December 17, 2010, the Central Policy Unit of the HKSAR government and the Applied Social and Economic Research Centre, Hong Kong University of Science and Technology held a seminar entitled "Youth and Social Change" to discuss the issues of the territory's post-1980s generation.

[6] *Apple Daily* (a Hong Kong Chinese newspaper), July 10, 2010.

[7] See Joseph Y.S. Cheng, "Introduction: Causes and Implications of the July 1 Protest Rally in Hong Kong", in his edited book, *The July 1 Protest Rally: Interpreting a Historic Event*, Hong Kong: City University of Hong Kong Press, 2005, pp. 13–24.

its difficulties as the decline in the share of the vote took place when the HKSAR government was increasingly unpopular.

Hong Kong's economic development and its prospects influenced the community's demands. If the economy continued to grow, the Hong Kong people would desire stability, and hope to solve their problems by their own efforts.[8] When the economy stagnated, the demand for income redistribution would be strengthened. For example, in the early 2010s, before the release of the government budget, political parties made demands for various sweeteners for the community, like one extra monthly payment of social security allowances and old-age pensions, waiver of one or two months of public-housing rents, transport subsidies for low-income earners, etc. In the long term, the HKSAR government had to comprehensively consider its commitments regarding all types of social services.

II Changes in the Structure of Hong Kong's Social Stratification and Their Impact

In 2012, Hong Kong's per capita GDP reached US$37,352 per annum. Obviously, it was a developed economy. However, according to a report of the United Nations Development Programme, Hong Kong's income gap was the largest among all Asian cities in 2008 and 2009.[9] The statistics from the HKSAR government's Census and Statistics Department showed that the Gini coefficient stood at around 0.43 in the 1970s; it rose sharply from 0.453 in 1986 to 0.518 in 1996; and it continued to climb to 0.537 in 2011.[10]

In September 2010, Oxfam of Hong Kong published its report on poverty in the territory which showed that the number of working-poor families had been increasing, from around 172,600 at the beginning of 2005 to about 192,500, a rise of 12% in five-and-a-half years. The report

---

[8] Lau and Kuan, *The Ethos of the Hong Kong Chinese*.
[9] United Nations Development Programme, *Development Report 2009: M Economy and Inequality*, 2009, http://hdrstats.undp.org/en/indicators/161.htm.
[10] Hong Kong, Census and Statistics Department, *Half-Yearly Economic Report 2012*, www.tradingeconomics.com/hong-kong/gdp-per-capita.

also indicated that the incomes of the poorest one-fifth of the families had shown no improvement in the same period; and the median monthly incomes of the poorest one-tenth and one-fifth of families were HK$3,000 and HK$6,000, respectively. In comparison, the median monthly income of the richest one-tenth of families had increased by 16% to HK$80,900, about 27 times that of the poorest one-tenth of families, reflecting that the gap between the rich and poor had widened in the past five and a half years.[11]

In October 2010, the Hong Kong Council of Social Service released a research report indicating that in the first half of the year, the population of "poor families" in the territory reached 1.26 million, amounting to 18.1% of the population, a record high. The report also revealed that the median monthly income of the high-income household group had risen from HK$31,000 in 2009 to HK$32,950; while that of the low-income household group had basically remained unchanged at HK$9,000. The income gap between the two groups had been maintained at the ratio of 3.4:1 in the past four years; but in the first half of 2010, it rose to 3.7:1. Apparently, the income gap worsened in the economic recovery after the recent global financial tsunami.[12]

According to the Census and Statistics Department of the HKSAR government, in the quarter September–November 2009, the number of households with a monthly income of HK$25,000 and above had dropped from that in the corresponding period of the previous year; while the number of households in various groups with a monthly income of below HK$10,000 had risen, with growth rates ranging from 2.4% to 9.7%.[13]

---

[11] *Ming Pao* (a Hong Kong Chinese newspaper), September 20, 2010. A "working-poor family" refers to a household with at least one member employed, and its monthly income is below one half of the median monthly income of local households with the same number of family members.

[12] *Ming Pao*, October 4, 2010. A "poor family" is one whose monthly income is less than or equal to one-half of the median monthly income of local families with the same number of members; at that time, the median monthly income of one-member families was HK$3,275, two-member families HK$7,100, three-member families HK$10,000, and four-member families HK$12,000.

[13] *Ming Pao*, January 20, 2010.

Under such circumstances, grievances among the lower socioeconomic strata easily accumulated. The gap between the rich and the poor in Hong Kong was serious in the past. However, it was like China at this stage — the Hong Kong people felt that their living standards had been improving, and they also considered that their living standards would continue to improve. In other words, Hong Kong was a place full of opportunities; as long as one worked hard, one's efforts would be rewarded. Even those who had little education with very limited upward social mobility prospects could still pin their hopes on their younger generation. In the early-2010s, however, "inter-generational poverty" had emerged as a social issue, reflecting that many people in the territory no longer consider Hong Kong as a place full of opportunities. They grumbled that there had been no real improvement in their living standards since Hong Kong's return to the Motherland, and they were not optimistic about its economic future. Meanwhile, they felt that work pressure and the pressure of making ends meet had been increasing. The rise in discontent naturally meant an erosion of their identification with the territory's political and economic systems.

The HKSAR government understood that grievances in the community had been gathering and that its popularity was low. It therefore hesitated to introduce policies which would add to the people's burdens; instead, it often offered them sweeteners. Regarding the burdens, the Donald Tsang administration abandoned its plan of broadening the tax base and introducing a consumption tax. On the long-term financing of medical care, it also avoided any proposals demanding contributions from the people; it simply chose to encourage individuals to join private-sector insurance schemes. The C.Y. Leung administration would like to make an important contribution in the housing area; but other than that, it was in a difficult position to deliver as it was much handicapped by disunity within the establishment and its own scandals.

The various subsidies and waivers provided by the annual budgets during the Donald Tsang administration showed that it was eager to please all socioeconomic strata. At the grassroots level, the demand for more income redistribution through the government was strengthening. When the economy was in good shape and the government enjoyed a budget surplus, people asked for a reduction of their tax burden or more subsidies.

When the economy deteriorated, people at the grassroots level demanded assistance. When could the HKSAR government refuse these ad hoc subsidies and waivers? It was obvious that these budgetary measures would only have a very limited impact.

A more serious problem was the gradual loss of the HKSAR government's potential to increase taxation to improve social services and the community's quality of life. The Hong Kong people realized that the ageing population implied an increase in expenditure on medical care and other social services; environmental protection through energy conservation and pollution reduction demanded efforts from both individuals and the government; and an enhancement of the territory's long-term international competitiveness required more investment in infrastructure and education. They were reluctant, however, to accept an increase in their tax burden, and those at the grassroots level demanded further income redistribution by the government. Meanwhile, the government avoided increasing the people's tax burden, and was forced to reduce its commitments in various social services. The government's capability to redistribute income in fact had been weakened, and those at the grassroots level received less help. For example, the direct subsidy schools scheme, the introduction of sub-degree programs, and the encouragement of private universities all reflected the HKSAR government's attempts to reduce its commitment in the education sector; but they indirectly had a negative impact on the upward social mobility of the children of poor families and exacerbated the gap between the rich and poor.[14]

Poverty adversely affected political participation.[15] Before 1997, the Hong Kong people were not very enthusiastic about political participation, but they basically accepted and supported the existing political and economic systems, indicated a relatively high level of satisfaction with the government's performance, and articulated few demands on the government. At this stage, the Hong Kong people's political participation was still not very enthusiastic; but their identification with the existing

---

[14] Joseph Y.S. Cheng, "The Deep Structural Problems of Direct Subsidy Schools" (in Chinese), *Sing Tao Daily* (a Hong Kong Chinese newspaper), December 16, 2010.
[15] Amartya Sen, "Foreword", in *From Poverty to Power,* edited by Duncan Green. Oxford: Oxfam International, 2008, pp. xiii–xvi.

political and economic institutions had been in decline. They had a lower level of satisfaction concerning the government's performance, stronger grievances with various phenomena of social injustice, and more demands and protests *vis-à-vis* the government. The latter tended to react rather passively to these demands and protests; it tried to reduce the people's dissatisfaction and psychological expectations, but normally it could not tackle the roots of the problems.

The final years of the Tsang administration and the first year of the C.Y. Leung administration witnessed many more protest activities. Very often, the radical young protesters were ready to confront the police, thereby leading to arrests. Worse still, an increasing number of protesters carried the old colonial flags in protest rallies to indicate their preference of the colonial administration over the HKSAR government, a phenomenon which caused considerable anger in Beijing and within the pro-Beijing united front.

III Meaningful Political Participation and Rational Deliberations

In the 1990s, theories on deliberative democracy were developed in Western political science, as a response to the perception and analysis of democracy as the articulation and aggregation of interests.[16] The latter theories were basically theories of rational choice, based on the premise that an individual citizen or voter would rationally consider the opportunities and restrictions of each option in making his/her decision. Democratic institutions therefore allow voters to pursue their interests freely and equally.

Deliberative democracy imposes a higher demand on citizens. Its theories are influenced by John Rawls' concept of political justice and the emphasis of John Stuart Mill on open debate in the 19th century. Deliberative democracy theories hold that citizens have the fundamental

---

[16] Shawn W. Rosenberg, "Introduction: Theoretical Perspectives and Empirical Research on Deliberative Democracy", in *Deliberation, Participation and Democracy*, edited by Shawn W. Rosenberg. Basingstoke, Hampshire and New York: Palgrave MacMillan, 2007, pp. 1–22.

cognitive capabilities to engage in rational debate; they would consider not only their individual needs, but also the public interest. The latter implies that individuals have ethical considerations; and they will reorder their priorities in the course of the debate. This kind of political participation brings its own satisfaction, and is in accordance with the belief that the full development of the individual can only be secured through meaningful political participation.

The Hong Kong people have a fine tradition of reason and moderation. Although a fully democratic political system has yet to be established, people enjoy freedom of speech, and the media offer platforms for free discussions. Self-censorship has certainly become more serious in the past two decades, but critics will not find it impossible to articulate their views.[17] Since the early 2010s, Internet media have been offering convenient, interactive discussion platforms for various small groups.

According to a survey conducted in the U.S. in February–March 2003, about two-thirds of respondents indicated that they had participated in some kind of regular political discussions in the past year, and a quarter of them had taken part in at least one organized forum.[18] It was likely that the Hong Kong people's participation rates would be substantially lower. On the one hand, their life was busier, and on the other, there were factors of political culture — the Hong Kong people often avoided political discussions in social gatherings.

In qualitative terms, however, the Hong Kong people should not do too badly. Local newspapers usually offered considerable space for commentaries and political columns; and their quality was respectable. The problem was that serious readers were few, and the discussions often only involved opinion leaders. In the past two decades, high quality in-depth investigative reports in newspapers and the electronic media became rare; budgetary considerations seemed to be the principal factor. Various types of civic groups organized many open forums and seminars;

---

[17] Joseph M. Chan and Francis L.F. Lee (eds.), *Media and Politics in Post-Handover Hong Kong*, London: Routledge, 2008.

[18] Fay Lomax Cook, Michael X. Delli Carpini, and Lawrence R. Jacobs, "Who Deliberates? Discursive Participation in America", in *Deliberation, Participation and* Democracy, edited by Shawn W. Rosenberg, pp. 25–44.

the quantity was impressive, and the quality was acceptable. Again, participants were few; and their major purpose seemed to be to attract media attention rather than to offer platforms for the public to articulate its views.

An encouraging development was the emergence of a number of private think-tanks in the past twenty years. Their scale and resources obviously could not compare with those in the Western advanced countries — there was even a considerable gap between them and those in Taiwan — but at least this was a healthy beginning. Given the financial resources of the local major business groups, they really should do more to build a better research foundation for policy discussions.

At this stage, the more prestigious, pro-establishment local think-tanks included the Business and Professionals Federation of Hong Kong, the Better Hong Kong Foundation and the Bauhinia Foundation; the latter was generally perceived to be in active support of the previous Chief Executive, Donald Tsang. The incumbent Chief Executive, C.Y. Leung, had very close ties with the One Country, Two Systems Research Institute. Two key members of his government team, Cheung Chi-kong and Shiu Sin-por, were formerly key leaders of the institute. The Hong Kong Policy Research Institute was no longer very active, though it attracted a lot of attention in the early years of the C. H. Tung administration; and the Social and Economic Policy Institute had ceased operation. Maintaining a think-tank of considerable scale on a long-term basis was certainly very challenging.

The Lion Rock Institute and Synergy Net were politically neutral; while the political stand of the Hong Kong Democratic Foundation and the Civic Exchange was close to the pro-democracy camp.[19]

As political parties in Hong Kong had limited resources for policy research, think-tanks' research outputs offered serious policy options different from those of the government. They served to promote meaningful policy discussions which were an important channel of political participation. There was still ample room for further development of think-tanks in the territory. In the controversy on the construction of

---

[19] See Tony Latter, *Hands on or Hands off? The Nature and Process of Economic Policy in Hong Kong*. Hong Kong: Hong Kong University Press, 2007, pp. 125–128.

high-speed railways, the work of proposing an alternative option challenging the government plan mainly fell upon two or three professionals; and it demonstrated the lack of policy research resources outside the government.

A serious handicap in promoting rational deliberations in political participation in Hong Kong was the deep ideological schisms within the political elites. The chances of accepting the other side's views were low, and the discussions centred on the publicity effects generated. Policy debates in the Legislative Council and its hearings seldom attracted the community's attention. Legislators emphasized securing sound bites in the media; and policy research was obviously not their priority. The vast majority of legislators depended on their respective small staff teams with limited policy research capabilities and resources. Top government officials tended to be cautious, and they wanted to make sure that they made no mistakes in public. Their strategy was to lobby for the support of the pro-establishment legislators; and the most effective way is to make concessions to satisfy their respective constituencies' demands. This pattern of parliamentary politics did not contribute much to meaningful political participation.

Theories on deliberative democracy stress adjusting the priorities of one's own interests in debates as well as balancing one's own interests with those of the public. However, the existing political cleavages had been exacerbated because, given the "executive-led" system of government, the HKSAR government was well protected by the electoral system as stipulated by the Basic Law, and there was no genuine political competition. The Chief Executive was picked by the Chinese leadership; and on important policy issues, the pro-establishment legislators would support the HKSAR government once Beijing had taken a stand. They would challenge the HKSAR government on minor policy issues like landfill though, so as to demonstrate that they were also ready to fight for the people's interests.

Political reforms were certainly one of the most significant concerns of the Hong Kong community. However, in the decade before the Occupation Campaign in 2014, there was only political mobilization, and almost no rational debates. Members of the pro-democracy movement understood that the Chinese leadership had no intention of allowing genuine democracy in the territory, hence their arguments were aimed at mobilizing people to support the democratic cause in elections and protest activities. At the same time, the defence put forward by politicians of the pro-Beijing united front was far from convincing; nobody realistically believed that the conditions in Hong Kong were not yet ripe for democracy. But the united front had substantial mobilizing power; it captured the government and a majority in the legislature and the District Councils.

Apparently there was no broadly-based political participation concerning important livelihood issues on which there were no well-defined political cleavages. The Donald Tsang administration raised the important question of broadening the territory's tax base. This was related to the level of the government's revenues, and the future financial resources in support of various types of social services. Hence, this was an issue with a significant impact on Hong Kong people's future welfare. Yet, there were not many serious discussions on the issue; the general response was that people were reluctant to accept an increase in tax burden, and the Donald Tsang administration abandoned the idea.

Long-term financing of medical care was a severe challenge for an ageing population. In the U.S. during the Clinton and Obama administrations, reform of the medical insurance system was hotly debated among all stakeholders, i.e., the entire population. However, in Hong Kong, most people were reluctant to contribute; they believed that the government had respectable fiscal reserves and therefore it should assume the responsibility for health care. The Tsang administration finally opted to encourage people to acquire their medical insurance policies from the private sector with financial incentives provided by the government.

In the final years of the British administration, especially during the administration of Governor Chris Patten, it tried hard to establish mutual trust with all political parties. On financial and economic policies, the British administration attempted to secure the votes of the pro-establishment legislators; on political reforms and human rights issues, it turned to the pro-democracy legislators for support.[20] This required

---

[20] Joseph Y.S. Cheng, "Sino-British Negotiations and the Challenges of the British Administration in the Final Transition Years" (in Chinese), in *Transition in 1997: Hong Kong's Challenges*, edited by Joseph Y.S. Cheng and Sonny S.H. Lo, Hong Kong: The Chinese University Press, 1997, pp. 23–24.

superb political skills; but all political parties felt that they had a constructive role to play in the government's policy-making process.

During the HKSAR government era, as Donald Tsang himself declared, there would be "differential treatment" depending on one's degree of support for the government. Political cleavages deepened in the absence of political competition, i.e., the opportunity for the government to be replaced by the opposition. As the pro-democracy groups were pushed outside of the political establishment, they felt they had no chance to influence government policies and therefore had little incentive to engage in a meaningful dialogue with top government officials. This "differential treatment" phenomenon gradually spread to the government's advisory committee system.

The government advisory committee system was an important channel for formal political participation. The traditional British model was to involve representatives from all representative, concerned groups in the relevant advisory committee in the policy sector. The British colonial administration was under no pressure to be accountable, and the appointees were appointed on an individual basis. The pressure on the British administration was quite limited, although in the 1970s and 1980s it began to actively involve some critics of the government.[21]

The HKSAR government made no attempt to improve the system further, instead there had been some serious backsliding. The first issue was the membership, which tended to be the same group of four or five hundred people. They mainly came from among the senior executives of major corporations and the top professionals with strong business ties with them. As more and more young family members of local tycoons received appointments, the suspicion of top government officials trying to curry favour with the tycoons was strengthening.

Senior government officials already spent considerable time on handling the media and the legislators, few of them were still willing to make good use of advisory committees to engage in serious consultation. As a result, most advisory committee members felt neglected. Those who were ready to offer critical views considered themselves cold-shouldered

---

[21] Joseph Y.S. Cheng, "Political Modernisation in Hong Kong", *The Journal of Commonwealth & Comparative Politics*, Vol. 27, No. 3, 1989, p. 306.

by government officials, who only welcome those members who were ready to defend government policies in public and who would not make their jobs more complicated.

IV Civil Society and Social Movements

Political participation offers opportunities for citizens to develop their full potential, and makes them realize that they can make an impact on the government; in the words of Premier Wen Jiabao, "to let people live happily with dignity".[22] From the government's point of view, low-level political participation would not exert pressure on the government, but it would not give the government a high level of legitimacy either. A politically apathetic population gave the government no trouble, but the latter could not achieve much either; this was the kind of situation Donald Tsang faced in his initial years. However, as his popularity declined, he gradually lacked the support and the political will to engage in serious policy reforms or even tackle controversial policy issues.[23] Due to the split of the establishment in the dirty electoral campaign fought between Henry Tang and C.Y. Leung, whose administration was subsequently tarnished by his own scandals and those of his team members, Leung's plight was even worse than that of Donald Tsang in his final years; even though Leung had intended to push for reforms.

In modern society, work pressure is high and life is busy, people's enthusiasm for political participation easily falls. Even in European countries with a long tradition of democracy, declining enthusiasm for political participation is still a challenge. Hence the concept of "participatory engineering" has emerged in the academic literature.[24] The concept largely refers to the efforts of political elites to promote political participation

---

[22] Jing Dongyu, "Wen Jiabao retires in a hidden way, the Development and Reform Commission finds it hard to suppress inflation" (in Chinese), *Cheng Ming Monthly*, No. 398, December 2010, p. 18.

[23] See, for example, Joseph Y.S. Cheng (ed.), *Evaluating the Tsang Years 2005–2012*, Hong Kong: City University of Hong Kong Press, 2013.

[24] Thomas Zittel, "Participatory Democracy and Political Participation", in *Participatory Democracy and Political Participation*, edited by Thomas Zittel and Dieter Fuchs, London and New York: Routledge, 2007, pp. 9–28.

through reforms of democratic institutions. In 2002, the ruling coalition of the Social Democratic Party and the Green Party in Germany proposed an amendment of the national constitution in parliament to introduce direct democracy measures at the federal level. Its purpose was to revive the nation's declining interest in political participation.

Hong Kong has yet to establish a democratic political system, and "participatory engineering" is beyond the community's horizon. The pro-establishment political parties normally believed that low voter turnout rates were in their favor; and the government naturally hoped that few people would take part in protest activities. On the other hand, pro-democracy political parties and a vast majority of NGOs were concerned about the development of civil society and the promotion of political participation among the people. However, they had limited resources, and tended to concentrate on issues which could attract people's attention.

Some Western political scientists hold different views. Their research reveals that people who have higher educational qualifications and incomes are more interested in politics and can better cope with the modern world's complicated political life. They therefore consider that economic development will have a greater positive impact on political participation than political institutions.[25] There had been no specific study on Hong Kong in this area, hence only some superficial observations could be offered at this stage.

In the District Boards (later District Councils) elections in the 1980s and 1990s, voter turnout rates in the New Territories were higher than those in the urban areas, with the highest rates in districts where there were high concentrations of indigenous villagers. In the urban districts, there were usually higher voter turnout rates in areas of high concentrations of public housing estates; voter turnout rates were lowest in upper-middle-class residential districts like Tsim Sha Tsui, Yaumati, Happy Valley, and Mid-levels.[26] This pattern had not changed much in the

---

[25] *Ibid.*, p. 10.

[26] Joseph Y. S. Cheng, "The 1988 District Board Elections — A Study of Political Participation in the Transitional Period", in *Hong Kong: The Challenge of Transformation*, edited by Kathleen Cheek-Milby and Miron Mushkat, Hong Kong: Centre of Asian Studies, University of Hong Kong, 1989, pp. 116–149.

early 2010s. Naturally, voter turnout rates were just one indicator of political participation, and the above pattern mainly reflected network mobilization power. However, voting in elections is considered the most important act of political participation; and the general explanation for the low voter turnout rates among the upper-middle socio-economic strata in Hong Kong was that they had nothing to ask for in terms of social services provided by the government, hence they had low motivation to vote. On the other hand, leaders and members of the most influential business and professional groups in Hong Kong were all well-educated with high incomes. They played important roles in the government's policymaking process, and often participated in the government's advisory committees. They were the political elite in Hong Kong.

In the early 1980s, when Beijing and London began to prepare and mobilize for the negotiations on Hong Kong's future, the pro-Beijing united front also actively approached community leaders in all socioeconomic strata and sectors. There was a major setback during the Tiananmen Incident and its aftermath, but united front work soon recovered. After the establishment of the HKSAR government, its development had become even more prominent. Joining these united front organizations was then perceived as a channel to become a member of the establishment; activists in these organizations had a good platform to stand for District Council elections, and had a chance to be appointed to the government's advisory committees. Those who were interested in pursuing a political career, especially those who did not come from rich families, were strongly tempted to consider these organizations. Appointments as political assistants and deputy heads of policy bureaus were apparently very attractive.

For many small businessmen and professionals who were not interested in politics, united front organizations were valuable for establishing useful economic contacts. In view of the rapid economic integration between Hong Kong and the Mainland, many owners of small- and medium-sized enterprises and professionals believed that membership of the united front organizations would bring them convenience and opportunities in developing their businesses in the Mainland, and the latter was increasingly important to them.

Since Hong Kong's return to the Motherland, civic groups outside the establishment had also been enjoying healthy development, in line with political theories on the relationship between economic development and political participation. The Hong Kong people enjoying respectable living standards sought satisfaction in life through social and political participation. In the same period, social and political participation in Taiwan showed remarkable progress. At the end of the Chiang Ching-kuo regime in the late 1980s, political liberalization — symbolized by the termination of the ban on political parties and newspapers — led to an outburst of enthusiasm for political participation that had been suppressed during the previous decades of authoritarian rule. This enthusiasm probably reached a peak in the presidential election in 2000. After that, corruption and the emotional, non-rational elements in the elections led to a return of political apathy among a segment of the electorate.

The development of civil society maintained its momentum nevertheless. Various religious groups, philanthropic bodies, environmental NGOs, etc., all demonstrated substantial resources and mobilization power. A considerable proportion of the people felt that their participation in the civil society brought them satisfaction.

The overthrow of Presidents Ferdinand Marcos and Joseph Estrada by "people power revolutions" in the Philippines was indeed impressive. Although corruption in politics continued to be a serious problem, and political and economic power was captured by a small number of families, the development of civil society was healthy, and the Filipinos were enthusiastic in social and political participation. In Indonesia, since the downfall of President Suharto in the wake of the Asia-Pacific financial crisis in 1998, political democratization and the development of civil society had been remarkable too so much so that commentators considered that Indonesia was the most democratic country in Southeast Asia. The performance of the student movement and the women's rights campaign was especially outstanding; within a short period of time, its media, in both qualitative and qualitative terms, made significant improvements.

Hong Kong's traditional political culture neglected participation and emphasized tackling one's problems through one's own efforts. Since the turn of the century, various types of civic groups had emerged, attracting many young participants and grassroots activists. These groups were usually small in size with very limited resources, but they often articulated issues not taken up by the major political parties.

The campaigns to preserve the Queen's Pier, Lee Tung Street (Wedding Cards Street) and Choi Yuen Village; the protest against the government's high-speed railway plan, and so on, to a considerable extent caught the government and the major political parties by surprise. The participants were social activists of the "post-1980s" generation. These social movements or campaigns demonstrated that the younger generation felt that the existing political parties did not represent them; and some of the young activists may not be keenly interested in the struggle for democracy. They wanted to choose their own issues, and campaigned in their own style; to them, participation itself was probably more significant than achieving the objectives of their campaigns.[27]

These activists of the "post-1980s" generation had their own networks and modes of mobilization. They were not much motivated to get themselves organized, apparently they did not seem to be active in establishing their own organizations; and they wanted to maintain a distance from the pro-democracy political parties. Their activities attracted a lot of media attention, and they were very active in the new Internet media, thus they had a considerable influence on the younger generation. A new star among these activists was the Scholarism group which successfully blocked the introduction of "Moral and National Education" as a subject in the school curriculum in the autumn of 2012. This group of senior high school students and young university students soon won the admiration of the community. In the July 1 protest rally in 2013, they raised more money than any other pro-democracy group or political party.

From an academic point of view, this type of political participation did not focus on the establishment of constitutional, democratic institutions, but much more on mobilization and participation, thus securing agenda-setting power through the articulation of issues at the community level. This type of participation concentrated on the community; participation itself brought satisfaction, and participation itself was the meaning and objective. In the long-term, this type of participation might serve to promote more inclusive and accountable political institutions, develop

---

[27] See Note 3 above.

a participatory political culture, and cultivate political talents outside the establishment. The social movements concerned were careful to avoid capture by political parties or political elites, so as eventually would go against their original purposes.[28] This reflected the weaknesses of existing political parties and political elites, and highlighted the danger of political fragmentation.

V Differences within the Pro-Democracy Movement

Even in democratic countries, coalitions of opposition parties or opposition parties not in alliance or coalitions find it difficult to maintain cooperation on a long-term basis if there is no chance for them to capture government together. There is a natural tendency to cooperate with the governing party, especially when it suffers from a setback in a general election and no longer controls an absolute majority in the legislature. The New Komeito in Japan is a good example. Another tendency is to become radicalized, and downgrade the importance of parliamentary politics, as is often the case with small communist parties in European countries.

Since Hong Kong's return to the Motherland, the pro-democracy parties had been in decline; further, they were kept outside the political establishment by the HKSAR government. Both of these tendencies were strengthening at the same time. In the first place, arguments on the party line first emerged in the DP, whose appeal was in decline due to other factors as well. Under such circumstances, the CP was established in early 2006, followed by the League of Social Democrats.

Intense competition among the pro-democracy political parties in Legislative Council elections became the norm; and this was largely related to the electoral system. In the direct elections to the geographical constituencies in the Legislative Council elections, voters had one vote each in the five multi-member constituencies. There were no incentives for the pro-democracy parties to cooperate; in fact, pro-democracy

---

[28] John Gaventa, "Foreword", in *Mobilizing for Democracy: Citizen Action and the Politics of Public Participation*, edited by Vera Schattam, P. Coelho and Bettina von Lieres, London and New York: Zed Books, 2010, pp. xiii and xiv.

candidates within the same constituency were in competition for the same pool of voters who were in support of the democracy cause.

In contrast, in District Council elections, which adopted the "single-member constituency, simple-majority" system, pro-democracy parties understood that it was a case of political suicide if two or more of their candidates competed in the same constituency. In fact, they would be severely criticized by the voters in support of the pro-democracy movement for their disunity. In the District Council elections in 2003, the pro-democracy parties initiated a formal co-ordination mechanism and secured a major victory, though the pro-establishment parties' support for "the Article 23 legislation" was the principal cause of their considerable fall in support. In the District Council elections in 2007, the coordination mechanism was basically maintained. Although the League of Social Democrats withdrew from the mechanism in the District Council elections in 2011, the other pro-democracy political parties still worked hard to uphold the coordination mechanism. To ensure that only one pro-democracy candidate competed in each District Council constituency was an arrangement of mutual benefit, that was why the coordination mechanism largely worked despite the differences among the pro-democracy parties.

As they were in perpetual opposition without effective participation in the government's policy-making processes, the pro-democracy parties had limited appeal to various types of interest groups. The business and professional groups were important enough to have frequent direct contacts with the government to influence its policies, and they did not maintain a dialogue with the pro-democracy parties. The limited contacts between the two sides were mainly for public relations purpose; in fact, within the "executive-led" system of government, the business and professional groups did not feel much need to have a meaningful dialogue with the pro-establishment political parties either.

The civic groups outside the political establishment were usually very cautious in their co-operation with the pro-democracy political parties. One reason was the traditional political culture; the groups concerned did not want to involve political parties in their negotiations with the government. There were unhappy experiences in cooperation in the 1980s and 1990s between the pro-democracy political parties and some grassroots pressure groups; the latter felt that they had been exploited by the former for publicity. Basically, civic groups outside the political establishment jealously guarded their independence and purity, they wanted to fight for their own unique missions and avoid being involved in the political interests and considerations of political parties.

Civic groups which valued an effective dialogue with the government naturally desired good relations with it; and anti-establishment pressure groups wanted to grasp the initiative of their political struggles in their own hands and refused to allow the initiative to pass to the pro-democracy political parties.[29] This alienation and mutual distrust between the latter and the anti-establishment pressure groups had perhaps been exacerbated since the second half of the first decade of the century. As dissatisfaction with the HKSAR government grew, some radical groups perceived all political parties as part of the political establishment and refused formal co-operation even with the pro-democracy political parties. In contrast to the European countries, there were very few issues and movements in Hong Kong that generated close cooperation between the anti-establishment political parties and civic groups.

To some extent, as the cause of fighting for democracy had been dominated by the pro-democracy parties, most civic groups of young people tended to find issues of their own interest. They were therefore not too keen concerning the struggle for democracy. In 2007, the protest movement to preserve the Queen's Pier seemed to have surprised the government and all major political parties. Apparently, the pro-democracy movement was not able to satisfy the younger generation's social demands. Admittedly, the pro-democracy movement failed to win the trust and wholehearted support of the people regarding the most significant livelihood issues ranging from housing, education, medical care to minority rights, environmental protection, and animal rights. As the community realized that the Chinese leadership opposed genuine democracy for the territory and significant breakthroughs could not be achieved in the foreseeable future, it was difficult to maintain a high

---

[29] Francis L.F. Lee and Joseph M. Chan, "Making Sense of Participation: The Political Culture of the Pro-Democracy Demonstrations in Hong Kong", *China Quarterly*, No. 193, March 2008, pp. 84–101.

level of enthusiasm for fighting for democracy among a majority of Hong Kong people.

Despite all these serious obstacles, the pro-democracy parties still secured about 55%–60% of the votes in the direct elections to the Legislative Council. The community counted on them to provide effective checks and balances *vis-à-vis* the HKSAR government; it appreciated the significance of checks and balances, and it understood that power corrupts. The Hong Kong people's political wisdom balanced the increasing political mobilization capability of the pro-Beijing united front. The latter through its political groups and grassroots organizations offered important services at the grassroots level. Their distribution of rice, edible oil, mooncakes, etc., organization of snake-soup banquets and holiday trips, and assistance in handling applications to various government departments were valuable to families with low incomes and limited education. These services helped the united front build effective networks; and the networks in turn became important mobilization instruments in elections and political campaigns.

At the same time, the HKSAR government placed a lot of emphasis on propaganda and image-building since the early-2010s, as reflected by the significant increase in resources spent in these fields. Senior civil servants often complained that their superiors paid too much attention to the criticisms of the media. Certainly, the HKSAR government's propaganda was one type of political mobilization, it was not very effective at this stage, but it was difficult to assess its impact on the community's political participation in the long term.

VI General Observations

In the past, the colonial administration successfully secured the Hong Kong people's support and its legitimacy through its performance in economic development and social stability. Since the territory's return to the Motherland, most people had not perceived any obvious sustainable improvement in living standards on their part, instead they considered that the gap between the rich and poor had been widening, upward social mobility opportunities had been in decline, and the government had been favouring major business groups in various ways. As reflected by the published opinion surveys, the community's evaluation of and support for the HKSAR government had been deteriorating, and there was a crisis of "legitimacy deficit" on its part. Lack of progress in democratization certainly disappointed the supporters of the pro-democracy movement.

Apparently, the Donald Tsang administration was aware of its "legitimacy deficit", hence, it avoided controversial policy issues like a consumption tax and mandatory contributions to a medical insurance fund. In the first year of the C.Y. Leung administration, there was already speculation that he might soon have to step down. While serious controversies and setbacks had been avoided, the Hong Kong people realized that they could not expect major policy reforms from the government. The latter gradually lost the appeal to persuade the community to take some " bitter pills", instead it became accustomed to distribute "candies" to please the public.

Within the framework of an "executive-led" system of government, the role of political parties was relatively limited. The difficulties and inadequacies of the pro-democracy movement have been considered above, the effectiveness of the government's advisory committee system had also been in decline; under such circumstances, the room for normal expansion of meaningful political participation for Hong Kong people was not obvious.

While there had been considerable accumulation of grievances in the community, so far, the Hong Kong people's general response had been a sense of resignation, disappointment, and helplessness, not anger. The economy of Hong Kong was a mature one, its middle class probably enjoyed one of the highest living standards in Asia, and families at the grassroots level benefitted from a fairly generous social security net. Since the negotiations on the territory's future in the early-1980s, Hong Kong people had well understood that they needed to maintain an attractive investment environment, and social stability was essential to such an environment.

On the other hand, in view of the Chinese leadership's rejection of genuine democratization, the community's sense of political impotence in the colonial era continued, and might perhaps have been exacerbated.

The vast majority of the Hong Kong people had no intention of confronting the Chinese authorities, and they were proud of China's rising international status; further, they were grateful for Beijing's support of the territory's economy in terms of policy concessions. In contrast to the years before 1997, Hong Kong people's trust for the central government was sometimes even higher than their evaluation of the HKSAR government's performance. The trend, however, had been reversed since 2008, the Chinese leadership's interferences in Hong Kong and the deteriorating human rights conditions in China resulted in a decline of this trust, and the fall was more significant in 2012 and 2013.

Radical political participation in general had a limited market in Hong Kong. There were considerable worry and resentment in the community against the mode of political articulation and expression on the part of the League of Social Democrats, People Power, and some young radical activists of the "post-1980s" generation. At this stage, the territory's moderate political culture was still an effective deterrence against radical political action, but there was a worry that as young people became more frustrated with their career prospects, the number of young radical activists would grow rapidly.

In the existing electoral system, the target of the radical political parties was one seat in each of the five geographical constituencies based on the support of 10% of the electorate. This was quite an achievable target, as was demonstrated in the 2012 Legislative Council elections, but the ceiling might soon be reached. Radical young activists usually did not amount to more than a few thousand; moreover, they were not interested in getting organized. Obviously, their radical political actions were moderate by European standards.

In the early 2010s, the local media observed "a resentment against the rich" among Hong Kong people which might have an impact on political participation in the territory. There was on the other hand, widespread expression of envy of the rich; newspapers and magazines were full of reports of the lifestyles of the rich, and apparently they were popular reading. This "resentment against the rich" probably reflected a dissatisfaction with the widening gap between the rich and poor and the government's policies favouring the major business groups and real estate tycoons. The latter and the government felt the pressure, hence the gesture of the establishment of a Community Care Fund.[30]

The challenge was not so much the resentment, but the perception of lack of fair competition. The early promulgation of a fair competition law would contribute to a reduction of the resentment. A more significant issue was the government's commitment in social services which represented income redistribution. This is probably the most important political question in all politically stable countries. Medical insurance was probably the domestic policy issue that had attracted the most attention in the U.S. in recent years, while in the wake of the global financial tsunami the impact of budget cuts on social security was at the top of the policy agenda in most European countries.

The situation in Hong Kong was rather unusual because the government enjoyed frequent budget surpluses and substantial fiscal reserves. The community was therefore reluctant to absorb extra taxation burden, and only asked the government to assume the financial responsibility for improvements in social security. To avoid controversies, the Donald Tsang administration dodged the issue of expanding the tax base through the introduction of a consumption tax, and refused to propose a mandatory contributory medical insurance scheme. The C.Y. Leung administration did not have the political support to engage in such testing policy reforms. The political reform issue would keep its hands full. Hong Kong people therefore did not feel that there were many serious policy issues to engage in community-wide deliberations, and this had a negative impact on political participation.

The political reform issue in 2013 and 2014 was a severe test. The Chinese leadership failed to satisfy Hong Kong people's demands for democratization, and the HKSAR government suffered a severe "legitimacy deficit"; the latter would hardly have the necessary political support to promote the reforms the territory needed. All parties would suffer from the policy paralysis and political polarization.

---

[30] See the comments made by the local tycoons about the resentment against the rich at http://uk.reuters.com/article/2014/02/28/hongkong-li-idUKL3N0LX2GO20140228 and http://www.chinadailyasia.com/opinion/2013-11/06/content_15096734.html accessed on April 2, 2014.

Under these circumstances, the Hong Kong people focused on their work and families. Work pressure was usually high, and leisure time was limited. Therefore, theoretically, there was ample scope for religious activities, neighbourhood social interactions, voluntary service, etc., to develop, as in the case of Taiwan. After all, human beings are social animals, and political and social participation brings satisfaction in life.

Acknowledgement

This chapter is originally published in *New Trends of Political Participation in Hong Kong,* ed. Joseph Y.S. Cheng, © 2014 City University of Hong Kong. Used by permission of City University of Hong Kong Press. All rights reserved.

Chapter 22

Democratization in Hong Kong: A Theoretical Exception

I Introduction

Hong Kong is a rather unique case in the discussion of democracy/democratization in East Asia. In the first place, it is not a sovereign state, but a special administrative region under the sovereignty of the People's Republic of China (Hong Kong Special Administrative Region of the PRC, HKSAR), which has pledged to maintain a high degree of autonomy in the territory in the Sino-British Joint Declaration of 1984. It has an "executive-led" system of government meaning that power is highly concentrated in the Chief Executive, and the selection process is tightly controlled by the Chinese leadership, as well demonstrated in the elections in 2012 and 2017. The legislature, to a certain extent, plays an effective checks-and-balances role, as new legislation and financial appropriations must be approved by the Legislative Council. However, the electoral system was designed so that the pro-democracy camp cannot secure a majority of seats, despite the fact that it consistently manages to secure about 50% to 60% of the votes in the direct elections to the legislature.

Most academics categorize Hong Kong's political system as a hybrid regime with varying levels of democracy in various political institutions. At the same time, there is a common understanding inside and outside the territory that unless there is genuine democracy in China, there can be no real democracy in Hong Kong. Theoretically, Hong Kong therefore offers an interesting example of how soft authoritarianism works, and what are the general challenges ahead.

This chapter traces the political development in Hong Kong and, in the next section, identifies its salient features. The third section attempts to explain the apparent theoretical contradictions, and the last section considers the challenges ahead in the context of the demands for change.

II Political Development in Hong Kong after 1997

The Tung administration was seen to be willing to sacrifice Hong Kong people's freedoms to please Beijing. Democratization came into the picture because people were dissatisfied that they had no part in selecting C.H. Tung as the Chief Executive; and when he performed poorly, there was no way to get rid of him. Various arguments against the premature introduction of full democracy, i.e., universal suffrage, as articulated by the pro-Beijing united front, fell flat because in the final years of the Tung administration, the community believed that any candidate would be better than he was.

The Chinese leadership was acutely aware of that, and was anxious to help to maintain the territory's political and social stability. Chinese leaders understood that they had to soften the opposition to Tung at least within the pro-Beijing united front and the business community. They therefore chose to help Hong Kong solve its economic problems. Assistance included a sharp increase in the number of tourists allowed to visit Hong Kong (the Individual Travel Scheme), the Closer Economic Partnership Arrangements (CEPA) which gives Hong Kong better access to the China market,[1] and political pressure on Guangdong to improve cooperation with the territory. People in Hong Kong appreciated the economic support from the central government and, in general, had a very good impression of the leaders in China then, namely, Hu Jintao and Wen Jiabao.

The Chinese leadership still considers that economic growth remains the key to the territory's social and political stability. Since the status quo is still satisfactory to the community which has no intention to challenge

---

[1] For details of CEPA, see all major newspapers in Hong Kong on September 30, 2003.

the Chinese authorities, moderate economic growth is adequate to dampen grievances to and maintain stability. However, the government lacks the legitimacy to redefine the priorities even in the economic and social services field. In view of Beijing's perception of threats from the pro-democracy movement, it is unlikely that it will release a timetable and a roadmap to democracy based on universal suffrage.

Twenty years after the territory's return to China, there has been no significant progress in democracy. In fact interferences from Beijing have been increasing since July 2003 when compared with the first three years after 1997. The Chinese authorities' dogmatic insistence on an "executive-led" system of government means that the systemic difficulties in the executive-legislature relationship have not been tackled. Meanwhile, the absence of serious civil service reforms has resulted in declining performance of the system as well as accumulating frustration.

III Explaining the Theoretical Contradictions

Dankwart Rustow argues that democratization is a long process which may take several generations.[2] Samuel Huntington, however, considers that a linear model "does not necessarily represent the matter in democratic transition".[3] Huntington proposes that there may be another "cyclical model of alternating despotism and democracy" in which regular elections cannot lead to the defeat of the government in power. In the developing countries, there may be a third model which is the oscillation between authoritarian regimes and democratic ones. According to Huntington, the expansion of middle class participation in politics may eventually bring about the collapse of authoritarian regimes and the installation of democratic ones.

The general literature of comparative democratization assumes that the role of the middle class is a key variable linking economic development and democracy. Modernization theory considers that economic

---

[2] Dankwart A. Rustow, "Transition to Democracy: Toward a Dynamic Model", *Comparative Politics*, Vol. 2, No. 3, April 1970, pp. 337–363.
[3] Samuel P. Huntington, "Will More Countries Become Democratic?", *Political Science Quarterly*, Vol. 99, No. 2, Summer 1984, p. 210.

development promotes political democracy because it transforms a traditional society into a modern society that constitutes a necessary and sufficient condition for democratic politics.[4] The societal transformations include the spread of education, urbanization, increase in upward social mobility opportunities, and so on. In line with economic growth, a modern society becomes more diversified and sophisticated, and cannot be easily controlled by an authoritarian regime. Some scholars argue that economic development destabilizes an authoritarian regime by cultivating a politically autonomous and empowered middle class.[5] It is generally expected therefore that the middle class would not accept authoritarianism and instead would demand political participation. Modernization theory considers that the expansion and strengthening of the middle class would enhance the pro-democracy forces. According to the structural-functional school of the modernization theorists, the middle class is the agent needed for bringing about the changes leading to a democratic polity. In sum, economic development transforms the social environment, giving rise to the middle class, who in turn promotes democratization which establishes a political arrangement serving its interests.[6]

---

[4] See, for example, Samuel P. Huntington, *The Third Wave: Democratization in the Late Twentieth Century*, Norman, Oklahoma: University of Oklahoma Press, 1991; and Seymour Martin Lipset, *Political Man: The Social Basis of Politics*, New York: Doubleday, 1960.

[5] See, for example, Robert Dahl, *Polyarchy: Participation and Opposition*, New Haven, Connecticut: Yale University Press, 1971; Francis Fukuyama, "Capitalism and Democracy: the Missing Link", in Larry Diamond and M. F. Plattner, *Capitalism, Socialism and Democracy Revisited*, Baltimore: The Johns Hopkins University Press, 1993, pp. 94–105; R. Glassman, *The Middle Class and Democracy in Socio-Historical Perspective*, Leiden: E.J. Brill, 1995; Samuel P. Huntington, *The Third Wave: Democratization in the Late Twentieth Century, op. cit.*; Seymour Martin Lipset, *Some Social Requisites of Democracy: Economic Development and Political Legitimacy*, American Political Science Review, Vol. 53, No.1, March 1959, pp. 69–105; and Barrington Moore, *Social Origins of Dictatorship and Democracy: Lord and Peasant in the Making of the Modern World*, Boston: Beacon, 1966.

[6] Carles Boix, *Democracy and Redistribution*, Oxford: Cambridge University Press, 2003; and Gongqin, Xiao, "The Rise of the Technocrats", *Journal of Democracy*, Vol. 14, No. 1, January 2003, pp. 60–65.

Hong Kong goes against these tenets of the modernization theory; and it is not the only exception.[7] When the core values and basic rights of the people of Hong Kong were seen to be threatened as in the cases of the Tiananmen Square Incident in June 1989 and the "anti-Article 23 legislation" protests in 2003, the community showed a strong demand for democracy, with political participation reaching extremely high levels. This forced the British colonial administration, the U.K. government and, in fact, the international community to respond in 1989–1990 and the Chinese leadership to seriously adjust its Hong Kong policy in 2003–2004. Subsequently, when the political situation calmed down, Hong Kong people's political passion also declined.

(a) *Cost-benefit Analysis*

One explanation is a cost-benefit analysis. In view of the maintenance of the rule of law, the protection of basic human freedoms and the impressive economic growth during the British administration era from the 1950s to the 1980s, the people of Hong Kong were generally satisfied with the status quo. At the same time, the risks of confronting the colonial authorities were substantial. There were also opportunities for emigration to Western countries. Pursuit of democracy might have led to intervention by Beijing or the recovery of the territory by China, which the bulk of the population feared. On balance, the demand for political participation and democracy was dampened because the costs and risks were considerable, while the benefits were neither obvious nor significant.

Similar analysis and conclusion probably exist today in Hong Kong. The *status quo* is still acceptable. The rule of law and the protection of fundamental human freedoms have been basically maintained, though there have been criticisms of increasing self-censorship and censorship, as well as certain erosion of the independence of the judiciary. Economic growth in the past decade has not been very impressive in the eyes of Hong Kong people, but still respectable (see Table 22.1). At the same

---

[7] R. Robison and David S.G. Goodman, *The New Rich in Asia: Mobile Phones, McDonald's and Middle-class Revolution*, London: Routledge, 1996; and Garry Rodan (ed.), *Political Oppositions in Industrializing Asia*, London: Routledge, 1996.

Table 22.1: Gross Domestic Product (GDP) of Hong Kong, 1997–2016

Year	GDP At Current Market Prices HK$ Million	Year-on-Year % Change	In Chained (2016) Dollars HK$ Million	Year-on-Year % Change	Implicit Price Deflator of GDP Year 2016=100	Year-on-Year % Change	Per capita GDP At Current Market Prices HK$	Year-on-Year % Change	In Chained (2016) Dollars HK$	Year-on-Year % Change
1997	1,373,083	11.2	1,361,881	5.1	100.8	5.8	211,592	10.2	209,866	4.2
1998	1,308,074	-4.7	1,281,766	-5.9	102.1	1.2	199,898	-5.5	195,878	-6.7
1999	1,285,946	-1.7	1,313,896	2.5	97.9	-4.1	194,649	-2.6	198,879	1.5
2000	1,337,501	4.0	1,414,586	7.7	94.6	-3.4	200,675	3.1	212,241	6.7
2001	1,321,142	-1.2	1,422,520	0.6	92.9	-1.8	196,765	-1.9	211,864	-0.2
2002	1,297,341	-1.8	1,446,086	1.7	89.7	-3.4	192,367	-2.2	214,422	1.2
2003	1,256,669	-3.1	1,490,283	3.1	84.3	-6.0	186,704	-2.9	221,412	3.3
2004	1,316,949	4.8	1,619,938	8.7	81.3	-3.6	194,140	4.0	238,806	7.9
2005	1,412,125	7.2	1,739,623	7.4	81.2	-0.2	207,263	6.8	255,331	6.9
2006	1,503,351	6.5	1,861,966	7.0	80.7	-0.5	219,240	5.8	271,538	6.3
2007	1,650,756	9.8	1,982,339	6.5	83.3	3.1	238,676	8.9	286,618	5.6
2008	1,707,487	3.4	2,024,522	2.1	84.3	1.3	245,406	2.8	290,972	1.5
2009	1,659,245	-2.8	1,974,738	-2.5	84.0	-0.4	237,960	-3.0	283,206	-2.7
2010	1,776,332	7.1	2,108,382	6.8	84.3	0.3	252,887	6.3	300,160	6.0
2011	1,934,430	8.9	2,209,894	4.8	87.5	3.9	273,549	8.2	312,503	4.1
2012	2,037,059	5.3	2,247,469	1.7	90.6	3.5	284,899	4.1	314,327	0.6
2013	2,138,305	5.0	2,317,174	3.1	92.3	1.8	297,860	4.5	322,776	2.7
2014	2,260,005	5.7	2,381,184	2.8	94.9	2.9	312,609	5.0	329,370	2.0
2015	2,398,280	6.1	2,438,043	2.4	98.4	3.6	328,924	5.2	334,377	1.5
2016	2,490,776	3.9	2,490,776	2.2	100.0	1.7	339,500	3.2	339,500	1.5

Notes: Figures in this table are data released on 16 November 2018.

Source: Census and Statistics Department, The Government of the Hong Kong Special Administrative Region, "Hong Kong Statistics — Statistical Tables." http://www.censtatd.gov.hk/hong_kong_statistics/statistical_tables/index.jsp?charsetID=1&subjectID=12&tableID=030.

time, the community understands that the local economy has been increasingly dependent on that of China (see Table 22.2), and it lacks the political will to confront the Chinese authorities over the issue of democratization. Nationalism has become a more important factor in the values of the people of Hong Kong, who appreciate the rising status of the Chinese nation and China's achievements in the economic, scientific and technological, sports, and other arenas.

They realize that the Chinese leadership is reluctant to grant genuine democracy to the territory, i.e., accepting the outcomes of democratic elections without exerting any influence in the electoral processes. Although a significant majority of them is in support of democracy, as reflected by opinion surveys, in view of Beijing's hardline position on political reforms, the community tends to return to its traditional political apathy as it is reluctant to sacrifice stability and prosperity in the pursuit of democracy. Since 2003, the pro-democracy movement has been organizing a protest rally on July 1 every year, with the main theme of realizing democracy in the form of direct elections of the Chief Executive and the entire legislature on the basis of universal suffrage. There are other themes depending on the political issues of the times, and the turnout depends on the general level of dissatisfaction with the HKSAR government. Apparently this cost-benefit calculus exists among the middle class in China today too.[8]

Somewhat in contrast to Taiwan, the development of civil society remains relatively limited in Hong Kong in the sense that the proportion of citizens taking part in civil groups of various kinds and engaging in voluntary work is still comparatively low. S.K. Lau argues that in the 1960s and 1970s, the Hong Kong people realized that they could solve their problems through their own efforts without having to exert pressure on the government by political participation; he describes this culture as "utilitarian familism."[9] The community's values have undergone some changes which will be discussed below, but the "utilitarian" aspect certainly remains strong.

---

[8] Min Tang, "The Political Behavior of the Chinese Middle Class", *Journal of Chinese Political Science*, Vol. 16, No. 4, December 2011, pp. 373–387.

[9] Siu-kai Lau, *Society and Politics in Hong Kong*, Hong Kong: The Chinese University Press, 1982.

Table 22.2: Trade, investment and tourism between Mainland China and Hong Kong, 1978–2011

	Trade (US$ billion)			Entrepôt Trade			Investment (US$ billion)		Tourism (1,000 persons)	
Year	Mainland Exports to HK	Mainland Imports from HK	Total	Main-land Exports to HK	Main-land Imports from HK	Total	Mainland Investment in HK	HK Investment in Mainland	No. of Mainland Visitors to HK	No. of HK Visitors to Mainland***
1978	1.35 (—)	0.04 (—)	1.39 (—)	—	0.03	—	—	—	—	1,562
1981	3.78 (8.99)	1.41 (2.12)	5.19 (11.11)	—	1.03	—	—	—	15	7,053
1986	10.47 (9.78)	7.55 (5.61)	18.02 (15.39)	—	5.24	—	—	—	44	21,269
1991	37.61 (32.14)	26.63 (17.46)	64.24 (49.60)	51.77*	19.66	71.43	—	— (1.33)	112	30,506
1996	73.13 (32.91)	61.46 (7.83)	134.59 (40.73)	87.63	53.56	141.19	2.59** (—)	6.94** (2.58)	2,311	44,229
2001	87.43 (46.54)	70.02 (9.42)	157.45 (55.96)	103.64	63.66	167.30	4.94 (—)	8.50 (20.87)	4,449	74,345
2002	91.93 (58.46)	78.62 (10.73)	170.55 (69.19)	110.77	73.32	184.09	4.06 (—)	15.94 (16.72)	6,825	80,808
2003	100.72 (76.27)	95.20 (11.12)	195.92 (87.39)	123.99	90.49	214.48	4.87 (1.15)	7.68 (17.86)	8,467	77,527
2004	117.73 (100.87)	113.92 (11.80)	231.64 (112.67)	145.57	109.06	254.63	7.95 (2.63)	18.56 (17.70)	12,246	88,421
2005	134.53 (124.47)	129.82 (12.23)	264.35 (136.70)	168.36	124.09	292.45	9.35 (3.42)	16.71 (19.00)	12,541	95,928
2006	152.94 (155.31)	148.23 (10.78)	301.17 (166.09)	187.35	143.07	330.42	13.94 (6.93)	21.36 (17.95)	13,591	98,318
2007	170.47 (184.44)	167.74 (12.80)	338.20 (197.24)	204.84	162.53	367.37	13.36 (13.73)	36.40 (20.23)	15,486	101,136
2008	180.86 (190.73)	175.70 (12.92)	356.56 (203.64)	218.94	171.24	390.18	23.04 (38.64)	27.59 (27.70)	16,862	101,317

(Continued)

Table 22.2: (Continued)

	Trade (US$ billion)			Entrepôt Trade			Investment (US$ billion)		Tourism (1,000 persons)	
Year	Mainland Exports to HK	Mainland Imports from HK	Total	Mainland Exports to HK	Mainland Imports from HK	Total	Mainland Investment in HK	HK Investment in Mainland	No. of Mainland Visitors to HK	No. of HK Visitors to Mainland ***
2009	160.83 (166.23)	3.44 (8.71)	164.27 (174.95)	—	—	159.18	—	(46.08)	17,957	100,054
2010	196.62 (218.30)	4.01 (12.26)	200.63 (230.56)	234.06	201.41	435.47	37.04 (38.51)	37.21 (60.57)	22,684	102,495
2011	218.10 (267.98)	3.95 (15.49)	222.05 (283.48)	259.00	220.57	479.57	— (35.65)	— (70.50)	28,100	103,048

Notes: 1. Figures may not add up to the totals due to rounding.
2. "—" indicates that statistical data are unavailable, unknown, or negligible.
3. Statistics from mainland Chinese sources are given in brackets.
4. Figures for mainland imports from HK exclude HK's re-exports to China.
5. * Figure for 1992.
6. ** Figures for 1998.
7. *** No. of Hong Kong visitors to the mainland includes visitors from Macau.

Sources: Census and Statistics Department, The Government of the Hong Kong Special Administrative Region, "Hong Kong Statistics," http://www.censtatd.gov.hk/hong_kong_statistics/index.jsp; *A Statistical Review of Tourism* (1981, 1986, 1991, and 1996 issues), Hong Kong, Research Department, Hong Kong Tourism Association, 1982, 1987, 1992, and 1997; Hong Kong Tourism Board, *Visitor Arrival Statistics* (published monthly), http://partnernet.hktourismboard.com; State Statistical Bureau, People's Republic of China (comp.), *China Statistical Yearbook* (1983, 1987, 1992, 1997, 2003, 2004, 2006, 2008, and 2009 issues), China Statistics Press, Beijing,1983, 1987, 1992, 1997, 2003, 2004, 2006, 2008, and 2009; and Ministry of Commerce, National Bureau of Statistics, and State Administration of Foreign Exchange, People's Republic of China. *2008 Niandu Zhongguo duiwai zhijie touzi tongji gongbao (2008 statistical bulletin of China's outward foreign direct investment)*, September 2009, http://hzs.mofcom.gov.cn/accessory/200909/1253868856016.pdf.

In general, political parties in Hong Kong are cadre parties, not mass parties. The pro-Beijing Democratic Alliance for the Betterment (DAB) and Progress of Hong Kong is now the largest political party in Hong Kong, and it has a membership of over 10,000 with a large number of professionals including lawyers. As the flagship pro-Beijing party in the territory, it offers a good platform to build networks with government officials and businessmen. In a way, it serves the same purpose as the Rotary Clubs or the Lions Clubs. Card-carrying members believe they have a certain advantage working in China; as more and more professionals have to engage in business activities in the Mainland — they consider that the benefits of joining the party far outweigh the small costs. For the more ambitious, dedicated service for the party is often rewarded by senior government appointments, such as appointments to prestigious official advisory committees, and official honors. Appointments as deputies to the National People's Congress and their local counterparts, as well as delegates to the National Committee of the Chinese People's Political Consultative Conference and their local organs, are also possible rewards for party services and donations. These are significant honours with high political and social status; for example, deputies to the National People's Congress can ask to meet provincial governors and central ministers, and one can easily imagine what the privilege means for those doing business in Mainland China.

On the other hand, the pro-democracy parties are much less attractive to those who consider political participation from a cost-benefit analysis point of view. It is significant that the Civic Party, which is a pro-democracy party with considerable appeal to the middle class, does not even have one middle-level or senior executive of a major business corporation among its members. The pro-democracy parties consistently manage to secure as a group 55%–60% of the votes in the direct elections to the legislature; they manage to attract many middle class voters who offer them donations too, as reflected by the successful street fundraising efforts during the annual June 4 candlelight vigils and July 1 protest rallies. Admittedly, employees of major business groups do not want to be seen belonging to the pro-democracy parties, though some of them vote for these parties and offer them small donations.

In the 2011 elections of the Election Committee, which has the power to nominate and elect the Chief Executive, the pro-democracy movement did very well in the social welfare, legal, higher education, and education sectors. The design of the electoral system is such that the pro-democracy groups can only hope to secure seats in the professional functional constituencies as the business groups are expected to support the pro-Beijing, pro-establishment candidates. The pro-democracy groups remain competitive in those sectors which do not have many ties with the establishment and the major business groups, and they do very well in those sectors which do not accord a high priority to their respective sectoral interests and instead consider the core values of the community most important.

Satisfaction with the status quo on the part of the Hong Kong people is related to their comparing Hong Kong with its neighbors. Though the community found the three Chief Executives, C.H. Tung, Donald Tsang, and C.Y. Leung, far from satisfactory, it is in general happy with the performance of the civil service which is highly efficient and free from corruption. This satisfaction also helps to tilt the balance of the cost-benefit analysis towards the acceptance of the status quo.

(b) *The Refugee Mentality and Utilitarianism*

In the immediate post-war years, many people in Hong Kong who came from Mainland China shared a refugee mentality. Some also perceived emigration to Western countries as a way to improve their opportunities. This wave of emigration gradually increased when, in the 1980s, the Hong Kong people became concerned about the future of the territory. According to the figures given by the Security Branch of the British administration, the outward emigration flow stayed at a level of about 20,000 people per annum between 1981 and 1986, and then rose to 30,000 in 1987, 45,000 in 1988 and 42,000 in 1989. The Sino-British negotiations were an obvious cause of more people leaving Hong Kong. The delay in the statistics was because families needed at least two or three years to deliberate, decide, apply, and then finally move. The Tiananmen Incident in 1989 prompted more people to depart, and the figures further rose to

61,700 in 1990; 59,700 in 1991; 66,200 in 1992; 53,400 in 1993; 61,600 in 1994, 43,100 in 1995, and 40,300 in 1996.[10] The return flow of former emigrants also expanded as Hong Kong approached 1997. It was reported that for every 100 emigrants leaving Hong Kong in 1995, 60 former emigrants returned to the territory from overseas. The corresponding proportions in previous years were 27.9% in 1994, 29.1% in 1993, 16.2% in 1992, 7.7% in 1991, and 7.2% in 1990.[11] As expected, many Hong Kong families found it difficult to settle in the West. Those in their mid-careers encountered considerable difficulties starting second careers in other countries; adjustments required to begin from the bottom ranks were often too hard to swallow. Hence, when political stability was restored in the territory, many returned after securing their insurance policies, i.e., their new passports. Attempts to secure insurance policies have not ceased after 1997, hence, a substantial segment of the middle class in Hong Kong possesses foreign citizenships or rights of abode in foreign countries. A senior Canadian consular official informed the author at the end of 2011 that she believed that up to half a million Hong Kong residents held Canadian passports.

This phenomenon also helps to explain why most people in Hong Kong support democracy in principle but are unwilling to fight or sacrifice for it. Their cost-benefit calculus is that they have the exit option, but Hong Kong is the place where they can best develop their careers. The same element of utilitarianism applies here. Arguably, a segment of the middle class in Taiwan has also secured foreign passports, and there are many scandals concerning politicians' foreign passports and rights of permanent residence abroad. In contrast to Hong Kong, the pro-democracy movement in Taiwan during the era of authoritarian rule until the late 1980s had strong emotions of being suppressed, which was absent from Hong Kong. The territory's pro-democracy movement also lacked the passion of its counterpart in South Korea in the period of the 1960s–1980s.

The people of Hong Kong work very long hours. This applies to those in the lower socioeconomic strata who are under pressure to make ends meet as well as to the middle and upper-middle classes who are keen to

---

[10] *South China Morning Post*, February 15, 1997.
[11] *Ming Pao*, September 11, 1996.

advance their careers. The community often complains that there is insufficient time to spend with family. This fatigue adversely affects political participation and reinforces the utilitarian attitude. An interesting observation is that while Hong Kong parents are very serious about their children's education, they are reluctant to attend parent–teacher meetings and take part in their children's school functions.

(c) *Perceptions of China and the Sense of Political Impotence*

During the colonial era, people in Hong Kong did not have any strong incentive to fight for independence partly because they valued the refuge and were largely satisfied with the conditions of the colony relative to those in mainland China, and partly because they realized that independence was not a realistic option. This explained the absence of a strong emotion of being suppressed and a sense of political impotence on the part of the community.

At this stage, the Hong Kong people are acutely aware that the territory still enjoys better conditions than those on the Mainland and that the Chinese authorities would not allow independence, which has never been seriously considered an option. During the panic in the wake of the Tiananmen Incident, there were suggestions of buying an island for the resettlement of the population, but the proposal was soon abandoned for obvious reasons. As the community understands that decisions on democratization in Hong Kong are made in Beijing,[12] and that there is unlikely to be genuine democracy in Hong Kong until there are serious political reforms in China, the feeling of political impotence is natural.

In the long term, the Hong Kong people realize that the territory's economy is increasingly dependent on that of the Mainland (see Table 22.2). This rising dependence has been accompanied by a relative decline in Hong Kong's international economic competitiveness. By the turn of the century, the leaders of Shanghai no longer looked to the

---

[12] Protest rallies organized by the Pro-democracy movement usually start from Victoria Park in Causeway Bay and end at the government offices in Central. On January 1, 2010, the protest rally began in Central and ended at the Central Liaison Office in Sai Wan. See all major newspapers in Hong Kong on January 2, 2010.

territory as a model for emulation; they have turned their eyes to New York and London. At the time of Hong Kong's return to China in 1997, the Guangdong authorities were keen to establish closer economic ties with the HKSAR, but Hong Kong's top civil servants wanted to avoid a high degree of economic integration with the Mainland and were cool to Guangdong's overtures. In recent years, Guangdong has been following the footsteps of Shanghai, trying to attract investment from multinational corporations listed in the Fortune 500. The value of Hong Kong as an economic partner has thus been falling. In sum, dependence on the Mainland and the decline in relative bargaining power have exacerbated Hong Kong people's willingness to accept Beijing's position on the territory's electoral reforms.

At the same time, their confidence in China's future continues to strengthen (see Table 22.3). Apparently, this is related to their increasingly positive perception of China's international standing. A public opinion survey conducted by the New Youth Forum in March 2009, for example, revealed that 86% of the respondents thought that China had considerable international influence; about 77% believed that China would definitely or possibly overtake the U.S. as a world superpower within 50 years; 80% felt that China was a peace-loving country; and 60% believed that China's development would not threaten the Asia-Pacific region.[13] The successful Beijing Olympics certainly helped, and various space and military technology achievements also impressed Hong Kong people. The community believed that China, in contrast to the U.S., emerged from the global financial tsunami in 2008–2009 with its international status improved.

Apparently, the local economic difficulties and political controversies in the recent decade have weakened the Hong Kong community's trust in the central government and its confidence in "one country, two systems" (see Table 22.3). Given that the territory's economy is heavily dependent on the Mainland economy and the central government's policy support, and that the HKSAR government was chosen by China's leaders, Hong Kong people might have held the central government responsible for the performance of their economy and government. The power of the electoral

---

[13] *South China Morning Post*, March 30, 2009.

Table 22.3: Hong Kong people's confidence in China and trust for the Chinese leadership as reflected by public opinion surveys, 1997–2017 (half-yearly average)

Date of Survey	Confidence in China's Future (A) Confident	Not Confident	Trust in the Central Government (B) Very trust/ Quite Trust	Quite distrust/ Very Distrust	Confidence in "One Country, Two Systems" (C) Confident	Not Confident
7–12/2017	64.5%	27.4%	35.7%	44.6%	49.2%	45.7%
1–6/2017	64.9%	28.2%	38.6%	38.7%	50.8%	43.3%
7–12/2016	61.3%	29.7%	34.4%	42.0%	47.5%	43.9%
1–6/2016	57.2%	34.8%	29.9%	43.3%	43.4%	49.9%
7–12/2015	59.9%	30.0%	35.2%	39.9%	46.4%	46.5%
1–6/2015	65.8%	26.9%	34.4%	42.1%	47.3%	47.0%
7–12/2014	60.7%	31.3%	31.5%	46.6%	41.6%	51.8%
1–6/2014	65.0%	28.1%	35.1%	38.9%	47.5%	45.7%
7–12/2013	67.7%	24.0%	36.1%	36.8%	52.1%	41.0%
1–6/2013	66.6%	23.8%	30.9%	38.9%	51.3%	41.1%
7–12/2012	68.7%	22.2%	29.2%	37.4%	50.2%	40.9%
1–6/2012	72.7%	18.9%	35.2%	35.7%	53.1%	37.6%
7–12/2011	73.0%	19.2%	33.9%	32.4%	55.0%	36.6%
1–6/2011	78.7%	12.2%	37.3%	27.5%	60.5%	32.8%
7–12/2010	79.2%	14.3%	39.4%	26.9%	61.6%	30.8%
1–6/2010	84.4%	11.6%	44.7%	30.4%	60.6%	35.0%

(*Continued*)

Table 22.3: (Continued)

Date of Survey	Confidence in China's Future (A) Confident	Confidence in China's Future (A) Not Confident	Trust in the Central Government (B) Very trust/ Quite Trust	Trust in the Central Government (B) Quite distrust/ Very Distrust	Confidence in "One Country, Two Systems" (C) Confident	Confidence in "One Country, Two Systems" (C) Not Confident
7–12/2009	87.2%	8.5%	49.7%	18.8%	68.1%	26.0%
1–6/2009	88.2%	8.2%	52.6%	15.4%	72.5%	21.7%
7–12/2008	88.1%	7.9%	53.1%	14.5%	71.8%	21.6%
1–6/2008	87.9%	7.9%	54.9%	13.4%	74.6%	18.7%
7–12/2007	87.6%	7.8%	54.4%	15.6%	74.9%	18.8%
1–6/2007	87.5%	8.1%	49.9%	15.6%	72.9%	20.8%
7–12/2006	85.7%	9.3%	44.6%	19.7%	70.4%	23.6%
1–6/2006	85.0%	9.3%	48.5%	18.7%	69.4%	22.6%
7–12/2005	82.0%	11.0%	46.8%	24.4%	65.1%	25.3%
1–6/2005	79.0%	11.4%	43.1%	24.7%	57.2%	28.2%
7–12/2004	83.4%	9.2%	47.0%	20.9%	59.3%	28.4%
1–6/2004	82.6%	8.8%	40.0%	25.6%	51.7%	33.1%
7–12/2003	82.7%	8.3%	45.6%	20.6%	53.7%	30.9%
1–6/2003	79.1%	11.0%	37.6%	29.4%	49.2%	38.4%
7–12/2002	81.7%	9.6%	41.0%	26.2%	52.7%	34.3%
1–6/2002	81.1%	8.6%	48.7%	20.6%	58.7%	28.3%

(Continued)

Table 22.3: (Continued)

Date of Survey	Confidence in China's Future (A) Confident	Confidence in China's Future (A) Not Confident	Trust in the Central Government (B) Very trust/ Quite Trust	Trust in the Central Government (B) Quite distrust/ Very Distrust	Confidence in "One Country, Two Systems" (C) Confident	Confidence in "One Country, Two Systems" (C) Not Confident
7-12/2009	87.2%	8.5%	49.7%	18.8%	68.1%	26.0%
1-6/2001	78.6%	10.5%	33.7%	31.1%	56.7%	30.4%
7-12/2000	71.0%	15.0%	31.5%	31.0%	58.2%	27.5%
1-6/2000	73.1%	11.8%	31.9%	27.3%	62.0%	22.5%
7-12/1999	64.5%	27.4%	29.3%	29.7%	56.3%	29.6%
1-6/1999	64.9%	28.2%	27.3%	27.3%	57.7%	28.3%
7-12/1998	61.3%	29.7%	30.5%	30.8%	66.6%	21.9%
1-6/1998	57.2%	34.8%	28.7%	30.1%	64.5%	20.8%
7-12/1997	59.9%	30.0%	32.4%	29.8%	64.0%	18.7%

Note:
1. Question asked for (A) — Do you have confidence in China's future? The other option was "don't know/hard to say", which is not included in this table.
2. Question asked for (B) — On the whole, do you trust the Beijing Central Government? The other options were "half-half" and "don't know/hard to say", which are not included in this table.
3. Question asked fir (C) — On the whole, do you have confidence in "One Country, Two Systems"? The other option was "don't know/hard to say", which is not included in this table.

Source: Public Opinion Programme, The University of Hong Kong, http://hkupop.hku.hk/, retrieved November 18, 2018.

machinery of the pro-Beijing united front as demonstrated in the District Council and Legislative Council elections, and the competition among the pro-establishment candidates in the Chief Executive election campaigns in 2012 and 2017, also revealed Beijing's heavy-handed intervention in the territory's politics. Partly as a result, while Hong Kong people's trust in the central government and their confidence in "one country, two systems" had been strengthening from 1997 to 2008; since then, both trends have reversed.

In 2008, the Hong Kong people's trust in the central government was at its peak. It was considerably higher than its trust in the Hong Kong government, in contrast to the situation in the 1990s before the return of the territory to China. In a survey conducted in December 2008 (one of the series recorded in Table 22.3 and 22.4), 53% of the respondents said they trusted the central government. By comparison, 43% of the respondents indicated that they trusted the HKSAR government, and 19% indicated that they distrusted it. The 14% gap between those who trusted the central government and those who trusted the HKSAR government was the greatest since the end of 2003.[14]

In contrast, in early 1996, an opinion poll conducted by the Chinese University of Hong Kong revealed that 42% of the respondents trusted the British administration; those who trusted the British government amounted to less than 20%, while only 12% trusted the Chinese government.[15] A similar pattern emerged in various polls on the same subject in the 1990s. Hence, the Chinese authorities should be satisfied with the achievements of its united front charm offensive in the territory. This trust in the central government and confidence in "one country, two systems" implied that the Hong Kong people were less inclined to demand democracy as a mechanism of checks and balances against Beijing, in contrast to the mentality of "the exploitation of democracy as a bulwark against Communism", which hit its peak in the wake of the Tiananmen Incident in June 1989.[16]

---

[14] *Ibid.*, January 7, 2009.

[15] *Sing Tao Evening Post* (Hong Kong), February 5, 1996.

[16] See Joseph Y.S. Cheng, "Prospects for Democracy in Hong Kong", *op. cit.*, pp. 278–295.

Table 22.4: Hong Kong people's trust in the HKSAR government as reflected by public opinion surveys, 1992–2017 (half-yearly average)

Question: On the whole, do you trust the Hong Kong Government?
Collapsed data

Date of Survey	Total Sample (Half-Yearly)	Sub-sample (Half-Yearly)	Trust	Half-half	Distrust	DK/HS	Total	Net Value
7–12/2017	11196	8319	47.8%	17.2%	33.6%	1.5%	100.0%	14.2%
1–6/2017	14205	8604	42.9%	17.5%	38.0%	1.5%	100.0%	4.9%
7–12/2016	13075	7792	38.7%	19.9%	39.3%	2.1%	100.0%	–0.6%
1–6/2016	14096	8684	37.5%	18.7%	42.2%	1.6%	100.0%	–4.7%
7–12/2015	14135	8665	37.7%	22.8%	37.7%	1.7%	100.0%	–0.1%
1–6/2015	14376	8844	39.1%	21.9%	37.7%	1.2%	100.0%	1.4%
7–12/2014	13161	8107	38.9%	20.4%	39.0%	1.8%	100.0%	–0.1%
1–6/2014	14304	8269	41.2%	20.9%	35.8%	2.1%	100.0%	5.4%
7–12/2013	14176	8532	40.2%	19.6%	38.2%	2.1%	100.0%	2.0%
1–6/2013	14287	8635	39.4%	26.6%	31.9%	2.1%	100.0%	7.5%
7–12/2012	14241	8445	39.8%	24.8%	33.0%	2.3%	100.0%	6.8%
1–6/2012	2025	1150	35.5%	27.8%	34.1%	2.7%	100.0%	1.4%
7–12/2011	2043	1046	39.4%	28.1%	29.7%	2.8%	100.0%	9.7%
1–6/2011	2037	1076	38.3%	31.7%	28.2%	1.9%	100.0%	10.1%
7–12/2010	2024	2024	48.7%	31.1%	18.7%	1.5%	100.0%	30.1%
1–6/2010	2009	2009	43.8%	26.4%	28.7%	1.1%	100.0%	15.1%
7–12/2009	3033	3033	46.6%	31.2%	20.8%	1.4%	100.0%	25.8%
1–6/2009	3046	3046	48.2%	33.8%	17.0%	1.0%	100.0%	31.2%
7–12/2008	3102	3102	42.8%	36.9%	18.7%	1.6%	100.0%	24.1%
1–6/2008	3039	3039	62.6%	27.4%	8.3%	1.8%	100.0%	54.3%
7–12/2007	3035	3035	59.7%	28.2%	9.8%	2.3%	100.0%	49.8%
1–6/2007	3040	3040	57.3%	33.4%	7.2%	2.1%	100.0%	50.1%
7–12/2006	3036	3036	52.5%	34.0%	11.9%	1.6%	100.0%	40.6%
1–6/2006	3045	3045	62.4%	28.0%	7.6%	2.0%	100.0%	54.8%
7–12/2005	3029	3029	59.3%	25.1%	13.1%	2.6%	100.0%	46.2%
1–6/2005	3061	3061	47.1%	29.4%	18.6%	4.9%	100.0%	28.5%
7–12/2004	3063	3063	38.7%	28.4%	28.8%	4.0%	100.0%	9.9%
1–6/2004	3090	3090	32.5%	30.3%	31.7%	5.5%	100.0%	0.8%

(*Continued*)

Table 22.4: (Continued)

Date of Survey	Total Sample (Half-Yearly)	Sub-sample (Half-Yearly)	Trust	Half-half	Distrust	DK/HS	Total	Net Value
7–12/2003	3058	3058	29.9%	29.8%	34.9%	5.3%	100.0%	−5.0%
1–6/2003	3109	3109	29.9%	21.3%	42.8%	6.0%	100.0%	−12.8%
7–12/2002	3072	3072	34.4%	24.1%	35.2%	6.2%	100.0%	−0.8%
1–6/2002	3182	3182	47.4%	25.0%	22.1%	5.5%	100.0%	25.3%
7–12/2001	3169	3169	40.3%	26.5%	27.8%	5.4%	100.0%	12.5%
1–6/2001	3126	3126	44.2%	27.4%	25.1%	3.3%	100.0%	19.1%
7–12/2000	3145	3145	39.3%	26.1%	28.3%	6.4%	100.0%	11.0%
1–6/2000	2152	2152	41.5%	30.8%	20.2%	7.4%	100.0%	21.3%
7–12/1999	1627	1627	39.1%	31.0%	22.8%	7.1%	100.0%	16.3%
1–6/1999	2110	2110	38.7%	36.1%	18.0%	7.3%	100.0%	20.6%
7–12/1998	1624	1624	38.2%	34.9%	21.0%	5.8%	100.0%	17.2%
1–6/1998	1600	1600	37.1%	37.6%	16.5%	8.8%	100.0%	20.6%
7–12/1997	2602	2602	52.1%	27.9%	9.5%	10.4%	100.0%	42.6%
1–6/1997	3276	3276	63.2%	18.8%	13.5%	4.5%	100.0%	49.8%
7–12/1996	3177	3177	60.6%	22.2%	12.7%	4.5%	100.0%	48.0%
1–6/1996	3380	3380	54.5%	24.1%	16.0%	5.5%	100.0%	38.6%
7–12/1995	3395	3395	48.4%	22.0%	22.1%	7.5%	100.0%	26.3%
1–6/1995	3505	3505	48.4%	22.4%	23.3%	6.0%	100.0%	25.1%
7–12/1994	3165	3165	46.6%	22.8%	24.0%	6.6%	100.0%	22.6%
1–6/1994	3160	3160	47.7%	23.7%	21.5%	7.0%	100.0%	26.1%
7–12/1993	3607	3607	54.8%	16.8%	21.8%	6.6%	100.0%	33.0%
1–6/1993	3965	3965	53.9%	17.5%	20.7%	7.9%	100.0%	33.2%
7–12/1992	640	640	56.9%	14.7%	23.8%	4.6%	100.0%	33.1%

Note: DK means "don't know". HS means "hard to say".

Source: Public Opinion Programme, The University of Hong Kong, https://www.hkupop.hku.hk/english/popexpress/trust/trusthkgov/halfyr/datatables.html, retrieved on November 26, 2018.

Previous studies of the Hong Kong people's political attitudes revealed that the middle class shares a stronger democratic orientation in terms of its appreciation of the Western liberal democracy model and its support for due process and democratic political procedures.[17] This is

---

[17] See, for example, various public opinion surveys conducted by the Public Opinion Programme, The University of Hong Kong, http: //hkupop.hku.hk/; and the Hog Kong

especially so when a high level of education is considered an important attribute of the middle class. At the same time, people of the grassroots socioeconomic strata have a stronger sense of patriotism and identification with China. However, the middle class's stronger democratic orientation has not been an adequate motivating force prompting it to fight for democracy. Instead, a majority of the middle class at this stage has jobs related to China businesses, and this business connection has probably weakened its intention to challenge the Chinese authorities' position on the progress of democratization in Hong Kong.

Democracy is premised on the ideal that life is meaningful through political participation in the community to which one belongs. An individual realizes his or her full potential only through this participation in running the community's affairs. In the political calculus of most Hong Kong people, this is too demanding an ideal for them and they instead opt for economic power at the micro-level to secure an optimal measure of control over the socioeconomic aspects of their own lives. Even in democracies, for the less politically active, political participation remains a demanding ideal. The voter turnout rates at various levels of elections in the U.S. are good evidence of the less-than-enthusiastic response to the demands of political participation. In view of the Hong Kong people's hectic lives, political participation is perceived to be even more demanding and less appealing.

While every individual would like to have a good measure of control over his or her own life, this objective has been proven extremely difficult to fulfill because of the asymmetry in power between the individual, on one hand, and authoritarian regimes, big businesses, organized interest groups, and so on, on the other. This asymmetry in power is often reflected in the asymmetry in information held, which in turn is a result of the lack of transparency on the part of the powerful. The Hong Kong people are acutely aware of this asymmetry when they complain about the "hegemony" of real estate developers and when they felt cheated by the financial institutions' various derivative products during the global financial crisis in 2008–2009.

In the recent decade, the Hong Kong people have gradually come to realize the extremely limited control they enjoy over their own life. This realization has prompted them to emigrate again, especially after the

Occupation Campaign in 2014, though as they understand that the situations in democracies are not significantly better.[18] They were more inclined to take part in the increasingly frequent protest activities to vent their anger and frustration, especially the younger generations. This was one type of response found under authoritarian regimes and in democracies. Some would raise their level of political participation and seek to redress the asymmetries in power through collective action. This was in line with the general theory of democratization. However, obviously only a small number of people chose this option. Since the Occupation Campaign in 2014, political participation and protest activities have declined as people in support of democracy become frustrated and they understand that they cannot achieve any significant concrete political objectives in the foreseeable future.

IV The HKSAR Government's Legitimacy Deficit and the Demands for Change

The British administration secured its legitimacy by performance. The HKSAR government's unsatisfactory performance means that it suffers from a legitimacy deficit. The Hong Kong people are worried about the widening of the gap between the rich and the poor, the reduction in opportunities for upward social mobility, and the decline in the territory's international competitiveness. They do not believe that the C.H. Tung, Donald Tsang, and C.Y. Leung administrations have offered any effective policy programmes; in fact, they doubt whether they have made any serious efforts to come up with relevant policy programs.

In 2001, the Gini coefficient in Hong Kong had already reached 0.525; it was expected to be even later.[19] It actually reached 0.539 in 2016. In fact, Hong Kong at this stage has the largest gap between rich and poor among the major cities in the world. In September 2010, Oxfam of Hong Kong published its report on poverty in the territory, which showed that

---

[18] Albert O. Hirschman, *Exist, Voice and Loyalty: Responses to Decline in Firms, Organizations and States*, Cambridge, Massachusettes, 1970.

[19] See Legislative Council Factsheet FS07/04-05, compiled by the Research and Library Services Division of the Legislative Council Secretariat.

the number of working poor families had been increasing, from around 172,600 more than five years ago to about 192,500, a rise of 12%. The report also indicated that the incomes of the poorest one-fifth of the families had no improvement in the past five-and-a-half years; and the median monthly incomes of the poorest one-tenth and one-fifth of the families were HK$3,000 and HK$6,000, respectively. In comparison, the median monthly income of the richest one-tenth of the families had risen by 16% to HK$80,900, about 27 times that of the poorest one-tenth of the families, reflecting that the gap between the rich and the poor had been widening in the past five-and-a-half years.[20]

Earlier, in August 2009, the Life Quality Research Centre of the Chinese University of Hong Kong released a set of statistical and survey data which demonstrated that the overall quality of life of the Hong Kong people in the previous year had deteriorated to approximately the level in 2003, when the territory suffered from the Severe Acute Respiratory Syndrome (SARS) epidemic; the overall index declined by 3.5% when compared with that in 2007. The community's evaluation of the economy and its ability to purchase an accommodation through mortgage had dropped most sharply, falling by 30% and 33% respectively; the index on satisfaction with the government's performance also dropped by 29%.[21]

In September 2010, a survey revealed that among the fourth-generation Hong Kong people (born between 1976 and 1990) interviewed, 20% had experienced downward social mobility in the past five years, i.e., moving down the occupational ladder. This downward movement was more conspicuous among the low-skilled and unskilled workers' strata, which constituted 44% of the affected interviewees group. Over half of the respondents admitted that they had no opportunities for upward social mobility because of low educational qualifications.[22]

---

[20] *Ming Pao*, September 20, 2010. A working poor family is one which has at least one employed member; and its monthly income is less than half of the median monthly income of families in Hong Kong with the same number of members.

[21] *Ibid.*, August 14, 2009.

[22] *Ibid.*, September 13, 2010. The survey was conducted by a consultancy firm commissioned by the Hong Kong Association of Professionals and Senior Executives in May–July 2010.

In this connection, the group which was just above the social security net attracted the most attention. The number of workers earning a monthly income of between HK$10,000 and HK$20,000 each had increased from 1.02 million in 2007 to 1.17 million at the end of 2011.[23] For a two-person family, if its monthly income exceeded HK$12,000, its members would not qualify for transport subsidy, and if its monthly income was over HK$14,100, it would not qualify for public housing. In the beginning of the 2010s, a professor of sociology told the author that a recent university graduate expressed doubt whether he could be considered a member of the middle class. Given his educational background, by traditional standards, he would definitely be considered as such; but in view of his income and low expectations of future improvement, he realized that he would not be able to buy private housing and would indeed have difficulty raising a family.

In view of the above, it was natural that people should lament (or deplore) the widening socioeconomic gap. An opinion survey report released in early December 2011 showed that 76% of the respondents considered that the gap between the rich and the poor in Hong Kong was "serious or very serious"; and only 5% believed that the problem was "not serious or not very serious". Moreover, 56% of the respondents were dissatisfied with the government's performance in handling the issue, and 59% thought that the government "comparatively took care of the rich".[24]

In the early 2010s, the local media observed much resentment against the rich among the Hong Kong people, which might have an impact on political participation in the territory. Normally, there was much envy of the rich, with newspapers and magazines full of reports of the lifestyles of the rich, which apparently made for popular reading. This "resentment against the rich" probably reflected dissatisfaction with the widening socioeconomic gap and the government's policies favoring the major business groups and real estate tycoons. The government felt the pressure; hence, the gesture of the establishment of a Community Care Fund.

---

[23] *Ibid.*, October 6, 2011.

[24] *Ibid.*, December 2, 2011. The poll was conducted by the Chinese University of Hong Kong and the Hong Kong Association of Professionals and Senior Executives between September 26 and October 7, 2011.

Dissatisfaction in the society was accumulating in the beginning of this decade, but most people's response was a sense of helplessness, not anger. Radical political actions symbolized by the protests of the League of Social Democrats, though far from radical by Western European standards, could only attract the support of a minority, normally estimated to be around 10% of the public. Most Hong Kong people resented its protest activities, and it (together with its splinter group, People Power) lost badly in the District Council elections on November 6, 2011.[25] The community's value orientations tend to be conservative, and it favors the maintenance of the status quo. It selectively supports gradual reforms, and is worried that radical political campaigns may destabilize the society. The most popular political leaders attract public support by moderate images, and are perceived to have been articulating the voices of the silent majority. They are definitely not revolutionary leaders.[26]

The Chief Executive election of 2012 helped to illustrate some of the issues raised above. In contrast to 1997, when the Hong Kong people were anxious to avoid major changes, they seemed to welcome a new Chief Executive who was ready to introduce reforms. C.Y. Leung fully exploited this demand for change to establish a solid lead in popular support over Henry Tang, who was broadly perceived to be status quo-oriented. Tang was the candidate favored by Beijing initially.

The scandals and "dirty tricks" in the campaign prompted the Chinese authorities to intervene and assume almost full control of the electoral process. Beijing was suspicious that the two candidates had been collecting information against each other, and it considered that such exposures and adverse publicity would discredit the entire establishment. The Hong Kong people had vivid experiences of a "small circle election" as they acutely felt that they had no part in the election of their leader. In contrast, the business community wielded considerable influence; and worse still, it was ready to defy public opinion when almost all the local tycoons openly nominated Henry Tang at the peak of his scandals.

---

[25] See all major newspapers in Hong Kong on November 7 and 8, 2011.
[26] Joseph Y.S. Cheng, "Hong Kong Since Its Return to China: A Lost Decade?", in his edited volume, *The Hong Kong Special Administrative Region in Its first Decade*, Hong Kong: City University of Hong Kong Press, 2007, pp. 35–47.

The support from Beijing proved costly for the popularity of C.Y. Leung, and the legitimacy of his electoral victory was considerably compromised. There is substantial worry regarding the increasingly blatant influence of Beijing in local politics, but people in Hong Kong avoid open confrontation with the Chinese authorities. The latter will continue to support the territory economically to contain the community's grievances.

The challenges facing Hong Kong at this stage require a paradigm shift in policymaking. Beijing hopes to see a more visionary Chief Executive leading a proactive administration. However, the absence of democracy and the exacerbating social and political polarization deprive the administration of the legitimacy to push for reforms. This legitimacy deficit on the part of the Donald Tsang administration led to a mentality of avoiding major issues and focusing on gestures to win popularity. From its very beginning, the C.Y. Leung administration also suffered from many scandals, as well as from the community's deep suspicious of it. It had considerable difficulties establishing a consensus and generating sufficient support. The withdrawal of the national education program in September 2012 was a good example. Meanwhile, it was obvious that the Chinese leadership was not satisfied with governance of Hong Kong, and Chinese officials no longer tried hard to avoid any public comments on the Hong Kong situation which might generate a perception of compromising the territory's high degree of autonomy.

The rising discontent among the voters as reflected in the Legislative Council elections in September 2012 again demonstrated the demand for a new approach and innovative policies. The performance of the radical pro-democracy movement was impressive. People Power and the League of Social Democrats collected a 14.6% share of the votes in the direct elections. In terms of seats, they improved from three to four. The rise of the radical wing of the pro-democracy movement reflected a gradual change in the political culture and also the exacerbation of grievances and dissatisfaction at the grassroots level and among young people. They supported strong protest acts to air their grievances, and had no intention of pursuing policy changes through compromises. This certainly made coordination among the pro-democracy groups increasingly difficult.

The political orientation of the Xi Jinping administration in China was a significant variable. If it intended to pursue political reforms in China, it would likely allow Hong Kong to experiment with genuine democracy. If not, the Chinese authorities' prevalent frustrations with the Hong Kong situation continue to encourage them to intervene to ensure political stability and economic prosperity.

In 2013, political reforms emerged as the dominant issue in democratization in the coming years. The Chinese authorities promised that Hong Kong could elect its Chief Executive in 2017 and all seats in the legislature in 2020 by universal suffrage. The pro-democracy movement was mobilized to demand that this promise be implemented, and threatened to mobilize massive protests if its demands were not met. Whether genuine democracy would be granted in Hong Kong would depend on many factors including the political reform orientations of the Chinese leadership, the resistance of the local business community, and the appeal and mobilization power of the pro-democracy camp in Hong Kong. The outcome would be another significant test of the political wisdom of all parties concerned.

V Conclusion

The democratization, or the lack of it, in Hong Kong presents an interesting case study posing challenges to modernization theory. There are unique features in the Hong Kong case, mainly in the context of its special relationship with the Mainland. However, the behavior patterns and value orientations of its middle class are not unique. The first major question is whether political participation is part of a meaningful life. Under a soft authoritarian regime like the British colonial administration, the HKSAR government, the Singaporean government, and perhaps even the Chinese government today, a considerable segment of the respective populations probably does not believe that political participation is a significant source of satisfaction in life. In the years in Taiwan, there is a sense of disillusionment regarding democracy among a part of the concerned public, the people affected avoid political participation through established parties, and instead opt for voluntary work in civil society. Similar disillusionment exists among minorities in established democracies too. In the hectic life of modern society, political participation has to compete with many other demands even for those who cherish democracy.

Hong Kong people have tended to derive their satisfaction from family life and career development because of their political alienation and also, historically, a refugee mentality in a colonial setting. A stable government providing the rule of law and a basic level of services would satisfy them. If they do not have to fight for it, they would be happy to support the democracy. If they have to struggle for it, they would have to consider the cost. There is the option of emigration, and there is also the choice of simply securing essential services like housing, children's education, pension, and so on, through one's own efforts. There is no intention to strive for democracy at all costs.

There is also an element of utilitarianism and cynicism regarding democracy on the part of Hong Kong people. About 60% of the electorate vote for the pro-democracy political groups in direct elections to the legislature in Hong Kong; most of these voters perceive the pro-democracy groups as checks-and-balances against the soft authoritarianism of the HKSAR government. They do not, however, believe that the pro-democracy movement would provide a credible alternative government; and they are doubtful whether a democratic government would offer a more effective and efficient administration. Moreover, Hong Kong's pro-democracy political parties do not succeed in attracting many voluntary workers and substantial donations. Even in established democracies, more and more voters see their votes as a means to punish governments that have not performed, while they have low expectations of all political parties and politicians.

In Hong Kong, the cynicism is perhaps stronger because even in the 1960s, the community was critical of the "British disease", i.e., strong trade unionism and the over-generous welfare society. Today, it has little sympathy for the European welfare states suffering from excessive national debts. The Hong Kong people typically prefer to keep money in their own pockets, and do not trust income-redistribution and the welfare state. Their values have been changing in recent decades, but the change is still inadequate to persuade them to fight for democracy in a costly way. There is an increasing sense of helplessness especially in confronting the

Chinese authorities and big business groups. However, this feeling of political incompetence is also spreading to some extent in established democracies, as symbolized by the "Occupy Wall Street" campaign.

Acknowledgement

Originally published as: Cheng, Joseph Yu Shek, "Democratization in Hong Kong: a theoretical exception", *Democracy in East Asia: Issues, Problems and Challenges in a Region of Diversity*, eds, Edmund S.K. Fung and Steven Drakeley. London and NY: Routledge, 2014, pp. 224–245. Reproduced with permission of The Licensor through PLSclear.

Chapter 23

The Emergence of Radical Politics in Hong Kong: Causes and Impact

In the first year of the C.Y. Leung administration, the Hong Kong people in general were very frustrated with the unsatisfactory performance of the government and the deterioration in the political culture. Political polarization had been exacerbated, and reaching a consensus on policies became increasingly challenging. Social schisms were deepening, diluting the pragmatism and moderation that were significant characteristics of the territory's political culture. In this context, the emergence of radical politics in Hong Kong and the frustrations of the "post-1980s generation" attracted much attention. There was an awareness that radical politics was a symptom rather than the cause of Hong Kong's political problems. As long as the establishment remained united, it still enjoyed the control of the policymaking processes.

This chapter examines the literature on the deteriorating living standards and the widening of the gap between the rich and the poor in the territory that were perceived as the root causes of the community's grievances and dissatisfaction, and as the factors which had contributed to the rise of radical politics. It then considers the responsibilities of the HKSAR government in terms of both its political philosophy and its performance. In this context, the author studies the emergence of new social movements, their characteristics, modes of operation, and so on. An assessment of their impact on effective governance follows. The limitations of depending mainly on secondary data and the existing publications of academics are obvious. A satisfactory explanation for the variety of political radicalism would require information and original research on the formation, objectives, organization, modes of mobilization, leadership, and strategies of different radical groups.

I The Deteriorating Living Standards and the Widening of the Gap between the Rich and the Poor

Political stability in China may perhaps be explained in this simple way — people do not see a credible alternative to the Communist Party regime; more important still, a vast majority of the Chinese population has experienced substantial improvement in living standards in the four decades, and most of them still expect further improvement in the years to come. In contrast, most people in Hong Kong believe that their real incomes have fallen since the territory's return to China in 1997; and a majority of the population is pessimistic about its future. Young people have acutely felt a decline in their opportunities for upward social mobility. These factors are generally regarded as the root causes of the community's dissatisfaction and the emergence of radical politics.

As Leo Goodstadt observes, "For the first time in decades, poverty became widespread."[1] The HKSAR government admitted that the number of workers who, "despite working hard", "consistently cannot earn reasonable salaries to satisfy the basic needs of themselves and their families" was to reach almost 200,000.[2] By 2005, the government reluctantly conceded that more than a million people (15% of the population) were living in poverty.[3] A government-sponsored study stated

---

[1] Leo F. Goodstadt, *Poverty in the Midst of Affluence — How Hong Kong Mismanaged Its Prosperity*, Hong Kong: Hong Kong University Press, 2013, p. 1.
[2] In 2001, there were 176,000 employees in this category, 6% of the workforce.
[3] They had risen to 195,800 by 2007. See Commission on Strategic Development, "An Overview of the opportunities and Challenges of Hong Kong's Development" (CSD/6/2008, October 2008), p. 6, and "Table 2: Characteristics of Working Poor in Hong Kong, 2001–2007," p. 24; and Economic Analysis and Business Facilitation Unit, "Legislative Council Subcommittee to Study the Subject of Combating Poverty: Indicators of Poverty — An Update for 2005" (CB(2)2727/05-06(03), July 2006), "Annex 2: Indicators of Poverty — An Update for 2005," p. 3.

that the "post-1980s generation" was the best educated in Hong Kong history, yet they encountered worse employment opportunities, lower earnings, and less hopeful lifetime prospects than their parents' generation.[4] Even when the economy improved, the community did not consider that they had benefitted. When Donald Tsang, C.H. Tung's successor, visited Beijing for an official visit in December 2006, he told central government officials that "Hong Kong's economy is the best it has been in almost twenty years."[5] The message was clear — the economy was in good shape, there should be no severe political challenges, and the Chinese leadership should be satisfied with his administration.

At the end of September 2013, the C.Y. Leung administration released its definition of the local poverty line, that is, families with incomes equal to or less than half of the median income of families in Hong Kong with the same number of members. In concrete dollar terms, this definition referred to one-person families with monthly incomes of HK$3,600 or less in 2012, two-person families with monthly incomes of HK$7,700 or less, three-person families with monthly incomes of HK$11,500 or less, four-person families with monthly incomes of HK$14,300 or less, five-person families with monthly incomes of HK$14,800 or less, and families of six persons or more with monthly incomes of HK$15,800 or less. According to these criteria, people in poverty amounted to 1.31 million, which is 19.6% of the population. With the intervention of social security and various benefits, people in poverty still reached 1.02 million. The government promised to help the "working-poor" families, but it has been criticized for the absence of policy objectives and policy programs meant to reduce poverty.[6] A study by the Bauhinia Foundation, a think-tank close to Donald Tsang, revealed that the median household income in 2005 was still 15.8% lower than that in the peak year of 1997. More serious still, between 1996 and 2005, the number of households with a monthly

---

[4] Xiaogang Wu, "Hong Kong's Post 80s Generation: Profiles and Predicaments: A CPU Commissioned Report," Centre for Applied Social and Economic Research, Hong Kong University of Science and Technology, Central Policy Unit, May 2010, p. 40.
[5] *South China Morning Post*, December 28, 2006.
[6] *Apple Daily*, September 29, 2013.

income below HK$8,000 rose by 76.5%, to more than 500,000, and their proportion of the total number of households rose from 13% to 22%.[7]

Obviously, the Chief Executive felt pressure to respond. Speaking in a question-and-answer session at the Legislative Council in January 2007, Donald Tsang admitted that some low-income households had failed to benefit from the stronger economy, but the most important thing was to create jobs through a stronger economy. He indicated that at least wage levels had stopped declining; in the last quarter of 2005, those earning HK$15,000 or more per month accounted for more than one-third of the labor force, compared with a quarter during the same period a decade ago. Furthermore, the proportion of workers earning less than HK$9,000 per month also dropped from 42% in 1996 to 36% in 2005, while the lowest income group, earning less than HK$5,000 per month, represented only 5% of the working population. The Chief Executive also pointed to the falling unemployment rate, which stood at 4.4% at the end of 2005.[8] However, he had obviously not taken into consideration inflation and the rise of housing prices.

The post-war generation in Hong Kong enjoyed satisfactory salary increases on the basis of hard work. Dr. Ohmae argues that this could not be expected in Japan at this stage, where employees' salaries would probably peak when they hit 40. Further raises would be difficult, and Hong Kong's situation was probably similar. Dr. Ohmae suggests that the Japanese should adjust their lifestyles, since not everyone would join the middle class. They might have to forget about owning cars and houses in the suburbs, and paying expensive tuition fees to prepare their children for top universities.

Furthermore, in an aging society with a sharply falling fertility rate, the financial burden of social services would increase. Taxation would rise in the absence of administrative reforms. At this stage, Hong Kong's Mandatory Provident Fund (MPF) was inadequate to provide for the community's retirement, and the Hong Kong people had yet to tackle the

---

[7] *South China Morning Post*, January 10, 2007; and *Ming Pao*, January 10, 2007.

[8] *Ming Pao*, January 12, 2007. See also Joseph Y. S. Cheng, "Hong Kong since Its Return to China: A Lost Decade?," in *The Hong Kong Special Administrative Region in Its First Decade*, edited by Joseph Y.S. Cheng, Hong Kong: City University of Hong Kong Press, 2007, pp. 3 and 7.

long-term financing of their medical services. Employees would have to wait another 20 years at least before their MPF accounts were large enough to contribute in an important way to their retirement incomes. Since their birth, MPF accounts had been managed by private-sector financial institutions whose fees were considered excessive and returns rather disappointing.[9] Most people did not consider their MPF accounts a significant part of their savings for retirement.

Meanwhile, the gap between the rich and the poor had been widening. In 2001, the Gini coefficient in Hong Kong already reached 0.525; and it rose to 0.539 in 2016. Normally, a level exceeding 0.4 provokes caution, and the territory's level was comparable to that in some Latin American countries. According to a document prepared by the local legislature, the Gini coefficients were 0.249 in Japan in 1993, 0.326 in Taiwan in 2000, 0.316 in South Korea in 1998, and 0.425 in Singapore in 1998.[10] In September 2010, Oxfam in Hong Kong published its report on poverty in the territory, which indicated that the incomes of the poorest one-fifth of families had shown no improvement in the past five and a half years, and the median monthly incomes of the poorest one-tenth and one-fifth of families were HK$3,000 and HK$6,000, respectively. In comparison, the median monthly income of the richest one-tenth of families had risen by 16% to HK$80,900, about 27 times that of the poorest one-tenth of families, reflecting that the gap between the rich and the poor had been widening since 2004.[11]

In October 2010, the Hong Kong Council of Social Service released a research report revealing that the median monthly income of the high-income household group had risen from HK$31,000 in the previous year to HK$32,950, while that of the low-income household group had basically remained unchanged at HK$9,000. The income gap between the two groups had been maintained at the ratio of 3.4:1 in the past four years, but in the first half of 2010 it rose to 3.7:1. Apparently, the income gap worsened in the economic recovery after the global financial tsunami in

---

[9] Goodstadt, *Poverty in the Midst of Affluence*, p. 14.

[10] The data come from the Legislative Council Factsheet FS07/04-05, complied by the Research and Library Services Division of the Legislative Council Secretariat.

[11] *Ming Pao*, September 20, 2010. Their monthly income is less than half of the median monthly income of families in Hong Kong with the same number of members.

2008–2009.[12] According to the Census and Statistics Department of the HKSAR government, in the quarter from September to November 2009, the number of households with a monthly income below HK$25,000 and above dropped from the corresponding period of the previous year; while the number of households in various groups with a monthly income of below HK$10,000 rose, with growth rates ranging from 2.4% to 9.7%.[13]

Earlier in August 2009, the Life Quality Research Centre of the Chinese University of Hong Kong released a set of statistical and survey data which demonstrated that the overall quality of life of the Hong Kong people in the previous year had deteriorated to approximately the level of 2003, when the territory suffered severely from the SARS epidemic. The community's evaluation of the economy and its ability to purchase accommodation through mortgage had dropped most sharply, falling by 30% and 33% respectively; the index on satisfaction with the government's performance also dropped by 29%.[14]

In the past, the gap between the rich and poor in Hong Kong was substantial. In the beginning of the 1970s, the governor, Sir Murray MacLehose, made an important commitment to the public housing and education sectors, offering significant improvements in the quality of life at the grassroots level. However, neither the British administration nor the community was attracted to the "welfare society" model. Most important of all, before the Asia-Pacific financial crisis in 1997–1998, the Hong Kong people considered the territory a place full of opportunities, where individuals' efforts would be rewarded. Even those who lacked the educational qualifications and prospects for upward social mobility would still pin their hopes on their second generation, who hopefully would

---

[12] *Ming Pao*, October 4, 2010. Poor families in this research report are defined as those with incomes equal to or less than half of the median incomes of families in Hong Kong with the same number of members, for example, one-person families during the survey period with monthly incomes of HK$3,275 or less, two-person families with monthly incomes of HK$7,100 or less, three-person families with monthly incomes of HK$10,000 or less, and four-person families with monthly incomes of HK$12,000 or less.
[13] *Ming Pao*, January 20, 2010.
[14] *Ming Pao*, August 14, 2009.

become professionals and business executives through tertiary education. The alleviation of intergenerational poverty had become a social issue only since the middle of the first decade in the new century.

In view of the globalization process, Hong Kong understood that it had to become a knowledge economy. Hence, the competitiveness of the low-education, low-skill labor force had been in sharp decline, and the income gap within the labor force had been widening. In the economic integration between Hong Kong and the Mainland, the former's labor-intensive industries moved to the Pearl River Delta in the early 1980s, and the labor-intensive services followed. Meanwhile, the inflow of immigrants from the Mainland expanded the supply of unskilled laborers with a low level of education, contributing to the phenomena of an increased population of "working-poor" families, the lack of improvement in incomes during the economic recovery after the financial crisis in 2008–2009, and so on.

In September 2010, a survey revealed that among the fourth-generation Hong Kong people (born between 1976 and 1990) interviewed, 20% had experienced downward social mobility in the past five years, that is, moving down the occupational ladder. This downward movement was more conspicuous among the stratum of low-skilled and unskilled workers, which constituted 44% of the group of affected interviewees. Over half of the respondents admitted that they had no opportunities for upward social mobility because of their low educational qualifications. According to this survey, 51.9% of the fourth-generation Hong Kong people (assuming those who arrived in Hong Kong in 1949 or before were the first generation) interviewed believed that they had failed to secure upward social mobility opportunities because of their "low educational qualifications"; 38.9% of the respondents blamed the Hong Kong economy; and 33.3% considered the fact that they had not worked hard enough and that faulty government policies were the root causes, respectively.[15]

It was relatively easy to understand that those with "low educational qualifications" lacked upward social mobility opportunities; but what

---

[15] *Ming Pao*, September 13, 2010. The survey was conducted by a consultancy firm commissioned by the Hong Kong Association of Professionals and Senior Executives from May to July 2010.

about those with high educational qualifications? In the beginning of the 2010s, there was much media discussion on the frustration and anger of the "post-1980s generation," including university graduates who were regarded as the social elite. Naturally, the supply of university graduates had been increasing, and they had to adjust their expectations to avoid the scenario of "the higher the expectation, the bigger the disappointment".

The values of the Hong Kong people had been changing gradually. Before 1997, unemployment was not a concern. The community believed that anyone who was willing to work should have no difficulty finding a job. In the first half of the 2010s, it had to accept that the territory's unemployment rate at one point was higher than those in the U.S. and the U.K. Hence, even those who were gainfully employed worried about the employment of their next generation.

The HKSAR government, think-tanks like the Bauhinia Foundation, and non-governmental organizations such as Oxfam and the Hong Kong Council of Social Service had produced a substantial body of statistical data demonstrating the deteriorating living standards and the widening gap between the rich and poor in the territory. However, the collection of such data had not been guided by any theoretical framework, and such data had not yet been systematically analyzed by academics. Hence, the causal linkage between the deterioration in living standards and the widening income gap on one hand, and the emergence of radical politics in Hong Kong on the other had not been meaningfully established. Furthermore, the above phenomena were not unique to Hong Kong; they were quite common among the other three "little dragons of Asia", countries at a similar level of development as Hong Kong, and even among developed countries. There was a rich body of literature on the subject, but detailed and systematic comparisons between Hong Kong and other relevant countries were very few in number. The territory had not yet been able to benefit from comparative studies.

II The Responsibility of the HKSAR Government

Naturally, the HKSAR government had to assume responsibility for the deteriorations in living standards and the widening of the gap between the rich and the poor. The first chief executive, C.H. Tung, was widely believed to have been forced to step down for health reasons by Beijing in mid-2005 because of his unsatisfactory performance. In the final year of the Donald Tsang administration, according to the opinion survey series conducted by The University of Hong Kong, his popularity ratings fell sharply.[16] In the very first year of the C.Y. Leung administration, it already faced difficulty partly because of various scandals surrounding the Chief Executive and his team and partly because of the accumulating grievances in the community.

Goodstadt places the blame on the leadership and values of C.H. Tung. Tung emphasized financial stringency; as a result, austerity budgets, reductions of the civil service establishment, and salaries tended to exacerbate deflation when the economy went into recession; cutbacks on social security and social services too naturally affected their quality and supply.[17] According to Goodstadt, Tung and the top civil servants believed that the "business model" should be followed, that is, to reduce expenditure, avoid debts, and generate budget surpluses. Since the late 1980s, the British administration and its successor had also been attracted by the "new public management" philosophy that enjoyed the support of the international community.[18] The philosophy basically called for a smaller public sector. Budgetary savings secured through reducing the government bureaucracy were perceived as improvements in efficiency. Social services were adversely affected because health, education, and social welfare were all highly labor-intensive. The complacency on the part of the British administration and the business and professional elite supporting it were to blame as well. Goodstadt observes that the crisis faced by the C.H. Tung administration was exacerbated by the colonial administration's past inaction; and this delay in investment in social development was deliberate.[19]

---

[16] See Joseph Y.S. Cheng (ed.), *Evaluating the Tsang Years 2005–2012*, Hong Kong: City University of Hong Kong Press, 2013.

[17] See Goodstadt, *Poverty in the Midst of Affluence*, especially the introduction, pp. 1–27.

[18] In 1988, the governor, Sir David (later Lord) Wilson, stated that growth in the civil service was to be restricted and its "ministerial" structure was being reviewed by international management consultants. Sir David Wilson, *Hong Kong Hansard*, October 7, 1987, p. 46.

[19] Goodstadt, *Poverty in the Midst of Affluence*, p. 5.

This reluctance to invest in social services and welfare was influenced by the government's own philosophy, but was also reinforced by the Chinese leadership's Hong Kong policy. During the Sino-British negotiations on the territory's future and in the transition toward 1997, the Chinese authorities were eager to demonstrate their respect for investors' interests, and reduce the concern that "Hong Kong people administering Hong Kong" would lead to an increase in expenditure on social services and welfare, and therefore rises in taxation. The Chinese authorities were acutely aware that money could depart from Hong Kong easily, and investors were uneasy about its future.[20] In addition, Chinese leaders' suspicions against the British administration included a conspiracy theory that it would spend generously to please the local people, secure popularity, and leave the financial problems to its successor, the HKSAR government. This conspiracy theory gained greater currency in view of the deteriorations in Sino-British relations during the Chris Patten administration in the aftermath of the Tiananmen Incident in June 1989. The strenuous negotiations on the financing of the new airport and the revenues gained from land sales were vivid illustrations of such suspicions.

Under such circumstances, both the British administration and the business and professional elite were reluctant to improve Hong Kong's social services and welfare. The pro-democracy camp as well as the trade unions and grassroots NGOs were also deterred from demanding for significant improvement in social services. This deterrence effect remained in force throughout the transition period and well into the early years of the HKSAR government.[21]

The first chief executive, C.H. Tung, declared that Hong Kong had lived in "a bubble economy" for many years.[22] In his meetings with the

---

[20] Joseph Y. S. Cheng, "Towards the Establishment of a New Order," in *Hong Kong SAR: In Pursuit of Domestic and International Order*, edited by Beatrice Leung and Joseph Y. S. Cheng, Hong Kong: Chinese University Press, 1997, pp. 271–299.

[21] Chan Yuen-han, probably the most respected politician in the pro-Beijing united front, for example, supported self-help on behalf of the Hong Kong Federation of Trade Unions as a solution for unemployment and suggested allowing the jobless to become street food vendors. See Chan Yuen-han, Federation of Trade Unions, *Hong Kong Hansard*, November 16, 2005, p. 2,059.

[22] C.H. Tung, *Government Information Services*, June 15, 1998.

community leaders before his assumption of office, he clearly indicated that he was very concerned with the decline in the territory's international competitiveness due to its high cost structure, especially the exorbitantly high property prices. He therefore made it clear that he wanted to bring housing prices down, and indirectly wages down, though he did not make the latter explicit. Hong Kong's return to the Motherland coincided with the Asia-Pacific financial crisis, and the C.H. Tung administration began to preach financial stringency, which intensified deflation. By 2011, the government had accumulated net assets amounting to HK$1.4 trillion; but it was significant that successive administrations had offered no serious plans to make good use of the assets to enhance the territory's future international competitiveness nor to improve social services to raise the people's quality of life.

Though the community's grievances and protests finally forced C.H. Tung to step down, his successor did not seem to have learnt the lesson. In June 2005, Donald Tsang insisted that efforts to narrow the gap between the rich and the poor were bound to do more harm than good. In his final policy address, he admitted that "the wealth gap has given rise to the demand for income redistribution," and it "has become a structural cause for social tension". However, he immediately jumped to the conclusion that it "is simply not feasible to support a significant increase in recurrent welfare expenditure by raising taxes or issuing bonds."[23] It was exactly this arrogance, laziness, and unwillingness to engage the community for discussion that made the Hong Kong people angry. The older generations embraced a self-reliance spirit; they believed that through their own hard work, they would be able to solve their own problems. At this stage, the younger generations considered that the government had a significant role in helping them meet their challenges ahead, ranging from housing to their children's education, hospital services, provisions for their retirement, and so on.

The Hong Kong people understood that they could not expect a Scandinavian welfare society model, but it was only natural that they compared their welfare with what their counterparts in Singapore and

---

[23] Donald Tsang Yam-kuen, Chief Executive, *Hong Kong Hansard*, June 27, 2005, pp. 8, 944 and 8,945.

Macau received. They realized that the government could not raise taxes by a big margin, but they had reason to doubt why Donald Tsang had to promise the business community to lower the corporate tax rate in his re-election bid.[24] His administration's stubborn refusal to re-launch the Home Ownership Scheme and its cutting back of the supply of public rental housing were especially criticized for the neglect of people's livelihood and serving the interests of the powerful real estate tycoons.

On the other hand, during the tenure of the Donald Tsang administration, distributing small gifts to various segments of the population became routine. These usual "candies" included payment of one or two months rents for public housing tenants, an extra one-month allowance for recipients of Comprehensive Social Security Assistance, Old Age Allowance, and Disability Allowance, rates waiver, electricity rate subsidies, and so on. These "candies" obviously pleased various socioeconomic groups, though with diminishing returns. However, the path-dependence impact was significant; and whether they liked it or not, Donald Tsang's successors would find it difficult to terminate these supposedly one-off measures. In years of prosperity when government budget surpluses were substantial, people asked the government to share the community's wealth; and in years of economic difficulties, people asked for help from the government to ease their plight. Political parties reinforced these demands as they also presented their requests in their consultations with the administration to please their respective supporters.[25] These "candies" could not play a significant role in minimizing the community's grievances. Increasingly, the Hong Kong people believed that the inaction of the HKSAR government to tackle their livelihood issues was related to its eagerness to please the business community. Their anger grew because, on one hand, the previous measures dissuading investors from leaving the territory had been diminishing in impact, and

---

[24] In his re-election policy platform in early 2007, Donald Tsang indicated that he aimed to reduce both the profit tax rate and salary tax rate to 15%. In the following October, he reduced the profit tax rate from 17.5% to 16.5% and the salary tax rate from 16% to 15%. See *The Standard*, October 9, 2007.

[25] See Kam Wah Chan, "Rethinking Flexible Welfare Strategy in Hong Kong: A New Direction for the East Asian Welfare Model?," *Journal of Asian Public Policy*, Vol. 5, No. 1, March 2012, pp. 71–81.

on the other hand, more and more people realized that their own efforts might no longer be adequate to solve their problems, housing being an obvious example.

The British colonial administration used to assume the role of aggregating interests. While major British business groups were given privileges like having representatives in the Executive Council, their influences in both the government and the market had been in decline since the 1970s in view of the rise of local business groups. Since the return of the territory to the Motherland, the latter had become increasingly influential in the HKSAR government's policymaking processes.

In the first place, their assets grew and some of them had gradually emerged as world-class business groups. They also had substantial investment projects in mainland China. As local business leaders remained the key targets of the Chinese authorities' united front, the Chief Executive and leading government officials understood that local business leaders had more chances of meeting Chinese leaders than they did. The latter often consulted local business leaders on the performance of the HKSAR government and the potential candidates for the future Chief Executive position. The Hong Kong people naturally became suspicious when many senior government officials joined major corporations upon retirement.

There had been increasing concern of a "collusion between top government officials and the tycoons." After decades of consumer demand, the real estate industry had still failed to disclose the exact measurements of the flats they sold. Families that spent their life earnings on a property were given measurements of "constructing areas", with actual usable space amounting to 65% to 85% of the given "construction areas". The HKSAR government had only issued guidelines which had been implemented only since the beginning of 2013 and they are not legally binding regulations for the industry. The arrogance of the industry was further demonstrated by its refusal to allow prospective buyers to take actual measurements and photographs of the model flats. After years of charging excessive management fees for MPF (pension fund) contributions, the financial services industry finally agreed to reduce its charges by a small margin. There was obvious room for further reductions, but the government had not exerted pressure on the industry. Finally, in late-2011, small shopkeepers revealed that major suppliers had threatened to cut off supplies if they sold a certain brand of quick noodles at prices below those of two major supermarket chains. Without an effective competition law, consumer rights could not be safeguarded.

This increasing concern of a "collusion between top government officials and the tycoons" was most vividly exposed in the government's housing policy. Since the bulk of the wealth of the territory's richest tycoons had come from the real estate industry, land supply and the public housing policy were perceived to be related to these tycoons' fortunes. After the initial years of the C.H. Tung administration, the HKSAR government greatly reduced its commitment in the provision of public housing and became more relaxed in preparing new land supply for the private sector. These policy orientations had driven up housing prices significantly since their recovery from the SARS epidemic in 2003.[26] The Hong Kong people acutely realized that Singaporeans had been enjoying much better housing conditions, and the significant difference could be explained only in terms of government policy. Even middle class families who had no financial difficulties understood that their housing conditions could have been considerably improved if the government had performed better in land supply. When the C.Y. Leung administration pledged to improve housing for the people, it could not do much for at least four or five years because of the time lag between increasing land supply at the policy level and the actual delivery of housing units to meet the people's demand.

In the eyes of ordinary people, the legitimacy deficit of the HKSAR government had been deteriorating, not only because of its unsatisfactory performance, but also because of its lack of concern for the interests of ordinary people who did not think that the government was accountable to them. This legitimacy deficit in turn created new problems. In the first place, this legitimacy deficit led to the government's general reluctance to tackle controversial policies. For example, at this stage, the MPF was inadequate as a pension system for retirement. While the Hong Kong people are accustomed to relying on their savings, the improvement in life

---

[26] See Goodstadt, *Poverty in the Midst of Affluence*, Chapter 3, "Housing: Unending Crisis," pp. 87–110; and Ngai Ming Yip, "Housing Policy in the Tsang Administration," in Cheng, *Evaluating the Tsang Years*, pp. 319–346.

expectancy and the crises in the financial markets were causes for worry. Middle class families were also concerned with the provision of hospital services in the public sector as their savings might not be adequate for long-term serious illnesses.

The Donald Tsang administration did not offer any plans to strengthen the MPF scheme as additional payments from employers and employees were bound to be unpopular. Instead, it merely offered incentives to encourage people to acquire private sector health insurance. The proposal was not well received as people in general could not afford it and believed that public hospitals had to serve them. Middle-class families welcomed the limited incentives, but would rather the government assume the burden of running the insurance system.[27] The C.Y. Leung administration was in political trouble since its inauguration and was in no position to tackle these major policies.

The legitimacy deficit of the HKSAR government generated the need for Beijing to support it often, and its unpopularity spread to the central government. In 2013, the lobbying of legislators to support the C.Y. Leung administration by the Central Liaison Office (the central government's agency in Hong Kong) became an open secret, so much so that the pro-Beijing media had to defend it as legitimate.[28] This constant interferences in Hong Kong had its adverse impact. From 1997 to 2008, Hong Kong people's identification with the Chinese nation and their trust for the central government had been strengthening, according to public opinion surveys; but both trends had been reversed since then, and the respective declines had been sharpening in the middle of the 2010s. The intermediate-term and long-term impact of the central government's support for the HKSAR government at critical moments might well be weakened.

Finally, in the first year of the C.Y. Leung administration, its low popularity resulted in a few of its team members keeping a distance from it, including the convener of the Executive Council, Eden Lam Woon-kwong, in the controversial issue of free-to-air television licences.

---

[27] Joseph Y.S. Cheng, "The 2012 Chief Executive Election in Hong Kong and the Challenges for the Chinese Authorities," *East Asian Policy* (Singapore), Vol. 5, No. 2, April/June 2013, pp. 92–95.

[28] See *Ta Kung Pao* and *Wen Wei Po*, November 8, 2013.

This was undeniably a sign of weakness on the part of the HKSAR government.[29] In sum, these problems represented a vicious circle indicating that the legitimacy deficit of the government further weakened it and its ability to deliver, leading to a worsening of its legitimacy deficit.

Criticisms against the HKSAR government and the three administrations since 1997 had become normal, but constructive proposals were rare. In the Chief Executive election in 2012, the campaign strategies of both C.Y. Leung and Henry Tang focussed on their respective opponents' scandals; unfortunately the focus of the media was the same, and there were no meaningful deliberations on policy measures to arrest the deteriorating living standards and the widening of the gap between the rich and poor. In his second policy address delivered on January 15, 2014, Chief Executive C.Y. Leung offered a policy package amounting to HK$20 billion of recurrent expenditure per annum to help various underprivileged groups. The package on the whole was well received, though there were arguments on the impact of the aging society and slower economic growth rates on the depletion of fiscal reserves.

There was no serious community-wide discussion on the impact of such policy measures on radical politics in the territory. Meanwhile, there was considerable media discussion on the increasing political polarization in the community and, to a lesser extent, the political fragmentation within the establishment and the pro-democracy camp. Quarrels among political groups within each camp and within individual political parties were common phenomena.[30] The Legislative Council electoral system had facilitated the election of radical candidates through the multi-seat, single-vote constituencies with up to nine seats up for grabs in New Territories West. There were some analyses of election results and election strategies.[31] However, the relationship between political fragmentation and the Legislative Council electoral system on one hand and the emergence of radical politics on the other deserved more original research.

---

[29] *Wen Wei Po*, November 11, 2013; see especially *Ta Kung Pao* editorial on the same day.
[30] Cheng, "2012 Chief Executive Election," p. 103.
[31] See, for example, the 13 articles published in *Ming Pao* between August 23 and October 4, 2012 by Ivan Tsui Chi-keung on the Legislative Council elections in the same year.

While the emergence and exacerbation of political radicalization in Hong Kong attracted a lot of attention and generated considerable concern, there was also a strong view that local political radicalism was not radical at all, compared with that in the stable Western democracies and that in other developing countries. While the popularity of political leaders and the legitimacy of the government had been in decline, the social policy programs articulated by the pro-democracy parties were still quite conservative by European standards. In many protest rallies, there were calls for the resignation of the incumbent Chief Executive and related ministers, but the political demands were for democratization of the electoral systems and not the overthrow of the existing socioeconomic system. Concern about the territory's political radicalism mainly centred on the ineffective governance and failure to introduce new policy programs on the part of the administration because of the political polarization and fragmentation.

III The Emergence of New Social Movements

The body of literature on the emergence of new social movements (NSMs) in Hong Kong is still developing; there is naturally the argument that their "newness" has been exaggerated.[32] Their ideological orientation is perhaps the most important characteristic differentiating them from their predecessors; this ideological orientation is reflected by the NSMs' objectives, organizational structures, and action patterns. Post-materialism and libertarianism are considered to have an important influence on them.[33]

In the case of Taiwan, the educated segment of the population realizes that the chances of ordinary people becoming rich are often limited, and

---

[32] Grant Jordan and William Maloney, *The Protest Business?*, Manchester: Manchester University Press, 1997, pp. 46–74; and Alan Scott, *Ideology and the New Social Movement*, New York: Unwin Hyman, 1990.

[33] Russell Dalton, Manfred Kuechler, and Wilhelm Burklin, "The Challenge of New Social Movements," in *Challenging the Political Order: New Social and Political Movements in Western Democracies*, edited by Russell Dalton and Manfred Kuechler, New York: Oxford University Press, 1990, pp. 3–20. See also Ka-ying Wong and Po-san Wan, "New Evidence of the Postmaterialist Shift: The Experience of Hong Kong," *Social Indicators Research*, Vol. 92, No. 3, July 2009, pp. 497–515.

it has sought satisfaction through active participation in civil society activities in the recent or three two decades. Despite some disappointment with the performance of political parties and political leaders after the achievement of democracy, this participation has not been adversely affected. These phenomena have not yet appeared in Hong Kong, though university students seem to be politically more active in the 2010s.

C.H. Tung, the first Chief Executive of the HKSAR, understood the limitations of materialism — that is, in a mature economy, people could not expect respectable growth in per capita incomes continuously. He attempted to appeal to Confucianism with limited impact. More realistically, there might well emerge a new type of neighborhood groups. Given the acute need for emotional support in a highly competitive society where work pressure was substantial, a sense of loneliness and alienation was widespread. Single parents, retirees, young people who are well educated and ready for some volunteer work, and others, formed a substantial pool of potential members ready to group together in service of the neighborhood. These people were distinct from members of the existing grassroots groups in that they were financially better off and did not plan to seek help directly from the government. They did not intend to take an active part in politics, but they wanted a meaningful interaction with the community through which they sought mutual help, emotional support, and satisfaction through service. At this stage, religious organizations came closest to satisfying this demand, but obviously, there was much room for similar secular groups to develop.[34]

The abovementioned type of neighborhood groups had not yet emerged in Hong Kong in any significant scale; the pro-Beijing united front had, to some extent, filled this gap. The Chinese authorities began publicly building their Hong Kong community network and influence in 1985 when the Hong Kong branch of the New China News Agency opened three district offices in Hong Kong Island, Kowloon, and the New Territories. Pro-Beijing political forces mounted a campaign to block the introduction of direct elections to the Legislative Council in 1988. They also mobilized their supporters, identified candidates, and

---

[34] Joseph Y.S. Cheng, "Postscript: Towards the Establishment of a New Order," in Leung and Cheng, *Hong Kong SAR*, pp. 297–298.

isolated political opponents in the district board elections in March 1988. The pro-Beijing united front suffered a severe setback because of the Tiananmen Incident, and this was reflected in the sweeping electoral victory of the pro-democracy political groups in the 1991 elections to the Legislative Council.[35] Since then, the pro-Beijing political groups had gradually recovered. These groups did not perform well in the 1995 Legislative Council elections in terms of seats won, but they altogether secured 34% of the vote and their mobilization power was impressive in a number of ways.

In subsequent years, the performance of the Democratic Alliance for Betterment and Progress of Hong Kong (DAB) and the Hong Kong Federation of Trade Unions (HKFTU) showed that the community services offered by the pro-Beijing groups had been rewarded. Given their financial resources, they continued to gradually expand their grassroots network. Moreover, the pro-Beijing united front could also reward their supporters with honours such as memberships in the National People's Congress, the Chinese People's Political Consultative Conference, and their provincial counterparts as well as appointments to the HKSAR government's advisory committees. By the mid-1990s, the Chinese authorities had already established their system of honors for the Hong Kong community. Such efforts and resources laid a good foundation for the pro-Beijing political groups.

Since the massive protest rallies in 2013 and 2014, the pro-Beijing united front had gradually built a very sophisticated electoral machinery similar to the People's Action Party in Singapore. The services delivered at the grassroots level were sometimes summed up as "snake-soup banquets in winter, vegetarian meals for the elderly, moon-cakes during the Mid-autumn Festival, and rice dumplings during the Dragon Boat Festival." District councillors of the united front arranged visits to the poor elderly in the public housing estates almost monthly with a bag of rice, a bottle of cooking oil, and a bottle of soy sauce for each. These visits

---

[35] See Joseph Y.S. Cheng, "Hong Kong's Legislative Council Elections: Review of 1991 and Planning for 1995," in *25 Years of Social and Economic Development in Hong Kong*, edited by Benjamin K.P. Leung and Teresa Y.C. Wong (Hong Kong: Centre of Asian Studies, The University of Hong Kong, 1994), pp. 291–313.

brought warmth and comfort to the elderly. As a result, the pro-democracy camp held slightly over a quarter of the seats in the HKSAR's 18 District Councils out of a total of over 400, and they were in the minority in every District Council. This situation left very little room for service-oriented moderate civil groups to develop at the grassroots level.

Hence, radical civil groups developed at the other end of the political spectrum. These social activists were disappointed with the pro-democracy parties too, partly because they resented electoral politics that had to accommodate considerations of pleasing voters, seeking publicity, and making compromises so as to secure partial results and avoid failures. There were unhappy experiences of past cooperation because of the above. Since the design of the Basic Law normally provides a safe majority support for the administration in the legislature, the pro-democracy political parties have not been involved in the policymaking process in a meaningful way since 1997, cooperation with them was not very helpful in securing concessions from the government. The NSMs therefore tended to contest individual issues on their own.[36]

The NSMs wanted to develop loose non-hierarchical forms of organization, and they valued the experiences of participation and the community spirit almost as much as achieving their policy objectives. Typically, they developed collective decision-making processes, appealed to the community through skilful media strategies to win public opinion support, rejected the mediation of political parties and politicians, demanded direct dialogues with the government and power holders, and were willing to engage in confrontational action.[37] As observed by Ma Ngok, they sought to avoid the contamination of partisan politics and co-optation by the government in order to maintain the purity of their causes.[38]

---

[36] Tai-lok Lui and Stephen Wing-kai Chiu, "Introduction — Changing Political Opportunities and the Shaping of Collective Action," in *The Dynamics of Social Movements in Hong Kong*, edited by Stephen Wing-kai Chiu and Tai-lok Lui, Hong Kong: Hong Kong University Press, 2000, pp. 1–19.

[37] Kai Hon Ng, "Social Movements and Political Capacity in Hong Kong: An Alternative Perspective," *Issues & Studies*, Vol. 49, No. 2, June 2013, pp. 185–186.

[38] Ma Ngok, "Social Movements and State-Society Relationship in Hong Kong," in *Social Movements in China and Hong Kong*, edited by Khun Eng Kuah-Pearce and Gilles Guiheux, Amsterdam: Amsterdam University Press, 2009, p. 50.

In the middle of the first decade of the new century, the annual number of reported protests increased from under 100 before the millennium to around 200.[39] One explanation naturally was the deteriorating living standards and the widening of the gap between the rich and the poor discussed in section 1 of this chapter. Dissatisfaction and grievances accumulated in society, especially among young people, who also suffered from the decline in opportunities for upward social mobility.

Takis S. Pappas observes the significance of another factor in his study of the emergence of radical mass movements in democracies.[40] Hong Kong is not a democracy. However, beginning in the 1970s, the British administration gradually established a system of advisory bodies to absorb interest groups into the policymaking process.[41] The moderate political culture in the territory encouraged policy grievances and controversies to be settled within the formal institutional framework. The decline in legitimacy on the part of the HKSAR government discussed in section 2 had adversely affected the effectiveness of this "administrative absorption" process, giving rise to radical mass movements.[42]

Pappas attempts to link radical action at the mass level with strategic choices at the elite level, explaining the former in terms of the symbolic-cum-strategic action of individual political entrepreneurs employing specific frames to mobilize the masses. He examines three cases: (i) Andreas Papandreou in Greece in the 1970s, (ii) Slobodan Milosevic in Serbia in the 1980s, and (iii) Hugo Chavez in Venezuela in the 1990s. He analyzes how they were able to construct subversive ideological messages and mobilize radical political action, that is, how creative symbolic power could become a powerful political resource. "When this creativity is particularly original," argues Abner Cohen, "when it helps to articulate or

---

[39] Kai Hon Ng, "Social Movements and Political Capacity in Hong Kong," p. 181.

[40] Takis S. Pappas, "Political Leadership and the Emergence of Radical Mass Movements in Democracy," *Comparative Political Studies*, Vol. 41, No. 8, August 2008, pp. 1,117–1,140.

[41] Joseph Y. S. Cheng, "Political Modernisation in Hong Kong," *Journal of Commonwealth & Comparative Politics*, Vol. 27, No. 3, November 1989, pp. 306–307.

[42] Ambrose Yeo-chi King, "The Administrative Absorption of Politics in Hong Kong," *Asian Survey*, Vol. 15, No. 5, May 1975, pp. 422–439.

objectify new groupings and new relations," we are faced with charismatic leaders.[43]

Most Hong Kong people were very ignorant about the above three cases, but young people in the territory were familiar with the charisma of radical political leaders like Long Hair Leung Kwok-hung and Raymond Wong Yuk-man. In the Legislative Council elections in September 2012, People Power, led by Raymond Wong, and the League of Social Democrats, led by Leung Kwok-hung, won 264,000 votes, compared with 255,000 votes for the Civic Party and 247,000 votes for the Democratic Party.[44] Leung and Wong had replaced Emily Lau Wai-hing as radical political leaders attracting the support of the angry young people, though Lau was perceived as the anti-Beijing firebrand or the most radical legislator when she first entered the Legislative Council in 1991.

Conservative Hong Kong people were not happy with the frequent protests, and the pro-Beijing media lamented this phenomenon and labelled the territory as "the capital of protests". Then Secretary for Security Ambrose Lee Siu-kwong criticized the young activists for "seriously undermining" the rule of law.[45] Yet, the community understood that the territory's protest activities were mild compared with those in major Western cities. At the academic level, Chantal Mouffe argues that when a society lacks a dynamic public space allowing for agonistic confrontation among diverse political identities, a more nefarious space may open, where alienation generates alternative identifications along antagonistic divides like nationalism, religion, and ethnicity.[46] At this stage, rule of law and freedom of the media had been well maintained in the territory because all parties concerned realize that their maintenance

---

[43] Abner Cohen, *Two-Dimensional Man: An Essay on the Anthropology of Power and Symbolism in Complex Society*, Berkeley: University of California Press, 1974, p. 30.

[44] Eddie Luk, "Even More Radical," *Standard*, September 14, 2012.

[45] *HK Online*, http://hk-magazine.com/feature/post-80s-boom (accessed October 2, 2013).

[46] Chantal Mouffe, "For an Agonistic Public Sphere," in *Radical Democracy: Politics between Abundance and Lack*, edited by Lars Tonder and Lasse Thomassen, Manchester: Manchester University Press, 2004, pp. 123–132; see also Simon Springer, "Public Space as Emancipation: Meditations on Anarchism, Radical Democracy, Neoliberalism and Violence," *Antipode*, Vol. 43, No. 2, 2011, pp. 525–562.

was essential to the functioning of Hong Kong as an international financial centre and international business services centre. There were concerns regarding some signs of deterioration, but all civil society groups believed they enjoyed ample freedom to articulate their causes and grievances. The real issues were increasing political polarization and the grave doubts regarding the political will of the administration to tackle the controversial policy challenges.

It had to be admitted that the existing literature had not been able to establish the organic linkage between poverty, social inequalities, and so forth, on one hand, and actual radical political actions on the other, though incidents of protest activities and related minor conflicts with the police had been on the rise. Arguably, a correlation could be established, but the causal effect had not been well analyzed. After all, the number of radical political activists in the territory remained very small. There were some in-depth interviews of university students and young people at the postgraduate theses level, but published works were almost absent.

(a) *Dockers' Strike, 2013*

Not all NSMs in Hong Kong were post-materialist; in the general climate of radicalization, trade unions were also emboldened. In early May 2013, a 40-day strike involving hundreds of crane operators and stevedores inside the Kwai Tsing Container Terminal ended with a small victory for the workers, securing a 9.8% wage increase. The dockers' strike was the largest industrial action in the new century. It was significant in that it attracted a lot of media attention and public support on an unprecedented scale. The strike collected public donations of more than HK$8 million; and student organizations, both in high schools and tertiary institutions, actively showed their support. The donations helped the dockers on strike to hang on. The community normally did not show a strong support for trade unionism and tended to believe in market forces. Moreover, the dockers' wages were not low by Hong Kong standards. However, this time, civil society and members of the public were mobilized to attend demonstrations and rallies in support of the striking workers. For the latter, it was also a significant moment of political re-engagement; after the strike, the workers continued participating in other political events such as the July 1 demonstration to demand collective bargaining rights and democracy.

Collective bargaining rights of trade unions are not recognized in Hong Kong, reflecting their weaknesses and the power of capital. One of the last acts of the Patten administration was to legislate such rights; and the provisional legislature of the HKSAR immediately revoked them in its first months. It reflected the political contradictions in Hong Kong when the Communist Party regime in Beijing cared more for investors' interests than workers' rights, and when the HKFTU dared not speak for the very basic right of trade unions after becoming part of the political establishment. Hence major employers could still simply ignore workers who grouped together to make demands.

Legally, the striking workers were negotiating with the contractors of the container terminal, but the workers and their supporters protested against the major business group Hutchison Whampoa Ltd. and the richest man in Hong Kong, Li Ka-shing. Li was a folk hero in the 1970s, as he was perceived to make his own fortunes and take over from the British hongs on behalf of the local business community. In the eyes of the protestors, he was then seen as a very rich man exploiting the workers.[47] This changing perception was sometimes labelled as the "hate the rich" syndrome, and was obviously a reflection of the anger over the disparity between the rich and the poor. The pro-democracy movement certainly used this as a good example to illustrate the strong linkage between democracy and people's livelihood.

(b) *Hong Kong Autonomy Movement*

Orthodox ideologies often have a limited appeal in Hong Kong. Leung Kwok-hung was a rare example of a political leader who put his cause within a socialist frame. As Europe entered a significant phase of reintegration of East and West, it faced an increasing problem with the

---

[47] Chen Te-ping, "Hong Kong Strike Hits Tycoon's Image," *Wall Street Journal*, April 8, 2013, http://online.wsj.com/article/SB10001424127887323550604578410233885297880.html.

rise of far-right political parties.[48] Immigration was often the major controversy triggering riots. As can be expected, there are no far-right political groups in this cosmopolitan metropolis. But the rising tensions between Hong Kong people and Mainlanders had given rise to the Hong Kong Autonomy Movement and a similar group called Hong Kong Nativism Power.[49]

As two communities interact closely, misunderstandings easily arise. Naturally, when more than 40 million tourists from Mainland China visited Hong Kong every year, the territory became very crowded, causing resentment among the locals.[50] While tourism was a major pillar of the economy, most Hong Kong people did not feel they had benefitted directly from it. Instead, they believed that this influx caused considerable inconveniences. Commercial premises in districts most frequented by tourists tended to command higher rents, driving up prices and forcing the relocation of small businesses serving the locals. Mainland tourists' massive purchases of baby formula caused a shortage of supply for mothers with infants, resulting in an uproar and embarrassment for the HKSAR government. Some Hong Kong people were upset that workers at expensive luxury goods outlets treated Mandarin-speaking customers better. In the extreme cases, some angry Hong Kongers called Mainlanders "locusts", and a Beijing University professor Kong Qingdong called Hong Kong people "dogs".

There were materialistic issues of public sector resources too. The Donald Tsang administration's promotion of the medical care sector providing services for foreign visitors as an export of service produced some undesirable side effects. Thousands of pregnant women came to Hong Kong to give birth to babies in private hospitals so that their children

---

[48] Cas Mudde, *Populist Radical Right Parties in Europe*, Cambridge: Cambridge University Press, 2007.

[49] Chin Wan, "Uphold Hong Kong's Autonomy, Safeguard the City State's Freedom — General Programme of the Hong Kong City State Autonomous Movement (in Chinese)," http://hkam2011/blogspot.com/2011/06/blogpost_25.html. See also the Hong Kong Nativism Power Facebook page, https://www.facebook.com/pages/Hong-Kong-Nativism-Power/204516669578487.

[50] See the statistics provided by the Census and Statistics Department, HKSAR government, partnernet.hktb.com/tc/research_statistics/index.html?print=1.

would secure Hong Kong resident status. Private hospitals had to recruit pediatric doctors and nurses from public hospitals, resulting in a deterioration of services in the public sector for the locals. Subsequently, these children came to Hong Kong for their education, causing a shortage of places in kindergartens in the northern New Territories near the border.

With the emergence of organizations like the Hong Kong Autonomy Movement, the grievances and emotions were raised to the political level. Chin Wan, the principal theoretician of the movement, argued in May 2011 that the Tiananmen Incident aroused Hong Kong people's fear of China, and the pro-democracy movement proposed the idea of "democratic resistance against Communism". However, Chin criticized the Democratic Party for its conciliatory approach towards Beijing at this stage, and appealed for a strong stand on Hong Kong autonomy. He and his supporters then blamed the Individual Visit Scheme, the National Education project, and so on, for the escalation of tensions between mainland China and Hong Kong.

Support for the movement had been considerably enhanced by the opposition to the increasing interferences in Hong Kong on the part of the Chinese authorities. There was a serious concern that these interferences threatened the freedom and lifestyle that Hong Kong people cherished. The movement obviously touched on the sensitivities of Beijing, which was worried about the separatist movements in Tibet and Xinjiang, as well as the independence orientations in Taiwan and Hong Kong. The pro-Beijing united front was particularly angry with the movement's lion and dragon flag, adopted and modified from the British colonial flag. The explicit anger, however, seemed to have been encouraging more such flag bearers in the territory's protest rallies in the 2010s.

(c) *Occupy Central Movement*

Supporters of the pro-democracy movement in Hong Kong had been angry and frustrated in the past two or three decades with the lack of progress in democratization; and this anger and frustration were vividly reflected in the Occupy Central Movement. The Standing Committee of the National People's Congress released its decision on December 29, 2007, in response to the pro-democracy movement's demand for a timetable and a road map. It states, "appropriate amendments may be made to the specific method for selecting the fourth Chief Executive and the specific method for forming the fifth term Legislative Council of the HKSAR in the year of 2012. The election of the fifth Chief Executive of the HKSAR in the year 2017 may be implemented by the method of universal suffrage; that after the Chief Executive is selected by universal suffrage, the election of the Legislative Council of the HKSAR may be implemented by the method of electing all the members by universal suffrage."[51] The decision thus offers the Hong Kong people the hope that the earliest possible dates to practise universal suffrage in the election of the Chief Executive and the entire Legislative Council would be 2017 and 2020 respectively.

The pro-democracy movement did not feel reassured by this offer, and there is a strong worry that though the Hong Kong people might be granted the right of electing the Chief Executive by universal suffrage by 2017, they might be able to elect only from a list of candidates approved by the Chinese authorities. This fear was much exacerbated by the remarks of Qiao Xiaoyang, chairman of the Law Committee of the National People's Congress, in a closed-door seminar on the Hong Kong Basic Law, attended by the pro-establishment legislators in Shenzhen on March 24, 2013. Qiao declared that "any members from the opposition camp who insist on confronting the central government cannot become the Chief Executive of Hong Kong."[52] Qiao seemed to be suggesting that a screening mechanism would be in place to select the candidates for the Chief Executive in 2017. Qiao further elaborated that "Chief Executive candidates must be persons who love the country and love Hong Kong" and that "those who confront the central government would fail to qualify."[53]

It was in this context that Benny Tai from the Law School of the University of Hong Kong proposed the idea of the Occupy Central

---

[51] HKSAR Government, *Consultation Document: Methods for Selecting the Chief Executive and for Forming the Legislative Council in 2012*, November 2009, p. 42.
[52] Joshua But and Collen Lee, "Opponents of Beijing Ineligible to be C.E.," *South China Morning Post*, March 25, 2013.
[53] *Ibid.*

Movement in his *Hong Kong Economic Journal* column in January 2013, Tai further reiterated the idea in the *South China Morning Post* in early February 2013 about his plan to rally tens of thousands of protesters to block the roads in Central in July 2014. Tai hoped that the protest would rally support from the public and exert pressure on Beijing to allow democracy for the territory. Tai's proposal was based on the belief that unless the Hong Kong people were willing to sacrifice and engage in political struggle, the Chinese authorities would not concede democracy to them. The campaign ignited the enthusiasm of the pro-democracy supporters, and the idea developed into a movement exactly because the participants were convinced that democracy was not a gift bestowed from above.

The philosophical paradigm of the Occupy Central Movement came from the concept of deliberative democracy advocated by James Fishkin. Tai and his team emphasized rational discussion through deliberation day exercises to find a consensus on the method of electing the Chief Executive while the civil disobedience campaign would serve as a last resort. According to Fishkin, deliberative democracy offers the entire nation the opportunities for thoughtful interaction and opinion formation that are normally restricted to small-group democracy.[54] Deliberative democracy brings the face-to-face democracy of ordinary citizens who can participate on the same basis of political equality as that offered by the ancient Athenian Assembly.[55] The most important element of deliberative democracy is to identify the "refined public opinion" that would result from more thoughtful interactions. This certainly was a significant attraction and a rewarding experience to those in Hong Kong who sought meaningful political participation.

The movement, as expected, attracted severe criticisms from the pro-Beijing united front, and it was perceived as a direct challenge to the Chinese authorities. The latter probably had the "Arab Spring" in mind and were concerned with the movement's demonstration effect in China. The entire united front was mobilized to condemn it. According to a series

---

[54] James Fishkin, *Democracy and Deliberation*, New Haven: Yale University Press, 1991, p. 4.
[55] *Ibid.*

of public opinion surveys by *Ming Pao*, support for the movement rose from 25% of the respondents in April 2013 to 32% in July and fell back to 25% in October, while those who opposed fell from 51% in April 2013 to 46% in July and increased again to 55% in October.[56] Given the territory's moderate political culture, support for a civil disobedience campaign severely condemned by Beijing was not expected to be high; even a support rate of 25% already deserved close attention by the Chinese authorities and the HKSAR government.

The emergence of NSMs and radical politics was a relatively new political development in the territory, and more research outputs were anticipated in the coming years. Detailed and systematic research on the formation, objectives, organizations, modes of mobilization, leadership, and strategies of different radical groups was still rare. Two specific areas probably deserved more attention. The ideas and strategies of their leaders and activists were much influenced by Western philosophers; this influence and the local adaptation processes were significant in a better understanding of NSMs and radical politics in the territory. In-depth interviews of these leaders and activists would be valuable. Comparisons between NSMs and radical politics in the territory and those in East Asia as well as those in relevant countries should be illuminating; and this work probably had not yet begun. NSMs in Hong Kong might also have a potential impact on the development of civil society in China, which would have much more significant global effects. Research in this area was related to the future democratization process in Hong Kong as this impact was a concern on the part of the Chinese leadership.

IV Radical Politics and Effective Governance

In the early 2010s, the Hong Kong people were complaining in unison about local politics as their frustrations grew. Their dissatisfaction was centring broadly on the decline in Hong Kong's international economic competitiveness and the inefficiency of the government. Both had been gradual processes since 1997 or so, and were related to the "legitimacy deficit" of the HKSAR government discussed in section 2 of this chapter.

---

[56] *Ming Pao*, October 15, 2013.

As observed by Ian Scott, policy stalemate or, even worse, policy inertia in the sense that the administration tended to avoid initiating major policy proposals or controversial ones, became increasingly frequent.[57]

The pro-Beijing united front severely blamed the pro-democracy camp and the radical political movements for the problems of the administration, focusing on their protest activities and the filibustering, and other delaying tactics in the legislature. However, in view of the design of the Basic Law and the actual distribution of seats in the Legislative Council, if the administration and the political establishment could get their act together, the pro-democracy camp could not effectively block the policymaking process. After all, it too had to respect the trends of public opinion.

The scandals surrounding C.Y. Leung and the resignations and scandals of several members of his team gave rise to a lot of rumors about quarrels at the top of the government. Those who had supported Leung's candidacy wanted to see reforms and improvements, but the old guards of the civil service accorded a priority to preserving proper procedures and their way of doing things. These internal divisions had affected the administration's ability to deliver; for example, it had to back down even on a simple plan to restructure the government.

Top Chinese leaders appealed for reconciliation immediately after the 2012 Chief Executive election, and certainly C.Y. Leung would like to secure the support of the entire establishment. However, the appeal seemed to have limited success. Even the strong bond of the pro-Beijing united front seemed to have been eroded. The staunchly pro-Beijing monthly *The Mirror* severely criticized Rita Fan Hsu Lai-tai in its December 2012 issue for attacking the Chief Executive. Cheng Yiu-tong of the HKFTU revealed that members had withdrawn from the federation because they were disappointed by the position of popular legislator Chan Yuen-han on the proposed extra allowance for the elderly.

A weak administration naturally depended more on support from the Chinese authorities. However, the Hong Kong people's attitude toward the central government and their identity with the Chinese nation had been

---

[57] Ian Scott, *Public Administration in Hong Kong: Regime Change and Its Impact on the Public Sector*, Singapore: Marshall Cavendish, 2005, p. 24.

deteriorating. Actually, from 1997 to 2008 (according to public opinion surveys), the Hong Kong people's trust in the central government and their identity with the Chinese nation were strengthening; both trends, however, had reversed since then, and the declines became even sharper in the first half of the 2010s. In May 2013, a poll by the University of Hong Kong indicated that Hong Kong people who held negative attitudes toward the central government increased from 25% in November 2012 to 37%, those who held positive attitudes decreased from 29% to 20% in the same period.[58] In the following month immediately after the June 4 candlelight vigil, another survey by the University of Hong Kong revealed that the community's identification with the Chinese nation dropped to a 14-year low. Respondents who identified themselves as "Hong Kongers" amounted to 38%, 11% higher than six months ago; those who identified themselves as Chinese rose 2% to 23% in the same period; while those who identified themselves as "Chinese of Hong Kong" or "Hong Kongers of China" reached 36%, showing a decline of 13%.[59]

The vast majority of Hong Kong people, however, had no intention to confront the Chinese authorities, and they were proud of China's rising international status; furthermore, they were grateful for Beijing's support of the territory's economy in terms of policy concessions. As usual, it was the moderation and pragmatism of ordinary Hong Kong people that had contributed to political stability by punishing, through public opinion, the groups that were out of line.

Radical political participation in this sense had a limited market in Hong Kong. There were considerable worry and resentment in the community against the mode of political articulation and expression on the part of the League of Social Democrats, People Power, and some young radical activists of the "post-1980s" generation. At this stage, the territory's moderate political culture was still an effective deterrent against radical political action, but there was worry that as young people became more frustrated with their career prospects, the number of young radical activists would grow. On the other hand, tolerance was the best way to contain radical political participation. Suppression tended to be

---

[58] *Ming Pao*, June 5, 2013.
[59] *Apple Daily*, June 19, 2013.

counter-productive in the long term, especially when it was implemented by an unpopular government in "legitimacy deficit".

In the eyes of most Hong Kong people, political reform became the endgame. The old arguments that political reform had to be gradual and that conditions might not yet be ripe had, by this stage, lost all credibility. The widening gap between the rich and the poor, the decline in opportunities for young people to move up the socioeconomic ladder, the worsening housing problems, and the increasing inadequacy of the community's pension and healthcare systems not only exacerbated the community's frustrations and grievances but also made people realize that the C.Y. Leung administration lacked the political support needed to tackle such issues. Worse still, people did not believe that the administration could get back this support.

All parties concerned increasingly realized that the failure of reaching an agreement on political reform would hurt Hong Kong badly. The incumbent Chief Executive and the person elected in 2017 would lack legitimacy in the eyes of most people, and he or she would not have the mandate or political support to implement badly needed reforms. Effective governance might become difficult. The pro-democracy groups would not benefit from such difficulties. They would, in all likelihood, be divided and would be unable to play any constructive role. Such worries had generated renewed talk of emigration which had subsided after the mid-1990s, especially among young professionals.

In the 2012 Chief Executive election, there was a view that whoever elected would have great difficulties governing Hong Kong. It reflected the concern about the political polarization and the accumulated grievances in the community. With regard to the NSMs, the HKSAR government was no longer able to contain or absorb the politics of policymaking. The NSMs offered new values, issues, and demands which had not been well-anticipated by the government and the established political parties, including those of the pro-democracy camp.[60]

The impressive protest rally on October 20, 2013 against the C.Y. Leung administration's refusal to issue a free-to-air broadcast licence to

---

[60] Ian Scott, *The Public Sector Reform in Hong Kong*, Hong Kong: Hong Kong University Press, 2010, pp. 177, 190–194.

Hong Kong Television Network was a good demonstration of the influence and mobilization power of the Internet in building ad hoc united fronts without the involvement of established groups.[61] It was also a good example of the HKSAR government's failure "to aggregate demands and to gauge possible public responses to policy initiatives" in situations where "objections to its proposals often arouse after the formal period of consultation had taken place."[62]

The difficulties encountered by the HKSAR government had been considered by several academics. Anthony B.L. Cheung observes that "the conventional methods of administrative absorption and advisory politics began to give way to outright political agitation, protest and bargaining," and that the NSM groups were "also taking the issues to the courts and using judicial review as an extended political arena for agenda setting and bargaining."[63] Agnes Shuk-mei Ku argues that the ideological divergence between government officials and civil society groups had been widening; and that the latter were "looking for and articulating a new mode of state-society relations that outgrows the conventional mode of citizenship."[64]

On the whole, however, the NSMs and the pro-democracy camp still found it hard to challenge the government because the policy process "remains in the hands of a centralized bureaucracy."[65] If the establishment maintained solidarity and could get its act together, the policy capacity of the HKSAR government should not seriously suffer. Kai Hon Ng reaches the conclusion that the extent to which NSMs could challenge the government's "policy capacity depends on the meso-level political structures in which social activists have to operate."[66]

---

[61] See all major newspapers in Hong Kong on October 21, 2013.

[62] Scott, *Public Sector Reform in Hong Kong*, pp. 213 and 219.

[63] Anthony B. L. Cheung, "Policy Capacity in Post-1997 Hong Kong: Constrained Institutions Facing a Crowding and Differentiated Polity," *Asia Pacific Journal of Public Administration*, Vol. 29, No. 1, June 2007, p. 58.

[64] Agnes Shuk-mei Ku, "The Development of Citizenship in Hong Kong: Governance without Democracy," in *Repositioning the Hong Kong Government: Social Foundations and Political Challenges*, edited by Stephen Wing-kai Chiu and Siu-lun Wong, Hong Kong: Hong Kong University Press, 2012, p. 123.

[65] Elisa Wing-yee Lee, "Civil Society Organizations and Local Governance in Hong Kong," in Wing-kai Chiu and Siu-lun Wong, *Repositioning the Hong Kong Government*, p. 164.

[66] Kai Hon Ng, "Social Movements and Political Capacity in Hong Kong," p. 208.

The administrative absorption of politics has been a main theme in the study of the territory's political development;[67] but the administrative absorption of radical politics probably had not yet been studied both at the policy level and the academic level. In Western democracies, there have been many examples of radical environmental groups evolving into green parties and eventually joining governing coalitions. Apparently, these processes have not been examined by the establishment at the policy level nor by the local academic community. To contain the political fragmentation discussed above, the administrative absorption of radical politics calls for political vision preceded by research and public deliberations at the community level.

The influence of radical politics in the local democratization process was significant; the role of the Occupy Central Movement and the radical political groups in the campaign for genuine democracy in 2013–2014 was obvious, and would probably be examined in the research on the campaign in the near future. How the emergence of radical politics in the first half of the 2010s would shape a segment of the future political leadership of Hong Kong would likely be a research topic in the intermediate-term future.

V Conclusion

This chapter surveyed the rich body of literature that local academics had already produced on the emergence of radical politics in Hong Kong. Evidence on the deteriorating living standards and the widening of the gap between the rich and the poor was substantial. Apparently, the issue of poverty emerged in the final years of the last century and had been attracting increasing attention in the social welfare field as well. A literature review by the Legislative Council Secretariat in 2005 on poverty issues listed 27 major articles; only one of them was published before 1990, while 16 appeared between 1995 and 1999.[68]

---

[67] Yeo-chi King, "Administrative Absorption of Politics in Hong Kong."
[68] Simon Li, "Information Note. Causes of Poverty in Hong Kong: A Literature Review" (IN16/04-05), Hong Kong: Legislative Council Secretariat, January 10, 2005, pp. 5–7.

Poverty generates grievances especially in the context of the widening of the gap between the rich and the poor, and the perception of the collusion between top officials and big businesses. Under such circumstances, people naturally blamed the government. In the eyes of the community, the performance of all three Chief Executives failed to meet its expectations. Their respective philosophies were not in accordance with the people's values. Worse still, while most Hong Kong people believed that C.H. Tung's heart was in the right place, they did not think that Tung's successors had such qualifications. They were especially angry with government policies favoring the business community, and the phenomena of "greed" and corruption of the Donald Tsang and C.Y. Leung administrations reported by the media. The "legitimacy deficit" of the HKSAR government was a root cause giving rise to radical politics. This chapter admittedly was not able to cover the massive and interesting materials on the people's grievances against the Hong Kong government.

The local academics' analyses of the rise of NSMs owed much to Western theories, which had offered useful theoretical frameworks. There were some comparisons between the local groups and their counterparts in Western and Asian countries; but these were not systematic. The consensus on the origins, characteristics, modes of operation, and so on of the NSMs was strong; and the same applied to the failure of the government to anticipate and absorb their challenges.

While the literature surveyed revealed a common concern about political polarization as well as the decline in legitimacy and effective governance of the HKSAR government, the degree of pessimism varied. Confidence in the maintenance of social stability remains high, but there was little optimism that the performance of the government would soon improve.

Acknowledgement

Originally published as Cheng Joseph Y.S., "The Emergence of Radical Politics in Hong Kong: Causes and Impact", *The China Review*, Vol. 14, No. 1, 2014, pp. 199–232. Reproduced with kind permission from the Chinese University Press, Hong Kong.

Chapter 24

Assessing the C.Y. Leung Administration

I Introduction

On December 9, 2016, C.Y. Leung held a press conference and announced his decision not to seek re-election. The announcement came as a surprise to all concerned.[1] Carrie Lam, his successor, had let it be known that she would retire at the end of C.Y. Leung's first term as chief secretary for administration, as she anticipated that Leung would seek re-election. Indeed, C.Y. Leung had indicated upon his election as chief executive in 2012 that he would seek a second term. The community, therefore, expected him to seek re-election, and the political opposition had been organizing the "Anyone But C.Y." campaign.

There were no indications of Leung's stepping down within and outside the establishment until his public announcement. Leung explained that his decision was due to family reasons: "If I run my family will suffer unbearable pressure due to my electioneering…I must protect them."[2] However, just like C.H. Tung's resignation in 2005, very few people in Hong Kong accepted the official version. There were subsequently many

---

[1] Jeffie Lam and Joyce Ng, "Hong Kong Chief Executive CY Leung will not seek re-election due to family reasons," *South China Morning Post*, December 9, 2016, http://www.scmp.com/news/article/2053258/hong-kong-chief-executive-cy-leung-not-seek-re-election.

[2] *Ibid.*

reports that the central leadership in Beijing had asked him to step down because supporting his re-election would politically be very costly. Many groups within the pro-Beijing camp had revealed their dissatisfaction with C.Y. Leung to the Chinese authorities who had been monitoring the performance of the Leung administration. It was widely reported that the Chinese authorities had been consulting leaders of the pro-Beijing camp and the business community on the 2017 chief executive election in the final months of 2016, many of whom indicated that they would find it difficult to support C.Y. Leung's re-election.[3]

Having made the wrong choices regarding all three of Hong Kong's chief executives was naturally embarrassing for the Chinese leadership. The arrangement made was aimed at saving face for the Chinese authorities as well as C.Y. Leung. The latter offered not to seek re-election due to family reasons, and he was able to claim that "Beijing has always supported me and said I have done a good job."[4] He was subsequently elected as a vice-chairman of the National Committee of the Chinese People's Political Consultative Conference (CPPCC) in March 2017, a prestigious though largely ceremonial position which was also offered to C.H. Tung — but not to Donald Tsang, who was jailed almost five years after retirement on charges of misconduct in office. Leung's election to the National Committee was unusual because it took place before the end of his term as chief executive.

It seemed that Beijing was satisfied with C.Y. Leung's toeing its hard line on political reforms and political suppression, though it was unhappy with his failure to maintain the unity of the pro-Beijing camp. This was why at the very beginning of her election campaign Carrie Lam stated that she would follow Leung's policy line — even though she also admitted that she had to repair the political polarization of society.[5]

Repairing the political polarization of society was probably the most significant theme among the candidates in the 2017 chief executive

---

[3] See, for example, Lau Yui-siu, "為何不爭連任? 香港會和諧嗎?" [Why NOT compete for re-election? Will Hong Kong be Harmonious?], *Ming Pao*, December 10, 2016.
[4] *South China Morning Post*, December 9, 2016.
[5] *Ta Kung Pao*, January 19, 2017, http://www.takungpao.com.hk/hongkong/text/2017/0119/54832.html

election. Financial Secretary John Tsang Chun-wah even said that his candidacy was prompted by his wish that the Hong Kong people could avoid having to consider emigration.[6] With the benefit of hindsight, Chinese leaders likely agree that they had been prudent to refuse to endorse C.Y. Leung's re-election.

II The expanding Gap Between the Rich and Poor Amid Slow Economic Growth

Chinese leaders believe that if the economy in Hong Kong is doing well, then the people's grievances can be contained. According to government statistics, the territory's GDP grew from HK$1.934 billion in 2011 to HK$2.491 billion in 2016; and its per capita GDP grew from HK$273,549 in 2011 to HK$339,531 in 2016.[7] The respective annual growth rates in this period amounted to 5.2% and 4.4%, which were very respectable growth rates for a mature economy like Hong Kong. Yet, in general, most Hong Kong people feel that their real incomes have been in decline since the territory's return to China in 1997.

An important reason has been the substantial and expanding gap between the rich and the poor in the territory. Among the major cities in the world, Hong Kong has the largest gap between the rich and the poor. Its Gini coefficient rose from 0.45 in 1981 to 0.52 in 1996 to 0.537 in 2011 and 0.539 in 2016.[8]

---

[6] Joyce Ng, "John Tsang formally declares bid to lead Hong Kong and vows to 'restore hope in time of great uncertainty'," *South China Morning Post*, January 19, 2017, http://www.scmp.com/news/hong-kong/politics/article/2063523/john-tsang-officially-announce-chief-executive-bid-despite.

[7] Census and Statistics Department, Hong Kong Special Administrative Region (HKSAR), *Hong Kong Annual Digest of Statistics 2017,* Hong Kong: Government Printer, 2017, xi, https://www.statistics.gov.hk/pub/B10100032017AN17B0100.pdf.

[8] "Gini Coefficient," *Social Indicators of Hong Kong*, https://www.socialindicators.org.hk/en/indicators/economy/11.6; Census and Statistics Department, "Press Release: Census and Statistics Department announces results of study on household income distribution in Hong Kong [9 June 2017]", https://www.censtatd.gov.hk/press_release/pressReleaseDetail.jsp?pressRID=4180&charsetID=1.

The stagnation in ordinary people's incomes is perhaps best illustrated by the real wage index. Using September 1992 as the base (i.e., 100), it rose slowly to 116.4 in 2006 and remained stagnant at 120.7 in 2016.[9] The Hong Kong people often make comparisons with their counterparts in Singapore and Macau; and they are rather disappointed to discover that at current market prices, per capita GDP in Hong Kong stood at US$42,066 in 2015, while the corresponding figure for Singapore is US$52,889 and Macau US$71,984.[10] Indeed, this comparison with Singapore emerged in the chief executive election campaign in early 2017.

Up until the end of the last century, university graduates expected that eventually they would get married, have two children, and possess their own cars and accommodation — that was the middle class dream. Today, young people in Hong Kong realize that they have to make hard choices among these goals, as they can hardly expect to fulfill the entire dream. In most cases, they have lost the incentive to save on a long-term basis; they simply save enough to go on short holidays, spend the money, and save again.

In contrast to China, social mobility in the territory is more brittle in two key aspects. The vast majority of people in China experienced very substantial improvements in living standards in the era of economic reforms and opening to the external world after 1978, and they expect further improvements in the years ahead. In the case of Hong Kong, most people believe that their living standards have deteriorated since 1997, and they are pessimistic about improvements in the foreseeable future.

Regarding the issue of poverty, the C.Y. Leung administration publicly claimed that it had made an important contribution to its reduction. In 2015, 569,800 families and 1.345 million people lived under the poverty line, and the poverty rate was 19.7%. After the government's policy interventions, only 392,400 families and 971,400 people remained

---

[9] Census and Statistics Department, *Hong Kong Annual Digest of Statistics 2017*, x.

[10] See Chen Li Ailun, "香港經濟形勢分析與展望" [Analysis and Prospect of the Economic Situation in Hong Kong] and "Research Group of the Analysis and Prospect of the Economy in Macao, "澳門經濟分析與展望" [The Analysis and Prospect of the Economy in Macao] in Li Yang *et al.* (eds)., *2017 年中國經濟形勢分析與預測* [Economy of China Analysis and Forecast (2017)], Beijing: Social Sciences Academic Press (China), 2017, pp. 312–335 and pp. 336–351 respectively.

under the poverty line, and the poverty rate was reduced to 14.3%.[11] Obviously, the C.Y. Leung administration highlighted the fall in poverty rate due to its policy interventions. However, the government's policy interventions merely lifted some people living under the poverty line to living standards just above the poverty line, through various subsidies. The fact is that for a relatively prosperous city like Hong Kong with a per capita GDP of HK$338,806 in 2016, the number of people living under the poverty line either before or after government policy interventions is unacceptable.

By comparison, in 2011 — before C.Y. Leung took office — 530,000 families and 1.295 million people lived under the poverty line and the poverty rate was 19.6%. After government policy interventions, 399,000 families and 1.005 million people remained below the poverty line, and the poverty rate was reduced to 15.2%. Hence, the poverty rate actually slightly increased from 19.6% to 19.7% under the C.Y. Leung administration; and after new policy measures were introduced by the new administration, the poverty rate was only reduced from 15.2% to 14.3%.[12] In view of the ageing population and the decline in the average household size, reducing the poverty rate will only become more challenging in the future.

Hong Kong, however, has frequent budgetary surpluses; and it has accumulated government reserve balances amounting to about HK$840 billion (US$109 billion) at the end of March 2016, exceeding 35% of its annual GDP, and enough to pay for 23 months of government expenditure.[13] This certainly means that the government enjoys a sound fiscal position, and can overcome challenges arising from unfavorable external conditions and crises. However, increasingly, critics have raised questions as to how the government can employ its fiscal reserves in a more constructive manner.

---

[11] Commission on Poverty, "2009–2015 年的貧窮情況及趨勢" [Poverty Conditions and Trends in 2009–2015], *2015 年香港貧窮情況報告 [2015 Report on the Poverty Conditions in Hong Kong]*, Chapter 2, 15–17.
[12] *Ibid.*
[13] Chen Li Ailun, "Analysis and Prospect," 320.

There is a consensus that they should not be used to subsidize routine government expenditure; but there is no strong opposition to using the reserves to enhance the territory's long-term international competitiveness. The government, however, has not come up with any major policy programs towards this end.

The government has often indicated that it has to make preparations for the territory's ageing population. People aged 65 years and above constituted 16% of the population in 2015, and this proportion will rise to 36% in 2064. However, in its 2016 consultation exercises on a universal pension scheme, the C.Y. Leung administration adamantly refused to accept the financial responsibility for such a scheme and instead opted for various policy measures to help the elderly on a means-tested basis.[14] The government's position was disappointing in the eyes of the social service sector and the pro-democracy movement, and reflected a fiscal conservatism on the part of the political establishment.

Hu Angang, a leading economic scholar at Tsinghua University in Beijing, examined Hong Kong's economic difficulties and offered the following set of statistics. From 1970 to 1994, per capita GDP in Hong Kong rose from US$925 to US$21,421, maintaining double-digit growth every year with the exception of 1985. From 1997 to 2010, per capita GDP in Hong Kong increased from US$27,170 to US$31,758, a nominal rise of only 21.4% in 14 years.

In 1997, GDP in mainland China amounted to US$265.926 billion, while that of Hong Kong reached US$177.353 billion. Guangdong's GDP at that time was about one-tenth that of mainland China, and one-sixth to one-seventh that of Hong Kong. From 1998, mainland China enjoyed a 15-year period of double-digit growth. In 2014, mainland China's GDP reached US$10.36 trillion, about 38 times that of Hong Kong, which amounted to US$273.667 billion. Guangdong's GDP in 2014 exceeded US$1 trillion, more than three times that of Hong Kong. Among China's provincial units, Hong Kong ranked 15th in terms of GDP that year.[15]

---

[14] See the final policy address delivered by Chief Executive C.Y. Leung on January 8, 2017 and the media commentaries on the following day.

[15] Hu Angang, "香港—如何發展之定位? 怎樣融入之挑戰?" [Hong Kong — How to Position Itself for Development? The Challenges of How to Integrate with China?], in He

Hu's views are representative of those of think-tanks in mainland China engaging in research on Hong Kong. They consider that the Hong Kong economy has not been performing well, and they often believe that the HKSAR government has to be more proactive in its economic policies. They also tend to hold the view that the Hong Kong economy has been more and more dependent on the mainland Chinese economy, and the territory's contribution to China's economic modernization has been in decline.

Hong Kong's economic dependence on mainland China has been a controversial issue, and has been raised often by leaders of the pro-Beijing camp in Hong Kong, as well as by ordinary people in mainland China and its tourists coming to the territory. This is usually considered humiliating by the Hong Kong people. Hence, in terms of economic performance, the C.Y. Leung administration failed to satisfy Hong Kong people — the gap between the rich and the poor was perceived to be widening; the territory was falling behind Singapore and Macau economically; and even in the eyes of China's experts on Hong Kong, the C.Y. Leung administration had not been proactive enough to promote economic growth — an unfavorable comparison with its counterparts in most coastal cities in China.

The following statistics serve to illustrate Hong Kong's economic dependence on China. In 2015, Hong Kong's merchandise imports amounted to HK$4.064 trillion, with HK$1.984 trillion (49%) of them coming from China. In the same year, its domestic exports amounted to HK$46.861 billion, with HK$20.433 billion (43.6%) of them going to China. Hong Kong's re-exports reached HK$3.558 trillion in the same year, with HK$1.916 trillion (53.8%) going to China, and HK$2.163 trillion (60.8%) originating from China.[16]

In 2014, direct investment inflow into Hong Kong amounted to HK$876.5 billion, with HK$221.8 billion (25.3%) coming from China,

---

Yiwen and Liu Lanchang (eds.), 十三五規劃與香港—定位、機會與挑戰 [*The Thirteenth Five Year Programme and Hong Kong — Positioning, Opportunities and Challenges*], Hong Kong: City University of Hong Kong Press, 2016, p. 26.

[16] Census and Statistics Department, Hong Kong Special Administrative Region (HKSAR), *Hong Kong Annual Digest of Statistics 2016,* Hong Kong: Government Printer, 2016, 66, https://www.statistics.gov.hk/pub/B10100032016AN16B0100.pdf.

HK$476.7 billion (54.4%) from the British Virgin Islands, and HK$16.7 billion (1.9%) from the Cayman Islands.[17] It is considered that a large proportion of the investment from the British Virgin Islands and the Cayman Islands actually originates from China. In the same year, direct investment outflow from Hong Kong reached HK$962.2 billion with HK$637.9 billion (66.3%) going to mainland China, HK$64.9 billion (6.9%) to the Cayman Islands, and HK$26.2 billion to Bermuda (2.7%).[18] Investment outflow from Hong Kong to the Caribbean is similarly believed largely to originate from China.

Mainland China has become, by far, the principal source of tourists to Hong Kong. In 2015, 59.308 million visitors arrived in the territory, with 45.842 million (77.3%) coming from mainland China.[19] The large tourist inflow from mainland China has been a source of friction between Hong Kong and mainland China, and many people in Hong Kong have raised the issue that the territory has to consider its capacity to serve tourists and whether a limit should be set so as to better regulate the tourist inflow.

Hong Kong's economic dependence on mainland China has also been reflected by its inclusion in China's economic and social development planning processes. The 11th Five-Year National Economic and Social Development Plan (2006–2010) simply discussed Hong Kong's direction of development. In the following 12th Five-Year Development Plan (2011–2015), a special chapter was dedicated to Hong Kong and Macau, defining Hong Kong's position and role in China's development strategy as well as its own development program. Many in Hong Kong, especially those in support of the pro-democracy movement, were dissatisfied with this inclusion in the national development plan without consulting the local community.

This dissatisfaction was ignored, and the process was repeated in the 13th Five-Year Development Plan (2016–2020). Some commentators observed that in the 12th Five-Year Development Plan, the Chinese authorities indicated that they would "support Hong Kong and Macao to consolidate and raise their competitive edge"; but in the following plan,

---

[17] *Ibid.*, 109.
[18] *Ibid.*, 110.
[19] *Ibid.*, 332.

they stated that they would "support Hong Kong and Macao to raise their economic competitiveness," reflecting a recognition that Hong Kong no longer enjoyed much of a competitive edge. [20]

In the spring of 2017, Chinese leaders highlighted the development of the Greater Bay Area (of Guangdong–Hong Kong–Macau), i.e., the integration of the Pearl River Delta including Hong Kong and Macau. The project had already been under discussion for a few years, but the inclusion of Hong Kong was emphasized only then. The C.Y. Leung administration worked hard to promote the project, prompting speculation that this might become Leung's area of specialization in his capacity as a vice-chairman of the National Committee of the CPPCC after stepping down as the chief executive.

The Greater Bay Area development project has been based on the Chinese leadership's recognition that urbanization would be significant in China's development at this stage, as this would stimulate domestic consumption and investment to serve as the major components of sustainable economic development, in view of the declining importance of infrastructural investment and exports. From the Guangdong authorities' point of view, the project would allow the province to better compete with the Yangtze River Delta and the Beijing–Tianjin–Hebei Area around Bohai. As Guangdong intends to step up its development of modern service industries, it has realized the advantages of the development of a substantial metropolitan area centered on the Pearl River Delta.

Despite the government's rhetoric, the Hong Kong community has raised questions concerning the role of the HKSAR in the planning process and the lack of consultation of Hong Kong people by the HKSAR government. At the root of these questions is concern about the maintenance of the "One Country, Two Systems" model as well as the core values and lifestyles of the Hong Kong community in the integration process. If Hong Kong becomes just an ordinary coastal city of China or part of one of its major metropolises, is this to the advantage of Hong Kong?

---

[20] He Yiwen, "前言" [Foreword], in He Yiwen and Liu Lanchang (eds.), *The Thirteenth Five Year Programme and Hong Kong*, xxiii.

Even the territory's major business groups realize the severe challenges ahead, given that the Pearl River Delta plans to concentrate on its modern tertiary sector and relocate its manufacturing industries to the eastern and western parts of Guangdong. C.Y. Leung's claim that Hong Kong would serve as the "super connector" for Guangdong and China has been ignored: the Guangdong authorities wish to eliminate the province's dependence on connectors through the development of the province's modern tertiary sector, developing direct ties with the world's top corporations and the international markets. Guangdong's emphasis on finance, banking, insurance, logistics, maritime and air transport, tourism, etc., obviously poses serious competition to Hong Kong. The C.Y. Leung administration's rhetoric on the advantages of integration appeared unconvincing in the eyes of Hong Kong people.

As housing prices rise rapidly and real incomes stagnate, there is a worry on the part of the lower socioeconomic strata in Hong Kong that they may eventually have to move to the Pearl River Delta where the cost of living is lower, while elements of the business and professional elites of China would move to Hong Kong. This is certainly not the kind of economic integration which appeals to them.

Despite relatively slow economic growth, the unemployment rate remains low in Hong Kong and naturally contributes to social stability. In the period 2011–2015, the unemployment rate stayed at a level of 3.3%–3.4% and underemployment 1.4%–1.7%.[21] Though Hong Kong people can no longer say that anyone who is willing to work should have no difficulty finding a job, the tertiary sector still offers many job opportunities. Job satisfaction presents a serious challenge though, as jobs in the lower end of the tertiary sector do not offer job security, benefits, and career development opportunities. Hence, young people frequently change jobs.

Hong Kong will continue to function as an international financial center and business services center. Though the territory's unique position in the China market will decline, the China market is expected to maintain its growth in the foreseeable future — hence, the absolute size of a declining share of an expanding pie (the China market) may still expand.

---

[21] Census and Statistics Department, *Hong Kong Annual Digest of Statistics 2016*, p. x.

The territory will have to work hard to improve its productivity and competitiveness so that its share of the pie will not shrink too much.

Hong Kong will continue to seek new niches to prosper, which has been its typical mode of operation. An increasing share of the accumulated wealth of the major business groups in the territory will go to mainland China and overseas — this partly explains why while Hong Kong's GDP has continued to grow, the lower socioeconomic strata has not experienced an improvement in living standards. There must be more investment in education and human resources development; the major challenge is to ensure that the education system encourages creativity and innovation.

The development of high-tech industries in Hong Kong has not made much progress, in contrast to the other three "little dragons of Asia". Meanwhile, the reallocation of manufacturing industries to the Pearl River Delta in southern China and beyond was completed by the turn of the century. The employment situation may well deteriorate because the service industries will continue to adopt automation and other cost-cutting measures to maintain their competitiveness and profit margins.

In the past, there was a suggestion that high-tech industries might be developed in the territory using Hong Kong's capital, marketing skills, and international network, as well as scientific and technological talents from mainland China and its advanced industrial base. Unfortunately, nothing much has been achieved so far. Hong Kong's only connection with high-tech industries is its financial institutions, which serve to raise venture capital supporting their development.

Hong Kong is the fourth global financial center; and according to the International Institute for Management Development in Lausanne, Hong Kong was ranked the most competitive economic entity in 2016.[22] Among the cities in China, according to the Chinese Cities Competitiveness Research Association, Hong Kong has lost its leading position and was ranked second in 2016 after Shanghai. Without doubt, Hong Kong has highly advanced financial and business service sectors, but they cannot provide satisfactory employment for the city's entire labor force (3.9 million in 2015); and this partly explains the widening gap between the rich and the poor in the territory.

---

[22] Chen Li Ailun, "Analysis and Prospect," 332.

III Chinese leaders' Hong Kong Policy and Exacerbating Contradictions Between Hong Kong and Beijing

In the initial years after Hong Kong's return to the motherland in 1997, the Chinese authorities attempted to show respect for the "one country, two systems" model. The first test came with the Article 23 legislation, which was seen as a threat to Hong Kong people's core values and lifestyles. The SARS outbreak and the economic difficulties it brought further raised the anger of the public. As a result, more than half a million people participated in the July 1, 2003 protest rally.

The victory of the pro-democracy camp in the District Council elections in November 2003, and its being perceived to have a small chance of securing half of the seats in the Legislative Council elections in September 2004, symbolized the revival of the pro-democracy movement, as well as the extent of public dissatisfaction with the Tung administration — a threat towards Beijing's fundamental policy towards Hong Kong. The Chinese authorities, therefore, believed that they had to intervene.

The heavy involvement of the Chinese authorities in Hong Kong affairs subsequently further weakened the legitimacy and effectiveness of the HKSAR government. Business leaders likely felt that if they needed anything, they should lobby Beijing. Once the firewall had been broken, the involvement became deeper and broader in scale. The most conspicuous has been the grassroots service network of the Democratic Alliance for the Betterment and Progress of Hong Kong and other pro-Beijing groups, which have visited elderly people as well as families in need with monthly gifts of rice, noodles, edible oil, etc., and offered other benefits such as weekend outings with seafood lunches and mooncakes for Mid-Autumn Festival, etc. These networks have facilitated these groups to establish strong support bases able to deliver votes in elections.

Journalists have also observed by that the pro-Beijing united front has established thousands of civic groups with substantial mobilization power. The pro-Beijing camp in recent years can easily mobilize hundreds of thousands of supporters in rallies articulating support for its political causes and opposing those of the pro-democracy camp; it can easily collect hundreds of thousands of signatures in petitions too. Some of these groups do not hesitate to disrupt the political activities of the pro-democracy movement, leading to mildly violent conflicts. These disruptions began in 2013 when the pro-democracy camp initiated public discussions and seminars in support of political reforms. There is no evidence linking these "patriotic" groups to the C.Y. Leung administration, but it at least tolerated them and made no attempt to dissuade the pro-Beijing united front and the Chinese authorities from these somewhat violent altercations. The disruptions of these "patriotic" groups compromise the territory's political culture, and exacerbate political polarization and confrontations in society.

With the backing of a powerful machinery, the pro-Beijing united front has been able to infiltrate almost every pro-democracy group. Most pro-democracy activists believe that their emails and mobile phones have been hacked or tapped; in recent years, they have taken to leaving their mobile phones outside meeting rooms when participating in political discussions. At the same time, the HKSAR government has been exercising its powers of appointment to reward its supporters with positions in the official system of advisory committees. Without the voices of the opposition, government officials have an easier task, but the entire system of advisory committees has lost its value and legitimacy.

The weakness of the C.Y. Leung administration and the divisions within the pro-Beijing camp led the Central Liaison Office to frequently intervene. When the C.Y. Leung administration lobbied unsuccessfully for majority support in the Legislative Council to endorse its policy proposals, it had to rely on the Central Liaison Office to do the lobbying. When pro-Beijing legislators made a serious tactical mistake while voting on the political reform bill on June 18, 2015, they immediately went to explain their error to the Central Liaison Office; they then apologized to the public while ignoring the C.Y. Leung administration.[23] Central Liaison Office officials and HKSAR government officials publicly acknowledged that lobbying the Legislative Council had become a regular part of the Liaison Office's work.[24] Journalists in the territory also understand that the

---

[23] See the major newspapers in Hong Kong on June 19–20, 2015.
[24] Shiu Sin-por, head of the Central Policy Unit, admitted that the Central Liaison Office had consistently participated in lobbying work in the Legislative Council because some

Central Liaison Office coordinates election campaigns on behalf of the pro-Beijing camp.[25] All these cast doubt on the maintenance of Hong Kong's high degree of autonomy within the "one country, two systems" framework.

The major confrontation between the Chinese authorities and the pro-democracy movement finally arrived with the political reform deliberations and the Occupy campaign of 2013–2014. In 2007 the Chinese authorities had promised to consider universal suffrage for the chief executive election in 2017 and further democratization of the Legislative Council electoral system afterwards. The pro-democracy movement therefore initiated consultations and presented its proposals in early 2013, while Benny Tai and others planned the Occupy Central campaign, modelled after the Occupy Wall Street campaign in the U.S. The Chinese authorities agreed to grant universal suffrage, but only while maintaining tight control over the nomination process within the establishment-dominated Election Committee; in other words, the Hong Kong people would be permitted to choose the chief executive from a list of candidates endorsed by the Chinese authorities.

The Chinese authorities essentially refused to negotiate, and the Occupy campaign started in late September 2014. The confrontation hardened the Chinese leadership's position on Hong Kong. In the first place, it realized that conciliatory promises of "gradual progress in democratization", "democratic elections when conditions are ripe", and so on, would no longer work; the Hong Kong people would have to be taught to accept the parameters of the "one country, two systems" model as defined by the Chinese authorities. At the same time, the pro-Beijing united front had been spreading the argument that the Hong Kong economy was now highly dependent on that of the mainland, and not the other way around. The implicit message was that Hong Kong's bargaining power has been in decline and it should not make excessive demands.

---

lawmakers would only listen to the Central Liaison Office. C.Y. Leung also stated that the HKSAR government was responsible for lobbying the Legislative Council, but the Central Liaison Office had a definite role in the process. See *AM730*, March 12, 2014.

[25] See, for example, *Hong Kong Economic Journal*, March 2, 2017.

Chinese leaders and the HKSAR government have both appealed to the Hong Kong community to concentrate on the economy and make good use of the opportunities offered by Beijing's "One Belt, One Road" initiative. They blame the pro-democracy movement for delaying the administration's policy programs through its obstruction tactics; however, the executive branch of the government has ample powers, and the establishment controls a comfortable majority in the legislature through an undemocratic electoral system. The pro-democracy camp remains in the minority, despite capturing 55%–60% of the popular vote in the Legislative Council elections.

In the aftermath of the Occupy campaign, support for the pro-democracy movement has been maintained and, in fact, slightly improved despite setbacks in political reforms and internal divisions, as reflected by the results of the District Council elections in November 2015, the Legislative Council elections in September 2016 and the Chief Executive Election Committee elections in December 2016. The support for pro-democracy candidates and the high voter turnout rates reflected that the Hong Kong people value the opportunity to articulate their demands and maintain some form of checks and balances.

The alleged abductions of booksellers to mainland China in 2016 and the similar abduction case of Xiao Jianhua in early 2017 eroded the confidence of Hong Kong people in the firewall provided by the "one country, two systems" model. In the eyes of the Hong Kong people, intense power struggles in Beijing may well prompt Chinese leaders to ignore the autonomy granted to the Special Administrative Region. Hong Kong may increasingly become just another coastal city in mainland China; this worry supports sentiments opposed to the "Mainlandization" of Hong Kong.[26]

Naturally, the Chinese leadership perceives advocacy for independence or even an official referendum on the territory's future as a political taboo, attracting a severe crackdown. The activists concerned with these activities now face many court cases and judicial attempts have been made to

---

[26] See Joseph Yu-shek Cheng, Jacky Chau-kiu Cheung and Beatrice Kit-fun Leung (eds.), *Mainlandization of Hong Kong — Pressures and Responses*, Hong Kong: Contemporary China Research Project, City University of Hong Kong, 2017.

remove pro-independence legislators. The crackdown has blunted the development of the radical groups, but dissatisfaction among the young people continues to accumulate.

No constructive dialogue now exists between the establishment and the entire spectrum of the pro-democracy movement; this means that political polarization will remain. It is difficult to ensure effective governance and the administration hesitates to initiate major policy programs. The result is the decline of Hong Kong's international competitiveness. It appears that Beijing is trying to renew contact with the moderates of the pro-democracy camp without making any substantial concessions; this is, however, not acceptable from the latter's point of view.

IV Evaluation of CY Leung's Performance

C.Y. Leung was obviously a very skillful politician to have secured election as chief executive in 2012. The Chinese leadership likely abandoned its previous endorsement of Henry Tang and switched its support to C.Y. Leung in the final month or so of the campaign. Henry Tang was groomed to be the chief executive after serving in the most important positions in government and being supported by the powerful business community. However, his incompetent handling of the illegal construction scandal in the campaign period likely eroded the Chinese leadership's confidence in him.

C.Y. Leung fully exploited his humble family background to win the sympathy and support of the Hong Kong people, posing himself as a typical success story of the community. As a politician, he had tried to maintain ties with the grassroots groups and the pro-democracy parties; and he had been more successful than other establishment figures in cultivating a dialogue.

Despite his initial good image and popularity, he soon suffered from his own illegal construction scandal at the very beginning of his administration.[27] In his first year in office, a number of his top officials had to step down because of various scandals. Executive Council member

---

[27] *South China Morning Post*, July 13, 2012.

Franklin Lam Fan-keung left the council due to allegations of profiting from real estate deals based on insider information. Another executive councilor, Barry Cheung Chun-yuen, departed because of police investigations into his struggling Hong Kong Mercantile Exchange.[28] Earlier, development minister Mak Chai-kwong resigned because he was accused of abusing civil service housing allowance by "cross-leasing" properties with a colleague in the 1980s.[29] Health minister Dr. Ko Wing-man, and Mak Chai-kwong's successor, Paul Chan Mo-po, however, survived their illegal structures and sub-letting scandals respectively.

The C.Y. Leung administration, therefore, started with a weak government plagued with scandals and a tarnished image. Leung's election owed much to the strong support of the Chinese authorities, which sent Politburo member Liu Yandong, then head of the Party's United Front Department, to Shenzhen to oversee the lobbying of support for Leung. It was reported that many business leaders still supported Henry Tang, in defiance of advice from Beijing; and Li Ka-shing openly declared his endorsement of Henry Tang. This explained the low level of support for C.Y. Leung (689 votes out of 1,200).

Leung found it hard to attract respectable figures to join his government, and his team included not a few pro-Beijing figures who had been neglected by previous administrations. Worse still, Leung gradually came to be perceived as an arrogant leader without much patience and skill to accommodate various vested interests — in sharp contrast to his earlier image. This resulted in his failure to maintain solidarity within the establishment.

In view of the shortage of housing and rising property prices, the C.Y. Leung administration accorded priority to housing policy, which was generally considered his area of expertise. His declaration that he would increase land and housing supply to suppress housing services and his subsequent measures to cool the property market certainly did not endear him to the major business groups. Unfortunately, his policy measures have not been effective, and property prices were higher at the end of his term in office than at the beginning. By then, most Hong Kong people believed

---

[28] *South China Morning Post,* May 23, 2013.
[29] *South China Morning Post,* July 6, 2012.

that housing prices could not fall. Despite the business community's difficult relations with C.Y. Leung, most Hong Kong people remained very critical of the "collusion" between the government and big business, although the latter's criticisms of Leung in front of the Chinese authorities had been an important factor in Beijing's refusal to support his re-election. One should also be reminded that it was actually Donald Tsang's inaction in increasing land supply which had been responsible for the territory's rising land prices.

Rural interests were hostile to the C.Y. Leung administration as well. The author was informed by a leader of the Heung Yee Kuk that the Central Liaison Office had to intervene in the quarrel between C.Y. Leung and rural interest leader, Lau Wong-fat, to ensure the latter's effective mobilization against the Occupy Central campaign. This is but one example of Leung's failure to unite the establishment, and reflects the validity of the criticism that his weakness and incompetence had called for interventions from the Central Liaison Office.

In early 2016, some radicals in the Heung Yee Kuk attempted to form a new party as they were reluctant to support the DAB in every issue.[30] Realizing that they could not articulate their rural interests effectively and that their influence was on the decline, they proposed the formation of a new party, the New Progressive Alliance, which would enable them to bargain with the Chinese authorities and the HKSAR government more effectively. The plan was to compete in the September 2016 Legislative Council elections. An interesting phenomenon was that the rural interests all negotiated with the Central Liaison Office, and the C.Y. Leung administration had no role to play. It was plain that the Central Liaison Office was the principal agent in coordinating elections in Hong Kong. In the end, the plan was shelved.

During the C.Y. Leung administration, government officials and Central Liaison Office officials were often invited to various public functions. The latter were even present in ceremonies and activities of many secondary schools. In the eyes of the community, the C.Y. Leung administration had been responsible for the erosion of the territory's autonomy under the "one country, two systems" model.

---

[30] *Apple Daily*, March 2, 2016.

The DAB and the traditional pro-Beijing groups were the most reliable supporters of the C.Y. Leung administration; this support, however, seemed to have been based on toeing the Beijing line faithfully rather than agreement with Leung's policy programs. Jasper Tsang Yok-sing, a senior leader of the DAB, often indicated his criticisms of Leung in a polite manner in his media appearances; and his brother Tsang Tak-sing resigned from his position as Secretary for Home Affairs, prompting plentiful speculation about his disagreements with C.Y. Leung. A few business leaders, such as Ricky Wong Wai-kay and James Tien Pei-chun, also a veteran Liberal Party leader, emerged as critics of the C.Y. Leung administration and became quite popular with the public.

The pro-democracy groups' relations with the C.Y. Leung administration were poor. It is understood that on issues such as political reforms and democratization, decisions are made by Beijing and not by the HKSAR government. However, a majority of the pro-democracy legislators supported 70% of routine government policies,[31] and most top government officials maintained a constructive dialogue with most pro-democracy parties. However, Beijing's hard line on political reforms destroyed the relatively amiable atmosphere. Filibustering became frequent in the Legislative Council, and no meaningful dialogue could be conducted between the pro-democracy legislators, on one hand, and government officials and pro-establishment legislators, on the other. Government officials simply braved the criticisms and filibustering of the pro-democracy legislators, and relied on the establishment's majority to pass bills. They then blamed the pro-democracy camp for obstructionism. Government efficiency was adversely affected, and it became very difficult for the C.Y. Leung administration to launch bold policy initiatives. Even a moderate party like the Civic Party refused to meet C.Y. Leung for his conventional consultation of all legislators on his upcoming policy address. Most pro-democracy groups resented what they saw as C.Y. Leung's arrogance, and considered meeting him futile and meaningless.

---

[31] Stuart Lau, "Hong Kong's pan-democrat lawmakers not as obstructive as you might think," *South China Morning Post*, July 18, 2016, https://www.scmp.com/news/hong-kong/politics/article/1991460/hong-kongs-pan-democrat-lawmakers-not-obstructive-you-might

A few of C.Y. Leung's top officials also became highly unpopular in the eyes of the public and the media. They included education minister Eddie Ng Hak-kim, environment minister Wong Kam-sing, and information coordinator Andrew Fung Wai-kwong. Shiu Sin-por became notorious for his perceived arrogance. His Central Policy Unit was seen as specializing in defending the administration instead of reflecting the community's views and critically reviewing the government's policies.

V The Pro-democracy Movement

The emergence of the localism groups during and after the Occupation Campaign in 2014 has been a significant development in the pro-democracy movement. Young people's general frustration with their socioeconomic conditions and their anger with the undemocratic and repressive C.Y. Leung administration have prompted them to advocate for the independence of Hong Kong. To some extent, this is a kind of youthful defiance rather than a serious independence movement. The groups involved have not developed credible political discourses, nor have they offered any action plans or timetables. The Hong Kong people are fully aware that independence is not a realistic option, yet, in the September 2016 Legislative Council elections, these localism groups secured 18% of the popular vote in an election with a record high turnout (58% turnout rate).[32]

In 2016, almost every student union in the tertiary institutions in the territory adopted a localism position, and many young people now declare that they are not Chinese, but Hong Kongers. The change of sentiment has taken place very rapidly, as public opinion surveys indicated that Hong Kong people's identification with the Chinese nation and their trust for the Chinese leadership reached a peak in 2008, the year of the Beijing Olympics.

The rapid increase of tourists from mainland China, amounting to 47.2 million in 2014 and 45.8 million in 2015, caused considerable resentment among the local population, especially because of the former's

---

[32] See all major newspapers in Hong Kong in the two days after the Legislative Council elections on September 4, 2016.

rude behavior and shopping patterns. The deterioration in human rights conditions in China, including the harsh suppression of human rights lawyers, autonomous trade unions, and autonomous underground churches also alarmed Hong Kong people. Above all else, increasing interference from Beijing in Hong Kong affairs and the rejection of political reforms by the Chinese leadership in 2013–2014 has put Chinese authorities in a bad light in the eyes of the local community, which now fears that its core values and lifestyles have been threatened. Hence, some critics have called the Chief Executive C.Y. Leung "the father of Hong Kong independence".

During the Occupy campaign in 2014, student activists seized the leadership and organization of the campaign from the original initiators — namely Benny Tai, Chan Kin-man, and Chu Yiu-ming. Differences emerged between the activists and the leaders of the pro-democracy political parties. In general, the former felt that the latter were too conservative, and they believed that the time had come for themselves to assume leadership. While some of these "umbrella groups" openly articulate support for Hong Kong independence, others like Demosist (the political wing which has emerged from student group Scholarism) adopt a more moderate stand, calling for an official referendum on the future of Hong Kong.

In the September 2016 Legislative Council elections, Democracy Groundwork, Land Justice League, Demosist, Civic Passion, and Youngspiration all won seats, demonstrating the appeal of their cause and the supporters of the pro-democracy movement's preference for new faces.[33] In these elections, the mainstream pro-democracy parties all faced the challenge of intergenerational leadership changes. The Democratic Party and the Civic Party, which had prepared well, achieved satisfactory results in the elections; while the Labour Party and the Hong Kong Association for Democracy and People's Livelihood, which had neglected the challenge, suffered badly.

While the espousal of the causes of Hong Kong independence and localism serves to distinguish the mainstream pro-democracy groups and

---

[33] *Ibid.* Another group, Hong Kong Indigenous, had its political star, Edward Leung Tin-kei, disqualified and could not take part in the elections.

the newly-emerging young radical groups, their differences in style, the lack of trust between them, and accumulated frictions have made it difficult for them to cooperate closely. They seem to enjoy the support of different constituencies — the mainstream groups receive support from liberals who are often 40 years of age and above, well-educated with middle class status; while the radical groups attract the support of the younger generations. The former uphold the principle of non-violent political campaign, and they share a concern for the development of China. The latter are sometimes tempted to engage in confrontations with the police, and believe that Hong Kong should maintain a separate identity as well as a certain distance from China.

After the September 2016 Legislative Council elections, the two Youngspiration legislators made controversial gestures in their oath-taking ceremony, resulting in the C.Y. Leung administration adopting a judicial review procedure in an attempt to deprive them of their legislator status. This was followed by an interpretation of Article 104 of the Basic Law by the Standing Committee of the National People's Congress in Beijing. The C.Y. Leung administration also adopted the same judicial review process to try to disqualify four other legislators who also had refused to follow the routine in their own oath-taking ceremonies. At the time of writing, the court cases are still in process for two legislators, the two Youngspiration legislators, and two others who had lost their seats.

The behavior of the Youngspiration legislators during their oath-taking aroused considerable resentment among the Hong Kong public, and their weakness in subsequent protest activities also disappointed their own supporters. Meanwhile, the C.Y. Leung administration adopted a tough line against the radical localism groups whose leaders had been bogged down by court cases; even the banks refused to allow these groups to open bank accounts. In early 2017, it appeared that the localism groups had lost some of their appeal, and their future development become uncertain. However, the crackdown has not reduced the levels of frustration and anger among young people, whose political identification and political participation patterns mean that the deep polarization in society is far from being healed.

While the pro-establishment candidates in the 2017 chief executive election all indicated recognition of the problems of political and social polarization, they still discussed Article 23 legislation and offered no promises of political reforms. Understandably, these issues are to be decided by the Chinese leadership; and unless it is willing to alter its Hong Kong policy, no resolution is in sight. Obviously, given the political climate in Beijing, Xi Jinping appears in no mood to engage in a constructive dialogue with the pro-democracy camp on democratization and political reforms.

The pro-democracy movement understands that it has entered a period of low tide, as it has no realizable short-term objectives and therefore it cannot effectively mobilize the community. The number of people taking part in demonstrations and protest activities has been in decline, but this is no consolation for the HKSAR government. Approval ratings for the government, the chief executive, and most top government officials were at a very low level during the years of the C.Y. Leung administration. Dissatisfaction had been accumulating while the legitimacy of the HKSAR government had been falling. In public opinion surveys in 2016 and 2017 evaluating the disciplinary forces, the Independent Commission Against Corruption, which used to be the pride of Hong Kong, ranked last — while the police force came second last.

At the end of the Occupy campaign, the author suggested that the HKSAR government should continue the dialogue on political reforms. It should also initiate community-wide consultations on one or two major livelihood issues. Finally, it should recruit some young pro-democracy activists into the advisory committee system. The gist of the proposals was to maintain dialogue, even in times of political confrontation. The proposals remain relevant for the new Carrie Lam administration.

In the second quarter of 2017, many pro-Beijing figures including Rita Fan indicated that the Chinese authorities would not be interested in altering the framework for political reforms in Hong Kong, defined at the end of August 2014 by the Standing Committee of the National People's Congress. In early May 2017, Zhang Dejiang, then Chairman of the Standing Committee of the National People's Congress, visited Macau, praising it for its early completion of the Article 23 legislation. This praise was broadly interpreted in Hong Kong as asking the territory to follow Macau's good example.[34]

In this context, a constructive dialogue between the pro-democracy camp and the Carrie Lam administration cannot be established. Without a dialogue, there will be no meaningful competition between the moderate wing and the radical wing within the pro-democracy movement, and the confrontation with the Carrie Lam administration will be dominated by the radical wing. Political apathy will spread among a larger and larger segment of the population. Mutual distrust will escalate; and in the sharpening political struggle, established rules and conventions will likely be violated.

During the second half of the C.Y. Leung administration, independence advocacy became a "straw man" which was conveniently used as an excuse for political suppression. The latter in turn eroded the cherished pluralism in society, exacerbated political polarization and enhanced mutual intolerance. All of these factors contributed to the popular statement: "This is not the Hong Kong I used to know."

Community-wide consultation on one or two important livelihood issues is a way to establish dialogue between all parties concerned, which would help to reignite pragmatism, cooperation, and compromise. Success will improve the Hong Kong people's welfare and bring credit to the government and the chief executive.

The C.Y. Leung administration did launch a broad consultation exercise on the issue of a universal pension scheme between December 2015 and June 2016, with Carrie Lam, the then chief secretary for administration, in charge. The issue was an appropriate one, and in the eyes of the public, the HKSAR government had the financial resources to act. However, Carrie Lam obviously was not interested in the introduction of such a scheme, and she set so many restrictions that even the social welfare sector soon lost interest in the discussions. Lam even openly quarreled with Professor Nelson Chow, who had been advising the

---

[34] See all the major newspapers in Hong Kong on May 10 and 11, 2017 on Zhang Dejiang's visit to Macao.

government on related issues for the past two or three decades. In the end, the C.Y. Leung administration only agreed to strengthen subsidies for some categories of the elderly in need. The process failed to convince the public that the Leung administration was eager to contribute to non-political social policy issues.

In the first half of 2017, even the pro-Beijing Hong Kong Federation of Trade Unions publicly asked C.Y. Leung to fulfill his electoral pledge on labor issues. The trade unions were dissatisfied with the delay in standard working hours legislation and the existing practice of allowing employers to draw from the employees' Mandatory Provident Fund accounts to pay for their severance payments. It was obvious that the pro-Beijing trade unions were frustrated that they could not deliver to their workers despite faithfully toeing the Beijing line to support the C.Y. Leung administration. They could easily raise donations to offer services to their members though; these services, in turn, helped them build grassroots networks for mobilization — including that for elections.

Government appointments were fully exploited by the C.Y. Leung administration. Leung set up a senior position in the Central Policy Unit to help him vet candidates for appointments, including those for the official advisory committee system. There were many media reports on "Leung fans" receiving offers based not on their merits, but on their close ties with Leung. These appointments appeared not only to be rewards for supporters of the Leung administration or the pro-Beijing united front, but they were also supposed to exercise influence, for example in public university councils.

There were no attempts made to recruit members of the new radical groups and the pro-democracy movement in general to the government's numerous advisory committees. The frequent prosecutions of pro-democracy activists after the Occupy campaign were seen as political suppression, and officials of the C.Y. Leung administration refused to attend functions of pro-democracy political parties; the latter found themselves unable to communicate with their pro-Beijing counterparts. The C.Y. Leung administration unnecessarily exacerbated political polarization in the society.

VI Conclusion

The Chinese leadership had probably intended to maintain the "one country, two systems" model in Hong Kong. Its desire to secure a high level of control to avoid risk, however, has proven to be a stronger motivation. As it has no intention to introduce political reforms in China, it cannot accept the existence of genuine democracy in Hong Kong. The contradictions between Beijing and the SAR, therefore, continue to sharpen.

Since C.Y. Leung owed his chief executive position to the Chinese leadership's support, he chose to be accountable only to the Chinese leadership and not to the Hong Kong people. In due course, his administration lost the support of the people and he had to rely more and more on the endorsement of the Chinese leadership and the lobbying work of the Central Liaison Office. However, in the exacerbation of the contradictions between Beijing and Hong Kong, endorsement by the Chinese leadership became a liability in securing legitimacy from the Hong Kong people.

The political reform deliberations and the Occupy campaign in 2013–2014 led to a showdown between the Chinese authorities and the Hong Kong people. C.Y. Leung's faithful toeing of the Beijing line maintained his support from the Chinese leadership. However, as the Chinese leadership moves to teach the Hong Kong people its baseline regarding the "one country, two systems" model and the territory's economic contributions to China's development decline, the status of the chief executive in the eyes of the Chinese authorities also drops. The chief executive's reporting visits to Beijing and the instructions from the Chinese leaders are now carefully scrutinized by the local media, who perceive that Hong Kong's chief executive has been treated increasingly like an ordinary provincial head. In recent years, Chinese leaders have tended to praise Macau's chief executive far more than his counterpart in Hong Kong.

While the maintenance of stability has largely succeeded, "the hearts of Hong Kong people have not returned", and this was most conspicuous during the years of the C.Y. Leung administration. Successive chief executives selected by Chinese leaders failed to deliver, and the HKSAR government, in contrast to the British administration, could not claim to have achieved legitimacy by performance. After all, times have changed. Young people cannot be persuaded to accept an authoritarian regime; they refuse even to accept the elderly leaders of the pro-democracy camp.

During the years of the C.Y. Leung administration, Hong Kong people realized that democracy could not be achieved in the foreseeable future, and they felt that their core values and lifestyles had been threatened. Under such circumstances, exit has re-emerged as an option.[35] Recent public opinion surveys indicate that over 40% of young people would like to emigrate.[36] It does not imply that they want to depart immediately, but it means that they are ready to go if opportunities arise. Around one million people in Hong Kong already have foreign passports or permanent resident status overseas, secured in the 1980s and 1990s. While the community's commitment weakens, Chinese leaders likely believe that professionals leaving Hong Kong can be replaced by talents from mainland China without much difficulty. Thus, the acceleration of "mainlandization" is the most conspicuous legacy of the C.Y. Leung administration.

Acknowledgement

The manuscript of this chapter was first submitted to the City University Press as "Overall evaluation of the C.Y. Leung Administration", to be published in Cheng, Joseph Y.S. ed., *Evaluation of the C.Y. Leung Administration*. Publication in process.

---

[35] Albert O. Hirschman, *Exit, Voice, and Loyalty: Responses to Decline in Firms, Organisations, and States,* Cambridge, Massachusetts: Harvard University Press, 1970.
[36] Hong Kong Institute of Asia-Pacific Studies, Chinese University of Hong Kong, "Press Release: Survey Findings on Views on Emigration from Hong Kong", http://www.hkiaps.cuhk.edu.hk/wd/ni/20170612-114605_1.pdf.